THE GLOBALIZATION OF
CORPORATE GOVERNANCE

In Memoriam
Michael Whincop
12/12/1968–25/6/2003

The Globalization of Corporate Governance

ALAN DIGNAM
Queen Mary, University of London, UK

MICHAEL GALANIS
University of Leeds, UK

ASHGATE

Published by
Ashgate Publishing Limited
Wey Court East
Union Road
Farnham
Surrey, GU9 7PT
England

Ashgate Publishing Company
Suite 420
101 Cherry Street
Burlington
VT 05401-4405
USA

www.ashgate.com

British Library Cataloguing in Publication Data
Dignam, Alan J.
  The globalization of corporate governance.
  1. Corporate governance. 2. Globalization.
  I. Title II. Galanis, Michael.
  658.4-dc22

Library of Congress Cataloging-in-Publication Data
Dignam, Alan J.
  The globalization of corporate governance / by Alan Dignam and Michael Galanis.
      p. cm.
  Includes bibliographical references and index.
  ISBN 978-0-7546-4625-9
  1. Corporate governance--Law and legislation. 2. Corporation law. 3. Globalization. I. Galanis, Michael. II. Title.

  K1327.D54 2009
  338.6--dc22

                                                            2008053461

ISBN 978-0-7546-4625-9

Reprinted 2010

Mixed Sources
Product group from well-managed forests and other controlled sources
www.fsc.org Cert no. SA-COC-1565
© 1996 Forest Stewardship Council
FSC

Printed and bound in Great Britain by
MPG Books Ltd, Bodmin, Cornwall.

Contents

List of Charts and Graphs

Charts

Graphs

List of Tables

Preface

The process of economic globalization, as product and capital markets integrate, places huge, and it is argued by some, irresistible pressures,[1] on the worlds 'insider' stakeholder oriented corporate governance systems. Insider corporate governance systems in countries such as Germany and Japan, so the argument goes, should converge or be transformed by global product and capital market pressures to the 'superior' shareholder oriented 'outsider' corporate governance model prevalent in the UK and the US.[2] What these pressures from globalization are, how they manifest themselves and whether they are likely to cause such a convergence/ transformation lies at the heart of our exploration in this book.

We began working on this book out of a common concern that there was a misunderstanding in the comparative corporate governance literature about the way pressures to change from the process of globalization, play out into real systemic change. Analysis of a competition between insider and outsider systems in terms of 'triumph' and 'failure', 'superiority' and 'inferiority', comparisons in natural selection terms or descriptions of outsider systems as the 'standard model' or the 'Top', in a race to the 'Top' analysis, seemed to us oddly misplaced given the complexity of the issues at hand. In one sense our aim in writing this book is relatively simple; we aim to show that change within corporate governance systems produces very uncertain outcomes even where the intention is to produce a uniform one. Observing, as much of the literature does, that outsider shareholder oriented rules are being adopted in insider systems does little, as we will demonstrate over the course of this book, to help us understand what effect this will have, as diversity of reaction should, in our view, be regarded as the norm. That does not mean we rule out convergence

---

1   Hansmann, H. and Kraakman, R. (2001) 'The End of History for Corporate Law', Georgetown Law Journal, 89, 439 at 468.

2   Corporate governance in this book refers to the product of an institutional balancing process whereby the sometimes conflicting interests of a corporation's stakeholders (shareholders, employees, creditors, government, local community and more recently the environment) are accounted for and/or prioritized in order to produce benefit for society. The insider and outsider models described here represent different institutional balancing processes whereby in outsider systems the process is designed to prioritize shareholders in order to maximize wealth for them and benefit other stakeholders indirectly as shareholders reinvest their wealth to create more jobs etc. Institutional arrangements in insider systems tend to weigh the balance of stakeholder interests differently and choose to benefit stakeholders through direct wealth transfers from the company's activities, for example through enhanced wages, better working conditions and job security for employees. We discuss these differences further in Chapter 1.

occurring, it is a possible outcome, but just one of many that might occur. In essence while we are interested in the cause of change and the effect of change in corporate governance systems, we are also interested in the gap between cause and effect.

Like all good lawyers we also begin with a *caveat*. In exploring the globalization of corporate governance we work across a number of disciplines, primarily – law, finance, economics, economic history and political history – in order to get a broader view of change and transformation related to the process of economic globalization. This has advantages in that it allows us to make links between disciplines that provides additional insight into the process of economic globalization and its outcomes in corporate governance terms. It also has its downside as it means we have to cover a lot of ground without necessarily going into detail everywhere. This is particularly risky where we enter highly contested territory within the five disciplines we cover. We acknowledge these limitations as the price we pay for our aerial view but we think the risk has been worth running. We would hope that those who read it bring to their reading a similar willingness to reach out from the confines of their discipline.

We owe a general debt of gratitude to Peter Alldridge, Cari Batenburg, John Birds, Roger Cotterrell, Giullio Fella, Martin Gelter, Harry Haramis, Yunjoo Lee, Norbert Lieckfeldt, Eva Lomnicka, John Lowry, Harry Mertzanis, Harilaos Metzanis, Charles Mitchell, Paul Mitchell, Chris Riley, Gerhard Sorger, Bob Thompson, David Tomkin, and Dirk Zetzsche for their assistance with parts of this book over the years. We thank the various members of staff at the *Deutsches Aktieninstitut* who were very helpful in responding to data queries. We would also like to thank Henry Hansmann and Ron Gilson for giving up their time to discuss some of the ideas in this book on visits to London and Cambridge in 2002 and 2004 respectively. We owe a specific debt of gratitude to John Armour, Brian Cheffins and Josh Getzler for always being available to discuss ideas. Particular thanks go to Bob Burns for his uncanny ability to find things when all else fails and to Leyanda Cocks for her unceasingly rigorous research assistance in the face of unreasonable deadlines. We also thank the editorial staff at Ashgate Publishing, in particular – Aimée Feenan, Sarah Horsley and Alison Kirk, who commissioned this book, waited patiently while we missed deadline after deadline and then ensured a smooth production process. Our gratitude as well to Joey Johnson, Sheila Shirley, Kaptan Miah and Nerys Evans at the School of Law, Queen Mary, University of London, for their tireless assistance over the years. As always we are indebted to our loved ones, Xanthippe, Liz, Grainne, Iris and Laurence, without whose support none of this would have been possible. We have dedicated the book to the memory of Michael Whincop, who before his untimely death in 2003, persuaded us that Ashgate would be a congenial home for an interdisciplinary work on comparative corporate governance. He was right, as usual, and his fellowship and scholarship are much missed by all who encountered him.

Alan Dignam and Michael Galanis
London and Leeds, March 2009

Overview

The book is divided into two parts with four chapters in the first and five in the second. In Part 1: Theorizing Corporate Governance Change, we set out the theoretical context for our examination of change and transformation in corporate governance systems as a result of globalization. We begin in the first chapter – *Corporate Governance Convergence and Corporate Theory* – by setting the initial corporate theoretical context for the debate, to illustrate the polarization within this context and its link to convergence/transformation scholarship. In doing this we explore the various theories that have been used to explain the nature of the corporation. Over the course of the twentieth century, as the managerial firm emerged, corporate theory focused clearly on the accountability gap created by the separation of ownership from control. As such, two broad conceptions of the corporation emerged in the literature, which we describe as shareholder supremacy and managerialism. The former advocates that the focus of managerial power should be the shareholder, while the latter advocates broader accountability for managers to stakeholders. Although these conceptions of the corporation are highly contested, shareholder supremacy has over the past 30 years come to ascendancy particularly in the United States (US) and the United Kingdom (UK). In turn as the globalization of financial markets has been driven by investors from US/UK Anglo/Saxon 'outsider' systems, this has been accompanied by an elevation of the contested theoretical accountability debate and the dominance of shareholder supremacy to the global stage, with some scholars claiming that the convergence of insider systems to a 'superior' shareholder oriented outsider system is preordained.

In Chapter 2 – *Institutional Analysis and Corporate Governance Systems* – we introduce institutional analysis as our preferred form of theoretical analysis for a forum in which change in the institutional context, whether national or global, is significant. We argue that managerial behaviour is shaped in an imperfect world, where the bounded rationality of economic agents and uncertainty give rise to positive transaction costs. Therefore, in comparing corporate governance systems at the national and global level, where institutional interactions are crucial to convergence claims, we consider institutional analysis to be more effective rather than other theories based on neoclassical equilibria that assume freedom from institutional interference. Thus in imperfect markets, whether a corporate governance system reflects shareholder supremacy or managerialism or indeed is moving from one to the other, is determined in our view by the institutional structure within which it is embedded. We then go on to identify certain key complimentary institutional sub-systems (corporate law, the financial system, the industrial relations system, and sub-systems related to the government demand function, particularly competition and effective demand), that are central to corporate governance outcomes and which we emphasize in our exploration of convergence/transformation in Part II of the book. We then continue to examine insider and outsider corporate governance models to demonstrate the coherence of both systems as workable combinations of complementary national institutional sub-systems.

In Chapter 3 – *Globalization and its Impact on Corporate Governance Systems* – we set out our theoretical view of globalization as a process. In doing so we consider that internationalization and regionalization, in so far as they facilitate a decoupling from the national arena, form part of the process of globalization. We then examine the process of globalization and its potential to cause change in corporate governance systems. We argue that through the process of economic globalization led by capital and product market liberalization, conditions that promote securitization of financial systems, externalization of labour markets, promote shareholder corporate law norms and introduce highly competitive product markets, have been created that could, in theory, cause workability problems for insider corporate governance models.

In Chapter 4 – *Theorizing the Possibility of Change in Insider Corporate Governance Systems: Divergence or Convergence?* – we set out the various theoretical approaches to institutional change and how they predict national institutional sets will respond to the pressures of globalization. In doing so we bring together the central elements of the previous three chapters to examine the potential dynamic responses of national corporate governance systems to the pressures from the process of globalization. We begin by discussing claims of a neoclassical origin that emphasize a clear uniform shareholder oriented outcome in response to the forces of globalization. We then examine theories of institutional change that emphasize the role of institutions in either facilitating or blocking change. In all we conclude that institutional dynamics within systems can vary considerably, so that national corporate governance models should be expected to react differently to common stimulants and not uniformly, as neoclassical theories of change and its associated scholarship would predict.

We then turn in Part 2: Observing Change and Transformation in the UK, US and Germany, to examine evidence of institutional change in the UK, the US and Germany. In Chapter 5 – *The Insider Corporate Governance Systems of the UK and the US: From Colony to Cold War* – we examine long-term change in the institutional corporate governance sub-systems of the UK and US in the period from their initial colonial relationship until the early 1970s. We focus on the outsider systems of the UK and US because their outsider status is exceptional within the world's corporate governance systems and so before examining changes to the German insider system, that might be leading to transformation to an outsider system of corporate governance, we need to understand more about how the UK and US came to their exceptional status. In all, the UK, over the time period we analysed in this chapter, did not in our view conform to a shareholder oriented outsider system of corporate governance. While the stock exchange was a source of finance which increased over time, at almost all points along the way families, banks, government and labour exerted significant influence over managerial discretion. Additionally, competitive pressures were negated by government instigated collusion or tolerance of collusion and from the 1930s protective tariff barriers diminished overseas competition. Similarly, the US did not conform to a shareholder oriented outsider system of corporate governance in this period. In the US, while the stock exchange grew in importance and dispersed ownership of large US companies emerged, managerial discretion was significantly influenced at various points by banks, government and labour, while dispersed shareholders were unable to exert control over management.

Competitive pressures were greater than in the UK, but US companies had much greater protection through tariff barriers than UK companies did prior to the 1930s. In all, the UK and US, conformed to an insider model more than an outsider one over this period. Indeed the economic shock of the Great Depression in the US and of WWII in Britain, caused institutional transformation in both countries to stronger insider systems. However, within the insider paradigm, change was generally constant in both the UK and US and the seeds of future corporate governance transformation were evident by the late 1960s, as institutional investors began to emerge as an influence and the hostile takeover began to squeeze managerial discretion.

In Chapter 6 – *The Emergence of Outsider Corporate Governance Systems in the UK and US: From the End of the Golden Age to Globalization* – we examine how the UK and US were transformed from insider systems to become the two shareholder oriented outsider systems they are today. In both countries the post war consensus between labour, business and government collapsed in the 1970s with the end of the Bretton Woods agreement, increased product market competition, stagflation and successive oil crises. Transformation came in the UK and the US with the introduction of ideologically driven monetarist and deregulatory policies by Margaret Thatcher and Ronald Reagan. At that point a domestic shock induced by these policies further facilitated change by softening up any remaining resistance to systemic transformation. By the end of the 1980s, both the UK and the US had emerged as shareholder oriented outsider systems, as the industrial relations and financial systems of both countries were transformed and the government's role in the marketplace was reduced. Corporate law did not seem to play much of a role in this, as it had a managerial orientation. In the vacuum created by the withdrawal of the state, the diminution of labour power and a deregulated financial market, the institutionalization of shareholding and the emergence of a market for corporate control in both countries allowed shareholders to become the major influence within the corporate governance systems and complete the transformation to outsider systems.

What is noteworthy in our long-term historical analysis of change in the role of government, industrial relations, financial systems and corporate law, is the fluidity of institutional change over time in the UK and US. Rather than static constellations of institutional systems, they have been engaged in constant rearrangement in response to stimulus. While broadly one would describe the UK and the US as insider systems up until the 1980s, that classification disguises a remarkable amount of change/transformation and diversity in reaction in the institutions affecting corporate governance outcomes over time. At various times up until the 1980s, management, families, labour, banks, competitive pressures and the government or combinations of these elements have been important influences on management discretion. Most of that change indicated diversity of reaction in institutional structure to stimulus until the 1980s, when in reaction to a similar shock both systems reoriented themselves to produce a similar outcome. The experience of the UK and the US may not be transferable generally to analysis of institutional systemic convergence/transformation as their shared institutional history may have played a role in the common response to shock. We explore this further in the final chapter.

In Chapter 7 – *The Traditional German Corporate Governance Model* – before we consider the evidence of convergence/transformation in Germany caused by the pressures of globalization, we must first establish a base against which we can judge the evidence of such convergence/transformation. In this chapter we set out the traditional German insider corporate governance model. We begin by examining the nineteenth century origins of the German corporate governance model and observe that it has not been based on the idea that managers act solely in the interests of shareholders. Labour co-determination, industry cross-shareholdings, family shareholding, state shareholding and bank shareholding indicate a strong insider bias to the corporate governance system. Externally a weak securities market, bank finance, deficient disclosure and minority shareholder protection rules, the absence of a market for corporate control and collusive relationships between companies are features of the traditional corporate governance system.

In all, managers within the traditional German corporate governance model have significant discretion upon which the major constraint is the interests of employees followed by the interests of families, banks, affiliated companies and the state, all sustained historically by a notion of long term commitment between the company and its various stakeholders. Thus, the German model of corporate governance has been based on the workable complementarity of its institutional components and has provided the foundations for a workable system which performed extremely well for most of the post war era and has achieved and maintained a high level of social welfare and cohesion. However, as the process of economic globalization picked up speed from the late 1980s onwards, greater pressures for change did start to emerge.

In Chapter 8 – *Economic Globalization and the German Insider Corporate Governance Model* – we examine the interaction between the forces of global corporate governance isomorphism and the traditional German corporate governance institutions described in Chapter 7. We examine in the first section how exposure to increased global and regional competition and the globalization of production created simultaneous pressures on management and labour. The result of this has been a formal protective path dependent reaction in Germany to strengthen co-determination, while at the same time the participants in the reinforced co-determined system have been engaged in introducing functional flexibility to reflect the weakened position of labour. Additionally developments at the EU level in the availability of the *Societas Europea* (SE), the *Centros* decision and the Lisbon 2010 agenda aimed at facilitating the single European market may have brought some formal erosion of co-determination and the introduction of a more flexible labour market. In all, co-determination has changed to accommodate a consensus in which labour is weaker in an increasingly global workplace. However, the institutions of co-determination, though altered, still remain a central part of the German system of corporate governance and significantly they are still highly valued by workers and the general public.

From the late 1980s onwards considerable reforms have taken place within the German financial system to enhance the role of securities markets in the mobilization of savings. As the liberalization of capital controls progressed over the 1980s the interaction between domestic and foreign financial markets through regulatory arbitrage, as Germany's largest companies and banks began to increasingly operate outside Germany, created a need to attempt a gradual reorienting of the German financial system to a more market oriented model necessary for *Finanzplatz Deutschland* ('Germany as a Financial Centre').

As a result of *Finanzplatz Deutschland*, capital gains tax changes, accountability and disclosure, insider dealing, prospectus requirements, pension reform, corporate law amendments, the introduction of a corporate governance code and accounting reforms have all clearly moved to introduce outsider oriented rules into the German corporate governance system or in the case of tax and shareholder voting changes, actively encourage insider disengagement. However, some of the reforms necessary to alter the German financial system created significant path dependent resistance. Takeover reform at both the EU and domestic level in the aftermath of the Vodafone/Mannesmann hostile takeover in 1999/2000, moved to allow management to protect themselves from hostile bids. Additionally, some of the outsider oriented reforms have not had the intended effect and may have operated to enhance managerial power and insider private rent extraction.

The most significant effects of the exposure of German companies to capital markets and the *Finanzplatz Deutschland* reforms has been on the shareholdings of German companies. The withdrawal of banks as liquidity providers and protectors of management has been a particular feature of the changes since the 1990s as the banks have stopped lending to German companies, sold their shares and given up their board positions. As some insiders have left, German institutional investors and foreign, mostly institutional, investors have taken their places. Private equity and hedge funds from the UK and US have also been buying stakes in medium and large German companies and have been emphasizing a shareholder oriented rather than a stakeholder approach to running those companies. However, a significant reaction by management to enhance their power, as banks have withdrawn, is evident in the increasing number of former managers on the supervisory board and attempts to find 'anchor' shareholders who are long-term investors. The stock market crash in 2001/2002, also seems to have had a damaging effect on an emerging equity culture as German institutional investors have been withdrawing between 2003 and 2007, while other blockholders, even banks, have been increasing their shareholdings. The upsurge in government, bank and non financial corporations' shareholdings between 2003 and 2007, may partly be a reflection of managers and labour seeking 'anchor' long-term shareholders and/or the enhanced ability of insiders to engage in private rent extraction. In all, over the past 20 years both functional and formal outsider norms have been introduced into the traditional German corporate governance model. There have though been significant path dependent reactions to these norms as well.

Whether the German insider corporate governance model is moving to or is transforming into an outsider system is a complex question that we consider in the final chapter.

In Chapter 9 – *The End of Globalization?* – we draw together our conclusions from the previous chapters and examine the future of globalization as a continuing agent of change. One of the features of our examination of change in the UK, US and Germany is that, in general, change within corporate governance sub-systems seems to be a constant process of stimuli and reaction within a complementary workable set of institutional sub-systems. However, as we discussed in Chapter 4, sometimes shocks to individual sub-systems or to the systems as a whole can align forces for change in a particular direction removing path dependent reactions and pushing it away from its original course. The interwar years in the UK culminating in the shock of WWII exerted transforming influence while in the US the combined shock of the 1929 crash and the Great Depression similarly caused a transformative reaction in the US. Successive economic shocks in the 1970s and early 1980s, brought about a period of unworkability for the corporate governance systems of the UK and US, as the government, labour and management consensus of the post war years broke down in the face of economic shock. The corporate governance system was then only capable of being transformed as the path dependent forces one would normally expect to resist severe change were overwhelmed by those successive shocks. This leaves us with two general observations which we explore further. First that the similarity of reaction in the UK and US in the 1980s, suggests to us, given our institutional critique, that shared institutions are playing a role in those reactions and second that diversity of reaction to similar economic pressures to change occurred in Germany.

While in a general sense diversity in reaction to change over time was the norm within the UK and the US, shared colonial history played a key role in transferring certain core econo-cultural values such as a mutual central respect for freedom of contract, protection of private property and arms length economic regulation. Over time, while the two countries have developed differing institutional sub-systems, the values upon which they were built were similar and were reinforced over the centuries by the strong trading relationship between the two countries. In terms of explaining why the UK and US react in such similar ways to shocks to their institutional structure over the course of the 1970s and 1980s, we consider that because these shared values form the background upon which formal institutions are embedded in both countries, economic institutions when faced with similar shocks end up with similar outcomes, because the values underlying the decision making in the realignment process were the same. In other words, the similar reaction of these two systems to shock is not likely to be transferable to the analysis of institutional change/transformation generally, as we consider that their shared institutional history has played a role in the common response to shock.

Indeed, diversity of reaction has been the German experience. In contrast to the UK and US over the 1970s and early 1980s Germany did not experience the dramatic shocks experienced by the UK and US, despite being exposed to the same events. Unemployment rose, but not near the levels of the UK and US and rampant inflation was not present, as the Bundesbank's historic emphasis on price stability was successful and the institutions of co-determination in the German insider model held wages down. By the 1990s as the process of globalization began to impact, co-determination came under severe pressure while securities market reforms and direct exposure by core companies to the global capital markets have introduced outsider norms into the traditional German insider model. The reactions to these changes have been interesting. Formal responses to the threat to co-determination have occurred to reinforce it, fear of hostile takeovers has spurred a formal protection of management and formal and functional reactions have occurred with regard to outsider based management incentives. One of the most significant changes has been the reaction of banks who have withdrawn from their traditional role as supporters of management and suppliers of liquidity, by selling their shares, giving up their board seats and ceasing to lend to client companies. The outsider reforms may not have had their intended effect as managerial power may have been enhanced by the withdrawal of the banks, in that management have been reacting by replacing the banks on the supervisory boards with former management and by seeking out anchor shareholders.

We consider this managerial reaction to be a crucial indicator of the rearrangements occurring within the German corporate governance model. The effects of the process of globalization in the 1990s and early twenty-first century, have weakened labour influence and caused banks to disengage at the same time as outsider shareholders have grown in number but are not yet a significant influence on management discretion. All this has enhanced management discretion. A reengaging of traditional insiders since 2003 also suggests that while the system has changed, the insider system is being reworked according to its internal logic and is not transforming into an outsider one. Of course that still leaves the possibility that the process of globalization could produce a future shock which does destabilize the system and because the system has already borne some of the adaptation costs of change, future transformation may cause less resistance from the forces of path dependent. We have reason to doubt this will occur in this form, as it is more likely that events bringing about the end of the current process of globalization could cause a destabilizing shock either moving Germany to a stronger insider system or to an outsider one.

Within the past decade the process of economic globalization has slowed and in 2008 the two pillars upon which it has been build, the liberalization of trade and capital markets, have been eroded by the collapse of the Doha trade talks and the sub prime and resultant global capital market crisis. Property crashes, runs on banks, nationalization and part nationalization of banks, massive coordinated government funding injecting liquidity into capital markets, IMF loans to fund nations in crisis and stock market crashes have all been features of the global economy since autumn 2008 as government intervention and demand management have swung back into vogue to prevent systemic collapse. Re-regulation of capital markets as a result of this experience with a new form of Bretton Woods Agreement to build a financial architecture to deal with unregulated capital markets seems likely as we write in early 2009. In turn as real introspection is brought to the process of increased liberalization and globalization of trade and capital markets, the legitimacy of the outsider shareholder model, designed by and for this process of globalization, also comes into question. In such a changed environment insider corporate governance models may come to be valued once more.

List of Abbreviations

ADR	American Depositary Receipts
AG	Aktiengesellschaft (German public corporation)
AGM	Annual General Meeting
AktG	Aktiengesetz (Stock Corporation Act)
AnSVG	Anlegerschutzverbesserungsgesetz (Act Improving the Protection of Investors)
APAG	Abschlussprüferaufsichtsgesetz (Accountants' Supervision Act)
APAK	Abschlussprüferaufsichtskommission (Accounting Supervisory Commission)
ASEAN	Association of Southeast Asian Nations
BA	British Aluminium
BaFin	Bundesastalt für Finanzdienstleistungsaufsich (Federal Financial Services Supervisory Institution)
BAWe	Bundesaufsichtsamt für den Wetpapierhandel (Federal Securities Trading Supervisory Office)
BBC	British Broadcasting Corporation
BEIC	British East India Company
BetrVerfReformG	Betriebsverfassungsreformgesetz (Works Council Reform Act)
BetrVG	Betriebsverfassungsgesetz (Enterprise Constitution Act)
BGH	Bundesgerichtshof (Federal Court of Justice)
BilKoG	Bilanzrechtskontrollgesetz (Accounting Control Act)
BilMoG	Bilanzrechtsmodernisierungsgesetz (Accounting Law Reform Act)
BilReG	Bilanzrechtsreformgesetz (Reform Act on Accounting Regulations)
BIS	Bank for International Settlements
BKartA	Bundeskartellamt (Federal Cartel Office)
BSK	Börsensachverständigenkommission (Commission of Stock Exchange Experts)
CalPERS	California Public Employees Retirement System
CDU	Christlich Demokratische Union (Christian Democratic Union)
CEO	Chief Executive Officer
CEPREMAP	Centre pour la recherché économique et ses applications
CME	Coordinated Market Economies
DAI	Deutsche Aktieninstitute

DAX	Deutscher Aktien Index (German stock index)
DCGK	Deutscher Corporate Governance Kodex
	(German Corporate Governance Code)
DGB	Deutscher Gewerkschafsbund
	(German Trade Union Federation)
DM	Deutsch Mark
DSW	Deutsche Schutzvereiningung für Wertpapierbesitz
	(Shareholder association)
DTB	Deutsche Terminbörse (German derivatives exchange)
EBLR	European Business Law Review
EC	European Community
ECB	European Central Bank
ECJ	European Court of Justice
EEC	European Economic Community
ERISA	Employment Retirement Income Securities Act
ESOP	Employee Stock Option Plan
ESRC	Economic and Social Research Council
EU	European Union
EUREX	European Exchange
FAO	Food Agricultural Organization
FDI	Foreign Direct Investment
GAAP	Generally Accepted Accounting Principles
GASB	German Accounting Standards Board
GATT	General Agreement on Tariffs and Trade
GDP	Gross Domestic Product
GmbH	Gesellschaft mit beschränkter Haftung
	(Large private limited liability companies in Germany)
GNP	Gross National Product
GWB	Gesetzgegen Wettbewebsbeschränkungen
	(Act against Restraints of Competition)
HGB	Handelsgesetzbuch (German commercial code)
IAEA	International Atomic Energy Agency
IAS	International Accounting Standards
IASB	International Accounting Standards Board
IBRD	International Bank for Reconstruction and Development
ICAO	International Civil Aviation Organization
IFRS	International Financial Reporting Standards
IG	Interessengemeinschaften (Pooling associations)
IMF	International Monetary Fund
IMO	International Maritime Organization
INSEAD	Institut Européen d'Administration des Affaires
IPO	Initial Public Offering
IZA	Institute for the Study of Labor

KAGG	Gesetz über Kapitalanlagegesellschaften
	(Investment Company Act)
KapAEG	Kapitalaufnahmeerleichterungsgesetz
	(Facilitation of Capital Raising Act)
KapInhaG	Kapitalmarktinformationschaftungsgesetz
	(Capital Market Information Liability Act)
KapMuG	Kapitalanleger-Musterverfahrensgesetz
	(Law on Example Procedures for Investor Suits)
KonTraG	Gesetz zur Kontrolle und Transparenz in Unternehmensbereich
	(Act on Control and Transparency in the Enterprise Sector)
LME	Liberal Market Economies
LSE	London Stock Exchange
LTCM	Long-Term Capital Management
M&A	Mergers and Acquisitions
MBA	Master of Business Administration
MC	Marginal Cost
MiFID	Markets in Financial Instruments Directive
MitbestG	Mitbestimmungsgesetz (Co-determination Act)
MNE	Multinational Enterprise
MP	Member of Parliament
MR	Marginal Revenue
NAFTA	North American Free Trade Agreement
NAIRU	Non-Accelerating Inflation Rate of Unemployment
NAPF	National Association of Pension Funds
NBER	National Bureau of Economic Research
NI	Northern Ireland
NLRB	National Labor Relations Board
NUM	National Union of Mineworkers
NYSE	New York Stock Exchange
OECD	Organization for Economic Co-operation and Development
OPEC	Organization of Petroleum Exporting Countries
PATCO	Professional Association of Air Traffic Controllers
PEP	Personal Equity Plan
PLC	Public Limited Company
RIETE	Research Institute of Economy Trade and Industry
SE	Societas Europea
SEC	Securities and Exchange Commission
SOFFEX	Swiss Options and Financial Futures Exchange
SPD	Sozialdemokratische Partei Deutschland
	(Social Democratic Party of Germany)
SSRN	Social Sciences Research Network
TESSA	Tax-Exempt Special Savings Account
TNC	Transnational Corporation

TransPuG	Transparenz- und Publizität Gesetz (Transparency and Disclosure Act)
TUG	Transparenzrichtlinie-Umsetzungsgesetz (Act for the Implementation of the Transparency Directive)
UBG	Venture capital firms
UK	United Kingdom
UMAG	Gesetz zur Unternehmensintegritat und Mondernisierung des Anfechtungsrechts (Act on the Improvement of Corporate Integrity and on the Modernization of the Regime)
UN	United Nations
UNCTAD	United Nations Conference on Trade and Development
UNESCO	United Nations Economic, Scientific and Cultural Organization
US	United States
USA	United States of America
USSR	Union of Soviet Socialist Republics
Ver.di	Vereinigte Dienstleistungsgewerkschaft (United Services Union)
VorstOG	Vorstandsvergütungs-Offenlegungsgesetzes (Vorstand Remuneration Disclosure Act)
WB	World Bank
WHO	World Health Organization
WMO	World Meteorological Organization
WpHG	Wertpapierhandelsgesetz (Securities Trading Act)
WpÜG	Wertpapiererwerbs- und Übernahmegesetz (Securities Acquisition and Takeover Act)
WTO	World Trade Organization
WWI	World War I
WWII	World War II
WZB	Wissenschaftszentrum Berlin für Sozialforschung (Social Science Research Center Berlin)

PART 1
Theorizing Corporate Governance Change

Chapter 1

Corporate Governance Convergence and Corporate Theory

Introduction to the Corporate Theory Debate

In this first chapter we attempt something both difficult and necessary – an overview of the major influences on the development of corporate theory. This is difficult because it involves distilling centuries of thought and numerous complex theories into a few pages. It is necessary because, as we will observe in Chapters 5 and 6, theory and subsequent change in the corporate governance systems of the US and the UK are closely linked. Additionally as we noted in the preface the theoretical approach of convergence scholars forms a large part of the assumptions they bring to their comparative work. So we start this chapter with a 'health warning' – while hopefully the following section provides an accessible overview of the progression of corporate theory over the past 200 years it is not complete or simple. In order to give it form we emphasize major influences and ignore minor ones even though they may have been important in their time. Where there is a choice of theorists to discuss we have chosen the one whose work we think epitomizes the theory best. Where we discuss a theory it is just an overview of its major contribution to corporate theory and not a complete description. This also applies to our theoretical discussions in other chapters. However, before we turn to the theoretical overview we need briefly to describe some key practical developments in corporate history that relate to our theoretical context.

The Emergence of the Managerial Firm[1]

In the eighteenth and nineteenth centuries despite the existence of few large joint stock companies created to promote foreign trade and colonization or to manage some utilities, all major economies were dominated by unincorporated business forms owned and controlled by individuals. The volume of firms' operations was

---

1 We use the terms 'corporation' and 'firm' interchangeably here as we will be examining economic theories of the firm later in this chapter and economists use the more generic term 'firm' which includes all types of production organizations irrespective of their legal nature.

limited and owners were generally able to manage their businesses.² As Bratton notes:

> [v]ery little tension arose between economic practice and individualist economic and legal theory in the early nineteenth century. The economy closely resembled the atomistic type described in Adam Smith's classical theory.³

Therefore, the managers of the firm could easily be regarded as its owners and *vice versa*.

During the nineteenth century the enactment of general incorporation statutes dispensed with the need for special state corporate charters and made the creation of incorporated companies much easier. Gradually, what Chandler has called the 'traditional enterprise' began to be replaced as a business form by the incorporated company.⁴ Initially, incorporated companies were still 'entrepreneurial' in their nature. Ownership and control were integrated since the owners of shares were also the managers of the company's business without the need for extra managerial input. Segregated economies, small productions and slow movement of goods generally meant that the operational workload was still manageable by the entrepreneurs themselves. So the use of salaried managers was minimal and even where it occurred those managers were acting under the guidance of the owner–entrepreneur.

The first big change came during the second industrial revolution at the end of the nineteenth century, with the emergence in the US and Europe of large infrastructure and utility ventures like the railways, the telegraph, and mining companies. These ventures could only be undertaken by large corporations run not by owners–entrepreneurs but by extensive salaried managerial hierarchies who provided very little capital. The finance for such large capital intensive projects was only available by pooling the funds of thousands of investors and financiers. The owners of stock had neither the knowledge nor the power to administer these pioneers of 'big business'.⁵ As Chandler, states:

---

2   Chandler, A. (1977) The Visible Hand: The Managerial Revolution in American Business, Cambridge, MA: Belknap Press of Harvard University Press, 14; and Berend, T. (2006) An Economic History of Twentieth Century Europe, Cambridge: Cambridge University Press.

3   Bratton, W. (1989) 'The New Economic Theory of the Firm: Critical Perspectives From History', Stanford Law Review, vol. 41, 1471 at 1483. Adam Smith famously observed that while 'a businessman intends only his gain, he is led by an invisible hand to promote an end which is not his intention'. See Smith, A. (1976) An Inquiry into the Nature and Causes of the Wealth of the Nations, in Campbell, R., Skinner, A. and Todd, W. (eds) Oxford: Clarendon Press, 456.

4   See Chandler, A., above n2, Chapters 1 and 2.

5   Adam Smith, himself acknowledged that in the early joint stock companies of the eighteenth century the involvement of shareholders in management was an imaginary presumption rather than a reality. The manager-controlled corporation was at that time an exception to the rule of integrated ownership and control. See Smith, A., above n3, 741.

[t]he building and operating of the rail and telegraph systems called for the creation of a new type of business enterprise. The massive investment required to construct those systems and the complexities of their operations brought the separation of ownership from management. The enlarged enterprises came to be operated by teams of salaried managers who had little or no equity in the firm. The owners, numerous and scattered, were investors with neither the experience, the information, nor the time to make the myriad decisions needed to maintain a constant flow of goods, passengers, and messages. Thousands of shareholders could not possibly operate a railroad or a telegraph system.[6]

Thus, the first management controlled or 'managerial', as they are commonly called, companies emerged as one of the by-products of the second industrial revolution. The significance of this development is twofold. First, these managerial corporations provided a previously non-existent managerial and administrative know-how, such as accounting and statistical controls, which emerged as the basis for modern business. The second contribution was the creation of the transportation and communication infrastructure that created the opportunities for mass production in many other industries that transformed the nature of capitalism – from classical to 'managerial' – and of markets – from rural, agrarian and commercial to industrial and urban. Fast and large volume transportation, created large integrated markets which presented vast opportunities for industrial growth in scale and scope.[7]

These growth opportunities that emerged from the enlarged markets and changing technologies during the late nineteenth and early twentieth century demanded new organizational structures similar to those that had been developed by railway companies. In the 1890s and early 1900s intense merger activity in the United States and to a lesser extent in Germany resulted in the dilution of the original entrepreneurs' stock ownership. Similar developments also occurred in Britain and Japan but at a slower pace which accelerated after World War II. By the 1940s commentators such as Burnham were claiming that this 'managerial revolution' would give rise to a new 'ruling class' of managers.[8] This dominance over industrialized economies led Chandler to claim that the 'visible hand' of the managerial hierarchy had come to replace Adam Smith's 'invisible hand' of the market.[9] Thus, the giant managerial corporation emerged, first in the United States and Germany and later in Britain and Japan, as the dominant economic player of the twentieth century.

---

6   Chandler, A. (1990) *Scale and Scope: The Dynamics of Industrial Capitalism*, Cambridge, MA: Belknap Press of Harvard University, 1.

7   Ibid.

8   Burnham, J. (1941) *The Managerial Revolution: What is Happening in the World Now*, New York: John Day.

9   See Chandler, A., above n2.

Differences of course did exist as each version of managerial capitalism reflected national institutional sets and historical events that also determined the time when the separation of ownership from control took place. Such national differences, according to Chandler, give rise to a distinction between 'competitive' and 'cooperative' managerial capitalism.[10] The US is an example of the former as the early prohibition of cartels, on the one hand, constrained close inter-firm cooperation and made merger combinations more attractive and, on the other, it enhanced competition between the large oligopolistic corporations that ensued. In contrast, as we will examine in Chapters 5 and 7, in the UK and Germany, cartelization was not illegal – at least not before the end of World War II – and consequently intra-firm cooperation was common in the home market, although in Germany's case competition between German companies was intense in the international market.[11] Additionally, in the somewhat peculiar case of Japan, manager controlled firms were allowed to cooperate closely by forming extensive group networks, but competition between those groups has been very aggressive both at home and abroad.[12]

Despite those differences, the common denominator in major capitalist economies has been the managerial corporation with *de facto* separation of corporate ownership from control. Obviously, this major socio-economic development did not go unnoticed. Keynes for example observed this practical departure from economic classicism in 1926 when he wrote that shareholders had dissociated themselves from company management.[13] However, the milestone work on the separation of ownership and control came from Berle and Means, a lawyer and an economist respectively. In 1932 they published *The Modern Corporation and Private Property* which was the first systematic study of corporate control in the United States.[14]

Berle and Means assumed that corporate control derives from the ability to select and appoint directors since the board of directors is the main decision-making body of the corporation. Their study of ownership structure of American corporations showed that shareholdings were so dispersed as to preclude shareholders from having sufficient interest in exercising their control rights over management. According to their analysis, 65 percent of the largest two hundred

---

10   See Chandler, A., above n6, 12.

11   Wengenroth, U. (1999) 'Germany: Competition Abroad – Cooperation at Home: 1870–1990' in Chandler et al. (eds) Big Business and the Wealth of Nations, Cambridge: Cambridge University Press, 139–175.

12   Morikawa, H. (1999) 'Japan: Increasing Organizational Capabilities of Large Industrial Enterprises, 1880s–1980s' in Chandler et al. (eds) Big Business and the Wealth of Nations, Cambridge: Cambridge University Press.

13   Keynes, J. (1931) 'The End of Laissez-Faire' in Essays in Persuasion, London: Macmillan, 314–315.

14   Berle, A. and Means, G. (1932) The Modern Corporation and Private Property, New York: Harcourt [revised edition, 1968].

American corporations were manager-controlled, which in their view signified the *de facto* separation of ownership and control.[15]

However, in most other countries the shareholding pattern is rather different than the US even for large firms. In both Germany and Japan, for instance, ownership has historically been much more concentrated, as banks, families, the state and, most importantly, other non -financial corporations are large shareholders. This could lead one to assume that due to these ownership patterns the separation of ownership and control thesis has *prima facie* no relevance.[16] However, the separation of ownership from control can occur in these insider systems through different means. A company with concentrated ownership can come within the managerial category due to the identity of its large shareholders, if the latter are not interested in controlling managers. For instance, as we note in Chapter 7 extensive cross-shareholding networks in Germany have this very effect since they are used as a shield against control oriented shareholders' influence. But even where families are still present in large companies, their ability to direct company affairs can be substantially reduced by the scale of operations that demands the delegation of control to a large managerial hierarchy. As Veblen noted in 1924 there had by necessity been a gradual transfer of corporate control from capitalistic owners to engineer-managers who had objectives that were different from those of owners.[17] Thus, concentrated shareholdings do not automatically imply the integration of corporate ownership and control.

The assertions of Berle and Means were not entirely original. Over a century earlier Adam Smith himself had made a similar observation about the joint stock companies of his time when he wrote:

> [t]he directors of such companies, however, being the managers rather of other people's money than of their own, it cannot well be expected, that they should watch over it with the same anxious vigilance with which the partners in a private copartnery frequently watch over their own.[18]

However, what made *The Modern Corporation and Private Property* a milestone was that, unlike in the eighteenth century, by 1932 the managerial corporation had emerged as a significant force in society, instead of being the exception to the rule. As Berle and Means explained:

> [a] society in which production is governed by blind economic forces is being replaced by one in which production is carried on under the ultimate control of

---

15 Ibid., 110. We discuss this period in US history further in Chapter 5.

16 See for example Pettet, B. (2000) Company Law, London: Longman, 55 and 59.

17 Veblen, T. (1924) The Theory of the Leisure Class: An Economic Study of Institutions, London: Allen & Unwin; and Veblen, T. (1921) The Engineers and the Price System, New York: Harcourt, Brace & World, 28.

18 See Smith, A., above n3, 741.

a handful of individuals. The economic power in the hands of few persons who control giant corporations can harm or benefit a multitude of individuals, affect whole districts, shift the currents of trade, bring ruin to one community and prosperity to another.[19]

As a result, the Berle and Means thesis not only gave a new spin to an old legal theory debate on the nature of the corporation but also attracted the interest of economic theorists. Both lawyers and economists searched for a solution to the problems of corporate legitimacy that the managerial corporation raised. The former examined the social legitimacy of managerial power over companies and the latter looked for the economic efficiency implications of the separation of ownership from control.

The Development of Corporate Theory

The corporation and its governance had been the subject matter of academic debate even before the rise of the managerial firm as the dominant economic actor in major economies. Incorporation and corporate personality raised legal and economic efficiency questions that gained importance as the company became a more common business form. As the following discussion will show, understanding the nature of the corporation is by no means a straightforward task. Different theoretical approaches can lead in a general sense either to viewing the corporation as being a real entity or as a pure fiction. These two perceptions of the corporation can broadly be categorized as corporate realism and nominalism respectively.

The choice between corporate realism and nominalism has important implications for corporate governance, because our views about the nature of the company reflect how we comprehend the concept of corporate ownership and its relation to control. If, for example, a company is a real person it has its own interests separate from the shareholders and the question moves to how to define those interests. However, if the nominalist approach is followed, the corporation resembles a legal object. As such, it has no rights or duties and can be owned by real persons who are vested with the corporate control rights in order to serve their own needs.

Legal theories of the corporation

During the early formative years of corporate law the theoretical debate essentially concerned the origins of the new business form and only indirectly its nature. What theorists looked for was the source from which the right for corporations to exist derived. The origins of the corporation can be traced in the Roman *societas*,

---

19   See Berle, A. and Means, G., above n14, 46.

an association of persons with a common purpose, and the medieval canon law which allowed religious foundations to incorporate as legal *personae fictae* in order to receive and own property as a mechanism for tax avoidance. These were the first forms of incorporated bodies with some legal capacity as persons, though not natural ones. Contract was the basis of such legally recognized bodies as it was for forms that evolved later such as common law partnerships and the civil law *société en commendite*, the ancestors of the incorporated company.[20] The existence of those bodies depended on the private initiative of individuals who were free to draft association agreements. This led to the belief that the very existence of corporations too derived from contracts between natural persons who could thus create fictitious persons with legal capacity.[21] In other words, the basis of the corporation's existence were contractual relationships between private individuals.

However, this contractual view was not left unchallenged. Until well into the nineteenth century full incorporation could not take place unless a special charter was granted by statute or decree. Such privileges conferred by the sovereign or the state were commercially exploited in the sixteenth century when the corporate form was used for the expansion of foreign trade and colonization or for the creation of national monopolies in utilities, transport, finance, etc. The state was heavily involved in the incorporation process. That is, for associations of individuals to become legal persons a concession from the state was necessary. Thus, according to this 'concession' theory the origins of the corporation lay in the regulatory power of the state rather than in the private initiative of contracting individuals.[22]

Concession theory was very influential so long as the state's participation in each and every incorporation was necessary. That was to change considerably with the adoption of general incorporation statutes. These instruments turned the act of incorporation into a private right rather than a privilege, since no special charter grants by the state were necessary any longer. Thus, with the enactment of general company statutes the state's micro-level involvement was transformed into macro-level regulation. The most important illustration of this is that the state gave up the power to designate what the objectives of a corporation would be as corporate charters were, and still are, drafted by and according to the needs of the private individuals applying to form the company. All the state can do to exert its influence is to formulate general macro-level rules that define the boundaries of corporators' freedom to draft charters.

20　Buckland, W. and McNair, A. (1965) Roman Law and Common Law: A Comparison in Outline, Cambridge: Cambridge University Press, 300–301.

21　Jacobson, A. (1980) 'The Private Use of Public Authority: Sovereignty and Associations in the Common Law', Buffalo Law Review, vol. 29, 599 at 662–63; Stokes, J. (1986) 'Company Law and Legal Theory' in Twining, W. (ed.) Legal Theory and the Common Law, Oxford: Blackwell Publishers, 162; and Angell, J. and Ames, S. (1846) A Treatise on the Law of Private Corporations Aggregate, 3rd edition, Boston: Little, Brown, 36.

22　Million, D. (1990) 'Theories of the Corporation', Duke Law Journal, 201 at 206.

Despite this change, concession theory has not entirely lost its relevance since incorporation is still based upon the enactment of company laws by the state.[23] In other words, the right of incorporation is still granted by the state. Thus the presence of general company laws may not necessarily imply a decrease of state influence. Indeed, some have argued that the state has had a dominant role even after the shift of incorporation regulation from the micro to the macro-level.[24]

In sum, by looking at who the actual corporators are, both concession and contract theories attempt to explain the origins of the corporation. The former contends that the state is the key corporator, while the latter tends to project the associated individuals who formed the company. Both theories have an inherent legitimation element in that they provide justifications for or against state influence on private individuals' ability to form corporate bodies. However, although their primary focus is on the corporators, these legitimation attempts also entail indirect implications about the nature of the company. Concession theory's centrality of law in the formation of a company strips the latter of any real, natural existence. The corporation is thus a mere construct of the mind and exists *artificially* simply because the law says so.

Due to these implications the concession approach has been associated with the 'fiction' theory which attempts to describe the company's nature rather than its origins. The most prominent exponent of this theory was the German Romanist Friedrich Karl von Savigny. His initial contention was that a legal relationship could only exist between persons as subjects.[25] However, in order for such a relationship to take place the persons involved should recognize each other as capable of assuming the role of a legal subject. Having established this as his starting point, Savigny then went on to determine who or what can be such a person. Firstly, he contended that humans should fall within the definition of a person because, due to their real corporeal existence, they can be recognized as the subjects in a legal relationship *naturally*. He then distinguished such human persons from numerous others that are recognized in law as persons but which are not real as they do not exist naturally. Such entities, according to Savigny, can also be legal subjects, or legal persons, but only because the law makes them so. The law gives them those attributes that allow them to be recognized as subjects in

---

23   Foster, N. (2000) 'Company Law Theory in Comparative Perspective: England and France', American Journal of Comparative Law, vol. 48, 573 at 583.

24   Hazen, T. (1991) 'The Corporate Persona, Contract (and Market) Failure, and Moral Values', North Carolina Law Review, vol. 69, 273, 297–298 for instance claims that, even though corporate charters were not created by the state, tight regulatory constraints on corporate activity gave a public element to company law. Similarly, see Millon, D., above n22, 211 who writes that 'extensive regulation indicated a conception of corporate law as public law'.

25   Von Savigny, F. (1884) Jural Relations: or, The Roman Law of Persons as Subjects of Jural Relations: Being a Translation of the Second Book of Savigny's System of Modern Roman Law, Rattigan, W. (transl.), London: Wiley & Sons, 1.

legal relations. Thus, such legal persons exist merely as fictitious ones rather than naturally and only with the essential contemplation of law.

Following this line of thought, the corporate entity, lacking a natural existence, falls within this second type of person. Thus, according to Savigny, the corporation is an entity that has an existence of its own which is distinct from its corporators but only as a fictitious legal person rather than as a natural being. It can effectively be a subject in legal relations and it is also recognized as such by other persons, but this is so only with the assistance of the law. As Iwai explains:

> the corporate personality is an inter-subjective concept which has been introduced into the legal system as a legal device to simplify the web of contractual relations between a group of individuals and a multiple of outside parties.[26]

Thus, the law appears to be a core element in the fiction theory as it is in concession theory. It is because of this observation that the two theories have been largely merged.[27] Since, according to concession theory, the corporation is a mere legal creation, it must only be an artificial construct, a fiction.

Although fiction theory attempts to define the nature of the corporate entity, its explanatory power regarding the relationship between ownership and control is minimal. Although it recognizes that a corporation can exist as an entity *in law*, it fails to determine the exact nature of this entity's relationship with the corporators. Thus, fiction theory's normative usefulness is more apparent in explaining the role of the state in corporate governance. Since the law is vital for the corporate entity's existence as a person, the state, being the main promoter of the law, can have an important interest and influence in corporate activity.[28] However there may be an indirect implication from this. If the state does have an influence this is to the detriment of the corporators' freedom to create associations without state interference. Thus, the corporate control role of corporators is weighted against the role of the state. In other words, there is a weighting between statism and nominalism in favour of statism.

Nevertheless, for the same reasons that the concession theory lost much of its significance with the decline of the state's chartering authority, the fiction theory's

---

26   Iwai, K. (1999) 'Persons, Things and Corporations: The Corporate Personality Controversy and Comparative Corporate Governance', American Journal of Comparative Law, vol. 47, 583 at 603.

27   Although this merging is not without controversy, see Maitland's criticisms in Gierke, O. (1900) 'Political Theories of the Middle Age' in Maitland, J. (transl. and ed.), Cambridge: Cambridge University Press, xxi; and Phillips, M. (1994) 'Reappraising the Real Entity Theory of the Corporation', Florida State University Law Review, vol. 21, 1061 at 1064.

28   See Phillips, M., above n27, 1082.

assertions about the nature of the company also lost ground to other less statist ones. These were the aggregate and corporate realism theories.[29]

The former is in fact based upon the contract theory presented above. It was originally developed by nineteenth century European theorists such as, von Jhering[30] and de Vareilles-Sommieres,[31] who shared a different view about the nature of the corporation founded on the individual freedom to form contractual associations without any state interference. The basis of the aggregate theory is the premise that human beings, being the only 'real' persons, have the ability to be legal subjects and have rights naturally without the prior operation of law. One such natural right is the freedom to establish contractual relations with each other in order to form business associations. Thus, corporations are seen as associations that are formed by aggregates of individuals and are comprised of the contractual relations between those individuals. The company being an aggregate of contracts becomes neither a real entity nor an artificial legal person independent of its members. In fact, as the corporate entity disappears completely from the picture – any corporate rights, duties or interests are in fact those of the corporators themselves.[32] By denying the corporation any 'real' existence separate from its members, aggregate theory represents the pure 'nominalist' view of the corporation. Viewed in this way the corporation is seen as something very similar to the contractual relationship between partners in a partnership.[33]

The normative implications of aggregate theory are very important from a corporate governance perspective. Firstly, by identifying the company with the contracting shareholders it legitimizes the norm of shareholder supremacy in corporate decision-making. Since there is no real and distinct corporate entity, it is the shareholders' interests, rights and duties, as expressed in the corporate contracts that need to be observed and enforced. Although later versions[34] of the theory have included other non-shareholder contractual relations e.g. of creditors, managers, and of other company officers, shareholders have generally been regarded as the core constituency.[35] This theoretical model fits the middle nineteenth century economic reality well as this period was characterized by stable concentrated ownership and small companies controlled by their shareholders. The

29   These theories are also known as group theory and real entity theory respectively. It should be noted here that corporate realism should be distinguished from the 'realist' movement in general legal theory.

30   von Jhering, R. (1913) Der Zweck im Recht (Law as a Means to an End), available at <http://socserv2.mcmaster.ca/~econ/ugcm/3ll3/ihering/LawMeansEnd.pdf>.

31   De Vareilles-Sommières, G. (1919) Les Personnes Morales, Paris: F. Pichon et Durant-Auzias.

32   Morawetz, V. (1886) A Treatise on the Law of Corporations, 2nd edition, Boston: Little, Brown, 2.

33   Schane, S. (1987) 'The Corporation is a Person: The Language of a Legal Fiction', Tulane Law Review, vol. 61, 563 at 568.

34   See the discussion on economic theories later in this chapter.

35   See Phillips, M., above n27, 1066.

second important implication stemming from aggregate theory concerns the role of the state. Since, as stated above, the corporation is formed by contract between private individuals, the state automatically becomes an outsider with no legitimate influence. Thus, nominalist theorists have been opposed to government regulation of corporate activity since that would be contrary to the principle of individual freedom of contract.

Around the end of the nineteenth century the aggregate theory began to lose its normative influence.[36] The emergence of the large managerial firm with a constantly fluctuating and fragmented ownership, as well as the reality of limited liability, did not sit well with the aggregate model. The identification of the corporation with its members was increasingly untenable.[37] It seemed that as companies were getting larger the influence of shareholders was diminishing and the corporation was acquiring a separate life of its own, this time as a real entity. Moreover, the corporation was losing its contractual nature in a legal sense as the judiciary confirmed the 'reality' of corporate personality and shareholders were automatically deemed bound by the articles of association.[38] As Hazen and others have argued, the consent requirement for the creation of a legally binding contract could not be realistically fulfilled in the case of large managerial firms with distant relationships with their shareholders.[39] An alternative theory not based on contractual considerations could accommodate these changes with more ease. Such an alternative was provided by corporate realism.

The main advocate of corporate realism was the German scholar Otto von Gierke, who viewed the corporation as an entity which was completely independent from its members.[40] The difference from Savigny's assertions was that Gierke's entity was not a legal fiction but a real person. The argument was that in all societies when individuals join together into groups and associations there is a trade off between individualism and collectivism. That is, in order for a group to persist, the individual has to make sacrifices. When this happens, the group's interests can be no longer identified with those of the individual *ante* association. Instead, the group acquires a will and goals of its own which do not necessarily fluctuate with membership changes. In fact, the opposite may be the most common situation; the individual will usually have to adapt in order to join the association. In this process the prescriptions of the law are irrelevant. Legal recognition is not necessary for the associated group's real existence to be established. Maitland's

---

36   See Bratton, W., above n3, 1490.

37   See Machen, A. (1910–1911) 'Corporate Personality', Harvard Law Review, vol. 24, 253 at 259, who claims and mathematically attempts to prove that 'any group whose membership is changing, is necessarily an entity separate and distinct from the constituent members'.

38   *Salomon v. Salomon & Co. Ltd.* (1896) [1897] A.C. 22 (H.L.); and Dignam, A. and Lowry, J. (2008) Company Law, Oxford: Oxford University Press, Chapter 8.

39   See Hazen, T., above n24, 299–302.

40   See Gierke, O., above n27.

description of the corporation in his introduction to the translated version of Gierke's work illustrates this:

> [The corporation is] no fiction, no symbol, no piece of the State's machinery, no collective name for individuals, but a living organism and a real person, with body and members and a will of its own. Itself can will, itself can act; it wills and acts by the men who are its organs as a man wills and acts by brain, mouth and hand.[41]

The normative value of these assertions is obvious since corporate realism provides theoretical legitimacy to managerial power. Being a real entity, the corporation can have its own interests and duties separately from its members, it can own property and employ a workforce, but most importantly it cannot itself be owned, just as all other real persons cannot. As a result there is a differentiation between corporate property and shareholder property. Shareholders cannot be regarded as the owners of the company and so it is not run solely for their benefit. Instead the corporate entity defines its own objectives and uses all its available inputs to achieve them through its officers. Consequently, the shareholder supremacy norm advanced by the aggregate theory loses its validity. All this fits well the managerialist paradigm, and so it is not surprising that corporate realism became dominant with the emergence of the managerial firm.[42] However, with regard to the role of the state corporate realism is somewhat contradictory. While Gierke and his followers were prepared to advocate for more regulation in order to ascribe a public character to the corporation, others used corporate realism to deny any state involvement in what they saw as strictly private bodies.[43]

The theory has two major flaws. The first is that, although it offers plausible arguments about the existence of the firm as a real entity, it stops short of attempting to define the nature of the corporate entity's interests. This is, in fact, one of the aggregate theory's strengths since it precisely defines the corporate interests by identifying them with those of the shareholders. Realism convincingly refutes this assertion, but it does so by creating an uncertainty. In effect there is a shift of the theoretical uncertainty from the company's nature to the company's interest.

The second flaw derives from the realist assumption that the corporate person is similar to the human person, in that they both seek to achieve their objectives without any internal tensions or conflicts of interest. In other words, officers such as managers and other employees, being the company's organs, are treated as an integral part of the corporate entity and have no will, interests or objectives

---

41   Ibid., xxvi. In the original text as translated by Maitland, Gierke uses the term 'German Fellowship'.

42   See Bratton, W., above n3, 1490–1493.

43   Hager, M. (1989) 'Bodies Politic: The Progressive History of Organizational "Real Entity" Theory', *University of Pittsburgh Law Review*, vol. 50, 575 at 630–632. See also Dodd's approach below, n45.

of their own. They only act in accordance to the corporate will – whatever that may be? Consequently, the realist model excludes the possibility of opportunistic behaviour on the part of any of the individuals involved with the corporation either as members or as officers. Although plausible in an ideal world, this premise is hardly sustainable in reality. Individuals even within the structure of commercial associations do not subject their self-interest to the common objective unless the two somehow coincide. Thus, even if one could define the corporate interest with precision, corporate realism does not provide any support for the assertion that they will be promoted by the company's organs, which are usually identified with management. Inherently an accountability problem arises.

Despite these flaws, the economic success of managerial capitalism remained largely undisputed for several decades, as did the justifications provided for it by corporate realism. However, this temporarily changed with the Great Depression.[44] It was in such a context of severe economic downturn that Berle and Means presented their thesis about the separation of ownership from control and the rise of unconstrained managerial power. These realizations pressed for answers to the problems of corporate realism presented above and sparked the famous debate between Adolf Berle himself and his fellow law professor Merrick Dodd. They summed up the essence of the issue in the question 'for whom are corporate managers trustees?'[45]

In his attempt to answer this question Dodd followed a novel pluralist approach as he sought to expand the theory of corporate realism to include corporate social responsibility. He accepted that the corporation is a real entity distinct from its shareholders but similar to any other real person that entity has a social role and should be subjected to the principles of citizenship. Thus, in the case of corporate citizens, purely economic self-interest, i.e. profit-maximization, may be subjected to other social objectives. The adoption of a realist stance is crucial for the plausibility of this assertion. Thus, when Dodd detached the corporate interest from shareholder interests, corporate social responsibility could be inserted. The implication from this is that social objectives can be integrated into the corporate interest so that ultimately there should be a balance between the two.

Having dealt with the definitional problem of the corporate interests in this manner, Dodd was then able to engage upon the accountability issue. Once again the theoretical basis for his claims was provided by corporate realism. Since

---

44   Galbraith, for instance, identified 'bad corporate structure' as one of the causes of the 1929 crash: Galbraith, J. (1961) *The Great Crash 1929*, London: Penguin and H. Hamilton, 183.

45   See Dodd, E. (1932) 'For Whom are Corporate Managers Trustees?', *Harvard Law Review*, vol. 45, 1145; Dodd, E. (1935) 'Is Effective Enforcement of the Fiduciary Duties of Corporate Managers Practicable?', *University of Chicago Law Review*, vol. 2, 194; Berle, A. (1932) 'For Whom are Corporate Managers Trustees: A Note', *Harvard Law Review*, vol. 45, 1365; and Berle, A. (1931) 'Corporate Powers as Powers in Trust', *Harvard Law Review*, vol. 44, 1049.

managers of large corporations had to discharge their duties in accordance with a socially responsible entity that is distinct from its shareholders, they should also be expected to have 'a sense of social responsibility toward employees, consumers, and the general public'.[46] In other words, Dodd's answer to the debate's question was that managers are trustees for the corporation as a socially responsible person rather than for the shareholders as Berle believed.[47]

Dodd's pluralist approach is very important from a corporate governance perspective because it entails ramifications for the nature of ownership and its relationship with control. Similarly to Gierke's realism, share ownership is distanced from the concept of control since the corporation pursues its own objectives and not those of its shareholders. By directing the element of management accountability towards the corporation as an independent entity the shareholders' aggregate is stripped of its control function. Therefore, Dodd provides a clear justification for the separation of ownership from control. The concept of shareholder supremacy legitimized by the aggregate theory loses its influence as managers can pursue goals that may even contradict it in order to achieve the principal corporate and social objectives. Moreover, although the original version of corporate realism was often used to oppose state regulation of corporate activity, Dodd's approach is different.[48] As Millon observed:

> [Dodd's] objective was a legal regime that encouraged managers to use their broad powers not only for the benefit of shareholders, employees, and other participants in the corporation's activities but also for the good of the general public [...] Here then was an argument for a public law of corporations [...] Far from assuring the triumph of big business, the natural entity theory itself contained implications that critics relied on to attack the large corporation's new-found position of privileged economic power.[49]

Dodd's corporate social responsibility argument had many strengths which were also recognized by Berle and Means who, in *The Modern Corporation and Private Property*, recognized in principle the possibility and desirability of a solution based upon a pluralist approach similar to Dodd's with:

> a purely neutral technocracy, balancing a variety of claims by various groups in the community and assigning to each a portion of the income stream on the basis of public policy rather than private cupidity.[50]

---

46   See Dodd, E. (1932), above n45.

47   Ibid., 1161.

48   Horwitz, M. (1985) 'Santa Clara Revisited: The Development of Corporate Theory', West Virginia Law Review, vol. 88, 173 at 221.

49   See Millon, D., above n22, 220.

50   See Berle, A. and Means, G., above n14, 356.

In practice, however, Berle felt that such a solution entailed hidden accountability weaknesses because of the lack of an effective enforcement mechanism. His concern was that the amorphousness of the beneficiaries' interests in the pluralist model diluted managerial accountability and granted managers more unconstrained power. In his reply to Dodd's proposition, Berle promoted the idea of a narrowly defined accountability mechanism with managers being trustees for the shareholders rather than the company itself.[51] In this way he assimilated the corporate interest with the shareholders' wealth maximization objective by disregarding the insights of corporate realism. In fact, though not expressly stated, underlining Berle's minimalist analysis is a version of the aggregate theory which also comprises a contractual relationship between shareholders and managers. Under that contract, the former entrusted their private property to the latter. The only issue to be dealt with is that of ensuring the enforcement of this contract by enhancing managerial accountability to the shareholders. Conceived in this way the corporation loses all the public characteristics attributed to it by Dodd's version of corporate realism and becomes an aggregation of private (shareholder) interests. Consequently, the legitimation arguments for corporate social responsibility collapse in favour of the shareholder supremacy principle as an expression of individualism.

In sum, the debate between Dodd and Berle transformed the old legal debate on the nature of the corporation by placing the focus on the legitimacy of managerial power and the role of corporations in society. Although both theorists have as their staring point the *de facto* separation of share ownership from control, their final propositions are antithetical. Dodd welcomed the ostracism of the shareholder from the centre of corporate control in order to give way to the possibility of 'socializing' the corporate entity. On the other hand, for practical reasons Berle regarded the rise of managerial power as a danger to society and sought to find mechanisms to bridge the accountability vacuum, as he saw it, which exists in the managerial corporation. Societal benefit, he believed, could be achieved, if the corporate objective were limited to shareholder wealth maximization as opposed to Dodd's vaguely defined social responsibility.

By the 1950s Dodd's pluralism/realism appeared to win the argument and this was even acknowledged by Berle himself as he converted to pluralism in his later writings.[52] The economic successes of managerial capitalism in major economies

---

51   See Berle, A., above n45.

52   See Berle, A. (1959) Power without Property, New York: Harcourt, Brace, 90–91 and 100; and Berle, A. (1954) The 20th Century Capitalist Revolution, New York: Harcourt, Brace, 169. Of course, critics of the social responsibility thesis were also present. The most prominent was Milton Friedman (Friedman, M. (1962) Capitalism and Freedom, Chicago: University of Chicago Press, 122, 133–36) who saw the shareholders as the real owners of the corporation as a *persona ficta*. He believed that allowing managers to promote social objectives amounted to giving them the right to impose social taxes on shareholders' property without having the necessary political authority. See also Fischel, D. (1982) 'The Corporate Governance Movement', Vanderbild Law Review, vol. 35, 1259 at 1269–70,

during the early WWII reconstruction era provided empirical justifications for socially responsible corporate realism and managerial autonomy (see *infra.* Chapters 3 and 5). It appeared that managerial self-interest coincided with societal objectives even without the imposition of mandatory company law constraints to establish corporate social responsibility.[53] The objectives of managerial companies were an amalgamation of private and social interests similar to that envisaged by Dodd. Managerial autonomy from shareholder supremacy enabled the corporation to accommodate diverse interests such as those of employees, the customers or even the state and the general public, and to be seen as a social institution rather than an aggregation of private interests.[54]

However, the nominalist approach did not disappear. Instead, it was taken up, expanded and refined, this time by economists rather than lawyers, beginning with Coase in the 1930s and continuing with Jensen and Meckling in the 1970s, to become the dominant theory by the end of the twentieth century, as managerialism began to lose its legitimacy first in the US and the UK and later in other countries and international fora. Aggregate economic theories slowly began to infiltrate and shape legal theory to such an extent that they came to offer a fully developed alternative to corporate realism.

Economic theories of the firm

The main concern in economics is whether available resources are allocated in an efficient manner. So, while legal theories of the corporation are based on arguments that have their roots in legal tradition and moral values, economics views the issues related to the nature of the firm through the prism of economic efficiency. Although, some have argued that efficiency can be a moral principle in itself since it increases general welfare.[55] However, despite its usage in media and government circles, as a technical concept efficiency is somewhat elusive. For

---

where Fischel argues that the corporation is a legal fiction and as such it cannot owe a social responsibility duty.

53   Although in some European countries there was indeed some legal institutionalization of non-shareholder interests, such as those of employees, with the enactment of worker participation laws. See Chapter 7 on the German example.

54   Although some theorists at the time attempted to integrate it into aggregate theory. Chayes, for instance, based his social responsibility argument on an aggregate model with expanded membership. See Chayes, D. (1959) 'The Modern Corporation and the Rule of Law' in Mason, E., The Corporation and Modern Society, Cambridge, MA: Harvard University Press, 25–44 at 25. The aggregate membership included non-shareholder constituencies, such as employees, who were entitled to participate in corporate decision-making.

55   Posner, R. (1980) 'The Ethical and Political Basis of the Efficiency Norm in Common Law Adjudication', Hofstra Law Review, vol. 8, 487 at 500–502.

example, Coleman identifies at least four efficiency-related notions.[56] However, the most commonly used version is Pareto efficiency/optimality, named after its originator, the nineteenth century economist and sociologist Vilfredo Pareto. This notion describes the state of affairs where resources cannot be reallocated so as to make one person better off without making someone else worse off. Moreover, apart from allocative efficiency, economics is also concerned with the notion of productive efficiency. Simply put, this describes the maximization of output from given inputs. These two aspects of economic efficiency are interrelated since it is the efficient allocation of resources that makes efficient production possible. Economics uses such criteria as a rule of thumb in order to determine when a particular type of conduct or institution is justifiable. Therefore, any arguments about the firm's nature are based on economic efficiency grounds rather than moral grounds.

What is striking, however, is that at least until relatively recently, traditional (neoclassical) economic theory virtually ignored the existence of the firm and concentrated on market operations or individuals' actions instead. In neoclassical economic theory, firms are simply considered as economic actors quite similar to individuals who transact in the market. This theory, based on the Walrasian and Marshallian tradition,[57] does not look into the internal operations of the firm, which resembles an 'empty box'[58] and thus has no complete analysis of the firm to offer. Neoclassicists study the firm by using a number of theoretical assumptions.[59] The first assumption is that the distribution of production factors within the firm is always coordinated according to the classical price theory, which also applies to market coordination.[60] This predicts that, if factor X is valued higher in A

---

56   Coleman, J. (1998) 'Efficiency, Utility, and Wealth Maximization' in Wiener-Katz, A. (ed.) Foundations of the Economic Approach to Law, Oxford: Oxford University Press, 11–18.

57   See Walras, L. (1954) Éléments d'Économie Politique Pure, Lausanne: Corbaz, 1874–1877, Jaffé, W. [transl.] (1954) Elements of Pure Economics, London: George Allen and Unwin; and Marshall, A. (1920) The Principles of Economics, 8th edition, London: Macmillan.

58   Jensen, M. and Meckling, W. (1976) 'Theory of the Firm: Managerial Behaviour, Agency Costs, and Ownership Structure', Journal of Financial Economics, vol. 3, 305 at 307.

59   Some prominent exponents of the theory are Machlup (Machlup, F. (1946) 'Marginal Analysis and Empirical Research', American Economic Review, vol. 36, 519); Oliver (Oliver, H. (1947) 'Marginal Theory and Business Behaviour', American Economic Review, vol. 37, 375); Friedman, M. (1953) Essays in Positive Economics, Chicago: University of Chicago Press; and Stigler (Stigler, G. (1947) The Theory of Price, London: Macmillan). Some classic neoclassical models of the firm have been developed by Hicks (Hicks, J. (1939) Value and Capital, 2nd edition, Oxford: Clarendon Press) and Arrow and Debreu (Arrow, K. and Debreu, G. (1954) 'Existence of an Equilibrium for a Competitive Economy', Econometrica, vol. 22, 265).

60   The assumption is that natural prices of goods are reflected by market prices which are determined by the matching of supply and demand.

than in B, then X will move to A until the price difference disappears. In this way the market determines the prices and automatically marks out what the best allocation choice is. This implies that the role of management, if any, is a passive rather than an active one. Thus, in neoclassical economics there is no theorizing about managerial coordination and the firm is assimilated to a factory without an administrative hierarchy.[61] Even where an administrative hierarchy exists, the neoclassical assumption is that it merely coordinates factors in the same way that the price mechanism would. Alternatively, the theory assumes that the firm is owned by a single entrepreneur. Again this single owner makes all management decisions according to the price-theoretic assumption.

The second assumption, based on the classic axiom that all economic actors seek to maximize profit, is that the firm pursues the single objective of profit maximization. This is achieved by applying the marginalist principle which assumes that the change in total revenue resulting from selling an additional unit of commodity (Marginal Revenue) equals the change in total cost resulting from a unit change in output (Marginal Cost). Profit maximization is attained when Marginal Revenue equals Marginal Cost (MR = MC). This occurs in series of independent time-horizon periods which are determined by technological change, capital intensity of production, product life, and so on. Profit maximization within all these independent short-term periods leads to profit maximization in the long-term as well. That is, the relation between short-term and long-term profit is harmonious. Moreover, when pursuing their goals firms act without being conscious of other firms' reactions.

Finally, the third main assumption of the neoclassical theory is that the firm operates in perfect certainty as it has full knowledge about all present and future circumstances that affect its operations. Irrespective of whether production factors are coordinated by an administrative hierarchy or by a single entrepreneur, the firm has unlimited information on production costs and revenues. The lack of informational asymmetries excludes any uncertainties and enables the firm to make all *rational* decisions in order to achieve its profit maximization goal.[62] In this way, all alternative strategies are evaluated and compared with certainty so that only the profit-maximizing ones are 'chosen'. In fact, as Loasby claims, firms and other economic agents' choices are absolutely predetermined:

> [i]f knowledge is perfect and the logic of choice complete and compelling then choice disappears; nothing is left but stimulus and response ... if the future is certain there can be no choice.[63]

---

61   See Chandler, A., above n2, 490.

62   This is the well-known 'global rationality' assumption of neoclassical economics.

63   Loasby, B. (1976) *Choice, Complexity and Ignorance: An Inquiry into Economic Theory and Practice of Decision Making*, Cambridge: Cambridge University Press, 5. See also Latsis, S. (1976) *Method and Appraisal in Economics*, Cambridge: Cambridge University Press.

The neoclassical theory of the firm is essentially a theory of equilibrium which is achieved in markets characterized by perfect competition.[64] It is in such markets that the price-theoretic assumption that firms are passive price-takers rather than active price-makers applies and where Pareto optimality is achieved. In the neoclassical equilibrium a single price prevails in the market according to which all rational profit-maximizers make their adjustments to their output in order to equate Marginal Cost with Marginal Revenue. Thus, profit-maximizing firms achieve their goals by using the prices formed by the market according to the law of supply and demand.

It should be noted here that subsequent formulations of the neoclassical theory have allowed for the possibility that non-profit maximizing firms may exist at least in the short-term. For instance, in a classic paper published in 1950 Alchian used the Darwinian natural selection example to claim that the achievement of long-term profit maximization is crucial for the firm's survival in a perfectly competitive market.[65] Profit maximizing firms enjoy an advantage over non-profit maximizing firms, since they have the financial resources to grow faster than the latter who will be out-competed and eventually eliminated. The significance of Alchian's model is that, although it allows the possibility of firm-level divergence from profit-maximization, the neoclassical objective applies at an industry-wide level through an evolutionary process and thus the neoclassical equilibrium holds. Profit maximization is then not a choice objective but it is one externally imposed on the firm's owner as a necessary precondition for survival.

The equilibrium assumptions of the neoclassical theory have some important implications for corporate governance. First, since both managerial hierarchy and sole entrepreneur ownership are treated as equivalent coordination mechanisms within the firm, the relationship between ownership and control and its organizational implications are rendered irrelevant. There is no difference between a non-owner manager and an owner-entrepreneur since both are simply assumed to make optimal decisions based on given (perfect) information. In such a theory where discretion is completely ruled out managerial innovation and motivation have no relevance. Irrespectively of who is in control of the firm the profit-maximization objective will be pursued. Secondly, the perfect markets assumption of the theory calls for the rejection of any non-market intervention. Since the allocation of resources in equilibrium is optimal, any regulatory or other interference would lead to inefficiency. Neoclassicism is therefore antithetical to the regulation of corporate activity by the state or any other regulator in favour of a laissez-faire approach.

---

64 Perfect competition describes a market where there are a large number of small firms who produce an identical (homogenous) product, where there are no entry-barriers for new competing firms and where all firms face the same costs.

65 Alchian, A. (1950) 'Uncertainty, Evolution and Economic Theory', *Journal of Political Economy*, vol. 58, 211.

Despite its undisputed influence, at least until the global financial crisis that began in 2008, in modern economic thinking, neoclassical theory has some obvious flaws. Particularly, the over-abstraction of global rationality, certainty and perfect market assumptions which constitute the basis of the theory. The problems stem from the fact that the neoclassical theory is based on optimal equilibrium conditions. This means that if its preconditions are relaxed with the introduction of elements of uncertainty or deviations from the perfect market models, then the price-theoretic assumptions begin to lose their predictive power and the neoclassical theory its normative significance. While in a utopian world markets can be perfectly competitive and economic agents (individuals and firms) can make their decisions having perfect knowledge about all current and potential eventualities, in reality these conditions cannot be met.

As already mentioned, traditional neoclassical theory probably fits best the pre-managerial era when markets resembled to a large extent the models of competition it assumes. It is in that era that the theoretical consensus about neoclassicism arose, after all, despite the fact that even then global rationality was far from a real circumstance.[66] However, in an economy dominated by managerial firms the neoclassical theory loses much of its relevance. The size of managerial firms indicates that markets are imperfectly competitive (oligopolistic) and that Alchian's evolutionary argument cannot apply. In addition, the separation of ownership from control appears to be in odds with the owner-entrepreneur assumption and reveals the gap left by traditional theory's failure to deal with the structure of the firm. So it is not a coincidence that it was in the 1930s, the heyday of managerial capitalism, that an intense debate arose on whether neoclassical theory was satisfactory or a new more realistic approach should be developed to deal with the firm as an organization that differs from markets or individuals.

The pioneering attempt to provide theoretical insights into the nature of the firm as a coordinator of resources was made by Coase.[67] In his famous article 'The Nature of the Firm' he sought to explain the firm's nature and existence by looking at the reasons for intra-firm as opposed to market coordination.[68] If as neoclassical theory assumes there is no difference between the two, he asked, then why is it that firm coordination sometimes supersedes price-mechanism coordination in the market?

In order to deal with this question Coase focused on the single exchange transaction or more simply the contract between two economic agents.[69] What he

---

66   Kirzner, I. (1997) How Markets Work: Disequilibrium, Entrepreneurship and Discovery, Hobart Paper No. 133, Institute of Economic Affairs.

67   See Campbell, D. and Klaes, M. (2005) 'The Principle of Institutional Direction: Coase's Regulatory Critique of Intervention', Cambridge Journal of Economics, vol. 29(2), 263–288.

68   Coase, R. (1937) 'The Nature of the Firm', Economica, vol. 4(4), 386.

69   In the economic literature the word contract has a less technical meaning than in legal texts as it is used to broadly describe an economic transaction.

found was that the use of the price mechanism entails what he called transaction costs.[70] Such costs can arise from drafting, negotiating and enforcing contracts because natural prices of goods are not automatically known to the transacting parties. The real world is one of uncertainty where, contrary to the global rationality assumption, economic agents do not and cannot have full knowledge about all relevant contingencies.[71] Thus, Coase argued, in order to economize on the costs of using the market and therefore of production or allocation, transacting parties allow an 'entrepreneur' to coordinate the distribution of resources by *command*. Within the firm contracts are not eliminated but are considerably reduced because they are replaced by cooperation. For the series of contracts between the entrepreneur and other agents required in market transacting one is substituted where the latter agrees to follow the directions of the former in return for some remuneration. So, Coase defined the firm's hierarchical structure as a 'system of relationships which comes into existence when the direction of resources is dependent on an entrepreneur'.[72] Optimal firm-size is determined by balancing the costs arising from market and entrepreneur coordination so the firm expands until the point where both types of costs are equal.[73]

Coase's insights gave a new spin to economic theories of the firm because he demonstrated that firms do exist and they are different from markets or individuals. Although, as himself admitted fifty years after his seminal work, his intention was to compare coordination by organizations with that by the market mechanism, his transaction cost approach provided the theoretical platform for an analysis of the firm as a governance structure.[74] The Coasean theory, however, did not catch on until several decades later when theorists, like Williamson, rediscovered and expanded it to form a new kind of economic analysis based on transaction costs.[75] As Zingales noted:

> [t]he link between theory of the firm and corporate governance is even more compelling ... The word "governance" implies the exercise of authority. But in a free-market economy, why do we need any form of authority? Isn't the market responsible for allocating all resources efficiently without the intervention of any authority? In fact, Coase (1937) taught us that using the market has its costs,

---

70   See Coase, R., above n68, 391.

71   These circumstances are responsible for what Simon has termed 'bounded rationality'. In rejecting the neoclassical hypothesis of global rationality he argues that the real world is one of uncertainty, where agents have incomplete knowledge. As such an agent's rationality is unavoidably bounded. See Simon, H. (1957) Models of Man: Social and Rational, New York: Wiley.

72   See Coase, R., above n68, 393.

73   Ibid., 394.

74   Coase, R. (1988) 'Lectures on The Nature of the Firm', Journal of Law, Economics, and Organization, vol. 4(1), 33 at 47.

75   We discuss Williamson's work later in this chapter.

and firms alleviate these costs by substituting the price mechanism with the exercise of authority. By and large, corporate governance is the study of how this authority is allocated and exercised. But in order to understand how this authority is allocated and exercised, we first need to know why it is needed in the first place. We need, thus, a theory of the firm.[76]

More influential at the time when Coase was writing was the empirical disputation of traditional neoclassical thought that came from the renowned Oxford Economists Research Group.[77] They presented evidence that real businessmen do not attempt to maximize profits according to the neoclassical marginalist principle and that oligopoly, rather than perfect competition, is the main market structure. In contrast to the neoclassical proposition, firms do not make decisions without regard to their competitors' actions and reactions but are subjected to oligopolistic interdependencies. Firms are not price-takers but instead they make conscious decisions about pricing. They prefer price stability because of customers' aversion to volatility, and so, contrary to the traditional theory's predictions, prices are adjusted to output rather than vice versa. Perhaps most importantly, the Oxford economists found that profit-maximization was not the only goal of firms, but other objectives like goodwill were also important. This constituted a direct empirical attack on the backbone of Walrasian neoclassicism which, due to its neglect of the firm and its nature, was unable to explain common business behaviour outside perfect market conditions.

This revisionist trend combined with the Berle and Means stipulation that managers were in control of large corporations set the stage for the theoretical examination of managerial behaviour in oligopolistic markets.[78] In fact, *The Modern Corporation and Private Property* was one of the first works to imply that managerial firms did not pursue the profit maximization objective. However, despite the undisputed theoretical influence of their thesis, Berle and Means did

---

76   Zingales, L. (2000) 'In Search of New Foundations', Journal of Finance, 55, 1623–1653.

77   See Hall, R. and Hitch, C. (1939) 'Price Theory and Business Behaviour', Oxford Economic Papers, vol. 2, 12. The publication of this paper gave rise to an intense debate on the profit-maximization assumption between marginalists and anti-marginalists. See Machlup, F., above n59 arguing that the neoclassical theory of the firm is not intended to yield predictions about individual firms it is only concerned about competitive market prices; Stigler, G. (1947) 'The Kinky-Oligopoly Demand Curve and Rigid Prices', Journal of Political Economy, vol. 55, 432; Friedman, M., above n59; and Nagel, E. (1963) 'Assumptions in Economic Theory', American Economic Review Papers and Proceedings, vol. 53, 211.

78   By oligopoly economists mean markets that are neither pure monopolies not perfectly competitive but anything in between. It is assumed that the economic agents in oligopolistic markets are large firms who produce identical or similar products. Entry barriers are also assumed to be present.

not attempt to develop an economic theory upon which to base this implication.[79] They merely assumed that, due to the divorce of ownership from control, management teams do not pursue the objectives of the neoclassical firm. As Bratton observes, the concept of the neoclassical entrepreneur was split between management and capital.[80] This split left a theoretical vacuum, arising from the fact that traditional economic theory treated the firm as a mere entrepreneur rather than as an organization, that economists were keen to fill.[81]

The first managerial theories of the firm, as they are known, begun to appear in the late 1950s and suggested a significant conflict between managerial objectives and profit maximization as envisaged in equilibrium theory. Broadly they argued that a conflict arises from the fact that in managerial firms decision-makers own no stock. So managerial theories, similarly to the neoclassical postulation, assume that shareholders are the owners of the firm who *would* maximize profit had they been in control. However, because managers are vested with the decision-making function, they pursue other goals that suit their own preferences. This implies that managerial theories share with neoclassicism a common assumption: individuals, whether owners or managers, are assumed to be self-interested persons who to seek to maximize their own welfare. So given that there may be a divergence between shareholder and management preferences, the crucial element that determines whether the profit maximization objective is pursued is managerial *discretion*. In other words, the basis of managerial theoretical models is the ability of managers to exercise their discretion and diverge from the neoclassical assumptions in order to maximize their own gains.

In an early attempt to examine managerial objectives and incorporate managerial preferences in the theory of the firm, Baumol hypothesized that managers are interested in sales revenue maximization as opposed to profit.[82] Of course, the two motives are not always conflicting for the obvious reason that profit is a by-product of sales revenue. So, the promotion of sales is a necessary precondition even for attaining the neoclassical objective. For example, because of declining sales consumers may shun a product when they feel it is falling in popularity, banks and money markets will be more reluctant to provide capital, distributors may be lost, and employment relations can deteriorate as firing rather than hiring can become the norm. However, Baumol's proposition is that managers out of self-interest see sales revenue as an end in itself rather than just a means.[83]

---

79   Sawyer, M. (1979) Theories of the Firm, London: Weidelfeld and Nicolson, 89–90.

80   Bratton, W., above n3, 1495.

81   For an early critique of the neoclassical theory on this point see Papandreou, A. (1952) 'Some Basic Problems in the Theory of the Firm' in Haley, F. (ed.) A Survey of Contemporary Economics, vol. II, Illinois: R.D. Irwin, 183–219.

82   Baumol, W. (1967) Business Behaviour, Value and Growth, New York: Harcourt, Brace & World.

83   Ibid., 46–47.

His argument is based on the fact that managers' salaries are often more closely linked to sales rather than profit (e.g. sales commissions) and often companies are ranked according to their sales performance. Moreover, large sales give prestige to managers, while large profits are most likely appropriated by the shareholders. Thus, firms use the sales objective as a 'rule of thumb' even at the expense of maximum profit by setting output at a level where Marginal Revenue is lower than Marginal Cost (MR < MC). In theory, sales maximization may lead to zero or negative profitability if it requires prices that are so low that costs are not covered; hence the potential conflict between the two objectives.[84]

Nevertheless, Baumol suggests that, although sales revenue is the ultimate managerial goal, a compromise is reached where a certain minimum acceptable profit level is laid down.[85] In other words, managerial discretion is not totally unconstrained. Sales' growth demands funds that are generated either internally through capital retentions or externally by borrowing or issuing equity. In the former situation the profit requirement is direct. If, on the other hand, the latter method is adopted, the minimum profit constraint is determined by external demands and expectations. Lenders are more willing to lend to a profitable firm. In the case of equity finance, the higher the profitability level, the more funds capital markets will be willing to provide. At the same time, the firm must ensure that its shares remain attractive to the capital market by providing a rate of return that is satisfactory to the current and potential investor. If this rate falls below the minimum acceptable level managers run the risk of being ousted, since shareholders may sell their shares to a hostile takeover raider who may be attracted by a falling share-price and acquire control of the firm. Since such transactions in the market for corporate control are usually followed by a replacement of incumbent management, they are assumed to constitute a force constraining managerial discretion.[86] The calculation of the difference between the minimum profit constraint and the maximum profit level provides a method of measuring managerial discretion; the larger the difference the greater the discretion managers enjoy.

What can be seen as an expansion of the sales-maximization model was presented five years after Baumol's exposition, by Williamson, who argued that managers use their discretion to maximize their own *utility* as opposed to that of shareholders.[87] The concept of managerial utility comprises pecuniary and non-pecuniary elements such as salary, security, power and status, prestige and professional excellence.[88] While salary is easily measurable in monetary terms all the remaining elements are non-pecuniary and therefore their monetarization is

---

84   Ibid., 48.
85   Ibid., 49.
86   See Manne, H. (1965) 'Mergers and the Market for Corporate Control', Journal of Political Economy, vol. 73(2), 110.
87   Williamson, O. (1964) The Economics of Discretionary Behavior: Managerial Objectives in a Theory of the Firm, Chicago: Markham.
88   Ibid., 32.

necessary for their inclusion in an economic theory of the firm. For this purpose Williamson developed the concept of 'expense preference' to describe the satisfaction that managers get from certain types of expenditures. In particular, there is a positive managerial preference for staff expansion expenditures, emoluments and discretionary profits.[89] Regarding the first type, managers have a preference for staff increases which are to a certain extent equivalent to promotion since they contribute to power and often to salary. Emoluments are defined as the portion of salaries which is discretionary in the sense that its removal would not influence managers' decision to keep their job. Such expenses can arise from company cars, luxurious offices, expense accounts and so on, and are believed to also add to managerial power, status and prestige. Finally, managerial utility can also derive from the attainment of profits above the minimum necessary for job security (discretionary profits). The implication here is that future expansion and therefore managerial satisfaction depend on such profits which are also a measure of success since they demonstrate the achievement of the firm's goal. According to Williamson, although there is a distinction between the purposes of the firm as an organization and the personal goals of managers, managerial utility can also derive from organizational achievement.[90] This is a deviation from the approach to the minimum profit constraint in Baumol's model, where it is assumed that managers gain no utility from profit *per se* and therefore are prepared to sacrifice any profit above this minimum necessary for an increase in sales revenue.[91] Nonetheless, managerial expense preference and the profit-maximization objective are by no means aligned. In his careful case-studies Williamson shows that in a sharp fall off of demand and therefore of profitability; the decline of managerial utility expenses is disproportionate to that of other expenditures. This, he argues, proves the ability of managers to exercise their discretion according to the expense-preference model.

Also in 1964, Marris presented a different approach to the behaviour of the managerial firm that focuses on growth as a management objective.[92] In this model, all the diverse objectives that can be pursued by managers are amalgamated into the single motive of 'sustainable long-run growth in size measured by assets, employment or real output'.[93] Although the starting point is similar to that in Williamson's model, in that managers are after prestige, power and security, Marris' claim is that these objectives are attained by pursuing a growth rate that is faster than would be optimal for shareholders in terms of profitability. The assumption here is that beyond a certain point the growth rate and the return rate do not increase proportionately. Thus, in contrast to the neoclassical theory where

89   Ibid., 34–37.
90   Ibid., 36.
91   Sawyer, M., above n79, 98–99.
92   Marris, R. (1964) The Economic Theory of Managerial Capitalism, London: Macmillan.
93   Marris, R. (1998) Managerial Capitalism in Retrospect, London: Macmillan, 113.

growth is merely an indirect outcome of pursuing maximum profit, in Marris'
model the managerial firm free from shareholder control can set its growth rate
independently from the neoclassical equilibrium objective. Growth, nevertheless,
is costly and thus requires cash flow. Marris identifies retained earnings as the
most important source of cash flow. He then argues that retention and reinvestment
can be justified from the maximization point of view since it can ensure long-term
profit maximization. In this case, shareholders are satisfied and the firm's stock is
seen as an attractive investment causing the market valuation of the firm to rise.
However, beyond a certain point the substitution of an expectation for larger future
profits/dividends for smaller current ones can cause shareholder dissatisfaction
and depress the firm's market value. This is where managerial preference for
maximum growth rates begins to contradict market valuation. Marris' prediction
is that managerial discretion leads to the maximization of growth rates subject to
a minimum market valuation constraint. This constraint arises from the fact that
as the market valuation falls the potential of the firm being taken over increases.
Thus, managers need to find a balance between the maximum growth rate and
the maximum market value in order to ensure their job security. In other words
a form of profit 'satisficing' occurs whereby a minimum amount is returned to
shareholders to keep them from selling their shares.

One observation that has to be made here is that all these managerial models are
based on the fact that, just like product markets, capital markets are also imperfect.
In other words, they assume that shareholders or potential takeover raiders do not
have perfect knowledge about the firm's actual and future profitability. If stock
markets were perfect in providing all necessary information about a firm's present
and potential profitability, then any firms who pursue growth beyond the current
profit maximization rate would be taken over as they would depress their market
value. Thus, the market for corporate control would be sufficient to ensure that
no other objectives than current market value maximization were pursued and the
need for alternatives to the neoclassical paradigm would automatically disappear.

Obviously the analysis of firm behaviour in managerial theories is useful in
understanding the ramifications of the separation of corporate ownership and
control. Manager-controlled corporations are different from owner-controlled
ones in that they are inherently prone to pursue objectives that are not only
different from those of shareholders but can also be antagonistic to them. In a
sense, by recognizing that managers and/or corporate organizational hierarchies
can actually pursue *their own* objectives as those of the firm, rather than of the
shareholders, managerial theories introduce some elements of corporate realism
into the economic theory of the firm. While ownership is detached from actual
decision-making and control, management input becomes the centre-point and the
main driving force of the firm as an *end* in itself. As a result, the shareholders'
interests are reduced to a mere constraint on the pursuit of the firm's own goals as
an organization and as an entity that has its own separate existence.

Regarding the two component elements of corporate governance, managerial
theories of the firm are mainly concerned with the nature of control and its

microeconomic effects. As regards the nature of ownership they do not provide any analysis, since they simply assume that shareholders are owners without any further elaboration. What may seem an arbitrary assumption can be explained by the fact that the primary purpose of managerial theories is not to determine and justify the metaphysical nature of the corporation and its ownership but simply to explain managerial motivation. Another explanation can perhaps be that managerial theories are not intended to displace neoclassical theory altogether. Rather, their purpose is to fill the theoretical gaps that it leaves in the sphere of imperfect markets where the organizational nature of the firm becomes important in understanding economic activity. Nevertheless, the mere fact that managerial theories visualize the firm as something different from the profit-maximizing economic agent constitutes a challenge to Walrasian neoclassicism and the universal applicability of its assumptions, just as the Coasian argument did to some extent.

However, as already mentioned, by the 1970s the legitimacy of the managerial firm was being called into question in the harsh economic environment prevalent in that decade.[94] This environment, as we will observe further in Chapter 6, provided a receptive context for theorists, such as Alchian and Demsetz or Jensen and Meckling, who sought to explain the behaviour of the managerial firm in neoclassical terms and argue against managerialism.[95] Alchian and Demsetz' starting point is similar to that in Coase's theory, namely the transaction within and outside the firm.[96] However, they conclude that Coase's argument that coordination within the firm is by command is unsatisfactory because it fails to explain where the entrepreneur's authority to coordinate production comes from. In order to provide an answer to this problem, they deviate significantly from Coase's theorization by arguing that the firm should not be seen as a mechanism where coordination of resources is by command. On the contrary, they claim that there are no authority-based relations within the firm which in turn has

> no power of fiat, no authority, no disciplinary action any different in the slightest degree from ordinary market contracting between two people ... To speak of managing, directing, or assigning workers to various tasks is a deceptive way of noting that the employer continually is involved in renegotiation of contracts on terms that must be acceptable to both parties.[97]

---

94   See Jensen, M. (1993) 'The Modern Industrial Revolution, Exit, and the Failure of Internal Control Systems', *Journal of Finance*, vol. 48(3), 833; and Jensen, M. (1989) 'The Eclipse of the Public Corporation', *Harvard Business Review*, vol. 67(5), 61.

95   The emergence of this anti-managerialist trend that appeared during the 1970s was almost simultaneous to a similar movement in law in the US and the UK. See Bratton, W., above n3.

96   Alchian, A. and Demsetz, H. (1972) 'Production, Information Costs, and Economic Organization', *American Economic Review*, vol. 62, 777.

97   Ibid., 777.

By viewing the firm in this way, Alchian and Demsetz deny that there is any difference between transactions that take place in the market and those that are concluded within the firm. In essence the firm *is* itself a market and therefore the management function is reduced to a mere contract renegotiation *process*. No hierarchy or authority-based relationships exist within the firm. To illustrate this stipulation they focus on the employer-worker relationship. They argue that, although it may appear that management has an authority over the worker, in fact the relation is a symmetrical one based on a 'quid pro quo' contract.[98] Just as the employer orders the worker to perform certain acts, the worker 'orders' the employer to pay him a wage in consideration. Similarly, the worker can 'fire' the employer by leaving the job in the same way that the employer can also terminate the employment agreement. Thus, the firm is a nexus of explicit and implicit contracts and within it there is the continual renegotiation described in the extract above. Because there are no power differentials (hence the lack of hierarchy) every (re)negotiation leads to outcomes that are satisfactory for both contracting parties so that there is always an equilibrium reached. To take the employer-worker example again, if either party to the employment contract does not like the terms offered they will seek a better alternative elsewhere. Where this results in a shortage of employees, (perfect) labour market forces will compel employers to offer better terms of employment until equilibrium is reached.

The only thing that distinguishes firms from markets, according to Alchian and Demsetz, derives from the fact that team production by workers is involved. This, they argue, involves 'metering' problems that make it difficult to determine workers' rewards according to their performance, i.e. their individual contributions to the collective effort. This is because individuals have the tendency to 'shirk' when they work as part of a team.[99] In order to overcome shirking in team production, firms assign a central agent, namely the shareholder, the role of monitoring. This monitoring party is himself discouraged to shirk by being made the ultimate risk-bearer as 'residual claimant' of the team's earnings after all the 'fixed' claims of other contracting parties e.g. creditors, are deducted. Thus, the residual claimant must be given 'property rights' over the firm's net-cash-flows and the ability to renegotiate contracts in order to carry out his coordination function efficiently. The precondition for efficient coordination is the alignment of each individual's rewards with his output.

The importance of Alchian and Demsetz's model for corporate governance lies in the fact that it justifies the role of shareholders as profit-earning entrepreneurs by using efficiency considerations. In other words, it provides theoretical legitimacy to the economic assumption that shareholders should be regarded as the ultimate controllers of the firm and therefore as 'owners' of the firm, or more precisely its

---

98   Ibid., 783.
99   Ibid., 779.

net cash-flow.[100] Not only are they the constituency that determines what objectives should be pursued by the firm if it is to be efficient, but they also have the necessary incentives to ensure that these objectives are *actually* pursued. The implication is that firms controlled by unconstrained managers are not efficient, because of the divergence between the objectives of managers and those of profit-maximizing shareholders.[101] Therefore, the argument goes, in order to promote efficiency and economic welfare, one would have to ensure that within the firm structure there are sufficient constraints on managerial discretion aligning management motivation to the profit-maximization objective which in turn leads to the maximization of the firm's market value.[102]

This line of thought is also followed by Jensen and Meckling who extended the nexus-of-contracts theory by including explanations about managerial motivation.[103] Their analysis is similar to that of Alchian and Demsetz in that they regard the firm as a nexus of equilibrating contracts similar to those concluded by self-interested economic agents in a market. To use their words, the firm is nothing more than

> a legal fiction that serves as a nexus for a set of contracting relationships [among individuals] and is also characterised by the existence of divisible residual claims on the organisation's assets and cash flows, which can generally be sold without permission of other contracting individuals ... Viewed in this way, it makes little or no sense to try to distinguish those things that are "inside" the firm from those things that are "outside" of it.[104]

However, their main contribution is their analysis of the motivational split between managers and owners by describing the relationship between them as one of agency. According to Jensen and Meckling, an agency relationship is a

---

100   Alchian and Demsetz define firm ownership as the combination of the right to be a residual claimant-monitor of the team, to be the central party common to all contracts with input providers, to observe input behaviour, to alter the membership of the team, and to sell all these rights. So even though they talk about 'ownership', they do not use the term as lawyers might mean it. See ibid., 783.

101   This has provided the theoretical basis for the view that corporations should be run solely in the interests of shareholders, to whom managers should be accountable. See Easterbrook, F. and Fischel, D. (1989) 'The Corporate Contract', Colombia Law Review, vol. 89, 1416; Easterbrook, F. and Fischel, D. (1983) 'Voting in Corporate Law', Journal of Law and Economics, vol. 26, 395 at 403; and Easterbrook, F. and Fischel, D. (1981) 'Takeover Bids, Defensive Tactics, and Shareholders' Welfare', Business Lawyer, vol. 36, 1733.

102   When dealing with this issue in this way the object of study changes from how to reconcile firm *behaviour* with neoclassical marginalist principles, to how to reconcile firm *structure* with marginalist principles.

103   Jensen, M. and Meckling, W., above n58.

104   Ibid., 311.

contract under which one or more individuals, the principal(s), engage another, the agent, to perform some service on their behalf by delegating to him some decision-making authority.[105] This relationship is based on an assumption that, because all individuals want to maximize their own utility, the agent will not always act in the interests of the principal. This divergence of interests gives rise to what they call *agency costs*. These accrue from the principals', i.e. the shareholders, efforts to align the interests of agents with their own as residual claimants, and are the sum of expenses for monitoring the agent's performance, of expenditure incurred so that the agent guarantees that he will act in the principal's interests ('bonding'), and of any residual loss caused by any remaining divergence. In effect, monitoring expenses are the product of information asymmetry between the principal and the agent, since the former does not have knowledge about the efficient allocation of resources that is equal to that of the agent. Obtaining all necessary information in order to exercise monitoring is inherently costly. Principals, therefore, will be willing to incur such costs only if the benefits accruing to them from monitoring are higher. This depends on the extent of residual claims owned; the higher the claims, i.e. of shares owned, the more motivated the principal, i.e. the shareholder, will be to exercise monitoring.

Having described the owner-manager relationship as one of agency, Jensen and Meckling state that agency costs are in effect the costs of the separation of ownership and control or of shirking in Alchian and Demsetz' terms. Consequently, they are related to the extent to which managers are also residual claimants; the higher the managers' claims and, therefore, the higher their interest in the firm's market value, the lower the agency costs. Where, on the other hand, managers have anything less than a controlling interest in the firm, as is the case in managerial firms, their residual claims are deemed insufficient to bridge the gap between ownership and control and as a result agency costs accrue.

Addressing this Jensen and Meckling suggest that constraints can arise from the market for managers within and outside the firm itself. Competition from other potential managers disciplines the incumbent management team who, as a result of the increased risk of losing their jobs, will be prevented from diverging from the market-value maximization objective. The effectiveness of this constraint depends on the cost of replacing the under-performing managers which in turn is related to the principal's ability to measure performance.[106]

Moreover, Jensen and Meckling[107] and subsequently Jensen[108] argue that managerial discretion can also be constrained by the financial structure of the firm. Increased debt, for instance, has the effect of reducing cash flow and thus

---

105   Ibid., 308.

106   See also Fama, E. (1980) 'Agency Problems and the Theory of the Firm', Journal of Political Economy, vol. 88(2), 288.

107   See Jensen, M. and Meckling, W., above n58.

108   Jensen, M. (1986) 'Agency Costs of Free Cash Flow, Corporate Finance and Takeovers', American Economic Review, vol. 76, 323.

makes the risk of bankruptcy more imminent. The more intense competition in the product market is, the higher the risk of bankruptcy and the more effective this constraint will be. On the other hand, excess cash-flow – that is, cash for which there are no profitable investment opportunities left within the firm – reduces the threat of default and therefore increases agency costs resulting from managerial discretion. For this reason, any excess cash flows should be re-distributed to the shareholders in the form of dividends or share-repurchases, so that managers are prevented from wasting it in 'inefficient' organizational spending and excessive growth beyond the market-value maximization point.

Obviously, the availability of relevant firm-specific information to the monitoring principal is the key for both these constraints to become operative. In the managerial firm, however, no shareholder has sufficient incentives for acquiring control-related information. The obvious problem that arises is how to ensure the operation of the above mechanisms in the absence of direct shareholder monitoring. Jensen and Meckling, in a similar manner to managerial theorists, regard the market for corporate control through the operation of hostile takeovers as a key managerial constraint. If, as it is assumed, capital markets are efficient – that is, if they are able to process all relevant information about the firm's investment opportunities so that the market value of the firm reflects the present value of the firm's expected future net cash flows, including those from future investment opportunities – then managerial effort will be fully reflected in the stock prices as determined by the market.[109] Poor managerial performance will lead to the undervaluation of the firm's stock in comparison to the market as a whole. The resulting reduction of the firm's market value is a measure for the 'residual loss' element of agency costs. Consequently, the higher the agency costs in a firm the more likely it is that a bidder will attempt a hostile takeover offer to the firm's shareholders. As a result managers will have the incentive to reduce agency costs in order to avoid their replacement after a change in ownership. They do so by implementing *ex ante* monitoring devices such as audits, independent directors, incentive compensation schemes etc. So ultimately it is managers who bear the costs of discretion, and the more efficient the market is, the stronger the managers' incentive to reduce agency costs will be. When firms do not structure their incentive contracts so as to minimize agency costs, the theory assumes that they

---

109   Jensen, M. (1983) 'Organization Theory and Methodology', Accounting Review, vol. 50, 323; Fama, E. and Jensen, M. (1983) 'Separation of Ownership and Control', Journal of Law and Economics, vol. 26, 301. This is the efficient markets hypothesis which generally holds that a market is efficient if it is impossible to make economic profits by trading on available information. For a general literature review on this hypothesis: see Fama, E. (1970) 'Efficient Capital Markets: A Review of Theory and Empirical Work', Journal of Finance, vol. 25, 383. Market efficiency also implies that, since the short-term price of a stock reflects the present value of the firm's long-term results, short-term values cannot be distinguished from long-term values. See Easterbrook, F. and Fischel, D. (1981) above n101.

will be selected out and disappear in a similar way to that described by Alchian.[110] Therefore, optimal resource allocation within and without the firm is directly related to capital market efficiency; hence the emphasis placed by advocates of the agency paradigm on ensuring that market efficiency is maintained, for example by rejecting any factors that may hinder the operation of the market for corporate control.

What is important in the 'nexus-of-contracts' and agency analysis is that in effect it introduces nominalism into the economic theory of the firm. It does so by dismantling the firm into a number of transactions between self-interested input-providers and by focusing on the monitoring role of shareholders as residual owners of the revenue generated. Private bilateral contracts between actors prevail over managerial command and, therefore, market constraints determine the allocation of resources in an efficient manner. Managerial input is reduced to a commodity, an agency service, acquired by the principals at a certain cost (agency costs).[111] In effect, management ceases to be an *end*, as predicted by managerial theories, and is reduced to a mere production *means*. By regarding intra-firm coordination as no different from market contracting the nexus-of-contracts/agency approach 'progresses' from the Walrasian 'black box' to a 'no-box' analysis, i.e. the microeconomic institutional analysis of the firm remains strictly neoclassical.

The theory also contains some other important implications of a normative character. Firstly, because of the firm's nexus-of-contracts nature, the role of law is only to provide 'mandatory' contractual terms supplementing those privately agreed with the only purpose of reducing agency costs. So legal rules are the 'products of a historical process in which there were strong incentives for individuals to minimize agency costs'.[112] The implication here is that, since only market forces and individual choice determine contractual and legal rules efficiently, there is no need for mandatory corporate law.[113] Secondly, related to the first point any corporate social responsibility assertions, such as those put forward by Dodd, are

---

110   See Jensen, M., above n108; Fama, E. and Jensen, M., above n109; and Alchian, A., above n65.

111   As Jensen and Meckling claim: 'Finding that agency costs are non-zero ... and concluding from this that the agency relationship is non-optimal, wasteful or inefficient is equivalent in every sense to comparing a world in which iron ore is a scarce commodity (and therefore costly) to a world in which it is freely available at zero resource cost, and concluding that the first world is "non-optimal"'. Jensen, M. and Meckling, W., above n58, 328.

112   See Jensen, M. and Meckling, W., above n58, 360.

113   On the argument that corporate law rules should not be mandatory so that individuals can exercise their contractual freedom and opt out if they consider them inefficient see Bebcuck, L. (1989) 'Foreword: The Debate on Contractual Freedom in Corporate Law', Columbia Law Review, vol. 89, 1395; McChesney, F. (1989) 'Economics, Law, and Science in the Corporate Field: A Critique of Eisenberg', Columbia Law Review, vol. 89, 1530; and Fischel, D., above n52, 1273.

unacceptable for two reasons.[114] Firstly, since the alignment of managerial behaviour to shareholder interests as a precondition for the reduction of agency costs is one of the main premises of the nexus-of-contracts analysis, any inclusion of non-shareholder interests in managerial decision-making constitutes a diversion from the market value-maximization objective and is therefore inefficient. Secondly, the nature of the firm as a mere fiction demolishes the foundations of Dodd's social responsibility argument which, as noted earlier, is built upon corporate realism.

From these inferences about the nature of the firm it becomes apparent that the nexus-of-contracts theory is to a large extent a reformulation of the aggregate theory in economic terms.[115] The neoclassical nexus-of-contracts approach provided economic efficiency justifications for the old legal assertion that contract was the basis of the firm's fictitious nature. Seen in this way, it is not surprising that the theory has had an enormous influence in legal literature too.[116] As Clarke observed, the 'theory now dominates the thinking of most economists and most economically oriented corporate law scholars who focus at all on the theory of the corporation'.[117] Perhaps the main driving force behind the almost immediate acceptance of the neoclassical nexus-of-contracts/agency paradigm was, as we will observe in Chapter 6, that it offered a very clear alternative in the context of the massive economic shocks experienced in the 1970s and early 1980s. However, the neoclassical version of the contractual theory of the firm has not found unanimous acceptance in economic analysis of the firm. The main source of dissent is its over-reliance on efficient markets and the global rationality of contracting parties when agreeing on the *ex ante* monitoring mechanisms.

In a series of articles and books since 1975, Williamson has expanded Coase's claim that firms supersede markets to fully explain the firm's nature and behaviour on a transaction cost basis.[118] Once again the initial point of reference is the

---

114   Jensen and Meckling state this expressly: 'The personalisation of the firm implied by asking questions such as, "what should be the objective function of the firm?" or, "Does the firm have a social responsibility?" is seriously misleading. *The firm is not an individual.* It is a legal fiction that serves as a focus for a complex process in which the conflicting objectives of individuals ... are brought into equilibrium within a framework of contractual relations.' See Jensen, M. and Meckling, W., above n58, 311.

115   See Phillips, M., above n27, 1090–1091; Millon, D., above n22, 232; and Bratton, W., above n3, 1513–1515.

116   See, for example, Gordon, J. (1989) 'The Mandatory Structure of Corporate Law', Columbia Law Review, vol. 89, 1549; and Easterbrook, F. and Fischel, D. (1989) above n101.

117   Clark, R. (1989) 'Contracts, Elites, and Traditions in the Making of Corporate Law', Columbia Law Review, vol. 89, 1703 at 1705.

118   See Williamson, O. (1985) The Economic Institutions of Capitalism, London: Collier Macmillan; Williamson, O. (1984) 'Corporate Governance', Yale Law Journal, vol. 93, 1197; Williamson, O. (1981) 'The Modern Corporation: Origins, Evolution, Attributes', Journal of Economic Literature, vol. 19, 1537; Williamson, O. (1979) 'Transaction Cost Economics: The Governance of Contractual Relations', Journal of Law and Economics,

contract. However, in contrast to the neoclassical model, Williamson accepts that markets are not perfect or efficient due to the presence of transaction costs. As discussed above, these arise during and from the process of negotiating as a result of the combination of bounded rationality and opportunism, and due to the impossibility/difficulty of predicting all future contingencies that may affect a contractual relation. Consequently, parties are unable to write complete contracts either because they are too costly or simply because it is humanly impossible. Contractual incompleteness imposes costs arising from renegotiations.[119] Moreover, Williamson claims that transaction costs are particularly high where efficiency requires that one or both parties invest in transaction-specific assets. This is because asset specificity has 'lock-in' effects that increase the vulnerability to the other party's opportunism.[120] Thus, where one party makes a transaction-specific investment, it will expect that adequate governance structures, i.e. institutions, exist to safeguard its investment. These can be realignment incentives e.g. termination penalties, a specialized governance structure to resolve disputes, trading regularities that support and signal intentions of continuity or in some cases full disclosure of transaction-specific information.[121] The hierarchical structure of the firm is assumed to provide such safeguards and is therefore itself seen as a non-market governance mechanism. So, within the firm contracting parties have the incentives to make transaction-specific investments and thus minimize the efficiency loss that would arise had they settled for the less efficient alternative of arm's length contracting in the market. This explains the economic significance of the firm and its survival against markets or other organizational forms in the adverse selection process.

Having recognized the firm as a governance mechanism, Williamson uses the transaction cost analysis in order to explain the potential role of corporate constituencies – such as labour, shareholders, managers, suppliers, creditors and customers, as well as the community's interest – in corporate governance through board-level representation.[122] His conclusion is that all constituencies, except for shareholders as a group, have opportunities to renegotiate their contracts and thus establish adequate safeguards for their investments without board representation.

---

vol. 22, 233; and Williamson, O. (1975) *Markets and Hierarchies: Analysis and Antitrust Implications. A Study in the Economics of Internal Organization*, London: Collier Macmillan.

119   These can be costly simply because of the time and resources spent in the bargaining process or because in the presence of informational asymmetry one party may be cheated and thus suffer loss.

120   This is because, contrary to general purpose assets, such transaction-specific assets cannot be redeployed without significant cost if the contractual relation is terminated or otherwise upset. As Williamson states: 'what was a competitive market with a large number of bidders at the outset is effectively transformed into one of bilateral monopoly thereafter', Williamson, O. (1984) above n118, 1202–1203.

121   Ibid., 1204–1205.

122   Ibid., 1207–1221.

On the other hand, (dispersed) shareholders bear the residual risk of the company's failure or success and their claims are 'located at the end of the queue should liquidation occur'.[123] For this reason, Williamson argues, the firm's governance structure and the board in particular should be seen as a mechanism to safeguard shareholders' investments from expropriation by other constituencies.[124]

Addressing managerial discretion, Williamson admits that it does exist and treats it as another type of transaction cost – after all he was one of the first to claim this. However, somewhat controversially he claims that the governance structure of the corporate hierarchy serves as an important constraint on managerial misconduct. More specifically, the managerial firm's multidivisional structure, where quasi-autonomous divisions are coordinated by a central office, has improved managerial incentives for 'longer-run strategic decision-making'.[125] This is achieved because the central office acts as an internal capital market that reallocates funds from low-growth divisions to high-growth ones favouring profit over other goals. Williamson admits that the multidivisional form alone does not eliminate managerial discretion. However, he claims that it enhances the effectiveness of the market for corporate control because acquirers can 'digest' their acquisition.[126] Thus, although the divergence between managerial and shareholder incentives does not disappear, organizational structure can 'relieve legitimate concerns with managerial discretion'.[127]

This neo-institutional transaction cost approach obviously departs from the neoclassical version of contractualism in certain significant ways.[128] Most importantly, in Williamson's and other neo-institutional models markets are not assumed to be efficient. It is for this reason that the firm, not as another market but as a governance structure, comes into play to alleviate the impact of market failure by eliminating transaction costs so that an efficient equilibrium is still reached as a result of the right mix of markets and non-market governance structures. Thus, although, contrary to Jensen and Meckling's assertion, in Williamson's model the firm has both authority and fiat as a meaningful entity rather than a mere

---

123   Ibid., 1210.

124   So agency costs as defined by Jensen and Meckling can be regarded as just one type of transaction costs. See Jensen, M. and Meckling, W., above n58.

125   See Williamson, O. (1981) above n118.

126   See Williamson, O. (1984) above n118, 1225.

127   See Williamson, O. (1985) above n118.

128   Institutional Analysis began in the early twentieth century as an attempt to explain why economic behaviour often departs from the laws of supply and demand. Its focus is on Institutions which consist of formal rules, informal constraints (norms of behaviour, conventions, and self imposed codes of conduct) and their enforcement characteristics. It was revived in the latter part of the twentieth century most notably by Douglas North and in this incarnation is referred to as 'new' or 'neo' institutional analysis. See Davis, L. and North, D. (1971) Institutional Change and American Economic Growth. London: Cambridge University Press; and North, D. and Thomas, R. (1973) The Rise of the Western World: A New Economic History, Cambridge: Cambridge University Press and Chapter 2.

fiction, the same result is reached with regard to the ultimate purpose of the firm, namely current market value maximization with shareholders enjoying a central role as residual claimants. In other words, both models provide arguments for the alignment of managerial decision-making with shareholder interests so as to reach an efficient equilibrium. However, whereas in the Jensenian agency version it is the firm's lack of real existence that excludes objectives other than market-value maximization, in Williamson's neo-institutional version of contractual theory corporate social responsibility claims are ruled out by the firm's organizational *existence*.

More recently attempts have been made to extend both the (neoclassical) contractual and neo-institutional models so as to legitimate the inclusion of non-shareholder interests in corporate decision-making. The excesses of the 1980s in the market for corporate control, especially in the US, and the resulting 1987 crash may have contributed to the general discontent with the hostile takeover as a mechanism for managerial discipline where markets are imperfect. Thus, in 1992 Hill and Jones reformulated Jensen and Meckling's agency model by excluding the element of market efficiency.[129] Their results were interesting since they claimed that market inefficiencies give rise to power differentials between the firm's stakeholders and managers and between stakeholders themselves that lead to a persistent disequilibrium at least in the short and medium run. Certain constituencies, such as management, exploit and entrench these power differentials to the detriment of stakeholders who lose their ability to enforce implicit or explicit contracts and as a result bear the residual risk. This gives rise to what they call 'contracting costs' which amount to the utility loss to all stakeholders resulting from managerial autonomy. In response, stakeholders seek to develop institutional structures that will align managerial motivation to their interests and thus lead to more efficient results as the power differentials diminish. In this way, Hill and Jones provide a theoretical paradigm, a 'stakeholder-agency theory', which legitimizes managerial accountability to all stakeholder interests rather than just the shareholders. In effect, this model provides a justification for departing from the Jensenian objective of current shareholder/market value maximization. Therefore, so long as this diversion from shareholders' interests is justified from an efficiency point of view, i.e. if it does not translate in managerial rent extraction, Hill and Jones' argument can be characterized as managerialism in disguise. Where markets are not efficient optimal equilibrium is reached only when managers are able to balance diverse stakeholder interests efficiently.[130]

129 Hill, C. and Jones, T. (1992) 'Stakeholder-Agency Theory', Journal of Management Studies, vol. 19(2), 131; Jones, T. (1995) 'Instrumental Stakeholder Theory: A Synthesis of Ethics and Economics', The Academy of Management Review, vol. 20(2), 404; and also Jones, T. and Wicks, A. (1999) 'Convergent Stakeholder Theory', The Academy of Management Review, vol. 24(2), 206.

130 See also Freeman, R., Wicks, A. and Parmar, B. (2004) 'Stakeholder Theory and "The Corporate Objective Revisited"', Organization Science, vol. 15(3), 346; and Damak-

There have also been similar extensions of Williamson's model with the most important being that developed by Freeman and Evan who claim that even non-shareholder constituencies can make transaction-specific investments that cannot be safeguarded any better than shareholder inputs.[131] Due to interdependencies that exist among stakeholder claims, it may be impossible for certain stakeholders to institute sufficient safeguards for their claims in bilateral agreements with the firm and therefore representation and voting rights are necessary.[132] Moreover, Freeman and Evan do not share Williamson's argument that shareholders have no renegotiation opportunities. They distinguish between small shareholders, who renegotiate their contracts on a daily or even quarterly basis, and shareholders with large blocks of stock that are not easily redeployed. Their claim is that it is only the latter type of shareholders that incur asset specificity and therefore deserve board representation. Thus, their main proposition is that the firm should be conceptualized as a 'set of *multilateral* contracts' and that 'governance rules could be devised to ensure that the interests of all parties are at least taken into consideration'.[133] In this way, Freeman and Evan use a transaction cost methodology similar to that of Williamson to integrate stakeholder interests into the theory of the firm. Thus, just like Hill and Jones do using agency theory, they provide efficiency based justifications for a pluralist approach similar to that advocated by Dodd.[134]

Polarization in Theory

The theories outlined above derive from two social science disciplines, namely law and economics, which differ significantly in the methods and criteria they use for analysis. While the former traditionally relies on moral principles and metaphysical or sociological arguments, in the latter, efficiency is the standard rule

Ayadi, S. and Pesqueux, Y. (2005) 'Stakeholder Theory in Perspective', International Journal of Business in Society, vol. 5(2), 5.

131   Freeman, R. and Evan, W. (1990) 'Corporate Governance: A Stakeholder Interpretation', Journal of Behavioral Economics, vol. 19(4), 337.

132   On this point they explain, 'A dividend payout to stockholders may well reduce product quality to customers, and put pressure on suppliers for lower prices. Consumer arbitration panels, pollution control machinery, and so on, may favour several stakeholders at the expense of stockholders or lenders.' Ibid., 349.

133   Ibid., 352.

134   On the history of stakeholder ideas see Schilling, M. (2000) 'Decades Ahead of Her Time: Advancing Stakeholder Theory Through the Ideas of Mary Parker Follett', Journal of Management History, vol. 6(5), 224. For a critical account of these stakeholder ideas see Antonacopoulou, E. and Meric, J. (2005) 'A Critique of Stakeholder Theory: Management Science or a Sophisticated Ideology of Control?', Corporate Governance, vol. 5(2), 22; and for a good collection of essays representative of the various theories discussed above see Clarke, T. (ed.) (2004) Theories of Corporate Governance: The Philosophical Foundations of Corporate Governance, London: Routledge.

of thumb. However, in the analysis above it is evident that, despite the divergence in the manner they approach the corporation (or the firm), both law and economics can produce similar results at least as far as the corporate entity and its governance power is concerned. For instance, fiction, aggregate and neoclassical contract theories on the one hand advocate a shareholder oriented model and corporate realism and managerialism on the other claim that the firm cannot be identified with its shareholders either directly because it's a real thing or because managers are the central *de facto* coordinating power within the corporation.

Thus, broadly two main conceptions of the corporation have emerged in the literature as solutions to the problems regarding the nature and governance of the corporation, which correspond to two basic underlying concepts, namely shareholder supremacy and managerialism. Shareholder supremacy refers to the recognition that current shareholders are the owners and therefore the only legitimate controllers of the corporation which has to be run in accordance to their preferences. This nominalist vision of the corporation then refers to what can be called shareholder-oriented corporate governance which calls for the alignment of managerial decision-making with the interests of shareholders. On the other hand, managerialism does not require the alignment of managerial objectives with shareholder interests but rather that managers use their discretion positively in order to promote the interests of all stakeholders including those of shareholders.[135] This model as we noted above encompasses economic managerial and realist conceptions of the corporation where diverse interests, which are often antithetical, are amalgamated through the managerial balancing process. The associational trade offs between shareholders' individualism and collectivism found in Gierke's realist argument are then extended to include similar trade offs between and among all types of stakeholders.[136]

By the final part of the twentieth century shareholder supremacy had come to hold sway, however as we noted throughout this chapter, debate in this area has remained highly polarized. In particular critics of shareholder theories have focused on their over abstraction. For instance, Jensen's agency theory is founded upon the existence of efficient markets. Indeed, where markets are efficient informational asymmetries between shareholders and managers are contained i.e. agency costs = 0, so that shareholders can always provide the firm with the necessary finance to pursue its profitable investment projects. Similarly, as Alchian and Demsetz argue, in the absence of bargaining power differentials between stakeholders no opportunistic expropriation takes place. To take a key contested example – the allocation of cash flow generated by the firm's activities. As already mentioned, neoclassicists or anti-managerialists, such as Jensen and Meckling, argue that

---

135   Aoki, M. (1984) The Cooperative Game Theory of the Firm, Oxford: Oxford University Press; and Blair, M. and Stout, L. (2001) 'Director Accountability and the Mediating Role of the Corporate Board', Washington University Law Quarterly, vol. 79, 403–447 for a similar claim.

136   See above n27 and text.

shareholder supremacy is a superior guiding principle because it reflects the ability of market forces to allocate resources efficiently. This means that cash flows must be invested only in order to maximize the market value of the firm, i.e. current shareholder wealth.[137] Moreover, any excess cash flows that may accrue after this objective is attained do not belong to the firm, since, in their view, it doesn't even have a real existence, and therefore should be returned to the firm's residual claimants, the shareholders, either in the form of dividends or share buy-backs. As Rajan and Zingales consider:

> [u]nless there is a strong complementarity between assets in place and growth opportunities from a technological point of view, there is no reason why new opportunities should be undertaken within the legal shell represented by the existing company.[138]

Excess cash retention by the firm is inefficient because it obstructs market allocation and, as a result, deprives other firms with profitable opportunities from obtaining the necessary finance to pursue them.

However, if markets are not perfect and thus short-term values do not reflect long-term expectations managerialists would argue that the alignment of managerial objectives with shareholders' expectations can translate into a preference for short-term returns with disastrous consequences for other stakeholders and the firm's long-term viability. This phenomenon, which amounts to excessive rent extraction by shareholders and is usually referred to as 'short-termism', has sensibly attracted the severe criticism of observers who do not adhere to the neoclassical paradigm.[139] As Greenfield notes:

---

137   More recently, however, Jensen has significantly moderated this claim by arguing that firms can only 'seek' to maximize market value, an objective that can be combined with what he calls 'enlightened stakeholder theory'. In this model Jensen seems at least partially to concede on the efficient markets hypothesis issue particularly since he admits that short-term profit maximization can destroy long-term market value. Moreover, contrary to his early arguments, he goes as far as to claim that 'companies, management systems, and economic systems are also like organisms'. Jensen, M. (2001) 'Value Maximization, Stakeholder Theory, and the Corporate Objective Function', European Financial Management Review, vol. 7, 154.

138   Rajan, R. and L. Zingales (2001) 'The Influence of the Financial Revolution on the Nature of Firms', Paper presented at the 2001 American Economic Association Meeting in New Orleans.

139   See Dickerson, A., Gibson, H. and Tsakalotos, E. (1995) 'Short-Termism and Under-Investment: The Influence of Financial System', Manchester School of Economic and Social Studies, vol. 63, 351–367; and Cosh, A., Hughes, A., Singh, A., Carty, J. and Plender, J. (1990) Takeovers and Short-Termism in the UK, Industrial Policy Paper No. 3, Institute for Public Policy Research, London. For an empirical investigation see Miles, D. (1993) 'Testing for Short-Termism in the UK Stock Market', Economic Journal, vol. 103, 1379.

all one can say persuasively is that a shareholder oriented model of corporate
law is better for shareholders. It is quite difficult to say it is better for society as
a whole, or for the economy, or for other stakeholders. It is even difficult to say
it is better for the firm itself.[140]

Therefore, for managerial theorists where markets are imperfect so that they
cannot allocate resources efficiently, the internalization of corporate finance
with the retention of cash flow, even if that's beyond the levels acceptable to
current shareholders, is a better outcome because managers are in the best
possible position to know what the firm's opportunities are and allocate resources
accordingly. Managerial discretion is necessary in these cases for the exploitation
of complementarities between the firm's assets and growth opportunities. Thus,
this view challenges the legitimacy of the claim that shareholders are the only
claimants of excess cash flows on the ground that other stakeholders may also
be residual risk bearers. In this case, if a balance between stakeholder interests
is to be achieved a minimum level of managerial discretion, i.e. diversion from
shareholder/market value maximization, is necessary and therefore legitimate.

On the other hand, managerial theories have a significant problem as we noted
above – that of managerial self-interest. Where, the concurrence of managerial
goals with the balanced promotion of the corporate interest as the amalgam of
all stakeholder interests does not arise, then managers are able to abuse their
discretion in order to promote their own self-interest to the detriment of all other
stakeholders and of course the firm.[141] Therefore, managerialist arguments that
managerial autonomy is the best guiding principle in imperfect markets needs to
be qualified by the fact that managerial autonomy can lead to managerial abuse.
Thus freedom from the 'rentier class' of shareholders would amount to slavery
to the managerial class who would be in a position to abuse their power, e.g.
by using retained earnings to build empires and awarding themselves excessive
salaries and other benefits, to the detriment of the firm and the economy at large.[142]
Furthermore, due to the existence of bargaining power differentials both within and
outside the firm, opportunistic behaviour by one or more powerful stakeholders
can be equally detrimental. Where one group of stakeholders is able to tilt the
balance of corporate decision-making to its side by dominating management, i.e.
by aligning managerial interests with the promotion of its own goals beyond what
the corporate interest would justify, a detrimental expropriation of the firm's cash
flow occurs.

---

140   K, Greenfield (2002) 'September 11th and the End of History for Corporate Law'
Tulane Law Review, vol. 76, 1409–1431.
141   See above n137 at 297.
142   Marris (1998), see above n93 at 159.

As we noted above the managerial corporation emerged in the US in the early twentieth century.[143] Its key features were a highly dispersed shareholding class accompanied by a controlling group of managers who had a great deal of discretionary power. It had a key accountability problem i.e. who were the managers accountable to? This accountability issue thus became the central focus for theoretical exploration resulting in a polarized contest in which eventually theories based on shareholder superiority came to dominate. In most of the rest of the world large scale corporations emerged with a managerial class but not accompanied by dispersed ownership. Instead, the original founding families, other companies, the state and banks held, and largely still hold, significant stakes in these companies. As such the underlying accountability issue was not as acute and as a result was dealt with in a notably different way.[144]

As we will explore in the course of this book, over the past 30 years changes in the macroeconomic environment as a result of economic globalization (primarily the effects of trade and capital liberalization) have placed great pressures on these jurisdictions to introduce Anglo/Saxon outsider shareholder norms.[145] In particular because of the dominance of Anglo/Saxon capital markets in Global capital markets as 'outsider' shareholder oriented capital has flowed into 'insider' systems accompanying this flow has been the extension of this highly contested theoretical Anglo/Saxon accountability debate to encompass the rest of the world.[146]

The convergence debate

Since the 1980s, scholarly interest in comparative corporate governance has increased enormously. Initially, this interest focused on classifying different types of corporate governance system. So called 'outsider' systems, according to the literature, tend to have a significant securities market, with uncommitted shareholders operating at arm's length and focused on financial return on equity.[147] 'Insider' systems on the other hand are characterized by the significance of the state, families, non-financial corporations, employees and banks as a source of funding

---

143   See Chandler, A. (1990) Scale and Scope: The Dynamics of Industrial Capitalism, Cambridge, MA: Harvard University Press.

144   See Roe, M. (1993) 'Some Differences in Company Structure in Germany, Japan, and the United States', Yale Law Journal, vol. 102(8), 1927–2003.

145   See Williams, C. (2002) 'Corporate Social Responsibility in an Era of Economic Globalization', University of California Davis Law Review, vol. 35, 705–778 at 741.

146   See for example Gilson, R.J. and Roe, M. (1993) 'Understanding the Japanese Keiretsu: Overlaps Between Company Governance and Industrial Organization', Yale Law Journal, vol. 102(4), 871–906.

147   Coffee, J. (1999) 'Privatization and Corporate Governance: The Lessons from Securities Market Failure', Journal Corp. Law, vol. 25, 1–39; and Berglöf, E. (1997) 'A Note on the Typology of Financial Systems' in Hopt, K. and Wymeersch, E. (eds) Comparative Corporate Governance: Essays and Materials, Berlin: Walter de Gruyter, 151–164.

and/or control.[148] The ownership of shares in insider systems are significantly more concentrated than in outsider systems, and employees, creditors, the state and shareholders often have an input into control. As a result, ownership and control are not separated. Outsider systems are associated with a core focus on the shareholder and so have a strong resonance with nexus of contracts theory,[149] while insider systems resonate more with managerial/realist theories as they are more responsive to stakeholder concerns because they often form part of a wider protective social infrastructure.[150] These two alternative systems of corporate ownership and control offer not just conflicting economic and legal models but also, it has been argued, political alternatives.[151] Roe for example has claimed that, broadly speaking, the more left-wing the government, the more likely it is that the corporate governance system will be an insider system and, the more right-wing a government is, the more likely it is that the system is an outsider one.[152] Over time however the comparative debate has become focused on the issue of whether insider corporate governance systems are unsustainable in an increasingly globalized world and will transform into allegedly 'superior' outsider shareholder oriented systems over time.[153]

At first this comparative corporate governance work was somewhat introspective. In the 1980s, commentators in the UK and the US (the two outsider systems) examined successful insider systems prevalent in countries such as Germany and Japan in order to draw lessons from them about the perceived

---

148   Berglöf, E. (1990) 'Capital Structure as a Mechanism of Control: A Comparison of Financial Systems' in Aoki, M., Gustafsson, B. and Williamson, O. (eds) The Firm as a Nexus of Treaties, London: Sage Publications, 237–262; and Hoshi, T. (1998) 'Japanese Corporate Governance as a System' in Hopt, K. et al. (eds) Comparative Corporate Governance: The State of the Art and Emerging Research, Oxford: Oxford University Press, 847–875.

149   Coffee, J. (1999) 'The Future as History: Prospects for Global Convergence in Corporate Governance and its Implications', Northwestern University Law Review, vol. 93, 641–708; and Stein, J. (1988) 'Takeover Threats and Managerial Myopia', The Journal of Political Economy, vol. 96, 61–80.

150   Porter, M. (1992) 'Capital Disadvantages: America's Failing Capital Investment System', Harvard Business Review, vol. 70, 65–82; and Edwards, J. and Fisher, K. (1996) Banks, Finance and Investment in Germany, Cambridge: Cambridge University Press, Chapter 2.

151   Amable, B. (2003) The Diversity of Modern Capitalism, Oxford: Oxford University Press.

152   Roe, M. (2000) 'Political Preconditions to Separating Ownership from Corporate Control', Stanford Law Review, vol. 53, 539–606.

153   Hansmann, H. and Kraakman, R. (2001) 'The End of History for Corporate Law', Georgetown Law Journal, vol. 89, 439 at 468. For a critical view of these claims see Ireland, P. (2005) 'Shareholder Primacy and the Distribution of Wealth', Modern Law Review, vol. 68(1), January, 49–81.

corporate governance problems within outsider systems.[154] In the recession that followed the end of the 1980s in the UK and the US, the German and Japanese insider systems were lauded for their long-term stability.[155] The nature of the debate began to change in the early 1990s, as part of a wider debate following the fall of the Berlin Wall in 1989, epitomized by Francis Fukuyama's work, 'The End of History', in which he claimed that all countries would converge to a western democratic model based on political and economic liberalism.[156] While Fukuyama's political claims were widely debated outside of academic circles his claims about the convergence to economic liberalism had a slow burning impact in the corporate governance literature. In the early 1990s commentators began suggesting that some form of worldwide convergence/transformation to an outsider system was occurring or would occur. Gilson and Roe, for example, expected some level of convergence to occur because certain institutions within the outsider models were efficient or simply because insider systems would mimic US leadership on economic matters.[157] In turn, just as Fukuyama's thesis had its opposing reaction in Samuel Huntington's 'The Clash of Civilisations', where he argued that the end of the cold war signified a new era of conflict based around cultural and religious conflict, so too did the convergence claims, in what is now known as the 'Varieties of Capitalism' literature.[158] In the Varieties analysis insider systems are geared towards funding companies in product markets that are capital intensive, safe and which innovate slowly over time i.e. traditional manufacturing. Outsider systems, by contrast, are geared towards innovative risk taking, so that capital and labour can be redeployed quickly should this be necessary i.e. high tech and financial services. In essence, both systems are efficient at what they do but, according to a Varieties analysis, insider systems have a level of coordination between institutions in the economy that makes them resilient to convergence.[159]

---

154   Scott, J. (1986) Capitalist property and Financial Power: A Comparative Study of Britain, the United States and Japan, New York: New York University Press; and Roe, M. (1990) 'Political and Legal Restraints on Ownership and Control of Public Companies', Journal of Financial Economics, vol. 27, 7–42.

155   Jacobs, M. (1991) Short-Term America: The Causes and Cures of our Business Myopia, MA: Harvard Business School Press; and Streeck, W. (1992) Social Institutions and Economic Performance Studies of Industrial Relations in Advanced Capitalist Economies, London: Sage.

156   Fukuyama, F. (1989) 'The End of History?', The National Interest, vol. 16, 3; and Fukuyama, F. (1992) The End of History and the Last Man, New York: Free Press.

157   Gilson, R. and Roe, M. (1993) 'Understanding the Japanese Keiretsu: Overlaps Between Company Governance and Industrial Organization', Yale Law Journal, vol. 102, 871–906; and Roe, M. (1996) 'Chaos and Evolution in Law and Economics', Harvard Law Review, vol. 109, 641–668.

158   Huntington, S. (1996) The Clash of Civilizations and the Remaking of World Order, New York: Simon & Schuster.

159   Hollingsworth, J. and Boyer, R. (1997) 'Coordination of Economic Actors and Social Systems of Production' in Hollingsworth, J. and Boyer, R. (eds) Contemporary

Despite this challenge in the theoretical literature, by the late 1990s, with a stock exchange boom in the outsider systems of the UK and the US and the insider systems of Japan, Germany and the Asian economies in varying degrees of crisis, the nature of the convergence debate changed significantly. The publication of a series of articles by La Porta et al. marked this turning point.[160] La Porta et al. examined levels of legal protection for shareholders in a large number of jurisdictions. They concluded from their study that strong corporate law protection for shareholders led to dispersed shareholding patterns, while weak shareholder protection led to more concentrated shareholder patterns. Strong legal protection and the emergence of a dispersed shareholding base is, they claimed, more likely to foster an environment attractive to private-sector investment. If strong legal protection for shareholders is not present, this has 'adverse consequences for financial development and growth'.[161] While La Porta et al. were not directly addressing the outsider/insider debate, their work contributed significantly to later claims for the superiority of the outsider system because they claimed that common law systems (the two outsider systems of the UK and the US being also common law systems) provided greater protection for shareholders than civil law systems (insider).[162]

The timing of the claims was also significant, coming soon after the Asian financial crisis in 1997, which was widely but incorrectly attributed to corporate governance failure in an insider system.[163] As a result, despite the La Porta et al. evidence being highly controversial, it sent a clear policy message to governments and international policy makers that law should be at the centre of investment policy, and spurred a debate about the role law has had in creating the outsider

---

Capitalism: The Embeddedness of Institutions, Cambridge: Cambridge University Press, 1–2.

160   La Porta, R. et al. (1998) 'Law and Finance', Journal of Political Economy, vol. 106, 1113–1155; La Porta, R., Lopez-de-Silanes, F. and Shleifer, A. (1999) 'Corporate Ownership Around the World', The Journal of Finance, vol. 54, 471–517. See also their later work, La Porta, R., Lopez-de-Silanes, F. and Shleifer, A. (2006) 'What Works in Securities Laws', Journal of Finance, 1; and Djankov, S., La Porta, R., Lopez-de-Silanes, F. and Shleifer, A. (2005) 'The Law and Economics of Self-Dealing', NBER Working Paper No. 11883.

161   Ibid. (1998), 1152.

162   Modigliani, F. and Perotti, E. (2000) 'Security versus Bank Finance: The Importance of a Proper Enforcement of Legal Rules', FEEM Working Paper No. 37.99 <http://ssrn.com/abstract=200559>; Scott, K. (1999) 'Corporate Governance and East Asia', Stanford Law School, John M. Olin Program in Law and Economics Working Paper No. 176 <http://ssrn.com/abstract=173369>; and Johnson, S. and Shleifer, A. (2001) 'Coase v. the Coasians', The Quarterly Journal of Economics, vol. 116, 853–900.

163   Singh, A., Singh, A. and Weisse, B. (2002) 'Corporate Governance, Competition, The New International Financial Architecture and Large Corporations in Emerging Markets', ESRC Centre for Business Research, University of Cambridge Working Paper No. 250 <http://ideas.repec.org/p/cbr/cbrwps/wp250.html>.

systems present today in the UK and the US.[164] La Porta et al. and their advocates viewed the shareholder-orientation of corporate law in the UK and US as central to the creation of outsider systems.[165]

As we noted above, the claims of La Porta et al. marked a change in the nature of the debate, from one of introspection and the possibility of convergence, to implicit claims of superiority for outsider shareholder-oriented norms. That is, that convergence/transformation will be to an outsider model. By 2001 the claims of superiority were no longer implicit, but explicit. For example, despite the collapse of the US stock market bubble between 2001 and 2002, Hansmann and Kraakman claimed, in a deliberately provocative borrowing of Fukuyama's 'End of History' thesis, that a range of factors, including the failure of alternative corporate governance models, logical/ideological pressures, and the globalization of product and financial markets, meant that '[the] triumph of the shareholder-oriented model of the corporation over its principal competitors is now assured'.[166] Notwithstanding the collapse of the US companies Enron and WorldCom in 2002 and the period of self-analysis and reform that followed, mainstream outsider advocates (mainly US commentators) have, at least until the global crisis in financial markets that began in autumn 2008, remained confident in the triumph of the outsider shareholder corporate model.[167] And so just as the US domestic corporate accountability debate has been dominated over the past 30 years by shareholder oriented solutions to corporate accountability issues, many convergence scholars have also associated non-shareholder oriented systems with the domestic US conception of the issue. As Ireland notes:

> [m]uch of the pressure for the adoption of rigorously shareholder-oriented corporate structures has, of course, come from the US, as part of the more general pressure exerted to compel governments worldwide to adopt neo-liberal economic and social policies. It has been US academics who have been largely responsible for developing the theories which try to rationalize and legitimate both neo-liberalism and Anglo-American style shareholder primacy. This is not insignificant ...[168]

---

164   Coffee, J. (2001) 'The Rise of Dispersed Ownership: The Roles of Law and the State in the Separation of Ownership and Control', Yale Law Journal, vol. 111, 1–82 at 25–29; and Cheffins, B. (2002) 'Corporate Law and Ownership Structure: A Darwinian Link? Contemporary Issues in Corporate Governance', University of New South Wales Law Journal, vol. 25, 346–378.

165   See above n160.

166   Hansmann, H. and Kraakman , R. above n153.

167   Ireland, P. (2005) 'Shareholder Primacy and the Distribution of Wealth', Modern Law Review, vol. 68, 49–81; and Greenfield, K. (2002) 'September 11th and the End of History for Corporate Law', Tulane Law Review, vol. 76, 1409–1429.

168   Ireland, P. above n167, 79–80.

Perspective is influential here as viewed through the prism of an Anglo/Saxon debate historically focused on what were perceived as unaccountable managers of dispersed shareholder corporations in which shareholder supremacy has come be expressed as an orthodox solution, one gets a distorted view of the rest of the world's corporate accountability mechanisms where systems have not historically produced dispersed shareholders and as a result have a different, often managerial focus, to internal accountability. Put simply, in our view analysing a corporate governance system as good or bad depending on its conformity to a shareholder orientation would lead one to a distorted view of the rest of the world's insider systems where accountability is often framed in a broader institutional context. As we noted at the start of this chapter the theoretical context is significant here in three ways. First, as we will observe in Part II of the book, real corporate governance transformation, in the US and the UK, was closely linked to changes in the theoretical landscape. Second, the convergence scholarship as we noted above, is in our view strongly driven by a theoretical 'shareholder superiority bias' which needs to be filtered for if we are actually to examine the likelihood of change and transformation in corporate governance systems. An understanding of this is essential for our further examination of neoclassical theories of change in Chapter 4. Third, as we will observe in Chapters 3 and 6 and to which Ireland alludes above, this shareholder superiority scholarship has also been influential in framing the rules upon which the process of globalizing capital markets has been based.

Conclusion

In the course of this chapter we have explored the various theories that have been used to explain the nature of the corporation. Over the course of the twentieth century as the managerial firm emerged corporate theory focused clearly on the accountability gap created by the separation of ownership from control. As such, two broad conceptions of the corporation emerge in the literature which we describe as shareholder supremacy and managerialism. The former advocates that the focus of managerial power should be the shareholder while the latter advocates broader accountability for managers to stakeholders. Although these conceptions of the corporation are highly contested, shareholder supremacy has over the past 30 years come to ascendancy, particularly in the United States. In turn, as the globalization of financial markets has introduced Anglo/Saxon 'outsider' capital into 'insider' systems such as Germany, this has been accompanied by an elevation of this contested theoretical accountability debate and the dominance of shareholder supremacy to the global stage with some scholars claiming that the convergence of insider systems to a shareholder oriented outsider system is preordained. In order to examine the viability of these claims and to explore change generally, in the next chapter we introduce institutional analysis as our preferred form of theoretical analysis for a forum in which change in the institutional context, whether national or global, is significant.

Chapter 2

Institutional Analysis and Corporate Governance Systems

Introduction

Having set out in the previous chapter the theoretical background to the claims made about the convergence of insider systems to outsider systems, in this chapter we begin our examination of these convergence claims. As we noted in the first chapter, in a perfect world where the neoclassical assumptions apply, the only determinant of corporate governance outcomes is the market. However, in reality managerial behaviour is shaped in an imperfect world, where the bounded rationality of economic agents and uncertainty give rise to positive transaction costs. Therefore, in comparing corporate governance systems at the national and global level, where institutional interactions are crucial to convergence claims, we will utilize institutional analysis rather than theories based on neoclassical equilibria that assume freedom from institutional interference. Where markets are not perfect, the orientation of a corporate governance system in terms of outsider shareholder or insider stakeholder outcomes, and the possibility of movement from one to the other, depends in our view on the institutional structure within which it is embedded. Additionally for us institutional analysis has an advantage when working, as we are, across a number of social science disciplines. As North stated when considering his aim in developing his ideas on institutional analysis:

> [a] useful theory of economic change cannot confine itself purely to economics but must try to integrate the social sciences and integrate them also with cognitive science.[1]

Institutional Analysis and Corporate Governance Outcomes

According to Alston's methodological proposition, institutional analysis can proceed in two different ways.[2] The first is one that focuses on the *effects* of

---

1   North, D. (2005) Autobiography, available at <http://nobelprize.org/nobel_prizes/economics/laureates/1993/north-autobio.html>.

2   Alston, L. (1996) 'Empirical Work in Institutional Economics: An Overview' in Alston, L., Eggertsson, T. and North, D. (eds) Empirical Studies in Institutional Change, Cambridge: Cambridge University Press, 25–30 at 26.

existing institutional configurations on economic agents' choices of action as a 'comparative statics' exercise. The second method concentrates on the dynamic analysis of institutional sets by examining the causes of institutional change. While the latter approach is central for the purposes of this work, this chapter is devoted to a static institutional analysis leaving the dynamic analysis for the chapters that follow. This is because, in order to identify the endogenous and exogenous dynamics as sources of a corporate governance system's change, a prior understanding of the determinant role of institutions is necessary.

Although institutionalist methodology has gradually gained wide acceptance over the years and now constitutes a significant element in economics and social science in general, there is no standard definition of institutions.[3] For instance, Veblen, one of the pioneers of institutional analysis, saw institutions broadly as 'settled habits of thought common to the generality of men'.[4] While versions of this 'common habits' approach can be found in several texts, more recently others have attempted to define institutions in more formal terms.[5] Thus, to North institutions are:

> the humanly devised constraints that shape human interaction. In consequence they structure incentives in human exchange, whether political, social, or, economic. ... In the jargon of the economist, institutions define and limit the set of choices.[6]

These behavioural constraints can be formal and informal. Formal institutions may include rules contained in constitutions, statute and common law, organizational by-laws, and even contracts. Informal institutions or norms, on the other hand, consist of accepted practices, customs and regularities that are not legally enforceable but which are, nevertheless, followed either for habitual reasons or because breaching them entails social and peer-group criticism as well as reputation costs. However, while they have an important influence on individuals' choices, these constraints do not determine human behaviour *completely*; they simply set the limits of action and define the opportunity set of economic agents, which may be broad or narrow depending on the nature and effect of institutional constraints.[7] As Parsons states,

---

3   See Hodgson, G. (1988) Economics and Institutions: A Manifesto for a Modern Institutional Economics, Cambridge: Polity Press; and Aoki, M. (2001) Toward a Comparative Institutional Analysis, Cambridge and London: MIT Press.

4   Veblen, T. (1919) The Place of Science in Modern Civilization and Other Essays, New York: Huebsch, 239.

5   Knight, F. (1947) Freedom and Reform: Essays in Economic and Social Philosophy, New York: Harper; Katona, G. (1951) Psychological Analysis of Economic Behavior, New York: McGraw-Hill; and Polanyi, M. (1967) The Tacit Dimension, London: Routledge & Kegan Paul. For a review of the literature see Hodgson, G., above n3, 124–134.

6   North, D. (1990) Institutions, Institutional Change and Economic Performance, Cambridge: Cambridge University Press, 3–4.

7   See Hodgson, G., above n3, 10–12.

institutions are 'normative patterns which define what are felt to be, in the given society, proper, legitimate, or expected modes of action or of social relationship'.[8] Since the behavioural choices of economic actors are not fully predetermined by the invisible hand of perfect markets, uniformity is not the norm. Zysman summarizes the determinant role of institutions as follows:

> national institutional structure shapes the dynamics of the political economy and sets the boundaries within which government and corporate strategies are chosen … Certainly, there will be variety within a particular polity; but its common national features give character and provide limits to that diversity.[9]

Institutions do not exist and operate in isolation from each other. On the contrary, viewed in a static way, they form coherent institutional webs the component elements of which are interconnected and complementary.[10] Complementarity can be vertical, i.e. between formal institutions and informal institutions, or horizontal, i.e. between institutions of the same type. For example, vertical complementarity occurs as legal rules often come into existence as a result of the crystallization of routines, conventions, traditions etc. and are therefore closely linked to the context of norms and values from which they derive. Moreover, informal institutions can be extensions, elaborations and qualifications of formal rules.[11] Horizontal complementarities come about as institutions, especially formal ones, are often shaped so as to be compatible and often reinforce each other. Such complementarities are more common between groups of institutions that are assigned with the task of regulating particular areas of activity, such as finance, industrial relations, social security, education, crime, property ownership, justice, contract, etc. These institutional groups collectively form *sub-systems* which are in a complementary relationship with each other as they make up a coherent institutional system.

Having identified the nature and role of institutional constraints, an important distinction that must be made is that between institutions and organizations, such as firms, unions, and regulatory or government agencies.[12] While the latter may also provide a structure for human activity, just as institutions do, they are essentially the creators of the institutional sets within which they act rather than

---

8   Parsons, T. (1940) 'The Motivation of Economic Activities', Canadian Journal of Economics and Political Science, vol. 6, 187 at 190.

9   Zysman, J. (1994) 'How Institutions Create Historically Rooted Trajectories of Growth', Industrial and Corporate Change, vol. 3(1), 243 at 271.

10   Ibid. and Amable, B. (1999) 'Institutional Complementarity and Diversity of Social Systems of Innovation and Production', Discussion Paper FS/99–309, Wissenschaftszentrum Berlin für Sozialförschung, Berlin.

11   North, D., above n6, 83.

12   Ibid., 4–5; and Amable, B., above n10. Some authors, however, tend to blur this distinction. See Alston, L., above n2.

parts of it. That is, just like humans, organizations are the players and institutions are the rules. This distinction is crucial for understanding not only the nature and role of particular institutional frameworks but also the interaction between rules and players. While organizations create institutions, at the same time they are shaped by the institutional sets within which they operate. Institutions determine the boundaries of organizations activities and, thus, shape their nature.

In a similar manner to Dewey's 'consequentialism' of the nineteenth century we take the view that to a large extent the nature of the corporate governance system is shaped by the institutional environment in which it operates.[13] By operating as constraints that affect economic agents' choices of action, institutions can affect corporate decisions. In a corporate governance system, each institution affecting the behaviour of managers, and, therefore, of the firm, has a particular dynamic which pulls firm behaviour in a particular direction. For instance, an institution that constrains managerial discretion forms an element in the institutional forces that pull the system towards a market oriented outsider shareholder model, whereas another that constrains the operation of the market for corporate control pulls it towards an insider system. In this way, institutions determine not only how much discretion, if any, managers can enjoy but can also set the limits of its use.

Thus, a corporate governance system can be described as a nexus of several such institutional forces. What then determines the nature of the system is the resultant force of this nexus, which drives firm behaviour towards either the insider paradigm or shareholder paradigm. So, while two separate national systems may bear several institutional differences, if the combined force of constraints limits managerial discretion significantly to the advantage of shareholders, then they can be categorized as *versions* of the outsider shareholder model.[14] If, on the other hand, the institutional constraints as a whole leave significant discretion to managers or directly favour stakeholders over shareholders, then the systems will essentially be versions of the insider paradigm.

However, one implication of institutional complementarity is that identifying all the institutions that may affect managerial behaviour, either directly or indirectly, can be very difficult.[15] This is even more so in a comparative analysis,

---

13   This claim was part of the early nineteenth century debate between legal theorists on the role of theory in determining the nature of the corporation. Dewey's position was that the theories of the corporation lead to conflicting implications as each theory can be 'used to serve opposing ends'. Instead, he claimed that the corporation is a concept which can only be determined by the consequences of its actions within the particular circumstances each time; see Dewey, J. (1926) 'The Historic Background of Corporate Personality', Yale Law Journal, vol. 35, 655.

14   Managers will always enjoy some discretion. Institutional sets, however, can enhance the role of market contracting *enough* to minimize the level of managerial discretion and so promote shareholder supremacy as the prevailing governance principle.

15   On the methodological difficulties of institutional analysis see Amable, B. and Pettit, P. (1999) 'Identifying the Structure of Institutions to Promote Innovation and Growth', Working Paper No. 9919, CEPREMAP, Paris; and Amable, B., above n10.

such as ours, due to the particular differences that exist between national institutional sets. Therefore, we rely in our analysis on the selection of particular elements or sub-systems that seem to have the largest influence on the strategic choices of organizations.[16] However, it is necessary to note that due to systemic complementarity and complexity, identifying and defining the precise boundaries of such sub-systems is not always possible and, as a result, some arbitrariness is unavoidably introduced. The general areas selected here as the most important in determining corporate governance outcomes are corporate law, the financial system, the industrial relations system and sub-systems related to the government demand function, particularly competition and effective demand. Due to the apparent centrality of corporate law in regulating corporate activity it seems appropriate to examine its role first.

Corporate Law and Corporate Governance Outcomes

Over the past decade there has been a resurgent interest in comparative company law. While in the past comparative corporate law studies have focused on the differences that exist between national legal rules governing corporate activity a feature of this recent wave of comparative work has been its emphasis on the similarities between major jurisdictions.[17] Indeed, to a large extent cross pollination of concepts has been a relatively common feature of major company law systems over time. As Hopt notes, taking the example of Japan:

> Japanese company law of 1893 (*Kyû-shôhô*) was based to a significant extent on a draft by the German scholar Carl Friedrich Hermann Roesler, and combined elements of the French *Code de commerce* (mainly as to its form) and of the German *Allgemeines Deutsches Handelsgesetzbuch* of 1861 (concerning many substantive principles). The later company law of 1899 (*Shôhô*) was close to the German company law revision of 1870 in its revised form of 1884, and the revised *Shôhô* of 1938 was closely modelled on the German Stock Corporation

---

16   Such a methodology resembles the 'Régulation' approach, which concentrates on certain standard institutional themes which can even be loosely connected with the subject of analysis, rather than a comprehensive analysis which would seek to identify all the institutions that are directly linked to the activities that are being studied. See, for instance, Aglietta, M. (1979) A Theory of Capital Regulation – The US Experience, London: New Left Books; and Boyer, R. (1990) The Regulation School: A Critical Introduction, New York: Columbia University Press.

17   See Reinier R., et al. (2004) The Anatomy of Corporate Law, A Comparative and Functional Approach, Oxford: Oxford University Press.

> Act of 1937. After World War II, Japanese company law reform closely followed
> the United States company law principles ...[18]

Here in this section we similarly observe that fundamental elements of corporate
law are very similar across most major capitalist models.[19] These elements have
significant implications for corporate governance as they are directly linked to the
elements of ownership and control and the relationship between them.

Corporate personality

The notion of corporate legal personality and its implications are perhaps features
that most corporate lawyers in all major jurisdictions now tend to perceive as given
and inseparable from the very existence of corporate law. While in nineteenth
century England the use of the trust enabled commercial associations to function
without the need for legal personality, in the absence of the trust, lawyers in
European Continental jurisdictions had to invent a vehicle that would serve the
needs of associations of entrepreneurs.[20] Thus, the *société en commandite* with a
legal personality distinct from its members, who enjoyed limited liability, became
the dominant business form in Continental jurisdictions relatively early. The need
to grant legal personality to such associations was more immediate on the Continent
than in England where deeds of settlement and partnerships continued to dominate
economic activity until well into the second half of the nineteenth century.[21]
Nevertheless, commercial reality revealed the weaknesses of the English legal
regime and inevitably led to the grant of limited liability and the recognition of
the company's autonomous legal persona even for small one-person companies.[22]

---

18   See Hopt, K. (2006) 'Comparative Corporate Law' in Reimann, M. and
Zimmermann, R. (eds) The Oxford Handbook of Comparative Law, Oxford, 1168.

19   By major capitalist models we refer primarily to the UK, US, Germany, France
and Japan. See ibid.; Hansmann, H. and Kraakman, R. (2004) 'What is Corporate Law?' in
Reinier, R. et al. above n17, 1–19; and Gepken-Jager, E., van Solinge, G. and Timmerman, L.
(2005) Voc 1602–2002: 400 Years of Company Law, Kluwer Law International.

20   See for instance *Child v. Hudson's Bay Co.* (1723) 2 P. Wms 207; *Harrison v.
Pryse* (1740) Barn. Ch. 324; and *Taylor v. Chichester Rly Co.* (1867) LR 2 Exch. 256.

21   When the Bubble Act of 1720 restricted dramatically the creation of joint stock
companies in England, entrepreneurs used the deed of settlement to establish unincorporated
associations in order to conduct their business operations. Those bodies were not separate
legal entities and their assets were held by trustees who could act on the associations'
behalf. This was not an ideal solution and the debate on whether the *société en commandite*
should be introduced into English law was long and intense. Foster, N. (2000) 'Company
Law Theory in Comparative Perspective: England and France', American Journal of
Comparative Law, vol. 48, 573 at 583.

22   See Joint Stock Companies Act 1856 and *Salomon v. Salomon Ltd.* [1897] AC 22
respectively. For a detailed overview see Gepken-Jager, E., van Solinge, G. and Timmerman,
L., above n19, 28–46.

So although English corporate law had different origins from other Continental European ones and followed a different path of evolution for several decades, over time the fundamental notions of corporate personality and limited liability became an indispensable element of both systems and their former colonies.

Additionally a significant change in the nature of the share had immense influence on the development of those notions. This change came with the growth of corporations, especially railway, mining and canal building companies, during the two industrial revolutions of the nineteenth century, combined with the increase in the number of shares with free transferability. Investors met in stock markets and bought, sold and liquidated their shares in companies in the same way that bonds were exchanged without affecting the companies themselves. The share as a unit of property was separated from the company's assets and acquired a market value of its own. The link between share ownership and corporate ownership was practically broken.[23]

So, in the most influential capitalist economies registered companies came to be regarded as autonomous legal entities or persons which are separate and distinct from their shareholders. As a legal person a company can sue and be sued. It can own property and enter into contracts with third parties, including other companies. Generally, a company can conduct its business in its own name and on its own behalf. It has a separate existence from its shareholders who may change or cease to exist without necessarily affecting the corporation.

Perhaps one of the most important consequences of corporate legal personality is in the sphere of ownership. All major corporate law systems stop short of attributing to any natural or legal person(s) full legal ownership of a corporation. So while under the doctrine of corporate personality a company may own property under its own name, even a controlling shareholder interest in a company, say 51–100 percent of all voting shares, this will not give rise to a proprietary interest in the company's assets.[24] The only property a shareholder owns is the shares themselves and the bundle of rights that their ownership carries.[25] This means that ownership of a company's shares is a matter distinct from corporate ownership.

Another fundamental attribute of the incorporated company is the doctrine of shareholders' limited liability.[26] In fact, limited liability and corporate personality

---

23   Ireland, P. (1996) 'Corporate Governance, Stakeholding and the Company: Towards a Less Degenerate Capitalism?', Journal of Law and Society, vol. 23(3), 287 at 303.

24   See for instance the English decision in *Macaura v. Northern Assurance Co. Ltd.* [1925] A.C. 619. Similarly, Article 529 of the French Commercial Code of 1807 acknowledged that a company (*société*) owned its assets in its own right. See Foster, N., above n21.

25   See Ireland, P., Grigg-Spall, I. and Kelly, D. (1987) 'The Conceptual Foundations of Modern Company Law', Journal of Law and Society: Critical Legal Studies, vol. 14(1) Spring, 149–165.

26   Hansmann, H. and Kraakman, R. (2004) 'What is Corporate Law?' in Reinier, R. et al. above n17, 8–10.

are the two sides of the same coin. It would be paradoxical to regard the corporation as a legal person distinct from its shareholders if the later were to be liable for the acts or liabilities of the former. Thus, corporate law allows for shareholders' liability to be limited to the amount of capital they provided for the purchase of their shares. So in a sense limited liability reduces the economic status of a shareholder to below that of a debenture holder. However, although a company has no owner in the strict legal sense, in most capitalist jurisdictions, corporate law recognizes in some form the body of shareholders in corporate control and governance. It is the shareholders as a body that approves significant transactions such as mergers and capital increases, has an input into who will be a director, and even decide on the company's dissolution and liquidation.

Organizing the separation of ownership from control

Another common feature of corporate law systems is the legal separation of share ownership from control in an organizational sense.[27] This is effected by the legally prescribed organizational structure of the company itself broadly divided between a shareholder body, the general meeting, and a management body, the board. The functions of the general meeting are regulated in a very similar fashion in all major corporate law systems.[28] For instance, general meetings vote by majority, appoint the company's auditors and decide upon important corporate transactions. Similarly, all national corporate laws provide some minimum safeguards against the exploitation of minority shareholders by the majority although some do so more effectively than others.[29]

What is more important, however, is that all corporate laws in one way or another call for the delegation of the powers and responsibilities of day-to-day management to a body which is separate from the General Meeting.[30] So there is a

---

27   Hansmann, H. and Kraakman, R. (2004) 'What is Corporate Law?' in Reinier et al. above n17, 11–13.

28   Baums, T. and Wymeersch, E. (eds) (1999) Shareholder Voting Rights and Practices in Europe and the United States, London: Kluwer International, 21–56.

29   According to La Porta et al. common law countries have tended to have higher levels of minority protection than their civil law counterparts. La Porta, R. et al. (1998) 'Law and Finance', Journal of Political Economy, vol. 106, 1113–1155; La Porta, R., Lopez-de-Silanes, F. and Shleifer, A. (1999) 'Corporate Ownership Around the World', The Journal of Finance, vol. 54, 471–517. Although for a more recent consideration of this issue see Armour, J., Deakin, S., Sarkar, P., Siems, M. and Singh, A. (2008) 'Shareholder Protection and Stock Market Development: An Empirical Test of the Legal Origins Hypothesis', University of Cambridge, CBR Working Paper; ECGI – Law Working Paper No. 108/2008 <http://ssrn.com/abstract=1094355>. See also Dunlavy, C. (2006) 'Social Conceptions of the Corporation: Insights from the History of Shareholder Voting Rights', Washington and Lee Law Review, vol. 63, 1347.

30   On the origins of the German delegation of control to management see Chandler, A. (1990) Scale and Scope: The Dynamics of Industrial Capitalism, Cambridge, MA: Belknap

significant delegation of corporate control from shareholders to a board of directors which can be through a unitary board or a two-tier structure comprising a non-executive supervisory board and an executive management board e.g. in Germany, Austria, the Netherlands, Denmark and Sweden.[31] The main link between those boards and the shareholders is that directors are generally appointed by the General Meeting.[32] This is the ultimate control function associated with share ownership. When the body of shareholders are not happy with the incumbent board members they can in theory dismiss or refuse to reappoint them as they think fit.[33] While this is a considerable theoretical power over the company granted by corporate law, the General Meeting's powers are of a 'residual' character, since the main decision-making body is the board. The management functions of a company are transferred on to the directors making the board the centre of the company's power structure.

This separation of (share-)ownership from control raises the issue of accountability of those in control of the company's affairs. So another standard feature of corporate law is the imposition of legal duties on directors with the purpose of ensuring that they meet certain standards of conduct and the prevention of abuses of power. Here there is diversity in the methods employed by different jurisdictions and their effectiveness for the enforcement of directors' duties. For instance, while many systems leave enforcement to adversarial private litigation, some corporate laws show a preference for internal negotiation and pressure from within the board structure.[34] However, there are broadly important similarities in the nature of those duties and their purpose in all major jurisdictions. Significantly, they all contain a duty that board members have to act in the best interests of the

---

Press of Harvard University, 591. On Germany, Britain and France see Whittington, R. and Mayer, M. (2000) The European Corporation: Strategy, Structure and Social Science, Oxford: Oxford University Press.

31   The supervisory board stands between the General Meeting and the management board. See Chapter 6 for a description of the German two-tier board structure.

32   In two-tier systems there are also employee directors.

33   Although the ability of shareholders to take action in large companies can be hampered by coordination problems. See Black, B. (1992) 'The Value of Institutional Monitoring: The Empirical Evidence', UCLA Law Review, vol. 39, 895–939; Stapledon, G. (1996) Institutional Shareholders and Corporate Governance, Oxford: Oxford University Press; and Brancato, C. (1997) Institutional Investors and Corporate Governance: Best Practices for Increasing Corporate Value, Illinois: Irwin Professional Publishing, Chapter 3.

34   For example, through supervisory board monitoring of the management board in the two-tier model.

company.[35] The duty is owed to the company itself as an autonomous entity and as a general rule it is the company that enforces it.[36]

Significantly from a normative perspective the formulation of the duty raises the question of what the interests of the company are? However, the law in most cases is insufficiently clear to provide an answer to this 'elusive concept'.[37] Indeed, most major corporate law systems give a broad meaning to the duty. In the United States, for instance, the enactment of corporate constituency statutes and some landmark court decisions balance outsider shareholder objectives with insider stakeholder objectives in the context of a takeover.[38] As a result the management of a target company have been able to take defensive action against a bid as long as it is broadly justified as being in the corporate interest.[39] In Germany, the concept of *Unternehmensinteresse* (interest of the enterprise) developed by the courts is also believed to integrate shareholder and non-shareholder interests.[40] Similarly, in France *l'intérêt social* (interest of the company) includes a plurality of interests apart from those of the shareholders.[41]

English corporate law provides a good example of how vague the concept of the interests of the company can be. Until 2006 the courts held that directors

35   Stengel, A. (1998) 'Directors' Powers and Shareholders: A Comparison of Systems', International Company and Commercial Law Review, vol. 9(2), 49–56; and Teubner, G. (1985) 'Corporate Fiduciary Duties and Their Beneficiaries' in Hopt, K. and Teubner, G. (eds) Corporate Governance and Directors' Liabilities – Legal, Economic and Sociological Analyses on Corporate Social Responsibility, Berlin: Walter de Gruyter, 149–177 at 155.

36   This is of course an incidence of separate legal personality.

37   Farrar, J. (1987) 'Ownership and Control of Listed Public Companies: Revising or Rejecting the Concept of Control' in Pettet, B. (ed.) Corporate Law in Change, London: Stevens, 55.

38   See *Revlon, Inc. v. MacAndrews & Forbes Holdings, Inc.*, 506 A.2d 173, 176 (Del. 1985); Karmel, R. (1993) 'Implications of the Stakeholder Model', George Washington Law Review, vol. 61, 1156; and Pinto, A. (1998) 'Corporate Governance: Monitoring the Board of Directors in American Corporations', American Journal of Company Law, vol. 46, 317–346.

39   Macey, J. (1998) 'The Legality and Utility of the Shareholder Rights Bylaw', Hofstra Law Review, vol. 26, 837. Note that managerial self interest is not a reason for a defensive action. See *Unocal Corp. v. Mesa Petroleum Co.*, 493 A.2d 946 (Del. 1985), at 955; *Cheff v. Mathes*, 41 Del. Ch. 494, 199 A.2d 548 (S. Ct. 1964) 508; and Gilson, R. and Kraakman, R. (1989) 'Delaware's Intermediate Standard for Defensive Tactics: Is There Substance to Proportionality Review?', Business Law, vol. 44, 247.

40   Kübler, F. (1985) 'Dual Loyalty of Labor Representation' in Hopt, K. and Teubner, G. (eds) Corporate Governance and Directors' Liabilities – Legal, Economic and Sociological Analyses on Corporate Social Responsibility, Berlin: Walter de Gruyter, 429–444.

41   Paillusseau, J. (1991) 'The Nature of the Company' in Drury, R. and Xuereb, P. (eds) European Corporate Laws: A Comparative Approach, Aldershot: Dartmouth, 31–38.

did owe a duty to act in the interests of the company and that the interests of the company are equivalent to the interests of present and future shareholders.[42] On the surface this may seem to have resolved the problem in favour of shareholder supremacy. However this formulation of the duty did not automatically preclude non-shareholder interests from being taken into account in directors' decision-making. As Bowen L.J. famously stated in the late nineteenth century:

> [a] railway company, or the directors of the company, might send down all the porters at a railway station to have tea in the country at the expense of the company. Why should they not? It is for the directors to judge, provided it is a matter which is reasonably incidental to the carrying on of the business of the company; and a company which always treated its employees with draconian severity, and never allowed them a single inch more than the letter of the bond, would soon find itself deserted – at all events, unless labour was very much more easy to obtain in the market than it often is. The law does not say that there are to be no cakes and ale, but there are to be no cakes and ale except such as are required for the benefit of the company.[43]

As a result, the duty was capable of expansion to provide justifications for significant diversion from what *current* shareholders may perceive as their interests.[44] Indeed, UK directors have tended to perceive the interests of non-shareholder constituencies as fully integrated in the interests of the company.[45] As Lord Wedderburn observed:

> a director whose legal duty is to make an honest business judgment balancing all these interests will rarely be open to challenge unless he is a crook who has been careless with the minutes. The field is full of fudge.[46]

However, the enactment of section 172 of the Companies Act 2006 in the UK has codified the duty to act in the interest of the company and now a director of a company must act in the way they consider, in good faith, would be most likely to promote the success of the company for the benefit of its members as a whole and

---

42   *Percival v. Wright* [1902] 2 Ch. 421; *Greenhalph v. Arderne Cinemas Ltd.* [1951] Ch. 286; *Lee Panavision Ltd. v. Lee Lighting* [1991] B.C.C. 620; Milner Holland Q.C. (1954) Report on the Savoy Hotel Ltd. and the Berkeley Hotel Company Ltd. Board of Trade.

43   *Hutton v. West Cork Railway Co.* (1883) 23 Ch D 654 at 672.

44   On the flexibility of English corporate law see Parkinson, J. (1993) Corporate Power and Responsibility, Oxford: Oxford University Press, 279–280.

45   See Hampel Committee (1998) Committee on Corporate Governance – Final Report, London: Gee, 12.

46   Lord Wedderburn (1993) 'Companies and Employees: Common Law or Social Dimension?', Law Quarterly Review, vol. 109, 220 at 231.

in doing so must have regard to the interests of employees, the environment, the local community, suppliers and customers.[47] While it is too early to say whether this formulation will be interpreted significantly differently by the judiciary, the guidance from the Government on the interpretation of this section clearly intends the stakeholder provisions to have impact. It considers that the words:

> "have regard to" means "think about"; they are absolutely not about just ticking boxes. If "thinking about" leads to the conclusion, as we believe it will in many cases, that the proper course is to act positively to achieve the objectives in the clause, that will be what the director's duty is.[48]

As a result, a broader concept of the interests of the company may emerge.

Overriding indeterminacy

As the preceding discussion has shown, national corporate law systems have important similarities in the way they deal with corporate ownership and control and the relationship between them. We turn now to examine the extent to which corporate law can pull a corporate governance system towards the outsider shareholder model or the insider stakeholder model.

One would expect that corporate law should provide some conclusive answers about the nature of ownership and control, given their significance as factors determining the governance of the corporation. More precisely, the law could potentially clarify the status of the shareholder either as the owner of the company or as a mere financier similar to a creditor. By doing so it would not only determine the nature of corporate ownership but it would also settle the issue of in whose interests it should be run. Nevertheless, it does neither with sufficient certainty. Corporate law accepts the centrality of shareholders in corporate control by technically giving the general meeting significant power in important matters. This seems to resemble the outsider shareholder view of the corporation. However, by stopping short of treating them as true legal owners corporate law also promotes indeterminacy.

In large management-controlled corporations, characterized by a *de facto* separation of ownership and control, the role of corporate law is potentially crucial as it could provide concrete governance solutions. For example, if legal rules awarded shareholders clearly defined ownership rights over the company as a whole the corporate governance issue would become a marginal one. That is, it would be reduced into a legal enforcement debate which would merely concentrate

---

47   Dignam, A. and Lowry, J. (2008) *Company Law*, 5th edition, Oxford: Oxford University Press, Chapter 16.
48   Department of Trade and Industry (June 2007) *Companies Act 2006: Duties of Company Directors: Ministerial Statements*.

on the effort of ensuring managerial accountability to shareholders in order to bridge the gap between ownership and control.

Fortunately for academics, corporate law seems to be incomplete from a corporate governance perspective. It does not provide the necessary link between ownership and control so as to resolve the governance issue either directly, by awarding a legal ownership status to the shareholder, or indirectly, by giving a limited meaning to the corporate interest. As Iwai observes, due to its inability to determine the nature of the company, all corporate law provides is a 'menu' ranging from the 'nominalistic' to the 'realistic'.[49] In other words, national corporate law systems seem to share a common characteristic of indeterminacy. They stop short of determining the orientation of corporate governance, since they do not define conclusively the nature of corporate ownership and its relationship with control.

The implications from this indeterminacy are significant. By avoiding the conclusive resolution of corporate governance issues, corporate law as an institution becomes flexible enough to allow diverse corporate policies according to the specific wishes of those capable of exercising control over the company. This flexibility derives from the gap created by the simultaneous recognition of corporate personality with a vaguely defined interest and of the shareholder merely as a 'virtual' but not legal owner of the company. In the case of large public corporations where managers are in control, incompleteness and flexibility translate into increased discretion. So, to a great extent managerial discretion is institutionalized in corporate law subject, of course, to the use of the legal control tools supplied to the shareholders, which, however, may not always be available in practice.[50]

As we noted in Chapter 1, for a large part of the twentieth century versions of a managerial insider corporate governance systems have been dominant in several major economies. However, this similarity did not persist. As we will explore in Chapter 5 institutional developments that occurred in the UK and the US during the 1980s transformed the orientation of the corporate governance systems in those jurisdictions even though corporate law remained fairly stable as a promoter of managerial discretion. Thus, while corporate law could be seen as a core factor affecting corporate governance, in practice its determining force as an institution is weak. In other words, the core of national corporate law rules alone is not sufficient to account for the fundamental differences in the nature of corporate governance outcomes between national systems. Other institutions have an important role as determinants of corporate governance that can even 'neutralize' the influence of corporate law. This does not mean, however, that the institutional complementarity considerations discussed earlier have no validity. On the contrary, the 'neutralization' of corporate law is an illustration of institutional interaction

---

49   See Iwai, K. (1999) 'Persons, Things and Corporations: The Corporate Personality Controversy and Comparative Corporate Governance', *American Journal of Comparative Law*, vol. 47, 583.

50   See Black above n33.

and complementarity. This is because, when other institutions determine corporate governance outcomes, they do not override corporate law but fill those doctrinal gaps that are responsible for its indeterminacy.

Having considered the function of corporate law as a promoter of the managerial paradigm, at least in the case of corporations that are de facto controlled by managers, the work now turns to examine the influence of other sub-systems on corporate governance. Of course, the analysis of constraints herein is by no means exhaustive since the sub-systems and individual institutions that shape firms' and managers' choices are enormous. However, the institutional configurations analysed here are, as we noted above, the most important, in our view, in terms of determinative influence. Without resorting to a detailed analysis of specific institutions, the main aim here is to provide illustrations of the role of fundamental institutional sub-systems and their complementarities as determinants of corporate governance outcomes. The areas selected here, the financial system, the industrial relations system and sub-systems related to the government demand function, particularly competition and effective demand are considered as fundamental, because they are directly related either to the two most essential inputs of the firm, namely financial capital and labour, or to the nature of product market competition. As a result these institutional sub-systems regulate the three most important sources of managerial constraints.

The Financial System and Corporate Governance Outcomes

Broadly speaking a financial system comprises the processes through which savings are channelled to the real economy. Schmidt et al. define a financial system as the 'interaction between the supply of, and the demand for, the provision of capital and other finance-related services'.[51] They distinguish between a financial system and the financial sector, with the latter being a component of the former.[52] However, they also claim that corporate governance is also *part* of the financial system. This

---

51   Schmidt, R. and Tyrell, M. (2001) 'Pension Systems and Financial Systems in Europe: A Comparison from the Point of View of Complementarity', Working Paper No. 65a, Fachbereich Wirtschaftswissenschaften, Goethe-Universität Frankfurt am Main; Schmidt, R. and Tyrell, M. (2004) 'What Constitutes a Financial System in General and the German Financial System in Particular?', Working Paper Series: Finance and Accounting 111, Department of Finance, Goethe University Frankfurt am Main <http://ideas.repec.org/p/fra/franaf/111.html>; and Schmidt, R. and Weiß, M. (2003) 'Shareholder vs. Stakeholder: Ökonomische Fragestellungen', Working Paper Series: Finance and Accounting 104, Department of Finance, Goethe University Frankfurt am Main <http://ideas.repec.org/p/fra/franaf/104.html>.

52   They define the financial sector as 'the part, or sector, of an economy which offers the economic units in the other sectors opportunities to invest and to obtain financing, together with associated advisory and intermediation services. Its principal constituent elements are banks, other financial intermediaries and the financial markets, in particular

is not entirely consistent with the view presented here which conceives corporate governance as the *product* of complex and diverse institutional arrangements, which include but also go beyond the financial system, and not as *part* of them. This divergence of opinion demonstrates how institutional complementarity makes the distinction between sub-systems a very difficult task. It also shows how the relationship between institutional structures and economic actors is based on interaction so that the former determines the latter and *vice versa*. Nonetheless, following the distinction between institutions and players we outlined earlier and since corporate decision-making in the view of this work is better defined as a player's *action* rather than as a *constraint*, corporate governance should in our view be differentiated from the financial system, or any other institutional sub-system.[53]

Financial allocation channels are numerous and diverse – the most important of which are banks, securities markets, pension funds and other non-bank financial intermediaries which collectively comprise the financial sector. In modern economies the regulatory environment in financial markets constitutes an extremely complex system of interwoven institutions which range from rules governing foreign exchange-capital controls, savings, securities markets and investor protection, taxation, etc. All these institutions combined determine the ways in which financial capital is mobilized and ultimately distributed to the corporate sector and, therefore, shape the financial system as a whole. Different historical contingencies require different institutional responses which in turn determine what types of channels are ultimately chosen for funding industrial investment. Thus, while all capitalist financial systems are similar, in that financial sectors therein consist of various allocation mechanisms, the role of particular channels differs.

In order to explain this divergence between financial systems it is important to emphasize the existence of relationships between savers, the financial sector and non-financial firms as channels of information flows.[54] The role of information is of crucial importance since it affects the nature, distribution and volume of transaction costs by defining the boundaries of each economic actor's rationality.[55] It is at this level that institutions come into play as they determine the types of financial relations by 'guiding' the flows of information between economic actors. For instance, institutions that facilitate the flow of information from a corporation towards public investors can decrease the level of uncertainty in securities markets and consequently reduce the transaction costs of securities finance. Mandatory

---

the securities exchanges as organised financial markets'. Ibid., Schmidt, R. and Tyrell, M. (2001).

53   See North n6, 4–5 and text.

54   See Schmidt, R. and Tyrell, M. above n51.

55   Leland, H. and Pyle, D. (1977) 'Information Asymmetries, Financial Structure, and Financial Intermediaries', Journal of Finance, vol. 32(2), 371.

disclosure rules are one such type of institutions.[56] Other rules, ranging from inadequate securities regulation to defamation laws, may also hinder public information flow. When sufficient public information is lacking, close and private rather than arm's length market-based financial relationships will emerge, as high transaction and agency costs will deter economic actors from using securities markets. Under such circumstances, financial intermediaries, the most important of which are banks, may be able to resolve informational asymmetries by pooling funds and thus internalizing financial transactions.[57] So, two fundamental parameters that characterize financial systems are the degree of financial *intermediation*, on the one hand, and *securitization* on the other. The former shows the importance of non-market mechanisms in channelling financial resources, while the latter is evidence for the relevance of market-based financial relationships.

Since the inevitability of at least some transaction costs in financial contracting makes the presence of some intermediation a characteristic of any financial system, it is inevitable that completely securitized systems cannot exist in the real world. Nevertheless, while securities markets and financial intermediaries are present in most systems, their significance and role are not equal in all financial systems as they depend on the manner in which institutional sets resolve informational asymmetries. Thus, where financial systems as a whole tend to reduce the costs of securities finance, securities markets should acquire a central role in the allocation of capital. In contrast, if systems hamper public flows of information, the importance of financial intermediation, and so the role of banks, families, non-financial corporations and the state should increase. In other words, institutional differences can give rise to two main types of financial systems. The first, which can be called 'market-based', is built around large and liquid public securities markets that constitute its centre. The second, which can be termed 'bank-based', is a financial system in which banks as financial intermediaries constitute the dominant channels through which financial capital reaches the non-financial corporate sector.

From the above discussion it is evident that the institutional constraints regulating the costs of using the securities markets are of central importance in determining whether a financial system is bank-based or market-based. Such institutions are numerous and diverse both in terms of function and of nature.

---

56   For a detailed analysis of specific institutions see Black, B. (2001) 'The Legal and Institutional Preconditions for Strong Securities Markets', UCLA Law Review, vol. 48, 781.

57   While other financial institutions, such as insurance companies, investment funds and pension funds may also have an intermediation role, banks are considered to be 'unique' in their function as financial intermediaries. James, C. (1987) 'Some Evidence on the Uniqueness of Bank Loans', Journal of Financial Economics, vol. 19, 217; and Diamond, D. (1984) 'Financial Intermediation and Delegated Monitoring', Review of Economic Studies, vol. 51, 393.

While some observers attach more importance to legal rules,[58] others claim that legal enforceability is not a necessary condition for a particular institution to exert determinant influence and that self-governance mechanisms can be at least as effective.[59] Irrespectively of what their type is, institutions promoting and supporting the role of securities markets have two specific functions. The first is to resolve information asymmetries between public investors and the corporate sector by increasing the volume of valuable information that is publicly available. Such institutions include mandatory disclosure rules for listed corporations and accounting standards, but also quality screening of securities issues by private investment banks, stockbrokers and rating agencies. Increased information flows facilitate the calculation of risk by those interested in investing in securities and related instruments and so they reduce uncertainty. Thus, the more public information such institutions produce, the less the transaction costs and the more efficient the markets.

The second function is to reduce the ability of those who possess non-public, privileged information to behave opportunistically to the detriment of market investors. Institutions such as insider trading prohibitions, takeover regulations and various other minority shareholder protection rules can minimize private rents that accrue from establishing close financial relationships. As a result, the transaction costs for arm's-length investors arising from insider investors' opportunistic behaviour decline. In the absence of private rents accruing, both types of investors are placed in a similar position *vis-à-vis* the corporate sector. Thus, the incentives for non-market financial relations diminish and the role of securities markets as an allocation mechanism of financial capital is enhanced, while that of intermediation declines.

Furthermore, apart from those institutions that directly regulate information flows, numerous other constraints may also exist that determine the role of securities markets in the financial system. For example, particular regulatory controls and government policies may be specifically designed to hinder the development of securities markets to the advantage of the banking sector and *vice*

---

58   La Porta, R., Lopez-de-Silanez, F., Shleifer, A., and Vishny, R. (2000) 'Investor Protection and Corporate Governance', Journal of Financial Economics, vol. 58, 2; La Porta, R., Lopez-de-Silanez, F., Shleifer, A., and Vishny, R. (1998) 'Law and Finance', Journal of Political Economy, vol. 106, 1113; La Porta, R., Lopez-de-Silanes, F., Shleifer, A., and Vishny, R. (1997) 'Legal Determinants of External Finance', Journal of Finance, vol. 52, 1131; and Shleifer, A. and Vishny, R. (1997) 'A Survey of Corporate Governance', Journal of Finance, vol. 52, 737.

59   See Coffee, J. (2001) 'The Rise of Dispersed Ownership: The Roles of Law and the State in the Separation of Ownership and Control', Yale Law Journal, vol. 111, 1–82 at 25–29; and Cheffins, B. (2001) 'Corporate Law and Ownership Structure: A Darwinian Link? Contemporary Issues in Corporate Governance', University of New South Wales Law Journal, vol. 25, 346–378; and Cheffins, B. (2001) 'Does Law Matter? The Separation of Ownership and Control in the United Kingdom', Journal of Legal Studies, vol. 30, 459.

versa.[60] The imposition of such institutional constraints can directly interfere with the competitive position of each type of financial resources allocation mechanism and thus determine the orientation of the financial sector. The manner of such interference varies significantly both in form and in influence from interest rate policies,[61] minimum reserve requirements[62] or tax burdens[63] to direct restrictions on the scale and scope of operations that financial institutions can undertake.[64]

On the surplus side of a financial system a number of institutional factors shape both the extent and the choice of savings according to the particular needs of each country. A particularly significant element of national savings is the system of pension provisions. Generally, there are two types of pension systems. The first and, at least until recently the most common is the 'pay-as-you-go' system where the working population undertakes to fund the retirement of pensioners by making compulsory contributions to state and corporate pension schemes in return for a guaranteed income ('defined-benefit') they will receive when their turn to retire comes. The important aspect of this system is that pension income distribution is simultaneous to the active population's contributions so that no significant asset accumulation takes place. The second type is the 'funded' system where wage earners make their own retirement provisions by contributing specified amounts ('defined-contributions') to public or private pension funds. Those pension funds invest the capital contributed in securities and other assets so that, when the pension policy of a particular beneficiary matures, the accumulated capital will depend on the asset prices at that time. Whether the pay-as-you-go or the funded system is the prevailing pension system depends on institutional factors, such as tax incentives and other pension-related regulations, that discourage or encourage households to invest in pension funds and similar savings vehicles – e.g. insurance funds, mutual funds, unit trusts etc.

---

60   Ibid. For an analysis of this view from a political perspective see Roe, M. (2000) 'Political Preconditions to Separating Ownership from Corporate Control', Working Paper No. 155, Columbia Law School, Center for Law and Economic Studies, Columbia University.

61   The interest rates are directly related not only to banks' profitability but also determine the attractiveness of bank saving as opposed to investment in other assets such as securities.

62   If these requirements are too high banks will be in a direct disadvantage, since they either have to shift the higher costs to their clients or face a decline in profits.

63   Most importantly, capital gains tax rates are one of the costs of securities transactions and thus have a direct impact on the liquidity of securities markets. Cheffins, B. and Bank, S. (2007) 'Corporate Ownership and Control in the UK: The Tax Dimension', Modern Law Review, vol. 70(5), 778–811.

64   See, for instance, the impact of the Glass-Steagall Act upon the US banking sector until its repeal in 1999. Yu, L. (2002) 'On the Wealth and Risk Effects of the Glass-Steagall Overhaul: Evidence from the Stock Market, AFA 2003 Washington, DC Meetings <http://ssrn.com/abstract=354389>.

What is important for the purposes of this discussion is that the way savings and most importantly pension provisions are organized has a major influence in role securities markets have in the financial system. Where the funded system is chosen, then a very large portion of household savings is directly channelled to the securities markets. In turn, pension funds and other institutional investors promote securitization rather than intermediation.[65] This is because they are market oriented financial institutions and most of their investment goes to securities and related instruments rather than taking the form of direct loans to corporations as banks do. At the same time, they rely on developed and liquid securities markets because they need to diversify their investments so that they can minimize their risk and avoid becoming locked in particular securities by over-investing in them. Thus, pension funds, similarly to other institutional investors, do not commit themselves to close financial relationships but prefer their investments to be as liquid as possible.

It is due to these factors that Schmidt and Tyrell conclude that the design of pension provisions as an integral part of a financial system is directly related to whether a system is market-based or not.[66] Where the financial system is designed to channel savings to securities markets via pension funds and other institutional investment vehicles, banks have a disadvantage in attracting savings, due to the historically higher long-term yields of stocks and bonds in comparison to bank deposits. Therefore, their role as providers of long-term finance diminishes as securitization progresses. So, pay-as-you-go pensions are complementary to financial intermediation since they shield banks from competition and thus warrant their role as long-term financiers of economic activity. Similarly, those institutions that promote a financial system's market orientation are complementary to the institutional arrangements that sustain a funded pension system and the securitization of savings more generally. However, it is important to note that in the latter case complementarity does not imply that securitization cannot exist without a funded pension system. Rather, it is the reverse causational sequence that reflects more accurately the link between developed securities markets and funded pensions. The institutional arrangements mentioned earlier that relate to information flows and investor protection can be sufficient for the development of securities markets. This, however, does not undermine the important role of pension funds and other market oriented collective savings vehicles as providers of liquidity.

In sum, two main types of financial systems can be identified. The first is the market-based system where securities constitute attractive investment opportunities for the surplus sector and an important source of long-term finance for the corporate sector. The function of banks in corporate finance is thus limited

---

65   See Davies, E. (1996) 'The Role of Institutional Investors in the Evolution of Financial Structure and Behaviour', Special Paper No. 0089, Financial Markets Group, London School of Economics.

66   See Schmidt, R. and Tyrell, M., above n51.

to providing diversified short-term loans that do not require the establishment of committed relationships with their clients. Moreover, institutional arrangements facilitate information flows in securities markets and thus reduce the costs of market transacting. So, generally, in the market-based system relationships between the financial sector and non-financial corporations are not necessarily committed and long-term but arm's length and determined by market forces.

The second type of financial system is bank-based, with securities markets that do not play a significant role either in pooling savings or in corporate finance. Instead, banks are dominant as channels of long-term financial flows from the surplus sector to the corporate sector. Since information does not become a public good and therefore transaction costs in securities markets are high, the financial sector needs to expend resources to acquire it privately. Long-term and committed relationships between financial institutions and corporations are then necessary for two reasons. Firstly, the acquisition of private information from the client requires significant relation-specific investment by the bank that, according to transaction cost theory, entails significant lock-in effects. Such relation-specific investment is possible only because the bank can use the acquired information for its own private benefit without sharing it with competitors. Secondly, the corporate sector is also interested in maintaining such financial relationships in order to prevent the opportunistic use by the banks of the private information it releases and to gain easy and stable access to the main external source of financial capital.

What is the significance of such differences in financial systems for corporate governance? To a large extent the answer to this lies in the differences in corporate finance that exist between the two types of financial systems. This is because there is a clear relation between corporate finance and patterns of share ownership. The presence of liquid securities markets means that financial claims are small and therefore dispersed. Otherwise they would not be liquid, since concentration of financial claims and the lock-in effects that characterize committed financial relationships are two sides of the same coin. Thus, subject to the forces of other institutional sub-systems, in a market-based financial system one expects to find a pattern of highly fragmented ownership of stock, whereas in a bank-based system shareholdings of listed corporations should be more concentrated and illiquid.[67]

This divergence in ownership structures between the two financial system types is highly significant for corporate governance outcomes because it is directly related to the corporate control channels that are available to shareholders. There are two such channels for dissatisfied shareholders, namely 'voice' and 'exit'.[68] The former describes the situation where there is direct intervention with managerial decision-making either formally through the General Meeting or informally by

67   See Berglöf, E. (1990) 'Capital Structure as a Mechanism of Control: A Comparison of Financial Systems' in Aoki et al. (eds) The Firm as a Nexus of Treaties, London: Sage, 237–262.
68   Hirschman, A. (1970) Exit, Voice and Loyalty: Responses to Decline in Firms, Organizations and States, Cambridge, MA: Harvard University Press.

face-to-face contact with managers. Shareholder exit, on the other hand, occurs where shareholders vote with their feet by selling their shares either directly to a takeover bidder or on the stock market and thus subject incumbent managers to the disciplinary forces of the market for corporate control. The choice of control mechanism is determined by a combination of two factors: the costs of exercising direct control ('voice') and the problem of collective action. In essence, these two factors are closely interlinked. The costs that accrue from exercising direct control constitute the resources expended by shareholders for obtaining sufficient firm-specific information as well as for assessing and improving managerial accountability. Whether a shareholder has sufficient incentives to incur such costs depends on his or her private gains as a result of the improvement in managerial performance. So, where private gains for all shareholders do not exceed their private costs, no *individual* shareholder will have the necessary incentives to exercise control, even if that were beneficial on a *collective* basis. It is at this point that the collective action problem becomes relevant.[69] The possibility of collective action is directly dependent on the degree of shareholder diffusion.[70] Provided that any improvement in corporate performance is reflected in the company's share price and/or dividends, private gains for the monitoring shareholder are directly related to the size of their shareholding. The higher the stake in the company the more the shareholder will capitalize on their monitoring expenditure and *vice versa*. So, concentrated share ownership automatically increases the likelihood of direct shareholder intervention whereas, if ownership is highly dispersed direct intervention is very difficult and so the ability to exit and the ensuing market effects e.g. hostile takeovers and the increased cost of capital to the company, become very important in constraining management discretion.

Thus, to the extent that the financial system can determine the structure of share ownership it has an immediate impact on the choice of corporate control. The bank-based system, on the one hand, creates significant incentives for financial capital providers, i.e. creditors and shareholders, to commit themselves to acquiring information about the value of the company's operations and thus become insiders. On the other hand, in the market-based system such incentives are virtually absent and financiers remain uncommitted outsiders to the firm reliant on market mechanisms to restrict managerial discretion.

An important issue that flows from this is whether there is any difference between the insider and the outsider system of corporate control in terms of the

---

69 For more extensive theoretical analyses of collective action see Olson, M. (1971) The Logic of Collective Action: Public Goods and the Theory of Goods, 2nd edition, Cambridge, MA: Harvard University Press; and Axelrod, R. (1984) The Evolution of Cooperation, New York: Basic Books. For applications to the shareholder behaviour see Easterbrook, F. and Fischel, D. (1991) The Economic Structure of Corporate Law, Cambridge, MA: Harvard University Press, Chapter 3; and Rock, E. (1991) 'The Logic and (Uncertain) Significance of Institutional Shareholder Activism', Georgetown Law Journal, vol. 79, 445.

70 See Rock, E., ibid.

incentives they create for managers. From a theoretical perspective, the answer to this depends on the combination of two things: the motives of shareholders and the degree of market efficiency. Different types of shareholders can have diverse and often conflicting expectations of their investment in a company. For instance, a founder shareholder whose entire wealth relates to his shareholding in the company may, once the company has reached maturity and is professionally managed, be risk averse. Institutional investors with a diversified portfolio, while not likely to encourage high risk, are likely to favour a higher risk/return ratio than a founder shareholder.[71] As such while the founder may want to retain excess capital within the company so that it can be used in difficult times or even for his or her personal benefit if need be, an institutional investor would want excess capital returned to shareholders.[72] Corporate cross-shareholdings also present a differing shareholder motive unrelated to financial returns and may simply be there to protect incumbent management or industrial strategy considerations may prevail over financial returns on equity. Shareholders who are also creditors may also hold their shares to give them influence over management primarily related to their creditor role i.e. to secure their lending and promote more loans. Again such a creditor-shareholder will be more risk averse than a diversified non-creditor shareholder and may allow the accumulation of undistributed excess cash flow.

Due to this divergence between the expectations of different shareholder types, even where share ownership is concentrated, shareholder value maximization may not be the prevalent corporate objective. On the contrary, as the share loses the attributes of a pure financial instrument to become something resembling a 'club membership' fee, shareholder commitment as a characteristic of the bank-based system can even translate into enhanced managerial discretion.[73] Since, in the absence of a liquid stock market, equity finance loses significance, bank-based systems seem to encourage the use of shareholdings for purposes other than financial income. That being so, strategic inter-firm cooperation, financial relationship building, and private rent extraction will be more important as an objective of owning shares where securities markets are not a central part of the

---

71   Investment fund expectations can differ depending on whether their investment policies are growth, or income-oriented or some combination of the two. They ethical funds may not even aim at maximum return on investment. See for instance Lewis, A. and Webley, P. (1994) 'Social and Ethical Investing – Beliefs, Preferences and the Willingness to Sacrifice Financial Return' in Lewis, A. and Warneryd, K. (eds) Ethics and Economic Affairs, London: Routledge, 171–183, and Mackenzie, C. and Lewis, A. (1999) 'Morals and Markets: The Case of Ethical Investing', Business Ethics Quarterly, vol. 9(3), 439.

72   In this case the founding shareholder's motives would be no different from those of unconstrained managers. Other cultural constraints, such as family heritage considerations, may also be important determinants of such shareholders' behaviour see Learmount, S. and Roberts, J. (2002) 'Meanings of Ownership of the Firm', Working Paper No. 238, ESRC Centre for Business Research, University of Cambridge, 9–10, available at <http://www.cbr.cam.ac.uk/pdf/WP238.pdf>.

73   See Chapter 6.

financial system. In contrast, in market-based financial systems, where stock markets are more important as a source of corporate finance, return on equity should be the prevalent criterion for investing in shares.

Nonetheless, whether this is in itself enough to pull corporate governance towards an outsider shareholder paradigm is not immediately clear. What still needs to be determined is whether outside shareholders in the market-based financial system have the *ability* to impose their expectations on managers. Since the key control channel for such shareholders is exit as a trigger for market discipline, market efficiency is of the utmost importance. As mentioned earlier, market-based financial systems rely heavily on institutional arrangements that facilitate public information flows which reduce the costs of market transacting. This does not mean that markets are *totally* efficient so that transaction costs are zero, but that they are *more* efficient than those in bank-based systems. Therefore, the existence of developed and liquid stock markets does not settle the issue of corporate control automatically in favour of an outsider shareholder orientation.

Since the major market controls on management in an outsider system are the market for corporate control and the discipline imposed by the need for listed companies to return to the capital markets for funds, a crucial element is how efficient the market is. As discussed above, market-based financial systems rely heavily on institutional arrangements that facilitate public information flow, because they reduce the cost of market transactions for dispersed shareholders.[74] However, if control-related information is unavailable or distorted, a market may tend towards intermediation. Even where control-related information is largely available, high transaction costs can arise if, because of a lack of sophistication or time, investors cannot process and use the information to make efficient investment decisions. This will be the position of small, individual shareholders who are not professional investors. For these shareholders, transaction costs can be so significant that exit is effectively unavailable. For instance, even in a 'hostile takeover' bid (that is, one opposed by management), where shareholders can directly show their approval or rejection of management, many individual investors find it difficult to decide whether the best option is to sell or to follow management and reject the bid. Unless there are clearly visible signs of managerial failure – such as repeated unsatisfactory dividend distributions, continuous share price drops or blatant private rent extraction by directors – individual investors often follow management guidance. In that case, the market for corporate control will not significantly restrain managerial discretion and may encourage a large shareholder to try to gain an input into control. As a result, small individual investors can become locked into a company because they can only sell on disadvantageous terms. At the same time they may be unable to exercise direct monitoring, since they lack the incentive and the resources to obtain or utilize information.

Thus diffuse ownership does not necessarily indicate an outsider system. A firm dominated by management, *a'la* Berle and Means, is one possible consequence

---

74   See Black, B., above n56.

of the powerlessness of small shareholders. Another possible consequence is that where diffuse ownership is combined with a large shareholder, an equivalent of an insider system may arise as that large shareholder has incentive to tie managers to their interests. Significantly those interests may not be the same as the dispersed shareholders.[75] However, there is a third possibility where a significant proportion of the shares are held by institutional investors. While in the UK and the US such investors generally operate on an arm's length basis, preferring market-based monitoring mechanisms,[76] they may intervene on major issues.[77] Institutional investors are different from small, individual shareholders as they have the sophistication and resources necessary to process and utilize the information that is publicly available. In effect, their presence significantly reduces the transaction costs that smaller individual investors have to bear. They are also different from blockholders because not only do they require liquidity and diversification, they also expect share value maximization. In other words, their investment policies are

---

75   This model is relatively common is Australia. See Dignam, A. and Galanis, M. (2004) 'Australia Inside/Out: The Corporate Governance System of the Australian Listed Market', Melbourne University Law Review, vol. 28(3), December, 623–653.

76   There are many examples of such market-based monitoring mechanisms. Awarding share-options as part of managers' remuneration creates a coincidence of interest between managers and shareholders. The market for corporate control disciplines managers: if they do not comply with shareholder wishes, the shareholders will start selling their shares and the share price will drop to a level where the company is subject to a takeover in which the managers will be replaced. Disclosure mechanisms ensure that information is given to shareholders and prevents managers from covering up their mistakes by hiding price sensitive information. Monitoring by non-executive directors acts as an immediate check on executive power at the board level. Additionally a discipline is also provided by the need to seek capital in the future. If management causes the company to perform poorly, it will be more difficult for it to raise funds by issuing new shares or borrowing money as investors and creditors will be less willing to invest in or lend to the company. Management thus has an incentive to make the company an attractive prospect to potential shareholders and creditors. See Dignam, A. and Lowry, J. above n47, Chapter 15.

77   In recent years, however, some large institutional investors – mostly Anglo-American public pension funds – have faced the 'lock-in' effects of concentrated ownership despite their broad diversification strategies, as their assets have grown to unprecedented levels. For those institutions, the 'voice' option – or what is most commonly referred to as 'institutional activism' is often the only economically rational option. Some funds also resort to corporate monitoring as a way to 'beat' the market. We discuss this further in the context of Chapters 6 and 8. The literature on this subject is substantial, see for example, Black, B. (1992) 'The Value of Institutional Monitoring: The Empirical Evidence', UCLA Law Review, vol. 89, 895; Stapledon, G. (1996) Institutional Shareholders and Corporate Governance, Oxford: Clarendon Press; and Brancato, C. (1997) Institutional Investors and Corporate Governance: Best Practices for Increasing Corporate Value, Chicago: Irwin Publishing, Chapter 3.

strictly driven by financial considerations.[78] While the combination of these two characteristics makes institutional investors inherently uncommitted shareholders, the fact that they face lower transaction costs also allows them to participate in corporate control contests more actively and to scrutinize the quality of information flow from companies.[79] Consequently, the institutionalization of financial assets and in particular corporate stocks increases the role of the market for corporate control as a disciplinary mechanism for managers and also increases the demand for free information flow to the market.[80] As we will observe in Chapters 5 and 6, institutionalization has an important role to play in restricting the discretion of directors and the ability of large non-financial shareholders to exercise control.[81] Thus, where a financial system combines a liquid stock market with a funded pension system or where generally long-term savings flow through the private financial sector – elements that, as it was shown earlier, are not unrelated – a strong tendency is created towards an outsider shareholder orientation as the prevailing principle in managerial decision-making.

Industrial Relations Systems and Corporate Governance Outcomes

While the financial system undoubtedly has significant determinative power over corporate governance outcomes by affecting the mode and force of shareholder influence in corporate decision-making, the industrial relations system can also give rise to managerial constraints by determining the governance role of labour, a production input as essential as financial capital. While industrial relations has gained broad recognition as an area of academic study, explicit and universally accepted definitions of what an industrial relations system actually is do not exist. For Hyman the subject is defined as 'the *process* of control over work relations' (emphasis added),[82] thus emphasizing the power and conflict factors between interested parties which give rise to complex informal institutional arrangements governing personal and collective employment relations.[83] Others have adopted a narrower definition that concentrates on a web of *generally* applicable rules that

---

78   Indeed, there may be a link between institutional ownership and dividend payout increases, see Short, H., Zhang, H. and Keasey, K. (2002) 'The Link between Dividend Policy and Institutional Ownership', Journal of Corporate Finance, vol. 8, 105.

79   Gorton, G. and Kahl, M. (1999) 'Blockholder Identity Equity Ownership Structures, and Hostile Takeovers', Working Paper No. 7123, National Bureau of Economic Research, available at <http://www.nber.org/papers/w7123>.

80   See Chapter 5.

81   See Lins, K. (2003) 'Equity Ownership and Firm Value in Emerging Markets', Journal of Financial and Quantitative Analysis, vol. 38, 159.

82   Hyman, R. (1975) Industrial Relations – A Marxist Introduction, London: Macmillan, 12.

83   Kochan, T. (1980) Collective Bargaining and Industrial Relations, Homewood: Irwin.

resolve conflict in employment.[84] For instance, in his influential work Dunlop identifies workers, managers and the state as the core players in industrial relations who interact to establish the institutions that determine the relationships between them.[85] Building on this, Flanders went on to define the industrial relations system as the set of all those institutions that can vary from statutory rules to collective agreements, arbitration awards, social conventions, accepted practice, and even managerial decisions.[86]

For the purposes of this work, Flanders' end product has the most resonance with the institutional analysis we have been engaged with here. Firstly, in a static analysis, like the present one, the process of institution making is irrelevant, since our quest is to identify institutional constraints and analyse their effect on the behaviour of labour and management. Secondly, placing the emphasis on rules rather than power differentials facilitates the comparative analysis of industrial relations systems, since it is differences in institutional arrangements resulting from historical contingencies[87] that are responsible for industrial relations systems' diversity.[88] By regulating transaction costs in labour markets, industrial relations systems determine the relationship between labour and the firm. Of course, the aim here is not to analyse the effect of specific individual institutions but to provide a general analysis of how an industrial relations system affects the orientation of a corporate governance system.

To begin with, in their endeavour to fulfil their human capital needs companies have two basic choices: they can either tap the external labour market to find the skills they require or develop their workforce internally through firm-specific training. The difference between these two choices is substantial not only regarding the nature and volume of resources deployed but also in respect of the type of employment relationships they create. The crucial elements that influence those industrial relations choices are asset-specificity and opportunism.

The former element describes the degree to which each party to the employment contract makes investments that are specific to the particular relationship. On the employer's side such investments can be the provision of on-the-job training, active reliance on the continuation of the employment relationship, redundancy pay promises, vested pensions and other benefits that enhance job satisfaction. What

---

84   Dunlop, J. (1958) Industrial Relations Systems, New York: Holt; and Bain, G. and Clegg, H. (1974) 'A Strategy for Industrial Relations Research in Great Britain', British Journal of Industrial Relations, vol. 12, 91.

85   See Dunlop, J., above n84, 7.

86   Flanders, A. (1965) Industrial Relations – What is Wrong with the System? An Essay on its Theory and Future, London: Faber and Faber, 10.

87   Zeitlin, J. (1987) 'From Labour History to the History of Industrial Relations', Economic History Review, vol. 40, 159.

88   Roche, W. (1986) 'Systems Analysis and Industrial Relations', Economic and Industrial Democracy, vol. 7, 3; and Streek, W. (1988) 'Industrial Relations in West Germany, 1980–1987', Labour, vol. 2, 3.

the employer relies on while making all these investments is that the employee will not unilaterally withdraw. Similarly, an employee can invest in a particular employment relationship by developing firm-specific skills and knowledge, by accepting to work more than they are being paid for, and by tying his present and future welfare to a particular company, e.g. by moving to a specific location and making non-transferable pension contributions. Since all these investments are relation-specific, if the employment contract is terminated, they automatically become liabilities.[89] The implication is that the larger such investments are, the greater the costs arising from the employment contract's termination, because relation-specific assets are not re-deployable. Consequently, each party that invests in such assets limits his or her exit option. Where both employers and employees face high exit costs, the likely effect is that the employment contract will be a long-term one based on mutual commitment and trust.[90] In other words, the two parties exclude the possibility of resorting to the external labour market by internalizing it.[91]

The choice between external and internal labour markets has important organizational effects. Firstly, long-term commitment goes side-by-side with cooperative relationships between managers as the firm's controllers and employees in order to deal with potential adverse economic conditions. In such situations it is employees who face the higher risk of not capitalizing on their investment by not receiving what is implicitly promised to them.[92] It is at this point that the fear of employer opportunism substantiates, since, unless employees have sufficient information about the firm's real economic situation, they may assume that their employer is breaching their implied agreement and discontinue their firm-specific investments. Resolving informational asymmetries between managers and the workforce when such circumstances arise is crucial in order to prevent the relationship from collapsing due to increased worker scepticism about whether to trust their employers.[93] So, the necessary governance mechanisms for

---

89   The costs arising to the employer from the lost production during the search for a replacement employee, and to the employee due to the lost wages as a result of the redundancy will also add to these liabilities.

90   Where relation-specific investment is unilateral, then the party making such investment will be vulnerable to the other side's opportunistic behaviour. In the absence of governance mechanisms safeguarding the disadvantaged party the result may be conflict and inefficiency.

91   This type of internal resource allocation should be distinguished from market transacting since it is not governed by the price mechanism. However, the term 'internal labour markets' is prevalent in the industrial relations literature and therefore we continue that practice here. See Hodgson, G., above n3, 176.

92   For instance, they may not get the training, salary and other benefits they expect or they may even lose their job if circumstances are very negative.

93   See Williamson, O. (1984) 'Corporate Governance', Yale Law Journal, vol. 93, 1197 at 1209; and Hart, O. (1983) 'Optimal Labour Contracts under Asymmetric Information: An Introduction', Review of Economic Studies, vol. 50, 3 at 23.

resolving disputes must be in place, which can vary from formalized employee consultation to board representation, both carrying the corresponding degree of influence in corporate governance outcomes.[94]

Moreover, since in internal labour market systems the threat of dismissal in case of underperformance is not easily used by the employer to motivate the workforce, other alternative motivational mechanisms are required. These usually take the form of internal promotion assessment schemes based on seniority and productivity as the main criteria, profit sharing arrangements and higher wages than those that can be obtained in the external labour market. Such institutions, however, make the sustainability of operating internal labour markets partly dependent on growth, because the size of the organizational hierarchy determines the promotion opportunities available.[95] The establishment of internal labour markets, therefore, creates a bias towards growth-maximization similar to that identified by managerial theorists. Thus, one can expect that those firms that choose such industrial relations policies are more prone to invest their cash flow in organizational expansion rather than distribute it to shareholders.[96]

On the other hand, where the external labour market option is chosen as a source of human capital, industrial relations will be diametrically different from those associated with internal labour market systems. Firstly, since no significant relation-specific investment takes place, the possibility of unilateral opportunism within the firm is minimal. In the absence of the significant lock-in effects that characterize internal labour markets, each party that is unsatisfied with the employment contract has the exit option more easily available. For instance, where the employer believes that the employee under-performs, they can replace the employee at a relatively low cost. Similarly, a dissatisfied employee will leave their job and look for another in a different company more easily if their skills are transferable and, therefore, do not become a liability outside the firm in question. As a result no information or power sharing mechanisms are necessary. The relatively unrestricted availability of exit is sufficient to ensure that neither party to the employment contract loses out as a result of unilateral withdrawal. Thus, in firms where external labour markets are the prevalent source of human

---

94   See Jirjahn, U. and Smith, S. (2006) 'What Factors Lead Management to Support or Oppose Employee Participation – With and Without Works Councils? Hypotheses and Evidence from Germany', Industrial Relations: A Journal of Economy and Society, vol. 45(4), 650–680. For a description of such governance mechanisms see Kershaw, D. (2002) 'No End in Sight for the History of Corporate Law: The Case of Employee Participation in Corporate Governance?', Journal of Corporate Law Studies, vol. 2, 34–81.

95   Rubery, J. and Wilkinson, F. (1994) Employer Strategy and the Labour Market, Oxford: Oxford University Press, 49.

96   Expansion may also include close cooperation with other similar firms resulting to group structures that encourage labour mobility between affiliated firms. This has been a common occurrence in Japan. See Odagiri, H. (1992) Growth Through Competition, Competition Through Growth – Strategic Management and the Economy in Japan, Oxford: Clarendon Press, 57, and other case-studies mentioned therein.

capital, industrial relations will tend towards an adversarial nature, as opposed to a cooperative one. Moreover, since no internal promotion mechanisms are needed these firms are more prone to shareholder distribution than investing their cash flow in organizational growth.

These differences between the two labour systems gain more substance in restructurings such as cost-cuttings and hostile-takeovers, two things that are often combined, because it is in such situations that the conflict between labour and shareholder interests becomes more apparent. As regards the former, employers that rely on internal labour market systems cannot easily use workforce reductions in order to cut their costs, because they would lose their ability to recoup their relation-specific investments. Moreover, because labour has an input into control there is an organizational bias against takeovers. Informal constraints are also present as extensive redundancies will be damaging for their reputation as 'good' committed employers and, consequently, their ability to attract the right employees in the future would be curtailed. For this reason, when cost-cuttings require the reduction of labour costs those companies that internalize labour markets face more pressure to find less drastic alternatives that are less disadvantageous to employees than companies which use external labour markets.[97] Thus, labour market internalization has further effects on corporate governance outcomes by placing constraints on managerial choices by creating a bias in favour of employee interests. Where this bias cuts into the expectation of shareholders that excess cash-flow is distributed to them instead of being used to 'subsidize' employment relations, a clear conflict arises. For instance, the company may have to favour employee satisfaction over dividend distributions, in which case shareholders will be asked to bear a higher share of the costs of a restructuring than they would have to, had the company been operating an external labour market.

The significance and extent of this conflict between shareholder and employee interests is then directly dependent on the shareholders' investment horizon. If shareholders are committed, because it is beneficial for the company and for them in the long-term, they will be more willing to sacrifice some of their current earnings in order to ensure long-term profitability.[98] If, on the other hand, they are more interested in receiving current returns than in capitalizing on the company's long-term prospects, i.e. if they are not locked into their financial relationship

---

97 Such less drastic measures can include overtime cuts, temporary lay-offs during which the employee receive a reduced salary, transfers of employees from unprofitable to profitable divisions or even affiliate companies, or even to postpone dividend distributions. See Odagiri, H., above n96, 56–64.

98 On the relationship between financial commitment and investment in human resources see Lazonick, W. and O'Sullivan, M. (1996) 'Organization, Finance and International Competition', Industrial and Corporate Change, vol. 5(1), 1; and Lazonick, W. and West, J. (1995) 'Organizational Integration and Competitive Advantage: Explaining Strategy and Performance in American Industry', Industrial and Corporate Change, vol. 4(1), 229.

with the company, the conflict becomes substantial and insurmountable. As the degree of shareholder commitment is determined by the financial system, labour market internalization is thus positively related to the degree of financial intermediation. Hence, the relationship between the industrial relations system and the financial system is a complementary one. As Amable et al. concluded in the context of labour/management relations: 'strong and influent financial markets are complimentary to a weak union and ... weak and less influent financial markets are complimentary to cooperative relations between union and management'.[99] As a result, as funding from the securities market becomes more important in a corporate governance system there should correspondingly be increased pressure to externalize labour markets.[100]

As we noted above, in the case of a hostile-takeover the divergence between the interests of employees and of shareholders becomes even more striking. Usually, in the absence of minimum safeguards the most disadvantaged corporate constituency after the completion of a takeover transaction are employees who often have to face redundancies as a result of operational overlaps between the merged entities or of cost-cutting policies so that post merger financial liabilities can be met.[101] Of course for employees who have not made any relation-specific investments and who can expect to be absorbed by other companies if they lose their job, the costs will be painful but relatively controllable. However, where at least one of the companies involved in a takeover operates an internal labour market system, the effects on the employees will be much greater. In effect, the completion of the transaction will constitute a wealth transfer from the workforce to the shareholders, since the latter will not accept an offer for their shares unless they receive a premium.[102] Thus in this scenario the interests of employees and managers may coincide as both are the ultimate losers on the completion of a hostile-takeover.[103]

Having shown that firms' industrial relations choices have significant implications for managerial decision-making by determining whether discretion is used in favour of employees or not, what requires examination are the factors that determine such choices in the first place. In other words, it needs to be clarified what external institutional constraints affect companies' employment policies. Firstly, as already mentioned, institutional constraints from the financial system are

99   Amable, B., Ernst, E. and Palombarini, S. (2005) 'How do Financial Markets Affect Industrial Relations: an Institutional Complementarity Approach', Socio-Economic Review, vol. 3, 312.

100   See Chapter 8 on the German experience of this.

101   See Coffee, J., above n59, 7, claiming that employment security and takeover activity cannot easily co-exist.

102   Ibid.

103   Where, of course, managers are awarded stock-options or are protected by golden parachutes this coincidence will not materialize. Such measures, therefore, are antagonistic to labour market internalization policies.

crucial in the formulation of a firm's employment system. The interaction between shareholder commitment, the degree of which is directly dependent on financial market efficiency, and industrial relations has already been mentioned.[104] As a more specific illustration of the interaction between the two sub-systems, takeover regulation, essentially part of the investor protection regime, regulates the ability of managers to resist unsolicited bids. It, therefore, constitutes an institutional factor indirectly affecting industrial relations and subsequently determining the governance role of employees.[105]

The skill-development system in a society can also affect firms' choice between internal and external markets. The extent to which formal education institutions and organizations – e.g. schools, universities, etc. – within a society are capable of providing a pool of specialized skilled labour from which firms can select their workforce will determine the levels of investment in intra-firm training.[106] Thus, where the skills required by firms are readily available in external labour markets, the incentive for hiring unskilled employees with the intention of providing them with in-house training will be low. However, where the supply of skills does not match the demand in terms of quality or quantity or both then firms will have increased incentives to provide additional training themselves.[107]

Furthermore, employment law and other employment-related rules also impose significant constraints on firms' industrial relations choices. A great variety of legal rules covering among other things issues such as job protection, part-time work, union recognition and power, collective bargaining, employee consultation and participation, and pension transferability regulate the availability of exit from employment contracts and shape industrial relations. Where such regulations as a whole raise considerably the costs of removing employees, they constitute externally imposed lock-in factors which are common to all companies operating within the same set of rules. Such regulatory environments, therefore, limit the discretion that firms have in the formulation of their internal employment policies and create pressures for labour market internalization with the corresponding implications for corporate governance as explained above.

Finally, other firms' labour policies may also give rise to external constraints by affecting labour supply and demand conditions. For instance, if most employers, especially large corporations whose choices carry more social weight, operate

---

104   Franks and Mayer have also made a similar claim on the complementarity between insider ownership and labour market internalization. See Franks, J. and Mayer, C. (1990) 'Capital Markets and Corporate Control – A Study of France, Germany and the UK', *Economic Policy*, vol. 10, 189.

105   The EU debate on the Takeover directive was highly controversial because of this element. See Dignam, A. (2008) 'The Globalization Of General Principle 7: Transforming The Market For Corporate Control in Australia and Europe?', *Legal Studies*, vol. 28(1), 96–118.

106   See Rubery, J. and Wilkinson, F., above n95, 51.

107   Osterman, P. (ed.) (1984) *Internal Labour Markets*, Cambridge, MA: MIT Press.

internal market systems, a firm that prefers the external market option will face more difficulties in finding and attracting the skills it needs. This illustrates how vertical complementarities between such informal constraints and formal employment rules operate.

Despite these institutional constraints that determine industrial relations systems, employers are often left with sufficient room to manoeuvre. At the micro-level a company can usually combine labour market internalization and externalization depending on its particular needs. For instance, for jobs that do not require any firm-specific skills, and therefore no additional internal training, tapping the external labour market can be preferable. In contrast, a core of jobs that needs to be carried out by employees with firm-specific training will require more committed relationships that external markets cannot provide.

However, the external institutional constraints mentioned here can be sufficient to determine whether a system *as a whole* creates pressures towards one direction or another. Thus, industrial relations systems can generally be dichotomized as those where labour market internalization and employment commitment prevail, and those where external markets and lack of commitment are most common. The mechanics of the former type of system pull corporate governance towards what can be described as an 'insider labour-oriented' system, where a coalition between managers and employees constitute a significant source of decision-making power. The latter type of industrial relations system can better sustain and be sustained by a more market oriented outside shareholder focused governance model.

The Government Demand Function:
Competition, Effective Demand and Corporate Governance Outcomes

The important role of competition as a determinant of managerial choice and performance has been widely recognized in the literature on corporate governance and the theory of the firm. For instance, Gilson and Roe state that 'the most elegant monitoring mechanism is intense product market competition'.[108] As we discussed in Chapter 1, according to the neoclassical model the existence of perfectly competitive markets can be sufficient to ensure that the profit-maximization hypothesis applies. The threat of bankruptcy is more imminent where competition is fierce and so managerial discretion is highly constrained. In a classic formal examination of the relationship between competition and managerial discipline, Hart has shown that competition *per se* is negatively related to managerial discretion.[109] Similarly,

---

108   Gilson, R. and Roe, M. (1993) 'Understanding the Japanese Keiretsu: Overlaps Between Corporate Governance and Industrial Organization', Yale Law Journal, vol. 102, 871, 891–895.

109   See Hart, O., above n93.

Mayer[110] claims that the degree of product market competition may function as a control over management decisions in that it provides clear performance benchmarks and 'swift retribution for erring managers'.[111] As Allen and Gale explain:

> competition is important … A firm can lose its entire market to a stronger competitor. In fact, this kind of competition may be seen as an alternative to the takeover. Instead of having a raider take control of the assets of a company with a weak management, replace the management, and change the target firm's strategy, a competing firm takes control of the market of a company with a weak management and dispenses with the whole firm.[112]

As we noted in Chapter 1, where managers are not fully constrained, firms will primarily pursue growth, and since the pursuit of growth usually translates into sales maximization, managerial firms will compete for market share and, thus, the agency costs for shareholders can be high. However, Odagiri has observed that competition is not absent in these situations as he argues competition can be complementary to the growth maximization objective.[113] However, to be sustainable, this type of competition requires either the continuous increase of existing markets' capacity or the penetration and, if possible, the creation of new markets usually through innovation or export.[114]

---

110   Mayer, F. (1997) 'Corporate Governance, Competition, and Performance' in Deakin, S. and Hughes, A. (eds) Enterprise and Community – New Directions in Corporate Governance, Oxford: Blackwell, 171–194.

111   See also Fama, E. (1980) 'Agency Problems and the Theory of the Firm', Journal of Political Economy, vol. 88(2), 288.

112   Allen, F. and Gale, G. (1998) 'Corporate Governance and Competition', New York University, available at <http://www.econ.nyu.edu/user/galed/papers.html>. Others such as Jensen do not view it as a powerful influence. See Jensen, M. (1993) 'The Modern Industrial Revolution, Exit, and the Failure of Internal Control Systems', Journal of Finance, vol. 48(3), 850.

113   See Odagiri, H., above n96, 316 claiming that for managers to feel the pressure of product markets competition does not necessarily have to be based on output prices.

114   This in effect constitutes a type of Schumpeterian competition based on continuous product, technological and organizational innovation in a process of 'creative destruction'. Schumpeter, J. (1942) Capitalism, Socialism and Democracy, New York: Harper & Brothers, 84. This has led some economists to talk about a trade off between the neoclassical static efficiency and the Schumpeterian dynamic efficiency (Nelson, R. and Winter, S. (1982) An Evolutionary Theory of Economic Change, Cambridge, MA: Harvard University Press, Chapter 14; and Klein, B. (1977) Dynamic Economics, Cambridge, MA: Harvard University Press). However, commenting on neoclassical and Schumpeterian competition, Langlois claims that in fact the distinction is not between two different *forms* of competition but between two *views* of it; one that sees competition as a *state of affairs* and another that regards it as a *process*. See Langlois, R. (ed.) (1986) Economics as a Process – Essays in The New Institutional Economics, Cambridge: Cambridge University Press, 11–12.

Thus, if Odagiri's product market conditions are met, one ends up with something approximating the marginal situation described in Chapter 1 where growth maximization mimics some of the effects of profit maximization. As Kester considers:

> [s]o long as growth opportunities were abundant and product and factor market rivalry was fierce, corporate managers were likely to deploy resources in a highly disciplined way. High rates of real growth, moreover, can do much to attenuate disputes among corporate stakeholders by relieving pressures to compare one [company's] gains to those of another from a zero-sum perspective ... [Shareholders] may tolerate agency costs associated with the separation of ownership from control ... if the offsetting gains from bearing such costs are greater efficiency in production arising from higher levels of relationship-specific investment and substantially reduced transaction costs arising from a greater use of flexible, implicit contracts; the mitigation of hazards associated with relationship-specific investment; reliance on non-legal dispute resolution techniques instead of costly legal adjudication; and so forth.[115]

The difference between Odagiri's competitive model and that of Hart seems to be that the former is associated with relatively high growth rates of market capacity without which excessive discretionary cash flows would accumulate, whereas the latter is a model that simply concentrates on the competitive allocation of resources according to a given or perhaps low rate of market growth. Indeed, expanding market capacity and new market creation, the ability of firms to increase the scale and scope of their operations, have been fundamental elements in Chandler's story about the success of managerial capitalism.[116] Chandler's account is also consistent with other theoretical studies presenting a causal link between innovation and large oligopolistic firms.[117]

Given these insights into the role of competition as a factor constraining managerial discretion, institutional arrangements that determine the structure of product markets as well as the nature and effects of competition can have a significant influence on corporate governance.[118] While competition policy

---

115   Kester, W. (1996) 'American and Japanese Corporate Governance: Convergence to Best Practice?' in Berger, S. and Dore, R. (eds) National Diversity and Global Capitalism, Ithaca: Cornell University Press, 107–137 at 127.

116   See Chandler, A. (1977) The Visible Hand: The Managerial Revolution in American Business, Cambridge, MA: Belknap Press of Harvard University Press.

117   See Fisher, F. and Temin, P. (1973) 'Returns to Scale in Research and Development: What Does The Schumpeterian Hypothesis Imply?', Journal of Political Economy, vol. 81, 56, claiming that large firms tend to innovate more that small ones.

118   On the important role of legal institutions in determining competition and market structure. See Demsetz, H. (1974) 'Two Systems of Belief about Monopoly' in Goldschmid, H., Mann, H. and Weston, F. (eds) Industrial Concentration: The New Learning, Boston, MA: Little, Brown.

within the legal literature usually has a narrow meaning comprising antitrust regulation, here we use the term broadly in order to encompass those institutions that shape the nature of competition as a determinant of corporate governance.[119] Such institutions can range from obvious ones such as express or implied cartel agreements between firms and antitrust regulation, to government demand policies such as full employment, public expenditure, export and import barriers. For example, full employment policy and public investment programmes have direct effects on demand for firms' products by ensuring that consumers have wages to spend on products and by the state being a consumer of private sector goods itself (for example, by building and running a hospital the state is a consumer in a wide range of industries from construction to stationery, as well as creating hospital and associated jobs). Trade policy at the macroeconomic level has a very big effect on the levels of competition firms face at the micro level.[120] If trade policy is open, then competition will normally be high at the micro-level, which in turn reduces the ability of managers to retain earnings, as resources are needed to compete.[121] If trade policy is protective, then levels of competition are reduced and the ability of management to retain earnings is enhanced. Ideally, to encourage demand, government trade policy should be an imbalance of protective home markets and open access to foreign markets.[122] In such a model the firm can expand abroad from a protected home base. By defining the structure of product markets, all these institutions determine the competitive conditions within national borders as well as outside of them.

Cooperative arrangements between companies can also have significant corporate governance effects as cartel agreements, where they exist, insulate firms from the effects of competition either between them or from potential

---

119   Hoekman and Kostecki define competition policy as 'the set of rules and disciplines maintained by governments relating either to agreements between firms that restrict competition or the abuse of dominant position'. Hoeckman, B. and Kostecki, M. (1995) The Political Economy of the World Trading System, Oxford: Oxford University Press, 252.

120   Instead of looking at individual markets, macroeconomics studies aggregate outcomes of decisions made by individuals, firms and government. As a result, macroeconomists are interested in areas of the economy, such as employment, trade, capital controls, growth and price stability, that do not appear on the radar if one focuses on the micro-level where the analysis is on individual markets and firms. See Miles, D. and Scott, A. (2002) Macro-economics: Understanding the Wealth of Nations, New York: Wiley, 390; and Begg, D., Fischer, S. and Dornbusch, R. (2005) Economics, New York: McGraw-Hill, 335.

121   Hart, O. (1983) 'The Market Mechanism as an Incentive Scheme', Bell Journal of Economics, vol. 14, 366–382; Gilson, R. and Roe, M. above n108, 891–895; Mayer, F. (1997) 'Corporate Governance, Competition and Performance' in Deakin, S. and Hughes, A. (eds), Enterprise and Community – New Directions in Corporate Governance, Oxford: Blackwell, 171–194.

122   We consider this issue in Chapter 3.

rivals. Of course, the extent, structure and sustainability of cartels fluctuate according to the wishes of participating companies as well as the influence of other institutions. For example, a cartel may be a loose agreement establishing rules for production quotas and prices in order to control the price mechanism and shift competition to other functions such as innovation. Such an arrangement is inherently vulnerable to unilateral opportunism, especially if the individual firm's benefits from breaching the agreement are larger than the costs of rival retaliation. However, a cartel may also be more rigid and stable by including formal and often state-supported governance structures and enforcement mechanisms or even the exchange of shareholdings and company board members, something that has the effect of increasing the costs of breaching the agreement and thus ensuring its stability.[123] Moreover, due to the cooperative nature of inter-firm relations where markets are dominated by cartels and cartel-like agreements, hostile takeovers may not operate as a management discipline. This is especially so where cooperative relationships crystallize as cross-shareholding arrangements which are a form of stable and committed ownership with minimal financial expectations in terms of distributed profits. For these reasons, different forms of cartelization can constitute a classic tool of managerial entrenchment. Additionally a lack of competition can also have a detrimental effect on management skills, in that a protected domestic environment may not be the best place to learn the skills necessary to operate in a competitive global market. Porter, while recognizing that there may be economies of scale in promoting large protected ventures, argues that a competitive domestic base is the best springboard for competing internationally.[124] For example he points out that Japanese companies operating in competitive domestic markets are also successful in international markets. However, a large number of Japanese industries have almost no domestic competition and in turn companies operating in those industries have almost no international success.[125]

However, formal institutions have a considerable role here in that the ability of corporations to create anti-competitive agreements depends heavily on whether

---

123   For an overview of the literature on this see Scott, J. (1985) 'Theoretical Frameworks and Research Design' in Stokman, F., Zeigler, R. and Scott, J. (1985) Networks of Corporate Power, Cambridge: Polity Press, 1–19; Scott, J. and Griff, C. (1985) Directors of Industry: The British Corporate Network, 1904–1976, Cambridge: Polity Press; Glasberg, D. (1987) 'The Ties that Bind? Case Studies in the Significance of Corporate Board Interlocks with Financial Institutions', Sociological Perspectives, vol. 30, 19–48; and Mizruchi, M. (1996) 'What Do Interlocks Do? An Analysis, Critique and Assessment of Research on Interlocking Directorates', Annual Review of Sociology, vol. 22, 271–302.

124   Porter, M. (1990) The Competitive Advantage of Nations, New York: The Free Press, Simon & Schuster.

125   Ibid., 413. See also Komine, K. (1991) 'Structural Change of Japanese Firms', Japanese Journal of Economic Studies, vol. 19, 82–84.

antitrust regulation is permissive or not.[126] Where there are strict regulations prohibiting anti-competitive practices, cooperative relationships between firms are difficult to establish or maintain and, as a result, the possibility of managerial insulation from either product or stock market control mechanisms is reduced. In contrast, if competition regulation does not prevent or even supports cartelization then, this will not provide a serious constraint on managerial discretion. Of course, this will also depend on the growth potential of product markets since, where Odagiri's competitive conditions are met, the impact of anti-trust regulation becomes less relevant.[127]

In order for this latter 'expansionist' competitive model to operate, however, institutional arrangements must at least not restrict the growth potential of product markets. For instance, where trade barriers of any sort and at any level segregate or restrain markets, to the extent that this is not offset by innovation, the growth preference of managerial firms will create a tendency towards overcapacity and inefficiency and an incentive to cartelize. Thus, a model where managers have a wide discretion needs an environment where institutional sets facilitate or promote the expansion of existing markets or the creation of new ones. In Keynesian terms, managerialist growth preference can be sustainable and indeed lead to increasing welfare only where there is sufficient *effective demand* to absorb growing output. For this reason, financial systems that have a tendency to insulate managers from the direct or indirect control of shareholders seeking profit maximization can operate effectively, as we described above, with institutional macro-level arrangements that guarantee growing demand. Where this type of complementarity exists managerial discretion can balance a wide range of interests as Kester described above.[128] In the opposite case where this coincidence of interests does not hold agency costs for shareholders may be high as managers may be able to abuse their discretion to use the firms' resources for their own benefit.[129] Thus, where, for example, trade barriers are significant, or where macroeconomic policy cannot guarantee that effective demand is sufficient, strict anti-trust rules and efficient capital markets may be necessary to ensure that product market competition as well as direct or indirect shareholder monitoring provide sufficient constraints on managerial discretion.

Finally, complementarities also exist between competition and industrial relations. As discussed in the previous section, a system that contains incentives

126   Whitley, R. (1999) Divergent Capitalisms: The Social Structuring and Change of Business Systems, Oxford: Oxford University Press, 18; and Chandler, A., above n30, 71–79.

127   Less relevant in the context of the orientation of the corporate governance system but obviously not irrelevant in terms of consumers who are paying higher prices for goods.

128   Kester, W., above n115.

129   This is the situation feared by Jensen when he dismisses managerialism altogether. See Jensen, M., above n112 and text.

for labour market internalization is more easily sustainable in the long-term if there is sufficient corporate growth potential. Thus the market/demand growth factor described here is an important variable in the maintenance of insider corporate governance systems where managerial discretion is shielded from strict shareholder accountability.

Insider and Outsider System 'Workability'

The analysis so far has demonstrated the significant role of institutional contexts in determining corporate governance outcomes. Outside the theoretical laboratory, where uncertainty and bounded rationality are the norm due to market imperfections an institutional system that is Pareto-optimal is not achievable. Although some corporate governance institutions may be efficient others are not, so that at least some stakeholders are bound to lose out while others gain. What is possible, however, is to establish an institutional system that balances out inefficiencies. In order to describe this characteristic of a corporate governance system, Schmidt[130] uses the term 'workability' which implies that, although a system is sub-optimal, as a whole, stakeholders' transaction costs are manageable and, therefore, there is a *better* welfare result in comparison to other systems where transaction costs are relatively high.[131] This gives workable systems a 'comparative institutional advantage' against those corporate governance systems which are unworkable.[132]

With regard to the workability of a corporate governance system the concept of institutional complementarity is important. As the above discussion has demonstrated, institutions in one subsystem are workable if institutional configurations in other sub-systems are compatible. As Eichengreen describes, in the European context:

> [c]ritically ... [institutions] were complementary. The effectiveness of one enhanced the effectiveness of the others. Without patient banks and cohesive employers associations, firms would not have been able to make extensive investments in vocational and apprenticeship training, whose payoff was delayed and would have otherwise been difficult to appropriate. And without a system of extensive vocation and apprenticeship training, the advantages of bank-based finance and cohesive employers associations would have been less. Thus, the

---

130   Schmidt, R. (1997) 'Corporate Governance: The Role of Other Constituencies', Working Paper No. 3, Fachbereich Wirtschaftswissenschaften, Goethe-Universität Frankfurt.

131   Of course, as North claims, the gap between 'better' and 'efficient' outcomes is still vast. See North, D., above n6, 109.

132   Soskice, D. (1999) 'Divergent Production Regimes: Coordinated Market Economies in the 1980s and 1990s' in Kitchelt, H., Lange, P., Marks, G. and Stephens, J. (eds) Continuity and Change in Contemporary Capitalism, Cambridge: Cambridge University Press, 101–134 at 102.

parts of Europe's economic and social model fit together in mutually supportive ways. For half a century and more, they enhanced the economy's capacity to deliver high-quality manufactured products, stable employment, incremental innovation, and an equitable distribution of income.[133]

As we discussed earlier a corporate governance system is a nexus of many institutional forces pulling and pushing for influence. Not all are pulling and pushing in the same direction at the same time and so not all parts of the workable system need be in place for the resulting force of the nexus to achieve a workable outcome in corporate governance terms. For example as we will observe in Part II of the book, the US has a very different history with regard to competition than the UK but without affecting the workability of its corporate governance system. Broadly however two general workable equilibria can be identified corresponding to the two main theoretical concepts of the firm outlined in Chapter 1.[134] The first is an outsider shareholder model of corporate governance which broadly relies on a market-based financial system with powerful institutional shareholders enhancing stock market efficiency, on flexible labour markets and on a strict competition policy regime that prevents managers from forming inter-corporate alliances to insulate themselves from market disciplines. The availability of the exit option in both the labour and the financial markets makes the system relatively flexible so as to accommodate price competition by allowing or even encouraging rapid and radical cost-cutting and restructuring strategies of firms.[135] That is, in the outside shareholder-oriented system the emphasis is on flexible arm's length, market-based transactions, so that the firm tends to lose its organizational nature and resemble the nexus-of-contracts model developed by Alchian and Demsetz or Jensen and Meckling. In accordance with the old tradition of nominalism, as the firm's entity disappears, its assets, i.e. what remains after all contractual obligations are met, become the property of the shareholders to whom managers should be directly accountable.

The second workable equilibrium is an insider model based on enhanced managerial discretion, and which broadly comprises a financial system that enhances long-term commitment between financial and productive capital, an industrial relations system that facilitates labour market internalization by providing formal and informal mechanisms for cooperation and conflict resolution between

---

133 Eichengreen, B. (2007) 'The European Economy Since 1945: Coordinated Capitalism and Beyond', Heritage Lectures No. 1023, Heritage Foundation, 2; and Eichengreen, B. (2006) The European Economy Since 1945: Coordinated Capitalism and Beyond, Princeton: Princeton University Press.

134 The term equilibrium is qualified by the word 'workable' in order to differentiate from the Pareto-optimal equilibrium.

135 See Cunningham, L. (1999) 'Commonalities and Prescriptions in the Vertical Dimension of Global Corporate Governance', Cornell Law Review, vol. 84, 1133 at 1144 emphasizing the flexibility and adaptability of the outside shareholder model.

employers and employees, and a competition policy regime that allows inter-firm cooperation. As already mentioned the government's role in the economy is important for expanding markets and effective demand. However, while we focus on the demand function of government as significant for insider systems, we will also refer at times to the government having an influence within an insider system as a direct result of a shareholding or a nationalization programme or externally through its regulatory function or indeed combinations of all these factors. Moreover, free from a shareholder orientation the emphasis in insider models is on organization building as there is a tendency to remove transactions from the market and place them within the firm as a governance hierarchy. Assets such as excess cash flow stay in the firm as corporate property to be invested internally. Other firm-specific assets, such as organizational commitment and know-how, are also created that are not externally redeployable because they tend lose their value outside the firm. In this fashion, the firm resembles the stakeholder or realist models described in Chapter 1. Significantly, the insider and outsider models of corporate governance are both workable as combinations of complementary institutional sub-systems.

Conclusion

In this chapter we introduced institutional analysis as our preferred form of theoretical analysis for a forum in which change in the institutional context, whether national or global, is significant. We argue that managerial behaviour is shaped in an imperfect world, where the bounded rationality of economic agents and uncertainty give rise to positive transaction costs. Therefore, in comparing corporate governance systems at the national and global level, where institutional interactions are crucial to convergence claims, we consider institutional analysis to be more effective rather than theories based on neoclassical equilibria that assume freedom from institutional interference. Thus in imperfect markets, whether a corporate governance system produces outsider shareholder outcomes or insider stakeholder outcomes or indeed is moving from one to the other, is determined in our view by the institutional structure within which it is embedded. We then identified certain key complimentary institutional sub-systems (corporate law, the financial system, the industrial relations system, and sub-systems related to the government demand function, particularly competition and effective demand) that are central to corporate governance outcomes and which we will emphasize in our analysis of change in the chapters that follow. We further continued to examine the insider and outsider corporate governance systems to demonstrate the coherence of both systems as workable combinations of complementary institutional sub-systems at the national level. In the next chapter we examine the process of economic globalization and try to identify the pressures within that process that might cause institutions in insider corporate governance systems to change.

Chapter 3

Globalization and its Impact on Corporate Governance Systems

Introduction

Having established in the previous chapter that the insider and outsider models are both workable as combinations of complementary institutional sub-systems, the purpose of this chapter is to examine the forces within the process of economic globalization that might be giving rise to pressures on institutions in insider corporate governance systems to conform to a shareholder orientation. As we see it, through the process of economic globalization led by capital and product market liberalization, conditions that promote securitization of financial systems, externalization of labour markets, promote shareholder corporate law norms and introduce highly competitive product markets, have been created which have the potential to cause change in insider systems. In doing so we examine in turn the economic history of globalization, to get a picture of the overall process we are dealing with, before then turning to examine the interaction between economic globalization and national institutional structures that determine corporate governance. However, before doing so, some conceptual clarifications are necessary.

Defining globalization

Although the phrase had been used much earlier, in 1983 Levitt popularized the term 'globalization' among key opinion formers in observing that increasing integration of product markets provided the opportunity for firms to offer globally standardized products.[1] Since then it has assumed a ubiquitous but vague status. As Cotterrell notes:

---

1   Levitt, T. (1983) 'The Globalization of Markets', Harvard Business Review, May-June, 92. For recent discussions of globalization in general, see Braendle, U. and Noll, J. 'On the Convergence of National Corporate Governance Systems' (August 2005), available at <http://ssrn.com/abstract=506522>; Abdelal, R. and Tedlow, R. (2003) 'Theodore Levitt's "The Globalization of Markets": An Evaluation after Two Decades', Harvard NOM Working Paper No. 03–20; Harvard Business School Working Paper No. 03–082, available at <http://ssrn.com/abstract=383242>; and Palepu, K., Khanna, T. and Kogan, J. (2002) 'Globalization and Similarities in Corporate Governance: A Cross-Country Analysis', Harvard NOM Working Paper No. 02–31; Strategy Unit Working Paper No. 02–041; Harvard Business School Working Paper No. 02–041, available at <http://ssrn.com/abstract=323621>.

the idea of globalization embraces so much, and entails such huge claims about social and economic forces and the movements of history that it is hard to grapple with. It is also widely seen as weighed down with valuations positive or negative. Attempted descriptions of phenomena associated with globalization usually carry with them arguments or assumptions about the causes of these phenomena. They are seen, for example, sometimes as the product of inevitable, almost natural forces (a global "invisible hand"), or as the result of more deliberate political, economic, cultural or other strategies (often seen as imperialistic). And judgments are made about the consequences of globalization.[2]

As a result before we can even begin writing about globalization we must take a position within contested territory as to the nature of globalization, as some regard it as a theory, others as a historical epoch or new paradigm, and others as a process.[3]

In this study we view it as a process as it appears to be the most accurate for a number of reasons. Firstly, globalization, it seems to us, cannot be a theory because it does not contain and prove any hypotheses that would help us understand or explain any phenomenon. On the contrary, globalization requires a theory or theories to aid our understanding of it as a socio-economic phenomenon. Secondly, globalization cannot be regarded as a specific historical epoch or a new paradigm, because as we will demonstrate it is a phenomenon that has occurred before and it can also be reversed as well as reoccur in the future. Finally, the grammatical ending of the word itself, although not determinative, signifies that it is a process rather than a static state of affairs. As such globalization should therefore be distinguished from the term 'globalism'. As Rosenau observes:

> [g]lobalisation is not the same as globalism, which points to aspirations for an *end state of affairs* wherein values are shared by or pertinent to all the world's five billion people, their environment, their roles as citizens, consumers or producers with an interest in collective action designed to solve common problems.[4]

---

2   Cotterrell, R. (2008) 'Transnational Communities and the Concept of Law', Ratio Juris, vol. 21(1), March, 1–18 at 2. On the vague meaning of globalization see Sugden, R. and Wilson, J. (2005) 'Economic Globalization: Dialectics, Conceptualisation and Choice', Political Economy, vol. 24, 13–32.

3   Reich, S. (1998) 'What is Globalization: Four Possible Answers', Working Paper No. 261, The Helen Kellogg Institute for International Studies, University of Notre Dame. See also van Der Bly, M. (2007) 'Globalization and the Rise of One Heterogeneous World Culture: A Microperspective of a Global Village', International Journal of Comparative Sociology, vol. 48(2–3), 234, available at <http://csi.sagepub.com/cgi/content/abstract/53/6/875>; Kolodko, G. (2006) 'Globalization and Its Impact on Economic Development', Working Paper No. 81, Transformation, Integration and Globalization Economic Research, Warsaw, available at <http://ssrn.com/abstract=961479>; and Held, D. and McGrew, A. (2002) Globalization/Anti-Globalization, Cambridge: Polity Press, 2.

4   Rosenau, J. (1996) 'The Dynamics of Globalization: Towards an Operational Formulation', International Studies Association Convention, San Diego, 3–4 (emphasis added).

The term should also be distinguished from the process of internationalization.[5] This term, which is also a process, contains the word 'nation' as one of its main ingredients whereas globalization does not. This is because internationalization describes a world of nations which increasingly act and interact with each other as separate and autonomous units, either directly or through their citizens. Similarly regionalization projects such as the European Union (EU) exhibits elements of both increasing internationalization and denationalization as partial sovereignty is passed to the EU regional level. Globalization on the other hand, does not contain this national element. This is because it inherently involves national units going through a process of becoming increasingly integrated, until they eventually disappear as separate entities and are replaced by the holistic state of affairs that globalism describes; that is, globalization contains the element of loss of national autonomy. However, internationalization, regionalization and globalization are processes that are closely linked with each other, because the former pair can ultimately lead to the latter. That is, increasing international and regional activity and interaction can cause and promote global integration. This perhaps explains why the terms are sometimes used interchangeably. As such because we view globalization as a process in which internationalization and regionalization play a part, in Part II of the book we regard, where appropriate, evidence of increased internationalization and regionalization as part of the process of globalization.[6] Ziltener, describing European regional integration, captured neatly the national, international and global nature of that project when he stated:

> [t]here is no convincing empirical evidence of European integration having let to either short-term or sustained economic growth effects. The regulatory changes of the Single Market project were part of a global process of economic restructuring and mainly served to enhance the competitiveness of world market oriented European countries.[7]

To add to the problems of working in such contested territory, the elements of internationalization, regionalization and globalization are also extremely complex and without rejecting the significance of other aspects of the processes, this study focuses only on the economic aspects of globalization. There are two reasons for

---

5 On the distinction between an 'inter-nationalized' and a 'globalized' world economy see Hirst, P. and Thompson, G. (1999) 'The Tyranny of Globalization: Myth or Reality' in Buelens, F. (ed.) Globalization and the Nation-State, Cheltenham: Edward Elgar, 140–141.

6 We recognize that 'regionalism' and 'internationalism' can also be individual outcomes of regionalization and internationalization respectively. They can also in our view further the process of globalization.

7 Ziltener (2004) 'The Economic Effects of the European Single Market Project: Projections, Simulations – and the Reality', Review of International Political Economy, vol. 11, 953.

this, one practical and one contextual. Firstly, globalization is a vast subject and so to keep some sort of focus on our central claims about corporate governance outcomes does not allow for a detailed consideration of all aspects of globalization, i.e. economic, social, cultural, political, etc. Secondly and most importantly, in the field of corporate governance, economic factors are by far the most dominant in the creation of determinant institutions such as those analysed in the preceding chapter.

In the previous chapter we focused on the *effects* of existing institutional configurations on economic agents' choices of action as a 'comparative statics' exercise in order to provide a base understanding of the role of determinative institutions that affect corporate governance outcomes. In this chapter and the next, as globalization is a process of change, rather than a static state of affairs, we concentrate on a dynamic analysis of institutional sets as we are exploring the potential causes of institutional change.[8]

Early Globalization and its Collapse

The popular literature on current economic affairs confers an impression that the current wave of globalization, which has its roots in the international economic settlement at the end of WWII, is an unprecedented phenomenon. However, this is not the case and to a certain extent history is repeating itself one century after the previous globalization wave of the late nineteenth and early twentieth century, which eventually started to reverse with the Great War in 1914.[9] Indeed, Baldwin and Martin have argued that in many respects global economic integration was more intense a century ago that it has been until relatively recently.[10]

For instance, in the 1860s and 1870s numerous predominantly bilateral treaties established a largely liberal international trade regime. Although there

---

8   Alston, L. (1996) 'Empirical Work in Institutional Economics: An Overview' in Alston, L., Eggertsson, T. and North, D. (eds) Empirical Studies in Institutional Change, Cambridge: Cambridge University Press, 25–30; and Day, R. (1994) Complex Economic Dynamics, Cambridge, MA: MIT Press, 12.

9   Nayyar, D. (2006) 'Globalization, History and Development: A Tale of Two Centuries', Cambridge Journal of Economics, vol. 30(1), 138.

10   Baldwin, R. and Martin, P. (1999) 'Two Waves of Globalization: Superficial Similarities, Fundamental Differences' in Siebert, H. (ed.) Globalization and Labour, Kiel: Institüt für Weltwirtschaft an der Unniversität Kiel – Mohr Siebeck. See also Sindzingre, A. (2004) 'Explaining Threshold Effects of Globalization on Poverty: An Institutional Perspective', The Impact of Globalization on the World's Poor – UNU-WIDER Conference, First Project Meeting on Conceptual Issues, Helsinki, 2 UNU-WIDER Research Paper No. 2005/53, available at SSRN: <http://ssrn.com/abstract=931559>; Wolf, M. (2003) 'Is Globalization in Danger?', The World Economy, vol. 26(4), 393; and Williamson, J. (2002) 'Winners and Losers Over Two Centuries of Globalization', Working Paper No. 9161, National Bureau of Economic Research, Cambridge, MA, 6, available at <http://www.nber.org/papers/w9161.pdf>.

was a reversal of trade liberalization between developed countries in the last two decades of the nineteenth century, by 1910 world trade as a proportion of GDP was impressively high with the only exception being the US, which was highly protectionist during this period (see Table 3.1).[11] Generally, the trend was for developing countries to specialize in exports of raw materials and imports of manufactures, while developed countries followed the opposite pattern.[12]

Table 3.1 Total trade as a percentage of GDP for selected developed countries

	circa 1870	circa 1910	circa 1950	1995
UK	41	44	30	57
France	33	35	23	43
Germany	37	38	27	46
Italy	21	28	21	49
Denmark	52	69	53	64
Norway	56	69	77	71
Sweden	28	40	30	77
USA	14	11	9	24
Canada	30	30	37	71
Australia	40	39	37	40
Japan	10	30	19	17

Source: See Baldwin, R. and Martin, P. (1999) 'Two Waves of Globalisation: Superficial Similarities, Fundamental Differences' in Siebert, H. (ed.) Globalisation and Labour, Kiel: Institüt für Weltwirtschaft an der Unniversität Kiel – Mohr Siebeck, Table 11.

Moreover, much of that trade was intra-firm trade, i.e. trade occurring within a single firm comprised of a parent and its foreign and domestic subsidiaries, as foreign direct investment (FDI) grew significantly during the pre-World War I (WWI) era, accounting for one third of total foreign investment flows and over nine percent of world output by 1913.[13] Most of these high FDI levels resulted either directly or indirectly from firms' efforts to gain access and exploit natural resources in developing countries. However, FDI flows towards developed countries, albeit smaller than those directed to developing countries, were often in the manufacturing sector therein, mainly as a result of rising tariffs around the

11   See Chang, H.J. (2002) Kicking Away the Ladder: Development Strategy in Historical Perspective, London: Anthem Press.
12   Bairoch, P. and Kozul-Wright, R. (1996) 'Globalization Myths: Some Historical Reflections on Integration, Industrialisation and Growth in the World Economy', Working Paper No. 113, UNCTAD, New York.
13   UNCTAD (1994) World Investment Report 1994, Geneva, United Nations, 130.

1900s forcing manufacturing formerly located outside the tariff zone to relocate inside.[14] By 1914, 55 percent of FDI stock was in the primary product sector, 20 percent in railroads (a sector linked to natural resources exploitation), 15 percent in manufacturing and only 10 percent in services.[15] Cross-border financial flows were also exceptionally large (see Table 3.2 below) during this first period of globalization, indicating that financial markets were highly integrated.[16]

A major contributing factor in global financial integration in this period was the institutional environment that was provided by the 'Gold-Sterling Standard' as a fixed exchange rate system of that era. This was a monetary system where most cross-border transactions were denominated in sterling as a world currency based on direct convertibility into gold. The hegemonic role of Victorian Britain as an enforcer of *Pax Britannica* and the position of the City of London (the City) as the world's clearing house were central to the sustainability of the system.[17] Although Britain ran a trade-balance deficit, the proceeds from the City's financial activity and the large inflows of short-term capital maintained a significant balance of payments surplus which supported the world's main currency.[18] In this environment capital flows grew rapidly seeking the highest returns mainly from long-term investments in railways, infrastructure, and industry.[19] However the Gold-Sterling standard was in no sense a global planned exchange system rather it was the creation of complementary state and private strategies operating in an economically and militarily dominant Britain during the late nineteenth and early twentieth century.[20]

---

14   Kenwood, A. and Lougheed, A. (1994) The Growth of the International Economy, 1829–1990, 3rd edition, London: Routledge.

15   Dunning, J. (1983) 'Changes in the Level and Structure of International Production: The Last One Hundred Years' in Casson, M. (ed.) The Growth of International Business, London: Allen & Unwin, 89.

16   See Nayyar above n9, 140.

17   See Harley, C. (2004) 'Trade, 1870–1939: From Globalization to Fragmentation' in Floud, R. and Johnson, P. (eds) The Cambridge Economic History of Modern Britain: Vol II Economic Maturity, 1860–1939, Cambridge: Cambridge University Press, 161–189; and Ingham, G. (1994) 'States and Markets in the Production of World Money: Sterling and the Dollar' in Corbridge, S., Martin, R. and Thrift, N. (eds) Money, Power and Space, Oxford: Blackwell, 32–39.

18   Ibid.

19   See Baldwin, R. and Martin, P., above n10, 16–21.

20   See Ingham, G., above n17, 38.

Table 3.2 Capital flows, 1870–1996 (average absolute value of current account as a percentage of GDP)

	UK	USA	CAN	FRA	GER	ITA	JPN	ARG	DNK	NOR	SWE	AUS	All
1870–1889	4.6	0.7	7.0	2.4	1.7	1.2	0.6	18.7	1.9	1.6	3.2	8.2	3.7
1890–1913	4.6	1.0	7.0	1.3	1.5	1.8	2.4	6.2	2.9	4.2	2.3	4.1	3.3
1919–1926	2.7	1.7	2.5	2.8	2.4	4.2	2.1	4.9	1.2	4.9	2.0	4.2	3.1
1927–1931	1.9	0.7	2.7	1.4	2.0	1.5	0.6	3.7	0.7	2.0	1.8	5.9	2.1
1932–1939	1.1	0.4	2.6	1.0	0.6	0.7	1.0	1.6	0.8	1.1	1.5	1.7	1.2
1947–1959	1.2	0.6	2.3	1.5	2.0	1.4	1.3	2.3	1.4	3.1	1.1	3.4	1.8
1960–1973	0.8	0.5	1.2	0.6	1.0	2.1	1.0	1.0	1.9	2.4	0.7	2.3	1.3
1974–1989	1.5	1.4	1.7	0.8	2.1	1.3	1.8	1.9	3.2	5.2	1.5	3.6	2.2
1989–1996	2.6	1.2	4.0	0.7	2.7	1.6	2.1	2.0	1.8	2.9	2.0	4.5	2.3

Source: Obstfeld, M. and Taylor, A. (1997) 'The Great Depression as a Watershed: International Capital Mobility Over the Long-Run', Working Paper No. 5960, NBER, Cambridge MA, Table 2.1.

This period ended in the devastation of WWI as the international system was destabilized and gradually abandoned in favour of a floating exchange rate regime. As Harley describes it:

> [t]he most important long-run economic effect of the war, however was the destruction of the international monetary equilibrium under the gold standard that had supported the previous half-century of globalization. At the outbreak of war prudent investors sold assets in belligerent countries and demanded foreign exchange or gold in order to move their assets from the war zones. Governments responded to the threatened loss of gold by *de facto* (although usually not *de jure*) abandonment of the gold convertibility of national currencies.[21]

In 1925 the British government attempted to re-join the Gold Standard by fixing sterling at its pre-WWI rate. However, Britain's loss of its hegemonic role in trade and finance over the course of the war made this untenable.[22] In the absence of a stable management regime, the world monetary system was flooded with speculative financial flows which stifled economic growth and challenged governments' efforts to control exchange rates. In effect, there was a passage from a managed international system to a denationalized global disorder. Eventually, the Great Crash of 1929 and sterling's departure from its peg in 1931 signified the dramatic end not only of the Gold-Sterling standard but also of the last remnants of this first period of globalization. Nations that had not already turned to protectionism after WWI, turned quickly to tariff barriers and the imposition of capital controls in the hope of regaining their autonomy from global financial markets and solve their huge socio-economic problems (see Table 3.2).[23]

From Post-War Internationalization to Contemporary Globalization

In this section we consider economic developments in world markets during the second half of the twentieth century. In doing so we describe how international cooperation at the end of WWII led to the institutionalization of an international regime for capital flows and trade but that eventually flaws inherent in that economic regime led to its partial collapse and the beginning of the current globalization process.

---

21   See Harley, C., above n17, 177.

22   Ibid., 176–180.

23   For an overview of the events see Obstfeld, M. and Taylor, A. (1997) 'The Great Depression as a Watershed: International Capital Mobility Over the Long-Run', Working Paper No. 5960, NBER.

The Bretton Woods-GATT regime

It took the devastation of WWII for powerful (winner) nations to act collectively to establish an international economic order of managed world trade and finance that would undo the international trend of uncontrolled protectionism. This task was undertaken by the United Nations Monetary and Financial Conference held at Bretton Woods, New Hampshire in July 1944. The major figures at the convention were Harry Dexter White and John Maynard Keynes, representing the US and Britain respectively, who had been developing ambitious plans for the world economy since the early 1940s, on the basis of exchange rate stability and international cooperation. There were, however, significant differences between the two sides' proposals; White's plan placed the emphasis on price stability, while Keynes' primary goal was fostering economic growth.[24] Eventually, the final set of agreements, collectively known as the Bretton Woods agreement, mostly reflected the views of the US, which had emerged from the two world wars as the largest economic and military power. Although it initially had an economy largely insulated from world markets, the US had become the world's economic hegemon due to its role as the largest creditor nation with a significant balance of payments surplus.

The institutional arrangements that emerged from the Bretton Woods agreements in 1944 aimed at a stable macroeconomic environment emerging from the post war devastation that would ensure continuous investment and growth. Within that international order, national governments were able to implement expansionary policies which ensured that effective demand was sufficient to absorb increasing industrial output.[25] This monetary system was based on a Gold-Dollar exchange standard where the American currency was fixed to gold, while all other currencies were pegged to the dollar, with only a very narrow margin of fluctuation.[26] Managed currency readjustments were allowed in cases where parities were not sustainable in the long-term. The management of payments difficulties by governments was to be facilitated by two international agencies, the International Monetary Fund (IMF) and the International Bank for the Reconstruction and Development (IBRD)

---

24   Ikenberry, G. (1992) 'A World Economy Restored: Expert Consensus and the Anglo-American Postwar Settlement', International Organization, vol. 46(1), 289.

25   Rajan, R. and Zingales, L. (2001) 'The Great Reversals: The Politics of Financial Development in the 20th Century', Working Paper No. 8178, NBER, Cambridge, MA.

26   To be precise, the Bretton Woods agreement simply provided for the flexible fixing of exchange rates. However, due to the dominant role of the US in the world economy the dollar emerged as the key currency for world payments. See Underhill, G. (2006) 'Introduction: Global Issues in Historical Perspective' in Stubbs, R. and Underhill, G. (eds) Political Economy and the Changing Global Order, 3rd edition, Canada: Oxford University Press; and Stubbs, R. and Underhill, G. (1994) 'Global Issues in Historical Perspective' in Stubbs, R. and Underhill, G. (eds) Political Economy and the Changing Global Order, London: Macmillan, 151.

which later became the World Bank (WB).[27] The former was responsible for the provision of financial relief to countries facing short-term payments difficulties and the latter's mission was to promote and fund the long-term development of less-developed economies.[28] Moreover, the Bretton Woods agreement legitimated the imposition of controls on capital movements that were not related to trade and most countries used this right in order to prevent speculative attacks on their currencies and retain control over their macroeconomic policies. Curbing speculation was seen as the antidote to the causes of the Gold-Sterling Standard's collapse, the Great Depression and the destabilizing currency speculation engaged in by militarily aggressive states in the 1930s.[29]

Additionally as part of this process of reconstruction, the General Agreement on Tariffs and Trade (GATT) was established in 1947 to regulate and promote the liberalization of international trade through the reduction of tariff barriers.[30] Generally, the Bretton Woods-GATT regime should be characterized as international in its initial phase, rather than global, since it was a product of government planning and was directly instituted through international government cooperation; it was a regime created by nations for nations, who retained considerable autonomy in the formulation of their economic policies either on their own or with the help of the IMF and the World Bank. The system promoted the managed liberalization of trade, on the one hand, but at the same time, departed from liberal orthodoxy, by restricting short-term financial flows within national borders. As Keynes himself observed:

> [n]ot merely as a feature of the transition but as a permanent arrangement, the plan accords every member government the explicit right to control all capital movements. What used to be heresy is now endorsed as orthodoxy.[31]

---

27   Boughton, J. (2006) 'American in the Shadows: Harry Dexter White and the Design of the International Monetary Fund', IMF Working Paper No. 06/6.

28   The US also implemented the European Recovery Programme (the Marshall Plan) between 1948 and 1952 which was aimed at providing $13.5 billion for the reconstruction of Europe after WWII – the funding provided by the Plan by far exceeded that available through the Bretton Woods Institutions. See generally Schain, M. (2001) The Marshall Plan: Fifty Years After, New York: Palgrave.

29   We discuss this period and these factors further in Chapter 5.

30   Bordo, M. and Eichengreen, B. (1993) A Retrospective on the Bretton Woods System: Lessons for International Monetary Reform, Chicago: University of Chigaco Press, Chapter 1.

31   Moggridge, D. (ed.) (1998) Collected Writings of John Maynard Keynes, Volume 26: Activities 1941–1946: Shaping the Post-War World, The Clearing Union, Cambridge: Cambridge University Press, 149. See also: Abdelal, R. (2005) Capital Rules: Institutions and the International Monetary System, 1–3, available at <http://www.princeton.edu/~smeunier/Abdelal,%20The%20Rules%20of%20Globalization.pdf>.

Moving to globalization

Although it took a few years to bed in, the Bretton Woods-GATT system was extremely successful in promoting stability and economic growth in the aftermath of WWII. However, it also contained flaws which eventually surfaced as the causes of the system's final collapse. Firstly, the unilateral character of the regime in the absence of the Soviet Union, meant large parts of the world's economy were excluded.[32] Secondly, the US as the systems main guarantor was problematic, as it meant that the perpetuation of American financial hegemony was necessary. Moreover, due to a failure of the negotiating parties to reach an agreement, the issue of payments imbalances was not sufficiently dealt with, despite Keynes' assertions that the accumulation of surplus by some countries could be as detrimental for the world economic system as the accrual of deficits.[33] The US, as a surplus country and a major creditor, did not want to compromise its advantage and so tried to ensure that the international economic system protected US interests as they were viewed at the time.[34]

Ironically, the very mechanisms that the US supported in order to perpetuate its economic dominance in the immediate post war period had the opposite effect as time wore on. As the European economies recovered and grew stronger, they began to challenge US economic superiority. By the late 1950s the US balance of payments surplus had been eliminated and had turned into a deficit which continued to expand well into the 1960s. By 1968 the US current account also went into deficit and the first signs of a devaluation of the dollar began to appear. Growing military spending for Cold War purposes further exacerbated the problem as American competitiveness *vis-à-vis* other western countries and Japan eroded.[35] The absence of a mechanism for dealing with payments imbalances proved to be the Achilles heel of the Bretton Woods system.[36] The American government was then faced with the impossible dilemma of how to adjust the dollar's parity to its real value against other currencies, while maintaining its status as the world's currency.

---

32   We discuss this further in Chapter 5.

33   Walter, A. (1991) World Power and World Money: The Role of Hegemony and International Monetary Order, New York: St. Martin's Press, 154–156.

34   Underhill, G. (2006) 'Introduction: Global Issues in Historical Perspective' in Stubbs, R. and Underhill, G. (eds) Political Economy and the Changing Global Order, 3rd edition, Canada: Oxford University Press; Simmons, B. and Elkins, Z. (2004) 'The Globalization of Liberalization: Policy Diffusion in the International Political Economy', American Political Science Review, vol. 98(1) 171–189; Harvey, D. (2003) The New Imperialism, Oxford: Oxford University Press, 128–132; and Walter, A., above n33.

35   Simmons, B. and Elkins, Z., above n34.

36   Stubbs and Underhill note that the Bretton Woods agreement was never fully implemented as the IMF and the World Bank were under-resourced and largely substituted by the Marshall plan so that the world economy was ultimately run by the US Treasury and the Federal Reserve, see Stubbs, R. and Underhill, G., above n34, 150–151.

The situation was further complicated by the fact that the strict capital controls that Keynes advocated were never fully implemented. Most importantly, the British government's aspirations to revive the role of the City as an international financial centre by allowing the operation of offshore markets dealing in dollars and other currencies gave rise to large unregulated financial flows.[37] These markets, known as the Eurodollar markets, first appeared in the 1950s and have grown enormously since then. The demand for such an offshore market was present in the 1950s as the Soviet Union and other Eastern Bloc countries, fearing a blocking of dollar balances in the US in the event of hostilities, sought to protect themselves. Once the market was established, the Soviet Union and satellite states moved their overseas dollar holdings into the City's offshore market.[38] They were soon joined by other governments and by companies engaged in international activities earning dollars. The motive for the latter was that the lack of regulation in the City's offshore markets permitted banks to pay higher rates of interest which were also not subject to the levels of taxation charged onshore.[39] The money from the Eurodollar markets was then available for lending to companies who sought to finance their international operations with cheap offshore money as the lack of regulation similarly allowed banks to charge borrowers less than they did in regulated markets. Additionally, developing countries were keen to tap this source of cheap money.[40] In 1964 the value of the Eurodollar market was $11 billion and by the end of that decade it had grown to $40 billion.[41] However, even these amounts were dwarfed by the huge inflows of petrodollars that flooded the Eurodollar markets as Organization of Petroleum Exporting Countries (OPEC) countries accumulated vast amounts during the oil crises over the course of the 1970s. By the 1980s the Eurodollar markets reached $4.5 trillion in value.[42] This was truly global capital which existed outside national borders. Significantly, it began to challenge national institutional sets through regulatory arbitrage.

The emergence of these denationalized global capital flows made exchange rate movements not only larger and more unpredictable, but increasingly uncontrollable even by the strongest central banks. In turn, the combination of speculative financial flows and the unsustainable parity of the dollar meant that the end of the fixed exchange rate regime was only a matter of time. In August 1971

---

37   See Walter, A., above n33.

38   For a more extensive discussion on the emergence of the Euromarkets see Burn, G. (2006) The Re-emergence of Global Finance, Basingstoke: Palgrave; and Pilbeam, K. (2006) International Finance, 3rd edition, Basingstoke: Macmillan, Part III.

39   See Hill, C. (1998) International Business: Competition in the Global Marketplace, Chicago: Irwin/McGraw and Hill, 331–332.

40   Ibid.

41   Martin, R. (1994) 'Stateless Monies, Global Financial Integration and National Economic Autonomy: The End of Geography?' in Corbridge, S., Martin, R. and Thrift, N. (eds) Money, Power and Space, Oxford: Blackwell, 257.

42   See Hill, C., above n39, 330.

the Nixon administration abandoned the gold-dollar standard and allowed the dollar to float. This effectively ended the Bretton Woods system. Other countries, challenged by currency speculators, soon followed the same path, so that by 1973 a new financial order of floating exchange rates was established and the Eurodollar market expanded to become the Eurocurrency market.[43] This in our view marked the beginning of the passage from the international financial order of the first three post war decades to the current wave of globalization.[44]

With the availability of global finance offshore, financial and non financial firms could easily sidestep national financial systems so that restrictions on capital movements became unsustainable as they were subjected to the pressures of arbitrage. The abolition of capital controls was therefore inevitable.[45] The first of the major countries to lift these measures were Canada, Germany[46] and Switzerland in 1973, who were then followed by the US in 1974, Britain in 1979 and Japan in 1980. The liberalization of capital controls led to an explosion of short-term financial flows. The value of average *daily* foreign exchange transactions rose from just $10–20 billion in 1973 to $80 billion in 1980 and to $1880 billion in 2004 (see Chart 3.1).

---

43   Simmons, B. and Elkins, Z. (2003) 'Globalization and Policy Diffusion: Explaining Three Decades of Liberalization' in Kahler, M. and Lake, D. (eds) Governance in a Global Economy: Political Authority in Transition, Princeton: Princeton University Press, 275–304.

44   Blyth, M. (2002) Great Transformations: Economic Ideas and Institutional Change in the Twentieth Century Cambridge, UK: Cambridge University Press.

45   Neely, C. (1999) 'An Introduction to Capital Controls', Federal Reserve Bank St. Louis Review, November/December, 81(6), 13–30.

46   Although Germany did retain some significant barriers to capital movement until the mid 1980s. This is discussed further in Chapter 8.

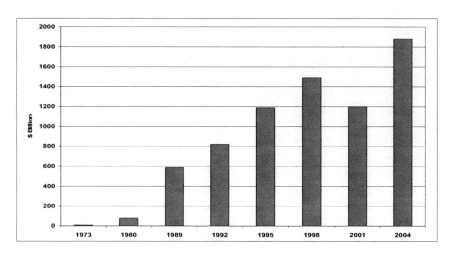

Chart 3.1 Average daily foreign exchange transactions
Source: BIS (2005) Triennial Central Bank Survey: Foreign Exchange and Derivatives Market Activity in 2004, Basel, 43, available at <http://www.bis.org/publ/rpfx05t.pdf> and BIS (1999) Central Bank Survey of Foreign Exchange and Derivatives Market Activity 1998, Basel, available at <http://www.bis.org/publ/r_fx98finaltxt.pdf>.

While foreign exchange markets now seem to be truly globalized, the globalization of securities markets has also progressed rapidly since the 1980s with the growth of the Eurobond and foreign bond markets, with the former accounting for the lion's share.[47] As with Eurocurrency markets, immunity from government regulation, tax advantages and adaptability to exchange rate expectations have been the most attractive features of Eurobond finance for corporate and sovereign borrowers. Over the years, the market has expanded not only in volume but also in scope with the introduction of a broad range of securities instruments such as warrants, global depository receipts, international floating rate notes and euro-commercial paper. Thus, by 2007 the gross value of international debt securities' issues amounted to $1.7 trillion.[48] Comparatively the global integration of equity markets has been slow but has accelerated significantly from the mid 1980s.[49] As of 2000 the total

---

47   Eurobonds are bonds issued in countries other than the one in whose currency they are denominated. Foreign bonds are sold outside the issuer's country but are denominated in currency of the countries where they are issued.

48   BIS (2007) 'Highlights of International Banking and Financial Market Activity', BIS Quarterly Review, 22 June.

49   Ayuso, J. and Blanco1, R. (2000) 'Has Financial Market Integration Increased During the 1990s?', BIS Conference Papers, vol. 8, 175. See also Bekaert, G., Harvey, C. and Lumsdaine, R. (2003) 'Dating the Integration of World Equity Markets', Journal of Financial Economics, vol. 65, 203.

value of cross-border equity issues was $316.7 billion (Chart 3.2). Overall, cross-border investment in securities has reached extremely high levels with its value by far exceeding most major countries' GDP (Table 3.3).

The dominant force behind global financial flows and integration of capital markets have been institutional investors who have been constantly increasing the share of total household assets under their control since the 1960s. As we described in Chapter 2, just as the emergence of institutional investors within the national arena was an important element in the promotion of securitization within a financial system, so too has the growth of institutional investors represented a critical element in the transformation of global financial markets. Increasing pressure on pay-as-you-go pension systems as a result of an aging population, higher unemployment and lower tax revenues, increased market pressures on governments to cut their spending[50] and the retirement of the baby-boomer cohort during the past two decades, has produced an incentive for governments to provide tax efficient retirement products managed by professional investors. As a result, the growth of institutionalized holdings has seen a dramatic rise in all OECD countries since the 1990s (see Table 3.4).[51]

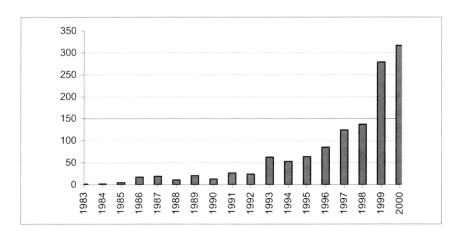

Chart 3.2 Value of announced cross-border equity issues (billion dollars)
Source: BIS, BIS Quarterly Review, Basel: Author, several issues.

---

50   These are pressures largely created by loss of autonomy at the macroeconomic level once capital controls had been removed. We discuss the phenomenon further later in this chapter.

51   OECD (2001) Financial Market Trends, No. 80, September, Paris, 46.

Table 3.3 Gross purchases and sales of securities between residents and non-residents in six major OECD countries (percentage of GDP)

	1975	1980	1985	1989	1990	1991	1992	1993	1994	1995	1996	1997	1998
US	4	9	35	101	89	96	107	129	131	135	164	213	230
Japan	2	8	62	156	119	92	72	78	60	65	84*	96	91
Germany	5	7	33	66	57	55	85	171	159	172	200	253	334
France	–	5	21	52	54	79	122	187	201	187	227**	313	415
Italy	1	1	4	18	27	60	92	192	207	253	468	672	640
Canada	3	9	27	55	65	81	113	153	212	189	258	358	331

Note: * Based on settlement data; ** January-September at an annual rate.

Source: BIS (1997) 67th Annual Report: 1 April 1996 – 31 March 1997, Basle, 9 June, table V.1, available at <http://www.bis.org/publ/ar67f01.pdf>; BIS (1999) 69th Annual Report: 1 April 1998 – 31 March 1999, Basle, 7 June, table VI.5, available at <http://www.bis.org/publ/ar99e.pdf>.

Table 3.4 Total financial assets of institutional investors (billion dollars)

| | Total | | Insurance companies and pension funds | | | | | | Mutual Funds | |
| | | | Total | | Insurers | | Pensions | | | |
	1995	2005	1995	2005	1995	2005	1995	2005	1995	2005
Australia	321	1,507	273	807	128	241	146	566	48	700
Canada	556	1,432	402	941	172	391	230	550	155	491
Euro Area	na	10,165	na	5,858	1,871	4,664	na	1,194	1,378	4,307
Belgium	114	344	85	226	76	212	9	14	29	118
France	1,176	3,008	642	1,646	642	1,614	0	32	534	1,363
Germany	1,057	2,152	919	1,856	779	1,573	140	283	138	297
Italy	na	1,007	na	557	120	528	na	29	130	451
Luxembourg	346	1,689	8	53	8	53	na	na	338	1,636
Netherlands	562	1,282	497	1,156	162	407	335	749	65	126
Spain	246	682	102	365	84	278	18	87	144	317
Japan	4,150	4,710	3,729	4,240	2,999	3,243	731	997	420	470
Korea	na	621	138	422	103	272	35	150	na	199
Mexico	na	132	na	84	na	21	na	63	na	47
Singapore	226	443	95	132	21	52	74	80	131	311
Sweden	na	506	90	387	na	268	90	118	35	119
Switzerland	na	681	na	565	na	227	na	338	48	117
United Kingdom	1,759	4,014	1,558	3,467	798	1,979	760	1,487	201	547
United States	10,546	21,811	7,020	12,906	2,804	5,601	4,216	7,305	3,526	8,905
Total		46,021		29,808		16,960		12,849		16,213

Source: BIS, Committee on the Global Financial System (2007) Institutional Investors, Global Savings and Asset Allocation, Committee on the Global Financial System, No. 27, 5.

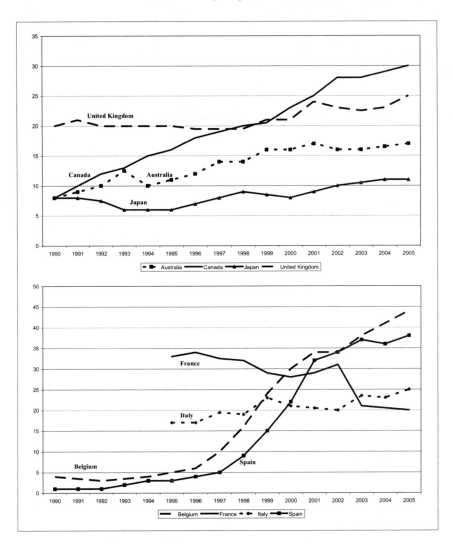

**Graph 3.1 Holdings of foreign securities by insurance companies
and pension funds (as percentage of total financial assets)**
Source: BIS, Committee on the Global Financial System (2007) Institutional Investors, Global
Savings and Asset Allocation, Committee on the Global Financial System, No. 27, 9.

Institutional investors allocation of assets vary from country to country but consistently the majority of assets have been held in equities and bonds.[52] Allocation also varies between type of institutional investor with pension funds holding almost 50 percent of their assets in equities and insurance funds generally holding 20–25 percent in equities.[53] Thus, in the absence of capital controls, the growth of institutional investment has become the driver behind the globalization of securities markets as a matter of necessity. While some national prudential regulations can restrict global portfolio diversification more than others and some investment products can be specialized and thus invest only in specific countries or regions, in general the vast expansion of assets under institutional control has meant the globalization of portfolios has become a necessary strategy for prudent fund managers who view the world as one large integrated market (see Graph 3.1).[54] In turn early mover funded pension financial systems such as the UK and US, dominated by institutional investors capable of shaping the process of the globalization of capital markets, elevates their bias towards securitization from national financial systems to the global. This then has the effect of promoting outsider system norms in companies from insider systems that avail of global capital markets.

The same also holds for non financial companies as this is indicated by the remarkable growth of FDI levels since the 1980s as Transnational Corporations (TNCs) began to play an increasing role of in the world economy.[55] During the 1960s and 1970s the growth rate of FDI more or less followed that of exports. However, since the mid 1980s FDI has accelerated dramatically so that by 1995 the world stock of FDI as a percentage of output had even exceeded 1913 levels.[56] Notably the quality of contemporary FDI differs from the earlier globalization period. Unlike the trend in the first period of globalization, a significant amount of FDI flows are now between developed countries and unlike the earlier FDI trend of the 1900s, contemporary investment in factors located in developing countries is predominantly directed to the manufacturing sector rather than primary resources.[57] Much of this

52   OECD, above n51, 52.

53   BIS, Committee on the Global Financial System (2007) Institutional Investors, Global Savings and Asset Allocation, Committee on the Global Financial System, No. 27, 6–7. More recently institutional investors have started to invest in hedge funds and private equity firms see BIS page 8.

54   On international portfolio diversification by institutional investors see Bartram, S. and Dufey, G. (2001) 'International Portfolio Investment: Theory, Evidence, and Institutional Framework', Working Paper No. 01–006, University of Michigan Business School, and Davis, E. (1991) 'International Diversification of Institutional Investors', Journal of International Securities Markets, Summer, 143.

55   The causes and effects of TNC activity are discussed later in this chapter.

56   Baker, D., Epstein, G. and Pollin, R. (1998) Globalization and Progressive Economic Policy, Cambridge: Cambridge University Press, 9.

57   See Kobrin, S. (2005) 'The Determinants of Liberalization of FDI Policy in Developing Countries: A Cross-sectional Analysis: 1992–2001', Transnational Corporations, vol. 14(1), 67–101; Blackhurst, R and Otten, A. (1996) Trade and Foreign

change in the pattern of FDI is attributable to TNCs pursuing the reorganization of their manufacturing production activities along global lines driven by labour cost reduction and mergers and acquisitions (M&A) in response to intense product market competition, this is something we return to later in the chapter.

GATT goes global

After consecutive rounds of GATT renegotiations and the almost universal expansion of signatory countries over the decades since 1947 a dramatic reduction in tariff barriers has been achieved. Eventually the World Trade Organization (WTO) was formed in 1995 as the main agency regulating global trade matters. The success of GATT can be seen in Table 3.5 which summarizes the effect of successive GATT agreements in reducing tariff rates in manufactured products. More specifically, Chart 3.3 shows the impact of successive international negotiations on US trade, historically one of the most protectionist among developed countries. As a result of these reductions on tariff barriers, total cross-border trade as a percentage of GDP has now exceeded the pre-WWI levels for almost all major economies.[58] All this evidence indicates that with the liberalization of world trade, the globalization of product markets has now progressed more than ever before. The creation of regional free trade areas, the most important of which are the European Union (EU), the North American Free Trade Agreement (NAFTA) and the Association of South East Asian Nations (ASEAN), has also been an important contributing factor in the globalization of trade.[59]

International trade in the post-WWII era can be divided into two main phases. During the first, between 1959 and 1979, trade flows were mainly between developed economies, with developing ones only playing a small role mostly limited to exporting primary goods. In the second phase, from 1980 onwards trade expanded and became global after the collapse of the Soviet Union in the early 1990s as developing countries increased their share of total international trade as a result of a significant increase in their role as exporters of labour-intensive manufactured goods.[60] As Baldwin and Martin report, the share of manufactured goods imports from developing countries for all OECD countries rose from six

---

Direct Investment – New Report by the WTO, Geneva: Information and Media Relations Division, Table IV.1; and UNCTAD (1994) World Investment Report 1994: Transitional Corporations, Employment and the Workplace, New York: United Nations, Table 1.5.

58   See Table 3.1.

59   Although some commentators argue this type of agreement has resulted in an observable regional bias a 'triadization' of trade rather than a globalization of trade see Cox, J., Ietto-Gillies, H. and Grimwade, N. (1997) Global Business Strategy, London: International Thomson Business Press, 99–100.

60   On the increase in total world trade see WTO (2007) International Trade Statistics, WTO available at <http://www.wto.org/english/res_e/statis_e/statis_e.htm>.

percent in 1970 to 13 percent in the late 1990s.[61] By 1994, manufacturing exports accounted for over 66 percent of total exports from developing countries, up from just 23.5 percent in 1980.[62] Notably the share of world manufacturing exports attributable to developing countries rose from 13 percent in 1980 to 16.6 percent in 1990 and to 26.8 percent in 2000.[63]

Table 3.5 Average tariff rates on manufactured products in major economies, 1913–2000 (percent of value)

	1913	1950	1990	2000*
France	21	18	5.9	3.9
Germany	20	26	5.9	3.9
Italy	18	25	5.9	3.9
Japan	30	–	5.3	3.9
Netherlands	15	11	5.9	3.9
Sweden	20	9	4.4	3.9
Britain	–	23	5.9	3.9
United States	44	14	4.8	3.9

Note: * Based on full implementation of 1994 Uruguay Agreement.
Source: Hill, C. (1998) International Business: Competition in the Global Marketplace, Chicago: Irwin/McGraw and Hill, Table 1.1.

In all the liberalization of financial markets and trade forms the essence of the current wave of economic globalization in that it has formed a *deepening* of capitalist integration in recent decades.[64] That integration has, as we will explore below, put national institutional arrangements determining corporate governance

---

61 See Baldwin, R. and Martin, P., above n10, 33.

62 Baker, D., Epstein, G. and Pollin, R. (1998) 'Introduction' in Baker, D., Epstein, G. and Pollin, R. (eds) Globalization and Progressive Economic Policy, Cambridge: Cambridge University Press, 7. IMF and World Bank (2001) 'Market Access for Developing Countries' Exports', available at <http://www.imf.org/external/np/madc/eng/042701.pdf> and IMF (2006) 'Intergrating Poor Countries into the World Trading System, Economic Issues, vol. 37, available at <http://www.imf.org/external/pubs/ft/issues/issues37/ei37.pdf>.

63 Lall, S., Weiss, J. and Zhang, J. (2005) 'The Sophistication of Exports: A New Measure of Product Characteristics', ADB Institute Discussion Paper No. 23. Figures after 2000 are divided up regionally for total figures in trillion dollars see World Bank (2007) World Development Indicators, Section 6: Global Links, 314, available at <http://siteresources.worldbank.org/DATASTATISTICS/Resources/WDI07section6-intro.pdf>.

64 Hoogvelt, A. (2001) Globalization and the Postcolonial World: The New Political Economy of Development, 2nd edition, Baltimore: Johns Hopkins University Press; and Hirst, P. and Thompson, G. (2007) Globalization in Question, 3rd edition, Cambridge: Polity Press.

under pressure to conform along specific lines. The purpose of the following section is to identify, explain and assess these pressures from continuing economic globalization.

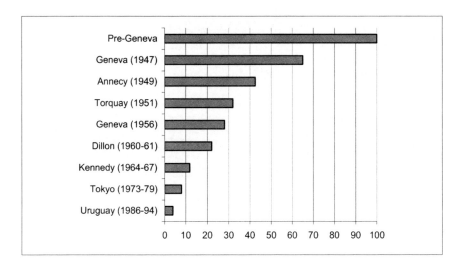

Chart 3.3 Weighted average US tariff rate after GATT rounds, 1947–1994
Source: Siebert, H. and Klodt, H. (1999) 'Towards Global Competition: Catalysts and Constraints', in OECD The Future of the Global Economy: Towards a Long Boom?, Paris. Figure 3, available at <http://www.oecd.org/dataoecd/42/0/35394025.pdf>. The Uruguay round was the last successful agreement. The Doha round of negotiations begun in 2001 has failed to reach an agreement as of yet. See Gallagher, P. (2005) The First Ten Years of the WTO, Cambridge: Cambridge University Press, 10; and Martin-Winters, The Uruguay Round, 2.

Understanding Globalization's Corporate Governance Impact: I

As was noted above the experiences of the Great Depression and WWII gave rise to an unprecedented consensus for the establishment of a stable international system, along Keynesian interventionist lines, which would provide the foundations for the reconstruction of devastated economies worldwide. The institutional arrangements that emerged from the Bretton Woods agreements ensured that a stable macroeconomic environment was in place to stimulate continuous investment and growth. Within that international order, national governments were able to implement expansionary policies which ensured that effective demand was sufficient to absorb increasing industrial output. This was combined, as we noted in Chapter 1, with the managerial corporation emerging as a significant force in society. Crucially, management exercised a wide discretion as to the allocation of retained earnings which played a key role in managers making long-term commitments to stakeholders.[65] Therefore, managerial autonomy from shareholders allowed managers to undertake a central coordinating role within the firm and deploy resources in a way that resolved conflicts among different resource providers within a macroeconomic frame work that allowed governments to pursue policies that complemented the managerial corporation. The result was a period of unprecedented economic growth, stability and wealth creation often referred to as the 'golden age of capitalism'.[66]

Some macroeconomic theory

In trying to understand the impact of globalization on corporate governance systems we draw upon aspects of macroeconomic theory that emphasize the connection between firm growth and government demand policy. In 1928, the economist Allyn A. Young departed from traditional equilibrium theory and argued that, contrary to the neoclassical assumption that an output increase is impossible without a proportional increase of costs, increases in scale also lead to increases in returns.[67] This is because the division of labour associated with increases in scale reduces the cost and price of commodities, which leads to an expansion of the market. In turn, a growing market makes further increases in the division of labour profitable, and starts a new circle of cumulative growth.[68] In other words, an increase in production creates a virtuous production cycle where the more you produce, the more demand you create, which in turn leads to a further increase in production. To use Young's terminology, growth, i.e. increasing output, creates 'reciprocal demand' that absorbs the growth and initiates a new cycle.

However, others recognized that there were weaknesses at the heart of this model because firms may lack the funds to increase production, and even if they do increase production, the element of reciprocal demand may not be triggered.

---

65   Baumol, W. (1967) Business Behaviour, Value and Growth, Princeton: Princeton University Press, 75–79. See also Lazonick, W. (1992) 'Controlling the Market for Corporate Control: The Historical Significance of Managerial Capitalism', Industrial and Corporate Change, vol. 1, 445–488; and Williamson, O. (1964) The Economics of Discretionary Behavior: Managerial Objectives in a Theory of the Firm, Prentice Hall, Englewood Cliffs, 169–170.

66   Marglin, S. and Schor, J. (1990) The Golden Age of Capitalism – Reinterpreting the Postwar Experience, Oxford: Clarendon Press; and Eichengreen, B. (2006) The European Economy Since 1945: Coordinated Capitalism and Beyond, Princeton: Princeton University Press.

67   Young, A. (1928) 'Increasing Returns and Economic Progress', Economy Journal, vol. 38, 527–542. For subsequent refinements of cumulative causation theory see Myrdal, G. (1957) Economic Theory and Underdeveloped Regions, London: Duckworth; Kaldor, N. (1996) Causes of Growth and Stagnation in the World Economy, Cambridge: Cambridge University Press; and Toner, P. (1999) Main Currents in Cumulative Causation: The Dynamics of Growth and Development, London: Macmillan.

68   See Young, A., above n67, 537.

To address these failings, Kaldor[69] argued that, provided that firms can retain and use their earnings,[70] higher profitability translates into increased investment in organizational and production technologies and results in an increase in productivity and output. To ensure that demand is present, Kaldor argued that government demand-management policies are crucial for the completion and perpetuation of this 'virtuous circle' of cumulative economic growth. If sufficient demand is ensured to absorb increased output, a new cycle can begin which will further promote growth and economic welfare. Kaldor argued, along Keynesian lines,[71] that demand was not only a key to sustainable economic growth but also the weak link which markets cannot always provide without intervention; hence the important role of government as a regulator of effective demand through the implementation of full employment policies, protective trade and public investment spending.[72] Ideally, for the cumulative causation model, government trade policy should be an imbalance of protective home markets and open access to foreign markets.[73] In such a model the firm can expand abroad from a protected home base. If these conditions were in place they should sustain a sequence of rising industrial growth leading to increased consumption, which would increase profitability, which would promote investment and ultimately lead to industrial growth.[74] Without government demand intervention, demand slumps can in turn lead to 'vicious circles' of diminishing output, investment, growth, and demand; with negative welfare consequences.[75]

Indeed, the post-WWII era saw national governments in most industrialized countries pursuing expansionary monetary and fiscal policies with the aim of

---

69   See Kaldor, N., above n67.

70   Kaldor and others have emphasized the vital role of retained earnings in financing industrial investment. See Kaldor, N. (1985) Economics Without Equilibrium, Cardiff: University College of Cardiff Press; Currie, L. (1981) 'Allyn Young and the Development of Growth Theory', Journal of Economic Studies, vol. 8, 52–60; and Cherian, S. (1999/2004) 'Internal Finance and Investment: Another Look', World Bank Policy Research Working Paper No. 1663, available at <http://ssrn.com/abstract=620672>.

71   The two major schools of macroeconomic theory are Keynesian economics which emphasizes the Government role in creating demand when needed and supply side neoclassical economics based on a limited role for government and a monetary policy based on the price of money as determined by the market. See Nicholson, W. (2005) Micro-economic Theory: Basic Principles and Extensions, Boston: South Western Educational Publishing.

72   See Marglin, S. (1990) 'Lessons from the Golden Age' in Marglin, S. and Schor, J. (eds) The Golden Age of Capitalism – Reinterpreting the Postwar Experience, Oxford: Oxford University Press, 1–38.

73   We consider this issue later in this chapter.

74   Kalecki, M. (1971) Selected Essays on the Dynamics of the Capitalist Economy, Cambridge: Cambridge University Press, Chapters 1–8.

75   See Myrdal, G. (1957) Economic Theory and Underdeveloped Regions, London: Duckworth.

sustaining effective demand. Institutional differences between national economic systems led to variations in both the methods and the extent of such policies.[76] For instance, systems which enhance labour power and create close ties between finance and industry are associated with more expansionary macro-policies,[77] whereas central bank independence and high international significance of national currencies are linked to more restrictive tactics.[78] However, more or less the general trend at least until the 1970s was for monetary and fiscal policies to aim for demand-led growth based on full employment. Characteristically, until the mid-1970s the objectives of US macroeconomic policy were set according to a mandate in the Employment Act 1946 which called for the fostering of 'conditions under which there will be useful employment opportunities ... for those able, willing, and seeking to work, and to promote maximum employment, production, and purchasing power'.[79] Such employment-growth policies, combined with an expansion of welfare state provisions, maintained high levels of consumption so that the major concern for some countries was how to ease effective demand rather than increase it.[80]

Crucial for the sustainability of such national policies was the relative macroeconomic stability at the international stage. Despite its flaws, which caused it to unravel during the late 1960s, the international economic order largely established by the Bretton Woods agreement was instrumental in the effectiveness of state-level Keynesian interventions. The key element was the restriction on capital mobility across borders which allowed national authorities sufficient financial autonomy to pursue their full employment and welfare state policies designed to maintain sufficient levels of effective demand. Moreover, in the absence of exchange rate fluctuations national authorities were able to adjust interest rates according to investment and growth targets. The IMF provided guarantees against short-term balance of payments problems and the World Bank, often supplemented by the Marshall Plan funding programme, ensured that high levels of long-term investment in reconstruction and development were maintained. When a national crisis occurred it tended to be short-lived and not contagious.[81]

---

76   Epstein, G. and Schor, J. (1990) 'Macropolicy in the Rise and Fall of the Golden Age' in Marglin, S. and Schor, J. (eds) The Golden Age of Capitalism – Reinterpreting the Postwar Experience, Oxford: Clarendon Press, 127–131.

77   On the former element see Lange, P. and Garrett, G. (1985) 'The Politics of Growth: Strategic Interaction and Economic Performance in Advanced Industrial Democracies 1974–1980', The Journal of Politics, vol. 47, 792–827. On the latter element see ibid. at 127–129.

78   See Epstein, G. and Schor, J., above n76, 127–129.

79   Meyer, L. (2000) 'The Politics of Monetary Policy – Balancing Independence and Accountability', BIS Review, 94/2000, available at <http://www.bis.org/review/r001027a.pdf>.

80   Glyn, A., Hughes, A., Lipietz, A. and Singh, A. (1990) 'The Rise and Fall of the Golden Age' in Marglin, S. and Schor, J. (eds) The Golden Age of Capitalism – Reinterpreting the Postwar Experience, Oxford: Clarendon Press, 60.

81   Epstein, G. and Schor, J. above, n76, 137.

Moreover, rising industrial output also led to the increase of international trade from the 1950s onwards with substantial increases after each successive GATT agreement. However, as Glyn et al. report, high domestic demand ensured that at least until the mid 1960s growth was mostly domestically based.[82]

In sum, as the data in Table 3.6 below indicates the stable macroeconomic environment during the golden age led to the achievement of impressive real growth rates for the world economy with low unemployment and an average of four percent inflation. An unprecedented consensus has been achieved within the corporation between capital and labour in which stable macroeconomic growth conditions nationally and internationally and a managerial microeconomic model based on the coincidence between stakeholder interests were complementary elements of a highly successful system versions of which were found in most major economies. As macroeconomic stability allowed for real interest rates to be kept at low levels, cash flow retention and internal reinvestment by firms provided higher returns for shareholders than its distribution and external investment in deposits, bonds, and other instruments. So, provided demand was sufficient, high growth rates of firms suited not only managers, shareholders and employees, but also society as unemployment was kept low and general welfare increased. A microeconomic corporate model with a high degree of autonomy from shareholders was combined with the establishment of a macroeconomic system which focused on demand management worldwide.[83] As the data below indicates, the performance results in this period are notable, and led for a time to a virtuous circle of cumulative growth with the interdependent elements of the Kaldorian model all in place.

Table 3.6 Post-war economic performance

Real GDP growth rates (percentage annual change)

	World	OECD Countries	Developing Countries*
1950–65	na	5.9	5.5
1966–73	5.1	4.8	6.9
1974–80	3.4	2.9	5.0
1981–90	3.2	3.1	3.3
1991–93	1.2	1.2	4.6
1994–95	2.8	2.6	4.7

---

82   Glyn, A., Hughes, A., Lipietz, A. and Singh, A., above n80, 51.

83   See Chandler, A. (1977) The Visible Hand: The Managerial Revolution in American Business, Cambridge, MA: Belknap Press of Harvard University; and Chandler, A. (1990) Scale and Scope: The Dynamics of Industrial Capitalism, Cambridge, MA: Harvard University Press.

Average growth rates of advanced capitalist countries 1820–1979
(percentage annual change)

	GDP	**GDP per capita**
1820–1870	2.2	1.0
1870–1913	2.5	2.5
1913–1950	1.9	1.2
1950–1973	4.9	3.8
1973–1979	2.5	2.0

Consumer prices (percentage annual change)

	1950–73	**1973–79**	**1979–83**	**1993–99**	**1999–2006**
US	2.7	8.2	8.2	2.5	2.8
UK	4.6	15.4	10.7	2.1	1.5
France	5.0	10.7	12.1	1.5	2.0
Germany	2.7	4.7	5.1	1.0	1.6
Italy	3.9	16.3	17.5	3.4	2.4
Japan	5.2	10.0	4.3	0.6	(0.4)

Average unemployment in OECD countries

	1951–59	**1960–69**	**1970–79**	**1980–89**	**1990–99**	**2000–06**
US	4.3	4.6	3.5	7.3	4.6	5.1
UK	2.1	2.7	4.4	9.9	8.0	5.0
France	1.8	1.7	3.8	9.0	10.6	9.2
Germany	4.6	0.7	2.3	6.0	7.6	8.5
Italy	7.0*	3.9	4.4	7.0	10.3	8.4
Japan	2.2	1.3	1.7	2.5	3.0	4.8
Australia	1.1	2.1	3.8	7.5	8.6	5.9
Belgium	4.3	2.3	4.8	10.8	8.5	7.7
Canada	3.9	4.7	6.6	9.3	9.6	7.0
Netherlands	2.1	1.2	3.9	9.7	5.4	3.5
Spain	2.2	2.4	4.3	17.7	15.9	10.3
Sweden	1.9	1.3	1.7	2.1	7.2	5.9
OECD av.	2.9	2.2	3.5	7.3	7.0	6.6

Volume of exports (percentage annual change)

	1950–73	1973–79	1979–83
US	6.3	4.9	(1.6)
UK	3.9	4.7	(0.1)
France	8.2	6.1	2.3
Germany	12.4	4.7	4.1
Italy	11.7	7.1	1.2
Japan	15.4	7.6	10.2

Note: * Excluding Eastern and Central Europe and former USSR countries. While we use OECD figures here for international comparative purposes it should be noted that OECD measures of unemployment tend to be lower than national measures. In the later chapters we use national measures.

Source: Marglin, S. and Schor, J. (1990) The Golden Age of Capitalism – Reinterpreting the Postwar Experience, Oxford: Clarendon Press, 42 and 47; Davidson, P. (2000) 'Capital Movements, Tobin Tax, and Permanent Fire Protection: a Response to de Angelis', Journal of Post Keynesian Economics, vol. 22(2), 197; Baker, D. (1998) 'The NAIRU: Is it a Real Constraint?' in Baker, D. et al. (eds) Globalisation and Progressive Economic Policy, Cambridge: Cambridge University Press, Table 1A; and OECD Factbook (2008) 'Economic, Environmental and Social Statistics: Unemployment Rates', 141, available at <http://titania.sourceoecd.org/pdf/factbook2008/302008011e-06-02-01.pdf>.

However, the collapse of the fixed exchange rate system between 1971 and 1973 signalled the beginning of a new era for the international economic order. As Eatwell noted, when governments and Bretton Woods agencies stopped bearing the full costs of currency management with the imposition of capital controls, foreign exchange risk was privatized.[84] Floating exchange rates not only created vast profit opportunities for currency speculators, but also made hedging against volatility risks a necessity for both financial and non financial corporations. As we discussed earlier, in order to deal with these new conditions governments removed exchange controls and financial regulations that restricted capital flows. The globalization of finance led to the construction of what has been described as 'the modern infrastructure of speculation'[85] as transactions in global financial markets are now not intended to finance trade or production but to capture gains from

---

84   Eatwell, J. (1996) 'International Financial Liberalisation: The Impact on World Development', ODS Discussion Paper Series 12, United Nations Development Programme, New York; and Eatwell, J. (2001) 'The Challenges Facing International Financial Regulation', DSC Conference: The Economies of Financial Market Regulation, San Francisco, available at <http://www.financialpolicy.org/DSCEatwell.pdf>.

85   See Eatwell, J., above n84, 3.

speculative predictions about a range of financial instruments based traditionally on currency, equity, commodities and bond movements.[86]

In particular the sheer size of capital flows has now made actual and potential movements in exchange rates much larger, more unpredictable, and uncontrollable. With so much capital available for speculation, apparent exchange rate problems can quickly turn into full-scale crises. Indeed, by 1973 speculators had challenged and defeated almost every central bank, including the US Federal Reserve.[87] Since the liberalization of capital controls, crises related to capital flows where waves of excessive optimism and speculation have been followed by excessive pessimism and withdrawal of funds have become relatively common.[88] For example the Latin American debt crisis of the 1980s, the 'Black Monday' stock market crash in 1987, the collapse of the Japanese 'bubble' in 1990, the speculative attacks on ERM currencies in 1992 and 1993, the Mexican balance of payments crisis in 1994, the Asian crisis in 1997, the Russian crisis in 1998, the Turkish crisis in 1999, the Argentinean crisis in 2001, the collapse of the internet bubble in 2001/2002 and the ongoing sub-prime and capital market crisis of 2007–2009. Additionally the increasing integration of financial markets has made these crises highly contagious so that problems in one economy can quickly spread across the globe due to the extensive financial exposures of global investors.[89]

Consequently, with the denationalization of financial capital, significant constraints have been imposed on national authorities' discretion to formulate macroeconomic policies.[90] As Martin notes, global financial integration has led

---

86 Nayyar, D., above n9, 141–142.

87 Harvey, J. (1995) 'The International Monetary System and Exchange Rate Determination: 1945 to the Present', Journal of Economic Issues, vol. 29(2), 493; and Moffit, M. (1983) World's Money: International Banking From Bretton Woods to the Brink of Insolvency, New York: Simon & Schuster, 71–92.

88 Gleason, K., Marthur, I, and Peterson, M. (2004) 'Analysis of Intraday Herding Behaviour Among the Sector ETFs', Journal of Empirical Finance, vol. 11, 681–694; Hirshleifer, D. and Hong Teoh, S. (2003) 'Herd Behaviour and Cascading in Capital Markets: a Review and Synthesis', European Financial Management, vol. 9(1), 25–66; Froot, K., Scharfstein, D. and Stein, J. (1992) 'Herd on the Street: Informational Inefficiencies in a Market with Short-Term Speculation', NBER Working Paper No. W3250, 1 February 1990, available at SSRN: <http://ssrn.com/abstract=273581>; and Scharfstein, D and Stein, J. (1990) 'Herd Behaviour and Investment', American Economic Review, vol. 80, 465.

89 See Guha, K. and Callan, E. (2007) 'Fed Comes to Markets Aid' Financial Times, Saturday, 18 August, 1; Stiglitz, J. (2003) Globalization and Its Discontents, Penguin, Chapter 4–5; Krugman, P. (ed.) (2000) Currency Crisis, Chicago: University of Chicago Press; Chang, R. and Velasco, A. (1998) 'The Asian Liquidity Crisis', Working Paper No. W6796, NBER; Sachs, G., Tornell, H. and Velasco, H. (1996) 'Financial Crisis', NBER Annual Bulletin; and Calvo, G. and Mentoza, E. (1996) 'Mexico's Balance of Payments Crisis: A Chronicle of a Death Foretold', Journal of International Economics, vol. 41(3), 235.

90 Simmons, B. (1999) 'The Internationalisation of Capital' in Kitschelt, H. et al. (eds) Continuity and Change in Contemporary Capitalism, Cambridge: Cambridge

to a loss of national autonomy, at least in the sphere of macroeconomic policy-making.[91] This loss of autonomy quickly shifted macroeconomic priorities from the objective of fostering employment and demand to maintaining given exchange rate parities or the levels of money supply. While such macroeconomic policymaking helped prevent capital flight, at least in the short-term, it has had a negative effect on growth rates and has caused an increase in real interest rates from the 1970s.[92] While within the Bretton Woods regime real interest-rates were deliberately kept low to promote growth, since the liberalization of capital controls in the late 1970s they have tended to exceed real Gross Domestic Product (GDP) growth even in the most developed countries such as the US (see Graph 3.2).

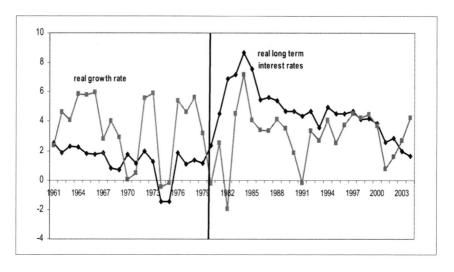

Graph 3.2 Real growth and real interest rates in the US, 1961–2004
Source: Data compiled from OECD Statistical Database. Real long-term interest rates calculations are based on the secondary market yields of 10 year bonds using the Fisher equation. The break in the pattern from 2002–2004 probably notes the point at where US interest rates were held at an artificially low level.

University Press, 36–69; and Keohane, R. and Milner, H. (1996) 'Internationalisation and Domestic Politics: an Introduction' in Keohane, R. and Milner, H. (eds) Internationalisation and Domestic Politics, Cambridge: Cambridge University Press, 3–24.

91   Martin, R. (1994) 'Stateless Monies, Global Financial Integration and National Economic Autonomy: The End of Geography?' in Corbridge, S., Martin, R. and Thrift, N. (eds) Money, Power and Space, Oxford: Blackwell, 253–278.

92   Christiansen, H. and Pigott, C. (1997) 'Long-term Interest Rates in Globalised Markets', OECD Economics Department Working Paper No. 175, OECD, Paris.

For our purposes there are a number of significant effects of this change in macroeconomic conditions on the Kaldorian model. Where real interest rates are high, cash retention and its reinvestment or distribution to stakeholders by management, is more difficult, as shareholders seek returns from management that outstrip less risky investments tied directly to interest-rates e.g. bonds or bank deposits. Moreover, in the aftermath of the collapse of Bretton Woods and the subsequent oil crisis, governments found that demand led spending policies failed to deal with unemployment and inflation. Disillusioned with demand led solutions and with being punished for those policies by nascent global capital markets, governments first in the US and the UK, moved strongly to 'monetarism' where the key goal is restraint of government spending in pursuit of controlling inflation.[93] As a result, government spending in the UK and the US was severely curtailed in the 1970s and 1980s in order to bring inflation under control.[94] Since then Governments have faced what has become known as the Mundell-Fleming 'trilemma' between the policy objectives of full capital mobility, a fixed exchange rate, and expansionary policies, of which only two can be pursued simultaneously if a crisis is to be avoided.[95] So, once commitment to capital mobility is made, demand led policies have to be carefully controlled if they are not to become antagonistic to currency stability.[96] In effect, for our purposes, the Kaldorian economic model was/is difficult to sustain because governments found/find it difficult to create demand at the macroeconomic level. Subsequently, monetarism has been adopted by all major central banks and has become part of financial market orthodoxy as the current global financial environment tends to punish expansionary policies with mass capital withdrawal and reward austerity with inflow.

In addition to the negative impact of high real interest rates and deflationary policies, since the collapse of the Bretton Woods exchange rate system, both financial and non financial corporations have had to commit portions of their cash

---

93   Goodfriend, M. (2002) 'The Phases of U.S. Monetary Policy: 1987 to 2001', The Federal Reserve Bank of Richmond: Economy Quarterly, vol. 88(4), 1–17.

94   See Simmons, B., above n90; and Stephens, J., Huber, E. and Ray, L. (1999) 'The Welfare State in Hard Times' in Kitschelt, H. et al., above n90, 164–193.

95   Mundell, R. (1963) 'Capital Mobility and Stabilisation Under Fixed and Flexible Exchange Rates', Canadian Journal of Economic and Political Science, vol. 29, 475; Fleming, J. (1962) 'Domestic Financial Policies Under Fixed and Under Floating Exchange Rates', IMF Staff Papers, vol. 9, 369–379; and Mundell, R. (1960) 'The Monetary Dynamics of International Adjustment Under Fixed and Flexible Exchange Rates', Quarterly Journal of Economics, vol. 74, 227. See also: Forssbaeck, J. and Oxelheim, L. (2006) 'On the Link Between Exchange-rate Regimes, Capital Controls and Monetary Policy Autonomy in Small European Countries, 1979–2000', The World Economy, vol. 29(3), 341–368.

96   Rodrik, D. (2007) 'One Economics, Many Recipes: Globalization, Institutions and Economic Growth', Princeton: Princeton University Press, 199–200. It was precisely the attempt by the British government to pursue all three objectives that led to the 20 percent devaluation of the pound against the German mark and its forceful exit from the Exchange Rate Mechanism on 'Black Wednesday' 16 September 1992.

flows or borrowed money to derivatives and other instruments in order to hedge against financial risk. By 2007 the total turnover of interest rate, currency and stock index derivatives reached \$533 trillion.[97] As a result an enormous amount of finance is now capitalized as pure finance rather than real asset creation through production. Moreover, trading risk-hedging instruments is itself an extremely complex and unpredictable activity that entails the possibility of very heavy losses if something goes wrong. The examples of Orange County, Barings Bank, Daiwa Bank, Metallgesellschaft, LTCM, Enron and the sub-prime and subsequent credit crisis from 2007/2009 illustrate the complexity of risks involved in derivative trading.[98]

Additionally the simultaneous liberalization of trade has exacerbated the problem governments face. Where governments are unable to stimulate domestic effective demand an obvious solution for domestic industries is to resort to export-led growth often with the assistance of governments. However, where there are imbalances within the coordination of international trade, such policies can lead to situations where exporting nations with low domestic demand grow at the expense of importing ones with higher demand, so that in the end there is no growth in overall global output.[99] In fact, it is this very effect, widely known as the 'balance of payments constraint',[100] which was a factor leading to the decline of the US economy in the late 1960s and its inability to support the Bretton Woods system.[101] In the absence of a system of coordinated trade[102] developed nations have tended to undermine the position of less developed ones with significant consequences for the global economy.[103] As Keynes himself states in his *General Theory*, if

---

97   BIS above n48, 24.

98   See Fay, S. (1997) The Collapse of Barings, New York: W.W. Norton & Company; Jorion, P. (1995) Big Bets Gone Bad: Derivatives and Bankruptcy in Orange County, Irvine: University of California at Irvine Academic Press; and Mello, A. and Parsons, J. (1995) 'Maturity Structure of a Hedge Matters: Lessons from the Metallgesellschaft Debacle', Journal of Applied Corporate Finance, vol. 8(1), 106; and Whalen, C. (2008) 'The Subprime Crisis – Cause, Effect and Consequences', Networks Financial Institute. Policy Brief 2008-PB-04, <http://ssrn.com/abstract=1113888>.

99   Toner, P. (1999) Main Currents in Cumulative Causation: The Dynamics of Growth and Development, Basingstoke: Macmillan, 142.

100   Thirwall, A. and Hussain, M. (1982) 'The Balance of Payments Constraint, Capital Flows and Growth Rate Differences Between Developing Countries', Oxford Economic Papers, vol. 10, 498.

101   See Marglin, S., above n72, 24.

102   GATT/WTO is not such a coordinated system.

103   On the negative effects of the unplanned world trade system see Wade, R. (2005) 'Failing States and Cumulative Causation in the World System', International Political Science Review, vol. 26, 17; Kaldor, N. (1981) 'The Role of Increasing Returns, Technical Progress and Cumulative Causation in the Theory of International Trade and Economic Growth', Economie Appliquée, vol. 34, 593 at 607; and Myrdal, G., above n75, Chapter 11.

appropriate demand management policies are adopted globally, such international trade conflicts should not arise:

> if nations can learn to provide themselves with full employment by their domestic policy ... there need be no important economic forces calculated to set the interest of one country against that of its neighbours. ... International trade would cease to be what it is, namely, a desperate expedient to maintain employment at home by forcing sales on foreign markets and restricting purchases, which, if successful, will merely shift the problem of unemployment to the neighbour which is worsted in the struggle, but a willing and unimpeded exchange of goods and services in conditions of mutual advantage.[104]

In effect while trade remained relatively uncoordinated governments in developed countries, who were restricted in most areas of macroeconomic policy, could still stimulate demand by creating imbalances in their trade with other usually less developed countries. Developed countries maintaining protective tariffs at home and providing domestic subsidies but gaining access to developing markets abroad has been a central problem with the GATT rounds over the past 40 years. As Nayyar has noted:

> [i]t must also be recognised that the spread of globalization is uneven. The exclusion of people and of countries, from the process, is a fact of life. Consider some evidence, for 2000, on international trade, international investment and international finance, which constitute the cutting edge of globalization. Industrialised countries accounted for 64 percent of world exports, while developing countries accounted for 32 percent and transitional economies for the remaining four percent. Industrialised countries accounted for 82 percent of foreign direct investment inflows in the world economy, whereas developing countries accounted for 16 percent and transitional economies for the remaining two percent. Industrialised countries accounted for 95 percent of cross-border mergers and acquisitions in terms of purchases, whereas developing countries accounted for just four percent and transitional economies accounted for a mere one percent.[105]

However, while this issue remains at the heart of imbalances in world trade and was a key factor in the collapse of the WTO Doha round in 2008,[106] the untrammelled ability of governments to stimulate domestic demand through unfair export led

---

104   Keynes, J. (1936) *The General Theory of Employment, Interest and Money*, London: Macmillan, 382–383.

105   Nayyar, D., above n9, 156.

106   The Doha round of trade talks began in 2001. We discuss the implications of this collapse in Chapter 9.

growth has been systematically reduced in each successive GATT round.[107] Thus a window where national governments in the developed world had some autonomy to pursue growth oriented policies has been slowly closing over the past 40 years. In sum, the era of globalization since the breakdown of the Bretton Woods agreement has moved in an antagonistic direction to insider systems reliant on a Kaldorian model.

The managerial governance of insider systems used as a process of balancing divergent stakeholder interests certainly faces challenges from economic globalization where trade barriers have been lowered – which increases competition in product markets and in turn squeezes management discretion – global capital is mobile and dominated by institutional investors – who promote securitization in financial systems – and governments are restricted in their ability to stimulate demand through spending.[108] As Eichengreen has argued in the context of European insider systems:

> the structures and institutions inherited from earlier periods and elaborated after World War II were better suited to incremental than radical innovation and to periods when the challenge for growth was to fine-tune and apply existing technologies rather than to fashion new ones out of whole cloth. They were tailored to a world of limited international competition and foreign investment, not to one of seamless integration and intense cross-border competition.[109]

Understanding Globalization's Corporate Governance Impact: II

The dramatic reduction of trade barriers after a series of GATT negotiations during the second half of the twentieth century has enabled firms to gradually view the world, rather than each particular country, as a single product market (see Tables 3.1 and 3.5 above). As a result FDI has grown enormously (see Table 3.7). As we noted in the earlier part of this chapter, one of the key differences between this current globalization period and the late nineteenth/early twentieth century one, has been the growth of FDI in the form either of locating manufacturing abroad or M&As in the developing world. These patterns need to be explained in detail if we are to draw some lessons about the impact of FDI on core institutions that affect

---

107   See Townsend, I. (2006) 'The WTO Doha Development Round: Where Next for World Trade?', House of Commons Library Research Paper 06/43. See above Table 3.5 on the dramatic reduction in tariff rates over the past 50 years.

108   Fazzari, S., Ferri, P. and Greenberg, E. (1998) 'Aggregate Demand and Firm Behaviour: a New Perspective on Keynesian Microfoundations', Journal of Post Keynesian Economics, vol. 20, 527–559.

109   Eichengreen, B. (2007) The European Economy Since 1945: Coordinated Capitalism and Beyond, Heritage Lectures No. 1023, Heritage Foundation, 3; and Eichengreen, B. (2006) The European Economy Since 1945: Coordinated Capitalism and Beyond, Princeton: Princeton University Press.

corporate governance outcomes. Indeed, these patterns at first sight contradict standard neoclassical theory of foreign investment which tends to regard trade and FDI as substitutes so that 'an increase in trade impediments stimulates factor movements and ... an increase in impediments to factor movements stimulates trade' and suggest something other than trade barriers is driving FDI.[110]

FDI in theory

Since the 1960s, when FDI rates began to grow, several alternative but not mutually exclusive theories have been developed to explain this seemingly puzzling relationship between trade liberalization and FDI. While none of them are able to fully explain the causes and illuminate all the aspects of FDI and the globalization of production, each theory has some useful insights into the effects these FDI patterns might be having in institutions crucial to corporate governance outcomes. It is for this reason that they should be regarded as complementary rather than as alternatives.[111] Generally, these theoretical approaches tend to focus either on the microeconomic or the macroeconomic factors that determine firms' strategic choices.

The pioneer of the microeconomic approach is Hymer whose path-breaking work provided the basis for modern theory of FDI and multinational production.[112] His main insight was that FDI, as a form of foreign factor *ownership*, encompasses the element of control by the investor over products and processes and this helps offset the investment risks involved when markets are imperfect. Thus, where an investment entails significant risks arising from information asymmetries between the investing firm and local competitors in the host country, from volatile exchange rates or from unfavourable host government interference with trade or production, FDI can provide sufficient control over the venture and thus reduce the overall costs. Moreover, according to Hymer, since in imperfect markets not all firms have the same capabilities, FDI may constitute a means of exploiting a particular oligopolistic advantage over specific processes such as production or distribution which foreign rivals lack.[113]

---

110   Mundell, R. (1957) 'International Trade and Factor Mobility', American Economic Review, vol. 47, 321.

111   For a good overview of FDI theories see Milberg, W. (2004) 'The Changing Structure of International Trade Linked to Global Production Systems: What are the Policy Implications?', International Labour Organization, Working Paper No. 33, 42, available at <http://sed-trade-forum.itcilo.org/Fre/Papers/ilo/changstruc.pdf>.

112   Hymer, S. (1960) The International Operations of National Firms: A Study of Foreign Direct Investment, Cambridge, MA: MIT Press.

113   See also Caves, R. (1996) Multinational Enterprise and Economic Analysis, 2nd edition, Cambridge: Cambridge University Press; Rugman, A. (1986) 'New Theories of the Multinational Enterprise: An Assessment of Internationalization Theory', Bulletin of Economic Research, vol. 38(2), 102; and Kindleberger, C. (1984) Multinational Excursions, Cambridge, MA: MIT Press.

Table 3.7 Inward and outward FDI stock (percentage of GDP)

	1980	1985	1990	1995	1997	2000	2004
World Total							
Inward	5.0	6.9	8.4	9.9	11.7	18.3	21.7
Outward	5.3	6.3	8.7	10.2	11.9	19.7	24.0
Developed Countries Total							
Inward	4.8	6.127	8.2	9.0	10.5	16.3	20.5
Outward	6.4	7.4	9.6	11.7	13.9	21.5	27.3
Developing Countries Total							
Inward	5.9	9.8	9.8	14.1	16.6	26.2	26.4
Outward	0.8	1.4	4.3	4.7	5.8	13.6	12.7
Latin Am. and Carib.							
Inward	6.4	10.5	10.5	15.1	17.2	24.7	34.1
Outward	0.4	1.1	5.5	1.7	2.3	10.3	13.1
S, E and SE Asia							
Inward	9.9	11.1	9.3	14.8	18.4	30.7	26.2
Outward	1.4	1.4	3.9	7.3	9.3	19.1	16.1
C and E Europe							
Inward	–	–	1.5	5.5	8.3	24.5	34.5
Outward	–	–	–	0.7	1.2	2.1	5.2

Source: UNCTAD (2005) World Investment Report 2005 – TNCs and the Internationalization of R&D, New York: United Nations; and UNCTAD (1999) World Investment Report 1999 – Foreign Direct Investment and the Challenge of Development, New York: United Nations.

Hymer's notion of control through factor ownership as an explanation of reducing risks bears a close resemblance to Coase's and Williamson's theory of the firm. In fact, Hymer has himself recognized a relation between the Coasean transaction cost theory in his own work.[114] Indeed, this common ground between the two theories has led others to develop the point further into a theory of FDI based on the *internalization* of transaction costs. The main proponents of this approach are Teece, Rugman and Buckley and Casson, and who regard the TNC as an organizational structure which has emerged to resolve international product market imperfections by bringing them within the firm, i.e. by internalizing them.[115] The main claim of the internalization school is that alternatives to FDI, such as subcontracting, outsourcing or licensing of intangible assets – managerial skills, technological know-how, etc. – involve significant transaction costs, because such assets are easily appropriable. Therefore, the nature of FDI as direct factor ownership abroad is a transaction cost economizing mechanism which ensures that assets remain under the control of the firm.[116] This approach, however, tends to regard the TNC as a more efficient alternative to international product market contracting (exports) and thus overlooks the fact that resource allocation by command is not always efficient. This is something Hymer was aware of as he recognized that FDI and the emergence of the TNC constitutes both a response to and a cause of market imperfections.[117] As we discuss later in this section, what is *regarded* as efficient from the firm's perspective is not always efficient in terms of general economic welfare.

Moreover, both Hymer's ownership theory and the internalization thesis suffer from a further deficiency. While they explain why FDI is preferred over other types of investment, such as non-controlling portfolio investment or licensing, they do not provide sufficient reasons for the multinationalization of investment. In order to deal with such theoretical deficiencies, Dunning developed his 'eclectic' approach to TNC activity which is more elaborate as it attempts to combine the

114   Hymer, S. (1968) 'La Grande "Corporation" Multinationale: Analyse de Certaines Raisons Qui Poussent à l'Intégration Internationale des Affaires', Revue Economique, vol. 14(6), 949.

115   Rugman, A. (1986) 'New Theories of the Multinational Enterprise: An Assessment of Internalisation Theory', Bulletin of Economic Research, vol. 35, 101; Teece, D. (1982) 'A Transaction Cost Theory of the Multinational Enterprise', Discussion Paper, International Investment and Business Studies, University of Reading; Teece, D. (1977) 'Technology Transfer by Multinational Firms: The Resource Cost of Transferring Technological Know-how', Economic Journal, vol. 87, 242; and Buckley, P. and Casson, M. (1976) The Future of the Multinational Enterprise, London: Macmillan.

116   Hennart, J. (1991) 'The Transaction Cost Theory of Multinational Enterprise' in Pitelis, C. and Sugden, R. (eds) The Nature of the Transnational Firm, London: Routledge.

117   Ietto-Gillies, G. (2005) Transnational Corporations and International Production: Concepts, Theories, Effects, Cheltenham: Edward Elgar, 62.

two theories above with considerations of locational factors.[118] The most important aspect of this approach is that internalization will occur only if certain locational advantages that are specific to the host country's economy are sufficient to attract the particular investment. So, according to Dunning's 'OLI' theory, for FDI to take place there must be a consummation of the ownership (O) of advantages enjoyed by the firm with locational (L) comparative advantages that the host economy has developed and it must be profitable for the firm to internalize (I) those advantages it owns rather than merely sell them on foreign markets.[119] To use Dunning's own words '[f]oreign production then, implies that location-specific endowments favour a foreign country, but ownership endowments favour the home country's firms'.[120]

Firms' 'ownership endowments' can include size and established position, product and process diversification, the ability to take advantage of division of labour, production technologies and managerial know-how, access to inputs (capital, labour, raw materials), market access, government protection and the ability to exploit differences between national and international/global markets. Countries' locational advantages, on the other hand, include natural and manmade resources, low taxes, low labour costs, high labour productivity, or state-supported monopolies and stable political environment, as well as favourable trade and financial regulations.[121]

While Dunning's OLI approach can be considered as an attempt to integrate micro and macroeconomic elements into a theory of FDI and multinational production, other theories tend to give more emphasis to the latter elements. Vernon's product life cycle approach for example regards the demand for a particular product as a central factor in a firm's decision to produce abroad.[122] More specifically, Vernon divides a product's life cycle into three phases. The

---

118   Dunning, J. (1980) 'Trade, Location of Economic Activity and the MNE: A search for an Eclectic Approach' in Ohlin, B., Hesselborn, P. and Wijkman, P. (eds) (1977) The International Allocation of Economic Activity, London: Macmillan.

119   Dunning, J. (1980) 'Explaining Changing Patterns of International Production: In Defence of the Eclectic Theory', Oxford Bulletin of Economics and Statistics, vol. 4(4), 269 at 275.

120   Dunning, J. (1980) 'Trade, Location of Economic Activity and the MNE: A Search for an Eclectic Approach' in Ohlin, B., Hesselborn, P. and Wijkman, P. (eds) (1977) The International Allocation of Economic Activity, London: Macmillan, 399; and Ietto-Gillies, G. (2004) 'The Nation-State and the Theory of the Transnational Corporation', available at <http://www.econ.cam.ac.uk/cjeconf/delegates/iettogillies.pdf>.

121   Dunning, J. (1981) International Production and the Multinational Enterprise, London: Allen & Unwin, 80–81; and Nachum, L. (2002) 'Firm-Specific Attributes and MNE Location Choices: Financial and Professional Service FDI to New York and London', ESRC Centre for Business and Research, University of Cambridge, Working Paper No. 223.

122   Vernon, R. (1966) 'International Investment and International Trade in the Product Cycle', Quarterly Journal of Economics, vol. 80, 90.

initial phase constitutes the introduction of the product to the market. At this stage, production takes place in the home market where the relevant technology and ideas originate. The product is still not standardized and there is an increased need for flexibility and adaptability to customer preferences, which makes spatial proximity to the market necessary. In addition, as product development is still a crucial element of the firm's activities, highly skilled labour is a necessary input. In the following phase as demand expands the product becomes increasingly standardized and its mass production becomes possible. Growing sales build up the product's reputation not only in the home market but also abroad so that in this second phase, to the extent that trade barriers permit, export markets begin to absorb an increasing portion of sales. Simultaneously, as product standardization progresses the need for skilled labour declines and the ability of rivals to copy the product in question increases. Price competition gradually tends to prevail over innovation and there is an increasing requirement for low-cost unskilled labour so that labour cost differentials between countries become increasingly relevant. Thus, Vernon argues, provided low-cost labour is available abroad, FDI becomes an inevitable cost-cutting strategy for firms with mature products who want to remain competitive. Similarly, the presence of tariffs and other trade measures affecting the product's price will also create an incentive for allocating production within foreign markets to capture demand therein.

However, as Vernon himself and others have acknowledged, in the new macroeconomic environment of increasing product market globalization the life cycle theory has lost some of its explanatory power.[123] Due to the dramatic reduction of tariffs, products can now be introduced in different national markets simultaneously, irrespectively of their life cycle stage. Moreover, the technological gap and income disparities in developed countries and leading developing countries have declined considerably since the 1960s when Vernon developed his theory, so that product life cycles not only have become significantly shorter but also they cannot explain high FDI levels between high per-capita income countries. Nonetheless, this approach can provide important explanations for the allocation of production facilities to developing countries, where labour is less skilled but abundant and cheap, as an attempt to combine the demand variable with the firms' cost-cutting strategies.

However, as Pitelis observes, Vernon's theory focuses on the demand for individual products and not on aggregate demand.[124] He has therefore proposed an alternative approach to explaining the multinationalization of production which is based on aggregate effective demand conditions and which should be

---

123   See Vernon, R. (1979) 'The Product Cycle Hypothesis in a New International Environment', Oxford Bulletin of Economics and Statistics, vol. 41, 255; Ietto-Gillies, G., above n117, 99–101; and Buckley, P. and Casson, M., above n115.

124   Pitelis, C. (1996) 'Effective Demand, Outward Investment and the (Theory of the) Transnational Corporation: An Empirical Investigation', Scottish Journal of Political Economy, vol. 43(2), 192 at 198.

seen as complementary to other theories focusing on microeconomic factors. In this way, Pitelis seeks to fill the gaps in the theories outlined so far by providing explanations for the cross-border element of FDI of all firms and irrespectively of their products' life cycle phases.

Pitelis' main premise is quite simply that the multinationalization of production can be attributed to deficient effective demand. As that deteriorates, say within one country, all firms therein, albeit in different degrees, will see the demand for their own products decline too with corresponding negative effects on rates of return on capital. That being so, firms will then have to face the dilemma mentioned earlier: they can either reduce prices to boost sales or cut production. In imperfect (oligopolistic) markets the former option may not be particularly attractive as it can lead to catastrophic price wars. If, on the other hand, the latter option is followed, the effect in the medium and long-term will be to further depress demand due to lower investment rates. What Pitelis' model, in a similar way to Kester and Kaldor, then suggests is that the way out of this 'no win' situation is for firms to exploit effective demand outside their national economic boundaries. In other words, where domestic demand is deficient, foreign markets can create the economies of scale and scope that domestic markets cannot and thus reduce the cost of internalization of foreign activities through outward investment. Of course, this model is not intended to and does not predict what form of foreign investment will be chosen by the demand constrained firm; its purpose is to illuminate the 'foreignness' of investment. As Pitelis puts it,

> [i]t provides a partial answer to the question "Why internationalisation?" but has little to say on "Why TNCs?" as opposed to exporting, licensing and/or subcontracting. To answer these questions, it is necessary to go back to the [microeconomic] theories. ... In this sense, a synthesis of supply-side micro reasons ... and demand side reasons represents a reasonably powerful ex ante reason for TNCs.[125]

In the light of the discussion in the section above on global demand conditions, this approach acquires particular value as it can explain the explosion of FDI flows since the 1980s, especially between developed countries. The demand slowdown since the liberalization of financial controls as governments have become restricted in terms of their spending and reductions of trade barriers which has increased competition in mature markets has led demand-constrained firms to expand their operations abroad mostly in the form of M&As in order to exploit opportunities arising in global product markets. Pitelis' empirical analysis of FDI data between developed economies since the Great Depression confirms his premise that flows have tended to follow favourable demand conditions.[126]

---

125   Ibid., 198–200.

126   Ibid., 198–203; and Pitelis, C. (2000) 'A Theory of the (Growth of the) Transnational Firm: A Penrosean Perspective', Contributions to Political Economy, vol. 19, 71.

As we noted above, the vast majority of FDI flows tend to be of two types, those from developed countries to developing ones in the form of locating manufacturing there and those between developed countries themselves in the form of M&A. In the light of the above theoretical analysis these two types of FDI flows reveal three main corresponding trends/strategies of TNCs. The first is cost-driven FDI, the second is demand-driven FDI, and the third is technology-driven FDI.

Cost-driven FDI flows are almost exclusively directed from the developed world to countries where inputs, mainly unskilled labour, are available at a low comparative cost. This is part of firms' efforts to exploit input price differentials between different countries. Thus, for production processes that require low-skilled labour, less developed countries with low labour costs in terms of wages and employment protection enjoy significant locational advantages over those countries where wages are high and redundancies are costly. Provided those low cost countries do not restrict trade, firms seeking to remain globally competitive will have an incentive to transfer their low-skill operations there which creates direct pressures on industrial relations systems that emphasize internalized labour markets. This explains the large flows of FDI from developed countries with high labour costs to less developed ones. Moreover, the closer those low labour cost countries are to the main 'demand markets', the better their locational advantage will be. It is not surprising, therefore, that Eastern European, Latin American and South East Asian countries have been significant hosts of cost-driven FDI. Their proximity to the trade 'Triad', i.e. the EU, North America and Japan, makes them particularly competitive as they can easily serve the major product markets. Of course, whether FDI actually takes place or another method of shifting production, such as licensing, outsourcing or sub-contracting, is preferred also depends on the internalization incentives of the firm.[127] It is reasonable to expect that such incentives will be higher, and thus FDI more likely, where the technological or managerial know-how involved in the production process is firm-specific and/or where high quality standards are required.

Demand-driven FDI, on the other hand, tends to flow mainly between developed countries. The higher the per-capita income and the larger the population, the more attractive a market is. In the current macroeconomic environment aggregate demand has become a locational advantage which can attract FDI from firms that face constraints in their home markets and who compete in the global marketplace. As Ohmae argues, firms have to establish themselves in all Triad countries constituting the major consumption powerhouses in order to become and remain competitive.[128] Much of this type of FDI has taken the form of M&As. Presence in these vast product markets carries significant internalization advantages, because

---

127   Viswanadham, N. and Balaji, K. (2005) 'Foreign Direct Investment or Outsourcing: A Supply Chain Decision Model ', ISB Working Paper Series, available at <http://www.isb.edu/faculty/Working_Papers_pdfs/Foreign_Direct_Investment_or_Outsourcing.pdf>.

128   Ohmae, K. (1985) Triad Power: The Coming Shape of Global Competition, New York: Free Press.

it enables TNCs to adapt their products to local tastes and needs as well as to exploit local distributional channels. Trade barriers, where present, may also be a significant reason for a local presence to avoid their penal effect. Simultaneously, another important factor affecting a country's locational advantage as a host of FDI is the growth potential of its economy. China is a clear case of a developing country of this kind due to its vast population and consistently high growth rates in recent years. It is then no surprise that TNCs from most Triad countries have been so keen to invest in Chinese industrial plants making China the largest developing country recipient of FDI.[129]

Finally, technology-driven FDI flows can be more mixed. Technology, of course, should be given a broad meaning so as to include not only scientific knowledge but also organizational and other capabilities. Given that patent or copyright laws can bar access to scientific knowledge and that know-how and capabilities tend to be highly firm-specific, the direct investment option contains significant internalization incentives. Obviously, developed countries score better in the area of technologies and therefore enjoy a clear locational advantage which makes them the largest hosts of this type of FDI. On the other hand, investment flows can originate from both developed and developing countries, since firms on either side have the incentives to acquire the highest technology available. However, subject to a few exceptional cases (China and India for example), firms from developing countries usually do not have the necessary resources to make such investment. This is shown by the low levels of FDI originating from such firms. So, just as in the case of demand-driven FDI, technology-driven investment flows mainly between developed countries and may be an additional response to competitive markets, as M&As may be driven by the need to capture a competitive technological advantage.

Although these three types of FDI can be considered as separate strategies, often they are interrelated and are pursued simultaneously by firms that compete in global product markets. This is because, faced with saturated competitive markets, firms need to *both* tap as much of global effective demand as possible *and* reduce their costs in order to remain price-competitive. At the same time, firms' struggle for global competitiveness may also require that they ensure their access to the latest technological capabilities.[130] The globalization of competition in product markets since the liberalization of world trade and finance has been exerting

129   Amiti, M. and Smarzynska Javorcik, B. (2008) 'Trade Costs and Location of Foreign Firms in China', Journal of Development Economics, vol. 85(1–2), February, 129–149; and Milberg, W. (2004) 'The Changing Structure of International Trade Linked to Global Production Systems: What are the Policy Implications?', International Labour Organization, Working Paper No. 33, 41, available at <http://sed-trade-forum.itcilo.org/Fre/Papers/ilo/changstruc.pdf>.

130   Howells, J. (2000) 'International Coordination of Technology Flows and Knowledge Activity in Innovation', International Journal of Technology Management, vol. 19(7–8), 806; and Howells, J. (1993) 'Emerging Global Strategies in Innovation

pressures not only towards the globalization of production but also towards the adoption of such integrated approaches in order to fully exploit OLI advantages. Indeed, the element of choice within competitive markets may not be present once a competitor starts pursuing a particular FDI strategy. As Knickerbocker has argued the strategic behaviour of firms operating in global oligopolistic markets tends to follow a pattern of action and reaction so that an aggressive FDI move by one firm can spark a defensive reaction by its competitors who seek to minimize the risk of being out-competed. In this way, a 'bandwagon effect' is created and FDI tends to 'bunch up' so that a move by one firm has the tendency to become amplified as rivals choose to mimic it.[131]

As a result of all these dynamics the global economic landscape has been transformed into one dominated by TNCs, industrial as well as financial, usually operating in oligopolistic markets that transcend national boundaries. Whether enabled or forced by the process of globalization, such corporations have been reorganizing their activities so as to reap diverse OLI advantages in multiple countries across the globe. As Gilpin observes, while in the early post war era multinationals pursued 'horizontal investment' strategies by establishing self-sufficient subsidiaries in foreign (developed) countries, since the 1980s they have moved to a 'vertical investment' tactic where different production facilities are scattered around the world as interdependent units heavily reliant on outsourcing in an integrated manner.[132] Goods can now be produced all around the world and ultimately be exported if necessary back to the country where the TNCs' head offices are based.

With the shift of assembly and other low-skill activities to low labour cost locations the old international division of labour, by which the role of underdeveloped countries in the world economy was to supply unprocessed raw materials to industrialized countries, has now largely come to an end. As Fröbel et al. predicted early in this period of economic globalization, a single world market for labour and industrial sites has emerged, encompassing all nations irrespective of their development stage.[133] Thus, production of both semi-processed and processed goods are being located in developing countries according to the demands of

---

Management' in Humbert, M. (ed.) The Impact of Globalization on Europe's Firms and Industries, London: Pinter Publishers.

131   Knickerbocker, F. (1973) Oligopolistic Reaction and Multinational Enterprises, Boston: Division of Research, Graduate School of Business Administration, Harvard University. See also Head, K., Mayer, T. and Ries, J. (2002) 'Revisiting Oligopolistic Reaction: Are Decisions on Foreign Direct Investment Strategic Compliments?', Journal of Economics and Management Strategy, vol. 2(3), 453–472.

132   Gilpin, R. (2000) The Challenge of Global Capitalism – The World Economy in the 21st Century, Princeton: Princeton University Press, 165–66.

133   Fröbel, F., Heinrichs, J. and Kreye, O. (1980) The New International Division of Labour, Cambridge: Cambridge University Press; and Fröbel, F., Heinrichs, J. and Kreye, O. (1978) 'The World Market for Labour and the World Market for Industrial Sites', Journal of Economic Issues, vol. 12(4), 1461.

global competitive forces. As a result such countries now export manufactured goods to the industrial world at competitive prices mainly due to low labour costs. In sum, international trade and capital liberalization and the revolution in transport and communication technologies have made such strategies possible and have given rise to what Flamm and Grunwald described as the 'global factory'.[134] In oligopolistic markets, this 'global switching' is not seen merely as a matter of choice but as a necessity for survival.[135] Just like financial capital, industrial capital has also become increasingly global.

FDI and its effect on corporate governance institutions

So far this discussion has concentrated on the impact of economic globalization on firms' strategies. However, it is particularly important for the purposes of this work to also examine the effect of these strategies, i.e. the global reorganization of production, on the economic environment itself to the extent that globalization entails a loss of national autonomy in key institutions. While the theoretical approaches to FDI and the globalization of production discussed above aim at explaining firms' adaptive reactions to their global environment, they fall short of exploring the ability of firms operating in imperfectly competitive markets to influence prices and their environment according to their own needs. The importance of this power of firms over macro and microeconomic pricing is even greater once the vast size of TNCs and their dominant role in product markets are accounted for. The United Nations estimated that in 2006 there were 78,000 TNC with 780,000 foreign affiliates.[136] It considered:

> [t]heir economic impact can be measured in different ways. In 2001, foreign affiliates accounted for 54 million employees compared to 24 million in 1990; their sales of almost $19 trillion were more than twice as high as world exports in 2000, compared to 1990 when both were roughly equal; and the stock of outward foreign direct investment increased from $1.7 trillion to $6.6 trillion over the same period. Foreign affiliates now account for one-tenth of world GDP and one-third of world exports.[137]

Thus TNCs rather than being the passive subjects of a globalization process may have the ability to bring international trade within their control, to influence

---

134   Flamm, K. and Grunwald, J. (1985), The Global Factory – Foreign Assembly and International Trade, Washington, DC: Brooking Institute.
135   Howells, J., above n130, 223.
136   UNCTAD (2007) World Investment Report, Geneva, xvi. There had been a notable decline in the number of foreign affiliates TNCs operated between 2001 and 2006. In 2001 65,000 TNC operated 850,000 foreign affiliates compared to 78,000 TNCs with 780,000 foreign affiliates in 2006. See UNCTAD (2002) World Investment Report, Geneva, xv.
137   UNCTAD (2002) World Investment Report, Geneva, xv.

government policy and weaken labour influence.[138] These points are important for understanding the nature and effects of TNC activity and therefore deserve a closer look.

The first issue, the ability of TNCs to subvert international trade, is a direct outcome of the globalization of production as described above. The very essence of this strategy is that numerous companies scattered around the world, affiliated and organized under the umbrella of a single TNC parent firm are able to exchange goods and services with each other for the purposes of completing the production and distribution of the final product. With the intensification of the globalization of production intra-firm trade has become a significant part of world trade especially in manufactured goods where it accounts for approximately 40 percent of world trade.[139] In the US and Japan, intra-firm trade figures run at approximately 50 percent and as much as 80 percent for the UK.[140] As Dicken describes it:

> TNCs account for around two-thirds of world exports of goods and services of which a significant share is *intra-firm trade*. In other words, it is trade within the boundaries of the firm – although across national boundaries – in the form of transactions between *different parts of the same firm*. Unfortunately, there are no comprehensive and reliable statistics on intra-firm trade. The "ballpark" figure is that approximately one-third of total world trade is intra-firm although, again, that could be a substantial underestimate. Unlike the kind of trade assumed in international trade theory – and in the trade statistics collected by national and international agencies – intra-firm trade does not take place on an "arm's length" basis. It is, therefore, subject not to external market prices but to the internal decisions of TNCs.[141]

As Dicken is suggesting high levels of intra-firm trade mean that TNCs have the potential to place international trade under their control. Consequently, Cowling and Sugden argue, increasing portions of trade flows are being managed in the interests of those firms and not of nation states so that 'a system of free international trade is

138   Cowling, K. and Sugden, R. (1994) Beyond Capitalism: Towards a New World Economic Order, London: Pinter Publishers; and Kottaridi, C. (2005) 'FDI, Growth and the Role of Governance: Changing the Rules of the Game', Contributions to Political Economy, vol. 24, 79.

139   European Commission (1995) A Level Playing Field for Direct Investment Worldwide, Brussels: The European Commission, 2; and Milberg, W. (2004) 'The Changing Structure of International Trade Linked to Global Production Systems: What are the Policy Implications?', International Labour Organization, Working Paper No. 33, 14, available at <http://sed-trade-forum.itcilo.org/Fre/Papers/ilo/changstruc.pdf>.

140   Dicken, P. (1992) The Internationalisation of Economic Activity, 2nd edition London: Paul Chapman, 49; and Milberg, W., ibid.

141   Dicken, P. (2007) Global Shift: Mapping the Changing Contours of the World Economy, London: Sage, 38.

in fact one of TNCs' subverted trade.'[142] As a result, increasing intra-firm trade can impose considerable constraints on government trade policies. In particular, the wide scope to manipulate transfer prices – i.e. the invoicing of internal transfers at non-market prices – by TNCs can affect governments' tax revenues, their ability to impose exchange controls, and to regulate the balance of payments and exchange rates, so that Keynesian demand management policies can become ineffective.[143]

Additionally the ability of TNCs to organize production on a global scale according to OLI advantages means that industrial capital can migrate towards countries with the best combination of locational advantages. In this way, national economic systems are placed in competition with each other in their efforts to attract FDI in manufacturing plants. This has increased TNCs' bargaining power *vis-à-vis* governments so that taxation, employment, education and infrastructure policies are often formed according to TNC needs.[144] Similarly, TNC global production strategies can weaken labour power as governments in response to TNC needs weaken employment rights or TNCs relocate production to low labour cost nations. Labour, like national governments, is usually immobile – as a result factor mobility gives significant bargaining power to TNCs in negotiating with labour and governments. More specifically, the availability of low labour cost production locations creates a downward pressure on employment protection and wages for less skilled labour in industrial countries.[145] Non-conformity can result in the relocation of production from high-cost to low-cost countries and thus create unemployment problems in the former. Conformity, on the other hand, leads to increasing wage disparities and the polarization of income distribution. Moreover, as the new international division of labour progresses, the global dispersion of a TNC's workforce limits the possibility for concerted internal labour action on behalf of the latter that would level the

---

142   Cowling, K. and Sugden, R., above n138, 69.

143   Ietto-Gillies, G. (2005) Transnational Corporations and International Production: Concepts, Theories, Effects, Cheltenham: Edward Elgar , 36, 169 and 181.

144   See Rodrik, D. (2007) One Economics, Many Recipes: Globalization, Institutions and Economic Growth, Princeton University Press, 201–203; Gordon, R. and MacKie-Mason, J. (1995) 'The Importance of Income Shifting in the Design and Analysis of Tax Policy' in Feldstein, M., Hines, J. and Hubbard, G. (eds) Taxing Multinational Corporations, Chicago: University of Chicago Press, 29–37; Kurzer, P. (1993) Business and Banking: Political Change and Economic Integration in Western Europe, Ithaca: Cornell University Press; and Frenkel, J., Razin, A. and Sadka, E. (1991) International Taxation in an Integrated World, Cambridge, MA: MIT Press. Additionally favourable conditions for TNCs are created by the requirements of international organizations such as the WTO, the World Bank and the IMF. See Rodrik, D. (2007) One Economics, Many Recipes: Globalization, Institutions and Economic Growth, Princeton: Princeton University Press, Chapter 1.

145   Geishecker, I. and Gorg, H. (2007) 'Winners and Losers: A Micro-Level Analysis of International Outsourcing and Wages', CEPR Discussion Paper No. DP6484, <http://ssrn. com/abstract=1138948>; Albo, G. and Roberts, C. (1998) 'European Industrial Relations: Impasse or Model?' in Meiskins-Woods, E., Meiskins, P. and Yates, M. (eds) Rising from the Ashes? Labour in the Age of 'Global' Capitalism, New York: Monthly Review Press.

bargaining position of employer and employee.[146] The repercussions of economic globalization and/or of TNCs' activities go beyond the drive for increased FDI and global reorganization of production as strategic choices. TNC reactions to increased competition as a result of globalization has also, as we described above, affected the form of such investments. Accordingly, Pitelis associates globalization with the tendency of FDI to take the form of cross-border mergers and acquisitions (M&A) rather than 'greenfield' investments.[147] For example the number and value of cross-border mergers and acquisitions has risen significantly since the mid 1980s and now easily accounts for most FDI.[148] Consistently in the past decade M&A activity made up more than half the FDI in most OECD countries.[149] In 2000 for instance, a peak year for cross-border investment, 81 percent of the value of all world FDI inflows was made up of cross-border M&A, the value of which exceeded $1.143 trillion, declining to 49 percent and $8.8 billion in 2007.[150] Additionally the number of 'mega' transactions with a value of over $1 billion has also risen significantly since the 1980s (see Table 3.8 below). Increasingly important within these overall FDI figures is the growing number of M&A transactions where the bidder is from the developing world (See Table 3.9). This form of FDI from the developing world has a very different pattern as it is split between 'Greenfield' investment (mostly investment in the developing world) and investment in existing factors (mostly developing world investing in the developed world for technology reasons).[151] Additionally, the globalization of product markets has increased competition in the developing world which in turn is playing a part in driving this increasing FDI from the developing world as firms can no longer wait to pursue a regional or global strategy.[152] As a result firms from the developing world are pursuing dual FDI strategies (Greenfield and acquisition) to gain commodities, brands, distribution outlets or technology, whereas firms from the developed world almost all pursue acquisition strategies in response to competitive pressures.

---

146   Fröbel, F., Heinrichs, J. and Kreye, O. (1980), above n133, 40.

147   Pitelis, C. (1991) 'The Transnational Corporation: Demand-side Issues and a Synthesis' in Pitelis, C. and Sugden, R. (eds) The Nature of the Transnational Firm, London: Routledge.

148   See Kang, N. and Johansson, S. (2001) 'Cross-Border Mergers and Acquisitions: Their Role in Industrial Globalization', OECD STI Working Papers 2000/1 (Paris: OECD, 2001), and UNCTAD (2006) World Investment Report: FDI from the Developing and Transition Economies: Implications for Development, New York: United Nations.

149   Christiansen, H. and Bertrand, A. (2006) 'Trends and Recent Developments in Foreign Direct Investment' in OECD, International Investment Perspectives, Paris, OECD, 26, available at <http://www.oecd.org/dataoecd/54/58/37010986.pdf>.

150   UCTAD (2008) Foreign Direct Investment, M&A by Region and Major FDI Indicators <http://stats.unctad.org/fdi/>.

151   Christiansen, H. and Bertrand, A., above n149, 12–19.

152   See Bonaglia, F., Goldstein, A. and Matthews, J. (2007) 'Accelerated Internationalization by Emerging Multinationals: The Case of White Goods', Journal of World Business, vol. 42(4), 369–383.

Table 3.8 Cross-border M&As with values of over $1 billion, 1987–2004

Year	Number of deals	Percentage of total	Value ($ billion)	Percentage of total
1987	14	1.6	30.0	40.3
1988	22	1.5	49.6	42.9
1989	26	1.2	59.5	42.4
1990	33	1.3	60.9	40.4
1991	7	0.2	20.4	25.2
1992	10	0.4	21.3	26.8
1993	14	0.5	23.5	28.3
1994	24	0.7	50.9	40.1
1995	36	0.8	80.4	43.1
1996	43	0.9	94.0	41.4
1997	64	1.3	129.2	42.4
1998	86	1.5	329.7	62.0
1999	114	1.6	522.0	68.1
2000	175	2.2	866.2	75.7
2001	113	1.9	378.1	63.7
2002	81	1.8	213.9	57.8
2003	56	1.2	141.1	47.5
2004	75	1.5	199.8	52.5

Source: UNCTAD (2005) World Investment Report 2005 – Transnational Corporations and the Internationalization of R&D, 9.

All this indicates that the intensification of economic globalization since the mid 1980s is gradually giving rise to a particularly active global market for corporate control. Current and potential leading firms across the world are striving to maintain or acquire those ownership advantages that will help them remain globally competitive and survive as independent firms. However, despite the vast sums involved, most of these transactions constitute investments in existing factors rather in the creation of new ones so that, although they can lead to an increase in the acquitting firms' capacity, they do not represent an equivalent net increase in the overall capacity of the world economy. Chaisnais describes this as follows:

> [t]he type of corporate behaviour which may prevail when there is room in the market for many rivals to develop is likely to change as soon as slow or very slow growth sets in. This of course is what has occurred since the 1980s.

Corporate growth and multinational expansion must now take place at the expense of other firms and thus FDIs occur principally in the form of mergers and acquisitions.[153]

Most importantly, studies have shown that, just like in other forms of FDI, M&A activity has an inherent propensity to create herding effects. In an argument that bears similarities with Knickerbocker's 'bandwagon effect', Gorton, Kahl and Rosen distinguish between aggressive and defensive acquisitions to show that firms may engage themselves in M&A as part of a strategy of discouraging other firms from launching hostile bids for them. This objective, of clear managerial origin, they argue, eventually leads to merger waves where efficiency is often sacrificed in the name of firm independence, so that M&A activity becomes itself an end rather than a means to exploiting OLI advantages.[154] This, of course does not undermine the importance of the latter as causes of increased M&A in recent years. In fact, one could combine the argument of Gorton et al. with OLI motives to argue that firms often pursue defensive M&As in order to create and maintain 'strategic comfort'.[155] The outcome, however, is similar; one deal leads to another as a response. However, whether driven by aggressive or defensive reasons there is no doubt that the evidence on M&A activity suggests that an enormous international merger wave has indeed been underway since the mid 1990s driven primarily by changes in product markets due to globalization (see Table 3.8).[156]

The effects of the emerging global market for corporate control are not negligible in creating pressures on institutions that effect corporate governance outcomes. On top of the general effects of cost-driven FDIs on industrial relations systems described above, M&A transactions in most cases lead to workforce reductions in merged entities and, unless other jobs are available elsewhere, they can result in additional downward pressures on employment and/or wage levels. In a restrictive macroeconomic environment where full employment policies are hard for governments to pursue due to all the factors analysed earlier in this chapter, international M&A activity can add to the pressures on internal industrial relations systems.

---

153 Chaisnais, F. (1993) 'Globalization, World Oligopy and Some of Their Implications' in Humbert, M. (ed.) The Impact of Globalization on Europe's Firms and Industries, London: Pinter Publishers, 17.

154 Gorton, G., Kahl, M. and Rosen, R. (2005) 'Eat or Be Eaten: A Theory of Mergers and Merger Waves', Working Paper, The Rodney L. White Center for Financial Research, University of Pennsylvania, available at <http://ssrn.com/abstract=713769>.

155 Schenk, H. (1999) Large Mergers a Matter of Strategy Rather than Economics, mimeo, Geneva: UNCTAD, 6, available at <http://www2.econ.uu.nl/users/schenk/WIR99.html>.

156 Black, B. (2000) 'The First International Merger Wave (and the Fifth and Last US Wave)', University of Miami Law Review, vol. 54, 799.

Table 3.9 M&As as share (percentage) of FDI by country/region, 1990–2001

Country/Region/Economy	1990	1995	1996	1997	1998	1999	2000	2001
Developed economies	81.60	80.60	85.30	86.60	91.50	81.10	86.00	98.60
European Union	68.90	65.70	74.20	89.60	71.60	73.20	72.50	65.90
Other Western Europe	79.50	103.80	120.60	69.80	52.20	69.40	102.50	121.00
United States	114.10	92.30	87.70	74.80	108.40	88.90	107.80	148.60
Developing Economies	42.73	14.66	23.40	35.07	44.06	32.87	29.68	41.90
Africa	19.53	14.63	30.93	40.45	28.90	24.10	36.80	90.44
Latin America and Caribbean	111.79	27.98	38.80	55.32	77.76	38.39	47.40	41.98
Asia	16.80	9.24	14.32	20.12	16.75	28.06	16.59	33.75
West Asia	5.28	74.00	13.91	6.52	1.22	103.40	140.99	32.01
Central Asia	na	30.32	124.36	60.87	5.52	2.96	5.65	0.42
South, East and South-East Asia	17.91	8.51	20.45	35.67	37.27	47.65	23.36	69.69
Pacific	na	9.42	6.94	171.33	14.80	48.03	5.68	na
Central and Eastern Europe	44.60	41.12	26.94	29.46	22.63	40.84	64.55	42.67
World	74.26	56.46	58.79	63.76	76.56	70.39	76.67	80.79

Source: Milberg, W. (2004) 'The Changing Structure of International Trade Linked to Global Production Systems: What are the Policy Implications?', International Labour Organization, Working Paper No. 33, 42, available at <http://sed-trade-forum.itcilo.org/Fre/Papers/ilo/changstruc.pdf>.

Of course additional pressures can be exerted because institutional sets that favour securitization over intermediation have an advantage when FDI takes the form of M&A, as they tend to encourage deep and liquid securities markets as described in Chapter 2. Institutional sets in the two leading outsider systems of the UK and US are conducive to takeovers and as a result of FDI being mainly corporate acquisitions, the US and the UK, being the countries with the world's two major equity markets, consistently top the OECD FDI league. If we take 2006 as an example the US was top of the FDI league with $184 billion in inflows, almost all of which represented the takeovers of existing businesses. The UK was second with inflows of $140 billion, which again was almost all takeovers.[157]

Significantly, this global market for corporate control demonstrates how capital mobility at the macroeconomic level can interact with organizational restructuring at the micro-level. Such transactions, especially when large corporations are involved, require enormous amounts of capital which often exceed not only the funds available within the company, but also the capacity of national financial markets. For large companies, however, this is not a significant constraint because in a world without capital controls they have the capacity to tap global capital markets in order to obtain the funds they may need.[158] Not only do they often enjoy credit ratings that are better than those of many governments, they also possess the necessary expertise to take advantage of global financial markets and thus bypass domestic banks as providers of external finance. Supranational markets such as Eurobond markets have been a source of trade and FDI finance for TNCs since the 1960s due to tax advantages and the lack of regulatory interference.[159] With the liberalization of capital controls during the 1980s, however, TNCs' financial options have increased dramatically. Although the globalization of equity markets is still at an early stage, large corporations in insider and outsider systems can effectively finance their activities through multiple-equity offerings, tapping most major stock markets simultaneously.[160] For example the following is but a small sample of the major companies that hold dual or multiple listings in the following countries; Royal Dutch Shell Plc (Netherlands, UK, United States), BP (UK, United States), Daimler AG (Germany, United States, Singapore, Canada, Argentina, Netherlands, France, Austria, Switzerland, UK), Toyota (Japan, United

---

157   Additionally two thirds of this US investment came from Europe. Christiansen, H., Goldstein, A. and Bertrand, A. (2007) 'Trends and Recent Developments in Foreign Direct Investment' OECD Financial Market Trends, June, 4.

158   Mellors, J. (1974) 'Multinational Corporations and Capital Market Integration' in Wilson, J. and Scheffer, C. (eds) Multinational Enterprises – Financial and Monetary Aspects, The Hague: Sijhoff, 235.

159   Burn, G. (1999) 'The State, the City and the Euromarkets', Review of International Political Economy, vol. 6(2), 225; and Mellors, J. (1974) 'Multinational Corporations and Capital Market Integration' in Wilson, J. and Scheffer, C., above n158, 235.

160   For a long list of the largest companies in the world and where they are listed see at <http://en.wikipedia.org/wiki/List_of_the_world%27s_largest_companies>.

States), Total SA (France, United States), AXA (France, United States), Allianz AG (Germany, France, United States), Volkswagen AG (Germany, Japan, United States, Luxembourg, Belgium, UK, Austria, Switzerland, France, Spain, Italy, Canada), Siemens AG (Germany, Italy, Canada, Austria, Belgium, Switzerland, Netherlands, UK, France, United States). In this way, firms in insider systems overcome the cost and volume restrictions imposed by the thinness of domestic markets on their ability to raise the capital required; this is especially so in large FDI M&A transactions driven by competitive pressures. Indeed, there is a strong correlation in the European context between companies that rely on export markets and the pursuit of expansionary strategies funded through cross-listing on global capital markets.[161]

Additionally, the privatization of former state industries in insider systems since the 1990s has also played a part in exposing some of the largest companies in those systems to global capital markets dominated by institutional investors. Ironically the more demand restricted a government finds itself in terms of spending because of economic globalization the more likely it is to find privatization of state industries an attractive revenue earner.[162] Additionally, where companies from insider systems raise equity from external capital markets or have been privatized into those markets, the dominant role of institutional investors in world financial markets and their expectation, once they have invested in a company from an insider system, that they will be able to enforce a shareholder-orientation, creates further pressures on managers in insider systems to rethink long-term commitments with non-shareholder constituencies.[163] Should a company from an insider system be the subject of a takeover by a UK or a US company, this brings obvious direct exposure to a shareholder-oriented corporate governance system. Indeed, even where a company from an insider system takes over a company from an outsider system this can act like a Trojan horse for shareholder orientation as many deals are completed involving a share swap between the merging firms.[164] In such as

---

161   Pagano, M., Röel, A. and Zechner, J. (2002) 'The Geography of Equity Listing: Why Do European Companies List Abroad?', Journal of Finance, vol. 57, 2651.

162   Belke, A. et al. (2005) 'The Different Extent of Privatisation Proceeds in EU Countries: A Preliminary Explanation Using a Public Choice Approach', IZA Discussion Paper No. 1741, 20.

163   In the year 2000, US and UK Institutional Investors held 35 percent of the outstanding shares in the 40 largest French companies listed on the Paris Stock Exchange and 41 percent of listed Dutch companies. See Tagliabue, J. (2000) 'Resisting those Ugly Americans', New York Times, New York, 9 January 2000, 1 and 10; and Chernoff, J. and Farnon, P. (1997) 'Governance Codes Vary by Market', Pensions and Investments, 16 September 1997, 16–32 at 16.

164   Mittoo, U. (1992) 'Managerial Perceptions of the Net Benefits of Foreign Listing: Canadian Evidence', Journal of International Financial Management and Accounting, vol. 4(1), 40, 43. On the increased use of ADRs listed on the NYSE as 'currency' for takeovers of US firms see 'American Depositary Receipts: More Size than Depth', Euromoney Magazine, October 1999, 80–82.

case the merged entity has a significant shareholding base of institutional investors within it, which creates additional pressures to conform to a shareholder model as it can, as we will observe in Chapter 8, make the company more vulnerable to a takeover. Additionally, raising capital through the UK or the US stock exchanges exposes insider companies to the shareholder-oriented regulations of those exchanges.[165] Thus, the opening of new funding opportunities in global financial markets constitutes direct challenges to the stability of stakeholder relationships in insider corporate governance systems by simultaneously promoting outsider shareholder-oriented norms.[166]

The Globalization of Corporate Law

While the above has given an indication of the effects of economic globalization on core institutional sub-systems such as finance, competition and effective demand and industrial relations we have not yet discussed the impact of globalization on corporate law. Obviously the lack of a global corporate law is one reason for this. Additionally our focus on economic globalization brings those institutions with primarily economic functions into closer focus but the effects of economic globalization are felt in corporate law too as international organizations have formulated strategies for the promotion of the shareholder supremacy principle and therefore deserve a mention.

The most important effort has been initiated by the Organization for Economic Cooperation and Development (OECD) with the formulation of its Corporate Governance Principles. These were the outcome of an Advisory Group set up in 1996 with the mandate of the OECD Ministers to review international corporate governance matters and propose minimum standards that should be followed in Member Countries. The Advisory Group reported in April 1998 and the following year a Task Force was set up to develop the final set of principles which were eventually adopted by the OECD Ministers in June 1999.[167]

Both the Advisory Group's Report and the Principles that sprung from it follow an approach that limits the meaning of corporate governance to the alignment of managerial decision-making to shareholder interests. Although the Principles recognize the importance of other stakeholders' rights, by advocating for managerial

---

165   Coffee, J. (1999) 'The Future as History: Prospects for Global Convergence in Corporate Governance and its Implications', Northwestern University Law Review, vol. 93, 665.

166   See Gilson, R. (2000) 'Globalizing Corporate Governance: Convergence of Form or Function', Stanford Law and Economics Olin Working Paper No. 192, 22, 23, available at <http://ssrn.com/abstract=229517>.

167   Dignam, A. and Galanis, M. (1999) 'Governing the World: The Development of the OECD's Corporate Governance Principles', European Business Law Review, vol. 10, 396.

accountability *solely* to current shareholders both directly and through the market for corporate control, they adopt an explicitly shareholder oriented model.

While the OECD Principles do not constitute a legally enforceable instrument they have had real effect because of their promotion as best practice by the OECD itself and other organizations such as the World Bank, the European Bank for Reconstruction and Development, the International Organization of Securities Commissions and the IMF. Indeed, the OECD Secretary General and the World Bank's President have signed a Memorandum of Understanding aiming for the 'improvement' of global corporate governance standards on the basis of the Principles. As part of this joint initiative, a Global Corporate Governance Forum and several Regional Policy Dialogue Roundtables have been formed to promote the acceptance of the Principles.[168] In other words there have been systematic efforts by international organizations to institutionalize an outsider shareholder orientation as a globally accepted corporate governance norm.[169] As Hansmann and Kraakman note:

> the pressures for further convergence [to a shareholder model] are now rapidly growing. Chief among these pressures is the recent dominance of a shareholder-centered ideology of corporate law among the business, government, and legal elites ...[170]

These pressures sometimes have a very direct effect on insider systems particularly those in the developing world. For example, in the aftermath of the 1997 Asian financial crisis the IMF, the WB and the US Government considered the root cause of the crisis to have been the insider nature of the Korean corporate legal model.[171] As a result, the financial assistance provided to Korea was conditional on the dismantling of the Korean insider model and the introduction of outsider legal norms.[172] Later, it became apparent that the root cause of the crisis was, somewhat ironically, changes in the macroeconomic environment, particularly instabilities

168   World Bank – IMF Reports on the Observance of Standards and Codes, Corporate Governance, available at <http://www.worldbank.org/ifa/rosc_cg.html>.

169   Can Atacik, M. and Jarvis, M. (2006) 'Better Corporate Governance: More Value for Everyone', World Bank Institute, Discussion Paper', February 2006, No. 2.

170   Hansmann, H. and Kraakman, R. (2001) 'The End of History for Corporate Law', Georgia Law Review, vol. 89, 439 at 468.

171   Greenspan, A. (1998) 'Testimony before the Committee on Banking and Financial Services', US House of Representatives, 30 January; and Ouattara, A. 'Globalization, Lessons from the Asian Crisis and Central Bank Policies', Réunion des Gouverneurs des Banques Centrales des Pays Francophones Ottawa, 23 June 1998, available at <http://www.imf.org/external/np/speeches/1998/062398a.htm>.

172   See Singh, A., Singh, A. and Weisse, B. (2002) 'Corporate Governance, Competition, The New International Financial Architecture and Large Corporations in Emerging Markets', ESRC Centre for Business Research, University of Cambridge Working Paper No. 250, 53, available at <http://ideas.repec.org/p/cbr/cbrwps/wp250.html>.

caused by the introduction of capital mobility. The result of this misunderstanding was the largest outflow of private capital ever recorded, resulting in the near collapse of a group of related economies.[173] Additionally for the developing world the 'conditionality' of loans from the IMF and WB further creates pressures to conform to shareholder-oriented norms.[174] Generally, the conditions on lending constitute pressures on borrowers to agree to institutional reforms that seek to enhance the role of markets, domestic and global, through prolonged austerity programmes, current and capital account liberalization, capital market de-regulation and enhanced outsider shareholder protection.[175] Further pressures are generated by institutional investors who will pay a premium for firms in the developing world with the right shareholder oriented governance practices.[176]

As we noted in Chapter 1, the academic literature on convergence itself has strong normative influence at the policy level.[177] In particular the work of La Porta et al. has been influential, despite its controversy, in seemingly providing evidence for the superiority of shareholder oriented corporate law norms. Within the European Union, policy focus, at least within the European Commission, is firmly on corporate governance reform with an outsider shareholder orientation.[178] All of these policy and ideological pressures create further pressures on key insider corporate systems to re-evaluate their corporate law.[179]

---

173   See Stiglitz, J. (2003) Globalization and Its Discontents, New York: W.W. Norton Company, 89–132; and Stiglitz, J. (1999) 'Reforming the Global Economic Architecture: Lessons from Recent Crises', Journal of Finance, vol. 54, 1508–1521.

174   Singh, A. and Zammit, A. (2006) 'Corporate Governance, Crony Capitalism and Economic Crises: Should the US Business Model Replace the Asian Way of Doing Business?', Corporate Governance: An International Review, vol. 14, 220–233.

175   Ibid.; Rodrik, D. (2007) One Economics, Many Recipes: Globalization, Institutions and Economic Growth, Princeton: Princeton University Press, 148; Pieper, U. and Taylor, L. (1998) 'The Revival of the Liberal Creed: The IMF, the World Bank, and Inequality in a Globalised Economy' in Baker, D., Epstein, G. and Pollin, R. (eds) Globalization and Progressive Economic Policy, Cambridge: Cambridge University Press; and Pauly, L. (1994) 'Promoting a Global Economy: The Normative Role of the International Monetary Fund' in Stubbs, R. and Underhill, G. (eds) Political Economy and the Changing Global Order, London: Macmillan. In 2003 US Treasury Undersecretary John Taylor stated to Congress that the US views free capital mobility as a fundamental right. See Wade, R., above n103.

176   See Can Atacik, M. and Jarvis, M., above n169, 4.

177   Roe, M. (2006) 'Legal Origins and Modern Stock Markets', Harvard Law Review vol. 120, 460 at 464.

178   On the Commissions corporate governance reforms see <http://ec.europa.eu/internal_market/company/modern/index_en.htm>.

179   Fremond, O. and Capaul, M. (2002) World Bank Policy Research Working Paper No. 2858, available at <http://ssrn.com/abstract=636222>; Williams, C. (2002) 'Corporate Social Responsibility in an Era of Economic Globalization', UCD Law Review, vol. 35, 705–777 at 741–742; and Bratton W. and McCahery, J. (1999) 'Comparative Corporate Governance and the Theory of the Firm: The Case Against Global Cross Reference',

Conclusion

We have sought in this chapter to identify within the process of economic globalization pressures on institutions in insider systems that might cause convergence/transformation to an outsider corporate governance model. We have identified significant pressures within the globalization process triggered primarily by the liberalization of trade and capital markets since the 1970s. With the lowering of trade barriers product markets have become highly competitive with the result that managerial discretion has been squeezed. This has two potential effects. First, the ability of managers to maintain commitments to stakeholders is reduced as resources are channelled into competitive survival. As Roe has observed:

> [p]art of the globalization pressure we see around the world is due to the shrinking of local monopolies as product market competition intensifies ... [T]he corporate governance implication here is that globalization presses firms to match wages closely to productivity: managers have less discretion over wages than when they faced less competitive product markets. That shrinking of local monopolies weakens stakeholder pressures on the firm's managers – because there is less available over which managers have discretion to share – and as those internal pressures to share diminish, this source of the demand for concentrated ownership might diminish as well, opening the way for a nation to develop deeper and wider securities markets.[180]

Second the response of managers to competitive markets has been to use global capital markets to expand into global product markets through M&As within the developed world, removing competitors, and/or through greenfield investments, usually manufacturing, in the developing world driven by labour cost reduction. Both of these reactions have significant negative effects on institutions in insider corporate governance systems, if firms from insider systems react this way, as commitments to labour are reduced and capital market funding introduces institutional investors with strong outsider shareholder oriented expectations into the company. Additionally, the shareholder-oriented rules of global stock markets introduce outsider norms such as enhanced disclosure into company behaviour and promote rules that encourage hostile takeovers.

The globalization of capital markets with the removal of capital controls in the 1970s has also had an effect on the ability of governments to pursue demand led policies as capital mobility has led to a loss of national macroeconomic autonomy. Governments over the course of the past 30 years have shifted policy from the

---

Columbia Journal of Transnational Law, vol. 38, 213–297; and Dore, R. (1999) 'Japan's Reform Debate: Patriotic Concern or Class Interest? Or Both?', Journal of Japanese Studies, vol. 25, 65–89 at 66.

180   Roe, M. (2003) Political Determinants of Corporate Governance, Oxford: Oxford University Press, 6.

objective of fostering employment and demand to maintaining given exchange rate parities or the levels of money supply. This not only has removed government demand support that has historically supported managerial-oriented insider systems but the knock on effects of this where governments have restricted spending, has been to promote the privatization of state industries and to promote private rather than state saving provision, both of which in turn promote securitization within the financial system as the privatized firms are capitalized on domestic and global capital markets and pension and insurance funds (institutional investors) pursue strict financial returns on their investments. Additionally, organizations at the global level have been promoting shareholder-oriented corporate governance norms which create further pressures to conform to a shareholder-oriented corporate governance system.

As the Kaldorian growth model of the golden age faded due to economic globalization, production systems that used to rely on high output growth and financial stability face increasing pressure to reorganize in order to deal with highly competitive markets. This reorganization can lead to the re-evaluation of established relationships between the firm and its main resource providers, i.e. financial capital providers and employees. However, the existence of pressures to change does not necessarily mean that the end result will be systemic institutional transformation i.e. convergence/transformation to an outsider system. As we will observe in the next chapter and in Part II of the book, institutions are remarkably resilient and outcomes when sub-systems change can be surprisingly diverse.

Chapter 4

Theorizing the Possibility of Change in Insider Corporate Governance Systems: Divergence or Convergence?

Introduction

In Chapter 1 we set out the highly polarized theoretical context which has resulted in the emergence of alternative corporate theories corresponding to managerial and shareholder corporate models. In turn we noted that this contested theoretical accountability debate has been elevated to the global stage with some scholars claiming that the convergence of insider stakeholder corporate governance systems to an outsider shareholder oriented system is preordained. In Chapter 2 we introduced institutional analysis as our preferred form of theoretical analysis for examining the effects of globalization and outlined the institutions and institutional sub sets (corporate law, industrial relations system, financial system and sub-systems related to the government demand function particularly competition and effective demand) that we considered were the most important in determining corporate governance outcomes. We then considered the insider and outsider corporate governance models to demonstrate the coherence of both systems as workable combinations of complementary national institutional sub-systems. In Chapter 3 we examined the process of globalization as a potential agent of change within these sub-systems. We concluded that the liberalization of trade and capital markets as part of this process has placed significant pressures on insider managerial systems. In this chapter we bring together all the central elements of those three chapters to examine the potential theoretical dynamic responses of national corporate governance systems to those pressures from the process of globalization to change. In doing so we will discuss claims of a neoclassical origin that emphasize a clear uniform shareholder oriented outcome in response to the forces of globalization. We then examine theories of institutional change that emphasize the role of institutions in either facilitating or blocking change. In all we conclude that institutional dynamics within diverse systems can vary considerably so that national corporate governance models should be expected to react differently to common stimulants and not uniformly as neoclassical theories of change and its associated scholarship would predict.

Theories of institutional change

In Chapter 2 we examined governance systems as static constellations of institutional sub-systems. Stability is, of course, a fundamental characteristic of institutional configurations. It is the stability of institutions that resolves transactional problems by introducing elements of certainty and predictability in markets that are full of uncertainty. Due to the existence of institutions, economic agents' behavioural patterns become more predictable, so institutional stability is 'a necessary condition for complex human interaction'.[1] This is because, by improving the predictability of available choices, established institutions facilitate the supply of information to economic actors and thus reduce the transaction costs even for highly complex transactions.[2]

However, institutional sets also react to change. The causes of institutional rearrangements are changes in the opportunities perceived by economic agents. These pressures to change tend to be the result of external changes in the economic environment.[3] The process of globalization and its accompanying pressures described in the previous chapter constitute a dramatic environmental change for firms and the national systems within which they operate. As the previous chapter shows, the opportunities and challenges stemming from economic globalization have significantly altered the nature of competition resulting in a shift in the preferences of corporations who want to adapt to the challenges of the evolving economic order and exploit the opportunities within it.[4] Financial and industrial capital mobility have altered the role of formerly nationally bound resources, such as unskilled labour and domestic savings, as well as of national institutional structures which are now subjected to competitive forces through the firms that are active in global markets.

As the globalization of economic activity has intensified, corporate governance isomorphism[5] is being transformed from one that is nationally embedded to a new type that is increasingly determined by global market forces and institutional arrangements that are not bounded within one nation. The opening of economic borders allows firms' operations to transcend national institutional systems and thus facilitates the interaction between national systems themselves and between national systems and the global economy. Predicting how these institutional

---

1   North, D. (1990) Institutions, Institutional Change and Economic Performance, Cambridge: Cambridge University Press, 84.

2   Hodgson, G. (1993) Economics and Evolution: Bringing Life back into Economics, Oxford: Polity Press, 132–133.

3   North, D., above n1, 73.

4   Baldwin, R. and Martin, P. (1999) 'Two Waves of Globalization: Superficial Similarities, Fundamental Differences' in Siebert, H. (ed.) Globalization and Labour, Kiel: Institüt für Weltwirtschaft an der Unniversität Kiel – Mohr Siebeck, 38–41.

5   The process whereby units within a population come to resemble each other. We discuss this process in detail later in the chapter.

changes may play out therefore becomes important and so once again we must enter contested theoretical territory between different theories of change to gain some insight here.[6] In doing so we first consider neoclassical theories of change and its associated corporate governance literature before turning to institutional theories of change.

Change and Convergence in Neoclassical Theory

As we discussed in Chapter 1, in a market where competition is perfect, prices are formed automatically by the market as firms are too small to influence them. Profit-maximizing choices are then made according to those given prices so that a Pareto-optimal equilibrium is achieved. When a price changes, e.g. due to an alteration in the availability of an input factor, an *optimal adaptation* of output occurs to accommodate the new equilibrium price. Similarly, if a new technology becomes available all firms will adopt it provided that is the profit-maximizing course of action.[7] This optimization process is traditionally based on the axiom that firms as entrepreneurs are fully informed and rational agents. How does institutional change fit into this paradigm?

The precise answer to this question is that it does not. The reason for this is that neoclassical theory assumes that where markets are perfectly competitive rational economic agents design perfect institutions which lead to optimality. As Coase describes it when transaction costs are zero, that is when there are no informational asymmetries and, therefore, no risk of unilateral opportunism, institutions do not matter.[8] So, when rational and well-informed agents perceive a new opportunity they immediately choose to take it *without being constrained by past institutional choices*. In order for such a market to exist competition has to be perfect so that price arbitrage and informational feedback can eliminate informational asymmetries thus enabling all agents to make optimal choices.[9]

As a result the possibility of mutual interaction between agents and institutions is excluded as it is only the former that shape the latter. So, given a change in the resources available or in market conditions, if any incumbent institutional constraints stand in the way of this process, they will be consciously abolished and replaced by others that are optimal so that a new optimal equilibrium is reached. In this sense, institutions are not seen as constraints but simply as efficient

---

6   For a good overview of the relevant theories here see Boyer, R. (2005) 'Coherence, Diversity, and the Evolution of Capitalisms – The Institutional Complementarity Hypothesis', Evolutionary and Institutional Economics Revew, vol. 2(1), 43.

7   For this condition to be satisfied it is assumed that intellectual property rights are imperfect and cannot prevent agents from ultimately having access to new technology.

8   Coase, R. (1960) 'The Problem of Social Cost', Journal of Law and Economics, vol. 3, 1.

9   North, D., above n1, 51.

transaction cost minimizing mechanisms.[10] They constitute integral elements of efficient markets by facilitating information flows between economic actors, and thus *support* the role of the market as a resource allocation mechanism. So, in this optimization process agents are the masters of institutions, since they are able to determine them according to their rational choices and expectations which in turn are independent of any institutional influence. To use Langlois' terminology, institutions are *instances* of market contracting between agents rather than as *alternatives* to market coordination.[11] Since institutions have no independent role or existence above and beyond the individual or the firm, they can be treated as irrelevant to the analysis of economic change. As Skott and Auerbach put it:

> [i]f institutional structures represented an optimal choice of instruments for the matching of exogenously given preferences and opportunities, then institutional change would have no more significance than, say, changes in consumption bundles as incomes increase; institutional change would be reduced to the status of epiphenomena.[12]

Similarly, all those factors that constitute sources of economic change are regarded as *exogenous* or given to the economic system so that ultimately economic analysis is limited only to resource allocation and exchange matters. Thus, just as the rationality premise excludes any discussion of agents' preferences, the availability of production resources is simply determined by *non-economic factors* – e.g. natural disasters, demographic changes, etc. – that are beyond the scope of economic science.[13] Production-related technology, i.e. scientific and organizational know-how, is also an exogenous non-economic variable, since it is assumed to be created outside the economic system and then uniformly disseminated across the market as a public good rather than being a private asset.[14] Any change in those

---

10   The firm and the market are complementary resource allocation mechanisms. See Coase, R., above n8.

11   Langlois, R. (1986) 'The New Institutional Economics: An Introductory Essay' in Langlois, R. (ed.) Economics as a Process – Essays in The New Institutional Economics, Cambridge: Cambridge University Press, 16.

12   Skott, P. and Auerbach, P. (1994) 'Cumulative Causation and the "New" Theories of Growth', Working Paper, Økonomisk Institut, Aarhus Universitet, 14.

13   Since the neoclassical 'economic man' can only be a rational utility-maximizer, the possibility of changing preferences as a result of institutional or other factors is by definition expelled from its analysis. See Knight, F. (1942) 'Some Notes on the Economic Interpretation of History' in Waldron-Long, P. (ed.) Studies in the History of Culture – The Disciplines of the Humanities, Menasha: G. Banta Publishing.

14   Hall, P. (1994) Innovation, Economics and Evolution – Theoretical Perspectives on Changing Technology in Economic Systems, London: Harvester Weatsheaf, 12–15. Technological progress has been incorporated in some neoclassical models as the product of research and development or the by-product of 'learning by doing'; see Arrow, K. (1952) 'The Economic Implications of Learning by Doing', Review of Economic Studies, vol.

exogenous factors, that is any external shock to the economic system, causes an automatic and optimally adaptive reaction within the system as agents pursue their ends in a competitive marketplace. As Hayek wrote, 'a *spontaneous order* results from the individual elements adapting themselves to circumstances'.[15]

Admittedly, when compared to the Walrasian static equilibrium, Hayek's thesis is indeed revolutionary, because it introduces a dynamic approach to institutional evolution that appears to break away from the strictly static tradition of general equilibrium theory. His model is one where an equilibrium occurs after self-interested agents form plans and strategies which eventually come into mutual consistency after an *adaptive process* of learning within a changing environment.[16] However, his insistence, though indirect, on the ability of agents to eventually make rational decisions and form correct expectations excludes any constraining influence of institutions on individual choices and thus defeats the advantage of analysing institutions in the first place. So, in essence Hayek's concept of 'spontaneous order' is not much different from Adam Smith's 'invisible hand'.

That conscious rational optimization constitutes a rather unrealistic postulate is not disputed even by some of the most faithful adherents to the neoclassical methodology. The requirement of conscious rational choices and expectations is too stringent to have a real application. So, as we noted in Chapter 1 Alchian's competitive selection argument has often been used to support the neoclassical analysis of the firm.[17] However, Alchian's theory is equally relevant to the macroeconomic analysis of institutional change and, therefore, neoclassical scholars, often identified with the Chicago School, have embraced it to defend the orthodox view that a free market economy is able to develop institutions that are efficient without non-market intervention.[18] Accordingly, in his classic essay on methodology, Friedman claimed that, although conscious optimization may be impossible in an uncertain and complex world, the maximization postulate could

---

29, 155; Levhari, D. (1966) 'Extensions of Arrow's "Learning by Doing"', Review of Economic Studies, vol. 33, 117. However, it is again assumed that even if a new technology is created endogenously it automatically becomes a public good so that all firms or nations can benefit from it irrespective of their own technology investment policies. In this way, increasing returns to scale in physical inputs become externalized so that, provided markets are competitive, equilibrium can occur. See Shaw, G. (1992) 'Policy Implications of Endogenous Growth Theory', Economic Journal, vol. 102, 611.

15   Hayek, F. (1982) Law, Legislation and Liberty: a new statement of the liberal principles of justice and political economy, London: Routledge & Kegan Paul, 36.

16   See Hayek, F. (1948) Individual Economic Order, Chicago: Chicago University Press, Chapter 2. Indeed the neoclassical evolutionary model is founded upon this revolutionary attempt to expand general equilibrium theory.

17   Alchian, A. (1950) 'Uncertainty, Evolution and Economic Theory', Journal of Political Economy, vol. 58, 211.

18   Bratton, W. and McCahery, J. (1999) 'Comparative Corporate Governance and the Theory of the Firm: The Case Against Cross Reference', Columbia Journal of Transnational Law, vol. 38(2), 214 at 243.

still hold because competitive selection forces agents to act *as if* their rationality was not bounded and therefore optimal institutional arrangements are established.[19]

The argument is that, just as firms who fail to maximize profit are selected out by the system, institutions that prevent firms from making rational profit-maximizing choices are out competed and eventually weeded out. In other words, those institutions that fail to deal effectively with transaction costs are eliminated and only optimal ones survive competition. Ultimately, institutional change as a result of exogenous shocks takes the form of a continuous evolution from one efficient institutional outcome to the next. The adverse selection process is usually indirect in the sense that it is agents that compete against each other rather than institutions.[20] So efficient institutional outcomes emerge because some firms are rational profit-maximizers *ex ante* and those firms who are not and are associated with inefficient institutions fail or *copy* the former by altering their institutional preferences.

Matthews identifies two possible ways in which competitive selection can operate. The first is one where uniformly defective knowledge prevails among economic agents so that conscious optimization is not possible. In this case, some firms, or groups of them, achieve optimal institutional results only because they happen to make the right choices by chance. Competition, then ensures that all other institutional choices are abandoned by those agents who chose them or are replaced by optimal ones. The second neoclassical version of competitive selection is one where there is differentially defective knowledge, i.e. informational asymmetries, among agents so that some can consciously make optimal institutional choices while others cannot.[21] Thus, while there is a difference in the cognitive features of agents in these two versions of competitive selection, the final institutional outcome in both is an efficient one.

So, if a general neoclassical approach can be constructed to deal with the process of institutional change, it would be founded upon a combination of optimization, conscious or fortuitous, and competitive selection. What restricts competition is non-market interventions in the form of government regulation

---

19   Friedman, M. (1953) 'The Methodology of Positive Economics' in Friedman, M. (ed.) Essays in Positive Economics, Chicago: University of Chicago Press. Nonetheless, Alchian himself was more hesitant in assimilating competitive selection with rational optimization: 'The economist may be pushing his luck too far in arguing that actions in response to changes in environment and changes in satisfaction with the existing state of affairs will converge as a result of adaptation or adoption toward the optimum action that should have been selected, if foresight had been perfect'. Alchian, A., above n17, 220.

20   As Matthews, R. (1984) 'Darwinism and Economic Change' in Collard, D., Dimsdale, N., Gilbert, C., Helm, D., Scott, M. and Sen, K. (eds) Economic Theory and Hicksian Themes, Oxford: Clarendon Press, 92 observes, '[o]ptimisation is direct choice by the economic agent, competitive selection is indirect social choice through changes in the relative weight of different decision-makers, brought about through the working of the system'.

21   Ibid., at 92.

that constrain individual choices and destroys the equilibrium of the market. In Hayek's view, a 'spontaneous order' cannot come about when governments impose price regulations, trade barriers, quality standards and so on, because markets are so complex that no central authority can acquire the necessary information and knowledge to make efficient institutional choices; decentralized decision making by individual agents is thus more efficient than government planning.[22] As Lachmann argued:

> [i]t would be wrong to think that a market economy ... could, or in the ordinary course of events would, find no answer ... History shows that whenever left sufficiently free from political interference to evolve its response to such challenges, the market economy has "grown" the institutions necessary to deal with them.[23]

This neoclassical evolutionary model has some very important implications for the direction of institutional change. Firstly, if agents within a single economic system face common problems and opportunities, the institutional adaptation process will result in one optimal structural solution that is common to all. Competitive selection will ensure that institutional choices which diverge from that new model will disappear, either due to the failure of those who chose them or because less successful agents imitate those whose performance is superior. That is, competition ensures that superior institutional technologies are disseminated evenly across the market so that a universal 'best practice' prevails.[24] This has given rise to the popular theory of *institutional convergence* which claims that, through the process just described, competition leads initially diverse institutional structures to converge towards a unique superior outcome that is adopted or supported by all (surviving) agents in a single market.[25] Ultimately, optimal

---

22   Hayek, F. (1945) 'The Use of Knowledge in Society', American Economic Review, vol. 35(4), 519 at 524.

23   Lachmann, L. (1978), 'Capital and its Structure', Kansas City: Sheed, Andrews and McMeel, 67.

24   Boyer, R. (1996) 'The Convergence Hypothesis Revisited: Globalization but Still the Century of Nations?' in Berger, S. and Dore, R. (eds) National Diversity and Global Capitalism, Ithaca: Cornell University Press, 46.

25   Originally the optimal convergence thesis was limited to economic growth rates; e.g. see Sala-i-Martin, X. (1996), 'The Classical Approach to Convergence Analysis', The Economic Journal, vol. 106(437), 1019–1036. However, once institutions are considered as relevant for economic performance, convergence of growth rates should also imply institutional convergence; this is a point not expressly made by neoclassical economists since they do not regard institutions as economic factors. An exception to this is North's early work on institutional evolution from which he retreated later in his career; see North, D. and Davis, L. (1971) Institutional Change and American Economic Growth, Cambridge: Cambridge University Press; and North, D. and Thomas, R. (1973) The Rise of the Western World: A New Economic History, Cambridge: Cambridge University Press.

institutional convergence will lead to the disappearance of economic performance disparities within each particular marketplace.

The optimal convergence thesis is founded upon a further sub-argument which springs from the neoclassical model of economic change outlined earlier; namely, the premise of institutional *reversibility*. This notion implies that markets can not only move freely from one institutional equilibrium to another but also they can as easily return to previous equilibria if that is an optimal choice. To illustrate this David has borrowed from physics the concept of 'ergodic systems', i.e. systems that are connected in such manner that 'it is possible to transit directly or indirectly between any arbitrarily chosen pair of states, and hence, eventually, to reach all the states from any one of them'.[26] As we noted earlier in a neoclassical framework institutions do not constitute constraints to agents' profit maximizing strategies, past institutional choices do not exhibit a controlling influence in present or future strategic decisions unless agents themselves so desire. In this fashion, institutional equilibria at any given moment are ergodic and can move both backwards and forward so that eventually concepts such as the past or the future become meaningless and *history is irrelevant*.[27]

Neoclassicism and corporate governance convergence

The influence of these theories of institutional change on the corporate governance convergence scholarship has been strong. The starting point has been that performance is directly linked to the efficiency of corporate governance techniques. Due to the determinant influence of institutions, the efficiency of these techniques depends on the effectiveness of related institutional arrangements in dealing with transactional and allocational issues and in enabling firms to fully exploit profit opportunities that may arise.[28] On the basis of this link between performance and corporate governance, competitive selection as described above ensures that from those institutions that determine firm behaviour only optimal ones survive. Furthermore, as the convergence thesis asserts, in a single perfectly competitive market one unique and efficient corporate governance model emerges as all other

---

26   David, P. (1997) 'Path Dependence and the Quest for Historical Economics: One More Chorus of the Ballad of QWERTY', Discussion Paper No. 20, Oxford University, 13.

27   David, P. (2007) 'Path Dependence: A Foundational Concept for Historical Social Science', Cliometrica, vol. 1, 2, 91–114; and David, P. (2001) 'Path Dependence, Its Critics and the Quest for Historical Economics', <http://www.econ.iastate.edu/tesfatsi/pathdep.pdavid.pdf>.

28   On the influence of institutional structures on economic performance see Myrdal, G. (1957) Economic Theory and Underdeveloped Regions, London: Duckworth. Accordingly, Boyer, R. (1996) 'The Convergence Hypothesis Revisited: Globalization but Still the Century of Nations?' in Berger, S. and Dore, R. (ed.) National Diversity and Global Capitalism, Ithaca: Cornell University Press, 41 states: 'Complex interactions between economic convergence and institutional diversity and, conversely, an inadequate institutional harmonisation may all induce economic divergence'.

inferior models are selected out and fade.[29] Of course, competition is the driving force towards optimality; therefore, any non-market intervention constitutes a distortion of the competitive selection mechanism and should be avoided. Thus, mandatory government regulation of corporate governance is inherently inefficient because it constitutes a constraint on rational individual choice and should, therefore, be avoided. Similarly, institutions that restrict competition by imposing direct and indirect barriers on economic activity are artificial imperfections imposed by governments. It is these non-market institutions that segregate national markets and distort competition between corporate governance systems at the expense of efficiency.

Thus, with the advent of globalization as an integration process of formerly segregated national markets into a single global marketplace, the emergence and universal adoption of a new and efficient corporate governance model is inevitable according to the neoclassical convergence literature. The argument is that, as the deregulation in financial, factor and product markets progresses and national economic borders erode, global competition will eventually drive costs and prices towards unique equilibrium levels. Thus, firms will not only compete on an equal footing but they will also face the same challenges and opportunities. Consequently, in order to survive they will have to develop and adopt the same optimal corporate governance solutions. Best practices will either be adopted as rational optimal choices of efficient firms or they will be 'imposed' by the market as inefficient corporate governance institutions and those firms associated with them are driven out by global competition. To the extent that rational firms' optimizing choices are constrained by inefficient national institutions that impose unnecessary costs, globalization has opened up the exit option so firms can choose the national systems they regard as efficient. As Bratton observes:

> [w]e come to a moment – whether in the immediate past, the present, or in the
> near future – at which intensifying competition in international product markets
> for the first time turns endowments derived from national governance systems
> into factors relevant to firms' competitive survival.[30]

Eventually, with the emergence of a global marketplace, competition is between different national institutional sets within which firms operate as promoters of change. As firms become increasingly mobile, regulatory arbitrage – e.g. through foreign listings, shifts of production operations or even re-incorporations in what firms regard as the best jurisdictions – results in an institutional 'race to the

---

29   For example, Easterbrook, F. (1997) 'International Corporate Differences: Markets or Law?', Journal of Applied Corporate Finance, vol. 9, 23, argues that free-market competition between corporate law and governance systems leads to a unique efficient outcome.

30   Bratton, W. and McCahery, J., above n18, 240.

top'.[31] Once globalization is complete – i.e. when a perfectly competitive global market is established – a process combining rational optimization and competitive selection between national systems will give rise to a unique, universal and optimal equilibrium model of corporate governance formed by market forces. According to Matthews, there will be:

> [i]mitation of the advancing country's institutions or its other modes of economic behaviour; adaptation by means of optimisation to changes in comparative advantage brought about by events in the advancing country; adaptation by means of competitive selection to those changes in comparative advantage; and achieved by emigration of entrepreneurship and management from the advancing country.[32]

Following this line of thought many observers have been suggesting that a process of global corporate governance convergence towards one 'best-practice' model is already underway.[33] Thus, Hansmann and Kraakman, as we noted in Chapter 1, follow the example of Fukuyama's 'end of history' claim[34] to categorically state that we have come to the end of history in the sphere of corporate law and governance with the universal acceptance of the shareholder oriented model's superiority over other models.[35] They contend that 'experimental' regulatory interventions by governments during the 1950s and 1960s reinforced

---

31   For classic expositions of the 'race to the top' argument in the context of US state competition for corporate regulation see Romano, R. (1998) 'Empowering Investors: A Market Approach to Securities Regulation', Yale Law Journal, vol. 107, 2359; Romano, R. (1993) 'Competition for Corporate Charters and the Lesson of Takeover Statutes', Fordham Law Review, vol. 61, 843; and Winter, R. (1989) 'The "Race for the Top" Revisited: A Comment on Eisenberg', Columbia Law Review, vol. 89, 1526. It is important to note, however, that as we noted in Chapter 1 there is a substantial 'shareholder bias' in this literature on corporate governance systems' competition as it takes as given the superiority of the shareholder model. In the absence of this assumption this interpretation of corporate governance developments can become much more complex and inconclusive. For instance, if one took the view that the insider model was superior, the race to the top argument would then have to be reversed. See also Howell, E. and Pan, E. (2001) 'Regulatory Competition in International Securities Markets: Evidence from Europe In 1999 – Part I', The Business Lawyer, vol. 56, 653.

32   Matthews, R., above n20, 114.

33   For an early exposition of this argument see Karmel, R. (1991) 'Tensions Between Owners and Managers: An International Perspective', Brooklyn Law Review, vol. 57, 55 at 90.

34   See Fukuyama, F. (1989) 'The End of History?', The National Interest, vol. 16, 3; and Fukuyama, F. (1992) The End of History and the Last Man, New York: Free Press, arguing for the final triumph of western free-market capitalism and its universal acceptance.

35   Hansmann, H. and Kraakman, R. (2001) 'The End of History for Corporate Law', Georgetown Law Journal, vol. 89(2), 439. Interestingly, Hansmann and Kraakman

managerial discretion and curtailed shareholder power in a way that hampered the efficient operation of product and capital markets.[36] Thus, the failure of managerial and stakeholder models in the 1970s and 1980s was not only inevitable, but also proved the superiority of shareholder supremacy as a guiding principle of corporate governance.[37] Therefore, Hansmann and Kraakman claim that, with the intensification of global competition, institutional systems supporting the insider managerial model, being the outcome of government intervention rather than market forces, are being selected out by investors and TNCs as locations for their investments and production activities due to their inefficiency as they contradict the market value maximization objective. Thus, institutional systems that have an outsider orientation enjoy a locational advantage. They provide firms with a more efficient organizational structure which ensures easier access to global capital markets and therefore give them a significant competitive advantage in the global marketplace. As a result of competitive pressures, all jurisdictions should be expected to develop similar locational advantages by converging towards what Hansmann and Kraakman call 'the standard model of the corporation', that is a shareholder oriented model. With the removal of government-imposed 'distortions', such as capital controls, markets will succeed in enhancing mechanisms of shareholder monitoring over managers, either directly or indirectly through the market for corporate control, global and national. Efficient corporate governance institutions will emerge through private market contracting rather than mandatory regulation of corporate activity.[38] Thus, the coming of globalization and the 'end of history' with the adoption of shareholder oriented corporate governance as the standard global and uniquely superior model has apparently brought the final efficient resolution to a long-standing debate.

In sum, given the emergence of globalization, if the global corporate governance convergence thesis is well-founded (although it looks somewhat tarnished given the massive market failures involved in the ongoing global financial market crisis since autumn 2008) an outsider-shareholder system should emerge which will not only be suitable to global economic trends, but will also create the necessary complementarities between global financial assets and investment opportunities so as to promote sustainable economic growth and prosperity. Free from government

---

acknowledge that national differences may in fact persist but they do not explain how this is reconciled with their end of history claim.

36   On the idea that government controls constitute barriers to convergence see also Ramseyer, J. (1998) 'Are Corporate Governance Systems Converging?; The Contextual Logic to the Japanese Keiretsu', Working Paper, Sloane Project on Corporate Governance at Columbia Law School, 544; and Berger, S. (1996) 'Introduction' in Berger, S. and Dore, R. (eds) National Diversity and Global Capitalism, Ithaca: Cornell University Press, 1.

37   For a forceful presentation of this 'superiority' claim see Macey, J. (1998) 'Measuring the Effectiveness of Different Corporate Governance Systems: Towards a More Scientific Approach', Journal of Applied Corporate Finance, vol. 10, 16.

38   Goddard, D. (1996) 'Convergence in Corporations Law – Towards a Facilitative Model', Victoria University of Wellington Law Review, vol. 26, 191.

interventions, global markets and firms operating in them will by themselves create a 'spontaneous order' establishing all institutions necessary for aligning the interests of managers with those of shareholders. Indeed, in accordance with the neoclassical theory's predictions, national corporate governance systems would converge to optimality.

On the other hand, outside the neoclassical lab, where markets are not assumed to be perfect or able to construct efficient spontaneous orders of the Hayekian type, a different picture emerges. This is because while the forces of globalization may push towards systemic convergence of some kind, a whole set of other institutional forces may simultaneously pull corporate governance systems towards their original position so that predicting where the resultant force will lead becomes difficult. However before we move to consider institutional theories of change we need to deal with an area of the corporate governance convergence scholarship that claims that both the outsider and insider models are equally fit.

Equal Fitness

However before doing so we need to introduce the concept of *isomorphism* which is important for our critique of equal fitness arguments. So far, either expressly or impliedly, this work has focused on systemic differences that exist at the national level. This constitutes a *de facto* recognition that an institutional system's dimensions are determined by national borders.[39] An important factor in the formation of institutions is the concept of isomorphism which Hawley defines as 'a constraining process that forces one unit in a population to resemble other units that face the same set of environmental conditions'.[40] To understand what drives isomorphism in corporate governance one has to begin with examining the environmental forces that shape the nature and behaviour of firms. First, existing and new firms under the umbrella of a particular institutional context automatically acquire several common characteristics, the elements of a particular governance model, so as to constitute a recognizable group. This mechanism of institutional determination is what DiMaggio and Powell term 'coercive isomorphism'.[41]

---

39   Admittedly, from a political science perspective there is a difference between a state and a nation. However, for the purposes of this work the two terms will be regarded as equivalent.

40   Hawley, A. (1968) 'Human Ecology' in Sills, D. (ed.) International Encyclopedia of the Social Sciences, New York: Macmillan, 328–337.

41   DiMaggio, P. and Powell, W. (eds.) (1991) The New Institutionalism in Organisational Analysis, Chicago: University of Chicago Press, 63–82 at 68, Holzinger, K. and Knill, C. (2005) 'Causes and Conditions of Cross-National Policy Convergence', Journal of European Public Policy, vol. 12(5), 775, and Delmas, M. and Toffel, M. (2004) 'Stakeholders and Environmental Management Practices: An Institutional Framework', Business Strategy and the Environment, vol. 13, 209.

Secondly, a governance model can be promoted through imitation as some firms, due to their own incapacity to innovate, model themselves by adopting the organizational innovations of others who appear more successful or compatible with the common institutional environment. DiMaggio and Powell call this 'mimetic isomorphism'.[42] It is important to emphasize that in this process, competitive or cooperative interaction between firms is crucial for the dissemination of organizational know-how. This means that mimetic isomorphism is more intense within a single marketplace. Since it is constraints, such as competition policy, trade barriers, and capital controls that to a great extent determine the boundaries of markets, the influence of institutional factors is once again very significant.[43]

Thus, it is shared institutional systems that, by promoting homogeneity in organizational structures, make firms not only look similar but also follow similar evolutionary paths so that generalizations about a model's evolution are possible.[44] Thus, the boundaries of a corporate governance model are broadly defined by the economic area that falls within the influence of an individual institutional structure. Given the above considerations, to make the standard link between corporate governance models and nations one has to establish that the boundaries of institutional sets tend to coincide with national boundaries. In a world where national governments constitute the central 'producers' of institutions this is not a particularly difficult link to establish. Additionally, private organizations are also important either as suppliers of institutions, such as contractual agreements, or as bargaining parties in political processes. However, so long as the legal system, as the core of an institutional framework, is the result of national government action, the coincidence between the boundaries of institutional systems and national territory should remain strong. So, coercive isomorphism is more intense within national borders due to the existence of national laws that are uniformly applied. Similarly, mimetic isomorphism is also more intense within national borders due to the higher interaction between agents within a national marketplace. Thus, the more nationally determined institutional sets are, the more firms within each national market will tend to acquire similar characteristics that differentiate them from foreign firms so that corporate governance models remain nationally embedded. In this case, competition remains national and therefore institutional differences between national systems lose their relevance. At least in theory, so long as a system is workable, institutional differences between different countries will have no effect and multiple nationally determined institutional equilibria can exist simultaneously.

---

42 See DiMaggio, P. and Powell, W., above n41, 69; and Frumkin, P. and Galaskiewicz, J. (2004) 'Institutional Isomorphism and Public Sector Organizations', *Journal of Public Administration Research and Theory*, vol. 14(3), 283.

43 Of course, this does not mean that the influence of geographical and other factors are not important as well.

44 The complex issue of institutional evolution will be discussed later in this chapter.

Significantly for our analysis here, this leaves open the possibility that differences in national corporate governance systems can become important if institutional barriers segregating national markets are removed. In this case, as firms actively or passively detach themselves from national institutional environments, the mechanisms of isomorphism lose their national character. This results in competition between corporate governance models within a *common economic context*.

Convergence and equal fitness claims

Several contemporary observers within the convergence scholarship have put forward an 'equal fitness' argument, i.e. that at any time or place the adoption of either the managerial or shareholder model is a corporate governance choice that is equally competitive. In the mid 1990s, a number of scholars began to analyse economies in terms of what they called 'social systems of production'.[45] They argued that, within each economy, layers of institutions, organizations, and social norms tend to form a coherent social system of production. In insider systems the layers are 'tightly coupled with each other into a full-fledged system'.[46] This in turn makes it unlikely that forces for convergence to an outsider model will have much effect because of the coherence of the system. In 2001, Hall and Soskice expanded the social systems of production ideas into what is now known as the 'Varieties of Capitalism' school.[47] In their work they distinguished two forms of economic system: 'liberal market economies' (LME) (which tend to encourage outsider corporate governance systems) and 'coordinated market economies' (CME) (which tend to encourage insider corporate governance systems). LME emphasize competitive market exchange where actors structure their interaction through arm's length bargaining and formal contracts funded by significant capital markets. CME on the other hand, facilitate non-market exchange with 'relational or incomplete contracting, network monitoring based on the exchange of private information inside networks, and more reliance on collaborative, as opposed to competitive, relationships to build the competencies of the firm'.[48] Financing is provided through the cooperative network of state, banks and strategic partners. LME emphasize flexibility and short-term commitments in relationships, while CME emphasize long-term commitments between actors. As a result, Hall

---

45   See Hollingsworth, J. and Boyer, R. (1997) 'Coordination of Economic Actors and Social Systems of Production' in Hollingsworth, J. and Boyer, R. (eds) Contemporary Capitalism: The Embeddedness of Institutions, Cambridge: Cambridge University Press, 1 at 2.

46   Ibid.

47   See Soskice, D. and Hall, P. (2001) 'Introduction' in Hall, P. and Soskice, D. (eds) Varieties of Capitalism: The Institutional Foundations of Comparative Advantage, New York: Oxford University Press, 1–68.

48   Ibid., 8.

and Soskice argue that each has a comparative advantage in different types of production. CME in the Varieties analysis are geared towards funding companies in product markets that are capital intensive, safe and which innovate slowly over time i.e. engineering and high quality consumer goods. LME are geared towards innovative risk-taking where capital and labour can be redeployed quickly should this be necessary i.e. high tech and financial services.

While these observations are useful when studying national institutional structures they become, in our view, difficult to sustain within an examination of globalization as the two models are designed, as our discussion of isomorphism above demonstrates, for specific national conditions. This renders comparison between them solely at a micro-level misleading when considering globalization which places the models in a new denationalized economic environment. Their competitive fitness can be tested only if the two models are placed within the same economic environment. So instead of treating the LME and CME as equally fit, one should, in our view, qualify this by regarding each of them as fit only *within its appropriate national context* and not necessarily equally fit for a global one. In other words comparative advantage at the national level may not have any application in a global context.

Hybrid optimal claims of equal fitness

Alternately others have tried to split the difference. Kester for example has argued that while competitive selection can lead to corporate governance convergence to best practice, the new global model will be neither the insider nor outsider model. Instead, a hybrid model will emerge which will combine the best elements of each system. Before the advent of global competition, national systems of corporate governance could maintain their diversity in the ways they dealt with the transaction costs of production processes.[49] This diversity, Kester argues, does not mean that one model is necessarily superior to the other. On the contrary, in a similar way to the Varieties literature he claims that both the shareholder model and the managerial model, though not optimal, have offsetting strengths and weaknesses that make them equally fit.[50] If the outsider model is more efficient in minimizing agency costs in the shareholder-manager relationship but less so in dealing with transaction costs in the production process, the insider model has exactly the opposite qualitative characteristics. However, where Kester differs from the Varieties literature is in his analysis of globalization. Where Varieties scholars see the systems as equally fit in a globalized as well as national setting, Kester argues that as globalization progresses and competition between systems intensifies, the two corporate governance systems will gradually merge by adopting

---

49   Kester, W. (1996) 'American and Japanese Corporate Governance: Convergence to Best Practice?' in Berger, S. and Dore, R. (eds) National Diversity and Global Capitalism, Ithaca: Cornell University Press.

50   Ibid., 127.

institutional arrangements that combine both production efficiency and agency cost minimization.[51]

While we think Kester is right to identify the complementary relationship between macroeconomic factors and corporate governance outcomes in that he recognizes the link between the insider model and growth we think he has made an error here in accepting the equal fitness premise in the context of globalization for the same reasons as we outlined in the Varieties section above.[52] Kester's claims also have a theoretical problem as one can either accept the efficient markets hypothesis or reject it, but cannot do both as he seems to do. It is difficult to explain how the insider and outsider model can be equal from an efficiency perspective within the *same* global macroeconomic context. Following the logic of Kester's equal fitness proposition, where markets are efficient, as Kester assumes, then shareholder supremacy should, if his analysis is to be consistent, be the only principle underlying corporate decision-making.

This is not however what Kester concludes as he goes on to outline a convergence scenario based on what Bratton and MacCahery call cross-reference, that is the exercise of selecting the best institutions from each model in order to combine them and construct a third model that is superior to the two original ones.[53] However, as the analysis in Chapter 2 has shown and as we will discuss further in the next section, due to the implications of institutional complementarity and its relation to systemic workability, convergence by institutional cross-reference is very difficult, if not impossible. So, even if the optimal convergence thesis were accepted, its final outcome would have to be a 'spontaneous order' that is workable. For these reasons, Kester's optimal convergence hypothesis based on institutional cross-reference is, we think, itself unworkable.

Institutional Analysis of Change

Viewed through the prism of institutional analysis, corporate governance developments can be interpreted in a way that is very different from the convergence claims discussed above. As already mentioned, institutionalist criticism of the neoclassical assumptions as unrealistic has gained momentum over the years. As we discussed in Chapter 2, the key element in an institutional critique of neoclassical analysis is that an institutional analysis departs from zero transaction cost-perfect market assumptions. As a result in an institutional analysis, institutions do matter as endogenous constraints on agents' behaviour and therefore their independent role in economic activity cannot be ignored.

Once the theoretical analysis of institutional change is modified to include market imperfections and deviations from the global rationality postulate, its

---

51   Bratton, W. and McCahery, J., above n18, 242.
52   Kester, W., above n49, 127.
53   Bratton, W. and McCahery, J., above n18.

predictions are significantly different from those of the neoclassical approach as institutionalists acknowledge that institutional systems may not always evolve efficiently. As Hodgson observes:

> [e]conomic evolution does not always proceed slowly and smoothly in Darwinian terms so that a permanent equilibrium is maintained. It can also proceed by succession of periods of stability and crisis, i.e. of apparent equilibrium and cumulative instability.[54]

This is because where transaction costs are positive, neither rational optimization nor competitive selection are capable of producing optimal outcomes. As regards the former, agents' bounded rationality prevents them from consciously designing optimal institutional sets. This is not denied even by neoclassicists who, as mentioned above, utilize competitive selection as a 'corrective' mechanism with results equivalent to those of rational optimization. Defending this utilization of competitive selection however is another matter.

To begin with, there is a fundamental difference between the two processes; while in rational optimization the choice of efficient institutions is made *ex ante*, competitive selection operates *ex post*. This means that the former, as a process of continuous and conscious optimal change, by definition excludes institutional imperfections. The retrospective nature of competitive selection, on the other hand, implies that there has to be a reversal or modification of past institutional choices which have become inefficient as a result of changes in prices and agents' preferences. For Friedman's claim that competitive selection can be regarded as equivalent to rational optimization in terms of efficiency to be valid, the costs generated during such institutional reversals or modifications must be zero. According to Matthews, this can be the case only if institutional adaptation is instantaneous, so that there is no loss of output during the change, *and* if institution-specific assets can be fully redeployed within the new optimal institutional framework.[55] Such a situation seems unlikely as institutional reversals or modifications may involve significant costs during the adjustment period and to '*ex post* non-malleability', i.e. the dumping of past investments that were specific to the old institutions.[56] This means that the process of competitive selection is itself subject to significant transaction costs, which can be called *adaptation costs*, and in our view therefore cannot be regarded as equivalent to rational optimization.

The significance of adaptation costs in institutional change is not exhausted with this observation. The most important consequence of these costs within an institutional analysis of institutions, as opposed to a neoclassical one, is that where they are above a certain level that agents are willing to bear, change may be delayed

---

54 Hodgson, G. (1988) *Economics and Institutions: A Manifesto for a Modern Institutional Economics*, Cambridge: Polity Press, 144.

55 Matthews, R., above n20, 103–106.

56 Matthews, R., above n20, 104.

or not pursued at all so that a situation of temporary or permanent institutional inertia can arise. In this case, the very nature of institutional evolution is altered, for it has to also encompass the scenario of a systemic failure to adapt to changing circumstances. The implication is that institutional change can become locked in an evolutionary path that not only diverges from optimal adaptation but from wealth-enhancing efficiency altogether.[57] In other words, the presence of adaptation costs makes possible the perpetuation of institutions that were built to serve needs of the past and which through their stability determine the path of systemic change. Thus, as stagnant and new institutions are mixed together, institutional choices of the past can have a direct impact on the form institutional change takes in the present and thus create historically rooted trajectories of evolution.[58] This process, described by the concept of path dependence, provides the theoretical basis for explaining the persistent diversity in form and performance between institutional systems[59] as well as for rejecting the notions of ergodicity and systemic reversibility due to the introduction of historical influences in institutional change, i.e. history is relevant.[60]

Thus, in a world of imperfect markets, where institutions can have a significant and independent role above the individual economic agent, the mechanics of change are fundamentally different from those in the neoclassical paradigm. Firstly, institutionalists reject the deterministic nature of neoclassical theory where agents' choices, actions and preferences are reduced to mere mechanistic reactions to external changes imposed by market forces.[61] As already mentioned, since institutional sets are not perfect, they never totally determine agents' economic behaviour. Instead, the significance of institutions lies in their role in shaping economic choice by simply defining its boundaries, which then allows sufficient freedom for real deliberative action.[62]

---

57   Eggertsson, T. (1996) 'A Note on the Economics of Institutions' in Eggertsson, T. and North, D. (eds) Empirical Studies in Institutional Chance, Cambridge: Cambridge University Press, 12.

58   Zysman, J. (1994) 'How Institutions Create Historically Rooted Trajectories of Growth', Industrial and Corporate Change, vol. 3(1), 243.

59   Boyer, R., above n28, 168; Boyer, R. (2000) 'The Embedded Innovative Systems in Germany and Japan – Distinctive Features and Futures', Working Paper No. 2000–09, CEPREMAP, Paris; North, D., above n1, 7; Soskice, D. (1999) 'Divergent Production Regimes: Coordinated Market Economies in the 1980s and 1990s' in Kitchelt, H., Lange, P., Marks, G. and Stephens, J. (eds) Continuity and Change in Contemporary Capitalism, Cambridge: Cambridge University Press; Whitley, R. (1999) Divergent Capitalisms: The Social Structuring and Change of Business Systems, Oxford: Oxford University Press; and Boyer, R. and Hollingsworth, J. (eds) (1997) Contemporary Capitalism – The Embeddedness of Institutions, Cambridge: Cambridge University Press, 51.

60   David, P., above n27, 198.

61   See Chapter 1.

62   Lewis, W. (1978) The Theory of Economic Growth, London: George Allen and Unwin, 142; and Hodgson, G., above n54, 12.

It is the interaction between the existing set of constraints and agents' purposeful activity, i.e. their effort to exploit the opportunities that arise and they perceive, that drives institutional change.[63] More specifically, while incumbent institutions will often permit and help the exploitation of available opportunities, there will also be instances where there are mismatches between agents' capacities, as shaped by institutional constraints, and tasks.[64] To put it differently, by operating as constraints on agents' choices of action, institutions simply determine which opportunities or preferences are 'exploitable' or legitimate and which are not. This means that some opportunities and preferences will be within the limits imposed by the existing institutional set and others will not, irrespective of whether this is efficient or not. It is when this situation arises that institutional adaptation may become necessary in order to expand or alter agents' capacities so as to match the new tasks. So, as North argues, dissatisfied agents will have an incentive to devote resources to changing the restrictive institutions.[65] Whether they eventually pursue this course of action or simply abandon the extra-institutional opportunities will depend on their subjective perception of the costs and benefits.

However, this is not a straightforward process. The presence of externalities gives rise to a conflict between the interests of those agents who would benefit from alterations in the institutional framework and of all others who have made institution-specific investments and who as a result would have to bear the adaptation costs if change occurred.[66] Thus, where transaction costs are positive, institutional change inevitably creates winners as well as losers. The efficiency of change, that is its wealth-enhancing effect, is then just a matter of how many winners as opposed to losers are created both in numerical and in value terms. Since informational asymmetries between agents as a typical characteristic of imperfect markets translate into power differentials, institutional change becomes dependent on the relative bargaining power of those seeking it and not on neoclassical rationality. As such institutional change may not proceed to serve general social needs but what Veblen calls 'vested interests' of the 'conservative class'; that is the group of agents interested in maintaining the status quo and who then become the 'carriers' of inertia and path dependence.[67] Accordingly, as van Tulder and Ruigrok

---

63   Unlike neoclassical theory, which ultimately treats these opportunities as the by-product of exogenous changes institutionalists claim that they can also be endogenously derived.

64   Zysman, J., above n58, 259.

65   North, D., above n1, 79. Certainly, agents might well pursue their objectives without prior alterations in their institutionally determined capacities, e.g. by violating a law or a convention. In this case the agents would have to balance the costs of punishment, if any, with the benefits of the violation. Such cases are not uncommon. However, they constitute exceptions rather than the rule.

66   The economic definition of externalities is that people involved in actions do not bear the full cost or receive the full benefit of their actions.

67   Veblen, T. (1924) The Theory of the Leisure Class: An Economic Study of Institutions, London: Allen & Unwin, Chapter 8.

have argued, 'core firms' in a particular economy have the ability to occupy a central position in the supply, distribution, financial and political networks and, thus, have a significant influence in the design of institutional frameworks.[68]

Furthermore, institutional change may not occur even when all leading agents, share a common perception that existing institutions are disadvantageous and that their change would be beneficial. The root cause of this type of inertia is the classic collective action problem as originally analysed by Olson and Hardin and then further enriched by Hirschman with the introduction of the 'exit' and 'voice' concepts.[69] Thus, in order to surmount inertia, a 'critical mass' of interested parties must be formed who are willing to engage themselves in voicing their dissatisfaction with the status quo and actively seek to change it.[70] The formation of stable constellations, such as lobby groups, trade unions and political alliances, may be necessary in order to overcome the free-rider problem which may frustrate the process.[71] Alternatively, change may also come indirectly as agents may exercise the exit option, provided institutional factors and relocation costs allow this, by leaving a system they regard as inefficient for another one and thus potentially cause the decline of the former.[72] Ultimately, systemic decline may raise the costs accruing from inertia relative to adaptation costs and therefore result in institutional change.

Furthermore, while, as mentioned above, institutional complementarity does not deserve specific analysis in a neoclassical context, where the independent role of institutional constraints is recognized, the notion becomes extremely important. As Amable et al. describe it in the context of labour relations:

> [m]ore precisely, the type of influence that labour market institutions have on the capital/labour compromise are partly determined by other important institutional features of the economy which, although not directly concerned with the social compromise, exert an influence on the outcome of this compromise. In other

---

68   van Tulder, R. and Ruigrok, W. (1997) 'The Nature of Institutional Change: Managing Rival Dependencies' in Amin, A. and Hausner, J. (eds) Beyond Market and Hierarchy – Interactive Governance and Social Complexity, Cheltenham: Edward Elgar, 131.

69   Olson, M. (1982) The Rise and Decline of Nations – Economic Growth, Stagflation and Social Rigidities, New Haven: Yale University Press; Hirschman, A. (1970) Exit, Voice and Loyalty: Responses to Decline in Firms, Organisations and States, Cambridge, MA: Harvard University Press; Hardin, R. (1968) 'The Tragedy of the Commons', Science, vol. 162, 1243; and Olson, M. (1965) The Logic of Collective Action, Cambridge, MA: Harvard University Press.

70   Gehlbach, S. (2006) 'A Formal Model of Exit and Voice', Rationality and Society, vol. 18(4), 395; and Granovetter, M. (1978) 'Threshold Models of Collective Behavior', American Journal of Sociology, vol. 83, 1620.

71   North, D, above n1, 87.

72   Obviously, the availability of alternative and competing institutional systems is a precondition for this.

words, institutions do not exert an influence on political economy equilibriums one at a time, but jointly. The joint influence of institutions on the labour and the financial markets cannot be reduced to their direct, individual effect on each market but have to be analysed as a system because of complementarities.[73]

The horizontal and vertical interactions between institutional forces that complementarity implies are crucial for the process of institutional change because they can affect both its direction and its speed. Generally, institutional complementarity can be regarded as having a dual role as a transmission mechanism of adaptation costs *as well as* of systemic change.[74]

Firstly, institutional interactions may constitute obstacles to adaptation by introducing rigidities into the system. For instance, even where a group of agents have the ability and incentives to design a new fully adapted institution to replace an old one, before its implementation the new institution will have to be modified so as to fit complementary institutions. Modification may be direct and prospective during the formation process or indirect and retrospective through enforcement after the institution's adoption. Ultimately, institutional change takes the form of a compromise between adaptation to environmental factors and suitability to existing institutional configurations. The significance of this is that, even if information were sufficient for an efficient adaptation to changed circumstances, new institutions as single units can eventually lose at least some of their optimal attributes. It is for this reason that the function and performance of one particular institution often vary considerably within different institutional contexts.[75] In a more extreme but not uncommon case, a desired institution may be totally unfit for the existing framework and as a result be abandoned altogether either before its implementation or after it by becoming unenforceable and obsolete. In fact, these complementarities create a significant rigidity bias in institutional change by establishing a link between the adaptation costs of institutions that change and of institutions that remain in force. This accumulation of adaptation costs creates important obstacles to institutional adaptation, hence the role of institutional complementarity as a factor of systemic stability and therefore of path dependence.[76]

73   Amable, B., Ernst, E. and Palombarini, S. (2005) 'How do Financial Markets Affect Industrial Relations: An Institutional Complementarity Approach', Socio-Economic Review, vol. 3, 312.

74   Crouch, C., Streek, W., Boyer, R., Amable, B., Hall, P. and Jackson, G. (2005) 'Dialogue on "Institutional Complementarity and Political Economy"', Socio-Economic Review, vol. 3, 359.

75   Amable, B. (2000) 'Institutional Complementarity and Diversity of Social Systems of Innovation and Production', Review of International Political Economy, vol. 7(4), 645.

76   Crouch, C., Streeck, W., Boyer, R., Amable, B., Hall, P. and Jackson, G. (2005) 'Dialogue on "Institutional Complementarity and Political Economy"', Socio-Economic Review, vol. 3, 359–382.

As Dulbecco and Dutraive affirm, once institutional complementarity is taken into consideration, the claims of efficient adaptation and 'spontaneous order' cannot hold.[77]

On the other hand, the other side of the compromise between institutional adaptation and suitability that complementarity implies is that the successful implementation of a change will have an effect on the function of existing complementary institutions. This is because the resulting functional change of an existing institution will almost inevitably affect its overall adaptation costs either directly or indirectly through an alteration in the relative bargaining power of agents who are interested in the stability of that institution. It is reasonable to assume that when the implementation of a new institution is successful, the tendency will be towards a net reduction of at least some complementary institutions' adaptation costs. Thus, during a process of this kind, institutional complimentarity has the potential to become the vehicle of change and cause a domino effect of alterations in the system.[78] This is what more than a century ago Veblen described as an ongoing process of cumulative causation.[79] This aspect of institutional complimentarity is often underplayed in the Varieties of Capitalism literature. In a Varieties analysis the links between institutions in a CME creates a systemic fortress in which, as long as firms continue to produce the products in which their system gives them a comparative advantage over LME, they remain impervious to the process of globalization.[80] However, if one recognizes that the complementarities within an institutional system can be a source of change as well as stability then the potential for systemic change should not, in our view, be ruled out.

Of course, the final outcome of a change will depend on the interaction between adaptation costs that are specific to existing institutions and the forces of change. In practice, these are normally very difficult to calculate in advance, so that predicting the speed and the direction of this cumulative process is almost impossible. Accordingly, Myrdal has outlined his cumulative causation model as follows:

---

77   Dulbecco, P. and Dutraive, V. (2001) 'The Meaning of Market: Comparing Austrian and Institutional Economics' in Garrouste, P. and Ioannides, S. (eds) Evolution and Path Dependence in Economic Ideas: Past and Present, Northampton: Edward Elgar, 58; and Dulbecco, P. (2003) 'The Dynamics of the Institutional Change and the Market Economy: Understanding Contemporaneous Market Development Processes', The Review of Austrian Economics, vol. 16, 231.

78   Boyer, R. (2005) 'Coherence, Diversity, and the Evolution of Capitalisms – The Institutional Complementarity Hypothesis', Evolutionary and Institutional Economics Review, vol. 2(1), 43.

79   Veblen, T. (1898) 'Why Is Economics Not an Evolutionary Science?', Quarterly Journal of Economics, vol. 12, 373; and Veblen, T., above n67, 201 and 208.

80   Soskice, D. and Hall, P. (2001) 'Introduction' in Hall, P. and Soskice, D. (eds) Varieties of Capitalism: The Institutional Foundations of Comparative Advantage, New York: Oxford University Press, 56–62.

[t]he point is not simply that "many forces are working in the same direction". They are, in fact, not doing so. In general there are periods when opposing forces balance one another so that the system remains in rest until a push or a pull is applied at one point or another. When the whole system starts moving after such a shock, the changes in the forces work in the same direction, which is something different.[81]

In the light of the discussion above one can read into Myrdal's statement the dual role of institutional complementarity as a factor of stability and change. Amable takes the argument further by drawing a distinction between 'destabilization' and 'change'. The former amounts to a breakdown in the pattern of a complementary system, whereas the latter describes institutional alterations that do not affect the general logic of relations within that system.[82] In this fashion, what Myrdal, perhaps somewhat metaphorically, regards as a 'balance' is Amable's 'change', i.e. a normal process of systemic evolution *along a pre-selected path*. Destabilization, on the other hand, is the result of a 'shock' which triggers a process of cumulative change and which pulls or pushes the system away from its initial path.

In order to elaborate on this distinction it is necessary to introduce into the equation the concept of workability as discussed in Chapter 2. As we discussed in that chapter, institutions in one sub-system are only workable if institutional configurations in other sub-systems are compatible. We then identified two broadly workable corporate governance systems. The first is an outsider shareholder model of corporate governance which relies on a market-based financial system with powerful institutional shareholders enhancing stock market efficiency, on flexible labour markets and on a strict competition policy regime that prevents managers from forming inter-corporate alliances to insulate themselves from market disciplines. Thus, a market oriented financial system, especially if it is dominated by institutional investors, is compatible with well-developed external labour markets. Moreover, product markets must not be dominated by monopolies or oligopolies, as the ensuing cooperative relations between firms would distort the disciplinary effect of the market for corporate control and of competition on managers.

The second workable equilibrium is an insider model based on enhanced managerial discretion, and which comprises a financial system that enhances long-term commitment between financial and productive capital, an industrial relations system that facilitates labour market internalization by providing formal and

---

81 Myrdal, G., above n28, 17.

82 See Amable, B., above n75. In a similar fashion, Hollingsworth claims that '[i]nstitutional arrangements are always changing, but with a logic that is system specific [...] Being path dependent, a social system of production continues along a particular logic until or unless or until a fundamental societal crisis intervenes'. Hollingsworth, J. and Boyer, R. (1997) Contemporary Capitalism: The Embeddedness of Institutions, Cambridge: Cambridge University Press, 267–8.

informal mechanisms for cooperation and conflict resolution between employers and employees, and a competition policy regime that allows inter-firm cooperation. If institutions start to change then the complementary institutional interaction may be lost and the system of corporate governance may become incoherent. Where the destabilization of a workable system occurs, there are two possible outcomes. The first is one where cumulative causation progresses until a new workable equilibrium is found. In this case there is full adaptation to the shock and destabilization is only temporary. The second possibility, however, is one where the initial shock is not radical enough so as to produce a complete overhaul of the system. This is where the concepts of path dependence, complementarity and workability come to meet. Change may progress so as to affect only a few less path dependent institutions or sub-systems and leave all other more path dependent ones unaffected. Due to strong complementarities that exist between institutions and sub-systems the result will then be a system that is unworkable. In this case, full adaptation fails to take place and destabilization becomes a more permanent condition with significant negative effects on the system's performance.

Finally, another important link can be made between path dependence and the concept of workability due to the effect the latter has on a system's adaptation costs. To a great extent adaptation costs arise as a result of the uncertainty about what effects the new regime will have. Shelpse argues that this uncertainty about the impact of structural change on economic outcomes is enough to stabilize a system.[83] Hence, the more workable a system is, the greater its path dependence and *vice versa*. In fact, this is simply another formulation of the argument that, subject to the path dependence issues described so far, good performers have less incentive to change than bad performers do.

Institutional analysis of institutional change places important limitations on the claim of efficient convergence of corporate governance systems as a result of globalization. Once it is accepted, as we do, that institutions play a significant role in economic development, claims of the certain adaptation of an institutional system in a particular direction become untenable. Whether it eventually occurs will depend on the nature and significance of overall adaptation costs. Of crucial importance will be the ability of systems to resolve collective action problems and to create mechanisms for compensating those parties who have to bear the costs of adaptation. North defines this quality of institutional systems as '*adaptive efficiency*' which he distinguishes from allocative efficiency.[84] Accordingly, he states:

> [institutions] will not only determine the kinds of economic activity that will
> be profitable and viable, but also shape the adaptive efficiency of the internal

---

83   Shelpse K. (1986) 'Institutional Equilibrium and Equilibrium Institutions' in Weisberg, H. (ed.) Political Science: The Science of Politics, New York: Agathon, 51–81.

84   North, D., above n1, 80–83.

structure of firms and other organizations by, for example, regulating entry, governance structures, and the flexibility of organizations. … It is essential to have rules that eliminate not only failed economic organization but failed political organization as well. … Moreover, the very nature of the political process encourages the growth of constraints that favor today's influential bargaining groups. But adaptively efficient institutional frameworks have existed and do exist, just as adaptively inefficient frameworks have existed and do exist.[85]

In sum, once the assumptions of neoclassical theory are relaxed so that institutions are not neutral, the idea of convergence towards a unique optimum model is not inevitable even given the forces of globalization discussed in Chapter 3. There are two reasons for this. Firstly, the fact that national systems adapt to the forces of globalization does not mean the result will inevitably lead to real productive and allocative efficiency as we have painfully observed over the course of the global financial crisis from 2008–2009. The globalization of financial and production capital may create inefficiencies that markets are unable to resolve without outside intervention. As many authors have acknowledged, where markets are imperfect free competition between states and jurisdictional arbitrage can lead to a regulatory race to the bottom rather than to the top.[86]

Secondly, globalization is a work in progress, at least in the foreseeable future it is unreasonable to expect that the boundaries defining national economies as distinct institutional systems will be totally eliminated. Indeed history demonstrates that it may even retreat. In the absence of a fully integrated global marketplace the focus remains on the reactions of national systems to the process of globalization. As our institutional analysis of change shows, even in the presence of such pressures, depending on their internal dynamics institutional systems may not adapt fully or uniformly. Of course, the possibility of convergence as a process cannot be completely excluded; but, before a truly global marketplace is established, if it occurs it is more likely that it will be incomplete and within the margins set by different national institutional systems. As already explained, these margins can be very different depending on the institutional complementarities and adaptation costs involved. As Boyer observed, 'a unique equilibrium is not

---

85   North, D., above n1, 81–82.

86   For a collection of essays on the topic see Bratton, W., McCahery, J., Picciotto, S. and Scott, C. (eds) (1996) *International Regulatory Competition and Coordination – Perspectives on Economic Regulation in Europe and the United States*, Oxford: Clarendon Press, especially Chapter 9. For an early exposition of the 'race to the bottom' argument in the sphere of corporate regulation see Cary, W. (1974) 'Federalism and Corporate Law: Reflections Upon Delaware', *Yale Law Journal*, vol. 83, 663. See also Bebchuk, L. and Cohen, A. (2001) 'Imperfect Competition and Agency Problems in the Market for Corporate Law', Working Paper, University of Chicago. However, the same caveat in respect of the shareholder model's superiority assumption also applies to the 'race to the bottom' argument; see above n31.

warranted: the multiplicity of equilibria in an institutionally rich economy is the rule not the exception'.[87] After the initiation of a convergence process, depending on the institutional dynamics within each system change may be slow or fast, complete or incomplete, and thus the final institutional outcomes can be workable or unworkable. Therefore, differences in the nature, extent and transmission mechanisms of adaptation costs within particular systems do not allow for general predictions of convergence or non-convergence without specific analyses of particular systems' internal dynamics.

Institutional theory and corporate governance

There have been several attempts to introduce institutional analysis to the corporate governance convergence debate. The pioneering attempt to introduce market imperfections as sources of systemic inertia and path dependence was made by Milhaupt who argued that, contrary to the belief of optimal convergence advocates, the evolution of corporate governance institutions is all but straightforward due to the persistence of inefficient institutions.[88] This claim has been taken further by Bebchuck and Roe who have predicted that path dependence as a force of diversity will probably prevail over the pressures of global competition for convergence at least in the short and medium-term.[89] Building upon earlier work by Roe arguing that corporate governance institutions are formed by historical and political factors that are country-specific, they came to the conclusion that rationality and optimality considerations may have less influence in the institutional choices of firms and states.[90] Instead, historically and politically rooted national institutions constrain institutional choices of the present and, thus, prevent the 'efficient' adaptation of corporate governance to modern challenges. This is because past institutional choices have created powerful interest groups of stakeholders, such as managers, workers, creditors and various types of blockholders who have an overriding interest in entrenching themselves by preserving the status quo and who are, therefore, determined to prevent the divergence of corporate governance evolution from the pre-selected path. The reason for those stakeholders' resistance to change is that under the current regime they enjoy privileges, mainly in the form

---

    87   Boyer, R., above n28, 55. See also Zysman, J., above n58, 268.
    88   Milhaupt, C. (1998) 'Property Rights in Firms', Vanderbild Law Review, vol. 84, 1145.
    89   Bebcuck, L. and Roe, M. (1999) 'A Theory of Path Dependence in Corporate Governance and Ownership', Stanford Law Review, vol. 52, 127.
    90   See Roe, M. (1996) 'Chaos and Evolution in Law and Economics', Harvard Law Review, vol. 109, 641; Roe, M. (1994) Weak Owners, Strong Managers: The Political Roots of American Corporate Finance, Princeton: Princeton University Press; Roe, M. (2000) 'Political Preconditions to Separating Ownership from Corporate Control', Stanford Law Review, vol. 53(3), 539; and Roe, M. (2003) Political Determinants of Corporate Governance, Oxford: Oxford University Press.

of private rents, and make firm-specific investments that would be lost or devalued if radical institutional changes were implemented.[91]

Due to these internal workings of institutional structures, Bebchuk and Roe are of the view that an external shock would not lead to an immediate 'destabilization' and reorientation of a national corporate governance system. The pervasiveness of rent extraction by those dominant stakeholder groups translates into high adaptation costs that eventually impede reform unless the aim of the reform is to 'strengthen' existing rules and thus perpetuate the existing system. In this situation less entrenched stakeholders lack the resources and the necessary bargaining power to push through their reforms against the will of dominant parties.

Moreover, Bebchuk and Roe argue, even if some path dependent corporate governance institutions were in fact replaced by non-path dependent ones, convergence would still not be inevitable, because rules that remained unchanged could ensure that established practices are perpetuated. This is, of course, the institutional complementarity argument reiterated. On the one hand, if firms decide to evade what they consider inefficient legal rules by using private contracts, they may find their plans being frustrated by courts' and other organizational structures. On the other hand, even if some formal institutions were altered, Bebchuk and Roe claim, other legal rules could still neutralize the impact of these changes as horizontal complementarities between equal institutions would maintain the system's stability.

However, by overemphasizing the stabilizing effect of institutional complementarity what Bebchuk and Roe fail, in our view, to recognize is its dual role as a mechanism transmitting *both* adaptation costs *and* systemic change. Schmidt and Spindler for example argue that, although the persistent diversity scenario is plausible, it is equally possible that corporate governance systems could converge to an inferior outcome.[92] The basis of this claim is the close relationship between (horizontal) institutional complementarity and the concept of workability as a significant characteristic of a system. As we discussed earlier in this chapter in the context of the hybrid optimal argument the link between the two concepts is the reason we rejected institutional cross-reference as unworkable. If one takes an optimal institution from one national system and add it to another optimal institution from another national system the result is in our view highly unlikely to be a workable system as part of the reason the institutions were optimal in their national systems was their complementarity with other nationally embedded institutions. Removed from this complimentary context these institutions are unlikely to operate as they did in their national context.

91   Bebchuk, L. (2005) 'The Case for Increasing Shareholder Power', Harvard Law Review, vol. 118(3), 833–914.
92   Schmidt, R. and Spindler, G. (2002) 'Path Dependence, Corporate Governance and Complementarity', International Finance, vol. 5(3), 311; Bratton, W. and McCahery, J., above n18.

Interestingly while recognizing this effect, Schmidt and Spindler consider that despite its negative impact, cross-reference is still a real possibility, mainly because in the presence of adaptation costs a leap from one workable system to another is highly unlikely – for this to happen all component sub-systems would have to be reformed simultaneously in an ergodic manner. Thus, competitive pressures may lead to the alteration of a less path dependent institution or subsystem – something that Bebchuk and Roe also accept – which would then make the system as a whole unworkable and therefore potentially inferior to the original. It is the unworkability of the new system that makes it unstable and thus reduces the adaptation costs of further changes.[93] Further change, Schmidt and Spindler argue, could take two directions: a reversal to the initial workable equilibrium as advocated by Bebchuk and Roe or further away from it towards a totally different workable system. However, nothing guarantees the latter scenario, which resembles the cumulative causation process outlined earlier, will be the most efficient solution. This is because systemic instability creates an emergency situation which demands 'some kind of order *immediately*' rather than 'the best order later'. In other words, Schmidt and Spindler assert that in the presence of horizontal complementarities the efficiency of convergence depends on how easy or difficult it is to establish the potentially superior system.

Others have attempted to demonstrate the potential of vertical complementarities to promote corporate governance change and convergence. The pioneer of this argument is Gilson who has distinguished between what he calls 'convergence of form' and 'convergence of function'.[94] Although he does not specifically define the terms 'form' and 'function', one can deduce from his analysis that the former comprises formal legal rules while the latter describes private inter- and intra-firm contracting within the general legal framework. The starting point of Gilson's argument is that corporate governance systems may allow sufficient margins for firms to adapt their behaviour and function in accordance to changing circumstances without alterations in formal institutional structures. This type of adaptation, which resembles Amable's 'institutional change', will not be sufficient to push a system away from its path.[95] Where competition is imperfect, different

---

93   See above, n20 and text.

94   Gilson, R. (2000) 'Globalizing Corporate Governance: Convergence of Form or Function', Working Paper No. 174, Center for Law and Economic Studies, Columbia Law School. For the sake of accuracy, it should be noted that Gilson regards convergence based on contractual agreements as a third type of institutional change. However, the nature and effect of this third type and of functional convergence as described in his paper allow for their treatment as equivalent. See also Gilson, R. (2006) 'Controlling Shareholders and Corporate Governance: Complicating the Comparative Taxonomy', Harvard Law Review, vol. 119(6), 1641.

95   Ibid., 12. See also Gilson, R. (1996) 'Corporate Governance and Economic Efficiency When Do Institutions Matter?', Washington University Law Quarterly, vol. 74, 327 at 334; and Gilson, R. (2004) 'Corporate Governance, the Equity Contract and the Cost of Capital: Incremental and Accretive Reform Strategies', Paper Delivered at – International

systems can develop diverse but equally effective institutional solutions to common problems without their destabilization or their convergence.[96] However, contrary to Bebchuk and Roe's view, Gilson accepts that functional convergence may also 'disarm' path dependent institutions and their supporting stakeholder coalitions even if no change in formal rules is effected.[97] For example he considers market based mechanisms may be a driver of change because:

> [i]n these systems, poorly managed companies and those from whom controlling shareholders have siphoned pecuniary private benefits of control may require additional capital, especially to respond to the globalization of their markets and to new, more efficient foreign competitors. For these companies, internally generated funds will be insufficient, requiring recourse to the capital market. In this context, external suppliers of debt or equity can be expected to insist on a means to dissipate the controlling shareholder's influence if poor performance threatens the new investment ... From this perspective, globalization, even without additional regulatory initiatives, will operate independently to undermine inefficient controlling shareholder systems.[98]

Once a formal institution is rendered obsolete, its adaptation costs are dramatically reduced so that convergence of function can eventually facilitate convergence of form.

Corporate Governance Meeting – Hanoi, Vietnam, available at <https://www.oecd.org/dataoecd/19/58/34081304.pdf> where he stresses incremental institutional change.

96   More specifically, Gilson, R., above n94 uses Kaplan's (Kaplan, S. (1994) 'Top Executive Rewards and Firm Performance: A Comparison of Japan and the US', Journal of Political Economy, vol. 102, 510) empirical findings on the relation between managerial turnover and firm performance to argue that different systems can provide equally effective managerial accountability measures. In a different study to Kaplan's, however, Abe (Abe, Y. (1997) 'Chief Executive Turnover and Firm Performance in Japan', Journal of the Japanese and International Economies, vol. 11, 2) found that variations in measuring firm performance affect CEO turnover differently, since some systems place more emphasis on sales and employment growth – two measures that are related more to managerial rather than shareholder objectives – than others. See also Kato, T. and Kubo, K. (2006) 'CEO Compensation and Firm Performance in Japan: Evidence from New Panel Data on Individual CEO Pay', Journal of the Japanese and International Economies, vol. 20, 1.

97   Amable, B., Ernst, E. and Palombarini, S. (2005) 'How do Financial Markets Affect Industrial Relations: An Institutional Complementarity Approach', Socio-Economic Review, vol. 3, 311.

98   Gilson, R. (2006) 'Controlling Shareholders and Corporate Governance: Complicating the Comparative Taxonomy', Harvard Law Review, vol. 119(6), 1677–1678. See also Gilson, R. (2000) Transparency, Corporate Governance and Capital Markets, Paper Delivered at the Latin American Corporate Governance Roundtable, available at <http://www.oecd.org/dataoecd/55/45/1921785.pdf>.

This link between vertical institutional complementarities and corporate governance convergence towards a global model has been further explored by Coffee.[99] In a three-stage argument, which follows a similar line to that of Gilson, Coffee argues that forces of path dependence in formal corporate governance institutional arrangements can be neutralized and eventually overcome by the pace of functional convergence which should eventually 'dominate formal convergence'. The main vehicle for this process, his argument goes, will be the increasing pressures on and incentives of large firms to list their stock on those stock exchanges that are most developed in terms of liquidity and investor participation. As securities transactions become more spatially concentrated to those countries which enjoy better locational advantages as hosts, a few major stock markets emerge as dominant in the trading of international stocks. Effectively, cross-border corporate securities' listings should be seen as a type of regulatory arbitrage between national financial systems and those dominant stock markets. If capital markets in one system are not suitable to a firm's needs, financial globalization has now opened the possibility of partial or total exit based on a balancing between the costs and benefits that such a move entails.

The listing of a firm's securities on a foreign market constitutes the subjection of that firm to different securities regulations, including financial disclosure and even corporate governance standards that apply therein. As we noted in Chapter 3 the orientation of such regulations in developed capital markets is towards enhancing transparency from the outsider shareholder's perspective. Thus, Coffee's first claim is that firms seeking to remain competitive in global markets are increasingly adopting more outsider shareholder-oriented governance policies without the need of formal institutional changes in their home systems. Indeed, cross-listings of securities are a good example of functional convergence pursued by firms seeking to remain competitive by exploiting advantages in the sphere of corporate finance.

However, contrary to Coffee's and to a lesser extent Gilson's contentions that functional convergence precedes and dominates formal convergence, foreign securities' listings, would not have been possible without prior changes of laws governing international capital movements and foreign exchange rules, to name but a few, which have opened the door to regulatory arbitrage. Moreover, without the growth of Euromarkets – themselves a creation of government policy decisions not to regulate international capital markets unilaterally when it was still possible – as sources of corporate finance, firms would not have had the bargaining power to push forward the abolition of financial regulations that restricted global securities investments. Therefore, convergence of function and form should be seen, in our view, as two interdependent aspects of one process, i.e. of institutional change, rather than two separate ones.

---

99   Coffee, J. (1999) 'The Future as History: The Prospects for Global Convergence in Corporate Governance and Its Implications', Northwestern University Law Review, vol. 93, 641.

In any case, according to Coffee, as regulatory arbitrage by firms seeking to optimize their financial structure gains momentum, competition between national securities markets across the world for international securities' offering should intensify. Therefore, Coffee's second argument is that the globalization of corporate finance creates pressures for securities regulation and disclosure standards' convergence with dominant stock exchanges providing the benchmarks. Thus, the deregulation of global corporate finance is an illustration of how institutional changes on one side of the financial system (cross-border capital movements) alters firms' opportunity sets and preferences so as to trigger further institutional changes on another side (securities regulation). Arguably, the change of securities regulation rules should entail relatively low adaptation costs for two main reasons. Firstly, as an increasing number of large and, therefore, 'core' firms are becoming subjected to higher investor protection standards, it should be reasonable to expect that they will be less inclined to oppose change and they may even use their bargaining power to promote it. Secondly, as Coffee claims, securities regulation convergence should be less politically sensitive and, therefore, less path dependent, because it comprises rules that are largely 'neutral and technocratic that does not, *on its face*, challenge long-established social policies'.[100]

The third stage of Coffee's argument is that progress in the sphere of corporate securities regulation and financial disclosure will eventually lead to corporate governance convergence without the implementation of changes in national company laws. To reach this conclusion, Coffee concurs, to some extent, with the view presented here in Chapter 2; that company law is a weak determinant of corporate governance outcomes. Recalling similar experiences with the interactions between state corporate laws and federal securities regulation in the US, he concludes that the harmonization of national securities laws will be the driving force behind global corporate governance convergence, even if diverse national corporate laws persist.

Even if one accepts the first stage of Coffee's convergence argument, the second and third stages are not satisfactory for two reasons. Firstly, regarding the third argument, Coffee overemphasizes the determinant role of securities regulation alone. Even though it is an important set of institutional constraints on corporate governance, without 'supporting' developments in financial markets, as well as in other sub-systems, the impact of securities regulation convergence alone may prove to be insufficient to push insider models towards an outsider shareholder oriented one. Secondly, institutional forces may not resolve things as Coffee predicts, even if securities regulation has the effect he predicts. As we examined in Chapter 2, disclosure rules and investor protection regulations are mechanisms for reducing transaction costs for outside shareholders. More specifically, they aim at reducing the ability of insiders to extract private rents to the detriment of outsiders. If insiders lost the private benefits associated with their incentive to make firm-specific investments, their incentive to diversify would increase causing

---

100   Coffee, J., above n99, 670.

the externalization of financial relationships. Hence, convergence to higher market transparency standards in securities markets constitutes a re-orientation of one set of financial rules towards the outsider corporate governance model. As already described in Chapter 1 share ownership dispersion in imperfect markets may not be able to constrain managerial discretion if shareholders are arm's length investors. In that case, securities rules' convergence may simply lead to a shift either from one type of insider system based on insider control to another through the de-concentration of insiders' shareholdings, i.e. a managerial insider model based on a *de facto* lack of shareholder control or by simply facilitating change within the existing insider system through a rearranging of the relative power whereby insiders are weakened but don't withdraw, to the benefit of management but not outsider shareholders. As we will observe in Chapter 8 outsider reforms in Germany exhibit some of these effects. Thus, for a more radical shift away from an insider system towards an outsider shareholder model further institutional changes would be needed, such as the growth in the percentage of corporate securities held by institutional investors, market enforcement through the market for corporate control and the increased bargaining power of the latter that results from this. However, this would involve a significant expansion of institutional change from low profile institutions such as securities regulation to highly politicized, pension, takeovers, industrial relations and social security reform and so would link to our third criticism of Coffee's claims.

That is, in respect of the second stage, even if financial re-regulation along the lines described above commences, adaptation outside the financial system may not progress. The reason for this is that, although securities regulation is more 'technocratic', institutional complementarities with other institutional sub-systems may make the impact of regulatory changes in securities markets more obvious to adaptation cost-bearing stakeholders. If complementarity is a carrier of change, it is also a carrier of path dependence, and this is something Coffee underplays. Therefore, path dependence in one sub-system can also prevent the complete re-orientation of another. One possibility is that the 'technocratic' changes that do get implemented are eventually reversed so that the system as a whole reverts to its original position. However, such a reversal to the old regime can be difficult, as new vested interests may have emerged supporting the new regulations. Therefore, when the complexity of dynamic institutional interactions is taken into account, un-workability might occur. Alternately the technical reforms may simply make no difference as they are neutralized by stronger institutional forces and so no overall change in the system occurs. The technical reforms may also impact but not as intended as necessary complementary adaptations don't take place. For example, as we noted above, if reforms encourage dispersal and insider withdrawal occurs leading to an enhancement of managerial power because path dependent resistance arises to stop further pension, takeover, labour and social welfare reform. In all, Coffee's three-stage convergence argument has to be qualified by the fact that adaptation depends on how institutional complementarities resolve themselves, either as carriers of change or of path dependence. When forces of change prevail systemic adaptation progresses, but when they are overcome by path dependence forces adaptation stops until the dynamics of change re-emerge.

Conclusion

In this chapter we sought to examine the potential theoretical dynamic responses of national corporate governance systems to the process of globalization as determined by their internal institutional forces. In doing so we examined and excluded claims of a neoclassical origin that emphasize a clear shareholder oriented outcome within national corporate governance systems to forces of change. We then examined theories of institutional change that emphasize the role of institutions as both facilitators and negators of change. In all we concluded that institutional dynamics within diverse systems can vary considerably so that national corporate governance models should be expected to react differently to common stimulants. The intensity, extent and final outcome of any process of institutional change and thus the degree of global convergence towards an outside-shareholder corporate governance model or not, will ultimately depend on the nature and strength of complementarities within institutional systems that are particular to each nation. Given that the convergence claims centre on a move from an insider to an outsider system we will examine in Part II: Observing Change and Transformation in the UK, US and Germany, how the outsider systems in the UK and US came to their current exceptional status and what evidence there is that Germany is undergoing change that might be an indicator of convergence/transformation to an outsider system.

PART 2
Observing Change and Transformation in the UK, US and Germany

Chapter 5

The Insider Corporate Governance Systems of the UK and the US: From Colony to Cold War

Introduction

As we discussed in the preface and elaborated on in Chapter 1, the outsider corporate governance systems prevalent in the UK and the US are unique among the worlds corporate governance systems and are characterized by the largest businesses being listed on a securities market with a very large shareholding base that tends to interact with management on an arm's length basis.[1] In other words shareholders tend not to engage internally in the running of the company instead leaving it to management to run the company on their behalf. In outsider systems, as we observed in Chapter 2, market forces are significant in determining labour relations and in focusing managerial discretion on shareholders.[2] This is in contrast to the 'insider' systems of most of the rest of the world.[3] These 'insider' systems are characterized generally by the relative unimportance of the securities market as a source of finance. The principal sources of finance are banks, families, non financial corporations and the government. Shareholdings tend to be more concentrated and shareholders, organized labour, government and creditors are more actively involved in the control of companies. In other words a significant feature of insider systems is that insiders or coalitions of insiders are more actively involved in exercising influence over managerial discretion. Insider corporate

---

1 Claims that the common law family generally gives rise to 'outsider' status are doubtful given only the UK and US have the features of a dominant securities market in which arm's length shareholdings are prevalent. For a good overview of this issue see Cheffins, B. (2008) Corporate Ownership and Control: British Business Transformed, Oxford: Oxford University Press, 53–55.

2 Coffee, J. (1999) 'The Future as History: Prospects for Global Convergence in Corporate Governance and its Implications', Northwestern University Law Review, vol. 93, 641–708; and Stein, J. (1988) 'Takeover Threats and Managerial Myopia', Journal of Political Economy, vol. 96, 61–80 .

3 La Porta, R. et al. (1998) 'Law and Finance', Journal of Political Economy, vol. 106, 1113–1155; and La Porta, R., Lopez-de-Silanes, F. and Shleifer, A. (1999) 'Corporate Ownership Around the World', Journal of Finance, vol. 54, 471–517.

governance systems are, as a result, more stakeholder[4] oriented and in some countries form part of a tightly woven protective social market infrastructure.[5]

As we have noted above, the outsider systems of the UK and US are exceptional rather than standard and so before examining changes to the German insider system that might be leading to transformation to an outsider system of corporate governance we need to understand more about how the UK and US came to their exceptional status. In this chapter we focus on long run change in the corporate governance systems of the UK and US up until the 1970s. We chose this time line because one of the features of the two systems is their continued interaction with each other over the very long-term. In turn, the early 1970s marks a significant tipping point in the two economies which in turn allows us to stop and draw conclusions about both the nature of institutional change and the type of corporate governance system operating in the UK and US until that point. In doing so, we consider the development of these systems both in terms of their exposure to external forces such as trade and capital movement, internal forces such as the growth of organized labour and government, and in terms of their interaction with each other over time. By analysing long run change in institutions, such as industrial relations, the financial system, corporate law and sub-systems related to the government demand function, particularly competition and effective demand, discussed in Chapter 2 as significant for corporate governance change, we demonstrate that fluidity of reaction to change has been an important feature of both the UK and the US corporate governance systems over time. In the previous chapter we observed that within diverse systems institutional dynamics could vary significantly and that this was likely to lead institutions to react differently to common stimulants. In this chapter we found that even though there is a shared institutional history, as the US was a former colony, this was broadly the case in most of the reactions of institutions in this period. As we will explore in the course of this chapter, the UK and US conformed broadly to an insider system of ownership and control for most of their history despite large US companies having a dispersed shareholding base. At various times banks, government, labour and managers came to exert strong influence in the insider models present in both systems as institutional dynamics rearranged in response to change and shock.

---

4   Incorporating interests more broadly including, shareholders, employees, creditors, the community and the environment.

5   Porter, M. (1992) 'Capital Disadvantages: America's Failing Capital Investment System', *Harvard Business Review*, vol. 70, 65–82; and Edwards, J. and Fisher, K. (1996) *Banks, Finance and Investment in Germany*, Cambridge: Cambridge University Press, Chapter 2.

The Historical Roots of UK/US Capitalism:
Colonialism to Early Globalization

British interest in what is now the United States of America began with the British new world settlement of Virginia in 1607, nearly a century after the original Spanish colonies were set up after the arrival of Juan Ponce de León in 1513.[6] Despite initial difficulties the colonies expanded and prospered, founded on the export of primary agricultural products such as tobacco and sugar back to Britain.

Table 5.1 British imports of American tobacco, 1620–1775 (million pounds)

1620	1640	1672	1688	1708	1723	1740	1760	1770	1775
0.1	1.3	17.6	28.4	30.0	34.0	41.0	85.0	78.0	102.0

Source: Scheiber, H., Vatter, H. and Faulkner, H. (1976) American Economic History, New York: Harper & Row, Part 1, 53, Table 4.1. Source: US Department of Commerce, Bureau of the Census (1960) 'Historical Statistics of the US, Colonial Times to 1957', Washington, DC: US Government Printing Office, 766.

Over the following two centuries Britain became the primary military and industrial power in the world through two industrial revolutions and the build up of a powerful navy and army. Over that period Britain was consistently at war which had a direct effect on its relationship with the US colonies.[7] The need to be able to fund these wars and/or defend the colonies drove the British to centralize control over trade, shipping and general colonial economic activity.[8] In 1660 an 'Act for the Encouraging and Increasing of Shipping and Navigation' placed extensive restrictions on independent colonial trade in that it required that goods carried to and from England be transported by English-manned and English or English-Colonial-built ships. The colonies were also restricted in terms of their imports as taxes were applied to goods imported from other European nations. These restrictions on the US colonies ability to trade independently were successfully evaded until Britain imposed further controls on inter-colony import/exports in

---

6   Zinn, H. (2003) A People's History of the United States: 1492–Present, Pearson, Chapter 1; Nobleman, M. (2005) Juan Ponce de Leon, Capstone Press, 8; and McCusker, J. and Menard, R. (1985) The Economy of British North America: 1607–1789, Chapel Hill.

7   See Wright, Q. (1965) A Study of War, Chicago: University of Chicago Press, 53 on Britain's consistent wars from 1480–1940.

8   Engerman, S. and O'Brien, P. (2004) 'The Industrial Revolution in Global Perspective' in Floud, R. and Johnson, P. (eds) The Cambridge Economic History of Modern Britain: Volume I, Cambridge: Cambridge University Press, 452.

1673.[9] Gradually, Britain increased the number of products that could only be exported to England by the colonies. By 1766 this number of products had grown so large that direct trade with other countries was hardly feasible for the American colonies.[10]

During the eighteenth century the volume of trade, both import and export, with Britain grew steadily. Between the 1700s and the 1760s the annual value of trade between the two grew from £550,000 to £2.8 million.[11] However, increasingly the restrictions imposed on trade by the British were causing significant problems for the US colonies. The Sugar Act 1764, had it not been ignored by the colonists and English officials, would have meant economic disaster for the colonists by collapsing key markets for US products.[12] Things deteriorated even further with the imposition of the first direct taxation measure in the Stamp Act of 1765 imposing tax on all legal documents, newspapers, commercial contracts, pamphlets and playing cards in order to pay for the defence of the American colonies. The tax provoked outrage in the colonies because of the lack of representation of the colonies in this decision.[13] However, in effect the tax was unworkable as a result of this mass opposition and was abolished in 1766. The British Parliament however passed the Declaratory Act 1766 which stated that Parliament 'had, hath, and of right ought to have, full power and authority to make laws and statutes of sufficient force and validity to bind the colonies and people of America ... in all cases whatsoever'.[14]

Charles Townsend's appointment as Chancellor of the Exchequer in 1767 brought an increased level of scrutiny to US colonial affairs. New taxes were imposed on a whole range of goods and evasion was made much more difficult with the creation of an American Customs Board. Colonial courts were given the power to issue general search warrants and courts of admiralty were created to try cases of smuggling. Relations with the American colonies reached a new low soon after when a number of southern colonies refused to trade with Britain so that by late 1769 American imports to Britain fell by a third. Alarmed by the reaction of American colonists Britain responded by repealing the Townsend duties except those levied on tea. Trade between the American colonies and Britain boomed as a result (Table 5.2).[15]

---

9   Scheiber, H., Vatter, H. and Faulkner, H. (1976) American Economic History, New York: Harper & Row, 61.

10   Ibid.

11   Robertson, R. (1973) History of the American Economy, 3rd edition, New York: Harcourt Brace Jovanovich International Edition, 84.

12   Indeed some scholars attribute the origins of the American revolution to this Act. See Robertson, R., above n11, 89–90.

13   Middlekauff, R. (2005) The Glorious Cause: The American Revolution: 1763–1789, Oxford: Oxford University Press, 60–62; and Greene, J. (1995) Understanding the American Revolution: Issues and Actors, University of Virginia Press, 1–9.

14   The Declatory Act 1766, 6 George III, c. 12.

15   Robertson, R., above n11, 92.

By 1773 the British East India Company (BEIC) had severe financial problems and no prospect of selling on a vast accumulation of tea because it was being undercut by tea smugglers, the most prominent of whom were American colonists. The British Parliament provided assistance by granting a loan to the company and attempted to cut out the illicit trade in tea by giving the BEIC a monopoly over the Tea trade and a tax break in the Tea Act 1773. This monopoly destroyed the American colonists' trade in tea (smuggled and legitimate) and eventually led to tea being sent back to England or famously being destroyed in the Boston Tea Party.[16]

This time there was no attempt to conciliate the American colonies and Parliament passed a series of Acts in 1774 termed collectively by the colonists as the Intolerable Acts. This led to the closure of the port of Boston until the BEIC had been paid for its tea. As a result of the Intolerable Acts the colonies unified in response and at the First Continental Congress they voted not to trade with England or the British West Indies. In turn the Southern Colonies joined the protest as restrictive land policies and poor tobacco prices had left them equally as disgruntled as the Northern colonists.[17]

In economic terms the events leading to the revolution according to Robertson centered on 'a basic conflict between English mercantile policy on the one hand and the Northern colonial merchants' need for independent expansion on the other'.[18] In turn colonial relations with Britain deteriorated as suspicions that Britain's intention with the succession of taxes and monopoly laws were just a first step in restricting the economic freedom of the American colonies. Hostilities broke out in 1775, the declaration of independence was issued in 1776 and the revolutionary war ensued until its formal end in British defeat with the signing of the Treaty of Paris 1784.[19] In 1787 the Constitution of the United States of America was adopted and the new nation began life outside the British Empire.[20]

From the British perspective this had little effect as trade continued with the United States but without the cost of maintaining the defence of the colonies and its trade. However, the post war period for the former colonies saw a period of two decades where trade with Britain declined as it was outside the protected trade area of the British Empire, agricultural prices particularly tobacco prices were low and the new country attempted to pay back its war loans.[21]

---

16   John Hancock for example. See Unger, H. (2005) John Hancock, Merchant King and American Patriot, 120.

17   Robertson, R., above n11, 93–99.

18   Ibid., Robertson, 94; and Thomas, P. (1991) Tea Party to Independence: The Third Phase of the American Revolution, 1773–1776, Oxford: Clarendon Press.

19   Lipset, S.M. (1991) Continental Divide: The Values and Institutions of the United States and Canada, New York: Routledge, 22; and Miller, J.C. (1959) Origins of the American Revolution, Stanford: Stanford University Press, 505.

20   Amar, A.R. (2005) '"In the Beginning", America's Constitution: A Biography', London: Random House.

21   North, D. (1966) The Economic Growth of the United States 1790–1860, New York: W.W. Norton & Company, 19.

Table 5.2 British trade with the US (estimated market value of British imports from the United States, 1770–1775, 1784–1792)

Year	Estimated market value (in $ thousands)	Value relative (1790 = 100)
1770	3,248	55
1771	5,978	86
1772	5,078	86
1773	4,960	84
1774	4,842	82
1775	6,555	111
American Revolution		
1784	4,429	75
1785	4,901	83
1786	4,134	70
1787	4,488	76
1788	4,901	83
1789	4,901	83
1790	4,905	100
1791	4,724	80
1792	4,311	73

Source: Bjork. G. (1964) 'The Weaning of the American Economy: Independence, Market Changes and Economic Development', Journal of Economic History, vol. 24(4), 541, 550, Table 2. Source: 'Estimated market value of British imports from the United States was obtained by converting British "Official" values into a volume series (1790 = 100) and valuing with Laspeyres price index (1790 = 100) weighted by the composition of US exports to Britain.'

The war between Britain and France over the period 1799–1815 initially had a positive effect on the US economy as it became the largest neutral nation trading with both sides. In fifteen years the tonnage of the US merchant marine increased enormously. However, Britain's attempts to disrupt US trade with France by stopping and searching US ships and conscripting US sailors (on the basis that many were originally British) eventually dragged the US into the war. The blockades as a result of the war between the US and Britain in 1812 destroyed US/British Trade until 1815.[22] The war did have a positive effect in that until this point the US economy was primarily an agricultural economy but starved of manufactured imports it started manufacturing goods at home. Through a combination of cotton exports and increasing manufacturing the US economy grew rapidly as trade with Britain, who by 1860 was the world's largest trading nation, boomed once again

---

22   Benn, C. (2002) The War of 1812, Oxford: Osprey Publishing, 56–57; and Robertson, R., above n11, 241.

(Table 5.3).[23] By the middle of the nineteenth century Britain was importing 25 percent of her total imports from the US and some 40 percent of US imports came from Britain in the first part of the nineteenth century.[24]

Table 5.3 Official value of imports of merchandise into the UK – annual average in each five year period (million pounds)

	Total	From USA	Imports from USA as a percentage of total
1816–20	31.7	3.3	11
1821–25	35.8	4.8	14
1826–30	43.6	6.7	15
1831–35	47.7	9.4	19
1836–40	60.5	13.5	20
1841–45	72.1	18.2	25
1846–50	85.2	21.7	25
1851–55	116.9	27.5	24
1856	131.9	32.7	22

Source: Potter, J. (1969) 'Atlantic Economy, 1815–1860: The USA and the Industrial Revolution' in Coates, A. and Roberston, R. (eds) Essays in American Economic History, London: Edward Arnold, 19, Table 1.

The second half of the nineteenth century saw an enormous expansion of the US economy behind a highly protected economy. At the beginning of the US civil war in 1861 the Morrill Act was passed imposing protective tariffs and despite the end of the war in 1865 tariff rates continued rising.[25] In 1861 average US tariffs were 20 percent, by 1864 47 percent, by 1890 50 percent and by 1897 60 percent. In tandem the number of imports eligible to pay duties increased enormously.[26] As Potter described it:

> [t]he imposition of the highly protective tariff of 1864, more than any single other act, announced the severance by the USA of her ancient commercial

23   Frieden, J. (1994) 'International Investment and Colonial Control: A New Interpretation', International Organization, vol. 48(4), 559 at 576.

24   Robertson, R., above n11, 243.

25   Weigley, R. (2000) A Great Civil War: A Military and Political History, 1861–1865, Indiana University Press, 203–204; and Robertson, R., above n11, 370.

26   Robertson, R., above n11, 371.

links with the old world and constituted a declaration of American economic independence.[27]

US trade with Britain, particularly the cotton trade, remained significant but US trade with the rest of the world expanded as well as the export of manufactured goods began to exceed primary goods.[28] Although there is some dispute about when it happened, at some point between 1880 and 1900 the US overtook Britain as the world's leading economy.[29] By 1913 for example total combined British and German exports were \$2.3 billion while total US exports were \$2.4 billion.[30] Significantly, key aspects of this economic success related to corporate governance change.

The rise of the managerial corporation in the US

The industrial revolution in Britain at the end of the eighteenth century and beginning of the nineteenth century had a particular effect on the US economy. As highly skilled workers moved to the United States in this period to exploit innovations such as the spinning mill and domestic American innovations such as the cotton gin, the products of this nascent US industrialization needed increased means of transportation. In the early nineteenth century the railway was only beginning to emerge as a means of transport. By 1825 there was for example only one short transport railway in Britain.[31] Technological innovations in the US in the 1830s turned the railways from a novelty into a potential mass transport system for the continent.[32] In 1830 there was only 23 miles of railroad track in the US, by 1840 it had reached 3000 miles and had outpaced rail building in Britain.[33] At State and Federal level vast amounts of funding and land were provided to the rail companies to build and run a mass transportation system across the continent.[34] However, even this combination of state generosity and traditional private debt

---

27   Potter, J. (1969) 'Atlantic Economy, 1815–1860: The USA and the Industrial Revolution' in Coates, A. and Roberston, R. (eds) Essays in American Economic History, Edward Arnold, 48.

28   Engerman, S. and O'Brien, P., above n8, 463.

29   Prados de la Escosura, L. (2000) 'International Comparisons of Real Product, 1820–1990: An Alternative Data Set', Explorations in Economic History, vol. 37(1), 1–41.

30   Frieden, J. (1994) 'International Investment and Colonial Control: A New Interpretation', International Organization, vol. 48(4), 559 at 576.

31   The Stockton and Darlington Railroad see May, T. (2000) The Victorian Railway Worker, Oxford: Osprey Publishing, 6–7.

32   Brinkley, A. (1993) The Unfinished Nation. A Concise History of the American People, New York: McGraw-Hill, Inc., 223–224.

33   Licht, W. (1983) Working for the Railroad, Princeton: Princeton University Press, 10.

34   Billington, R.A. (1967) Westward Expansion, New York: The Macmillan Company, 642–643; and Fogel, R.W. (1964) Railroads and American Economic Growth: Essays in Economic History, Baltimore: The Johns Hopkins Press, 3.

funding exhausted the existing market capacity and the public equity market sprang up to serve the enormous funding needs of the rail companies.[35]

Corporate law played a small part in the rise of the rail companies and in turn other large managerial companies modelled on them. One of the legacies of British colonial rule had been the key role government played in granting corporate status. As Berle and Means described it:

> in the Eighteenth Century negotiations for these contracts were carried on with the crown, so in America they were carried on with the sovereign power of the various states as successors to the crown. In practice this meant the state legislature.[36]

Each company therefore needed a specific piece of legislation and so incorporation was largely the preserve of those of power and influence. In the whole colonial period for example only seven corporate charters were granted to American businesses. In the aftermath of the revolutionary war a relative boom occurred in the granting of charters by American states and some 328 were granted to businesses between the end of the war and 1800.[37] However, while the rail industry was powerful enough to obtain state charters of incorporation, in a general sense companies were still relatively rare and it was not until the latter part of the nineteenth century with the advent of general incorporation statutes that the company became a common form of business in the US. Although late in introducing a general incorporation statute Delaware eventually became the predominant state of incorporation by adopting a less restrictive set of corporate laws.[38]

As we noted in Chapter 3 the nineteenth and early twentieth century saw a phase of globalization that lasted from circa 1860 until 1914. In this period the US largely stayed outside this process by, as we described above, trading with the rest of the world behind a highly protective economy.[39] However, in terms of Foreign Direct Investment (FDI), capital controls had not yet appeared and so capital flowed freely across borders in this period. As such the US was a major beneficiary of FDI in this period as investors sought out high growth cross border opportunities and

---

35   Englebourg, L. and Bushkoff, S. (1996) The Man Who Found the Money: John Stewart Kennedy and the Financing of the Western Railroads. It also served the general public excitement about investing in these companies see Licht, W., above n33, 7–8.

36   Berle, A. and Means, G. (1968) The Modern Corporation and Private Property, Revised Edition, New York: Harcourt, Brace & World, Inc., 121.

37   Friedman, L. (1973) A History of American Law, New York: Simon & Schuster, 186.

38   Winter, R. (1977) 'State Law, Shareholder Protection, and the Theory of the Corporation', Journal of Legal Studies, vol. 6, 251–92; and Romano, R. (1985) 'Law as a Product: Some Pieces of the Incorporation Puzzle', Journal of Law, Economics and Organization, vol. 1(2), 225–83.

39   Chang, H. (2002) Kicking Away the Ladder: Development Strategy in Historical Perspective, London: Anthem Press.

the rail companies needed foreign capital.[40] By the end of this period in 1914 more than a quarter of total world foreign investment went to the United States.[41] In turn London's pre-eminence as the world's financial centre meant that most of this investment was either British in origin or flowed through London into the US.[42] In 1899, 80 percent of all foreign investment in the US came from Britain. By 1914 that had reduced to 60 percent although British investment had almost doubled in the intervening period. The reduction in percentage terms was because foreign investment from other European countries had by 1914 increased significantly.[43] As the railway companies' capital needs grew in the late nineteenth century their shares were listed in increasing numbers on the London and New York Stock Exchanges (NYSE). As the capital needs of non-railway companies grew, as the railways opened markets for their products, it was on the London Stock Exchange (LSE), and not the more conservative NYSE, that they listed in order to get funding. This would change in the decade before the First World War as the NYSE caught up with the funding needs on US non-rail companies. Indeed, it also began to attract British companies to list on the NYSE. The mobility of capital and the competition between the London and New York exchanges to provide finance was a significant feature of the early globalization period.[44]

This factor had an important influence on the US corporate governance system in the nineteenth and early twentieth century. Overseas investors needed protection that was not provided by US law[45] and so British investors developed a range of corporate governance monitoring measures, such as having a place on the board for themselves or their US agent and offering advice, using a 'Protective Committee' – essentially a temporary or semi-permanent audit committee – to check on things, or enforcing their foreclosure powers and running the company themselves. However, probably the most successful protective measure utilized by British investors was often to encourage collusion on price fixing where possible.[46] In turn as the public equity market grew to feed the capital needs of the railways the NYSE developed in essence a mini legal system to provide the necessary

40   Coffee, J. above n2, 27.

41   Panic, M. (1992) *European Monetary Union: Lessons from the Classical Gold Standard*, London: Macmillan, 101.

42   Kenwood, A. and Lougheed, A. (1994) *The Growth of the International Economy: 1829–1990*, London: Routledge, 30; Foreman-Peck, J. (1983) *A History of the World Economy: International Economic Relations Since 1850*, Brighton: Wheatsheaf Books, 133; and Eichengreen, B. (1985) 'Conducting the International Orchestra: Bank of England Leadership under the Classical Gold Standard', *Journal of International Money and Finance*, vol. 6, 5–29.

43   Davis, L. and Cull, R. (1994) *International Capital Markets and American Economic Growth, 1820–1914*, Cambridge: Cambridge University Press, 18.

44   Ibid., 62–66.

45   Coffee, J. above n2, 29–30. Apart from the weakness of US corporate law generally in this period the US courts also considered securities contracts as akin to gambling.

46   Davis, L. and Cull, R. above n43, 59–61.

quality control to attract overseas, mainly British, investment.[47] In this sense the first globalization phase with its ease of capital mobility described in Chapter 3, had a direct effect on US corporate governance structures which as we observe later in this chapter became the focus of reform in the 1930s.

It was also in this period that the managerial companies pioneered by the railway company bureaucracies described in Chapter 1 emerged as a powerful force in the US economy. Industries had sprung up to serve the rail industry and the railways opened markets, which in turn caused other large companies to emerge to serve the greater scale of these new markets. However, in Britain similar developments, as we will see, did not give rise to large scale managerial companies as it did in the US. Legislation at the end of the nineteenth century designed to protect the public from the collusive activities of US industry seems to have marked a decisive difference in the UK and US corporate governance story in this period.

The US managerial railway companies had an enormous practical effect on people's lives in the nineteenth century which lead to fears in the US about their power and influence.[48] For example until November 18, 1883 Local Mean Time in the US was set according to the movement of the sun. Local Mean Time was effectively abolished on November 18, 1883 by the railway companies. Without any thought to consider the State or Federal Government's view, the companies divided the United States into four time zones for timetabling purposes and introduced a new standardized rail time.[49] Although in time people came to accept standardized railway time and indeed those time zones still stand today, it fed suspicions of corporate power.[50] By 1890 the 12 major rail companies employed 100,000 people while the entire US Federal Civil Service consisted of 20,000 people.[51] In the US given its revolutionary experience with British monopoly power as a restraint on trade and individual economic freedom, as we described above in the case of the BEIC's tea monopoly, it was ironic, given this distrust, that unlike other industrialized nations big business had evolved ahead of government. The combination of these two factors fuelled deep concerns about the power and legitimacy of large corporations in the US which remains to this day. In 1867 farmers, merchants and shippers concerns about price fixing in the rail industry led to individual states attempting to introduce legislation regulating fares.[52] The rail companies fought state and federal regulation of fares in the State and Federal

---

47   Coffee, J., above n2, 27–49; and Davis, L. and Cull, R., above n43, 72.

48   Gordon, S. (1996) Passage to Union: How the Railroads Transformed American Life, 1829–1929, Dee.

49   Laurie, B. (1989) Artisans into Workers, New York: Hill and Wang, 114.

50   Riegel, R. (1927) 'Standard Time in the United States', The American Historical Review, vol. 33(1), 84–89.

51   Revolution to Reconstruction Project (1991) An Outline of the American Economy, Chapter 3, 10, available at <http://www.let.rug.nl/~usa//ECO/1991/ch3_p10.htm>.

52   Billington, R. (1967) Westward Expansion, New York: The Macmillan Company, 728–729.

Courts with some success for decades but by 1916 a raft of Federal legislation covered most of the rail industry.[53] However, general public concerns about abuse of power by many companies across US industry brought about the passing of the Sherman Anti-Trust Act in 1890 resulting in 1911 in the break up of three of the largest and most powerful US companies, Standard Oil, the American Tobacco Company and the Du Pont Company.[54] Faced with a severe impediment to their collusive activities, a horizontal merger wave occurred across many industries.[55] In effect the collusive activities were brought in-house. This marked a key development in US corporate governance history as a merger of already large companies created vast managerial companies with an enormously dispersed shareholding base. In effect the managers had emerged from the merger wave as the only constituency capable of exercising control.

Although as we described above, the US overtook Britain as the world's leading economy by the end of the nineteenth century, Britain remained the dominant world power in the period from 1860 until 1914. British currency (sterling) underwrote international trade, its financial markets were the largest and most important in the world and it operated with an evangelical zeal for free trade.[56] Unlike the US it was a place capital flowed through and out of into the world and as a result large domestic businesses did not have the US feature of significant foreign investors to fuel corporate governance innovation.[57] Its rail companies' capital needs were smaller and although they became by a significant margin the largest businesses in the UK they offered an important refinement to existing markets rather than the continental scale market building operation that occurred in the US.[58] Additionally as we discussed earlier in this chapter, the British state had evolved in advance of large companies because of its need to control trade to raise taxes for its continual

---

53   Scheiber, H., Vatter, H. and Underwood Faulkner, H. (1976) American Economic History, New York: Harper & Row, 267–269.

54   Chandler, A. (1990) Scale and Scope: The Dynamics of Industrial Capitalism, Cambridge, MA: Harvard University Press, 78.

55   Ibid., 288–320; and Hannah, L. (1979) 'Mergers, Cartels and Concentration: Legal Factors in the U.S. and European Experience' in Horn, N. and Kocka, J. (eds) Law and Formation of the Big Enterprises in the Nineteenth and Early Twentieth Centuries, 306–315.

56   Britain generally imposed free trade on the developing world on terms which were favourable to it. Bairoch, P. and Kozul-Wright, R. (1996) 'Globalization Myths: Some Historical Reflections on Integration, Industrialization and Growth in the World Economy', Discussion Paper 13, Geneva, UNCTAD.

57   Coffee, J., above n2, 36. Although foreign, particularly Dutch, investors had provided the capital for the first industrial revolution, their proximity to their investments probably allowed them to monitor things themselves. See Brezis, E. (1995) 'Foreign Capital Flows in the Century of Britain's Industrial Revolution: New Estimates, Controlled Conjectures', The Economic History Review, New Series, vol. 48(1), 46–67 at 52.

58   Chandler, A., above n54, 253.

military endeavours. As a result fears about their power did not result in legislation, horizontal mergers and in turn highly dispersed ownership.

In Britain, as in the US, grants of corporate charters were available for large scale ventures such as canal or rail building but they were not a widely available form of doing business until the mid to late nineteenth century. The passing of general incorporation statutes in the mid nineteenth century meant incorporation was available but it was not until the late nineteenth century that incorporation became common for the UK's largest businesses and they began to use the stock exchange for finance.[59] Company law in turn offered weak protection of shareholders although by the end of this period the Companies Acts 1900 and 1907 did introduce some limited protection.[60] Over the course of the late nineteenth century, listed companies became much more common, and some notably railway and banking companies had largely dispersed shareholdings by the turn of the century. However, the mass of giant managerial companies that emerged in the US, did not have an equivalent in the UK where characteristically, the country's businesses were still controlled by founding families and their descendants through the nineteenth and early twentieth century.[61] And so at the end of the first period of globalization in 1914, the corporate governance landscape of the UK and US looked very different. Britain was largely dominated by traditional owner managed businesses, both incorporated and unincorporated, operating in an open competitive free trade environment with minimal government intervention. The US on the other hand was dominated by managerial companies operating internationally from a protected domestic environment in which government although small was actively involved in regulating collusive behaviour. Elements of change were however evident in both countries as organized labour was beginning to grow in influence from the middle of the nineteenth century onwards and government was moving to an active role in mobilizing a wartime economy.[62]

---

59   Gower, L. (1969) The Principles of Modern Company Law, Stevens, 22–51. Payne, P. (1978) 'Industrial Entrepreneurship and Management in Great Britain' in Mathias, P. and Postan, M. (eds) The Cambridge Economic History of Europe. Volume VII: The Industrial Economies: Capital, Labour and Enterprise, Part I (Britain, France, Germany and Scandinavia), Cambridge, 195; and Prais, S. (1976) The Evolution of Giant Firms in Britain: A Study of the Growth of Concentration in Manufacturing Industry in Britain 1909–70, Cambridge, 90.

60   Cheffins, B. above n1, 194–196.

61   Chandler, A., above n54, 235–294. More recently Hannah has argued that ownership of large British companies had separated from control in this period. See Hannah, L. (2007) 'The Divorce of Ownership from Control from 1900: Re-calibrating Imagined Global Historical Trends', Business History, 404. This claim however remains highly contested see Cheffins, B., ibid., Chapter 7.

62   On the rise of trade unions in Britain see Clegg, H., Fox, A. and Thompson, A. (1964) A History of British Trade Unions since 1889, Oxford: Clarendon Press, Chapter 2. On the response of employers in forming employer associations see Pelling, H. (1987) A History of British Trade Unionism, Penguin, Chapter 7. On the US experience see Tomlins, C. and King,

The End of Early Globalization: The Interwar Years 1914–1939

The First World War (WWI) proved not only the end of the first period of globalization described in Chapter 3 but the end of Britain as the world's leading economic power. While Britain's economy was in robust shape before and to a large extent during the war, there were certain crucial effects on its role as the leading economy that arose after the war. As Britain turned itself into a wartime economy and the war itself disrupted trade, former customers were picked up by US and Japanese companies or turned to their own industries to supply manufactured goods.[63] Britain returned after the war either to a crowded marketplace or a closed market as the rise of nationalism was accompanied by highly protective tariff walls.[64] While Britain retained it role as the world's largest foreign direct investor through the interwar years and its services sector produced world leading companies, the decline in manufacturing industries was precipitous.[65] The proportion of British national income attributable to exports was 33 percent in 1907, by 1924 this had fallen to 27 percent and by 1938 it was just 15 percent.[66] During the course of the war Britain borrowed large amounts from the US while at the same time lending even larger amounts to Russia, France, Italy and Empire countries to fund their war efforts. At the end of the war this left loans to repay to the US but with real difficulty collecting the loans made to its war allies. Imperial Russia being the largest recipient of British loans was especially problematic, as the revolution left an enormous unpaid debt. Additionally the trade deficit with the US grew significantly during the war as war goods were imported partly funded by the mass sale of UK assets in the US.[67] This was done initially by the government buying the US securities of UK investors but as the war continued and dollars were in short supply the Treasury was given power to requisition those US assets.[68] While Britain remained a significant economic power relative to the rest of the world,

A. (1992) 'Introduction: Law, Labor, History' in Tomlins, C. and King, A. (eds) Labor Law in America: Historical and Critical Essays, Baltimore: Johns Hopkins University Press, 1–19.

63   Wrigley, C. (2000) 'The War and the International Economy' in Wrigley, C (ed.) The First World War and the International Economy, Cheltenham: Edward Elgar, 1–33.

64   See Harley, C. (2004) 'Trade, 1870–1939: From Globalization to Fragmentation' in Floud, R. and Johnson, P., The Cambridge Economic History of Modern Britain. Volume II: Economic Maturity, 1860–1939, Cambridge: Cambridge University Press, 178.

65   See Wardley, P. (1991) 'The Anatomy of Big Business: Aspects of Corporate Development in the Twentieth Century', Business History, 268–296; and Dunning, J. (1988) Explaining International Production, Unwin, 74.

66   Pollard, S. (1983) The Development of the British Economy, London: Edwards Arnold, 116.

67   Howlett, W. and Broadberry, S. (2005) 'The United Kingdom During World War I: Business as Usual?' in Broadberry, S. and Harrison, M. (eds) The Economics of World War I, Cambridge: Cambridge University Press, 206–234.

68   Morgan, E. (1952) Studies in British Financial Policy: 1914–25, London: Macmillan, 326–329.

Britain's relationship with the US had changed fundamentally, leaving the US the dominant power.[69]

However, the situation Britain found itself in after the war was compounded by the ill-fated decision to re-enter the gold standard at Britain's pre-war level. As we discussed in Chapter 3 this re-entry level was too high as it did not take account of the changed economic circumstances Britain found itself in after the war. As a result British goods were uncompetitive and high levels of unemployment ensued. The problems of repaying US loans and of an uncompetitive economy dragged on Britain over the course of the 1920s as Europe generally declined economically as the aftermath of the war played out in a much contracted global economy. The great stock market crash in 1929 and ensuing depression in the 1930s were just further blows to an already depressed world economy. In a belated recognition of its changed economic circumstances Britain left the gold standard in 1931 and perhaps more symbolically, in a move away from free trade, also introduced tariffs to protect its industry.[70] The totality of all this economic displacement was that Britain and Europe generally in terms of output and living standards fell significantly behind the US in the first part of the twentieth century.[71]

Sterling's mispricing in the currency markets over the 1920s had also encouraged currency speculation and by the 1930s currency speculation became rife and extremely dangerous for governments. German military build up in the 1930s for example was accompanied by the use of speculative currency attacks on neighbouring countries and was particularly successful in the case of France.[72] By 1936 the UK, the US and France were all attempting to restrict capital flows.[73] As James describes it:

> [t]he lesson learnt from the experience was that controls were needed to defend France's national interest against the security dangers posed by hot money flows. The experience of the 1930s convinced many observers, not just in France, that speculative money was immoral and dangerous. By the late 1930s, and especially in the war years, a consensus emerged that the instability of the 1920s

---

69   Jones, G. (1997) 'Great Britain: Big Business, Management and Competitiveness in Twentieth-Century Britain' in Chandler, A., Amatori, F. and Hikino, T. (eds) Big Business and the Wealth of Nations, Cambridge, 105.

70   See Harley, C., above n64, 185; and Kindleberger, C. (1973) The World in Depression, London: The Penguin Press.

71   Eichengreen, B. (2006) The European Economy Since 1945: Coordinated Capitalism and Beyond, Princeton: Princeton University Press, 16.

72   Ironically, Adolf Hitler had himself often railed against the threat of international capital as a destabilizing force. As he wrote in 1925 'the hardest battle would have to be fought, not against hostile nations, but against international capital'. Hitler, A. (1925/1999) Mein Kampf, Boston, MA: Houghton Mifflin, 213.

73   Eckes, A. (1975) A Search for Solvency: Bretton Woods and the International Monetary System, 1941–1971, Austin: University of Texas Press, 162.

international economy, and thus also the way in which the financial sector served
as a transmitter of depression, was a consequence of unstable capital flows.[74]

This consensus would have its manifestation in the Bretton Woods agreement of
the post war period.

Corporate governance in the interwar years

WWI had a particular effect on corporate governance arrangements in Britain. Over
the period from 1914 to 1939 significant changes occurred within the institutional
structure of the economy as the state grew enormously, labour became a significant
force, free trade was abandoned and tariffs introduced, competitive forces were
stifled and the beginning of a move towards dispersed shareholdings occurred.
Prior to the war the British economy had been dominated by the private sector but
over the course of the war, state intervention began and accelerated over the course
of the 1920s and 30s as the social welfare system expanded.[75] As an indicator of
the rise of the state in facilitating demand in this period, public expenditure as a
percentage of GDP increased from 11.9 percent in 1913, to 20.5 percent in 1920,
to 33.2 percent by 1939. To fund this expansion standard rate taxation increased
from 5.8 percent in 1913 to 30 percent in 1920. Higher rate tax increased from
8.33 percent in 1913 to 52.5 percent by 1920. By 1939 standard rate taxation was
27.5 percent while the higher rate was 75 percent.[76] One particular effect of this
growth of the state was its direct intervention in industry. As Hobsbawm described
it, Britain 'turned from one of the least into one of the most trustified or controlled
economies'.[77] Industry mergers occurred on a large scale in this period either
forced by, or 'encouraged' by, the government. Across the board industries ranging
from iron, steel, chemicals, coal, rail, food, drink, tobacco, textiles, leather, china,
agriculture and glass became highly concentrated either through government
planned mergers or price and output controls.[78] Large firms dominating markets
and able, actively encouraged by government, to cartelize, often heavily subsidized

74   James, H. (2002) 'The End of Global Capital Flows During the Great Depression',
available at <http://www.crei.cat/activities/sc_conferences/15/james.pdf>.
75   Boyer, R. (2004) 'Living Standards, 1860–1939' in Floud, R. and Johnson, P., The
Cambridge Economic History of Modern Britain. Volume II: Economic Maturity, 1860–
1939, Cambridge: Cambridge University Press, 311–313.
76   See Middleton, R. (2004) 'Government and the Economy, 1860–1939' in Floud,
R. and Johnson, P. (eds) The Cambridge Economic History of Modern Britain. Volume II:
Economic Maturity, 1860–1939, Cambridge: Cambridge University Press, 462.
77   Hobsbawm, E. (1968) Industry and Empire: The Making of Modern English
Society, New York: Pantheon Books, 205–6.
78   Crafts, N. (1999) 'Economic Growth in the Twentieth Century', Oxford Review of
Economic Policy, vol. 15, 18–34.

by government, became the norm by the 1930s.[79] As one observer noted in 1937 'free competition has nearly disappeared from the British scene'.[80] In turn the tariff system favoured concentred markets over competitive ones so that even companies that might not favour mergers had clear incentives to do so.[81] In general there was little dissent among the political parties, general public or the media from the view that competitive forces had to be curtailed and British industry protected, first to aid war recovery and then to deal with the Great Depression.[82] Indeed, even the normally suspicious judiciary began to allow enforcement of collusive agreements and industry self-regulation became common.[83]

There is of course the temptation here to regard this merger wave as the equivalent of the late nineteenth/early twentieth century US wave. Hannah for example argues just this point but we believe that this is not the case.[84] Although collusive activity was a part of the reason for mergers in the US, such activity was heavily penalized unlike the British situation where it was encouraged. The markets in which US merged companies operated before and initially after WWI were also starkly different from the ones British firms faced in the 1920s and 30s, in that growth opportunities for US companies both domestic and internationally were abundant and so real benefits resulted from scale economies.[85] British firms on the other hand in this period, as we described earlier, were dealing with

---

79   On cartelization and concentration see Hannah, L. (1983) The Rise of the Corporate Economy, London: Methuen, 64; and on the growth of subsidies see Middleton, R. (1996) Government Versus the Market: The Growth of the Public Sector, Economic Management and British Economic Performance, c. 1890–1979, Cheltenham: Edward Elgar, 365–369.

80   Lucas, A. (1937) Industrial Reconstruction and the Control of Competition: The British Experiments, New York: Longmans, 2.

81   Eichengreen, B. (2004) 'The British Economy Between the Wars' in Floud, R. and Johnson, P. (eds) The Cambridge Economic History of Modern Britain. Volume II: Economic Maturity, 1860–1939, Cambridge: Cambridge University Press, 340.

82   Lucas, A. (1935) 'The British Movement for Industrial Reconstruction and the Control of Competitive Activity', The Quarterly Journal of Economics, vol. 49(2), 208; and Kirby, M. (1992) 'Institutional Rigidities and Economic Decline: Reflections on the British Experience', The Economic History Review, vol. 45(4), 637–660.

83   Cornish, W. (1979) 'Legal Control Over Cartels and Monopolization 1880–1914: A Comparison' in Horn, N. and Kocka, J. (eds) Law and the Formation of the Big Enterprises in the Nineteenth and Early Twentieth Centuries, Gottingen, 283–5, 288; and Cheffins, B. (2004) 'Mergers and the Evolution of Patterns of Corporate Ownership and Control: The British Experience', Business History, vol. 46(2), 256–284.

84   Hannah, L. (1974) 'Mergers in British Manufacturing Industry, 1880–1918', Oxford Economic Papers, vol. 26, 14.

85   Broadberry, S. and Crafts, N. (1990) 'The Impact of the Depression of the 1930s on the Productive Potential of the United Kingdom', European Economic Review, vol. 34, 599–607; and Broadberry, S. and Crafts, N. (1990) 'The Implications of British Macroeconomic Policy in the 1930s for Long Run Growth Performance', Revista di Storia Economica, vol. 7, 1–19.

declining markets abroad and carefully controlled markets at home. Additionally British companies were tied, as a matter of government policy, into slow growth Commonwealth markets.[86] British managers were also under increased demands from labour as union membership leapt from four million in 1913 to eight million by 1919 and collective bargaining spread, widely encouraged by government as a force for stability.[87] The rise of the parliamentary labour party went hand in hand with this increased labour activity which became increasingly militant over the 1920s and 30s.[88] Ironically, in a period of high unemployment (unemployment reached 17 percent in the 1930s)[89] which should have weakened labour bargaining, labour power grew significantly while management protected from competition through tariffs and collusion avoided introducing new technologies that would mean workforce reduction and capital expenditure.[90] As Clay commented in 1929 '[t]oday there are no unorganized industries in this sense; wages are held up, either by trade-union or government support'.[91]

Significantly, in the US the merger wave resulted in a separation of ownership from control while the British merger wave did not. As Chandler describes it they 'remained federations of small, personally managed firms that failed to rationalize facilities or to develop overall organizational capabilities thus increasing the productivity and competitiveness of the combined enterprises or the industry as a whole'.[92] This may have been because of the nature of the mergers themselves in that the British wave was not in a sense driven by normal commercial considerations but one in which the incentive of all was to retain the status quo including family and bank interests.[93] There were, however, indicators of future seeds of change in that changes in share ownership were occurring as more private individuals

86   Broadberry, S. (1997) The Productivity Race: British Manufacturing in International Perspective, 1850–1990, Cambridge: Cambridge University Press.

87   Harris, J. (1972) Unemployment and Politics 1886–1914: A Study of English Social Policy, Oxford, Chapter 5.

88   Beenstock, M. and Warburton, P. (1986) 'Wages and Unemployment in Interwar Britain', Explorations in Economic History, vol. 23(2), 153–172; and Beenstock, M. and Warburton, P. (1991) 'The Market for Labor in Interwar Britain', Explorations in Economic History, vol. 28(3), 287–308.

89   Boyer, G. and Hatton, T. (2002) 'New Estimates of British Unemployment, 1870–1913', Journal of Economic History, vol. 62, 643–675.

90   Lazonick, W. (1981) 'Production Relations, Labor Productivity and Choice of Technique: British and US Cotton Spinning', Journal of Economic History, vol. 41, 491–516.

91   Clay, H. (1929) 'The Public Regulation of Wages in Britain', Economic Journal, vol. 39, 323–343 at 332.

92   Chandler, A., above n54, 297.

93   Payne, P. (1967) 'The Emergence of the Large-scale Company in Great Britain, 1870–1914', Economic History Review, vol. 20, 534–536; and Sklar, M. (1988) The Corporate Reconstruction of American Capitalism, 1890–1916: The Market, the Law, and Politics, Cambridge, 164–165.

and financial institutions purchased shares through the stock exchanges.[94] In turn this led to increasing scrutiny of financial information by investors and calls for more accurate disclosure in companies' accounts. In response the Companies Act 1929 introduced improved disclosure requirements including an obligation on companies to produce accounts that were 'properly drawn up so as to exhibit a true and correct view of the state of the company's affairs'.[95] In all it constituted a minimal response to shareholder concerns and in the aftermath of the great crash it was the stock exchange that became increasingly active in regulating the issue of listed shares in order to regain the shaken confidence of investors.[96]

The beginning of a move to dispersed ownership in this period is however a patchy story in which unfortunate timing may have played a crucial role in maintaining the status quo. In the immediate aftermath of the war a boom occurred between 1919–1920 fuelled by a war related lag in demand and a rosy view of the future prospects for British industry. Many firms made large profits in this period and refinanced using combinations of bank debt and issues of new shares in the expectation of expansion. The classic example of this was the cotton industry where a huge refinancing programme was engaged in during the two years after the war. Demand for shares in these companies led to the banks financing this industry expansion with very large short-term loans designed to be repaid quickly by the company issuing shares. When the boom ended this left companies with enormous fixed interest bearing debts and unable to issue new shares at anything near the value of the loans. The cumulative effect of this was to leave the banks and shareholders with investments worth significantly less than their original value and severely depressed regional stock exchanges.[97]

In turn this had important longer term effects as the banks became by default long-term financiers of declining industries. In attempting to keep these companies going investment and innovation was stifled and firms in those industries colluded to protect themselves, while waiting for things to get better when shares could be sold and loans repaid at some reasonable value.[98] The dampening weight of these frozen loans on the development of British industry in the interwar years was a source of significant concern for the government in a number of ways. First, the major concern was the precariousness of the finances of industry generally

---

94   Bowden, S. and Higgins, D. (2008) 'British Industry in the Interwar Years' in Floud, R and Johnson, P. (2008) The Cambridge Economic History of Modern Britain. Volume II: Economic Maturity, 1860–1939, Cambridge: Cambridge University Press, 399–401.

95   Companies Act 1929 s.134 (1).

96   Cheffins, B., above n1, 278–281.

97   On the cotton industry experience see Higgins, D. and Toms, J. (2001) 'Capital Ownership, Capital Structure and Capital Markets: Financial Constraints and the Decline of the Lancashire Cotton Textile Industry, 1880–1965', Journal of Industrial History, 48–64. On the similar experience of the steel industry see Tolliday, S. (1987) Business Banking and Politics: The Case of British Steel, 1918–1939, Cambridge, MA: Harvard University Press.

98   Best, M. and Humphries, J. (1986) 'The City and Industrial Decline' in Elbaum, B. and Lazonic, W. (eds) The Decline of the British Economy, Oxford, 230.

which if conditions deteriorated further would lead to mass insolvency and further unemployment problems. Second, if the companies defaulted on the loans the banks would collapse.[99] Third, there was the conflicting concern that the banks were stifling future industrial development by maintaining old technology and nursing unprofitable firms beyond their natural life. In the end the government opted to support stabilization and protection of the companies and banks but there was significant criticism of the banks' moribund control of companies and in turn blame for industrial decline from all quarters.[100]

While the banks eventually managed to get their loans repaid in the 1930s the early post WWI boom followed by another equity boom in the run up to the great stock market crash in 1929 may for short periods afterwards have dampened both internal and external enthusiasm for shares as a source of finance and investment. Nevertheless, as the economy picked up in the aftermath of sterling's devaluation in the 1930s another stock market boom occurred in which new issues of shares featured strongly.[101] Despite the bumpy ride for shareholders the number of commercial and industrial companies that had shares listed on the stock exchange had increased from 571 in 1907 to 1,712 by 1939.[102] Despite the changed power relationship between the UK and the US, the UK was the major European recipient of FDI from the US and the UK was by a huge margin the largest provider of FDI to the US in the interwar years.[103] Overall protective government intervention seemed to be successful in stopping the collapse of the British economy over the interwar years but in doing so it removed incentives for organizational and technological change which perpetuated decline in the longer term.[104]

The US, on the other hand, had a very different experience in the immediate post war period. The war had allowed US firms to pick up British business across the board and the war had proved a fertile source of business, supplying goods and services to economies given over to wartime production.[105] In the immediate aftermath of the war fear of British business returning drove US business to internationalize as never before to retain and expand markets.[106] Additionally by

99   See Sayers, R. (1976) The Bank of England, 1891–1944, Cambridge, 319.

100   See Balfour, A. (1929) Final Report of the Committee on Industry and Trade, Cmd 3282, London: HMSO, 52; and Macmillan, H. (1931) Report of the Committee on Finance and Industry, Cmd 3897, London: HMSO.

101   Cheffins, B., above n1, 290–292.

102   Hart, P. and Prais, S. (1956) 'The Analysis of Business Concentration: A Statistical Approach', Journal of the Royal Statistical Society, vol. 119, 150–191.

103   Eckes, A. and Zeiler, T. (2003) Globalization and the American Century, Cambridge: Cambridge University Press, 265 and 267.

104   Gourvish, T. (1987) 'British Business and the Transition to a Corporate Economy, Entrepreneurship and Management Structures', Business History, vol. 29, 18–45.

105   Becker, W. (1992) The Dynamics of Business-Government Relations: Industry and Exports, 1893–1921, Chicago: Chicago University Press, 136–137.

106   This was done largely in cooperation with the US government. See Becker, W., above n105, 137–143.

the end of the 1920s the US had become the world's largest creditor nation with loans increasing from $2.2 billion in 1919, to $7.2 billion in 1931. Over the same period FDI flowing out increased from $3.5 billion to $8.0 billion.[107] However, domestically this world wide expansion by US big business was becoming the subject of some suspicion as US economic nationalism increased over the 1920s and a common theme was a belief that the US had been dragged into WWI by big business attempting to protect its interests abroad.[108] In turn the Wall Street Crash in 1929 and the Great Depression in the 1930s caused a decline in US GNP of 46 percent and manufacturing production fell by 50 percent between 1929 to 1933. Unemployment rose over the same period from 1.5 million to 13 million.[109] The reaction of the government to the economic shock of the crash and the Great Depression that began with Hoover's mass government spending and tax raising programmes, continued with the growth of the role of government in the economy under Roosevelt's New Deal.[110] Roosevelt was elected in 1932 and proceeded to focus on protecting the domestic economy rather than facilitating international trade.[111] As part of that process of turning inwards questions arose about the legitimacy of the US managerial corporation.

The emergence of companies with dispersed shareholdings, operating outside the US and run by unaccountable managers was seen by some as a serious threat to society. As we discussed in Chapter 1, in 1932 Berle and Means having observed somewhat controversially[112] that ownership and control of America's largest corporations were separated, expressed concern that managers were not only unaccountable to shareholders but exercised enormous economic power which had the potential to harm the community.[113] Others however, while recognizing managerial power were more concerned with protecting managers from the undue

---

107   Eckes, A. and Zeiler, T., above n103, 63.

108   Mowrer, E. (1928) This American World, London: Faber and Faber, 221 and 246.

109   Robertson, R. (1973) History of the American Economy, Harcourt, 699.

110   Barber, W. (1985) From New Era to New Deal: Herbert Hoover, the Economists, and American Economic Policy, 1921–1933, Cambridge: Cambridge University Press, 189–196.

111   Eckes, A., above n73, 85–88.

112   We say controversial as their claims have been contested and subsequently reaffirmed by scholars in every decade since they made the original claim. For a flavour of the back and forth nature of the debate as to whether dispersal was as extensive as Berle and Means claimed see Zeitlin, M. (1974) 'Corporate Ownership and Control: The Large Corporation and the Capitalist Class', American Journal of Sociology, vol. 74, 1073–1119; and Larner, R. (1970) Management Control and the Large Corporation, New York: Dunellen Publishing Company Inc. The most recent claim that dispersal was not as widespread as they claimed has been made by Holderness. See Holderness, C. (2009) 'The Myth of Diffuse Ownership in the United States', Review of Financial Studies, 3. For an overview of the literature and a response to Holderness see Cheffins, B. and Bank, S. (2009) 'Is Berle and Means Really a Myth?' forthcoming Business History Review.

113   See Berle, A. and Means, G., above n36.

influence of bankers (a legacy of British investment in US companies) and with harnessing managerial power for the general good.[114]

Indeed, the role of banks in exerting self interested influence over companies is a feature of both the UK and the US in the interwar years. In the UK the standard story of bank involvement in industry is one of distance and an unwillingness, unlike other countries such as Germany, to act as long-term funders of industry. However, recent evidence has caused a re-evaluation of this view. As Ross describes it:

> [t]his dichotomy between distant and aloof British banks and the closely integrated, managing and assisting German banks has been shown to be greatly exaggerated ... English and Scottish banks took great care to nurse their industrial customers through periods of difficulty, exploiting as they did so the accumulated expertise of long term close relationships which recognised the mutual benefits of continued co-operation.[115]

Banks, its seems, had a much more active role within British industry in good times and bad than has commonly been understood, ranging from assisting in crisis management involving restructuring or liquidation, to advising on mergers and share issues. As we have noted earlier in this section, the interwar period saw exactly this engagement with industry.[116]

In the US much of the target of reform during the 1930s focused on the divisive role of bank influence within companies. As an area of study, the literature on US fears about bank influence goes back to the mid nineteenth century.[117] That literature has consistently shown banks to be central to the US network of public company board interlocks.[118] Interlocking directorates have been the subject of general academic research since the beginning of the nineteenth century.[119] While

---

114   See Bell, D. (1960) The End of Ideology, Glencoe, IL: Free Press.

115   Ross, D. (2008) 'Industrial and Commercial Finance in the Interwar Years' in Floud, R. and Johnson, P. (eds) The Cambridge Economic History of Modern Britain. Volume II: Economic Maturity, 1860–1939, Cambridge: Cambridge University Press, 422. See also Collins, M. (1998) 'English Bank Development within a European Context, 1870–1939', Economic History Review, 1–24.

116   Ross, D. (1990) 'The Clearing Banks and Industry: New Perspectives on the Inter-War Years' in van Helten, J. and Cassis, Y. (eds) Capitalism in a Mature Economy: Financial Institutions, Capital Exports and British Industry, 1870–1939, Edward Elgar, 52–70

117   Ibid.

118   Brandeis, L. (1914) Other People's Money and How the Bankers Use It, Boston: Bedford; Mariolis, P. and Jones, M. (1982) 'Centrality in Corporate Interlock Networks: Reliability and Stability', Administrative Science Quarterly, vol. 27, 571–584; and Mintz, B. and Schwartz, M. (1985) The Power Structure of American Business, Chicago: University of Chicago Press.

119   For an overview of the early work on interlocks see Hilferding, R. (1910) Finance Capital, London: Routledge & Kegan Paul (reprinted 1981).

there are overlaps in the literature four broad categories can be identified.[120] The first category – *the social interlock* – emphasizes the positive aspect of interlocking networks. It tends to emphasize the benefits to society of having managerial controlled corporations with board members in common, which are, where dispersed ownership patterns are present, free to provide social benefits rather than focus on profit. Business lobby groups and sometimes government reports have tended to draw on this literature to justify inactivity with regard to interlocks. The second category – *the collusive interlock* – based around the work of Hilferding emphasizes the collusive aspect of the interlocks. Hilferding focused on the use of interlocks by banks to secure their interests.[121] He argued that the interlock network was a key part of a system of collusion between bankers and industrialists. The third category – *the mediating interlock* – also focuses on banks as central to the interlocking networks but does not emphasize the collusive aspect. Rather a mediating interlock allows the banks to make decisions as to capital allocation. Mintz and Schwartz also argue that the interlock network allows banks to mediate inter-firm disputes, minimizing their risk exposure and enabling the industry to present the state with a unified position.[122] In the US, interlocks between competing companies are prohibited because of their potential to lead to collusion.[123] Indeed, in the US they have historically been seen as a highly corrupting practice on many levels. As Brandeis, the architect of the Clayton Act which prohibited interlocks between competing companies, stated in 1913:

> [t]he practice of interlocking directorates is the root of many evils. It offends human law and divine. Applied to rival corporations it tends to the suppression of competition and to violation of the Sherman law. Applied to corporations which deal with each other it tends to disloyalty and to violation of the fundamental law that no man can serve two masters. In either event it leads to inefficiency for it removes and destroys soundness of judgement.[124]

The original purpose of the bank representation on boards was as a way of protecting the investments of overseas (mainly British) investment in those

---

120   For an overview of the literature see Scott, J. 'Theoretical Frameworks and Research Design' in Stokman, F., Zeigler, R. and Scott, J. (1985) Networks of Corporate Power, Cambridge: Polity Press, 1–19; Scott, J. and Griff, C. (1985) Directors of Industry: The British Corporate Network, 1904–1976; Cambridge: Polity Press; Glasberg, D. (1987) 'The Ties that Bind? Case Studies in the Significance of Corporate Board Interlocks with Financial Institutions', Sociological Perspectives, vol. 30, 19–48; and Mizruchi, M. (1996) 'What Do Interlocks Do? An Analysis, Critique and Assessment of Research on Interlocking Directorates', Annual Review of Sociology, vol. 22, 271–302.

121   Hilferding, R., above n119.

122   Mintz, B. and Schwartz, M. (1985) The Power Structure of American Business, Chicago: University of Chicago Press.

123   Clayton Act 1914, s.8.

124   Brandeis, L. (1913) Breaking the Money Trusts, Harpers Weekly, 6 December, i.

companies but over time they had developed to exhibit elements of mediating and collusive interlocks which became the focus of regulatory reform after the abuses evident in the stock market crash in 1929.[125] After the New Deal banking and securities reforms, bank influence diminished although the board interlocks still existed, as the banks still had control over short-term lending.[126] Similarly, by the late 1930 British banks influence was diminishing as the frozen loans from the early 1919–20 boom were at last repaid as prosperity returned.[127]

For the US Left driving Roosevelt's New Deal economic reforms in this period the emergence of dispersed shareholding was viewed as a positive development which had brought about the destruction of the family elites who had controlled American capital and indeed for some even the seeming end of capitalism itself.[128] The creation of the Securities and Exchange Commission and the raft of reforming banking and securities legislation in the early 1930s were in the words of its future Chairman William O. Douglas 'symbolic of a shift of political power. That shift is from the bankers to the masses; from the promoter to the investor. It means the government is taking the side of the helpless, the suckers, the underdogs'.[129]

For many others the manager dominated corporation was a positive development in American democracy whereby inherited wealth was no longer the determinant of success. Only in the US according to this view could one rise from the mail room to the board room based on talent and hard work alone. As Mizurichi comments:

> [r]ather than sharing Berle and Means' suspicion of managerialism as ushering in a dangerous era of concentrated economic power, American sociologists and other social scientists thus praised the new system as a further extension of democracy. This was reflected in statements about "peoples' capitalism", in which the widespread dispersal of stockholdings meant that corporations were, for practical purposes, publicly controlled, as well as in formulations about the "soulful corporation", concerned as much about its position as a respected member of the community as with its pursuit of profit. In fact, the pursuit of profit was deemed no longer necessary, as great size, market power, and weak

---

125   Coffee, J. (2000) 'The Rise of Dispersed Ownership', Columbia Law and Economics Working Paper No. 182, 31, available at <http://ssrn.com/abstract=254097>. See also Carosso, V. (1970) Investment Banking in America: A History, Cambridge, MA: Harvard University Press, 32–33.

126   The Glass-Steagall Act of 1933 separated commercial and investment banking until 1999 when most of it was repealed by the Gramm-Leach-Bliley Act of 1999. See Stearns, L. (1986) 'Capital Market Effects on External Control of Corporations', Theory and Society, vol. 15, 47–75, and Mintz, B. and Schwartz, M. (1985) The Power Structure of American Business, Chicago: University of Chicago Press.

127   See Best, M. and Humphries, J., above n98.

128   See Dahrendorf, R. (1959) Class and Class Conflict in Industrial Society, Stanford: Stanford University Press, 41; and Riesman, D. (1953) The Lonely Crowd, New Haven: Yale University Press, 242.

129   Douglas, W. (1934) 'Protecting the Investor', Yale Review, vol. 23, 521 at 522.

and disorganized stockholders allowed corporate managers to pursue goals other than profits ...[130]

Judicial protection of managerial discretion also increased markedly from the 1930s. Business judgement rules for example had been present in some US states from the mid nineteenth century but it was only from the late 1920s onwards that the Delaware courts developed the concept.[131]

A key moment in this period came in the public debate between Berle and Dodd.[132] As we discussed in Chapter 1, Dodd argued that companies have responsibilities to society which may involve unprofitable acts. The managers of such companies are as a result the ones who must exercise their powers to ensure the company's responsibility to a combination of shareholders, employees, consumers and the general public. Berle responded to Dodd's article agreeing with his general theme of corporate obligations to society but opposing Dodd's solution as too nebulous and a charter for managerial abuse. He argued that shareholders and maximizing wealth for shareholders should be the sole focus of managerial power and a channel for societal benefit.[133]

The tangible manifestation of these arguments about the obligations owed to society by US managerial companies were three pieces of employment legislation

---

130　Mizruchi, M. (2004) 'Berle and Means Revisited: The Governance and Power of Large U.S. Corporations', Theory and Society, vol. 33, 579 at 583.

131　See Nelson, L. (1980–81) 'Judgement Day for the Business Judgement Rule', Brooklyn Law Review, vol. 47, 1169–1204; and Towers, S. (1990) 'Ivanhoe Partners v. Newmont Mining Corporation – The Unocal Standard: More Bark Than Bite?', Delaware Journal of Corporate Law, vol. 15, 483–538. SEC proxy rules and the Williams Act also had similar effects see Hansmann, H. and Kraakman, R. (2001) 'The End of History for Corporate Law', Georgetown Law Journal, vol. 89, 439–468; and Brennan, B. (1991) 'Current Developments Surrounding The Business Judgement Rule: A "Race to the Bottom" Theory of Corporate Law Revived', Whittier Law Review, vol. 15, 299–326 at 302.

132　Berle, A. (1931) 'Corporate Powers as Powers in Trust', Harvard Law Review, vol. 44, 1049; Dodd, E. (1932) 'For Whom Are Corporate Managers Trustees?', Harvard Law Review, vol. 45, 1145; Berle, A. (1932) 'For Whom Are Corporate Managers Trustees: A Note', Harvard Law Review, vol. 45, 1365; and Dodd, E. (1935) 'Is Effective Enforcement of the Fiduciary Duties of Corporate Managers Practicable?', University of Chicago Law Review, vol. 2, 194. On the influence of the debate see Nesteruk, J. (2005) 'Response: Enriching Corporate Theory', American Business Law Journal, vol. 42(1–6), 91–95; Macintosh, J. (1999) 'The Issues, Effects and Consequences of the Berle-Dodd Debate, 1931–1932', Accounting, Organisations and Society, vol. 24(2), 139–153; and Weiner, J. (1964) 'The Berle-Dodd Dialogue on the Concept of Corporation', Colombia Law Review, vol. 64(8), 1458.

133　Bratton, W. and Wachter, M. (2007) 'Shareholder Primacy's Corporatist Origins: Adolf Berle and The Modern Corporation', Institute for Law & Economics, University of Pennsylvania Law School, Research Paper No. 07–24, available at <http://ssrn.com/abstract=1021273>. See also Tsuk, D. (2003) 'Corporations without Labor: The Politics of Progressive Corporate Law', University of Pennsylvania Law Review, vol. 151(6), 1861.

in the 1930s. The first piece of legislation was the Norris-LaGuardia Act which gave federal backing to the rights of workers to organize and pursue collective bargaining agreements. Significantly it removed the injunctive powers of Federal Courts in many employment disputes. In 1935 the National Labor Relations Act (NLRA) was passed allowing workers free choice of union, and the ability to pursue collective bargaining and concerted actions for their own protection. The National Labor Relations Board was also set up under the NLRA to oversee the operation of its provisions. In 1937 the Fair Labor Standards Act introduced a federal minimum wage and set maximum working hours.[134] In all the three Acts introduced minimum standards for all workers while providing a framework for workers and management to engage in collective agreements.

In Britain WWI had been a significant catalyst of institutional transformation as small government became large government, industrial relations were transformed as employment became a core focus of government policy, free trade was abandoned and tariffs and anti-competitive practices became the norm. None of this happened without resistance from path dependent institutions. The reflotation of sterling at too high a level, the return to free trade after the War until 1931 in the face of world wide protectionism and the almost disastrous flirtation with stock market financing that left banks as a major influence over a wide range of industries were all elements in resistance to or misunderstanding of the transformations that were occurring. The shock of the great crash and the following depression represented further stimulus to transformation as it ushered in, with UK currency realignment and protectionism in Britain, the beginning of the final period of this institutional transformation that would be completed by the further shock of WWII. In all Britain had entered a period of systemic unworkability in the interwar years. In the US institutional transformation also occurred beginning with the growth of the state in WWI and culminating with the raft of New Deal legislation in the 1930s again in the aftermath of the great crash and depression, which left the state and labour with enhanced roles within the marketplace and a concomitant reduction in managerial discretion.

Thus on the eve of WWII the corporate governance landscape of Britain and the US although different was beginning to show some similarities as they responded to war, stock market crash and depression. Both British and US companies operated from a protected home market and both faced declining markets as a result of economic nationalism around the world, as world trade dwindled. In both countries the state had grown significantly to exert a high degree of control over the economy. As managers in both countries faced increased labour bargaining power the internalization of job markets was becoming more common.[135] In both countries banks were a diminished influence. The key differences were that in

---

134   Stone, K. (2008) 'The Future of Labor and Employment Law in the United States', UCLA School of Law, Law and Economics Research Paper Series Research Paper No. 08–11, 3.

135   Ibid., 4.

Britain family control was still persistent although signs of change were present, while in the US ownership of large companies was separated from control.[136] Additionally in Britain, collusion was permitted while in the US such practices were not permitted although firms operating abroad were protected with high tariffs and subsidies to allow them to compete with companies from other countries who could collude.[137]

The Post War Settlement

In the immediate period after WWII, starting with the Bretton Woods agreement in 1944, international cooperation with the aim of promoting economic security became a priority. In 1945 the United Nations was founded as an agency of world governments facilitating cooperation in international law, security, economic development, and social equity.[138] Under its auspices a wide range of organizations devoted to economic cooperation came into being or were brought within its umbrella. These organization ranged from the World Bank (WB), the International Monetary Fund (IMF), the United Nations Economic, Scientific and Cultural Organization (UNESCO), the Food and Agriculture Organization (FAO), the World Health Organization (WHO), the International Labor Organization, the International Standards Organization (ISO), the World Meteorological Organization (WMO), the International Atomic Energy Agency (IAEA), the International Maritime Organization (IMO) to the International Civil Aviation Organization (ICAO). However, by 1946 it was clear that the multilateral vision of the post war intergovernmental landscape would not operate, as the beginning of the Cold War meant the carving up of the world into different spheres of influence.[139] This had a particularly distorting effect on the Bretton Woods agreement and the General Agreement on Trade and Tariffs (GATT). In the face of Soviet withdrawal from the Bretton Woods institutions and the General agreement on Trade and Tariffs plus the inability of many states in the immediate post war period to keep to their obligations under the Bretton Woods and associated agreements, Britain being the main defaulter, the US came to dominate these institutions and use them as

---

136   Bowden, S. and Higgins, D. (2004) 'British Industry in the Interwar Years' in Floud, R. and Johnson, P. (2004) The Cambridge Economic History of Modern Britain. Volume II: Economic Maturity, 1860–1939, Cambridge: Cambridge University Press, 399–401.

137   Wilkins, M. (1974) The Maturing of the Multinational Enterprise, Cambridge, MA: Harvard University Press, 52–53.

138   Basic facts about the United Nations: United Nations Deptartment of Public Information. News and Media Division (2004) About the United Nations, United Nations Publications, 3.

139   James, H. and James, M. (1994) 'The Origins of the Cold War: Some New Documents', The Historical Journal, vol. 37(3), 617.

an arm of US government policy.[140] Thus the period after the war, although it contained the roots of future globalization, is a story of further movement away from globalization towards the fragmentation of the world economy into different spheres of influence, whereby the United States and the Soviet Union emerged determined to exert economic and military power over the rest of the world.[141]

In the 'free world' the Bretton Woods agreement created, as we described in Chapter 3, the institutions to maintain a stable macroeconomic environment so that war torn countries could recover free from speculative capital flow attacks. However, in this initial period after the war even the Bretton Woods institutions could not handle the scale of the crisis the war torn economies of Europe and Asia found themselves in. As a result of this and the fear that economic instability particularly in Europe would lead to Soviet influence, the US set in place unilateral aid either directly to governments or through the Marshall Plan providing funds to rebuild the European economies.[142] Thus the trend was set whereby economics became a weapon in the cold war and globalization moved firmly off the agenda until 1986 when the US no longer perceived the Soviet Union as a threat.[143]

US corporate governance during the post war period

Over the course of WWII the growth of US government intervention in the economy continued and was viewed with suspicion by US business. Its continued role after the war and its attempts to construct a post war world in which governments came together to regulate international business through GATT and Bretton Woods, seemed to some initially at least not that much different than the Soviet model. As Eckes and Zeiler describe it:

> [w]hen Roosevelt and Truman talked about a "new deal" for the post war world –
> as they did in selling the Bretton Woods accords – the image of a world run by
> government regulators traumatized the private sector, especially among those
> with fiduciary responsibilities to weigh relative risks and gains in assessing
> investment opportunities.[144]

---

140   Milward, A. (1980) War, Economy and Society, 1939–1945, University of California Press, 364; Gardner, R. (1969) Sterling-Dollar Diplomacy: The Origins and Prospects of our International Economic Order, New York: McGraw-Hill, 71–95; and Vatter, H. (1985) The U.S. Economy in World War II, Columbia University Press, 159–163.

141   Gaddis, J. (1990) Russia, the Soviet Union and the United States. An Interpretative History, New York: McGraw-Hill, 151–176.

142   Ibid., 186; and Spero, J. (1985) The Politics of International Economic Relations, St Martins Press, 36–42. In Germany's case reparations payments to the allies outweighed Marshall Plan funding. See Giersch, H., Paqué, K. and Schmieding, H. (1992) The Fading Miracle: Four Decades of Market Economy in Germany, Cambridge: Cambridge University Press, 115.

143   Thatcher, M. (1993) The Downing Street Years, HarperCollins, 471 and 813.

144   Eckes, A. and Zeiler, T., above n103, 117.

Similarly, labour relations in the US became increasingly adversarial in the immediate years after the war as days lost to strike action rose dramatically.[145] However, the Soviet threat brought a change of attitude and while suspicions remained, the US government, business and organized labour formed a partnership which would last throughout the first part of the Cold War.[146] That partnership often led to actions being taken in the national interest but not in the interests of US industry or individual companies.[147] For example, the reintegration of the Japanese and German economies into the international economy was facilitated by enormous technology transfers from US companies.[148] In the cases of the car and consumer electronics industries those transfers would eventually create their major competitors.[149] For the same national security reasons, successive GATT rounds saw the US act specifically against the interests of its own domestic industry in allowing access by foreign companies to US markets without any reciprocal arrangement.[150] With the focus of the rest of the world on rebuilding behind defensive trade and capital barriers international trade was very slow to recover from the war, as was US private sector investment abroad. As late as the 1970s US government funding abroad ran at twice the amount provided by private industry.[151] The domestic US economy however grew solidly in the initial period after WWII. A significant part of this was the fact that government funding for military technology increased employment and had associated commercial civilian spin-offs for US companies. Similarly road, air and sea infrastructure improvements related to military needs also had enormous benefits

145   Ross, A. (1961) 'The Prospects for Industrial Conflict', Industrial Relations: A Journal of Economy and Society, vol. 1(1), 57–74 at 58; and on industrial relations generally in the post war period see Ross, A. and Hartman, P. (1960) Changing Patterns of Industrial Conflict, London: Wiley & Sons.

146   McQuaid, K. (1982) Big Business and Presidential Power: From FDR to Regan, Morrow, 122–168.

147   Although sometimes it worked out well despite the fact the company considered its actions uneconomic. IBM for example entered the computer business for largely patriotic rather than economic reasons. See Flamm, K. (1988) Creating the Computer: Government, Industry and High Technology, Brookings, 86–87.

148   To some extent though this was just making up for massive technology transfers from the defeated axis powers after the War. See Judt, M. and Ciesla, B. (1996) Technology Transfer Out of Germany After 1945, London: Routledge, 87.

149   Abegglen, J. and Stalk, G. (1985) Kaisha: The Japanese Corporation, Tuttle, 126–8; and Dobyns, L. and Crawford-Mason, C. (1991) Quality or Else: The Revolution in World Business, Boston, MA: Houghton Mifflin, 10.

150   Zeiler, T. (1999) Free Trade, Free World: The Advent of GATT, University of North Carolina Press, 167–190; and Eichengreen, B. above n81, 243.

151   Wilkins, M. (1970) The Maturing of the Multinational Enterprise: American Business Abroad from 1914 to 1970, Cambridge, MA: Harvard University Press, 285–324; and Kunz, D. (1997) Butter and Guns: America's Cold War Economic Diplomacy, New York: Free Press, 48–49.

for employment generally as well as goods and passenger movement. Crucially the US had emerged undamaged from the war which gave it a head start on most of the other major economies. These factors combined with the business, government and organized labour partnership had a virtuous circle effect as business expanded, employment increased as strike action diminished and wages increased.[152] Thus as we noted in Chapter 3 the golden age of capitalism in the US was premised on a stable macroeconomic framework provided by Bretton Woods institutions but supplemented by massive US government spending and active government control of the economy which created positive growth conditions in which cold war solidarity between capital and labour had a significant beneficial effect for all concerned. Additionally although collusion was heavily penalized, competitive conditions were relatively benign until the early 1960s, when the rebuilt European and Japanese economies began to make serious inroads into US markets.[153]

However, combinations of competitive issues were beginning to cause significant changes to the operation of the US managerial corporation. Over the course of the 1950s the US government had heavily restricted horizontal and vertical mergers.[154] Conflicting with this competition policy, tax incentives worked heavily in favour of mergers and acquisitions (M&A) as an engine of profitability. Beginning in the 1950s and peaking in the late 1960s companies who were restricted from pursuing M&A strategies in their own or related industries started to pursue M&A targets in unrelated industries, where the tax incentives would still operate but no anti-trust issues arose.[155] Managerial empire building was also no small part of the incentive to merge or engage in takeovers.[156] Thus companies grew in size and were operating in different often diverse industries where management had little experience. As Chandler has argued this had a serious negative effect on control within these new merged entities:

> [i]ncreasingly top managers at the corporate office ... lost touch with the middle managers responsible for maintaining the competitive capabilities of the operating divisions in the battle for market share and profits. This disconnection of corporate from operating management affected the competitive strength of

---

152   Eckes, A. and Zeiler, T., above n103, 152–154. On the link between economic growth and military spending see Kunz, D., above n151, 63.

153   Chandler, A. (1992) 'Corporate Strategy, Structure and Control Methods in the United States During the 20th Century', Industrial and Corporate Change, vol. 1(2), 263–284 at 273.

154   Fligstein, N. (1990) The Transformation of Corporate Control, Cambridge, MA: Harvard University Press, 30 and 163.

155   Chandler, A., above at n153, 276.

156   Mueller, D. (1969) 'A Theory of Conglomerate Mergers', Quarterly Journal of Economics, vol. 83(4), 643–659 at 644.

American companies and industries far more than the separation of ownership control and management ever had.[157]

As a result US companies suffered badly as competition from domestic and overseas rivals intensified. This merger wave also had a significant long-term effect on the operation of the stock market.

In the years after WWII American workers began saving for the longer term through pension and mutual funds. In turn institutional investors such as pension and mutual funds became significant holders of shares in US listed companies from the 1950s onwards.[158] This had two effects on the market for corporate control. First, institutional investors tended to trade shares regularly and in large blocks meaning that as institutional holdings increased a larger amount of shares were easily available for purchase on any given day, which facilitated M&A transactions. Second, in an environment where M&A activity could be described as a 'mania' – control rights in US companies began to have real importance, particularly as hostile takeovers began to emerge as a threat to management and the premiums paid for control rights became significant.[159]

In the 1950s there were a small number of high profile hostile takeovers which increased significantly over the course of the 1960s. Hayes and Taussig found for example that between 1956 and 1960 just 79 attempted hostile takeovers occurred. In the period 1964 to 1966 that number had increased to 156.[160] To put those numbers in context, Chandler estimates the total number of M&A in 1965 to be 2,000, in 1968 to be 4,500 and during the 'mania' year of 1969 to be 6,000.[161] Thus the number of hostile takeovers was small relative to the overall number of M&A. Nevertheless, despite their low numbers and the fact they were highly controversial, they were increasingly a threat to management and further enhanced the importance of shareholders. In response to the merger wave and resultant management fears, Federal and State level legislation was introduced to regulate M&A activities. In Delaware amendments to its General Corporation Law were made in 1967 that were designed to protect management increasingly worried about litigation arising from their defensive actions in M&A transactions. The effect of both the merger wave itself and this enactment was to cement Delaware's status as the incorporation state of choice as a wave of reincorporation from other

---

157   Chandler, A., above n153, 276.

158   Armour, J. and Skeel, D. (2006) 'Who Writes the Rules for Hostile Takeovers, and Why? The Peculiar Divergence of US and UK Takeover Regulation', ECGI – Law Working Paper No. 73/2006, 50, <http://ssrn.com/abstract=928928>.

159   Hayes, S. and Taussig, R. (1967) 'Tactics of Cash Takeover Bids', Harvard Business Review, vol. 45(2), 135–148 at 140.

160   Ibid., 137.

161   Chandler, A., above n153, 273; and The Harvard Law Review Association (1969) 'Cash Tender Offers', Harvard Law Review, vol. 83(2), 377–403.

states ensued as managers sought the most protective legal environment.[162] At the Federal level the Williams Act 1968 while designed to assist shareholders by ensuring disclosure and equality of treatment for shareholders, further protected management by slowing down the bidding process which provided management with time in which to mount a defence.[163] In all by the late 1960s the combination of government and labour partnership, new foreign entrants as a result of the newly revived European and Asian economies, the need to either plan or defend takeovers and mergers and the difficulties of running a large company operating in many different industries, introduced significant pressures on managerial discretion and produced negative performance outcomes by the 1970s.

British corporate governance during the post war period

The interwar years and the disruption of WWII did not leave Britain well prepared for the Golden age of capitalism.[164] While the US had a head start in not facing any rebuilding programme and cold war military spending had a positive civilian application for US companies, Britain had no such advantages.[165] As the devastated economies of Japan and Germany enjoyed an economic resurgence, Britain largely sat on the sidelines during this period.[166] While Britain's growth rate between 1950 and 1973 was historically high at 3 percent, the average growth rate experienced by the other big economies was 4.6 percent.[167] In 1950, Britain, despite the battering of another world war, provided 25 percent of world manufacturing exports. By 1975 it had been reduced to 9 percent as relative decline took effect. As Britain's historical Empire based markets shrank, continental European economies became more significant and GATT rounds slowly reduced British tariffs, the world became a more competitive place and the pattern of declining share of export markets accompanied by large scale import penetration was repeated across most

---

162   Dodd, P. and Leftwich, R. (1980) 'The Market for Corporate Charters: "Unhealthy Competition" Versus Federal Regulation', The Journal of Business, vol. 53(3), 259–83 at 268.

163   See Armour, J. and Skeele, D., above n158, 32–34.

164   Eichengreen, B., above n71, 122–126.

165   Hendry, J. (1990) Innovating for Failure: Government Policy and the Early British Computer Industry, Cambridge, MA: MIT Press, Chapter 13.

166   Broadberry, S. (1988) 'The Impact of the World Wars on the Long Run Performance of the British Economy', Oxford Review of Economic Policy, vol. 4(1), 25–37; and Crafts, N. (1982) 'The Assessment: British Economic Growth over the Long Run', Oxford Review of Economic Policy, vol. 4(1), i–xxi at viii.

167   Kitson, M. (1997) 'The Competitive Weaknesses of the UK Economy' in Arestis, P., Palma, G. and Sawyer, M. (eds) Unemployment and Economic Policy: Essays in Honour of Geoff Harcourt, London: Routledge, 133–149.

of Britain's manufacturing sector.[168] Over this period Britain's part of and influence in the international economy declined significantly.[169]

Wartime management of the economy by the state was generally deemed to have been a success and so the distinguishing characteristic of this period in Britain from the end of the war until the 1970s was a continued and expanded role for the state in co-coordinating the economy. Churchill's Conservatives had been rejected by the electorate because of their association with the hardships of both the 1930s and the war.[170] Under the new Labour government the public sector expanded enormously through innovations such as the National Health Service and the nationalization of a range of industries, as full employment became the central plank of government policy.[171] Industrial policy in this period favoured nationalization, industry concentration, collusion and national champions, which had significant long-term negative effects on the economy.[172] One important feature of the post war British economy was the emergence of a much enhanced labour movement from the wartime economy. The management of the economy had been a successful partnership of government, business and organized labour during the war. Indeed, in 1940 Ernest Bevin the general secretary of the Transport and General Workers Union became the minister for labour in the wartime cabinet, while Hugh Dalton his labour party colleague became minister for economic welfare. Bevin's position not only proved to be one of the key cabinet posts in managing the war time economy but also allowed Bevin to plan labour's role in the post war world.[173] In this period after the war with a new labour government in power this resulted in a state, labour and industry partnership characterized by a nationalization programme (coal, civil aviation, steel, transport, gas and electricity)[174] and by centralized bargaining which resulted in significant stability in wage and dividend restraint.[175] This consensus to some extent held together in the shadow of the Soviet threat throughout the 1950s, even though it was mostly a

---

168   Alford, W. (1988) British Economic Performance, 1945–1975, Basingstoke: Macmillan, 15; Elboum, B. and Lazonic, W. (eds) (1987) The Decline of the British Economy, Oxford: Clarendon; and Owen, G. (1999) From Empire to Europe: The Decline and Revival of British Industry Since the Second World War, HarperCollins.

169   Cairncross, A. (1995) The British Economy Since 1945, Oxford: Blackwell, 297.

170   Dallas, G. (2006) 1945: The War That Never Ended, Yale University Press, 501.

171   See Crafts, N. (2002) Britain's Relative Economic Performance 1870–1999, Institute of Economic Affairs: Research Monograph No. 55, 9.

172   Geroski, P. (1990) 'Innovation, Technological Opportunity and Market Structure', Oxford Economic Papers, 586–602; and Broadberry, S. (2001) Competition and Innovation in 1950s Britain, Business History, 97–118.

173   Taylor, R. (2000) The TUC: From the General Strike to New Unionism, Palgrave, 38.

174   Cheffins, B., above n1, 80–81.

175   Flanagan, R., Soskice, D. and Ulman, L. (1983) Unionism, Economic Stability and Incomes Policy: The European Experience, The Brookings Institute; and Eichengreen, B. (1996) 'Institutions and Economic Growth: Europe after World War II' in Crafts, N. and Toniolo, G. (eds) Economic Growth in Europe since 1945, Cambridge: Cambridge University Press.

period of conservative government.[176] Gower writing in 1955 in the Harvard Law Review and referring to the Dodd and Berle debate on the 1930s in that journal noted that:

> [s]o far at any rate as England is concerned public opinion seems to have hardened in favour of Dodd's view, so that it has become almost an accepted dogma that management owes duties to "the four parties to industries" (labor, capital, management, and the community) – a dogma which is repeated indiscriminately in the speeches of right-wing company chairmen and left-wing politicians.[177]

However, the partnership was increasingly questioned and over the course of the 1960s while successive governments attempted wage restraint through central bargaining, it was often subverted.[178] By the late 1960s and early 1970s strike action had become damaging to the economy as the number of working days lost through strike action rose enormously. In 1967 the number of working days lost to strikes was fairly representative of the average over the initial post war period at 2,787,000. In 1968 that figure rose to 4,690,000, in 1969 to 6,846,000, in 1970 to 10,980,000, in 1971 to 13,551,000 and by 1972 it reached 23,909,000 as the post war consensus broke down.[179]

One success story in the period after the war was the financial services sector. In the post war years as taxation incentives moved strongly in favour of holding long-term savings in collective investments, such as through pension and insurance providers, building societies grew as providers of mortgages, and banks expanded their services, the financial services sector grew rapidly.[180] In turn US FDI in Britain increased as did UK FDI in the US in this period after the war.[181] By the 1950s listed companies were a key part, if not the key part, of the British economy

---

176   Eichengreen, B., above n81, 124–125; and Tomlinson, J. (2004) 'Economic Policy' in Floud R and Johnson, P. (eds) The Cambridge Economic History of Modern Britain. Volume III: Structural Change and Growth, 1939–2000, Cambridge, 210.

177   Gower, L., above n178, 1190. See also Cheffins, B., above n1, 340–341 corporate ownership and control, on the widespread acceptance of a broad conception of the corporate interests at this time.

178   Broadberry, S. and Crafts, N. (1996) 'British Economic Policy and Industrial Performance in the Early Postwar Period', Business History, 65–91; and Broadberry, S. and Crafts, N. (1998) 'The Post-War Settlement: Not Such a Good Bargain After All', Business History, 73–79. On government attempts to restrain dividend in this period see Daunton, M. (2002) Just Taxes; The Politics of Taxation in Britain, 1914–1979, Cambridge, 247–256; and Gower, L. (1955) 'Corporate Control: The Battle for Berkeley', Harvard Law Review, vol. 68(7), 1176.

179   See Wrigley, C. (2002) British Trade Unions since 1933 (New Studies in Economic and Social History), Cambridge: Cambridge University Press, 43.

180   Wilson, K. (1983) British Financial Institutions: Savings and Monetary Policy, Prentice Hall, 16; and Cheffins, B., above n1, 802–807.

181   Eckes, A. and Zeiler, T., above n103, 265 and 267.

as equity finance grew in importance.[182] For example internal finance made up 94 percent of British corporate investment in the period 1952–1955. However, by 1971–1976 internal finance had reduced to 80 percent.[183] Slowly companies were increasing their reliance on long-term loans and equity.[184] Additionally, the Cold War had a paradoxical benefit for the financial services sector as we noted in Chapter 3. By the late 1950s international capital was once again flowing spurred by the new convertibility of European currencies.[185] While technically the UK government had implemented capital controls in the Exchange Control Act 1947, the Eurodollar market based in London but held through 'offshore' accounts grew enormously as the UK government, in a successful attempt to revive the financial markets in London, somewhat perversely allowed the Soviet Union and its satellite states to place its overseas dollar reserves in London.[186] The combination of its unregulated status, high interest rates on deposits and low lending rates proved very popular with companies and governments around the world.[187] As we discussed in Chapter 3, this allowed a huge pool of capital to exist outside the Bretton Woods system.[188]

The combined effect of new financing opportunities and a new competition regime had a particular effect on ownership and control in British companies in this period. Over the course of the 1950s and 1960s partly in response to new competition legislation but also as a result of managerial empire building a merger wave occurred in Britain resulting in increased concentration in most industries.[189]

---

182 Cheffins, B. (2001) 'Does Law Matter? The Separation of Ownership and Control in the United Kingdom', Journal of Legal Studies, vol. 30, 459–484.

183 Thomas, W. (1978) The Finance of British Industry, 1918–1976, London: Routledge & Kegan Paul, 315.

184 Paish, F. (1965) Business Finance, Pitman, 132–137; and Capie, F. and Collins, M. (1992) Have the Banks Failed British Industry?: Historical Survey of Bank/Industry Relations in Britain, 1870–1990, Institute of Economic Affairs.

185 Under the Bretton Woods Agreement currencies were convertible into gold or US dollars. Many countries in the aftermath of the war found this impossible to achieve, however by the late 1950s a number of countries including Britain tentatively introduced limited convertibility. See Fforde, J. (1992) The Bank of England and Public Policy, 1941–1958, Cambridge, 566 and Chapter 9 generally.

186 The Soviet union was concerned the US might impound its reserves as the Cold War grew more hostile so it moved its reserves out of the US and into London. For a more extensive discussion on the emergence of the Euromarkets see Burn, G. (2006) The Re-emergence of Global Finance, Palgrave; and Pilbeam, K. (2006) International Finance, 3rd edition, Basingstoke: Macmillan, Part III.

187 See Hill, C. (1998) International Business: Competition in the Global Marketplace, Chicago: Irwin/McGraw and Hill, 331–332.

188 Martin, R. (1994) 'Stateless Monies, Global Financial Integration and National Economic Autonomy: The End of Geography?' in Corbridge, S., Martin, R. and Thrift, N. (eds) Money, Power and Space, Oxford: Blackwell, 257.

189 See Jones, G., above n69, 128; and Singh, A. (1975) 'Takeovers, Economic

Unfortunately, the governments hoped for positive effects on the competitive environment of large size and increased competitiveness never materialized.[190] As Jones considered:

> [a] particular problem after 1945 was the uncompetitive home market of British industry. In the early 1950s between 50 and 60 percent of manufacturing output was regulated by cartels. The advent of a more assertive British competition policy led to their dismantling, only to be replaced by mergers leading to growing concentration. British governments between the 1940s and the 1970s continued to encourage and support actively collusive agreements in sectors as diverse as banking and agriculture, while in the 1960s and 1970s there was a series of ad hoc attempts to create "national champions" in manufacturing industry.[191]

In this anti-competitive setting British firms reaped huge profits and grew to large sizes.[192] In turn the move to dispersed shareholding accelerated rapidly as family shareholdings were diluted and they gave up their disproportionate representation on the boards of listed companies.[193] As was the experience in the US, whereby institutional investors such as pension funds, insurance companies and mutual funds became significant holders of shares, the same occurred in Britain.[194] In the UK though, this occurred on a much larger scale as the tax regime created an incentive for private individuals to sell their shares in this period and at the same

---

Natural Selection and the Theory of the Firm: Evidence from the Postwar Experience', Economic Journal, vol. 85(339), 497–515.

190   The literature on this concentration wave is large and consistent in its conclusion that increased firm size and industry concentration had a negative effect. See for example Hannah, L. (1980) 'Visible and Invisible Hands in Great Britain' in Chandler, A. and Daems, H. (eds) Managerial Hierarchies, Cambridge, MA: Harvard University Press, 71; Payne, P. (1990) 'Entrepreneurship and British Economic Decline' in Collins, B. and Robbins, K. (eds) British Culture and Economic Decline, Weidenfeld and Nicolson, 30–31; Prais, S. (1976) The Evolution of Giant Firms in Britain, Cambridge: Cambridge University Press; and Cheffins, B., above n1, 360–361.

191   See Jones, G., above n69, 130.

192   Eichengreen, B., above n71 125–126; and Crafts, N. and Mills, T. (2005) TFP Growth in British and German Manufacturing 1950–1996, Economic Journal, vol. 115(505), 649–670.

193   Families often held onto board seats even after they had ceased to hold significant shares in the company but this practice rapidly diminished in the second part of the twentieth century. See Franks, J., Mayer, C. and Rossi, S. (2004) 'Spending Less Time with the Family: The Decline of Family Ownership in the United Kingdom', NBER Working Paper No. W10628 9–10; and Hannah, L. (1983) The Rise of the Corporate Economy, Methuen, Chapter 10.

194   Armour, J. and Skeel, D., above n158.

time institutional investors had strong tax led incentives to purchase shares.[195] As a result private shareholding started to diminish as institutions took their place.

As the managerial corporation began to emerge in the 1960s, British managers began to exert their enhanced discretion in the same way as US managers were doing in the US by building larger and larger companies. Interaction between UK and US managers and labour was significant here. During the war the interaction of business leaders engaged in the joint prosecution of the war was strong and in the decade afterwards these informal interactions were formalized in the Anglo-American Council on Productivity. Through it British managers and trade unionists learned about US production techniques and tried, mostly unsuccessfully, to implement them.[196] However, while similar knowledge exchange occurred with German and Japanese managers in the post war period there were limits to the extent certain management strategies could be implemented in Japan and Germany in the absence of a comparable financial system.[197] These limits were not present in the UK because of the similarities in the UK and US financial systems. As a result the growth through M&A activity facilitated by the existence of a stock exchange in the US and described by Chandler as driven by '[m]anagerial hubris' was mimicked by UK managers.[198] As Kitson describes it:

> [a]lthough there was a rapid growth in mergers and takeovers during the 1950s and 1960s this primarily reflected managers pursuing their own interests, such as the desire to take control of a bigger business, rather than efficiency, the interests of shareholders and ultimately economic growth.[199]

The results were similar in that UK firms grew in size and senior managers lost touch with the operating divisions of the company.[200]

In a similar manner to the US experience, hostile takeovers also began to appear in the UK from the 1950s, attracting much media and government attention. While first the controversy was directed at the hostile bidder, whose behaviour, as in the initial phase of hostile bids in the US, was deemed unacceptable. However, as managers responded with, judged by the standards of the time, fairly aggressive

---

195   Cheffins, B. and Bank, S. (2007) 'Corporate Ownership and Control in the UK: The Tax Dimension', Modern Law Review, vol. 70(5), 778–811; and Cheffins, B., above n1, 344–349.

196   See Broadberry, S. and Wagner, K. (1996) 'Human Capital and Productivity in Manufacturing During the Twentieth Century: Britain Germany and the United States' in van Ark, B. and Crafts, N. (eds) Quantitative Aspects of Europe's Postwar Growth, Cambridge; and Hutton, G. (1953) We Too Can Prosper, British Productivity Council.

197   Eckes, A. and Zeiler, T., above n103, 182–183.

198   See Chandler, A., above n153, 276; and Singh, A., above n189.

199   Kitson, M. (2004) 'British Economic Growth since 1949' in Floud, R. and Johnson, P. (eds) The Cambridge Economic History of Modern Britain. Volume III: Structural Change and Growth, 1939–2000, Cambridge, 44.

200   Jones above n69.

anti-shareholder defences, public, media and government disquiet focused on the seemingly unfettered powers of managers.[201] While Companies Acts in 1948 and 1967 had improved disclosure standards for shareholders and the LSE has increased its oversight where self-interested transactions were at issue, managers still retained a very wide discretion under British company law.[202] However, unlike the US where hostile takeovers brought about legislative reform, in the UK industry itself provided the solution. In 1958 an attempt to fight off a hostile bid by management of British Aluminium (BA) was defeated by institutional investors tired of the manipulative behaviour of BA management.[203] Control rights, as in the US, from this point on really began to matter.

This high profile incident led to the formation, by the Bank of England, of a working party to draw up a set of guidelines for takeovers. Institutional investors were strongly represented on the working party while no management organization was included. In 1959 a self-regulatory set of guidance notes known as the 'Notes of Amalgamations of British Business' were issued, based around the principle that shareholders make the key decision on a takeover, However, they were often ignored and as a result of significant problems in the 1960s, the LSE and the Bank of England set up the Panel on Takeovers and mergers to oversee takeovers in the UK, through the administration of a code on takeovers and mergers.[204] Again institutional investors exerted a strong influence on the outcome, although this time management associations were involved in the process. The central guiding principle of shareholder decision making from the 'Notes of Amalgamations' was continued in General Principle No. 7 of the City Code, which enshrined the principle that management should not interfere with the bid and that shareholders will make the decision as to the merits of a bid. As Franks et al. described it:

> [f]or a brief period, the UK took on the appearance of Continental Europe with dual class shares, pyramids and discriminatory price acquisitions. But the takeover defences incurred the wrath of the institutions, which mounted a successful attack on them through the Stock Exchange and succeeded in devising the rules by which takeovers were to be conducted.[205]

---

201   Gower, L., above n178, 1176.

202   Gower, L., above n59, 55; and 515–599; and Cheffins, B., above n1, 328–333.

203   Cheffins, B., above n1, 363–364.

204   On the background to the formation of the Panel see Armour, J. and Skeel, D., above n158, 56–59; Davies, P. (1992) 'The Regulation of Defensive Tactics in the United Kingdom and the United States' in Hopt, K. and Wymeersch, E. (eds) European Takeovers: Law and Practice, Butterworths, 200; and Johnston, A. (1980) The City Takeover Code, Oxford, Chapter 1.

205   Franks, J., Mayer, C. and Rossi, S. (2004) 'Spending Less Time with the Family: The Decline of Family Ownership in the United Kingdom', NBER Working Paper No. W10628, 23.

The period between the war and the 1970s in the UK and US was a period of initial stability and then the beginnings of change. The continued growth of government control of the economy with a focus on demand led management fostering employment in the shadow of a new Soviet threat, was a strong feature of this period. Government, business and labour operated in partnership to initially produce stability in the UK and a 'golden era' in the US.

However, the seeds of change were also evident. In both countries competitive conditions began relatively benignly but as GATT reductions in tariffs and the recovered German and Japanese economies began to make inroads into UK and US markets, competition intensified. In both the UK and US responses to competitive pressures led to a wave of mergers and the beginning of the hostile takeover as a threat to managers. In the UK the growing influence of institutional investors ensured the response to regulating takeovers was to introduce a self-regulatory oversight focused on shareholders. In the US by contrast, where institutional investors were not as significant as the UK, the response was to protect management rather than shareholders. Increasingly competitive markets were also bringing about organizational change in both the UK and US. UK companies were rapidly moving to an arm's length relationship with their shareholders as families relinquished their shares and institutional shareholders took then up. In the US the merger wave led to companies growing in size and operating in diverse industries with a resulting loss of control of senior management over operations. The merger wave and nascent market for corporate control was also beginning to make control rights in corporations extremely significant. In the UK at the same time as shareholder power was growing, labour relations were deteriorating as the industry, government, labour partnership broke down.

Conclusion

As we described above the UK and the US have a shared history of trade and investment because of their former colonial relationship. However, despite this shared history, on the eve of war in 1914 Britain and the US looked very different in terms of their corporate governance systems. Britain still had traditional owner managed firms and operated in an open free trade environment in which the state and labour did not operate to constrain management discretion significantly. The US was dominated by managerial companies trading globally but from behind a protective tariff system. Labour was not a significant constraining influence on management and the dispersal of shareholders in these companies meant that managers were free from any sort of insider control. However, there was a higher level of state control of their activities than in Britain, as highly unusually the growth of big business preceded the growth of government in the US and so suspicion of US companies resulted in active state involvement in protecting the consumer against collusive behaviour by companies. These collusive issues were not a significant concern in the UK and would continue to mark a key difference between the two corporate governance systems for most of the twentieth century.

During the interwar years the corporate governance landscape changed significantly as the war disrupted trade and economic nationalism rose. Britain abandoned free trade and introduced a wide range of tariff barriers as world trade dwindled in the Great Depression. In both countries the role of government in the economy increased, as did labour bargaining power. Although in the 1920s banks had exerted significant influence over companies in the UK and the US, by the late 1930s banks were a diminishing influence. The major differences between the two countries remained that in Britain, family control still persisted, while in the US shareholding was dispersed and in Britain collusion was not only tolerated but coordinated by central government. As a result by 1939 banks had come and gone as influences on management, families persisted as an influence on British management, competitive pressures on management discretion were greater in the US and in both countries the state and organized labour had also come to exert pressure on management discretion.

The period between the end of WWII up until the mid 1960s was a period of stability in the face of the challenge of the Cold War. Macroeconomic stability was achieved through the Bretton Woods agreement whereby the rebuilding process necessitated by the WWII could be completed. The continued growth of the state's involvement in the control of the economy is a major feature of the period as government, business and organized labour coordinated their activities to ensure stability and growth and in Britain nationalization of industries occurred. However, as the German and Japanese economies recovered after the war, they began, due to favourable GATT treatment and massive financial and technological transfers from the US, to make serious inroads into US and UK markets. The response of companies in the UK and the US to this changed competitive environment was a merger wave and the beginning of the hostile takeover as a management threat. The merger wave in the UK resulted in families beginning to divest their shareholdings and institutional shareholders replacing them. Although competition legislation partly encouraged the merger wave in the UK, collusion still featured in the UK. In both the US and the UK, the merger wave had the effect of companies growing in size and operating in many different industries with the resultant loss of control by senior management.

In all the post war period is a tale of the further growth of influence of the state and labour on management discretion in the UK and the US. In Britain, families diminished in influence leaving a significant discretion for managers for a brief period which accelerated a merger wave. However, institutional investors who replaced families as major shareholders began to grow in influence as hostile takeovers emerged as a pressure on managerial discretion. In both countries competitive conditions had an influence on management discretion and the merger wave additionally damaged managerial performance as senior management lost control of operating units. By the 1970s the state, labour, business post war partnership was breaking down.

As we noted in the introduction to this chapter the corporate governance classification literature has settled on a neat generalization of insider and outsider systems. However, it is important to note that corporate governance systems may well be categorizable as insider or outsider but within that classification there are versions that differ significantly. Some insider systems may result in managerial dominance, some bank dominance, some state dominance or some may have representational models were a balance of stakeholder input is achieved.[206] Institutional transformation therefore can occur broadly within the insider paradigm as well as to an outsider system. For example, a bank based insider system might, as a result of a shock to its institutional structure, come as a result of institutional rearrangement to be dominated by the state.

The UK over the time period we have analysed here does not in our view conform to a shareholder oriented outsider system of corporate governance. While the stock exchange was a source of finance which increased over time, at almost all points along the way families, banks, government and labour exerted significant influence over managerial discretion. Additionally, competitive pressures were negated by government instigated collusion or tolerance of collusion and from the 1930s protective tariff barriers eliminated overseas competition. Similarly, the US does not conform to a shareholder oriented outsider system of corporate governance in this period. In the US while the stock exchange was important as a source of finance and dispersed ownership of large US companies was a feature throughout this period, managerial discretion was significantly influenced at various points by banks, government and labour while dispersed shareholders were unable to exert control. Competitive pressures were greater than in the UK, but US companies had much greater protection through tariff barriers than UK companies did prior to the 1930s.

In the previous chapter we considered Amable's distinction between 'change', which occurs within the general logic of an institutional system and 'destabilization' which results from a shock to the system that pushes institutional realignments in a new direction. In the US the wall street crash and the Great Depression seem to us to have caused an economic shock that led to institutional destabilization, unworkability and a reorientation of the role of the Government and labour in the economy. State intervention under Hoover and then the New Deal reforms were genuinely transformative of the US corporate governance system as the government demand function in the economy expanded enormously, labour power was significantly enhanced and the financial system reformed by the New Deal

---

206   See for example the difference between the Italian and German insider models, Bianchi, M. and Casavola, P. (1996) 'Piercing the Corporate Veil: Truth and Appearance in Italian Listed Pyramidal Groups', Fondazione Mattei, nota di lavoro, 6.96; and on Germany see Wengenroth, U. (1997) 'Germany: Competition Abroad – Cooperation at Home, 1870–1990' in Chandler, A. et al., above n69, 32.

securities and banking legislation.[207] This did not though transform it to an outsider system but rather moved it to a stronger insider model.

Beginning with the economic aftermath of WWI Britain suffered a series of institutional shocks in the interwar years and it entered a period of systemic unworkability as path dependent forces failed to recognize Britain's loss of economic power. Events related to the crash and the depression in the UK, eventually brought about a recognition of Britain's changed status in the world economy but the depression had a real impact in inflicting hardship in the 1930s that played a role in the outcomes caused by the further destabilizing shock of WWII.[208] The general election in 1945 saw the unexpected rejection of Churchill and the Conservative party after the war as the general populace abandoned the party they associated with the misery of the 1930s and had brought about a devastating war, however victorious they had been.[209] The labour government elected in 1945 introduced a nationalization programme, a comprehensive welfare state, the building of the National Health Service and represented, in effect, Britain's more socialist New Deal as path dependent forces collapsed. By the 1950s both countries moved deeper into the insider paradigm. However, the seeds of corporate governance transformation along a different path were evident by the late 1960s. We turn in the next chapter to examine the transformation of the UK and the US from insider to outsider shareholder oriented systems and what it tells us about change and transformation in insider systems.

207   Barber, W., above n110.
208   Kitson, M. and Michie, J. (2000) The Political Economy of Competitiveness: Essays on Employment, Public Policy and Corporate Performance, London: Routledge, 69–108.
209   Dallas, G., above n170.

Chapter 6

The Emergence of Outsider Corporate Governance Systems in the UK and US: From the End of the Golden Age to Globalization

Introduction

In this chapter we examine the transformation of the UK and the US corporate governance systems from insider systems, where the government, labour and in the case of the UK – families, exerted a significant influence on managerial discretion, to outsider systems with a core managerial focus on shareholders. Over the course of the 1970s as the post war consensus of state, labour and business partnership began to break down, competitive pressures increased and at the same time shareholders in the form of institutional investors challenged for influence. This changing environment coincided with the collapse of the Bretton Woods system and two external shocks in the form of oil crises which eventually brought about radical economic change in the 1980s and a dramatic change in the orientation of the corporate governance systems, as labour and government were significantly reduced as an influence on managerial discretion. Into this power vacuum stepped institutional investors, who held sufficient shares in listed companies by the 1980s, to ensure that through the reorientation of market rules managerial discretion focused on shareholder interests. By the end of the 1980s the UK and the US had emerged as shareholder oriented outsider systems and their integrated capital markets, based on an outsider shareholder orientation, assumed nascent global market status.

The End of the Golden Age and the Beginning of Globalization

As we discussed in Chapter 1, the 1970s marked a turning point for the corporate governance systems of the UK and the US. The combined effect of funding massive Cold War demand led programmes within and without the US, self-inflicted trade distortions that favoured European and Asian companies over US companies and competition from resurgent German and Japanese economies began to pose serious problems for the US by the 1970s. Rising unemployment, high inflation and high interest rates ensued in both the UK and the US as stagflation (unemployment problems, slow growth and high inflation) took hold.[1] Higher taxes, price and wage controls were introduced in the US but failed to have a positive impact.[2] Additionally, attempts to defend the dollar ranging from central bank intervention to capital controls failed and by 1971 the US has its first merchandise trade deficit since 1893.[3] In response as we discussed in Chapter 3, the US effectively ended the Bretton Woods institutional structure by withdrawing in August 1971 and removing capital controls in 1974.[4] However, inflation remained persistent in both Britain and the US in the 1970s and the oil crisis in 1973–74 as a result of a boycott of the West by the Organization of Petroleum Exporting Countries (OPEC) increased the sense of general economic crisis. As Greenspan describes it:

> [t]he Arab oil embargo of October 1973 only made inflation and unemployment worse – not to mention hurting America's confidence and self esteem. The consumer price index ballooned: the year 1974 gave rise to the expression "double-digit inflation" as the rate went up to a shocking 11 percent. Unemployment was still 5.6 percent, the stock market was in steep decline, the economy was about to sink into the worst recession since the 1930s, and the Watergate scandal cast a pall over everything.[5]

Although there were primarily political motives behind the oil boycott, the ending of the Bretton Woods Agreement was also a factor in drastically increasing the price of oil in the 1970s. As oil is priced in dollars the depreciation of the dollar as a result of the end of Bretton Woods had reduced the amount of real income the oil exporting nations received. In turn OPEC re-priced oil against gold which by the mid 1970s allowed their real incomes to catch up with the dollar depreciation.[6] The US was particularly hard hit by this readjustment because of its heavy reliance on oil.[7] A second oil crisis in the wake of the Iranian revolution in 1979 increased the sense of crisis. US vulnerability was also felt in terms of the Cold War as the Soviet Union had become the world's largest oil producer by the end of the 1970s

---

1   Yergin, D. (1991) The Prize: The Epic Quest for Oil, Money and Power, New York: Simon & Schuster, 694–698; and Doder, D. (1980) 'Soviet Production of Gas, Oil Set Records Over 6 Months' in Washington Post, August 14, A24.

2   Greenspan, A. (2007) The Age of Turbulance, Penguin, 61–63.

3   Calleo, D. (1984) 'Since 1961: American Power in a New World Economy' in Becker, W. and Wells, S. (eds) Economics and World Power: An Assessment of American Diplomacy Since 1789, Columbia University Press, 398–409.

4   James, H. (1996) International Monetary Cooperation Since Bretton Woods, Washingston, DC: International Monetary Fund, 203; and Calleo, D., above n3, 412–424.

5   Greenspan, A., above n2, 62–63.

6   Hammes, D. and Wills, D. (2005) 'Black Gold: The End of Bretton Woods and the Oil-Price Shocks of the 1970s', The Independent Review, vol. 9(4), 501–511.

7   Carroll, P. (1982) It Seemed Like Nothing Happened: The Tragedy and Promise of America in the 1970s, Holt, Rinehart and Winston, 118–119 and 252–296; and Wyant, F. (1977) The United States, OPEC and Multinational Oil, Lexington, 74–83.

and the Soviet invasion of Afghanistan meant the USSR threatened the major oil producing nations of the Middle East.[8] The combined effect of all this was to significantly weaken world trade and move monetary policy away from demand management.[9] However, crisis would lead to change as Margaret Thatcher and Ronald Regan came to power with agendas that would transform the economies of both countries.

Transformation in the US

Nearly a decade of rising unemployment, high interest rates, high taxes, wage and price controls, a seemingly permanent stock market crash, a trade deficit and successive oil crises, gave momentum to the ideas of free market economists who viewed government interference as the root cause of much of the instability.[10] In the corporate theory contest, discussed in Chapter 1, the mid 1970s marked the point where Alchian and Demsetz and Jensen and Meckling provided a nexus of contracts model that began to seriously undermine the legitimacy of the insider model of the corporation that had been operating in the US up until this point. The nexus of contracts claims gained real traction because their timing i.e. massive economic shock, was crucial. Similarly in 1976, Milton Friedman the leading intellectual economic theorist advocating small government and a move away from demand management was awarded the Nobel prize for economics.[11] His ideas were to have a significant influence in both the UK and the US, as indeed did the nexus of contracts model of the corporation. US Government implementation of Friedman's ideas had begun under Carter in 1977 but would reach their apotheosis under Ronald Reagan.[12] In 1981 Ronald Reagan came to office with a free market inspired economic agenda for change focused on continuing the move away from demand management and reducing the role of the US government in the market. Government assets would over the course of the 1980s be privatized, income tax cut, free trade pursued and regulation reduced as market forces and a shareholder orientation were emphasized as a force for good. Perceived US vulnerability in the

8   Yergin, D. (1991) The Prize: The Epic Quest for Oil, Money, and Power, New York: Simon and Shuster, 609 and 619–625.

9   Kitson, M. (2004) 'British Economic Growth since 1949' in Floud, R. and Johnson, P. (eds) The Cambridge Economic History of Modern Britain. Volume III: Structural Change and Growth, 1939–2000, Cambridge, 48.

10   On the combined impact of these factors see Baker, D. (2007) The United States Since 1980, Cambridge: Cambridge University Press, 44–48 and 56–59.

11   The Economist, 'Milton Friedman's Legacy', 17 November 2006, available at <http://www.economist.com/daily/news/displaystory.cfm?story_id=8190872>.

12   Friedman was an adviser to Reagan see ibid. and Joskow, P., Noll, R., Niskanen, W. and Bailey, E. (1994) 'Economic Regulation' in Feldstein, M. (ed.) American Economic Policy in the 1980s, NBER Conference Report, 371–72.

Cold War was addressed by a re-emphasis on winning the Cold War which also meant that military spending would increase significantly.[13]

In 1981 and again in 1986 personal income tax rates were cut at the same time as monetarist policies were pursued by the Federal Reserve. Initially, a recession ensued and unemployment soared but by 1983 recession had been turned into robust growth which averaged over four percent from 1983 until 1989.[14] The price of this growth was a complete change in the role of the government in the economy. While in a general sense government spending increased under Reagan, this was mostly due to a huge military spending programme, outside of this a wide range of social welfare initiatives from the minimum wage to housing assistance were rolled back.[15] Deregulation or the adoption of business friendly approaches to regulation if it was necessary, became the order of the day. Industries such as haulage, airlines, telecoms and electricity had lighter touch regulation or complete deregulation applied.[16] The US Justice Department also took a more relaxed approach to anti-trust enforcement and encouraged the privatization of government assets.[17] It was however in its use of administrative measures that Reagan was most successful in achieving his deregulatory goals. On taking office Reagan ordered Federal agencies to do a cost benefit analysis on the effect of any new regulation and to implement only the least costly measures. This introduced a significant barrier to any new regulation. Budget and staff cuts in Federal agencies viewed as anti-business, were also effective in making enforcement of Federal standards against businesses difficult. Presidential appointees to head Federal agencies were chosen either because they knew nothing about the agency or because they had deregulatory agenda. Securities, labour, health and safety, discrimination and environmental protection laws were all reduced in effect through these types of administrative measures. This had the further effect of alienating staff committed to the roles of these agencies who in turn left to pursue careers elsewhere.[18] In a relatively short time the Reagan administration succeeded in reducing the effect

---

13   Niskanen, W. (1988) Reaganomics: An Insider's Account of the Policies and the People, Oxford: Oxford University Press.

14   Eckes, A. and Zeiler, T. (2003) Globalization and the American Century, Cambridge: Cambridge University Press, 208; and Feldstein, M. (1994) 'American Economic Policy in the 1980s: A Personal View' in Feldstein, M. (ed.) American Economic Policy in the 1980s, NBER Conference Report, 1–80.

15   On the budget deficit see Reeves, R. (2006) President Reagan: The Triumph of Imagination, New York: Simon & Schuster, 80–81; and Baker, D. above n10, 39–41 and 73–75.

16   Peoples, J. (1998) 'Deregulation and the Labor Market', Journal of Economic Perspectives, vol. 12(3), 111–130

17   Eckes, A. and Zeiler, T., above n14, 210–211.

18   Baker, D., above n10, 75; and Andrews, R. (1999) Managing the Environment, Managing Ourselves: A History of Environmental Policy in America, Yale University Press, 255–283.

of government in the marketplace.[19] There were two dramatic effects of this in the industrial relations and financial system.

In the US since the New Deal labour legislation, employment protection in the private sector hinged on union membership. If a worker was not in a union then they were subject to an 'employment at will' contract which meant they could be fired at any time, without any cause. Over the course of the Reagan presidency union membership dropped drastically as Reagan appointees dominated the National Labor Relations Board (NLRB). Up until 1981 the NLRB played a crucial role in the operation of employment protection in the US as it acted as a neutral arbiter of disputes over the rights of unions to organize and bargain collectively. Under the Reagan administration the NLRB became significantly more pro-business and anti-union. Vogel for example found that under the Ford presidency (1974–1977) 35 percent of cases found in favour of the company rather than the Union. Under Carter (1977–1981) that figure was 46 percent but under Reagan (1981–1989) it rose to 72 percent of cases.[20] Administrative obstructions also played a significant role in diminishing union power as the NLRB maintained a two year backlog of cases under Reagan. The combined effect of removing the neutrality of the NLRB was to allow companies to fire employees organizing unions with impunity.[21] Crucially Reagan's aggressive approach to public sector unions set the tone for future private sector management/union relations. In 1981 the Professional Association of Air Traffic Controllers (PATCO), one of the few unions to support Reagan in his presidential campaign, went on an illegal strike.[22] The union clearly thought they had a cooperative relationship with the Reagan administration as Reagan had written to the union during his campaign stating 'I pledge to you that my administration will work very closely with you to bring about a spirit of cooperation between the President and the air traffic controllers'.[23] This was not to be the case as Reagan fired all the strikers, replaced them with military air traffic controllers and arrested the PATCO leadership on criminal charges. While it would take nearly ten years to replace all the air-traffic controllers the action he took proved extremely popular with the general public and organized labour and business got the message that strike action would risk job losses.[24] The combined effect of Reagan's industrial relations policy was that very quickly

---

19   On the impact of 'Reaganomics' see Stockman, D. (1986) The Triumph of Politics: Why the Reagan Revolution Failed, HarperCollins; and Lekachman, R. (1984) Greed is Not Enough: Reaganomics, London: Random House.

20   Vogel, D. (1989) Fluctuating Fortunes: The Political Power of Business in America, Basic Books, 270.

21   LaLonde, R., Meltzer, B. and Weiler, P. (1991) 'Hard Times for Unions: Another Look at the Significance of Employer Illegalities', University of Chicago Law Review, vol. 58, 953–1014.

22   It is illegal for Federal employees to strike. See Baker, D. above n10, 36–37.

23   Quoted in Reeves, R., above n15, 63.

24   Ibid., 80 and 86–87.

union membership dropped significantly as union organizers could not operate, replacement workers became standard practice where strike action was taken and in turn strike action declined dramatically.[25] To add to the reduced role of labour in the economy, the Reagan administration vigorously pursued a free trade agenda where older US labour intensive industries, that were predominantly heavily unionized, were allowed to decline in the face of competition from imports.[26]

In Chapter 2 we discussed the importance of funded pension provision in promoting an outsider corporate governance orientation. As we noted in the previous chapter, one of the features of the financial system in the post war period was the growth in importance of the institutional investor in the financial system. Over the course of the 1970s generous tax incentives were provided for collective savings and pension funds in particular.[27] Furthermore, regulatory restrictions that existed during the 1960s preventing pension funds and life insurance companies from investing in equities were significantly relaxed, while in the late 1970s the Carter administration eliminated interest rate ceilings.[28] At the same time, high inflation, mainly as a result of the two consecutive oil crises, meant that fixed income securities like bonds provided mediocre yields that could not cover the needs of the institutional investors' beneficiaries. This induced institutions to seek higher returns in riskier assets. With the steady growth of stock markets the obvious solution was investment in equities and other high-risk securities. Most importantly, institutions invested in low-value bonds (junk bonds) which are risky but high-yield securities issued by companies lacking an established or sound earnings history. Moreover, with the growth of institutional assets, the abolition of fixed commissions for securities transactions, which held up trading volume, became inevitable. The elimination of fixed commissions in the 1970s[29] dramatically increased trading volume and unleashed unprecedented amounts of

25   Baker, D. above n10, 68–71; and Goldfield, M. (1989) The Decline of Organized Labor in the United States, Chicago: University of Chicago Press.

26   Eckes, A. (1995) Opening the American Markets: US Foreign Trade Policy since 1776, University of North Carolina Press, 245–248.

27   See for example the Employment Retirement Income Security Act (ERISA) of 1974; and Eckes, A. and Zeiler, T., above n14, 216.

28   ERISA was amended in 1978 to permit the investment of substantial proportions of pension funds' and insurance companies' assets in stocks and other high-risk securities.

29   The Securities and Exchange Commission prohibited fixed commissions on May 1, 1975. This decision was enacted a month later by the Securities Acts Amendments 1975.

capital into equity markets.[30] In 1960 for example total transactions on the NYSE reached 3 billion, by 1985 there were 27.5 billion transactions.[31]

In turn as stocks and bonds were placed in direct competition with each other in terms of yields they could offer, a general preference for higher short-term returns on equity was created, which in turn created pressures for higher dividend distributions by listed corporations.[32] As we noted in Chapter 3 as real interest rates constantly exceeded real growth rates shareholders had little interest in cash retention by companies and preferred the distribution of cash-flows and their reinvestment in high-yield securities.[33] It was in the context of a rapidly changing financial market that the Reagan administration encouraged financial market deregulation and a focus on shareholders. In 1981 Reagan appointed John Shad, a Republican campaign supporter and vice-chairman of a brokerage firm to the post of Chairman of the SEC. Shad while not actively hostile to the role of the SEC was nevertheless committed to a much less proactive role for the SEC.[34] During the course of his Chairmanship he set about deregulating the financial system to encourage a focus on shareholder oriented market based solutions and as a result oversaw an enormous speculative boom that led to the market crash in 1987.[35] Indeed, some of his actions in rolling back SEC oversight contained

---

30   Lazonick, W. and O'Sullivan, M. (1996) 'Organization, Finance and International Competition', Industrial and Corporate Change, vol. 5(1), 1–49 at 22; Davis, P. (1996) 'The Role of Institutional Investors in the Evolution of Financial Structure and Behaviour', Paper presented in the Reserve Bank of Australia's Conference on 'The Future of the Financial System', held on 8–9 July 1996 in Sydney; and Blommenstein, H. (1998) 'The New Financial Landscape and its Impact on Corporate Governance' in Balling, M., Hennessey, E. and O'Brien,. (eds) Financial Markets and Global Convergence, The Hague: Kluwer Academic Publishers, 41–70 at 46.

31   Chandler, A. (1992) 'Corporate Strategy, Structure and Control Methods in the United States During the 20th Century', Industrial and Corporate Change, vol. 1(2), 263–284 at 279.

32   Jones, G. (1997) 'Great Britain: Big Business, Management and Competitiveness in Twentieth-Century Britain' in Chandler, A., Amatori, F. and Hikino, T. (eds) Big Business and the Wealth of Nations, Cambridge, 136; and Short, H., Zhang, H. and Keasey, K. (2002) 'The Link Between Dividend Policy and Institutional Ownership', Journal of Corporate Finance, vol. 8(2), 105–122.

33   Lazonick, W. (1992) 'Controlling the Market for Corporate Control: The Historical Significance of Managerial Capitalism', Industrial and Corporate Change, vol. 1(3), 445–488 at 456.

34   Seligman, J. (1995) The Transformation of Wall Street: A History of the Securities and Exchange Commission and Modern Corporate Finance, Northeastern University Press, 575–577; and Vise, D. and Coll, S. (1991) Eagle on the Street, New York: Charles Scribner's Sons, 24–25.

35   A series of Pulitzer prize winning articles were written about John Shad's SEC during this time. The articles were published as Vise, D. and Coll, S., above n34. See also Stewart, J. (1991) Den of Thieves, New York: Simon & Schuster. Shad Chairmanship is discussed at pages 12, 26, 42, 234, 245, 283, 297 and 425. See also Stein, B. (1992)

the seeds of the later Enron and WorldCom scandals.[36] Additionally in 1982, the Reagan administration initiated the Garn- St Germain Depository Institutions Act 1982 which permitted US banks including Savings and Loan Associations to hold high yielding but high risk junk bonds.[37] Fierce competition within the deregulated financial markets ensued which made investments in high-risk securities a very attractive activity for banks and institutional investors. The combination of deregulation and the earlier removal of capital controls also had a dramatic effect on capital flows. In 1982 US FDI amounted to $207.8 billion and by 1990 that figure had reached $430.5 billion. International transactions in equities and bonds increased from 9 percent of US GDP in 1980, to 89 percent in 1989. US foreign equity holdings also increased from $89 billion in 1984 to $314 billion in 1989 as outsider capital flowed abroad. Overseas holders of US equities and bonds also increased enormously from $268 billion in 1984 to $847 billion in 1989 as capital generally became global.[38] In 1980 there were only 37 foreign companies listed on the NYSE, that number increased significantly over the 1980s to reach 246 by 1995.[39]

Thus, by the 1980s both the demand and the supply were present for the establishment of a large market for equities and junk bonds. It was this market in the early 1980s that created the conditions for an unparalleled wave of hostile takeovers in the US with financial institutions being the main participants.[40] In particular, the high demand for junk bonds facilitated the financing of hostile

---

A License to Steal: The Untold Story of Michael Milken and the Conspiracy to Bilk the Nation, New York: Simon & Schuster. Shad is discussed on pages 23, 77, 154 and 176.

36   He removed SEC oversight of non-audit work by accounting firms at the point when even the accountancy firms themselves had recognized the potential for abuse. See Brewster, M. (2003) Unaccountable: How the Accounting Profession Forfeited a Public Trust, John Wiley and Sons, 167–168.

37   Cornett, M. and Tehranian, H. (1990) 'An Examination of the Impact of the Garn-St. Germain Depository Institutions Act of 1982 on Commercial Banks and Savings and Loans', Journal of Finance vol. 45(1), 95–111.

38   Eckes, A. and Zeiler, T., above n14, 216.

39   Ramos, S. (2006) 'Technological and Deregulation Shocks and Stock Market Development', CEMAF/ISCTE Business School, 46, available at <http://www.fep.up.pt/ conferencias/pfn2006/Conference%20Papers/475.pdf>.

40   Henwood, D. (1997) Wall Street, New York: Verso. A major turning point, at least in the US, was the successful takeover of Electric Storage Battery by International Nickel Company of Canada financed by Morgan Stanley in 1974. Allegedly this changed the attitudes of investment bankers who until then regarded hostile takeovers as 'dirty business'; Lipton, M. and Panner, M. (1993) 'Takeover Bids and United States Corporate Governance' in Prentice, D. and Holland, P. (eds) Contemporary Issues in Corporate Governance, Oxford: Clarendon Press, 115–134 and 117. For similar attitudes that persisted in Germany until well into the 1990s see Chapters 7 and 8.

takeover bids for even the largest corporations.[41] Whereas in previous decades M&A activity had been driven by managers' strategic or 'hubristic' desires, the 1980s M&A wave saw the rise of transaction oriented M&As. These were M&As driven by entrepreneurs and financial intermediaries who intended to make profits out of the transactions themselves, rather than any long-term desire to profit from the ownership of the target or merged company.[42] In this environment a very active market for corporate control was established where companies with excess cash flows became targets and where acquirer companies ended up with massive amounts of debt to pay off, after the transaction's completion.[43] As Armour and Skeel describe it:

> [f]ueled by a combination of Michael Milken's discovery of the financing potential of high yield debt, deregulation, and a gentler approach by the Reagan administration to antitrust regulation, takeover activity soared to a level not seen since the great merger wave at the end of the Gilded Age.[44]

In this environment hostile takeovers became common and in turn where litigation ensued the Delaware courts favoured managers' defences during a bid, as in turn did individual states who introduced management friendly anti-takeover statutes in response to the 1980s takeover wave.[45] However, these protective provisions seemed only to raise the price necessary to succeed in a bid rather than necessarily defeat a bid.[46] Managers therefore faced enormous pressures to boost the market value of their companies to retain control and where they did lose control often

---

41   According to an SEC study, junk bonds accounted for 33 percent of the financing in the largest tender offers in the US; Coffee, J. (1986) 'Shareholders Versus Managers: Strain in the Corporate Web', Michigan Law Review, vol. 85, 1–109. See also Yago, G. (1990) Junk Bonds: How High Yield Securities Restructured Corporate America, Oxford: Oxford University Press, and Taggart, R. (1988) 'The Growth of the "Junk" Bond Market and Its Role in Financing Takeovers' in Auerbach, A. (ed.) Mergers and Acquisitions: Causes and Consequences, Chicago: University of Chicago Press, 5–24.

42   Bhagar, S., Schleifer, A. and Vishney, R. (1990) 'Hostile Takeovers in the 1980s: The Return to Corporate Specialization', Brookings Papers on Economic Activity: Microeconomics, 55.

43   Goldstein, D. (2000) 'Hostile Takeovers as Corporate Governance? Evidence from the 1980s', Review of Political Economy, vol. 12(4), 381–402. On the SEC's role in the boom see Vise, D. and Coll, S., above n34, 171–206.

44   Armour, J. and Skeel, D. (2006) 'Who Writes the Rules for Hostile Takeovers, and Why? The Peculiar Divergence of US and UK Takeover Regulation' ECGI – Law Working Paper No. 73/2006, 35, available at <http://ssrn.com/abstract=928928>.

45   Ibid., 34–35.

46   See Comment, R. and Schwert, G. (1995) 'Poison or Placebo? Evidence on the Deterrence and Wealth Effects of Anti-Takeover Measures', Journal of Financial Economics, vol. 39, 3; and Schwert, W. (2000) 'Hostility in Takeovers: In the Eyes of the Beholder?', Journal of Finance, vol. 55, 2599. Others would however argue the evidence is mixed see

the implementation of downsizing or labour reduction strategies or a combination of both was needed to pay off the amassed debts in the aftermath of a bid.[47] Thus, the takeover boom of the 1980s led to mass speculation, fraud and eventually to the "Black Wednesday" stock markets crash in October 1987.[48] Beginning in 1986 and continuing into the 1990s the expansion of saving and loan organizations into risky assets led to a wave of collapses that would eventually cost the taxpayer $132.1 billion.[49] John Shad left office shortly before the crash in 1987 and in 1989 became Chairman of Drexel Burnham Lambert, the Wall Street investment bank that pioneered the use of junk bonds, shortly before it collapsed.[50] Michael Milken the driving force behind Drexel and the junk bond market of the 1980s was indicted on 98 counts of racketeering and securities fraud in 1989. He was eventually sentenced to ten years in prison but was released after two years. Although the cost of his fines, litigation and payments to creditors amounted to $900 million he emerged with his fortune mostly intact.[51]

Transformation in the UK

The 1970s in Britain was a similar experience to the US in that high inflation, rising unemployment, recession and high interest rates featured strongly. Britain's entry into the European Economic Community (EEC) in 1973 had also required the elimination of trade barriers with other EEC countries further fuelling increased import penetration.[52] Business investment was further restrained by the spectre of

---

Bebchuk, L., Bar-Gill, O. and Barzuza, M. (2006) 'The Market for Corporate Law', Journal of Institutional and Theoretical Economics, vol. 162, 134.

47   Lazonick, W, and O'Sullivan, M. (2000) 'Maximizing Shareholder Value: A New Ideology for Corporate Governance', Economy and Society, vol. 29(1), 13–35 at 18.

48   The literature on this period is vast and entertaining for example see Binstein, M. and Bowden, C. (1993) Trust Me: Charles Keating and the Missing Billions, New York: Random House; Burrough, B. and Helyar, J. (1990) Barbarians at the Gate: The Fall of RJR Nabisco, New York: Harper & Row; Day, K. (1993) S&L Hell: The People and the Politics Behind the $1 Trillion Savings and Loan Scandal, New York: Norton; Lewis, M. (1989) Liar's Poker: Rising Through the Wreckage on Wall Street, New York: Norton; and Lorsch, J. with MacIver, E. (1989) Pawns or Potentates: The Reality of America's Corporate Boards, Boston, MA: Harvard Business School Press.

49   U.S. General Accounting Office (1996) 'Financial Audit: Resolution Trust Corporation's 1995 and 1994 Financial Statements', 13.

50   Vise, D. and Coll, S., above n34, 353–381.

51   Vise, D. and Coll, S., above n34, 373–376; and Forbes Magazine (2007) 'The World's Billionaires #458 Michael Milken', available at <http://www.forbes.com/lists/2007/10/07billionaires_Michael-Milken_SSM6.html>.

52   Eichengreen, B. (2004) 'The British Economy Between the Wars', and Tomlinson, J. (2004) 'Economic Policy', both in Floud, R. and Johnson, P. (eds) The Cambridge Economic History of Modern Britain. Volume III: Structural Change and Growth, 1939–2000, Cambridge, 187 and 195.

a further programme of nationalization once the labour government came to power in 1974.[53] The oil crisis in 1973–4 also boosted inflation and in 1976 the collapse of sterling forced the government to seek IMF assistance.[54] Labour unrest was also a feature throughout the 1970s in Britain culminating in the 'Winter of Discontent'[55] in 1978–1979 where private and public sector strike action at government attempts at pay restraint, led to food shortages, electricity blackouts and streets piled with uncollected refuse.[56] Strike action reached a post war peak of 29,474,000 working days lost as a result of strike action in 1979.[57] In all, as in the US, a sense of cumulative crisis pervaded the decade.

Although the disruption that brought about the 'Winter of Discontent' was over by February 1979 it played a key part in the defeat of the labour government and the election of the Conservative Party in May 1979, led by Margaret Thatcher. Although the previous government had experimented with monetarism as a solution to inflationary woes, Thatcher, as with Reagan, had come to power inspired by a free market Friedman agenda of monetarism and reduced government involvement in the market.[58] The effect of using monetarism, combined with a contraction of world trade after the second oil crisis in 1979 and a very strong pound, had by 1981 brought about a short but deep recession during which a quarter of British manufacturing industry was wiped out and unemployment rose from 5 percent in 1979 to 10 percent in 1980.[59] The combined effect of this was not entirely unhelpful to the government's agenda as it weakened the unions and emboldened management to challenge the unions. As part of this agenda the government introduced a raft of employment legislation making it more difficult to strike and

53   Seldon, A. and Hickson, K. (2004) New Labour, Old Labour: The Wilson and Callaghan Governments, 1974–79, London: Routledge, 57–58.

54   Hickson, K. (2005) The IMF Crisis of 1976 and British Politics: Keynesian Social Democracy, Monetarism and Economic Liberalism: The 1970s Struggle in British Politics, I.B. Tauris.

55   The phrase was borrowed by many newspapers from Shakespeare's Richard III: ACT 1, SCENE 1, 1–4: 'Now is the winter of our discontent, Made glorious summer by this son of York; And all the clouds that low'r'd upon our house, In the deep bosom of the ocean buried.'

56   Seldon A. and Hickson, K., above n53, 57.

57   Wrigley, C. (2002) British Trade Unions since 1933 (New Studies in Economic and Social History), Cambridge: Cambridge University Press, 43.

58   Feinstein, C. (1994) 'Success and Failure: British Economic Growth since 1948' in Floud, R. and McCloskey, D. (eds) The Economic History of Britain Since 1700. Volume III, 1939–1992, Cambridge, 114; and Eichengreen, B. above n5, 278–282.

59   Jones, G., above n32, 130; Dow, J. (1998) Major Recessions: Britain and the World, Oxford: Oxford University Press, 304–305; Laidler, D. (1985) 'Monetary Policy in Britain: Success and Shortcomings', Oxford Review of Economic Policy, vol. 1(1), 36; and Cairncross, A. (1995) The British Economy Since 1945, Oxford: Blackwell, 244.

organize trade unions.[60] In 1980 a strike by the Iron and Steel Trades Confederation ended in union defeat, in 1983 a print strike by the National Graphical Association ended not only in defeat for the union but the union's assets including its head office confiscated. However, it was the miners strike in 1984 that sent the clearest signal by the Thatcher government to the private sector that organized labour was no longer a threat.[61]

In 1981 coal mining was a nationalized industry and the government had almost triggered a dispute with the National Union of Mineworkers (NUM) but realized it was unprepared for the dispute. In 1984 once unions rights had been weakened by legislation and preparations had been made to stockpile coal or to switch power stations to oil the government set about reforming the mining industry. It appointed Ian MacGregor (formerly of British Steel) as the head of the National Coal Board (the state body that managed the nationalized coal industry) and charged him with pushing through wholesale reform of the industry. MacGregor's role in defeating the Iron and Steel Trades Confederation while at British Steel made his appointment a particularly symbolic and provocative act. In turn he announced that 20 mines would be closed with the loss of 20,000 jobs.[62] Inevitably industrial action ensued. In August 1984 the strike was declared unconstitutional because of the lack of a national ballot and when the NUM refused to pay the resulting fine, its assets were sequestered for contempt of court.[63] The questionable legality of the strike had a crucial knock on effect as striking miners lost entitlement to social welfare payment. In turn the combination of poverty, heavy policing, the ability of power stations to continue production with coal stockpiles, as well as media and other union hostility to the strike, led to a return to work in 1985.[64] At the beginning of the 1980s NUM membership was more than 250,000, by the end of the 1980s it was less than 10,000 and the coal mining industry had been reformed to the point

---

60   Arthurs, A. (1985) 'Industrial Relations in the Civil Service: Beyond GCHQ', Industrial Relations Journal, vol. 16(2), 26; Ewing, K. (1982) 'Industrial Action: Another Step in the 'Right' Direction', The Industrial Law Journal, vol. 11, 209; Brown, W. and Wadhwani, S. (1990) 'The Economic Effects of Industrial Relations Legislation since 1979', National Institute Economic Review, vol. 131(1), 57–70; and Deakin, S. (1992) 'Labour Law and Industrial Relations' in Michie, J. (ed.) The Economic Legacy 1979–1992, Academic Press, 173–191.

61   Adeney, M. and Lloyd, J. (1988) The Miners' Strike, 1984–85: Loss Without Limit, London: Routledge, 205 and Chapter 10 generally.

62   Campbell, J. (2003) Margaret Thatcher: The Iron Lady, Jonathan Cape, 99–100.

63   Ibid., 366; and Thatcher, M. (1993) The Downing Street Years, HarperCollins, 374.

64   Adeney, M. and Lloyd, J., above n61, Chapters 6 and 11; Towers, B. (1985) 'Posing Larger Questions: The British Miners' Strike of 1984–85', Industrial Relations Journal, vol. 16(2), 8–25. On the strike generally see BBC On This Day, '1984: Dozens arrested in picket line violence', <http://news.bbc.co.uk/onthisday/hi/dates/stories/april/9/newsid_2903000/2903651.stm>.

of vanishing.[65] In the wider context, 1984 saw the second highest loss of working days to strike action since the war at 27,135,000 days lost but the defeat of the miners marked a turning point in the influence of unions and days lost to strikes have fallen to historically low levels since then.[66]

The policy of privatization was also linked to a wider programme of reducing both the size of the state in the economy and the influence of unions. Over the course of the 1980s and early 1990s the Thatcher government privatized a range of government owned industries. On a much larger scale than in the US, industries and companies ranging from telecommunications, British Airways, Steel, electricity, water, docks, parts of the defence industry, rail and bus were privatized raising some 33 billion pounds for the government between 1979 and 1990.[67] This had the virtuous combination of raising revenue for the government, damaging the unions as job losses quickly ensued and reducing the role of the state in the marketplace.[68]

One of the problems in privatizing the state industries was that many had a monopoly position in their markets. The government's solution was to introduce single person regulators with minimal powers to investigate, limited sanctions and a complex relationship with government departments and other agencies, for each industry, to mimic the effect of a competitive marketplace. The regulators could in theory remove the licence to operate of a regulated body but that was an unusable power as it would in effect shut down an industry providing a public service (gas electricity, telecommunications, water etc). Although the government had introduced the Competition Act 1980 to investigate monopolistic practices, in general the government's instinct with competition policy was to deregulate and let competition take place without government interfering.[69] The privatized companies presented a real dilemma for the Thatcher government as they could not be simply privatized as monopolies with no oversight. The solution to the dilemma was to create a regulatory system that encouraged bargaining.[70] As Stephen

65   Brown, W. (2004) 'Industrial Relations and the Economy' in Floud, R. and Johnson, P. (eds) The Cambridge Economic History of Modern Britain. Volume III Structural Change and Growth, 1939–2000, Cambridge, 416.

66   Wrigley, C., above n57, 44.

67   See Parkinson, J. (1993) Corporate Power and Responsibility, Clarendon, 01; and Hannah, L. (2004) 'The State Ownership of Industry' in Floud, R. and Johnson, P. (eds) The Cambridge Economic History of Modern Britain. Volume III: Structural Change and Growth, 1939–2000, Cambridge, 98.

68   Cairncross, A., above n59, 234–237.

69   Turner, J. (1984) 'The Need for an Effective Competition Policy', European Intellectual Property Review, 331; and Suzuki, K. (2002) Competition Law Reform in Britain and Japan: Comparative Analysis of Policy Network, London: Routledge, 116. European Union competition policy would not begin to impact until much later. Zahariadis, N. (2004) 'European Markets and National Regulation: Conflict and Cooperation in British Competition Policy' Journal of Public Policy, vol. 24, 49–73.

70   Hannah, L., above n67, 107–9.

Littlechild, the economist advising the government on the form of privatization, stated later, he considered that the regulatory agencies he created had greater scope for bargaining than other forms of regulation.[71]

The decision by the government, made largely out of panic as institutional investors were initially disinterested, to offer the shares in the newly privatized entities to the general public also had the unintended but welcome effect of turning the general public into shareholders.[72] In particular the high profile advertising campaigns[73] that accompanied the privatizations raised public awareness of not only the individual privatization at hand but of the privatization process generally.[74] This in turn led the public to buy shares in the newly privatized entities particularly after many had made money in the initial privatizations.[75] Similarly, when building societies were deregulated in 1986 it led to wave of demutualization and listing on the stock exchange. In this process a large part of the general public became shareholders as their memberships were turned into shares.[76]

While in a general sense the successive oil crises had damaged the British economy, it had a positive effect on the financial services sector as much of the wealth gains that flowed to OPEC countries ended up, as we noted in Chapter 3, in the London offshore market. Additionally tax incentives continued to favour institutional investors who had benefited from the uncertainties of the 1970s as the public put their money into safe long-term investments such as pensions. In all the Thatcher government came to power determined to free up the London financial markets from government control and remove anti-competitive barriers to trade. Beginning in 1979, a concerted effort was made to free up the financial system from government restrictions. In turn capital controls were removed which freed up British capital for investment abroad and allowed capital to flow in, banks reserve ratios were abolished, restrictions on hire purchase were removed, Buildings Societies were allowed to expand their businesses into a huge range of financial services and the stock exchange was deregulated in 1986, in what was

71   Beesley, M. and Littlechild, S. (1992) 'The Regulation of Privatised Monopolies in the United Kingdom' in Beesley, M. (ed.) Privatisation, Regulation and Deregulation, London: Routledge.

72   Dignam, A. (2000) 'Exporting Corporate Governance: UK Regulatory Systems in a Global Economy', Company Lawyer, vol. 21(3), 70–77; and Cheffins, B. (2008) Corporate Ownership and Control: British Business Transformed, Oxford: Oxford University Press, 81.

73   Sunday Times (1986) 'Government Determined to Press Ahead with Sale; Advertising Campaign Will Be One of the Biggest Undertaken by the Government', 25 May 1986, 53.

74   The sale of British Telecom was said at the time to have created '… a new army of shareholders', The Times, 12 December 1984, 1.

75   The Times (1986) 'Flotation Stampede', 14 October 1986, 2.

76   Tayler, G. (2003) 'UK Building Society Demutualisation Motives', Business Ethics: A European Review, vol. 12(4), 394–402; and Fry, J. (1990) 'Abbey National Becomes a Company', Long Range Planning, vol. 23(3), 49.

known as 'big bang'.[77] As Plender described it at the time deregulation became part of a strategy to attract international capital and ensure the future of the London financial markets.[78] The strategy seemed to work as the value of UK equity turnover increased enormously after 'big bang' (See Chart 6.1 below). Additionally, while the number of foreign companies listed on the LSE had been stable for decades the number grew steadily over the 1980s from 394 in 1980 to 553 by 1990.[79] By 1990 Britain had become not only the largest European recipient of US FDI but the world's largest recipient and the UK was still the largest provider of FDI in the US.[80]

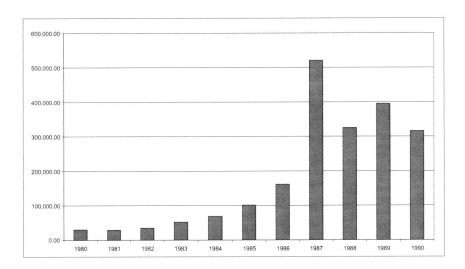

Chart 6.1 UK equity turnover (million pounds)
Source: LSE Historical Statistics, 15, available at <http://www.londonstockexchange.com/NR/rdonlyres/D02B7655-EBC0-4445-8C5B-97DDDF86198D/0/Historic2004.pdf>.

Despite the deregulatory instincts of the Thatcher government it was also keen to ensure legal protection for investors. As such Companies Acts in 1980, 1981,

77   Coakley, J. and Harris, L. (1992) 'Financial Globalization and Deregulation' in Michie, J. (ed.) The Economic Legacy, 1979–1992, Academic Press, 37–59; Cairncross, A., above n59, 269; and Michie, R. (1999) The London Stock Exchange: A History, Oxford: Oxford University Press, 543.
78   Plender, J. (1986–87) 'London's Big Bang in International Context', Journal of International Affairs, vol. 63, 41.
79   LSE historical statistics available at <http://www.londonstockexchange.com/NR/rdonlyres/D02B7655-EBC0-4445-8C5B-97DDDF86198D/0/Historic2004.pdf>, 3.
80   Eckes, A. and Zeiler, T., above n14, 265 and 267.

1985, 1989, a Financial Services Act in 1986 and two Insolvency Acts in 1985 and 1986 introduced further shareholder and creditor protections ranging from prospectus oversight to enhanced reporting, to insider dealing prohibition, to statutory minority protection.[81] The Thatcher government also introduced tax cuts and increased tax incentives for long-term savings that encouraged investment in the stock exchange, such as Personal Equity Plans (PEPs) and later Tax-Exempt Special Savings Accounts (TESSAs). Tax incentives also favoured employee share schemes.[82] The combined effect was similar to the US experience in that a boom ensued fuelled by deregulation and an M&A wave. The UK M&A wave again paralleled the US wave in that many were transaction driven rather than corporate strategy driven. Hostile takeovers had also become commonplace by the 1980s making up a quarter of all M&A tractions between 1970 and 1990.[83] Shareholder control rights in such a market for corporate control again increased in importance. In this frenetic environment it was only a matter of time before the legitimacy of the Panel on takeovers and mergers as a self-regulatory body was tested in court. In 1987 during the course of a bid, a decision of the Panel was challenged in the Court of appeal. While the court found that the Panel carried our a significant public function and was therefore in theory subject to judicial review it ultimately produced a decision highly protective of the Panel's jurisdiction in takeover matters by refusing to allow any legal challenge until the takeover is completed. As a result the panel's pro-shareholder approach was reinforced by the courts.[84] The UK FTSE index of 100 leading shares quadrupled in value between 1981 and 1987. The boom ended however in the stock market crash in October

---

81   Sealy, L. (2001) Cases and Materials in Company Law, Butterworths, 1–4; Authur, T. and Booth, P. (2006) 'Financial Regulation, the State and the Market: Is the Financial Services Authority an Unnecessary Evil?', Economic Affairs, vol. 26(2), 22; and Cheffins, B., above n72, 328–331.

82   Disney, R., Emmerson, C. and Smith, S. (2003) 'Pension Reform and Economic Performance in Britain in the 1980s and 1990s', NBER Working Paper No. 9556; Stillerman, B. (1990) 'PEP Talks and Piggy Banks' (1990) Director, vol. 43(12), 129; Currie, J. (1990) 'Protecting Investments', Management Today, 31; and Clark, T. and Dilnot, A. (2004) 'British Fiscal Policy Since 1939' in Floud, R. and Johnson, P. (eds) The Cambridge Economic History of Modern Britain. Volume III: Structural Change and Growth, 1939–2000, Cambridge, 392.

83   Jones, G., above n32, 128; Franks, J. and Mayer, C. (1996) 'Hostile Takeovers and the Correction of Managerial Failure', Journal of Financial Economics, vol. 40, 163–181; and Franks, J. and Harris, R. (1989) 'Shareholder Wealth Effects of Corporate Takeovers: The UK Experience 1955–1985', Journal of Financial Economics, vol. 23(2), 225–249.

84   See *R v. Panel on Takeovers and Mergers ex p Datafin PLC* [1987] QB 815, CA. Additionally the 'proper purpose' doctrine in UK directors duties also makes it difficult for directors to use their powers to frustrate a takeover. See Dignam, A. and Lowry, J. (2008) Company Law, Oxford: Oxford University Press, Chapter 14.

1987 when the UK market lost almost a quarter of its value in two days.[85] At the end of the decade a wave of corporate collapses demonstrated the weaknesses in internal corporate governance arrangements of British listed companies and lead once again to self-regulatory reform.[86] Nonetheless, by the end of the 1980s a shareholder oriented equity culture had been embedded in the UK. All in all some 15 million people were estimated to be shareholders in 1997 compared to 3 million in 1979, let alone the further millions whose long-term savings were invested through pension and long-term collective savings schemes.[87]

Institutional Investors Emerge

In both the UK and the US the combination of decline and internal and external shock had produced an unworkable corporate governance system as labour, government and shareholders competed for influence in an economic environment where successive external shocks in the form of the collapse of Bretton Woods, increased competition and the successive oil crises created huge uncertainty. The breakthrough from an un-workable to a workable system occurred because the unstable climate led to radical solutions and a final internal economic shock in the form of a deep but short recession in both countries in the early 1980s that further softened resistance to change. The result was the withdrawal of government from the marketplace and that labour ceased to have a significant impact on management discretion. This could of course have led to the emergence of managerial dominance in the absence of government and labour influence, rather than a shareholder oriented outsider corporate governance system and so in this section we focus in on the role of the institutional investor in bringing about that change in orientation.

As we explored in Chapter 5, up until the 1980s the UK and the US were more closely aligned to insider systems in that they lacked a shareholder orientation and the government, labour and, in the UK, families, had significant influence over managerial discretion. Nonetheless, shareholders were challenging for influence from the 1950s onwards. Florence, writing in 1961, identified a clear trend towards a divesting of family shareholdings in Britain's largest companies from the 1950s onwards.[88] Similarly, Hannah, writing in the 1970s, identified the 1950s as the

---

85   See Orr, R. (2007) 'The Winds of Change that Blasted Footsie', The Financial Times, 18 October 2007, available at <http://www.ft.com/cms/s/0/d12974ba-7d93-11dc-9f47-0000779fd2ac,dwp_uuid=0e98e476-7bdb-11dc-be7e-0000779fd2ac.html?nclick_check=1>.

86   See below on the committees on corporate governance.

87   See Department of Trade and Industry (1999) Modern Company Law For a Competitive Economy – The Strategic Framework, 12–13.

88   Florence, S. (1961) Ownership, Control and Success of Large Companies: An Analysis of English Industrial Structure and Policy 1936–1951, London: Sweet and Maxwell, 34.

decade when family influence really began to fall away.[89] However, it was not until the 1970s that the separation of ownership and control was completed.[90] Chandler claims that the separation of ownership from control finally emerged in the UK at the beginning of the 1970s.[91] Scott and Griffe, while agreeing that the change was occurring in the early 1970s, placed the point at which family ownership of shares finally gave way in the late 1970s.[92]

As we discussed in Chapter 5, until the late 1970s, social market issues such as industrial democracy, nationalization and partnership with government were a key aspect of the UK corporate governance system. Indeed, the initial response to UK concerns about managerial power, when ownership and control separated in the 1970s, was to seek to constrain management discretion by increasing the power and participation in the firm of the employees.[93] The high point in the industrial democracy debate came in the late 1970s with the report of the Bullock committee,[94] which advocated the benefits of increased employee participation. At this point, even the business lobby, represented by the Confederation of British Industry, accepted a more inclusionary stakeholder approach was needed.[95] Thus, as we have described in Chapter 5, the UK in terms of its industrial relations system, demand management by the state and financial system operated to produce an insider corporate governance system until its transformation in the 1980s.[96] As we will discuss below, its corporate law was also not particularly favourable to shareholders.

In the US, as we noted above, while dispersed ownership emerged much earlier, it did so with a management unconstrained by shareholders and with a greater

---

89   Hannah, L. (1974) 'Takeover Bids in Britain Before 1950: An Exercise in Business "Pre-History"', Business History, vol. 16, 65–77; and Hannah, L. (1976) The Rise of the Corporate Economy, London: Routledge, 130–131.

90   See Cheffins, B. (2001) 'Does Law Matter? The Separation of Ownership and Control in the United Kingdom', Journal of Legal Studies, vol. 30, 459–484.

91   Chandler, A. (1976) 'The Development of Modern Management Structure in the US and the UK' in Hannah, L. (ed.) Management Strategy and Business Development: An Historical and Comparative Study, London: Macmillan, 24–51, 45–46 and 49; and Chandler, A. (1990) Scale and Scope: The Dynamics of Industrial Capitalism, Cambridge, MA: Harvard University Press, 240.

92   Scott, J. and Griffe, C. (1984) Directors of Industry: The British Corporate Network 1904–76, Cambridge: Polity Press, Chapter 4; and Scott, J. (1997) Corporate Business and Capitalist Classes, Oxford: Oxford University Press, 89–90.

93   Hadden, T. (1972) Company Law and Capitalism, London: Weidenfeld and Nicolson.

94   Lord Alan Bullock (1977) Report of the Committee of Inquiry on Industrial Democracy, London: HMSO.

95   This view did not survive long once the Thatcher government was elected in 1979. See Clift, B., Gamble, A. and Harris, M. (2000) 'Social Democracy and the Company in the UK' in Parkinson, J., Gamble, A. and Kelly, G. (eds) The Political Economy of the Company, Oxford: Hart.

96   See Cheffins, B., above n90, 459–484.

discretion to share resources with stakeholders.[97] As state control of the economy grew in the aftermath of WWII an industrial partnership between organized labour, business and government emerged which was maintained until the 1970s. As such, as we described in Chapter 5, in a similar manner to the UK it operated to produce an insider corporate governance system.

Additionally, neither the US nor the UK have a corporate law that is particularly shareholder oriented. As we noted in Chapter 1, the 'law matters' thesis advocated by La Porta et al. claims that strong corporate law protection for shareholders played a crucial role in the emergence of outsider systems.[98] This is curious given that US corporate law has been somewhat anti-shareholder in its tendency to allow a much greater discretion to managers.[99] For example, the judicial allowance of corporate constituency concerns, and the enactment in numerous states of protective corporate constituency statutes,[100] management friendly proxy rules,[101] the allowance of staggered boards,[102] the use of protective business judgement

97   Roe, M. (2003) *Political Determinants of Corporate Governance*, Oxford: Oxford University Press, 6.

98   La Porta, R. et al. (1998) 'Law and Finance', *Journal of Political Economy*, vol. 106(6), 1113–1155; La Porta, R., Lopez-de-Silanes, F. and Shleifer, A. (1999) 'Corporate Ownership Around the World', *Journal of Finance*, vol. 54(2), 471–517; La Porta, R., Lopez-de-Silanes, F. and Shleifer, A. (2006) 'What Works in Securities Laws', *Journal of Finance*, vol. 6(1), 1–32; and Djankov, S., La Porta, R., Lopez-de-Silanes, F. and Shleifer, A. (2005) 'The Law and Economics of Self-Dealing', *Journal of Financial Economics*, vol. 88(3), 430–465.

99   On anti-shareholder US corporate law see Bebchuk, L. (2005) 'The Case for Increasing Shareholder Power', *Harvard Law Review*, vol. 118, 833–914 at 836.

100   *Revlon, Inc. v. MacAndrews & Forbes Holdings, Inc.*, 506 A2d 173, 176 (Del. 1985); Karmel, R. (1993) 'Implications of the Stakeholder Model', *George Washington Law Review*, vol. 61, 1156; and Pinto, A. (1998) 'Corporate Governance: Monitoring the Board of Directors in American Corporations', *American Journal of Comparative Law* (Supp. 1998), vol. 46, 317–346.

101   Hansmann, H. and Kraakman, R. (2001) 'The End of History for Corporate Law', *Georgetown Law Journal*, vol. 89, 439–468 at 468; and Burgess, K. and Grant, J. (2006) 'Investors "Lack Basic Rights" on US Board', *Financial Times*, 29 October 2006, front page.

102   A staggered board has differing classes of directors who are elected for different term lengths. They are generally regarded as operating to protect management. See Bebchuk, L., Coates, J. and Subramanian, G. (2002) 'The Powerful Antitakeover Force of Staggered Boards: Theory, Evidence, and Policy', *Stanford Law Review*, vol. 54, 887–951.

rules (particularly in Delaware),[103] and the allowance of takeover defences,[104] are all key anti-shareholder features of US corporate law.[105] Bebchuck, in considering the role of shareholders in the US, concluded that a basic element of US, corporate law was:

> [t]he preclusion of shareholders from intervening to adopt changes in the company's basic governance arrangements or to make major business decisions. This basic feature has a profound influence on the governance of US companies with dispersed ownership. The legal rules that tie shareholders' hands and insulate management from shareholder intervention partly account for the power of management and the weakness of shareholders in such companies.[106]

The UK is arguably more shareholder oriented in its corporate law, as it does in theory give shareholders the ability to remove the board. However, in larger companies coordination and apathy can be a significant barrier to shareholder control.[107] UK corporate law also accords a wide discretion to managers in their running of the company.[108] Dividends can only be declared by the board of

---

103   See Nelson, L. (1980–81) 'Judgement Day for the Business Judgement Rule', Brooklyn Law Review, vol. 47, 1169–1204; and Towers, S. (1990) 'Ivanhoe Partners v. Newmont Mining Corp. – The Unocal Standard: More Bark Than Bite?', Delaware Journal of Corporate Law, vol. 15, 483–538. SEC proxy rules and the Williams Act also had similar effects see Hansmann, H. and Kraakman, R., above n101; and Brennan, B. (1991) 'Current Developments Surrounding The Business Judgement Rule: A "Race to the Bottom": Theory of Corporate Law Revived', Whittier Law Review, vol. 12, 299–326 at 302.

104   *Unitrin v. American General Corporation* 651 A2d 1384 (Del 1995); Ferrell, A. (2004) 'Why Continental European Takeovers Law Matters' in Ferrarini, G. et al. (eds) Reforming Company and Takeover Law in Europe, Oxford: Oxford University Press, 8; Gilson, R. and Kraakman, R. (1989) 'Delaware's Intermediate Standard for Defensive Tactics: Is there Substance to Proportionality Review?', Business Law, vol. 44, 247–274; and Armour, J. and Skeel, D. (2006) 'Who Writes the Rules for Hostile Takeovers, and Why? The Peculiar Divergence of US and UK Takeover Regulation' ECGI – Law Working Paper No. 73/2006, available at <http://ssrn.com/abstract=928928>.

105   The US courts have also been prone to lift the corporate veil to the detriment of shareholders. See Hazen, T. and Markham, J. (2003) Corporations and Other Business Enterprises, New York: West Group, 124–144.

106   See Bebchuk, L. (2005) 'The Case for Increasing Shareholder Power', Harvard Law Review, vol. 18, 833–914 at 836.

107   Section 168 of the Companies Act 2006 allows shareholders to remove the board. On the problems of coordination see Rock, E. (1991) 'The Logic and (Uncertain) Significance of Institutional Shareholder Activism', Georgetown Law Journal, vol. 79, 445–506.

108   *Howard Smith Ltd. v. Ampol Petroleum Ltd.* [1974] AC 492 at 821 where Lord Wilberforce states 'it is established that directors, within their management powers, may take decisions against the wishes of the majority of shareholders, and indeed that the majority of shareholders cannot control them in the exercise of these powers while they remain in office'.

directors[109] and on key issues such as minority protection, it has historically been very shareholder unfriendly and even when reforms were introduced in the 1980s they were aimed at protecting shareholders in small private companies.[110] Similarly, directors' fiduciary obligations to shareholders have remained sufficiently vague so as to create a wide management discretion with regard to major decisions.[111] Additionally, the judicial interpretation of the directors' duty of skill and care has historically been maintained at a low level.[112] In all, as Cheffins has noted:

> [a]ccording to the "law matters" thesis, a country has the potential to develop a widely dispersed pattern of share ownership only if its legal system provides investors with sufficient protection against insider opportunism to allow them to be confident about owning a tiny stake in a publicly quoted company. The experience in the United Kingdom casts doubt on this line of reasoning. While the country currently has well- developed securities markets and an "outsider/ arm's-length" system of ownership and control, the law apparently contributed in only a marginal way to this outcome.[113]

We too remain unconvinced of the extent to which law, as La Porta et al. claim, played a role in the emergence of the outsider systems in the UK and the US, save that it may have been antagonistic to shareholders and needed to be subverted.[114] Indeed, as institutional investors emerged as a significant force in the 1970s and 1980s, this subversion seems to have occurred. By the late 1970s, the largest companies in both jurisdictions were listed on stock exchanges dominated not by small private investors, but by institutional investors who constructed accountability mechanisms, which have a very strong shareholder orientation.

For the purposes of the analysis that follows, it is important to note that the separation of ownership from control occurred in the UK and the US in

---

109 Dignam, A. and Lowry, J., above n84, Chapter 8.

110 Deakin, S. (2005) 'The Coming Transformation of Shareholder Value', Corporate Governance, vol. 13(1), 11; and Davies, P. (2003) Gower and Davies: Principles of Modern Company Law, London: Sweet and Maxwell, Chapter 17.

111 Dignam, A. and Lowry, J., above n84, Chapters 8 and 14. This remains the case even after the enactment of section 172 of the Companies Act 2006.

112 In the past two decades this has changed to hold directors to a higher standard but without much litigation ensuing. See Sealy, L. and Worthington, S. (2008) Cases and Materials in Company Law, Oxford: Oxford University Press, 300–308.

113 See Cheffins, B., above n90; and Cheffins, B., above n72, 330–331.

114 As we noted above there were changes to UK company law in the 1980s but not to the extent that those changes affected corporate governance outcomes. See Cheffins, B., above n90. Similarly, the separation of ownership from control in India, Taiwan, Mexico, Thailand and Malaysia was not the result of changes in corporate law but the result of changes in macroeconomic policy related to financial liberalization. See Singh, A. (1997) 'Financial Liberalisation, Stock Markets and Economic Development', The Economic Journal, vol. 107, 771–782.

very different forms. In the US, as we describe in Chapter 5, the separation of ownership occurred in its classic form, whereby the managerial firm emerged because shareholders were so numerous (and thereby dispersed) that they could exert little control on management. In the UK, the separation occurred much later when family ownership gave way mostly to institutional ownership. For a brief period in the 1960s arguably a form of the managerial corporation emerged in the UK in the gap created by family shareholders divesting and before institutional investors grew in size and influence. The merger wave in the 1960s as we noted in Chapter 5 was largely an exercise in managerial hubris which provides some evidence of the extent of managerial influence.

While the effect of both separations in the UK and US at the firm level is similar, in that institutional investors have, in a similar way to private investors also tended to be passive and find coordination difficult;[115] to classify both separations as giving rise to dispersed ownership is, we believe, a mistake, in that it underplays the sophisticated interventions institutional investors have made in reorienting the market-level rules that constrain management discretion. In this sense, the UK and the US moved in the 1970s towards a corporate governance system in which institutional-ownership began to compete for influence against labour and the state. In doing so the UK and the US, as we will observe below, moved a step closer to becoming outsider systems with a core focus on the shareholder.

The changed macroeconomic environment

As we have noted above, the world in which US and UK companies operated changed dramatically in the 1970s. The breakdown of the Bretton Woods system and the shock of the oil crisis were accompanied by a less protective trade policy in which foreign competition began to have a significant negative impact on domestic companies.[116] In turn, loss of autonomy at the macroeconomic level affected government ability over the 1970s and 1980s to support social welfare programmes, and led to reform, as the governments in the UK and the US cut spending in implementing monetarist policies to deal with these new macroeconomic conditions.[117]

The net beneficiaries of these cutbacks in government spending were institutional investors as tax incentives moved firmly towards private rather than government saving and pension provision in order to reduce government long-term spending.[118] In all, the institutional investor emerged as a significant force

---

115 See Rock, E., above n107.

116 Useem, M. (1996) Investor Capitalism, New York: Basic Books.

117 Meyer, L. (2000) 'The Politics of Monetary Policy – Balancing Independence and Accountability', BIS Review, No. 94/2000, available at <http://www.bis.org/review/r001027a.pdf>.

118 Davis, E. and Steil, B. (2004) Institutional Investors, Cambridge, MA: MIT Press, 38–41; and Black, B. and Coffee, J. (1994) 'Hail Britannia? Institutional Investor

in the UK and US equity markets by the 1980s.[119] While institutional investors meant a more concentrated shareholding base, they still remained largely passive investors as coordination remained problematic at the firm-level.[120] They were, however, more sophisticated in their approach to monitoring management at the market-level where individual institutional investors and organizations such as the Association of British Insurers, the National Association of Pension Funds in the UK, the Institutional Shareholders Committee and the Council of Institutional Investors in the US have been particularly successful in developing protective market-level mechanisms through their respective lobbying.[121] As we described in Chapter 2, institutional investors also operate as sophisticated information filters which ensures more accurate pricing information. These mechanisms focused management on key shareholder concerns without the shareholders having to become active within the company.[122] In other words, because coordination at the firm level was difficult, institutional investors focused on changing the rules of the stock exchange and its surrounding institutions to favour shareholders over management. A crucial element in that change has been the ability of institutional investors to relatively easily effect change at the market level and that in turn relates to the self-regulatory ethos present in the UK and the US.

The link between the US and the UK in terms of the development of their securities markets is their common law origin. It is clear that the US stock exchange, although nowadays viewed as having a much heavier-touch regulatory system than the UK, inherited in its key formative period British regulatory values based on freedom to contract, protection of property and a minimal state.[123] As coffee describes it:

Behaviour under Limited Regulation', Michigan Law Review, vol. 97(7), 1997–2087.

119   See Graphs 6.1 and 6.2 below. Tax incentives were not the only driver of institutional investors' interest in equities. Returns on equities had outstripped most other investments over time: see Jorion, P. and Goetzmann, W. (1999) 'Global Stock Markets in the Twentieth Century', The Journal of Finance, vol. 54, 953–980.

120   Black, B. (1992) 'The Value of Institutional Monitoring: The Empirical Evidence', UCLA Law Review, vol. 89, 895–939; Stapledon, G. (1996) Institutional Shareholders and Corporate Governance, Oxford: Oxford University Press; Brancato, C. (1997) Institutional Investors and Corporate Governance: Best Practices for Increasing Corporate Value, Illinois: Irwin Professional Publishing, Chapter 3.

121   Davies, P. (1997) 'Institutional Investors as Corporate Monitors in the UK' in Hopt, K. and Wymeersch, E. (eds) Comparative Corporate Governance: Essays and Materials, New York: Walter de Gruyter. On the US see Useem, M. (1993) Executive Defense: Shareholder Power and Corporation Reorganization, Cambridge, MA: Harvard University Press.

122   See Black, B. and Coffee, J., above n118.

123   Wilks, S. (1997) 'The Amoral Corporation and British Utility Regulation', New Political Economy, vol. 2(2), 279–298 at 280. We discuss this issue further in Chapter 9.

[e]ssentially, during the late 19th century, the US developed a functional substitute for strong minority legal protections through a self-regulatory mechanism (i.e. The New York stock exchange, which pioneered high disclosure standards) … these mechanisms largely closed the legal gap between the weak existing enforcement mechanisms and the necessary preconditions for dispersed ownership.[124]

Indeed, both Cheffins and Coffee have argued that the voluntary disclosure and self-dealing rules of the stock exchanges in the UK and the US have been crucial to the success of the stock exchanges in both those countries.[125] This is something we agree with and, in turn, we believe that the self-regulatory systems in the UK and the US, although different from one another, allowed institutional investors to construct an alternative set of norms that focused managerial discretion on them once the state and labour fell away in influence.

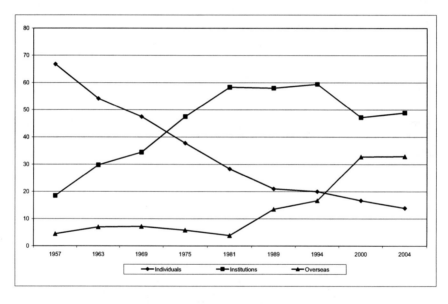

Graph 6.1 Share ownership patterns in the UK, 1957–2004
Source: Armour, J. and Skeel, D. (2006) 'Who Writes the Rules for Hostile Takeovers, and Why? The Peculiar Divergence of US and UK Takeover Regulation' ECGI – Law Working Paper No. 73/2006, 50, available at <http://ssrn.com/abstract=928928>.

---

124   Coffee, J. (2001) 'The Rise of Dispersed Ownership: The Roles of Law and the State in the Separation of Ownership and Control', Yale Law Journal, vol. 111, 1–82 at 25–29.
125   See Cheffins, B., above n90; and Coffee, J., above n124, 25–29.

In the UK, as we noted in the previous chapter, families began to divest their shareholdings and institutional investors took their place (see Graph 6.1) from the 1950s onwards.[126]

Between 1957 and 1969, the driver of this change seems to have been related, as we discussed previously, to favourable dividend taxation treatment for institutional investors compared to private shareholders.[127] This marked a significant turning point in the development of the UK's corporate governance system. First, the presence of institutional investors produced the beginnings of an important constraint on the ability of British management to retain earnings because institutional investors, in the absence of any real internal influence on management, looked to external verifiable measures such as dividends as an indicator of management performance.[128] By the mid 1960s, the sophisticated nature of institutional investor actions at the market level combined with advances in technology[129] was beginning to pose problems for the London Stock Exchange (LSE). As the LSE council noted in 1964 on the continuing loss of business to US brokers:

> [w]hile the total amount of investments held by UK nationals in the USA is greater than pre-war, they are now much more held by institutions than individuals. The institutions in their turn have formed their own USA connections and deal directly by means of the telephone.[130]

Indeed, the formation of the Panel on Takeover and mergers, in the late 1960s, was an exercise in institutional power over both British management and the LSE, which had in the past failed to deal effectively with the issue.[131]

In the period 1969–1981, institutional ownership accelerated rapidly (see Graph 6.1 above) because, as we noted above and in Chapter 3, macroeconomic conditions moved strongly against welfare state provision and led to pension reform.[132] The

---

126 Morgan, E. and Thomas, W. (1962) The Stock Exchange: Its History and Functions, London: Elek Books, 172–183; and Sir Harold Wilson (1980) Committee to Review the Functioning of Financial Institutions, London: HMSO, 208 and 214.

127 Cheffins, B. (2006) 'Dividends as a Substitute for Corporate Law: The Separation of Ownership and Control in the United Kingdom', ECGI – Law Working Paper No. 69/2006, available at <http://ssrn.com/abstract=906068>.

128 Ibid. Cheffins suggests this operated as an important precursor to a protective disclosure regime.

129 Phone calls between London and New York got much cheaper and the use of computers expanded. Eckes, A. and Zeiler, T., above n14, 158 and 216.

130 LSE Council, 16 March 1964.

131 See Armour, J. and Skeel, D., above n44; and Michie, R. (1999) The London Stock Exchange: A History, Oxford: Oxford University Press, 493.

132 Disney, R. And Emmerson, C. (2005) 'Public Pension Reform in the United Kingdom: What Effect on the Financial Well-Being of Current and Future Pensioners?', Fiscal Studies, vol. 26, 55–81.

major beneficiaries of this were the pension and insurance funds who provided the main alternatives and enhancements to the state savings and investment schemes.[133] The crucial tipping point in terms of the orientation of the LSE rules came in this period. In the early 1970s institutional investors were lobbying heavily, with limited success, for a reduction in the fixed-rate of commission. The breakthrough came in 1974 when the US gave up its capital controls entirely and UK institutional investors could deal through the US markets. This forced the LSE to revise its fixed-commission system, which up until this point had been used as a means to subsidize small investors, in favour of institutions who dealt in large volume.[134] As Michie noted:

> [a]s long as costs could be covered through overcharging large investors, who were increasingly financial institutions, then there was limited need to change. It was in the 1970s that this ceased to be as possible as in the past, as these institutions now had access to alternatives at home and abroad.[135]

In turn, the LSE disclosure regime was significantly enhanced as a result of institutional pressure which required management to push information to shareholders,[136] and defensive actions by management in takeovers were restricted by the operation of the panel on takeovers and mergers.[137] By the mid 1970s the LSE had come to the conclusion that its future was tied to the rise of the institutional investor.[138]

In October 1979, the UK removed its capital controls, and institutional investors became completely free to deal in UK and other securities in overseas markets. As a result, between 1979 and 1985, institutional investor overseas holdings increased from £12 billion to £100 billion.[139] At the same time, overseas capital began to flow into the UK equities market on a significant scale after capital controls were removed (see Graph 6.1 above). Foreign direct investment made up 7.2 percent of British GDP in 1967 but by 1990 that figure had increased to 21.2 percent.[140] Stapledon, taking an admittedly conservative view, estimates that half the overseas

---

133   Myners, P. (2004) 'Institutional Investment in the United Kingdom: A Review', HM Tresury, para 1.24, available at <http://www.hm-treasury.gov.uk/d/31.pdf>.

134   See Michie, R., above n77, 492–3.

135   Ibid., 493.

136   See Cheffins, B., above n127, 28.

137   Johnston, A. (1980) The City Takeover Code, Oxford: Oxford University Press, Chapter 1 (on the historical background to the Code); and Davies, P. (1992) 'The Regulation of Defensive Tactics in the United Kingdom and the United States' in Hopt, K. and Wymeersch, E. (eds) European Takeovers: Law and Practice, London: Butterworths, 200.

138   See Michie, R., above n77, 536–537.

139   Bond, S., Davis, E. and Devereux, M. (1987) Capital Controls: The Implications of Restricting Overseas Portfolio Capital, London: Institute for Fiscal Studies, 5; and Cheffins, B., above n72, 352–353.

140   Dunning, J. (1993) The Globalization of Business, London: Routledge, 290.

holdings on the LSE represent foreign institutional investors.[141] Davis, less conservatively, estimates the figure at two thirds.[142] Indeed, others estimate almost all of that figure to be institutional investors, with US institutions representing a half to two thirds of all overseas UK equity holdings.[143] In all, although domestic institutions increased their equity holdings on a more gradual scale over the course of the 1980s, the overall holdings of institutional investors continued to increase significantly, driven by foreign institutions. In the face of this, the LSE lost the ability to impose its more onerous and costly rules on its most powerful customers. While the 'big bang'[144] did not follow until 1986, the transforming event had already occurred. As the Chairman of the stock exchange commented at the time, 'the real impetus for change was the abolition of UK exchange controls in 1979. If anything should be called the "big bang" it was that'.[145]

The pattern of domestic and foreign, mainly US institutional investors, increasing their UK equity holdings continued (see Graph 6.1 above) until domestic pension funds started to divest part of their equity holdings to comply with more onerous rules on asset ratios and minimum funding requirements implemented by the UK Pension Act 1995.[146] Additionally, unfavourable taxation changes affecting the treatment of dividends for pension funds in 1997 also contributed to the divesting

---

141   Stapledon, G. and Bates, J. (2002) 'Reducing the Costs of Proxy Voting' in McCahery, J. et al. (eds) Corporate Governance Regimes: Convergence and Diversity, Oxford: Oxford University Press, 571.

142   Davis, E. (2002) 'Institutional Investors, Corporate Governance and the Performance of the Corporate Sector', Economic Systems, vol. 26, 203–229 at 209.

143   Lacaille, R. (2005) 'Globalization Shifts UK Company Ownership and Power', State Street Global Advisors, available at <http://www.ssga.com/library/esps/ricklacailleglobalizationshifts20050623/page.html>.

144   The 'Big Bang' refers to the changes to the rules of the LSE that took place on the 27 October 1986 which reformed the operation of the exchange by introducing single market makers rather than having separate stockbrokers and stockjobbers, completely ending fixed commissions, the introduction a screen-based quotation system used by brokers and the end of restrictions on ownership of UK stockbrokers. See Poser, N. (1991) International Securities Regulation: London's 'Big Bang' and the European Securities Markets, Boston: Little Brown and Company, 24–5.

145   Goodison, N. (1986) 'Chairman's Comments', Stock Exchange Quarterly, 8. See also Kay, J., Vickers, J., Mayer, C. and Ulph, D. (1988) 'Regulatory Reform in Britain', Economic Policy, vol. 7, 285–351 at 296; Goodison, N. (1988) 'London's Place in the Global Securities Market' (1988) International Affairs, vol. 4, 575–583; and Webb, D. and Tonks, I. (1986) 'The Reorganisation of the London Stock Market: The Causes and Consequences of Big-Bang', London School of Economics, Financial Markets Group Special Paper No. 20.

146   On the effect this had in switching pension fund holdings in equities into bonds see Davis, P. (2000) Regulation of Private Pensions, A Case Study of the UK, London: Pensions Policy Institute, No. Pi-0009, 11.

over this period.[147] While this marks a significant decline in domestic institutional shareholdings of 12 percent between 1994 and 2000, an important substitution effect occurred, with overseas shareholders increasing their UK holdings by 16 percent over the same period (see Graph 6.1 above). Taking Stapledon's more conservative estimate that only half that increase represented foreign institutions, then total institutional investor holdings declined from 68 percent in 1994 to 64 percent in 2000. Using the less conservative figure of two thirds, the decline is less marked, with total institutional shareholdings only declining from 70 percent in 1994 to 69 percent in 2000. If one assumes that almost all the overseas holdings are institutional investors, then total institutional investor holdings may actually have increased over this period. From 2000 onwards, domestic institutional investors started to increase their holdings again (Graph 6.1 above).

While in 1986 the big bang brought about a more formal state-regulatory role, in that a legislative framework was introduced for financial services, the self-regulating bodies, including the LSE, retained their autonomy.[148] Over the course of the 1990s, in a similar manner to the formation of the Panel on Takeovers and Mergers, the financial institutions in the City of London came together on a number of occasions to form committees on corporate governance (Cadbury, Greenbury and Hample)[149] to address failings in British management.[150] Most of the recommendations of the committees on corporate governance had been reforms that institutional investors had considered best practice for years.[151]

---

147   Bond, S., Devereux, M. and Klemm, A. (2007) 'Dissecting Dividend Decisions: Some Clues About the Effects of Dividend Taxation From Recent UK Reforms' in Auerbach, A., Hines, J. Jr., and Slemrod, J. (eds) Taxing Corporate Income in the 21st Century, Cambridge: Cambridge University Press, 41.

148   Financial Services Act 1986 section 142(6) and Watson, K. (2004) 'The Financial Services Sector Since 1945' in Floud, R. and Johnson, P. (eds) The Cambridge Economic History of Modern Britain. Volume III: Structural Change and Growth, 1939–2000, Cambridge: Cambridge University Press, 176–179.

149   Cadbury Committee (1992) Report of the Committee on the Financial Aspects of Corporate Governance, London: Gee. For an earlier example in the US see Riley, C. (1994) 'Controlling Corporate Management: UK and US Initiatives', Legal Studies, vol. 14(2), 244–265. See also Greenbury Report (1995) Directors' Remuneration: Report of a Study Group Chaired by Sir Richard Greenbury, London: Gee; Hampel Committee (1998) Committee on Corporate Governance – Final Report, London: Gee; Dignam, A. (1998) 'A Principled Approach to Self-Regulation? The Report of the Hampel Committee on Corporate Governance', Company Lawyer, vol. 19(5), 140–154; and Dignam, A. (2007) 'Lamenting Reform? The Changing Nature of Common Law Corporate Governance Regulation', Company and Securities Law Journal, vol. 25, 283–299.

150   Holland, J. (1996) 'Self Regulation and the Financial Aspects of Corporate Governance', Journal of Business Law, March, 127–164; and Amour, J., Deakin, S. and Konzelmann, S. (2003) 'Shareholder Primacy and the Trajectory of UK Corporate Governance', British Journal of Industrial Relations, vol. 41, 531–555.

151   See Business International Money Report (1987) 'Who's Running the Show? Why Institutions Are Blocking Equity Issues', May 11, 146; and Institutional Shareholders

Not only were these committees able to put in place accountability solutions designed to constrain the discretion of management of listed companies through further enhancing the disclosure and shareholder consent regime, the use of pre-emption rights and the abandonment of non-voting shares they were also powerful enough to intervene directly in the management structures of listed companies by creating a new direct monitoring mechanism by using the non-executive director (NED) and key board-scrutiny committees to supervise the executive directors.[152] In all, these key changes to the self-regulatory system promoted by the institutional investors operated to construct a shareholder oriented substitute to the more managerial UK corporate law, and push the UK, once the government and labour had been reduced in influence in the 1980s, towards what we now recognize as an outsider shareholder oriented corporate governance system.[153]

What occurred in the UK involved a combination of factors whereby macroeconomic change combined with deregulated capital markets, government withdrawal, industrial relations change and a self-regulatory ethos to effect a reorientation to a shareholder oriented outsider system. Many of those same elements were present in the US. In the US, the emergence of its outsider system took a different course initially. As we considered in Chapter 5, the emergence of a separation of ownership from control occurred in the US through dispersed ownership in the early part of the twentieth century. Additionally, in the 1930s, the intervention of the Federal government imposed a regulatory framework on the NYSE that did not exist in the UK. This would on one reading mean that the ability of institutional investors to reorient the rules to focus managerial discretion on institutional investors was more difficult, but this underestimates the historical resilience of the NYSE system of self-regulation and the effect of political patronage on leadership at the SEC.

The conditions under which the NYSE became, and maintained its status, as the premier US stock exchange, are significant here. The small size of the NYSE in the nineteenth century and the conservatism of its members led it to pursue a race to the top strategy in terms of its listing rules. The continual development of high disclosure standards and the rejection of risky listing applications gave it an exclusive status as the protector of the public investor.[154] However, that status was threatened by the collapse of the stock market in 1929, and the subsequent Great

---

Committee (1991) The Responsibilities of Institutional Shareholders in the UK, London: ISC.

152   Dignam, A. (2007) above n149; and Armour, J. and Skeel, D., above n44.

153   On the ability of institutional investors to also exert technological and structural change on markets see Davis, E. (1996) 'The Role of Institutional Investors in the Evolution of Financial Structure and Behaviour', Paper delivered at the Reserve Bank of Australia Conference: The Future of the Financial System, available at <http://www.zen13767.zen. co.uk/58-FINSTRU6.pdf>.

154   Michie, R. (1987) The London and New York Stock Exchanges, 1850–1914, London: Allen & Unwin, 198–273.

Depression. The legislative response produced by the New Deal banking and securities laws reshaped the regulatory environment by attempting to remove the influence of the investment banks from public corporations[155] and by introducing the Securities and Exchange Commission (SEC) to regulate the securities market. While this may look as if it marked the end of the self-regulatory system in the US, the story is more nuanced than it appears. While the New Deal Congress was united in its desire to strike at the influence of investment banks such as J.P. Morgan and Co.,[156] within public corporations its motivation to regulate the securities market was to protect shareholders and managers.[157] Indeed, although there is no doubt that the New Deal reforms were a traumatic event for the vested interests within Wall Street generally, the reality was not quite the draconian state takeover the rhetoric implied, primarily because the first Chairman of the SEC was a key business and Wall Street insider, Joseph P. Kennedy,[158] whose appointment was designed to reassure the business community that the SEC was not a threat. Geisst describes the appointment:

> Kennedy was renowned as an astute businessman who would not ruffle too many Wall Street feathers ... Kennedy's administration of the new SEC proved to be highly successful. He toed the line with Wall Street and the NYSE while actively setting up the mechanics of the commission so it could investigate and prosecute misdeeds by investment bankers and brokers.[159]

Indeed, vital parts of the disclosure regime such as accounting standards and the audit, remained self-regulating after 1934.[160] The changes also represented a time of opportunity for the NYSE's more reform-minded to make wide-ranging voluntary changes to its operation and personnel.[161] Additionally, even in the central reform of the banking industry, it is doubtful that the attempt to restrain bank influence was entirely successful. For example, J.P. Morgan and Co., the key villain in the Pecora Commission investigation of the Great Crash,[162] remained a central firm in the US

---

155   The Glass-Steagall Act 1933 split the US banking industry into commercial and investment banking.

156   The Pecora Commission investigating the cause of the Great Crash revealed wide scale fraud involving the banking industry. See Benston, G. (1990) The Separation of Commercial and Investment Banking: The Glass-Steagall Act Revisited and Reconsidered, Oxford: Oxford University Press.

157   Fraser, S. (2006) Wall Street: A Cultural History, London: Faber and Faber, 409–410.

158   The father of the future US President John F. Kennedy.

159   Geisst, C. (1997) Wall Street: A History, New York: Oxford University Press, 235.

160   On the history of the Audit in the US see 'A Brief History of Self Regulation', <http://thecaq.aicpa.org/Resources/Sarbanes+Oxley/Archive+-+A+Brief+History+of+Self+Regulation.htm>.

161   See Geisst, C., above n159, 252–253; and Fraser, S., above n157, 415.

162   Benston, G., above n156.

board interlock network until the 1980s, some 50 years after the New Deal reforms were supposed to strike a crippling blow to its power and influence.[163]

Of course the self-regulatory system had significant problems, and one of the key reasons the SEC was created was the failure of the NYSE to deal with market manipulation, despite the existence of rules forbidding such activity.[164] However, the end result of the securities reform process was not at all incompatible with one of the key historic aims of the NYSE in protecting investors through enhanced disclosure. Indeed, the New Deal securities reforms solved one of the problems the NYSE had when trying to improve disclosure standards. While it had proved relatively straightforward to force improved disclosure standards on new companies listing on the NYSE, once listed, the NYSE found it impossible to get the companies to abide by each new round of enhanced disclosure. As a result, there were differing levels of disclosure depending on the standards the company agreed to when it listed.[165] The New Deal securities legislation standardized disclosure across the board, and significantly, when the NYSE wished to raise disclosure standards to protect investors, they were pushing at an open door with the SEC. Indeed, by the 1960s as tensions arose between the NYSE and the emerging interests of institutional investors the SEC was widely viewed as the enforcement arm of the NYSE.[166] In all, the SEC and the New Deal reforms did not kill self-regulation but introduced an oversight function to the self-regulating role, which enhanced the operation of self-regulation in key areas thereafter.[167] As Grajzl and Murrell observed considering the New Deal regulatory reforms:

> [a] system of government-supervised self-regulation was established: "... many private economic associations became quasi-public in nature, for they were given public authority and an important role in making and implementing regulatory

---

163   Davis, G. and Mizruchi, M. (1999) 'The Money Center Cannot Hold: Commercial Banks in the U.S. System of Corporate Governance', Administrative Science Quarterly, vol. 44, 215–239.

164   Banner, S. (1998) Anglo-American Securities Regulation: Cultural and Political Roots, 1690–1860, Cambridge: Cambridge University Press, 278–280.

165   Fox, M. (1999) 'Retaining Mandatory Securities Disclosure: Why Issuer Choice is Not Investor Empowerment', Virginia Law Review, vol. 85(7), 1335–1419 at 1376–1379.

166   Stigler, G. (1964) 'Public Regulation of the Securities Market', Journal of Business, vol. 37, 117; Demsetz, H. (1969) 'Perfect Competition, Regulation and the Stock Market' in Manne, H. (ed.) Economic Policy and the Regulation of Corporate Securities, Washington, DC: American Enterprise Institute; West, R. and Tinic, S. (1971) 'Minimum Commission Rates on New York Stock Exchange Transactions', The Bell Journal of Economics, vol. 2, 577; Baxter, W. (1970) 'NYSE Fixed Commission Rates: A Private Cartel Goes Public', Stanford Law Review, vol. 22, 675; and Friend, I. and Blume, M. (1973) 'Competitive Commissions on the New York Stock Exchange', Journal of Finance, vol. 28, 795.

167   Coglianese, C. et al. (2004) 'The Role of Government in Corporate Governance', KSG Working Paper No. RWP04–045, 5.

policy". Trade associations and industry groups were authorized to establish codes of conduct that were exempt from antitrust laws. The Agricultural Adjustment Act decentralized regulatory decision-making in agriculture relying on farm associations for policy implementation. The Securities and Exchange Commission, established in 1934, played a critical role in giving the financial industry the authority to self-regulate and facilitated the creation of the largest self-regulatory body in the country, the National Association of Securities Dealers.[168]

As institutional investors became a force in the 1970s (see Graph 6.2), as in the UK, the pattern of increasing institutional orientation of NYSE rules to favour institutional investors became evident. As in the UK, in the late 1960s and early 1970s the NYSE fixed-commission system came under pressure from institutional investors who started trading shares off-exchange at cheaper prices.[169] The NYSE responded with small discounts on large transactions but this proved insufficient.[170] Within a year of the US eliminating capital controls in 1974, the fixed-commission system was eliminated and negotiated commissions were introduced by the NYSE amid fears of losing business abroad.[171] The growth in institutional investor importance can also be seen in the growth of block trades of over 10,000 shares by institutional investors which had increased from 3.1 percent of total sales on the NYSE in 1965 to 51 percent by 1985.[172]

One important difference between the UK and the US markets is that small retail investors have historically made up a much higher percentage of the US market than in the UK.[173] In turn, SEC policy was oriented towards those small unsophisticated investors. This became a point of tension as institutional investors began to lobby for more sophisticated disclosure standards in the 1970s. The swing away from the NYSE by the SEC in removing the fixed commission system proved to be an important turning point in the SEC's relationship with institutional investors.[174] By 1977 the SEC had come to the conclusion that institutional

---

168   Grajzl, P. and Murrell, P. (2005). 'Allocating Law-Making Powers: Self-Regulation vs. Government Regulation', available at SSRN: <http://ssrn.com/abstract=870888> 18.

169   See Geisst, C., above n159, 297–298; and Jarrell, G. (1984) 'Change at the Exchange: The Causes and Effects of Deregulation', Journal of Law and Economics, vol. 27, 278–279.

170   Jarrell, G., above n169, 280.

171   Geisst, C., above n159, 305–306.

172   Chandler, A., above n31, 279; and Jarrell, G., above n169, 277–279.

173   Seligman, J. (1994–1995) 'The Obsolescence of Wall Street: A Contextual Approach to the Evolving Structure of Federal Securities Regulation', Michigan Law Review, vol. 93, 649–702 at 664.

174   Stoll, H. (1979) 'Regulation of Securities Markets: An Examination of the Effects of Increased Competition', Monograph Series in Finance and Economics, New York University, Graduate School of Business; Tinic, S. and West, R. (1980) 'The Securities Industry under Negotiated Brokerage Commissions: Changes in Structure and Performance of New York Stock Exchange Member Firms', The Bell Journal of Economics, vol. 11, 29; Shaefer, J. and Warner, A. (1977) 'Concentration Trends and Competition in the Securities

investors were an important information filter for smaller investors and began to reform the disclosure regime to reflect that institutional role.[175] Additionally, by the early 1980s the elimination of capital controls in the UK in 1979 had also starkly illustrated how integrated the financial markets were becoming, as the NYSE was rapidly losing business to the London market.[176] Under pressure from the NYSE, and driven by the deregulatory instincts of its Chairman John Shad, the SEC acted. As Seligman noted:

> [c]umulatively, the general recognition of the mechanisms of an efficient market for information dissemination and the potential for significant export of U.S. securities sales persuaded the SEC in 1982 to adopt the current integrated disclosure system and shelf registration Rule 415.[177]

One can also observe the effect of the changed environment in which institutional investors became influential in the decline of bank influence in the early 1980s. Bank influence in the US in the period after the New Deal reforms is often overlooked in the corporate governance literature when discussing influences on management. The reason for the perceived decline of bank influence is that banks ceased to hold significant shares in US public corporations after the New Deal reforms in the 1930s.[178] However, while it is true that banks ceased to exert influence through their direct shareholdings, their influence, as we discussed earlier in this chapter, through board interlocks remained strong after the New Deal reforms. Significantly, for our purposes, by the mid-1980s the US commercial banks had almost ceased to be suppliers of loan capital to US companies, and their centrality in the board interlock network declined significantly.[179] The reason for this decline appears to have been their inability to compete with other newer forms of capital supplied by institutional investors.[180]

Industry', Financial Analysts Journal, vol. 33, 29 at 32; and Schwert, G. (1977) 'Public Regulation of National Securities Exchanges: A Test of the Capture Hypothesis', The Bell Journal of Economics, vol. 8, 128.

175   House Committee on Interstate and Foreign Commerce, 95th Congress, 1st Session, 618–652; Seligman, J., above n173, 685–686; and Gilson, R. and Kraakman, R. (1984) 'The Mechanisms of Market Efficiency', Virginia Law Review, vol. 70, 549–644.

176   Lohr, S. (1986) 'Rolling in Money in London', New York Times, 20 April 1986, part 3; and see Geisst, C., above n159, 310–313.

177   See Seligman, J., above n173, 687.

178   Roe, M. (1994) Strong Managers, Weak Owners: The Political Roots of American Corporate Finance, Princeton: Princeton University, 58.

179   See Davis, G. and Mizruchi, M., above n163.

180   James, C. and Houston, J. (1996) 'Evolution or Extinction: Where are Banks Headed?', Journal of Applied Corporate Finance, vol. 9(2), 8–23 at 11; and Kaufman, G. (1993) 'The Diminishing Role of Commercial Banking in the U.S. Economy' in White, L. (ed.) The Crisis in American Banking, New York: New York University Press, 139–159.

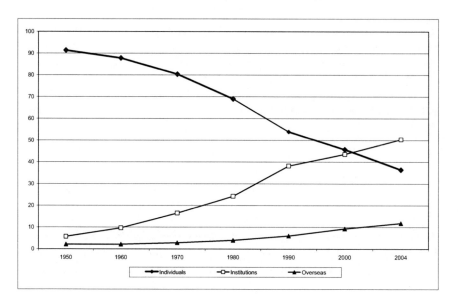

Graph 6.2 Share ownership patterns in the US, 1950–2004
Source: Armour, J. and Skeel, D. (2006) 'Who Writes the Rules for Hostile Takeovers, and Why? The Peculiar Divergence of US and UK Takeover Regulation' ECGI – Law Working Paper No. 73/2006, 50, available at <http://ssrn.com/abstract=928928>.

While we have emphasized the market level changes that institutional investors carried out in the UK and US and while as we described earlier, institutions do mostly remain passive at the firm level, they do also sometimes intervene directly in the management of companies. As institutional investors' holdings have grown in size they have faced 'lock-in' effects, as exit can be too costly or is not available at all.[181] For those institutions, the 'voice' option – or what is most commonly referred to as 'institutional activism' – is sometimes the only economically rational option.[182] In all, despite the difficulties of coordinated action, at times of crisis institutional investors in the UK and the US do sometimes form what Scott has described as a 'constellation of interests'.[183] At these times institutional pressure can build to effect policy change, as the board of directors of BT Group PLC

---

181   Cheffins, B., above n72, 370–381.

182   The literature on this subject is substantial: see Black, B., above n120; Stapledon, G., above n120; and Brancato, C., above n120, Chapter 3.

183   Scott, J. (1997) Corporate Business and Capitalist Classes, Oxford: Oxford University Press, 348–52. See also Stapledon, G., above n120, 121–22 and 125–27; Black, B. and Coffee, J., above n118; Holland, J. (1995) The Corporate Governance Role of Financial Institutions in Their Investee Companies, London: Certified Accountants Educational Trust, 34–36.

found in 1997 when it attempted to form an alliance with MCI Communications Corporation in the face of institutional disapproval.[184] Institutional investors can even effect the removal of a director, as Cedric Brown of British Gas PLC in 1996,[185] Charles Saatchi, the founder of Saatchi & Saatchi PLC in 1994,[186] David Montgomery of Mirror Group PLC in 1999,[187] and Michael Green of ITV PLC in 2003[188] found to their cost.[189] These removals were also followed by restructuring of the businesses. In the UK context, Stapledon has suggested that coordinated action to remove management requires a constellation of at least four institutional investors amounting to 20–30 percent of the equity.[190] Moreover, anecdotally, it seems that there is a large amount of institutional investor pressure brought to bear behind the scenes in the UK that does effect change.[191] This is less so in the US where coordination between institutions has historically been more difficult.[192] Additionally, there is less scope for coordination in the US than there is in the UK because large US institutional investors do not tend to own blocks of shares in companies that are as large as those held by their UK counterparts.[193] Despite these hurdles US institutional investors are not inactive but their methods of corporate governance activism are generally more formal and adversarial as they often resort to proxy fights and create target lists comprised of underperforming companies.[194] This type of institutional activism has been assisted by the fact that, apart from takeover regulation, all other important aspects of securities' regulation remains the responsibility of the SEC which has since the 1980s actively pursued, as we

---

184   Essick, K. (1997) 'BT's Abandoned Merger', InfoWorld, vol. 19(46) 76; and Essick, K. (1997) 'Snatching BT's Bride', Economist, vol. 345(8037), 19.

185   Rodgers, P. and Rentoul, P. (1996) 'Brown to Go as British Gas Splits Up', The Independent, 6 February, 21.

186   See Marckus, M. (1994) 'Saatchi Anger at "Takeover"', The Times, 4 January 1994, Business, 21.

187   Crawford, A. (1999) 'Mirror Group to Pursue Merger as Monty Goes', Marketing, 29 January 1999, 1.

188   See Randall, J. (2003) 'Why Michael Green had to Go', BBC News (UK Edition), 21 October 2003, available at <http://news.bbc.co.uk/1/hi/business/3210372.stm>.

189   Cheffins, B., above n72, Chapter 11.

190   Stapledon, G., above n120, 106–116.

191   Rock, E., above n107; Black, B. and Coffee, J., above n118.

192   Coffee, J. (1997) 'The Folklore of Investor Capitalism', Michigan Law Review, vol. 95, 1977–78 and 1983–1984; Black, B. (1998) 'Shareholder Activism and Corporate Governance in the United States' in Newman, P. (ed.) The New Palgrave Dictionary of Economics and the Law: Volume 3, Basingstoke: Macmillan, 461; and Stapledon, G., above n120, 271–272.

193   Stapledon, G., above n120, 106–116; and Bainbridge, S. (2003) 'A Comment on the SEC Shareholder Access Proposal', UCLA School of Law, Law & Econ. Research Paper No. 03–22, <http://ssrn.com/abstract=470121> 11–12.

194   MacAvoy, P. and Millstein, I. (2004) The Recurrent Crisis in Corporate Governance, Stanford University Press, 19–20; and Taylor, W. (1990) 'Can Big Owners Make a Big Difference?', Harvard Business Review, vol. 70–82 (Sept–Oct), 74.

noted earlier, the involvement of institutions on corporate governance issues. For instance, since 1992 the SEC has amended its proxy rules a number of times, which had previously increased the costs of coordinated activism, to allow easier communication between institutional investors and protect shareholders coordinating proxies.[195] Another significant incentive for pension fund activism was provided in 1988 in a letter from the Department of Labor – known as the 'Avon Letter' – in which it advised that pension funds obligations to beneficiaries also applied to the decision to exercise the right to vote at General Meetings.[196] Additionally, despite the greater difficulty in doing so, institutions can bring about the removal of board members as the removal a number of board members at General Motors and American Express in the early 1990s and of Michael Eisner from the Chairmanship of Disney in 2004 and his early retirement in 2005 indicates.[197] In all since the 1980s, a key feature of the corporate governance systems in the UK and the US has been the emergence of a body of institutional investors sufficiently large to engage in both market level restructuring and to sometimes outweigh the difficulties of coordinated action to effect a managerial focus on their interests in the absence of government and labour influence.[198]

By the time Reagan and Thatcher left office in 1989 and 1990 respectively, the Cold War had been won, Levitt had considered that the 'globalization of markets is at hand' and the 'end of history' had been somewhat prematurely declared by Fukuyama.[199] Domestically a transformation had occurred in the economies of both countries. The role of government had been reduced, capital was global and flowed freely in and out of the deregulated capital markets in New York and London, monetarist policies had become orthodoxy, labour markets were

---

195   Goodman, A. and Olson, F. (2001) A Practical Guide to Sec Proxy and Compensation Rules, Aspen Publishers Online, 10.10 and 10.11; and SEC (2007) SEC Adopts Proxy Rule Amendments Encouraging Electronic Shareholder Forums, available at <http://www.sec.gov/news/press/2007/2007-247.htm>.

196   The Deputy Assistant Secretary of the Pension Welfare Benefits Administration (PWBA now known as EBSA) issued the Avon letter to Mr. Helmuth Fandl, Chairman of the Retirement Board of Avon Products, Inc., on 23 February 1988.

197   Macavoy, P. and Millstein, I., above n194, 27–31; and Norris, F. (2004) 'Shareholder Power: Do Institutional Investors Deserve New Authority?', The New York Times, 23 April 2004, 713, available at <http://www.nytimes.com/2004/04/23/business/23norris.html?ex=1235019600&en=80bac643561d2289&ei=5070>.

198   For analytical accounts of US and UK institutional investor activism see Brancato, C. (1997) Institutional Investors and Corporate Governance – Best Practices for Increasing Corporate Value, Chicago: Irwin Professional Publishers; Useem, M. (1996) Investor Capitalism – How Money Managers Are Changing the Face of America, New York: Basicbooks; and Stapledon, G. (1996) Institutional Shareholders and Corporate Governance, Oxford: Oxford University Press.

199   Levitt, T. (1983) 'The Globalization of Markets', Harvard Business Review, vol. 61(3), 92–102; and Fukuyama, F. (1989) 'The End of History?', The National Interest, vol. 16, 3.

flexible. Trade in the absence of the Soviet threat and the opening up of former soviet states, had begun to take on a global character. As a result a transformation also occurred in the corporate governance systems of both countries as in the absence of the influence of government and labour, shareholders became the most powerful influence on management and an outsider shareholder oriented system emerged.[200] Consequently, a re-orientation has occurred in managerial motivation towards creating value for the shareholders.[201] An indication of how significant this change in managerial motivation has been is the fact that equity finance in the 1980s eventually became negative in both the US and the UK mainly as a result of extensive cash redistributions to shareholders in the form of share repurchases.[202] In addition, dividend payouts rose to unprecedented levels despite a decline in profit.[203] These developments have often led to allegations that the system now forced managers to pursue short-term profit to the detriment of long-term performance.[204]

Conclusion

In both countries the post war partnership between labour, business and government collapsed in the 1970s with the end of Bretton Woods, increased competition, stagflation and successive oil crises. Transformation came in the UK and the US with the introduction of monetarist and deregulatory policies by Margaret Thatcher and Ronald Reagan. Initial further shock induced by these policies further facilitated change by softening up any remaining resistance to change. By the end

---

200   On the influence of institutional investors on dividend and investment policy see Davis, E. (2002) 'Institutional Investors, Corporate Governance and the Performance of the Corporate Sector', Economic Systems, vol. 26, 203.

201   See Rappaport, A. (1986) Creating Shareholder Value – The New Standard for Business Performance, London: Collier Macmillan. Major consultancy firms gradually developed their own metrics for shareholder value, such as Economic Value Added (EVA™), Market Value Added (MVA), Cash Flow Return on Investment (CFROI), Total Shareholder Return (TSR), and so on. For a comparative overview of such metrics see Froud, J., Haslam, C., Johal S. and Williams K. (2000) 'Shareholder Value and Financialization: Consultancy Promises, Management Moves', Economy and Society, vol. 29(1), 80–110.

202   The aggregate value of shares repurchased by NYSE listed corporations was $1.1 billion in 1975 and $6.3 billion in 1982, by 1985 it had reached $37.1 billion: Brudney, V. and Chirelstein, M. (1987) Corporate Finance, 3rd edition, New York: Mineola, 541; and Corbett, J. and Jenkinson, T. (1996) 'The Financing of Industry 1970–1989: An International Comparison', Journal of the Japanese and International Economies, vol. 10, 71–96.

203   Lazonick, W. and O'Sullivan, M., above n30, 22–23.

204   Cosh, A., Hughes, A., Singh, A., Carty, J. and Plender, J. (1990) 'Takeovers and Short-Termism in the UK', Industrial Policy Paper No. 3, Institute for Public Policy Research, London and Coffee, J. (1986) 'Shareholders Versus Managers: Strain in the Corporate Web', Michigan Law Review, vol. 85, 1–109 at 104.

of the 1980s both the UK and the US had emerged as shareholder oriented outsider systems as the industrial relations and financial systems of both countries were transformed and the government's role in the marketplace was reduced. Corporate law did not seem to play much of a role in this as it had a managerial orientation. In the vacuum created by the withdrawal of the state, the diminution of labour power and a deregulated financial market, the institutionalization of shareholding and the emergence of a market for corporate control in both countries allowed shareholders to become the major influence within the corporate governance systems and complete the transformation to outsider systems. In turn from 1979 onwards, the NYSE and the LSE have been engaged in a constant regulatory competition.[205] In essence both markets had, after 1979 when UK capital controls were removed, lost the ability to have truly national corporate governance systems once capital was mobile and could engage in regulatory arbitrage.[206] As we noted in Chapter 3, the emergence of these denationalized nascent global capital markets proved an important driver of the process of economic globalization and the outsider shareholder oriented rules upon which it would be based.

What is noteworthy in our long-term historical analysis of change in the role of government, industrial relations, financial systems and corporate law, is the extent of institutional change and transformation over time in the UK and US. Rather than static constellations of institutional systems, they have been engaged in constant rearrangement in response to stimulus. While broadly one would describe the UK and the US as insider systems up until the 1980s, that classification disguises a remarkable amount of change, transformation and diversity in reaction in the institutions affecting corporate governance outcomes over time. At various times up until the 1980s management, families, labour, banks, competitive pressures and the government or combinations of these elements have been significant influences on management discretion and at one point in both systems, shock caused systemic transformation within the insider paradigm. Most of that change indicated diversity of reaction in institutional structure to stimulus until the 1980s when in reaction to the same stimulus both systems reoriented themselves to produce a similar outcome. The shared institutional history of the UK and the US may have played a role in that common response to stimuli. While we will return to this commonality of response in the final chapter, we turn, bearing in mind our observations on UK and US systemic corporate governance change and transformation, in the next two chapters to consider the evidence of systemic change in Germany as a result of the pressures exerted by the process of globalization we described in Chapter 3.

205   See Michie, R. above n77, 479–542.

206   On regulatory arbitrage see Lütz, S. (1996) 'The Revival of the Nation-State? Stock Exchange Regulation in an Era of Internationalized Financial Markets', MPIFG Discussion Paper 96/9, 9.

Chapter 7
The Traditional German Corporate Governance Model

Introduction

In Chapter 3 we identified the dynamics of isomorphism in world markets during the current globalization process and in Chapters 5 and 6 we observed the transformation from insider to outsider corporate governance systems in the UK and US in the 1980s. Our intention in considering the impact of the process of globalization on the German insider corporate governance model is to evaluate whether it is indeed converging/transforming into an outsider shareholder oriented model. However, before we turn to examine change within the German model we first need to map out the traditional German insider model that is said to be changing or have changed. We do this in this chapter. In doing so, although we begin with the nineteenth century roots of the German corporate governance model, our focus is on the German corporate governance model between the end of WWII and the mid 1990s, after which we believe the model comes under observable stress. As such in this chapter we provide an analytical overview of the main institutions of the German insider system of corporate governance before turning in Chapter 8 to consider evidence of institutional change that has resulted from the process of globalization.

The Origins of the German Corporate Governance Model: An Overview

The roots of the German system of corporate governance lie in the late nineteenth century. As the Germany states industrialized in the mid to late nineteenth century, companies drew on a number of sources of funding from equity to bank finance.[1] However, German banks became central to the financing of a newly unified German corporate sector after 1871. For example Deutsche Bank and Commerzbank were both formed just prior to the unification of the German states in 1870 and grew to develop close working associations with individual companies and industries. George von Siemens for example was on the management board of Deutsche bank

---

1 Throughout this book we refer simply to 'Germany' rather than to specific incarnations of the Germany state e.g. Imperial, Weimar, Nazi or West. Apologies to purists but we would hope the context we provide at particular points makes clear the limits of our assumptions about the German state.

when it was formed in 1870 and Siemens in turn developed an important working relationship with Deutsche Bank.[2] A key development in the formation of the German corporate governance system occurred in the period after the unification of Germany in 1871 and the defeat of France in the Franco-Prussian war of 1871. In the immediate aftermath, a wave of incorporations and a stock market boom occurred, fuelled by the flows of reparations payments from France.[3] In 1873 the German stock market collapsed in what became know as the *Grunderkrise* and a depression known as the 'Long Depression' ensued.[4] Although the German economy had recovered by the 1880s this crash and depression had a significant long-term effect on German corporate governance outcomes for a number of reasons. First, it cemented the close working relationships between the banks and industry as they sought to raise finance and survive in a difficult climate. The banks themselves at times ended up providing equity to companies or were stuck with stock overhangs, when no-one else would subscribe for shares or they had to convert loans into shares because companies where struggling to pay. For large financing projects the banks themselves developed close working relationships and worked together to pool their lending. By the beginning of the twentieth century it was common for banks to be involved in the founding of companies and their continuing management, as board members and shareholders.[5] Second, it moved the German state away from liberal economic policies such as free trade and competition, to protectionism, a distrust of stock exchange finance and the encouragement of cartelization. The collapse of a number of companies leading up to the stock market crash and in its aftermath, led to a concern to protect the public interest from managerial corruption and managerial exploitation of stakeholders, particularly employees.[6] By 1884 corporate law reform led to the supervisory board being introduced with employee representation on it and the shareholders' meeting had its supervisory power transferred to the supervisory board.[7] The most significant reform though, in discouraging the growth of external capital markets, was a requirement for the minimum nominal capital for shares to be set at an extremely high level. This had the intended effect of specifically discouraging small shareholdings and favouring banks, rather than the stock exchange, as the

---

2   Kurzrock, H. (1970) 'Aus der Geschichte der Commerzbank' in Commerzbank AG (ed.) 100 Jahre Commerzbank: 1870–1970, Frankfurt: Fritz Knapp Verlag, 39–125.

3   Masur, G. (1970) Imperial Berlin, New York: Basic Books, Inc., 63–65.

4   Marek, G. (1974) The Eagles Die. Franz Joseph, Elisabeth, and their Austria, New York: Harper & Row, 181–182.

5   Gall, L. (1995) 'Die Deutsche Bank von ihrer Gründung bis zum Ersten Weltkrieg 1870–1914' in Gall, L. et al. (eds) Die Deutsche Bank 1870–1995, München: Beck, 1–135.

6   Eyck, E. (1964) Bismarck and the German Empire, New York: W.W. Norton & Company, Inc., 223–236 and 252–261.

7   Jackson, G. (2004) 'Contested Boundaries: Ambiguity and Creativity in the Evolution of German Codetermination', RIETI Discussion Paper No. 04-E-022, available at SSRN: <http://ssrn.com/abstract=569541> or DOI: <10.2139/ssrn.10.2139/ssrn.569541>.

suppliers of external capital and large family blockholders as the exercisers of internal control. As Jackson described it:

> German lawmakers viewed the shareholders meeting sceptically for several reasons: its uncertain composition might lead to dominance by minority shareholders; it failed to provide continuous monitoring; and "democracy" that would give voice to small shareholders was widely considered undesirable due to their short-term interests and ability to exit.[8]

The Government also moved to protect struggling industries by introducing high tariffs and the government actively encouraged industry wide cartelization facilitated by the formation of business associations.[9] By 1914 the supervisory boards of the largest German companies had both an internal control function and a business network/cartelization function as their membership consisted of families, banks, other companies and the government.[10]

However, the banks' influence declined significantly as companies grew and became more self-reliant during the early twentieth century as they generated their investment funds internally and in turn their dependence on bank finance diminished considerably.[11] The influence of banks in the formulation of corporate policies was also undermined by the high inflation crises during the interwar years, as extremely high interest rates rendered bank finance unattractive compared to retained earnings.[12] As a result although the interwar period saw a continuation of the links between businesses and the banks, often again this was because German companies were in crisis for much of the 1920s and 1930s as the aftermath of defeat in WWI led to hyperinflation and mass unemployment and was followed by the depression era of the early 1930s.[13] Banks as a result became active in advising on reconstruction and refinancing with bad debts again being turned in to equity holdings for the banks. According to Chandler, their role diminished over this period to one of facilitating cooperation among their corporate clients rather than controlling them.[14]

---

8   Jackson, G. (2001) 'The Origins of Non-Liberal Corporate Governance in Germany and Japan' in Streeck, W. and Yamamura, K. (eds) The Origins of Non-Liberal Capitalism: German and Japan, Ithaca: Cornell University Press, 121–170.

9   Höpner, M. and Krempel, L. (2004) 'The Politics of the German Company Network', Competition and Change, vol. 8(4), 339–356 at 342.

10   Jackson, G., above n8, 132–133.

11   Fohlin, C. (2001) 'The Balancing Act of German Universal and English Deposit Banks', Business History, vol. 43(1), 1–24.

12   Chandler, A. (1990) Scale and Scope: The Dynamics of Industrial Capitalism, Cambridge, Mass.: Belknap Press, 419, 495 and 512–513.

13   Ferguson, N. (2002) Paper and Iron: Hamburg Business and German Politics in the Era of Inflation, 1897–1927, Cambridge: Cambridge University Press, 1–30.

14   Chandler, A., above n12.

The cartelization process also began to take a more formal structure in the interwar years as companies began to hold cross-shareholdings in one another. Inter-company cooperation in Germany had been emerging since the late nineteenth century and beginning of the twentieth century. As the German business landscape was increasingly dominated by large oligopolistic companies that were no longer entrepreneurial or family-controlled but managerial in terms of their ownership and control, cooperation was more preferable to price competition that could threaten stability. Inter-company contractual agreements and cartels became common and were enforceable in the German courts.[15] However, as the threat of arbitrageurs circumventing those arrangements could never be totally eliminated, many companies began to form profit pooling associations (*Interessengemeinschaften* or 'IGs') and corporate groupings (*Konzerne*) that were commonly accompanied by an interchange of share blocks and interlocking directorates.[16] These exchanges formalized the cartelization process by making it difficult if not impossible to depart from the cartel. During the economic downturn in the interwar years such arrangements became even more common and to some extent even substituted at times for bank borrowing as a source of corporate finance. As a result, by 1930 representatives of affiliated industrial corporations outnumbered bankers on company boards.[17] The supervisory board had by the 1930s come to function as a mechanism for cooperation between companies in an industry and their financiers.[18] The Nazi period between 1933–1945 saw a greater degree of state control. Fears of labour unrest in the period after WWI had led to the introduction of works councils to provide for employee consultation and representation in the Works Councils Act of 1920 (*Betriebsrätegesetz*).[19] Concern that the works councils were too left-wing led the Nazis to abolish them in the 1930s. However, by and large, apart from the diminution of labour, the structure of German industry remained the same during this period. The main initial Nazi interest was in reforming the German banking system but while they confiscated Jewish holdings in the banking sector and placed capital flows under government direction no major structural changes occurred.[20] Restrictions on dividends from 1934 onwards played an important part in making internal funds available for reinvestment and further discouraging equity as a form of finance for companies.[21] In the immediate aftermath of the war, although some of the very largest cartels were broken up, the realization by

---

15   Höpner, M. and Krempel, L., above n9, 342.

16   Feldman, G. (1977) Iron and Steel in the German Inflation: 1916–1923, Princeton, 256.

17   Chandler, A., above n12, 512–513 and 590–591; and Pohl, M. (1982) Konzentration im Deutschen Bankwesen (1848–1980), Frankfurt: Fritz Knapp Verlag., 302–303.

18   Jackson, G., above n8, 134.

19   Du Plessis, J. Großfeld, B. Luttermann, C. Saenger, I and Sandrock, O. (2007) German Corporate Governance in International and European Context, Springer, 112–114.

20   Kurzrock, H., above n2, 73.

21   Pohl, M., above n17, 405.

the Allies, as we noted in Chapter 5, that the rebuilding of the German economy was essential to counterbalance Soviet influence, meant that they maintained the ownership and control structure of German industry as a stabilizing force.[22] As a result the post war German corporate governance model we describe in the rest of this chapter has clear roots in its late nineteenth century predecessor.

Cooperative corporate governance

The German corporate governance system has historically been characterized by internal and external cooperation rather than rivalry within and among companies.[23] Höpner and Krempel found, for example, that 60 of the largest 100 German companies in 1996 formed a single network made up of cross-shareholdings and interlocking directorates.[24] A significant impact of this cooperative system is managerial insulation from external capital market pressures, particularly the market for corporate control, that could have placed the emphasis on dividend distribution as opposed to cash-flow retention. Retained earnings provided most of the financial capital for the investments necessary for the growth and competitiveness of German industry.[25] Moreover, banks, who historically provided most of the external finance, have been committed financiers that preferred cooperative arrangements that ensured stability and long-term profitability to adversarial confrontation.[26] As Chandler observed drawing a comparison with the UK and US:

> [i]n both the United States and Germany by the 1930s managerial capitalism had replaced personal capitalism in major sectors of the economy, in ways that were only beginning to be evident in Britain. The difference between the two brands of managerial capitalism was that one was oriented towards competition and the other towards cooperation.[27]

An important building block of the German model has also been the cooperative nature of intra-company relationships, especially between employers and employees.[28] The presence at an early stage in its development of employee

22   Höpner, M. and Krempel, L., above n9, 346; and Jackson, G., above n8, 137.

23   Wenger, E. and Kaserer, C. (1998) 'German Banks and Corporate Governance: A Critical View' in Hopt, K. et al. (eds) Comparative Corporate Governance: The State of the Art and Emerging Research, Oxford: Clarendon Press, 499–536.

24   Höpner, M. and Krempel, L., above n9, 341.

25   Forsyth, D. (1997) Regime Changes: Macroeconomic Policy and Financial Regulation in Europe From the 1930s to the 1990s, Ton Notermans: Berghahn Books, 284.

26   Wengenroth, U. (1997) 'Germany: Competition abroad – Cooperation at Home, 1870–1990' in Chandler, A., Amatori, F. and Hikino, T. (eds) Big Business and the Wealth of Nations, Cambridge, 142.

27   Chandler, A., above n12, 592.

28   Wengenroth, U., above n 26, 172.

input into the exercise of control ensured that German managers emphasized the importance of long-term investment in human capital which had benefits for workers but also for the full exploitation of technological and organizational opportunities.

While, as we will discuss in the next section, the current co-determination regime of mandatory labour representation on company boards did not come until after WWII, as we discussed earlier, the basis for this formal institutionalization of balancing capital and labour interests was already present. For example the influence of the German *Soziale Marktwirtschaft*[29] (Social Market Economy) model on managements' attitude and German corporate governance in general has been emphasized by a number of commentators. Streeck, for instance, in analysing the origins of the economic institutions in Germany, finds that they are the result of an:

> historical compromise between liberal capitalism [...] and two different countervailing forces, Social Democracy and Christian Democracy – as well as between traditionalism and two alternative versions of modernism, liberalism and socialism, and of course between capital and labour.[30]

As we observed earlier in this chapter, the initial origin of this compromise was in the late nineteenth century when Bismarck introduced corporate reform including employee representation on the supervisory board as a reaction to a stock market crash and to the growth of socialism and trade unions.[31] However, the most important industrial democracy measures present today, such as the compulsory inclusion of labour representatives on the boards of large German companies, were implemented during the reconstruction efforts initiated after the two World Wars

---

29   On the origins of the German social market see Nicholls, A. (2000) Freedom with Responsibility: The Social Market Economy in Germany, 1918–1963, Oxford: Oxford University Press. Some commentators have placed particular emphasis on the influence of the Hegelian vision of a socially responsible free market economy as well as the concepts of an 'economic constitution' developed by the renowned Freiburg School. See Hegel, G. (1942) Philosophy of Right, trans. by Knox, T., Oxford: Oxford University Press; Emmons, W. and Schmid, F. (1998) 'Universal Banking, Control Rights, and Corporate Finance in Germany', Federal Reserve Bank of St. Louis Review, July/August, 19–42 at 22–25; and Smith, E. (1994) The German Economy, London: Routledge, 16–20.

30   Streeck, W. (1996) 'German Capitalism: Does It Exist? Can It Survive?', Working Paper 218, 5–6, available at <http://www.nd.edu/~kellogg/publications/workingpapers/ WPS/218.pdf>.

31   Smith, E., above n29, 3–5 and 19; Wood, S. (1997) 'Weakening Co-determination? Works Council Reform in West Germany in the 1980s', Discussion Paper FS 1 97–302, Wissenschaftszentrum Berlin für Sozialforschung, Berlin and on the social policies generally see Holborn, H. (1982) A History of Modern Germany – 1840–1945, Princeton: Princeton University Press, Chapter 8.

and aimed at the stabilization and mobilization of the workforce.[32] These policies played a crucial role in the balance of interests within and without companies as well as in the evolution and success of the German post war economic model.[33] Additionally, due to the central role of universal banks (the big three being – Deutsche Bank, Dresdner Bank and Commerzbank, known as the *Großbanken*) in Germany's financial system many commentators have characterized the German model of corporate governance as bank-based – i.e. with banks being the main controlling and disciplinary force on management.[34] As we will examine later in this chapter, this mainstream view is not completely accurate as the banks have less incentive to exercise control than is often assumed.

Institutional Building Blocks of the German Managerial Governance Model

Given the socio-economic background described above, it is not surprising that the German system of corporate governance has not evolved around the stock market. Moreover, shareholder interests have not enjoyed the priority they now do in the US and the UK. The German model has been built upon long-term relations both between employers and employees as well as between shareholders, creditors, industrial partners, and the company. The fact that all these interests are represented and amalgamated on a typical company board, supports the characterization of the German corporate governance system as insider rather than outsider. In the sections that follow we analyse the German model by assessing the nature and effect of the main institutional arrangements in which it is embedded and which determine corporate governance outcomes.

Board structure and composition

The board structure of German public companies is a two-tier one, comprised of a supervisory board (*Aufsichtsrat*) and a separate management board (*Vorstand*). This structure has its roots in the *Verwaltungsrat*, a body on which shareholders, bankers and other entrepreneurs were represented, and which was instituted for the first time in the late nineteenth century by a mandatory requirement for a

---

32 Smith, E., above n29, 300–301.

33 On the evolution of the German model see Berghahn, V. (ed.) (1996) German Big Business and Europe, 1918–1992, Berg Publishers, and on post WWII developments see Dyas, G. and Thanheiser, H. (1976) The Emerging European Enterprise: Strategy and Structure in French and German Industry, London: Macmillan.

34 Shonfield, A. (1965) Modern Capitalism: The Changing Balance of Public and Private Power, London: Oxford Press, 246; Deeg, R. (1999) Finance Capitalism Unveiled: Banks and the German Political Economy, Ann Arbor: University of Michigan Press; and Zysman, J. (1983) Governments, Markets and Growth: Financial Systems and the Politics of Industrial Change, Ithica: Cornell University Press, 261–265.

supervisory board separate from management with members appointed by the shareholders. As we considered earlier, the original reason behind the creation of such a body was not only to provide a mechanism for management control by the shareholders but also to protect the public interest because of fears of managerial corruption and exploitation of stakeholders.[35] From its origins and design therefore one can observe that the German two-tier structure constitutes a "representational" model of corporate governance, where different interests are expected to be present on the *Aufsichtsrat* as a body assigned to counterbalance the *Vorstand's* power.

Aufsichtsrat

Under the German *Aktiengesetz* (Stock Corporation Act ('AktG')) a public corporation (AG) is obliged to have a supervisory board (*Aufsichtsrat*) strictly separate from management. Large private limited liability companies (GmbH) with over 500 employees are also required to have a supervisory board because they are subject to the co-determination regime (see below) and many private companies with less than 500 companies often choose to have a supervisory board.[36] The *Aufsichtsrat* is responsible for the appointment and dismissal of the *Vorstand* members[37] as well as exercising a continuing supervision over it.[38] However, there is a strict separation of the two bodies' functions since the day-to-day management of the company is exclusively the responsibility of the *Vorstand*.[39] *Aufsichtsrat* tenure may last for a maximum of five years before a renewal becomes necessary. *Aufsichtsrat* members are not full time employees and often take on multiple positions in several companies. The *Aufsichtsrat* operates in practice with relatively infrequent meetings, restricted time dedicated by the members, and limited flow of information between the two boards. Accordingly, Baums and Frick[40] consider that, except in times of financial distress, in practice the *Aufsichtsrat* acts more like

---

35   As we noted earlier this board structure came as a response to a severe market crash in 1873 which set the stage not only for the subsequent marginalization of the stock market but also for the dominant role of banks who then took over the financing of early industrial development. Jackson, G. above n8, 131.

36   Hopt, K. (1997) 'The German Two Tiered Board (Aufsichtsrat)' in Hopt, K. and Wymeersch, E. (eds) Comparative Corporate Governance: Essays and Materials, Walter de Gruyter, 7; and Third Part Act (*Drittelbeteiligungsgesetz*) 2004.

37   Section 84 AktG.

38   Section 111 AktG.

39   Sections 111(4)(1) and 76 AktG.

40   Baums, T. and Frick, B. (1996) 'Co-determination in Germany: The Impact on the Market Value of the Firm', Paper presented at the conference on 'Employees and Corporate Governance', Columbia University Law School, New York, November, 3, available at <http://www.jura.uni-frankfurt.de/ifawz1/baums/Bilder_und_Daten/Arbeitspapiere/a0197.pdf>.

an advisory, rather than a supervisory body.[41] Indeed, since 1976 the number of transactions requiring the supervisory board's approval has been decreasing.[42]

In the mid 1990s the average number of members on the supervisory board was between nine and 13 members.[43] The *Aufsichtsrat* size for co-determination companies is legally prescribed depending on the size of the workforce. Thus, in companies with a workforce between two thousand and ten thousand the *Aufsichtsrat* has twelve members, in companies with a workforce between ten thousand and twenty thousand the number rises to sixteen, and those companies with more than twenty thousand employees, have twenty *Aufsichtsrat* members.[44] A 1999 survey of the twenty-five largest companies in a number of European countries found that German boards are by far the largest in Europe.[45] The reason for the large size of the boards is that the *Aufsichtsrat* members' represent wider constituencies than board members in other European countries. The most significant constituency represented is labour. This again is legally prescribed by the labour co-determination regulations which, as we noted earlier, require that a number of employee representatives be appointed to the *Aufsichtsrat* of large corporations.

There are three board-level co-determination regimes in which the number of labour representatives varies according to the actual number of employees in the company. The first is the full-parity regime. It concerns only the '*Montan*' coal and steel industries and was introduced for the first time in 1951 with the enactment of the *Montanmitbestimmungsgesetz* ('Montan Co-determination Act') which provides for eleven *Aufsichtsrat* members, five of whom are labour representatives and the eleventh member is elected by a three-fifths majority of all members. The second is the one-third co-determination system which was created by the *Betriebsverfassungsgesetz* (Enterprise Constitution Act ('BetrVG')) 1952 and applies to corporations with more than five hundred and under two thousand employees. It provides for one-third employee representation on the supervisory board. Finally, the third regime was created with the enactment of the *Mitbestimmungsgesetz* 1976 (Co-determination Act ("MitbestG") 1976) which extended full parity co-determination to all companies with two thousand

41　The depleted role of the Aufsichtsrat as a monitoring body has attracted criticism which eventually led to legislative intervention. We discuss these changes in full in Chapter 8.

42　Bremeier, E., Mülder, J. and Schilling, F. (1994) 'Praxis der Aufsichtsratstätigkeit in Deutschland – Chancen zur Professionalisierung', AMROP International, Düsseldorf, cited in Prigge, S (1998) 'A Survey of German Corporate Governance' in Hopt, K., et al. (eds) Comparative Corporate Governance: The State of the Art and Emerging Research, Oxford: Clarendon Press, 57–60.

43　Prigge, S., above n42, 955; and Hopt, K., above n36, 8.

44　Section 7(1), sentence 1 of the Co-determination Act 1976 (Mitbestimumungsgesetz 1976 ('MitbestG') and Hopt, K., above n36, 241–242.

45　Russell Raynolds Associates (1999) Corporate Governance at the Dawn of Monetary Union – 1999 European Board Practices Survey, New York: Russell Raynolds.

employees or more. As described above, the size of the *Aufsichtsrat* depends on the number of workforce and labour representatives must comprise half the members of it. Generally each *Aufsichtsrat* member irrespectively of his background has one vote. However, in case of a stalemate in a vote by the board, the chairman, who is not a labour representative but is nevertheless elected by a two-thirds majority of the board, has a casting vote. In all these co-determination regimes the majority of labour representatives are elected directly by employees through the works councils (discussed later in this chapter) and the rest are trade union delegates.[46]

The remaining *Aufsichtsrat* members are elected by the General Meeting and are shareholder representatives. In practice, however, it is not uncommon for these members to be suggested by the management of the company.[47] Prigge notes that the connection between supervisory boards and management is often manifested by the influence of CEOs and chairmen on the selection of *Aufsichtsrat* members and the frequency of cases where retiring CEOs become chairmen.[48] Even though there is a legal requirement that the *Aufsichtsrat* be a body independent from management, independence under German law is not necessarily perceived in the same way as in the UK and the US.[49] In Germany independence is understood as the prohibition on current company managers sitting on the supervisory board. Thus, a study in 1996 has shown that 43 percent of German supervisory boards include a former manager.[50] Moreover, independence may also be compromised by personal links that can arise from the possibility of a company's managers and *Aufsichtsrat* members sitting together on boards of other companies, a common practice in Germany.

The relationship between management and *Aufsichtsrat* members compromises the supervisory role of what on paper should be shareholder representatives but instead are strongly linked with management. Indeed, Hopt emphasizes that one of the main historical functions of supervisory board representation is to create and maintain business networks; perhaps an indication of the wider insider nature of the traditional German corporate governance model's cooperative character.[51] Hopt claims that often appointments on the *Aufsichtsrat* have a relationship dimension, in the sense that they constitute a formalization of relations between the company and its business partners, resource providers, advisers and former managers. A good indication of this is that in 1996, 13 percent of all *Aufsichtsräte*

46　Baums, T. and Frick, B., above n40, 3–5.

47　Hopt, K. (1998) 'The German Two-Tier Board: Experience, Theories, Reforms' in Hopt, K. et al. (eds) Comparative Corporate Governance: The State of the Art and Emerging Research, Oxford: Clarendon Press, 250.

48　Prigge, S., above n42, 957–958.

49　See Dignam, A. and Lowry, J. (2008) Company law, Oxford: Oxford University Press, Chapter 16 on the Higgs definition of board member independence.

50　Korn/Ferry International (1996) Board Meeting in Session: European Board of Directors' Study, London.

51　Hopt, K., above n47, 233–235.

had at least one retired executive from another company, 70 percent a commercial banker, 13 percent a government official and 96 percent a worker representative – the latter being unavoidable due to the mandatory co-determination provisions.[52] Thus, one observation that can be made, bearing in mind the preceding discussion on the origins of German corporate governance, is that the German model has been remarkably consistent throughout its history in providing mechanisms for accommodating a range of stakeholders' interests.

Vorstand

The *Vorstand* is responsible for the day-to-day management and represents the company in business and legal affairs. The appointment of its members is usually for five-year terms with the possibility of renewal every five years and dismissals are allowed only when there is just cause.[53] Managing directors' remuneration is set by the *Aufsichtsrat*, which is perhaps one of the reasons why management pay in Germany has not historically been at the levels of the US or the UK.[54] Managing directors have a variety of duties to comply with, such as a duty of skill and care and a duty of loyalty.[55] Of central importance with regard to corporate governance is that managing directors owe their duties to the company itself, as in most company law systems. However, the corporate entity's interests are not identified solely with those of the shareholders. Historically, the *Aktiengesetz* of 1937 provided originally that management was explicitly responsible for shareholder interests *as well* as for the workforce and the public good – a view of the corporation that closely resembled Dodd's stakeholder model. Even though its replacement in 1965 does not make such a specific reference to non-shareholder interests, Hopt and many other authors believe that this is because the inclusion of employee and social considerations are legally self-evident.[56] In terms of enforcing the duty the AktG provides that the right to bring an action against management rests with the *Aufsichtsrat* which represents the company and not the shareholders vis-à-vis the managers.[57] This right has historically rarely been exercised.[58] However,

---

52   Korn/Ferry International, above n50.

53   Section 84 (3) AktG. Such a 'just cause' ('wichtig grund') may arise when there is a material breach of duty, a withdrawal of confidence by the General Meeting on objective grounds or an incapacity to manage.

54   Prigge, S., above n42, 966–967.

55   For a general discussion of directors' duties in German company law see Baums, T. (1996) 'Personal Liabilities of Company Directors in German Law', International Corporate and Commercial Law Review, vol. 9, 318–324.

56   See Hopt, K., above n47, 230–231 and 237. On employee interests see the next section 'Works Councils and Collective Bargaining'.

57   See section 112 AktG and, for example, the decision of the Bundesgerichtshof (Federal Supreme Court) of 21 April 1997, Betriebsberater, 1169.

58   Hopt, K. (1992) 'Directors' Duties to Shareholders, Employees and Other Creditors: A View from the Continent' in McKendrick, E. (ed.) Commercial Aspects of

the *Aufsichtsrat* or a court appointed representative respectively can be asked by a General Meeting resolution or by a large shareholder to commence an action against managers.[59]

In all though, German management wield significant power. As Raiser describes it:

> [u]nder German law, in the public company the power of the managing board is rather strong, because Section 76 rules directors to guide the company under their own responsibility, free from any binding instructions of either shareholders or supervisory board. Only fundamental changes require approval of the shareholder meeting, and the supervisory board may exercise a veto in certain cases where the by-laws provide such a veto. This widely discretionary power of the managing board favours a bias towards managerial "absolutism" which sometimes can hardly be stopped.[60]

Thus, in contrast to the nominalist conception of the corporation where shareholders are the only constituency to which directors are accountable and therefore the company should be run in their interests, German company law does not provide any similar obligation. At least in law, German managers have the ability to channel company cash flow to projects and schemes that do not necessarily create value for current shareholders without running the risk of being removed for breach of duty.

Works Councils and Collective Bargaining

While board-level co-determination means that labour has a significant input into decision making other labour market co-determination institutions are designed to further enhance labour 'voice' within and without the corporate organization. The *Betriebsverfassungsgesetz* (Enterprise Constitution Act ('BetrVG')) of 1952 re-institutionalized the role of works councils, which as we discussed earlier, were first introduced during the Weimar years in order to isolate the radical left in Germany's labour movement but were then abolished by the Nazis.[61] While the original intentions behind the works councils was to fragment labour power by cutting the link between the shopfloor and unions, eventually the latter managed

---

Trusts and Fiduciary Obligations, Oxford, 115.

59   The minimum holding to make such a request was at least 10 percent of the nominal capital. As we will discuss in Chapter 8, the area has been reformed to make it easier for shareholders to bring an action.

60   Raiser, T. (1992) 'The Legal Constitution of Business Enterprises in the Federal Republic of Germany', Annals of the Institute of Social Science, vol. 34, 27–46 at 37.

61   Thelen, K. (1991) Union of Parts: Labour Politics in Postwar Germany, Ithaca: Cornell University Press, 63–71.

to dominate works councils and thus increase their influence inside German companies.[62]

Initially the powers of works councils were strictly defined, reflecting the aims of the 1952 Act. However, over the years the measure proved to be highly successful and accepted by employers who began to recognize the value of consensus based employment relations. In 1970 this was reinforced by the findings of the *Biedenkopf Kommission* set up to assess the impact of co-determination in the *Montan* industries, which found that increased labour voice within companies had resulted to a peaceful compromise between employers and employees without any negative effects on productivity and profitability.[63] Cooperation between management and labour was important for the efficient setting of wage levels without conflict and the smooth implementation of new technologies, e.g. by facilitating the coordination of training and re-skilling programmes.[64]

These findings were thus followed by the enactment of the *Betrieb-sverfassungsgesetz* of 1972, which expanded the role of works councils and removed any barriers between them and the unions. This law granted a right to the election of works councils in all plants with five permanent employees or more by a direct vote and for a maximum term of three years. Candidates for Works Council membership have to be supported by at least 10 percent of the plant's workforce. According to Wood, this gives the German Trade Union Federation (Deutscher Gewerkschaftsbund ('DGB')) significant influence over the selection of candidates and therefore increases the leverage of unions within works councils.[65] What is of importance in understanding the cooperative nature of the corporate governance system in Germany, is that, even though they represent a particular constituency within the firm, council members are legally bound to act for the promotion of the welfare of the corporation as a whole.[66] This can be explained by the broad spectrum of issues in which works councils are involved. More specifically, they have extensive *co-determination* rights over working hours, bonus rates, working conditions, employment transfers and dismissals, and *information* rights regarding personnel planning, financial matters and major strategic changes. Obviously, these legal rights provide an institutional framework for an enhanced micro-level governance role for employees.

---

62   Wood, S., above n31.

63   Biednkopf Kommission (1970) Bericht der Sachverständigenkommission zur Auswertung der Bisheringen Erfahrungen bei der Mitbestimmung, Bochum: Bundestag-Drucksache VI/334.

64   Backes-Gellner, U., Frick B., and Sadowski, D. (1997) 'Codetermination and Personnel Policies of German Firms: The Influence of Works Councils on Turnover and Further Training', International Journal of Human Resource Management, vol .8(3), 328–347.

65   See Wood, S., above n31.

66   Müller-Jentsch, W. (1995) 'Germany: From Collective Voice to Co-Management' in Rogers, J. and Streeck, W. (eds) Works Councils: Consultation, Representation and Cooperation in Industrial Relations, Chicago: University of Chicago Press.

Besides co-determination channels, labour voice is also influential at a macroeconomic level due to the important role of unions in collective bargaining. Unionization levels have traditionally been high in Germany providing a virtual monopoly of interest representation due to the dominant position of DGB unions and the marginalization of non-DGB ones. Collective agreements between unions and employers' organizations, once concluded, are legally binding on all members of the signing associations and usually cover matters that do not fall within the scope of works councils with the focus being on wage determination. Generally, the law promotes the centralization of industrial relations policy as it gives higher status to collective agreements than to firm level co-determination arrangements unless the former expressly delegate matters to the latter.[67] However, there is no specific legislation governing collective bargaining which is simply guaranteed by the freedom of association provisions, Art. 8, para.3, of the *Grundgesetz* (German Constitution), although in turn the courts have formulated a general code on collective bargaining through their rulings. In 1980 for example 80 percent of workers in Germany were covered by a collective bargaining agreement.[68]

In sum, company-level co-determination through *Aufsichtsrat* representation and works councils and macro-level collective bargaining agreements between unions and employers' associations complement each other as channels of labour voice in industrial coordination. Moreover, the link between the two channels because of the dominant role of DGB unions in works councils, has ensured the coherence of the system. The complex web of German industrial relations institutions has been a significant force behind the incentives of managers to use their discretion in order to balance shareholder and employee interests. Comparative studies have shown that human capital related investment in German companies has been significantly more than in most other developed countries operating without a co-determination regime.[69] Moreover, such firm-specific investment has made labour market internalization policies highly significant in Germany. Trainee apprenticeship schemes undertaken by German companies, for instance, have constituted one of the major institutions in German socio-economic life combining both formal vocational education and on-the-job training (*Duales Ausbildungssystem*).[70]

---

67   Hassel, A. (1999) 'The Erosion of the German System of Industrial Relations', British Journal of Industrial Relations, vol. 37, 483–505 at 486–487.

68   OECD (2004) OECD Employment Outlook, Table 3.3.

69   Smith, S. (1991) 'On the Economic Rationale for Codetermination Law', Journal of Economic Behaviour and Organization, vol. 16, 261–281 at 276.

70   Smith, E., above n29, 268–273, and Jackson, G. (2004) 'Toward a Comparative Perspective on Corporate Governance and Labour Management', Discussion Paper, Research Institute of Economy, Trade and Industry (RIETI), 58.

Share Ownership

The share ownership structure of German companies has also played a part in the evolution of the German corporate governance model. Accurate historical figures on shareholdings are difficult to find, as transparency is a problem here.[71] Until 1995, equity stakes below 25 percent were not subject to mandatory disclosure. Since the mid 1990s this has improved as legislation implemented as part of the *Wertpapierhandelsgesetz* (Securities Trading Act 1994 ('WpHG'))[72] has made it obligatory for listed AGs to disclose equity stakes of five percent and above of outstanding equity. Nevertheless, difficulties in determining the ownership structure of German corporations still exist.

Despite this several studies have attempted to explore the structure and identity of German shareholdings. Generally, their results show that corporate ownership in Germany is highly concentrated and that the market for corporate control, such as it is, is dominated by large blockholders. A study conducted by Becht and Boehmer has shown that more than 50 percent of all listed companies have a single majority shareholder and that only 17.4 percent have no blockholder with a 25 percent stake or above.[73] In total they found that 85 percent of listed companies have at least one dominant blockholder.[74] Moreover, Franks and Mayer found that concentration in the largest 200 German companies is even higher since such a blockholder is present in almost 90 percent of them.[75] In addition, Goergen documented that ownership structure tends not to fluctuate significantly over time and that, even after German companies list on the stock exchange, their semi-private ownership structure is maintained due to the strong presence of large blockholders.[76]

Particularly interesting is the identity of shareholdings. Table 7.1 provides a good snapshot of the identity of the largest blockholders in a sample of two hundred large German companies in 1993. In almost half (96) of them the largest blockholder is another domestic non financial corporation. The second largest group is that of families with 43 largest blocks, followed by foreign non financial companies (21), banks (16) and the German government (11). These figures also reflect the size of shareholdings owned by each shareholder type. In Table 7.2 one

---

71   Becht, M. and Boehmer, E. (1999) 'Transparency of Ownership and Control in Germany', Working Paper, European Corporate Governance Network, 1999, available at SSRN: <http://ssrn.com/abstract=149774 or DOI: 10.2139/ssrn.10.2139/ssrn.149774>.

72   This piece of legislation is discussed more extensively in Chapter 8.

73   Becht, M. and Boehmer, E. (2002) 'Ownership and Voting Power in Germany' in Barca, F. and Becht, M. (eds) The Control of Corporate Europe, 128–154.

74   Becht, M. and Boehmer, E., above n71.

75   Franks, J. and Mayer, C. (1992) 'Corporate Control: A Synthesis of the International Evidence', IFA Working Paper, 165–192.

76   Goergen, M. (1995) 'The Evolution of Ownership and Control in German IPOs: A Dynamic Analysis', Working Paper, School of Management Studies, Keble College, University of Oxford.

can see the historical patterns of figures for blockholders in listed companies from 1960 to 1990 reflects a similar pattern.

Table 7.1 Significance of blockholders in traditional German governance

Largest blockholders in a sample of 200 large German companies in 1993

	Number of companies
Companies without a blockholder	9
Companies with a blockholder	189
Total	198

Type of largest blockholder	Number of blocks
Domestic non-financial company	96
Foreign non-financial company	21
Families (incl. trusts)	43
Domestic banks	16
Domestic government entities	11
Domestic insurance companies	2
Foreign government entities	1
Non-profit organisations	1
Total	200*

Largest blocks held by domestic non-financial companies (percent of total voting stock)

Size (percent)	Number of blocks
0–25	4
25–50	14
50–75	32
75–100	46
Total	96

Note: * Two companies had blockholders of equal size.
Source: Saling Aktienführer 1993 and 1994, Darmstadt: Verlag Hoppenstedt & Co.; Emmons, W. and Schmid, F. (1998) 'Universal Banking, Control Rights, and Corporate Finance in Germany', Federal Reserve Bank of St. Louis Review, July/August, 19–42, Tables 2 and 3.

Table 7.2 Distribution of shareholdings in German listed companies by owner type (percent)

Owning sector	1960	1970	1980	1990
Non-financial companies	40.7	37.4	42.8	39.0
Private households	30.3	31.3	21.2	20.0
Public sector	12.0	9.6	8.5	4.4
Banks	8.0	9.1	11.6	14.0
Insurance	3.4	4.2	4.8	7.8
Other financial*	–	–	–	–
Foreign investors	5.6	8.5	11.1	14.8

Note: * Due to a classification change in 1992 mutual funds, which were before then accounted for in other groups, from 1992 onwards have accounted for the bulk of 'other financial' owners.
Source: Vitols, S. (2005) 'German Corporate Governance in Transition: Implications of Bank Exit from Monitoring and Control', International Journal of Disclosure and Governance, vol. 2, 357–367.

With regard to the high level of non financial company ownership it is important to note that to a great extent it is explained by the high level of cross-shareholdings. Given the fact that the most common type of shares in Germany have historically been bearer shares and that disclosure avoidance was common, revealing with accuracy the exact level and structure of cross-shareholdings in German corporations is not an easy task.[77] Nevertheless, the *Deutsche Bundesbank* has estimated that cross-ownership accounts for about three-quarters of all blockholdings controlled by the non financial sector.[78] Moreover, in their analysis of listed companies in 1997, Wegner and Kaserer found that the amount of cross-shareholdings is between 27 percent and 36 percent of gross market capitalization.[79] On the other hand, as Table 7.3 below shows, the degree of cross-ownership is even higher in the banking sector. Also important is the link between different segments of the financial sector. For instance, in 1996 the insurance conglomerate Allianz and certain banks, Bayerische Hypotheken-und Wechselbank, Dresdner Bank and Münchener Rückversicherung, held stakes in each other of between 28 percent and

---

77 Wegner, E. (1996) 'Expert Opinion for the Monopolkommission, Part III: Überkreuzverflechtungen und die Blockade des Marktes für Unternehmenskontrolle', Frankfurt.

78 Deutsche Bundesbank (1997) 'Shares as Financing and Investment Instruments', Monthly Report, vol. 49(1), 27 at 38.

79 Wenger, E. and Kaserer, C. (1998) 'The German System of Corporate Governance – A Model Which Should Not Be Imitated' in Black, S. and Moersch, M. (eds) Competition and Convergence in Financial Markets: The German and Anglo-American Models, North Holland, 40–47.

42 percent.[80] In the 1980s the Bundesbank estimated that the big banks appear to account for almost half of all bank holdings in all sectors,[81] while in 1995 Allianz and Deutsche Bank controlled 4.87 percent and 3.43 percent respectively of total stock market capitalization in Germany.[82] However, most of the equity owned by banks is not in non financial companies but in other financial institutions.

Table 7.3 Share in voting rights of five largest private banks at their own general meetings in 1992 (percent)

	Deutsche Bank	Dresdner Bank	Commerz-bank	Bay. Vereinsbank	Bayr. Hypo	Total
Deutsche Bank	32.07	14.14	3.03	2.75	2.83	54.82
Dresdner Bank	4.75	44.19	4.75	5.45	5.04	64.15
Commerz-bank	13.43	16.35	18.49	3.78	3.65	55.70
Bay. Vereinsbank	8.80	10.28	3.42	32.19	3.42	58.11
Bayr. Hypo	5.90	10.19	5.72	23.87	10.74	56.42

Note: Percentage of present shares, including majority-controlled bank subsidiaries and investment companies.
Source: Prigge, S (1998) 'A Survey of German Corporate Governance', in Hopt, K., et al (eds) Comparative Corporate Governance: The State of the Art and Emerging Research, Oxford: Clarendon Press, Table 18.

Perhaps even more significant is the way voting rights are exercised. There, despite their relatively small amounts of equity in non financials, banks, particularly the *Großbanken*, are able to act as proxies and thus control voting majorities in many large companies. This is because historically under Section 135 AktG in order to have an exercisable voting right, shareholders must either deposit their shares with the company or give a proxy to a credit institution, a professional shareholder agent or a shareholder association. For holders of bearer shares, who normally want to remain anonymous, bank proxy voting is most preferable. Banks as a result have the potential to wield very large numbers of shares at General meetings. As the data in Table 7.4 shows the banks on average constituted more than 80 percent of total votes present at the General Meetings of the largest German companies in 1986, with the Big Three accounting for more than half of that 80 percent (45.44 percent of total banks votes present). Share depositors can if they wish instruct their bank on how to vote in a general meeting, but in practice such instructions

---

80   In April 2001 Dresdner Bank was taken over by the insurance conglomerate Allianz AG.
81   Deutsche Bundesbank (1987) 'Longer-Term Trends in the Banks', Monthly Report (May), 24–33.
82   Wegner, E., above n77.

are rare and usually banks vote as they think fit. Indeed, because of this apparent dominance of banks some observers regard German corporate governance as bank based. However, this is an area of controversy, as a closer analysis of the banks' role shows this view of the German corporate governance system to be open to a number of different interpretations. We will return to this important point later in the chapter once we have examined other equally significant aspects of the German corporate governance system. In sum, ownership of large German companies is highly concentrated with other non financial companies, families, the government and banks as the most significant blockholders.

Table 7.4 Voting blocks of banks at shareholder meetings of the largest German companies in 1986

Company and ranking		Percent of shares present at the AGM	Percent of shares voted by				
			Deutsche Bank	Dresdner Bank	Commerz-bank	All big three	All banks
1	Siemens	60.64	17.84	10.74	4.14	32.52	79.83
2	Daimler-Benz	81.02	41.80	18.78	1.07	61.66	69.34
3	Mercedes-Holding	67.20	11.85	13.66	12.24	37.75	57.35
4	Volkwagen	50.13	2.94	3.70	1.33	7.98	19.53
5	Bayer	53.18	30.82	16391	6.77	54.50	95.78
6	BASF	55.40	28.07	17.43	6.18	51.68	96.64
7	Hoechst	57.73	14.97	16.92	31.60	63.48	98.18
9	VEBA	50.24	19.99	23.08	5.85	47.92	98.18
11	Thyssen	68.48	9.24	11.45	11.93	32.62	53.11
12	Deutsche Bank	55.10	47.17	9.15	4.04	60.36	97.23
13	Mannesmann	50.63	20.49	20.33	9.71	50.53	95.40
18	MAN (GHH)	64.10	6.97	9.48	13.72	30.17	52.85
21	Dresdner Bank	56.79	13.39	47.08	3.57	64.04	98.16
27	Allianz-Holding	66.20	9.91	11.14	2.35	23.41	60.08
28	Karstadt	77.60	37.03	8.81	33.02	78.86	87.27
29	Hoesch	45.39	15.31	15.63	16.73	47.67	92.39
34	Commerz-bank	50.50	16.30	9.92	34.58	60.81	96.77
35	Kaufhof	66.70	6.29	13.33	37.18	56.80	98.45
36	Klöckner-Werke	69.13	17.30	3.78	3.55	24.63	53.00

Table 7.4 continued

Company and ranking	Percent of shares present at the AGM	Percent of shares voted by				
		Deutsche Bank	Dresdner Bank	Commerz-bank	All big three	All banks
37 KHD	72.40	44.22	3.82	1.50	49.54	85.29
41 Metallgesell-schaft	90.55	16.42	48.85	0.35	65.62	75.95
44 Preussag	69.58	11.15	5.60	2.59	19.34	99.68
51 Degussa	70.94	6.86	33.03	1.89	41.79	67.09
52 Bayr. Vereinsbank	62.40	11.42	2.71	3.59	17.72	68.69
56 Continental	35.29	22.77	9.99	6.04	38.81	95.55
57 Bayr. Hypobank	67.90	5.86	7.05	1.20	14.11	92.09
59 Deutsche Babcock	67.13	7.58	9.67	5.29	22.54	97.01
67 Schering	46.60	23.86	17.46	10.17	51.50	99.08
68 Linde	52.99	22.76	15.73	21.36	59.87	90.37
73 Ph. Holzmann	82.18	55.42	0.91	6.49	62.82	74.81
94 Strabag	83.02	6.80	19.15	1.37	27.32	95.24
96 Bergmann	99.12	36.89	-	-	36.89	62.15
98 Hapag-Lloyd	84.50	48.15	47.82	0.39	96.36	99.50
On average	64.49	21.09	15.30	9.05	45.44	82.67

Source: Gottschalk, A. (1988) 'Der Stimmrechtseinfluß der Banken in den Aktionärs-versammlungen von Großunternehmen', WSI-Mitteilungen, vol. 41, 294–304.

The Traditional Role of the Securities Market in Germany

As we discussed at the beginning of this chapter the German stock market has historically remained largely underdeveloped in comparison to the UK and US. However, there are eight stock exchanges in Germany with the *Frankfurter Wertpapierbörse* being by far the largest and most important of them with approximately 90 percent of total turnover of transactions.[83] Nevertheless, the total market capitalization as a percentage of GDP has historically been very low. For example in 1995 it was 23.9 percent compared to 95.2 percent in the US and 121.6 percent in the UK (Chart 7.1). The number of listed companies has also been very small. At the end of 1997, of the 3,000 AGs in Germany there were only 700 that had listed shares. The respective numbers of listings on the London and the New

---

[83] On the Frankfurter Wertpapierbörse see <http://deutsche-boerse.com/dbag/dispatch/en/kir/gdb_navigation/about_us>.

York Stock Exchanges were 2,046 and 2,271 (Chart 7.2). Given the institutional strength of labour representation and the importance of bank finance perhaps this is unsurprising but lack of investor protection may have played a role in making equities unattractive where blockholders still retain significant shares on listing. Indeed, a number of studies have found that German initial public offerings' (IPOs) post-issue performance was negatively related to the degree of ownership that is retained by the original owners.[84]

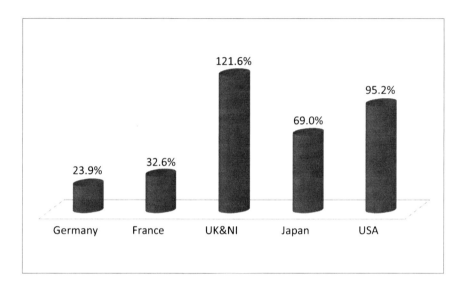

**Chart 7.1 Stock market capitalization as a percentage of GDP in
                 major economies, 1995**
Source: Authors own research using Deutsches Aktieninstitut Database (2008) Factbook: Statistiken, Analysen und Grafiken zu Aktionären, Aktiengesellschaften und Börsen, Frankfurt: DAI.

---

84   Ljungqvist, J. (1996) 'Can Firms Outwit the Market? Timing Ability and the Long-Run Performance of IPOs' in Levis, M. (ed.) Empirical Issues in Raising Equity Capital, Oxford: Elsevier. See also Bessler, W., Kaen, F. and Sherman, H. (1998) 'Going Public: A Corporate Governance Perspective' in Hopt et al., above n42, 569–605. For a similar general study with a different outcome but which does not examine the size of blockholding retained see Goergen, M. (1998) 'Insider Retention and Long-Run Performance in German and UK IPOs', European Corporate Governance Institute, Working Paper Series, available at SSRN: <http://ssrn.com/abstract=149780 or DOI: 10.2139/ssrn.10.2139/ssrn.149780>.

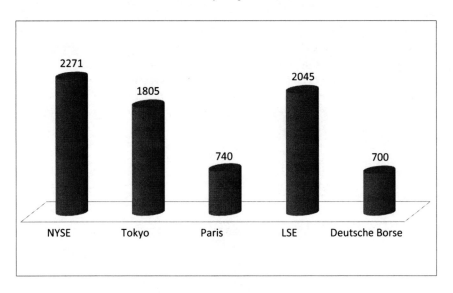

Chart 7.2 Listed industrial corporations in five major exchanges in 1997
Source: Authors own research using Deutsches Aktieninstitut Database (2008) Factbook: Statistiken, Analyses und Grafiken zu Aktionären, Aktiengesellschaften und Börsen, Frankfurt: DAI.

Historically, the largest percentage of finance for German corporations is generated internally in the form of retained earnings. Although this is not a distinctive characteristic for Germany, the use of internal funds by German companies has been above average and much more significant than equity or bank finance.[85] As regards external finance, issues of equity have not been as significant as in the UK and US. The same can be said about securitized debt in the form of bonds. This can partly be explained by similar factors as those that have hampered the development of the stock market, i.e. information asymmetries between inside and outside investors but also by lack of demand. As we noted earlier, the percentage

---

85   Vitols, S. (2001) 'The Origins of Bank-Based and Market-Based Financial Systems: Germany, Japan, and the United States' in Streeck, W. and Yamamura, K. (eds) The Origins of Nonliberal Capitalism: Germany and Japan in Comparison, Ithaca/London: Cornell University Press, 171–199 at 181; Mayer, C. and Alexander, I. (1990) 'Banks and Securities Markets: Corporate Financing in Germany and the United Kingdom', Journal of Japanese and International Economies, vol. 4, 450–475; Holtfrerich, C. (1995) 'Die Deutsche Bank von Zweiten Weltkrieg über die Besat-zungsherrschaft zur Rekonstruktion 1945–1957' in Gall, L. et al. (eds) Die Deutsche Bank 1870–1995, München: Beck, 409–578 at 574; and Corbett, J. and Jenkinson, T. (1996) 'The Financing of Industry 1970–1989: An International Comparison', Journal of the Japanese and International Economies, vol. 10, 71–96.

of intermediated debt, i.e. bank borrowing, as part of external finance has been high constituting the second most important source of corporate finance.[86]

Tax advantages for intermediated debt finance, particularly due to high securities transfer taxes, may also provide an explanation for the historically low level of corporate finance securitization.[87] Moreover, unlike the US banking system, where banks were forcibly split in the 1930s into deposit and lending institutions and separate investment banking institutions, historically German banks have not faced any significant regulatory restrictions on their activities.[88] This allowed them to grow into large all-purpose financial institutions that could provide more financial capital than their counterparts in some other countries, and therefore an alternative source of industrial finance to securities.

Takeovers

As we observed in Chapters 5 and 6 hostile takeovers played an important part in focusing managerial discretion on shareholders in the UK and US. Historically hostile-takeovers in Germany have been virtually non-existent in comparison to the US and the UK.[89] Two factors in particular, persistent ownership concentration and deficient outsider shareholder protection, have been instrumental in the absence of hostile takeovers and the subsequent insignificant role of the market for corporate control as a mechanism for aligning German managers' interests with those of shareholders.[90] We turn now to consider each of these factors.

The consequence of ownership concentration

Prima facie it seems that, at least partially, the absence of hostile takeovers can be explained directly by ownership concentration. Edwards and Fischer argue that simply the existence of a 25 percent blockholder can put off a potential

---

86   Hackethal, A. and Schmidt, R. (2004) 'Financing Patterns: Measurement Concepts and Empirical Results', Working Paper No. 125, Fachbereich Wirtschaftswissenschaften, Johann Wolfgang Goethe-Universität, Frankfurt am Main, Table 6, available at SSRN: <http://ssrn.com/abstract=254463 or DOI: 10.2139/ssrn.10.2139/ssrn.254463>.

87   Edwards, J. and Weichenrieder, A. (1999) 'Ownership Concentration and Share Valuation: Evidence from Germany', Working Paper No. 193, CESifo, Ludvig-Maximillian-Universität München. Available at SSRN: <http://ssrn.com/abstract=175333>.

88   The Glass-Steagall Act of 1933 separated commercial and investment banking and prevented US banks from expanding beyond their individual states until 1999 when most of it was repealed by the Gramm-Leach-Bliley Act of 1999.

89   Underhill, W. and Austmann, A. (2002) 'Defence Tactics' in Payne, J. (ed.) Takeovers in English and German Law, Hart Publishing, 867–90.

90   Coffee, J. (1991) 'Liquidity Versus Control: The Institutional Investor as Corporate Monitor', Columbia Law Review, vol. 91(6), 1277–1368.

hostile bidder from making an offer for the target company.[91] This is because the
acquisition of a stake below 75 percent by the bidder would not be enough to
remove the incumbent supervisory board members and pass successful resolutions
regarding important matters such as mergers, acquisitions and changes to the
Articles of Association.[92] Moreover, buying out a blocking minority stake may
be rather costly because the blockholder would normally require a premium that
would render the cost of the takeover too high or indeed they might not sell at all,
especially if the block in question is owned by a founding family.

An additional takeover barrier with relation to shareholder structure is the high
level of cross-ownership between German companies. As we discussed above,
inter-firm cooperative arrangements often led over time to the exchange of stock.
Even if not all of those cross-shareholdings have been used for management
entrenchment, a large number of them have indeed been created for this sole
purpose. A characteristic example is that of Mercedes Automobil Holding which
held a 25 percent stake in Daimler-Benz and was created by the latter with the help
of some of Daimler's main shareholders, namely Deutsche Bank, Dresdner Bank,
Commerzbank and Allianz Holding, for the sole purpose of preventing unwanted
hostile-takeover attempts.[93] As Wenger and Kaserer have noted:

> [t]he most effective way for management to stave off capital market pressure is
> to build a network of mutual shareholdings financed with retained earnings or
> coordinated capital increases serving the sole purpose to exchange equity among
> colluding companies.[94]

Consequently the possibilities of finding a potential takeover target in Germany
have historically been limited (Table 7.5 below). After a detailed examination of
all German listed companies, Jenkinson and Ljungqvist found a maximum of only
77 companies with a free float of 50 percent or more and therefore capable of
being taken over.[95]

91   Edwards, J. and Fischer, K. (1994) Banks, Finance and Investment in Germany,
Cambridge: Cambridge University Press, 192.
92   Sections 103 and 179 AktG.
93   See discussion in Wenger, E. and Kaserer, C., above n79, 7–15; and Höpner, M.
and Krempel, L., above n9, 343.
94   Wenger, E. and Kaserer, C., above n79, 21.
95   Jenkinson, T. and Ljungqvist, A. (1997) 'Hostile Stakes and the Role of Banks in
German Corporate Governance', Working Paper, Centre for Economic Policy Research,
Oxford, available at SSRN: <http://ssrn.com/abstract=33678>.

Table 7.5 Takeovers, pay and ownership: Germany and the UK

		Germany	UK
a) Takeovers (1988–1996)		4	1190
b) CEO compensation structure (1998)			
Total remuneration (average in US $)		398,430	645,540
Variable bonus as a percentage of annual basic compensation		27%	22%
Options/long-term incentive plans as a percentage of annual basic compensation		2%	38%
c) Ownership concentration of listed companies (1994–95)			
	>50%	68%	7%
Main Shareholder	25–50%	21%	12%
	<25%	11%	81%
d) Share ownership structure (1995)			
Private households/Individuals		14.6%	20.3%
Public sector		4.3%	0.8%
Insurance companies		12.4%	21.9%
Pension/Investment funds		7.6%	36.6%
Banks		10.3%	0.4%
Enterprises/commercial corporations		42.1%	1.1%
Rest of the world		8.7%	16.3%

Source: Data compiled from Schmidt, H. (1999) 'Differences between Financial Systems in European Countries: Consequences for EMU', Universität Frankfurt Working Paper No. 35, Table A2.

However, the minimal role of the German stock market and the hostile-takeover in corporate governance cannot be explained by the ownership structure alone. A number of other management entrenchment devices have also been introduced over the years. For instance, voting caps have historically been quite common particularly where founding families wished to retain control or in companies that felt threatened by increasing foreign ownership, mainly from oil producing countries, during the 1970s.[96] Furthermore, non-voting preference shares as well as shares with transferability restrictions (*Vinkulierung*) have also been common

---

96   Gordon, G and Schmid, F. (2000) 'Universal Banking and the Performance of German Firms', Journal of Financial Economics, vol. 58, 29–80; and Baums, T. (1993) 'Takeovers Versus Institutions in Corporate Governance in Germany' in Prentice, D. and Holland, P. (eds) Contemporary Issues in Corporate Governance, Oxford: Clarendon Press, 156.

types of publicly traded stock.[97] Multiple voting rights have generally been prohibited subject to the exception that state authorities could grant their approval for the use of this type of shares when deemed necessary to protect the overriding interest of the economy as a whole.[98]

Another very significant takeover barrier with regard to voting arises from the ability of German banks to act as custodians of shares and proxy-voters. As already mentioned, the number of votes banks exercise in General Meetings of large German corporations is substantial. Their attitude towards management has usually been supportive because of the long-term relationship between the banks and their corporate clients and also so that they could protect their investments as risk averse creditors.[99] Indeed, the introduction of restrictions on voting rights has usually been supported by the banks. The involvement of Deutsche Bank was instrumental in the implementation of a five percent voting cap during two respective hostile takeover bids for Feldmühle Nobel AG by Veba AG and the Flick family in 1988.[100] Mercedes Automobil Holding mentioned above was also an illustration of how banks have been helping corporate managers protect themselves from hostile takeovers. Thus, the banks' proxy-voting function has constituted a significant mechanism of managerial insulation from outside financial pressures over the years rather than operating as a disciplinary mechanism for shareholders. Finally, another structural impediment to hostile takeovers arises from the corporate board structure itself. More specifically, the labour representatives on a co-determined *Aufsichtsrat* will normally be fierce opponents of hostile bids because of the risks involved for the workforce in such transactions. Government shareholdings and restrictions on shareholders voting rights in certain important companies has also played a role here. The most famous restriction on voting rights is on shares in Volkswagen AG whereby a shareholder can wield only a maximum of 20 percent of the voting rights in the company no matter how many shares they actually own. The government also holds a 20 percent blocking minority of shares.[101] In all the influence of management, labour, banks, the government and the presence of cross-shareholdings have historically made it very difficult to takeover a German company.

97   Becht, M. and Boehmer, E., above n71.
98   Section 12(2) AktG. We discuss the reform of this area in Chapter 8.
99   See Goodhart, D. (1998) 'Banks Hold Key that Would Unlock the Door to Reform', Financial Times, 13 July, Survey, 4, on the policy of German banks not to participate in hostile bids mainly due to reputation reasons among their large corporate customers. We discuss the role of banks as exercisers of control later in this chapter.
100 Franks, E. and Mayer, C. (1998) 'Bank Control, Takeovers and Corporate Governance in Germany', Journal of Banking and Finance, vol. 22, 1385–1403 at 1389.
101 We discuss the Volkswagen restrictions in full in Chapter 8.

Deficient outside shareholder protection

At this stage it is useful to distinguish between two types of shareholders. The first is the committed inside shareholder who makes a large and therefore firm-specific investment in the company and who has the incentive to engage in active monitoring of management, and the second is the shareholder who lacks monitoring incentives and prefers to remain an uncommitted 'outsider'. If one general observation can be made from our description of the German Corporate governance system's institutional design so far, it is that the German system has been specifically designed to encourage the former type of shareholder and discourage the latter. This 'systemic' bias against the latter type of shareholder also has a reflection in a historically deficient investor protection regime when it comes to minority shareholder rights and disclosure.

Firstly, a minority investor in a German company faces a real and significant risk of wealth appropriation by insider blockholders or banks who may use their proxy votes against the interest of those outsider shareholders.[102] Edwards and Weichenrieder for example found evidence for this appropriation of private benefits by the largest shareholders in German companies. Interestingly the appropriation diminishes as the equity held by the second largest shareholder increases.[103] However, the ability of large blockholders to acquire private benefits to the detriment of minority shareholders is more pronounced with regard to changes of control. This has been attributed to the historical lack of effective takeover regulation in Germany.[104]

The traditional approach of takeover regulation in Germany followed the path of ex-post protection of minority shareholders, that is, *within* the merged entity, rather than the *ex-ante* protection, i.e. before the takeover transaction is complete.[105] It is widely believed that this form of regulation does not provide a minority shareholder sufficient protection. Thus, the dilution of minority shareholdings by controlling majority shareholders has been both possible and

---

102   Schmidt, H., Drukarczyk, J. and Honold, D. (1997) Corporate Governance in Germany, Baden-Baden: Nomos, 77–93.

103   Edwards, J. and Weichenrieder, A. (1999) 'Ownership Concentration and Share Valuation: Evidence from Germany', Working Paper No. 193, CESifo, Ludvig-Maximillian-Universität München, available at SSRN: <http://ssrn.com/abstract=175333>.

104   A set of 'Guiding Principles' were instituted in 1979 but only constituted some non-binding general recommendations. Again we discuss the reform of this area in Chapter 8.

105   Section 311ff. AktG. The most important rule of ex-ante protection is the requirement for a mandatory offer to all shareholders once certain thresholds (e.g. 30 percent of share-capital) are met. See Baums, T. (1996) 'The New Draft Proposal for a Directive on Takeovers – The German Perspective', Working Paper, Institut für Handels – und Wirtschaftsrect, Universität Osnabrück, <http://www.jura.uni-frankfurt.de/ifawz1/baums/Bilder_und_Daten/Arbeitspapiere/a1096.pdf>, and Schmidt, H., Drukarczyk, J. and Honold, D., above n102, 77–93.

common in German takeovers. This is because tender offers to minorities, when they occur, have historically been at a discount to the large blockholders. Wegner and Hecker for example found that in 45 cases between 1983 and 1992 such offers were 27.1 percent below the market price.[106] Similarly, Jenkinson and Ljungqvist show that in three out of four cases in their sample, discounts ranged from 15 percent to 64 percent.[107]

In addition, the absence of effective insider trading regulation, at least until the mid-1990s, has also acted as a deterrent for outside investors.[108] Although in 1970 the Voluntary Insider Trading Guidelines were adopted, their voluntary character and the lack of specific criminal or even administrative sanctions as well as of an effective enforcement mechanism rendered them ineffective and insider trading a common and even accepted practice. For instance, Standen reports a case where in 1986 a member of the AEG AG *Aufsichtsrat* purchased 700 shares in the company just before it was made publicly known that the company would be acquired by Daimler-Benz AG. After an investigation by the Frankfurt Stock Exchange, the board of inquiry characterized the event as a 'minor infraction' and found that there was no infringement of the rules.[109]

As regards disclosure, it is, as we noted above, because of the widespread use of bearer shares it is difficult to identify the exact ownership in terms of ultimate control of German corporations. This means that an 'outside' shareholder faces increased uncertainty and therefore higher risk due to the possibility that an externally invisible controlling blockholder or externally invisible coalition of blockholders may have the ability to extract private benefits. For the company's prospects of raising capital from the equities market this becomes a vicious circle as the increased risk to outsider shareholders of investing in a company increases the cost of equity finance for the company making it less attractive. Obviously, the higher the level of information provided in the market about ownership is, the lower the costs of raising equity and securitized finance in general should be.

In this respect, German accounting standards (German GAAP) had not been designed on the basis that they should provide the highest possible level of information and transparency that is required for outside-shareholder protection.[110] On the contrary, they have historically been manager and creditor rather than

---

106   Wenger, E. and Hecker, R. (1995) 'Übernahme- und Abfindungsregeln am Deutschen Aktienmarkt – Eine Kritische Bestandsaufnahme im Internationalen Vergleich', ifo Studien, vol. 41, 51–87.

107   Jenkinson, T. and Ljungqvist, A., above n95.

108   It was only in July 1994 that the passage of the Second Financial Markets Promotion Act (Finanzmarktförderungsgesetz) rendered insider trading a criminal offence. See section 38 Wertpapierhandelsgesetz (Securities Trading Act ('WphG') and the discussion in Chapter 8.

109   Standen, D. (1995) 'Insider Trading Reforms Sweep Across Germany: Bracing for the Cold Winds of Change', Harvard International Law Journal, vol. 36(1), 177–206 at 198.

110   There has been significant reform of this area and we discuss it in Chapter 8.

shareholder oriented.[111] This is because they have allowed managers extensive discretion to undervalue company assets (usually land and shares) and overvalue liabilities and thus create significant hidden reserves which are often used to smooth earnings in less profitable years. The accumulation of hidden reserves is clearly not in the interests of outside investors as it distorts the accurate picture of investment risks for them and has a negative effect on dividend distribution.[112] However, it suits creditor banks, because the existence of such funds minimizes the risk of loan default. It also suits managers because the cushion of hidden reserves reduces the risk of bankruptcy. And, of course, it suits labour because hidden reserves can be used to avert redundancies and other wage-related cost-cuttings during adverse financial circumstances. In general, it would be fair to say that the German GAAP has traditionally been less informative and less detailed than the International Accounting Standards (IAS), the subsequent International Financial Reporting Standards (IFRS)[113] or the US GAAP and therefore of more limited value for the outside investor.

An additional factor of significance for the liquidity of German listed stocks has until relatively recently been the high capital gains tax imposed on stock trades and income tax exemption on large shareholdings.[114] A rate levied as high as 52 percent on capital gains resulting from trading has historically acted as a significant hurdle to stock market liquidity. Many shareholders, even if they were prepared to divest their holdings in German corporations, were prevented from doing so because of the prohibitive tax rate that would be imposed on their proceeds. In turn a complimentary income tax policy further encouraged the holding of large blocks of shares as dividends on a holding of 25 percent, later reduced to 10 percent in the 1980s, were completely exempt from taxation.[115] Thus, unless the tax burden could be significantly overcome due to some other economic or strategic reasons, holding large stakes for a long time was the only rational choice for German shareholders.[116]

As we have already encountered with takeovers, co-determination also plays a role in discouraging outsider shareholders. Roe has observed that control of half *Aufsichtsrat* seats by employees undermines diffused ownership because in

---

111 Baetge, J. and Thiele, S. (1998) 'Disclosure and Auditing as Affecting Corporate Governance' in Hopt, K. et al., above n42, 701–741, and Schmidt, P. (1998) 'Disclosure and Auditing: A German Auditor's Perspective' in Hopt, K. et al., above n42, 743–756.

112 Nonetheless, it can also be in the shareholders' interest to undervalue the company's assets because of the so-called 'conformity principle' which links commercial and tax accounting. See Schmidt, P. above n111, 745–746.

113 In April 2001 the International Accounting Standards Board (IASB) changed the name of the standards from the International Accounting Standards (IAS) to the International Financial Reporting Standards (IFRS).

114 The tax regime for capital gains has been reformed, see discussion in Chapter 8.

115 Höpner, M. and Krempel, L., above n9, 346–348.

116 Monks, R. and Minow, N. (2003) Corporate Governance, Oxford: Blackwell, 325–326.

such a case the bargaining position of shareholders *vis-à-vis* employees is always likely to be inferior as other members are not unified and the Chairperson is neutral.[117] According to Roe, a consequence of this capital-labour clash is that the 1976 extension of co-determination has encouraged increased managerial power through the degrading by management of the monitoring functions of the *Aufsichtsrat*, mainly through reductions of information flows and of decisions requiring its approval. Within the German system this board is a body whose quality and constructive influence is essential for dispersed owners of German stock who do not have the necessary information to exercise control and thus entrust the *Aufsichtsrat* members with the function of management discipline. As it does not function in this way and indeed was not designed to do so, shareholders in Germany need to acquire large and therefore costly equity stakes in order to ensure they have the necessary influence to protect their investment.

This, nevertheless, does not mean that the market for corporate control in Germany was historically completely inactive. The market just operated differently, in that, there is convincing empirical evidence that large equity-block trades, which are not always friendly, have occurred with relative frequency. Jenkinson and Ljungqvist for example, writing in 1997, identified 17 such trades aimed at hostile stake building and 139 companies that could become targets for such activity.[118] However, they distinguish such transactions from the Anglo-American takeover where management turnover is the classic outcome, because the buyer's motive in Germany is usually to gain influence or cooperation rather than acquiring majority control in the target company. It is indicative that from the seventeen identified cases only two involved a complete dismissal of incumbent management. In sum, the securities markets have not had a significant role in corporate finance or governance in Germany. Hostile takeovers have not played a constraining role in managerial decision-making since the position of outside-shareholders has been too weak to exert any pressure through the market for corporate control. As a result many observers have argued that large blockholders, in particular banks, are the key players in corporate control and therefore they constitute an 'alternative' to the market for corporate control in aligning the interests of management with those of shareholders. As we touched upon earlier and will explore in more detail in the next section, blockholder motives are complex and so this hypothesis needs to be treated cautiously.

Insider Control

In terms of influence, the significance of blockholdings in Germany is analogous to the size of the block. Thus, a block of at least 25 percent carries with it veto powers

---

117   Roe, M. (1999) 'German Codetermination and German Securities Markets' in Hopt, K. et al. (eds.), above n42, 361–372.

118   Jenkinson, T. and Ljungqvist, A., above n95.

for significant company decisions such as charter amendments, supervisory board changes as well as profit- and control-transfer agreements. In companies with otherwise dispersed ownership such a stake should normally have even greater influence. A block of at least 50 percent plus one share gives majority control and therefore control over management subject to the existence of a blocking minority with a 25 percent stake. A block of 75 percent and over means that the blockholder has absolute control over all company activities apart from preventing a 10 percent minority bringing a corporate action against management.[119] Consequently, the role of blockholders is clearly of some significance within the corporate governance system in Germany.

Certainly, one possible outcome of concentrated ownership is that the shareholder-manager 'agency' problems that arise in companies with dispersed ownership may become irrelevant. Blockholders, due to the size of their stakes in the company, may have the incentives to control management because the costs of free-riding may be higher than monitoring costs.[120] As we noted in Chapter 1, the larger the stake, the more firm-specific the shareholder's investment and, therefore, the higher his/her incentive to establish the necessary institutional mechanisms to safeguard it. However, one needs to be careful about concluding from this that management will be constrained by blockholders in a system like Germany's where blockholders may have diverse incentives for holding shares.

Blockholders because of the size of their shareholding have the ability to intervene in the affairs of management. Outsider shareholders, interested in maximizing share value, might technically benefit from blockholder intervention if that is also the aim of the blockholder. However, as we discussed in Chapter 2, that may not be the blockholder's aim. A founder of a company or their descendants whose entire income is tied to one company is likely to be more risk averse than a diversified institutional investor. Moreover, in some cases prestige and family heritage considerations may be important determinants of family blockholder behaviour. Where a non financial corporation has a strategic blockholding in another company – such as where it is a major supplier, competitor or customer – industrial strategy considerations or simply management entrenchment will tend to prevail over the desire to maximize financial returns on equity. A blockholder that is also a creditor of the company may be more interested in securing the prompt repayment of loans plus interest than the maximization of shareholder returns. In all of these cases, outsider shareholders could be disadvantaged if the blockholder makes self-serving interventions in the management of the company or defers to management because non financial motives prevail.[121]

---

119   Again there has been reform of this area. See section 147(3) sentence 1 AktG and discussion on KonTraG in Chapter 8.

120   Shleifer, A. and Vishny, R. (1997) 'A Survey of Corporate Governance', Journal of Finance, vol. 52, 737–783.

121   See Learmount, S. and Roberts, J. (2002) 'Meanings of Ownership of the Firm', ESRC Centre for Business Research Working Paper No 238, University of Cambridge,

In the case of German companies this particular point is also emphasized by Edwards and Fischer:

> [i]t is not obvious that the existence of a large shareholder – one with a holding of 25 percent or more – will result in sufficient monitoring of the management of the AG to ensure that it acts in the interests of the suppliers of equity finance when the large shareholder in question is another AG with widely-dispersed share ownership. In such a case it cannot be assumed that the managers of the latter AG will necessarily use the large shareholding in the former AG in the interests of suppliers of equity, since these managers may themselves not be subject to monitoring and control.[122]

Accordingly, Edwards and Fischer rely on the evidence produced by Schreyögg and Steinmann in their study of a sample of 300 non financial companies which has shown that about 50 percent of them were manager-controlled and therefore could not be presumed to have sufficient incentives to monitor management of other companies in which they owned equity.[123] Thus, Edwards and Fischer claim that these manager controlled companies create a web of agency problems between shareholder and managers across a large number of companies.[124]

It is not surprising therefore that the degree of influence of different blockholder types in corporate governance and performance has become the subject matter of extensive discussion. Edwards and Weichenrieder for example found that the existence of some blockholder types, such as individuals or families, banks and foreign companies, has a positive impact on the company's market value and that the benefits of close monitoring for minority shareholders outweigh the costs of private benefit extraction by blockholders.[125] However, other types of blockholders, more specifically, non-bank companies and public sector bodies have, they claim, a negative effect. Edwards and Weichenrieder explain this as resulting from the fact that these blockholders lack the necessary incentives to monitor for the benefit of shareholders. Thus cross-shareholdings seem to operate in Germany as a significant management insulation device.

Although Edwards and Weichenrieder found that banks were among the block holders who had a positive effect, their role is the subject of considerable controversy in the literature. As already mentioned universal banks are not only the main providers of external corporate finance, but sometimes hold equity stakes as well as controlling a very large number of proxy-votes. Allegedly, this gives them

---

9–10, available at <http://www.cbr.cam.ac.uk/pdf/WP238.pdf>.

122   Edwards, J. and Fischer, K., above n91, 187.

123   Schreyögg, G. and Steinmann, H. (1981) 'Zur Trennung von Eigentum und Verfügungsgewalt – Eine Empirische Analyse der Beteiligungsverhältnisse in Deutschen Grossunternehmen', Zeitschrift für Betriebswirtschaft, vol. 51, 533–558.

124   Edwards, J. and Fischer, K., above n91, 189.

125   Edwards, J. and Weichenrieder, A., above n103.

great power and influence with regard to corporate control particularly as there are bank representatives sitting on German company boards. The traditional view therefore is that, despite being manager controlled institutions themselves, due to this two-fold relationship with their client companies, banks are actually able and willing to commit themselves to corporate monitoring and, as a result, mitigate any shareholder-manager agency problems arising from the separation of ownership and control.[126] This form of relationship banking internalizes capital markets and thus reduces the costs of information asymmetries that exist in external capital markets due to deficient disclosure and transparency. That is, companies with a bank which is a permanent partner in financial matters (so-called '*Hausbank*') have relatively easy access to intermediated finance in the form of bank loans, as opposed to market finance, and also because of the banks shareholding, enjoy the long-term commitment of their creditors even in situations of financial distress.[127]

Nonetheless, banks motivations are not necessarily aligned purely with those of shareholders and it has been suggested that they mainly use their voting power to further their interests as creditors rather than as shareholders and, thus, do not act in the interests of shareholders.[128] Banks because of their dual role in the company may lack the incentives to enhance current profit maximization (shareholder value) because it carries no direct financial benefits for them as creditors or often as shareholders as most of the shares they exercise in non financial corporations are proxy votes and so any benefit would flow to the owners of the shares not the banks. An example of this type of behaviour we have already touched upon earlier is the banks' historical role in supporting management in a takeover situation. Additionally, *Hausbanken* commitment to a long-term relationship with a client company comes at a price, in that the bank expects to receive adequate returns in the form of private gains such as customer loyalty and rent extraction. For example, *Hausbanken* tend to require more collateral from their companies in order to increase their bargaining power and exclusivity as creditors.[129]

---

126 According to Bayhurst, Fey and Schreyögg, 100 percent of banks are manager-controlled. See Bayhurst, A., Fey, A. and Schreyögg, G. (1994) 'Wer Kontrolliert die Geschäftspolitik Deutscher Großunternehmen? Empirische Ergebnisse zur Kontrollsituation der 350 größten Deutschen Unternehmen der Jahre 1972, 1979 und 1989 im Vergleich', Discussion Paper No. 213, Faculty of Economics, Fernuniversität Hagen.

127 Elsas, R. and Krahnen, J. (1998) 'Is Relationship Lending Special? Evidence from Credit-File Data in Germany', Journal of Banking and Finance, vol. 22, 1283–1316; and Elston, J. and Albach, H. (1995) 'Bank Affiliations and Firm Capital Investment in Germany', Ifo-Studien: Zeitschrift fur Empirische Wirtschaftsforschung, vol. 1, 1–15 at 3.

128 Wenger, E. and Kaserer, C., above n79; and Edwards, J. and Fischer, K., above n91, 214; and on the historical risk aversion of banks when involved with companies see Fohlin, C., above n11.

129 Elsas, R. and Krahnen, J. (1999) 'Collateral, Default Risk, and Relationship Lending: An Empirical Study on Financial Contracting', Working Paper Institut für Kapitalmarktforschung, Johann Wolfgang Goethe-University, Frankfurt am Main, available at <http://www.ifk-cfs.de/papers/99_13.pdf>.

Accordingly, two studies have shown that two-thirds of short and medium-term loans are collateralized and that for long-term loans the degree of collateralization can be even higher.[130] Banks may have also benefited historically from being able to insider deal.[131]

Over the years there have been a number of studies on the impact of universal banking and relationship-lending on corporate performance.[132] The evidence on this issue, is though, anything but conclusive. The first empirical study was conducted by Cable who found that in his sample, comprised of the 100 largest German companies in 1974, ownership concentration and bank voting power were positively related to company performance.[133] However, two subsequent studies by Edwards and Fischer and Gordon and Schmid have disputed Cable's results due to flaws in his methodology and find no significant connection between bank involvement and corporate performance.[134] Edwards and Fischer, in particular, interpret Cable's findings more as evidence of a positive relation between performance and ownership concentration rather than monitoring by banks. Indeed, they cast serious doubt on the notion that Banks would have any incentive to exercise proxy votes to benefit equity holders.[135] Moreover, Edwards and Fischer's study shows no significant connection between banks' proxy-voting rights and the appointment of bank representatives on the *Aufsichtsrat,* which may indicate that banks are not using their proxy voting power to monitor management.[136] This does not appear to be the case, however, when banks are also shareholders, rather than just exercising proxy votes, since direct ownership of shares is positively related to *Aufsichtsrat* representation.[137] Nibler, in a further study found a significant negative relationship between bank influence and corporate performance.[138] Similarly, Dittmann et al. found that bank presence was bad for performance and

---

130   See: Drukarczyk, J. (1993) Theorie und Politik der Finanzierung, 2nd edition, München: Vahlen; and Drukarczyk, J., Duttle, J. and Rieger, R. (1985) 'Mobiliarsicherheiten: Arten, Verbeitung, Wirksamkeit' in Rechtstatsachenforschung, Köln: Bundesministerium der Justiz.

131   Standen, D., above n109.

132   On the debate see Mülbert, P. (1998) 'Banks' Equity Holdings in Non-Financial Firms and Corporate Governance: The Case of German Universal Banks' in Hopt, K. (ed.) Comparative Corporate Governance: The State of the Art and Emerging Research, Oxford: Oxford University Press, 445–498 at 483.

133   Cable, J. (1985) 'Capital Market Information and Industrial Performance: The Role of West German Banks', Economic Journal, vol. 95(1), 118–132.

134   Edwards, J. and Fischer, K., above n91, 221–226, and Gordon, G. and Schmid, F., above n96.

135   Edwards, J. and Fischer, K., above n91, Chapter 9 and 226–227.

136   Edwards, J. and Fischer, K., above n91, 198 et seq.

137   Franks, J. and Mayer, C. (1997) 'Ownership, Control and the Performance of German Companies', Working Paper, London Business School.

138   Nibler, M. (1995) 'Bank Control and Corporate Governance in Germany: The Evidence', Working Paper No. 48, University of Cambridge.

that they only held their shares to defer taxes.[139] Additionally, Gerum, Steinmann and Fees claim that banks' *Aufsichtsrat* representation is rather insignificant in terms of real influence, firstly, because even if all bank representatives acted in concert they would still be a small minority against other representatives, and, secondly, because they would still have to rely on management-controlled inside information.[140] This is illustrated by the case of Karstadt AG where two of the *Großbanken* could not remove the CEO, even though they held a 20 percent stake between them in the company and were also represented on the *Aufsichtsrat*.[141]

Thus, if one conclusion can be drawn from the evidence available so far, it should be that the mainstream view about the corporate control role of German universal banks is less clear than it seems. While Table 7.4 above on the face of it seems to show that banks exert a very large amount of influence through their control of shareholdings, there is no clear connection between control rights exercised by banks and shareholder value maximization. Banks motives in exercising share votes are complex. However, a plausible explanation for the conflicting evidence on bank monitoring may simply be that banks do not intervene unless there is clear evidence of a crisis. This point has been emphasized by Hackethal and Tyrell who argue that the strong creditor orientation in German insolvency law gives banks, at least theoretically, the incentives to involve themselves in corporate rescue operations and reorganizations.[142] The banks holding of shares in companies may be part of a cooperative strategy of focusing management on keeping them happy as creditors in return for support for management in times of trouble. Indeed, private benefit acquisition as a result of a reorganization may constitute an additional incentive for bank involvement. Thus, the role of *Hausbanken* may be to 'sell' liquidity insurance rather than maximize corporate performance through continuous monitoring. For large and established companies, however, the value of *Hausbank* relationships should be lower than it is for smaller ones, because the ability of one bank to insure the company's liquidity diminishes as the company grows. Additionally the risk of insolvency for such companies is smaller (e.g. due the diversification of projects). Support for this contention can be found in Harhoff and Körting's study of company-bank relationships where they show that smaller

139   Dittmann, I., Maug, E. and Schneider, C. (2008) 'Bankers on the Boards of German Firms: What They Do, What They Are Worth, and Why They Are (Still) There', ECGI – Finance Working Paper No. 196/2008, 12, available at SSRN: <http://ssrn.com/abstract=1093899>.

140   Gerum, E., Steinmann, H. and Fees, W. (1988) Der Mitbestimmte Aufsichtsrat: Eine Empirische Untersuchung, Stuttgart: C.E. Poeschel Verlag. In 1979 bank representatives occupied 16.4 percent of shareholder Aufsichtrat seats and 8.2 percent of all Aufsichtsrat seats in AGs with 2,000 employees and over.

141   André, T. (1998) 'Cultural Hegemony: The Exportation of Anglo-Saxon Corporate Governance Ideologies to Germany', Tulane Law Review, vol. 73, 69–171.

142   Hackethal, A, and Tyrell, M. (1998) 'Complementarity and Financial Systems – A Theoretical Approach', Working Paper Finance and Accounting No. 11 Johann Wolfgang Goethe – Universität, Frankfurt am Main.

companies tend to rely more heavily on exclusive lending relationships than larger ones.[143] More significantly, Edwards and Fischer found that in the case of large listed companies competition amongst creditors is higher and a *Hausbank* is 'seen as the first among equals in a group rather than a monopoly supplier of financial services'.[144] This means that, even where there are no alternative external sources of capital to bank finance, banks' leverage over management is much less than some observers would like to believe. Thus, as the synthesis of the empirical evidence in this and the previous section has indicated, banks have historically, in our view, behaved more as manager-controlled organizations who are willing to provide support to their industrial clients and co-members of the German big business network rather than as their watchdogs acting in the interests of shareholders.

A Demand Oriented Institutional Structure

In the managerial insider models presented in Chapter 1 effective demand conditions were projected as a vital element that complements the microeconomic structure. What makes Germany particularly interesting, however, is that while its basic corporate governance structure, as described above, is clearly an insider managerial model, contrary to 'textbook' Keynesianism the role of government agencies in macro-management has been less significant than one would normally anticipate. In fact, demand targeting has not been a central feature of German macroeconomic policy-making during the post war era as it has in the UK and US. A general aversion to excessive statism due to the experiences of the totalitarian Nazi rule and the Allied occupation, gave rise to a preference for an institutional economic structure *within* the general framework of the *Soziale Marktwirtschaft* (Social Market Economy).[145] To balance this a powerful and independent Bundesbank remained focused on inflation rather than full employment and so it followed a tight monetary policy with a focus on keeping money supply stable.

However, it is misleading to assume that, since demand management has not been a fundamental goal for the Federal government, the German insider model operated in the absence of a demand environment. Firstly, the very essence of the *Soziale Marktwirtschaft* has been a well-developed social welfare system which benefited workers and tempered the effects of joblessness.[146] Secondly, while unemployment in the immediate post war years was high, gradually high annual

---

143 Harhoff, D. and Körting, T. (1998) 'Lending Relationships in Germany – Empirical Evidence from Survey Data', Journal of Banking and Finance, vol. 22, 1317.

144 Edwards, J. and Fischer, K., above n91, 142.

145 Allen, C. (1989) 'The Underdevelopment of Keynesianism in the Federal Republic of Germany' in Hall, P. (ed.) The Political Power of Economic Ideas: Keynesianism Across Nations, Princeton: Princeton University Press, 263–289.

146 For a detailed overview of the evolution and main features of the German welfare system see Smith, E., above n29, Chapter 5.

GDP growth rates until the late 1960s not only increased employment but also raised wages. The role of co-determination and collective bargaining institutions has been instrumental in this as they provided the basis for the setting of wages at appropriate levels linked to overall productivity. Thirdly, some focused direct government spending on infrastructure, education and business subsidies has been generous and contributed greatly to the reconstruction and competitiveness of industry. Well targeted Marshall Plan assistance also played a role in this.[147] Fourthly, managerial discretion combined with other fiscal measures, gave the private sector the incentive to plough profits back into production as the financial system encouraged savings, which were channelled to industry mainly through banks.[148] Last but not least, great emphasis was placed by the authorities on export-led growth, in that Germany promoted and relied on the post war liberalized regime of international trade under GATT and later the EU in order to tap effective demand in the US and other European countries for its products so that current account and trade surpluses have been the norm since WWII.[149]

In sum, while textbook Keynesianism tends to concentrate on *external* government intervention in the market mechanism in order to temper its destabilising effects, the German system has provided an institutional framework facilitating demand coordination from *within* the private sector.[150] As Streeck describes it, the state in Germany:

> acts in a variety of ways as a supporting, facilitating, encouraging force in the formation and preservation of broad, encompassing, internally heterogenous interest organisations. Ironically, but hardly unintended, the interventionist policy of the German State on the organizational forms of social interests enables it in many cases to abstain from direct economic intervention since it provides interest groups with a capacity to find viable solutions between and for themselves.[151]

Hence, full-employment and demand targeting by monetary authorities did not materialize in Germany, in large part, because it was not necessary. On the contrary, due to the expansionary tendencies of the managerial microstructure the independent Bundesbank and its restrictive policies were important constraints balancing expansive economic forces within the system. Thus, high industrial investment and growth, wealth redistribution through a complex system of fiscal, labour and welfare institutions of the *Soziale Marktwirtschaft*, and a combination

---

147 Smith, E., above n29, 117–118.
148 Allen, C., above n145.
149 Giersch, H. et al. (1992) The Fading Miracle: Four Decades of Market Economy in Germany, Cambridge: Cambridge University Press, 12–15.
150 Allen, C., above n145.
151 Streeck, W. (1984). Industrial Relations in West Germany, London: Heinemann, 145.

of domestic and foreign effective demand led the German economy to a Kaldorian virtuous circle of cumulative causation for most of the post war era.

Competition policy has also been complementary to this type of coordination of the German economy, in that it has generally allowed cooperation between companies. Indeed, cartelization and market concentration in vital industries became widespread during the late nineteenth century and continued into the first half of the twentieth century as successive German governments, in a similar manner to the UK, were concerned about the detrimental effects of excessive competition.[152] Even after the legislative programmes of decartelization and deconcentration implemented by the Allies after World War II, competition law enforcement was lax in accordance with the German notion of 'workable competition' developed during the early 1960s.[153] Price competition was not seen as a central goal of competition policy and this was reflected in the *Gesetz gegen Wettbewerbsbeschränkungen* 1957 (Act against Restraints of Competition ('GWB')) which protected resale price maintenance and this did not change until 1973. Similarly, until the 1973 amendments to the GWB came into force, merger control was virtually non-existent and did not prevent inter-firm cooperation and the development of extensive cross-shareholdings. According to Smith, even after 1973 few mergers have been prohibited by the German competition authorities.[154] Subsequent amendments during the 1980s and 1990s have widened the scope of the GWB and combined with parallel developments in EU merger control have established a more restrictive competition environment, but they came far too late to prevent concentration in German industries.[155] It is not surprising therefore that German industrial strength has not been built on price competitiveness in world markets, but on the superiority of German products in terms of quality. As Wengenroth explains the leitmotif of German manufacturing has traditionally been 'competition abroad-cooperation at home'.[156]

Conclusion

We have shown in this chapter that the traditional German corporate governance model has not been based on the idea that managers act solely in the interests of shareholders. The lack of a significant stock market, deficient disclosure and minority shareholder protection rules, industry cross-shareholdings, bank proxy

---

152   Smith, E., above n29, Chapter 8; and Holborn, H. (1982) A History of Modern Germany – 1840–1945, Princeton: Princeton University Press, 385–386.

153   Hoffmann, D. and Schaub, S. (1983) The German Competition Law: Legislation and Commentary, Kluwer Law, 105.

154   Smith, E., above n29, 426.

155   Smith, E., above n29, 430; and Monti, M. (2002) 'Germany and the European Competition Policy', Perspektiven der Wirtschaftspolitik, vol. 3(4), 409–416.

156   Wengenroth, U., above n26.

votes as well as labour co-determination provisions indicate a strong insider bias to the corporate governance system. As the shareholdings' analysis shows, the most common blockholders, especially in larger corporations, are other non financial companies whose presence is for strategic purposes and is not necessarily tied to equity value. Moreover, banks, despite their strong presence in financial markets and in General Meetings as custodians of proxy-votes, do not seem to have been exercising the corporate control role that has sometimes been attributed to them. As we discussed in Chapter 2, where banks are a significant presence within a corporate governance system their role tends to support management and their interests as creditors. In Germany this has been the case as their role has been more as a support for management and as liquidity insurance providers rather than as management monitors. As neither outsider shareholders, either directly or through the market for corporate control, or banks as proxy-vote custodians or non financial companies holding cross-shareholdings, seem to be able or willing to enforce outsider shareholder interests, managers in large German corporations have traditionally been able to pursue their policies with relative independence from outsider shareholder pressures. If shareholders wished to have a voice they needed to hold a very large block of shares in order to secure it. The major shareholders other than banks and non financial corporations are families, who have, as we discussed earlier, non financial considerations such as prestige and heritage or when they do have financial considerations are capable of engaging in rent extraction and therefore may not be useful proxies for outsider shareholders return on equity. In all managers within the traditional German corporate governance model have significant discretion upon which the major constraint is the interests of employees probably followed by the interests of families, banks, affiliated companies and the government, which has been sustained historically by a notion of long-term commitment between the company and its various stakeholders. As Mayer argues, this element of insider commitment is important for productive activities, such as complex manufacturing processes, that require involvement and investment by a large number of stakeholders.[157] This difference in culture between German and UK industry was commented upon by Lawrence when writing in 1980 comparing British and German management, he considered that while British management goals focused on making money, German managers considered their goal largely to be 'about making three-dimensional artefacts'.[158] It is not surprising therefore the traditional German corporate champions come from the manufacturing sector (e.g. high-precision electrical machinery, industrial chemicals and road vehicles).

At the same time, competition policy encouraging inter-firm cooperation has been crucial for the German system's workability. As Streeck claims, the German model's success has not been based on its ability to withstand price competition

---

157 Mayer, C. (1997) 'Corporate Governance, Competition and Performance', *Journal of Law and Society*, vol. 24(1), 152–176.

158 Lawrence, P. (1980) *Managers and Management in West Germany*, Croom Helm, 142.

or on fast product turnover. Stakeholder commitment cannot easily accommodate either.[159] On the contrary, German industry was successful because of its ability to 'evade' price competition by relying on product quality and innovation instead. Hand in hand with this, by following a pattern of export-led growth, exploiting regional and global trade agreements, German industry has relied on the quality of its products to compete abroad and on global demand conditions. So long as those remained strong, the German insider model was able to sustain its high investment-high growth levels.

Thus, the German model of corporate governance has been based on the workable complementarity of its institutional components as described above. The interaction between underdeveloped capital markets, corporate ownership concentration, co-determination provisions and collective bargaining, and the role of universal banks has provided the foundations for a workable system which performed extremely well for most of the post war era and has achieved and maintained a high level of social welfare and cohesion.[160] While managers have enjoyed considerable discretion vis-à-vis shareholders as a corporate constituency, the set of institutional constraints and incentives in the four major sub-systems – corporate law, the financial system, the industrial relations system and the government demand function, particularly competition and effective demand – have ensured that managerial autonomy was used to balance a range of stakeholder objectives. As we will examine in the next chapter, the process of globalization has brought about significant alterations to the traditional German insider corporate governance model.

---

159   Streeck, W., above n30.
160   Schmidt, R. (1997) 'Corporate Governance: The Role of Other Constituencies', Working Paper No. 3, Fachbereich Wirtschaftswissenschaften, Goethe-Universität Frankfurt, available at <http://www.finance.uni-frankfurt.de/wp/759.pdf>.

Chapter 8
Economic Globalization and the German Insider Corporate Governance Model

Introduction

Having outlined the traditional German Corporate Governance model in the previous chapter, we turn now in this chapter to assess how the model has been affected by pressures emanating from the process of globalization as described in Chapter 3. In doing so we consider developments in industrial relations resulting from the globalization of product market competition and the globalization of production, that indicate that formal protections have been increased while functional changes and potentially some formal EU level reforms, are affecting the traditional micro- and macro-level consensus between capital and labour resulting in a more flexible form of co-determination. We then consider financial market globalization, which has caused a gradual reorientation of the German financial system that has also affected the traditional German model. This reorientation of the financial system is associated with a series of legal changes which are closely related to corporate governance outcomes and which have the effect of promoting outsider norms within the traditional German corporate governance model. We then assess the impact of these legal reforms on relationships between traditional stakeholders and follow simultaneous changes in non-legal institutional arrangements in which corporate governance is also embedded. In sum the evidence of reaction to pressures from the process of globalization within differing sub-systems was clear, in that a redefinition of intra- and inter-firm relations has occurred and indeed is still occurring but perhaps not necessarily in the way intended.

The Changing Economic Context

In the 1980s unemployment began to take on a new character in Germany. It rose significantly in the mid 1980s and has remained persistently high since then by post WWII standards (see Graphs 8.1 and 8.2). In turn it has placed a very direct pressure on the traditional German corporate governance model in which co-determination is an important element. As part of the consequence of the collapse of the Soviet Union, East and West Germany were reunited in October 1990. The process of reunification involved the substitution of the German mark for the East German currency at full parity and the extension of wages, social welfare benefits and working conditions from the West across to the East. The total wealth transfer from West Germany to East Germany from 1991–2004 has been estimated to have been approximately \$1.6 trillion.[1] Despite this wealth transfer, after the introduction of a capitalist economy in East Germany unemployment reached 50 percent in some regions of former East Germany after reunification and has remained remarkably high in some eastern regions.[2] While the reunification of Germany played a part in the persistence of high unemployment and, as we will see, has affected the way co-determination operates, the process of globalization has also been playing a role in changing the way co-determination functions as key traditional German industries faced increased competition at home and abroad from the 1970s onwards.[3]

The emergence of foreign competitors, such as the Japanese and later the Koreans and other 'Asian Tigers' after the GATT Tokyo and Uruguay negotiating rounds in 1973 and 1986, who were able to produce high quality products faster and cheaper, meant that German producers could no longer rely on their quality competitiveness to outweigh higher production costs. The intensification and transformation of competition began to directly challenge the superiority of German manufacturers in traditional industries, such as iron and steel, coalmining, shipbuilding, consumer electronics, and motor vehicles.[4] In other words, German companies were beginning to lose their export markets to foreign rivals, an issue with very direct impact on an export based economy. By 1983 about 40 percent of the jobs in the German consumer electronics industry that existed during the 1970s had been lost. The German model was beginning to face a competitiveness crisis.[5] Indeed, as Germany's exposure to world trade and in turn global competition increased, Germany's share of total world exports began a decline in the 1980s, which would not be reversed until the beginning of the twenty-first century. By the mid 1990s its current account balance turned negative (see Table 8.1).[6]

1   Library of Congress (2008) Federal Research Division: Germany, April, <http://lcweb2.loc.gov/frd/cs/profiles/Germany.pdf>.

2   Kucera, D. (2001) Gender, Growth, and Trade: The Miracle Economies of the Postwar Years, London: Routledge, 155; and Cook, B. (2001) Europe Since 1945, Taylor & Francis, 1275.

3   Merkl, C. and Snower, D. (2008) 'East German Unemployment: The Myth of the Irrelevant Labor Market', Kiel Working Paper 1435, available at <http://www.ifw-members.ifw-kiel.de/publications/east-german-unemployment-the-myth-of-the-irrelevant-labor-market-1>.

4   Bosch, G. (1990) 'Retraining not Redundancy: Innovative Approaches to Industrial Restructuring in Germany and France', Geneva: International Institute of Labour Studies, 54; and Esser, J. and Fach, W. (1989) 'Crisis Management 'Made in Germany': The Steel Industry' in Katzestein, P. (ed.) Industry and Politics in West Germany, Ithaca: Cornell University Press, 240.

5   O'Sullivan, M. (1998) 'The Political Economy of Corporate Governance in Germany', Working Paper No. 226, INSEAD and Centre for Industrial Competitiveness, University of Massachusetts Lovell.

6   See also Streeck, W. (1996) 'German Capitalism: Does It Exist? Can It Survive?', Working Paper No. 218, <http://www.nd.edu/~kellogg/publications/workingpapers/WPS/218.pdf>.

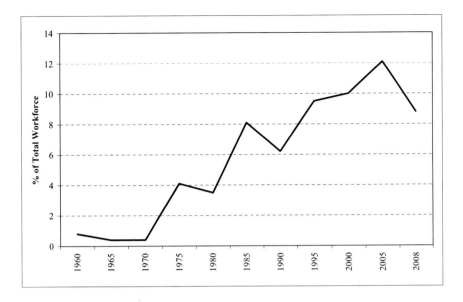

Graph 8.1 Unemployed persons as a percentage of total workforce (non-adjusted)

Source: German Federal Statistical Office. Part of the fall between 2005–2008 is attributable to the application of a new method of determining unemployment in Germany.

Table 8.1 Trade and export performance of Germany, 1988–2004

	Trade in goods and services % of GDP*	Visible exports % of total world exports**	Trade balance % of GDP	Current account balance % of GDP
1988	54.9	12.0	6.5	4.0
1994	51.0	10.1	2.7	-1.1
2004	59.2	9.4*	3.9	3.5

Note: 1998 West Germany, 1994 unified Germany. * Data calculated in a balance of payments basis. ** Exports calculated on an international transactions basis.
Source: Streeck, W. (1996) 'German Capitalism: Does It Exist? Can It Survive?', Working Paper No. 218, <http://www.nd.edu/~kellogg/publications/workingpapers/WPS/218. pdf>; and Deutsche Bundesbank (various years) 'Special Statistical Section', Frankfurt: Bundesbank. <http://www.bundesbank.de/statistik/statistik_veroeffentlichungen_sonderve roeffentlichungen.en.php#sonder11>.

One possible solution for German industry could have been to place more emphasis on product development and turnover in order to meet the standards of foreign rivals. However, the institutional arrangements of the traditional German model did not encourage such an approach, because commitment to long-established relationships between resource providers, especially between employers and employees, did not allow sufficient flexibility. As Herringel describes it:

> [e]ach time a new product or a new technology is introduced – as opposed to an old one that is customized for a customer – the various roles that each of the categories of skill and management will play in the production and development of the new product must be bargained out ... Few producers, large or small, have had success up until now in being able to overcome the opposition of entrenched groupings of skilled workers threatened with the loss of status through incorporation into teams that deny the boundaries of former jurisdictional specializations or of independent departments, reluctant to have their functional areas of power within the companies redefined and diluted through recomposition with other areas. It is difficult, after all, to tell workers and managers who with considerable legitimacy understand themselves as having contributed significantly to the traditional success of high quality manufacturing in Germany that their roles have become obstacles to adjustment.[7]

Thus, due to key path dependence problems, the general inability of German companies to restructure their basic organizational methods by adopting techniques such as lean production, and exploiting new business opportunities in high technology sectors affected their chances of reversing the decline in profitability and investment rates. The very strengths of traditional organizational arrangements in Germany which in the past contributed to the creation of accumulated organizational knowledge became a key aspect of competitive decline.[8]

Thus, in 1993 Germany entered its worst and longest recession in the post war era where slow growth and persistent unemployment problems became endemic characteristics of the German economy. From 1981 to 1991 although the German Economy was struggling with competitiveness issues it managed a fairly robust growth rate of 4.1 percent. However, from 1992 to 2004, growth in the German economy was persistently slow at 1.3 percent (Chart 8.1) and as we observed above it has been accompanied by high unemployment. At the same time, as we noted in the previous chapter, the institutional arrangements of the German state are not designed to facilitate demand targeting and so an institutionally constrained government, already financially stretched by reunification, could not easily fill the investment gap.

---

7   Herringel, G. (1996) 'Crisis in German Decentralised Production', European Urban and Regional Studies, vol. 3(1), 33 at 42–43.

8   Block, T. (2002) 'Financial Market Liberalization and the Changing Character of Corporate Governance' in Eatwell, J. and Taylor, L. (eds) International Capital Markets: Systems in Transition, New York: Oxford University Press, 207–230.

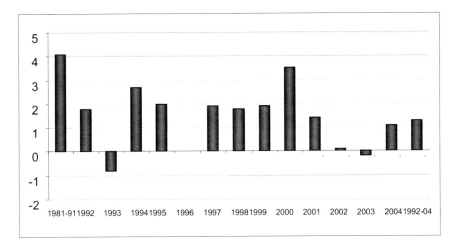

Chart 8.1 Real GDP growth (Germany annual percentage change)
Source: OECD Economic Outlook 78 Database.

In the 1970s and for most of the 1980s German companies had been able to smooth the pressures from global competition by taking advantage of the European Community's protectionist measures against non-Community exporters and by resorting to reductions in working time, leisure allowances, retirement and hiring-freeze policies.[9] However, in the early nineties what flexibility there was within the system had already reached its limits as the process of globalization including the European single market project began to impact.[10] Thus, German employers began to abandon their commitment to stable employment relations by resorting to mass dismissals. According to an estimate by the Kiel Institute of World Economy, as much as 1.3 million jobs accounting for 15 percent of Germany's manufacturing employment was lost between 1991 and 1996.[11] As Charts 8.2 and 8.3 show, even after the early 1990s recession, unemployment placed a damper on domestic demand growth as it remained low averaging a mere 0.6 percent from 1993 to 2005, while reliance on foreign demand has not been able to offset domestic conditions and sustain the higher GDP growth rates of the past. Persistent unemployment problems and job insecurity in this period created enormous pressures on the German social market model (*Soziale Marktwirtschaft*) and in turn the traditional German corporate governance model as a whole.

---

9   Tsoukalis, L. and Strauss, R. (1987) 'Community Policies on Steel 1974–1982: A Case of Collective Management' in Mény, Y. and Wright, V. (eds) The Politics of Steel: Western Europe and the Steel Industry in the Crisis Years (1974–1984), New York: de Gruynter.

10   As we explained in Chapter 3 we regard internationalization and regionalization as building blocks in the process of globalization.

11   Cited in O'Sullivan, M., above n5.

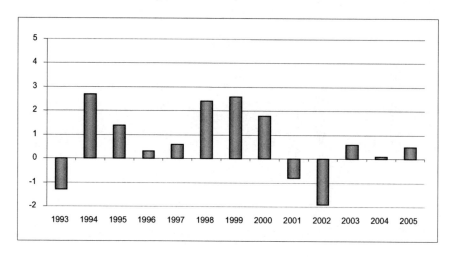

Chart 8.2 Domestic demand (percentage change from previous year)
Source: Bundesbank, various annual reports; German Federal Statistical Office; Ifo Institute, OECD.

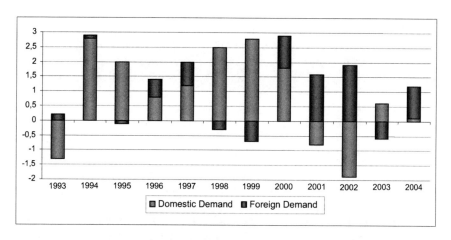

**Chart 8.3 Domestic and foreign demand conditions in Germany
(percentage contribution to GDP growth)**
Source: Bundesbank, various annual reports; German Federal Statistical Office; Ifo Institute, OECD.

As we discussed generally in Chapter 3 an important development in the process of globalization has been the globalization of production and its effects on labour. The globalization of production has since the early 1990s added to the pressures on the German insider model as national boundaries have become less significant for economic activity and the mobility of production factors in turn more intense. German employers have as a result become less dependent on their domestic workforce. Thus, low labour-cost locations, especially in the post-communist Central and Eastern Europe, have become more attractive for the allocation of production plants by German companies. For instance, countries like the Czech Republic, Slovakia, Poland and Hungary which are close enough for just-in-time production and can also offer labour skills similar to those in Germany but at a much lower cost, have become particularly attractive production locations for low and semi-skilled operations.[12] As the scientific advisory board to the German Ministry of Economic Affairs in its somewhat prophetic analysis of 'long-term unemployment' in Germany recognized in 1993:

> [s]ustained unemployment is above all a concomitant of increasing competition in a rapidly-integrating world economy. [...] Germany as a location (*Standort Deutschland*) competes internationally with its institutional framework and its factor cost for mobile capital that creates new jobs. Those countries that fall short in competition have to face unemployment, a declining propensity to invest and lower growth rates.[13]

As a result the German problem of persistent unemployment as a result of the globalization of competition has been made more acute because of the option of transferring labour intensive production abroad which free trade, technology change and capital control liberalization has opened up for German employers rather than follow the traditional route of investing in domestic German production innovation.[14] The rising gap between inward and outward FDI Stock flows in favour of the latter is indicative of the global production strategies undertaken by German companies since the late 1980s (Graph 8.2).

---

12   Streeck, W., above n6; and Nunnenkamp, P. (2004) 'The German Automobile Industry And Central Europe's Integration into The International Division Of Labour: Foreign Production, Intra-Industry Trade, and Labour Market Repercussions', Kiel Institute for World Economics, <http://www.ucm.es/BUCM/cee/papeles/09/pape0404220004a.pdf>.

13   Bundesregierung (1993) 'Bericht der Bundesregierung zur Zukunftssicherung des Standorts Deutschland', Deutscher Bundestag, 12 Wahlperiode, Drucksache 12/5620.

14   Welge, M. and Holtbrügge, D. (1997) 'Germany' in Dunning, J. (ed.) Governments, Globalization and International Business, Oxford: Oxford University Press, 337.

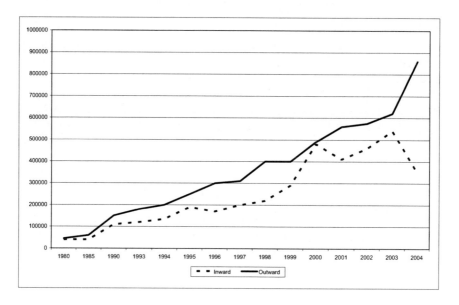

Graph 8.2 German FDI inward and outward stock, 1980–2004
Source: UNCTAD, World Investment Report (several editions).

This phenomenon is also reflected in the increasing significance of employment in foreign affiliates as a percentage of total employment. While much of German FDI outflows are demand driven, as they are directed towards other developed economies in order to secure export markets, cost-driven FDI has become increasingly significant. In a 1996 poll of 7,000 German companies, mainly from the industrial sector, 62 percent of those industrial companies who intended to expand their production abroad identified high domestic labour costs as their main motive.[15] In a similar survey in 2007, again costs formed the most significant motivation for relocation of economic activity by German companies.[16] In 1985 foreign workers as a percentage of German companies' total workforce amounted to 6.6 percent, by 1996 it had risen to 13 percent as companies reacted to increased competitive pressures in the 1990s by taking up the production exit option.[17] For instance, Veba, RWE and Thyssen, three of the largest domestic conglomerates in Germany, in the 1990–1997 period dramatically changed the ratio of their domestic

---

15   Deutsches Institut für Herrenmode (1996) <http://www.deutschesmodeinstitut. de/index.php?id=319>.

16   German Federal Statistics Office (2008) 'Methods – Approaches – Developments', 1/2008, 5–7, available at <http://www.destatis.de/jetspeed/portal/cms/Sites/destatis/Internet/ EN/Content/Wissenschaftsforum/MethodsApproaches/Infos/mad1__2008,property=file.pdf>.

17   UNCTAD (1999) World Investment Report 1999 – Foreign Direct Investment and the Challenge of Development, New York: United Nations, Annex Table A.1.7.

to international employment in favour of the latter.[18] It is worth noting that for Veba and RWE, in particular, this was combined with the first workforce reduction in their entire history. Siemens, Germany's largest company, also followed a similar trend by reducing its employees in Germany from 203,000 in 1996, to 194,000 in 1998 and increasing its international workforce from 176,000 to 222,000 in the same period.[19] In 2006 Siemens announced plans to 'de-localize' its business involving large scale job losses in Germany.[20] Compounding the problem, while German companies' investments abroad accelerated, foreign companies seem unwilling to offset these outflows by investing in German factors due to high wage and non-wage labour costs and prefer other low cost locations.[21]

The combination of intense competition domestically and the possibility of relocation outside the national boundary has provided a major bargaining chip for management negotiations with unions on working conditions and wages. For example in 1996 the management at Viessmann negotiated an increase in the number of working hours a week for no extra wages, when the company threatened to move production abroad. In 2004 Siemens negotiated a wide range of changes to pay and working conditions in return for maintaining production in Germany. Likewise, in 2005 BMWs threatened move to locate a new manufacturing plant outside Germany resulted in an agreement on increased working time and lower wages.[22] In the case of Siemens this made little difference as competitive conditions declined further and massive job losses followed.[23] In sum increased competition, persistent unemployment and production exit have a negative effect on domestic demand and can give rise to a vicious circle of economic slowdown and thus encourage further cost-driven FDI, lower wages, more unemployment and so on.[24] In the next section we explore the effect of these pressures on the co-determination aspect of the German corporate governance system.

---

18   Bendt, C. (1998) 'Corporate Germany at the Crossroads? Americanisation, Competitiveness and Place Dependence', Working Paper No. 98, ESRC Centre for Business Research, University of Cambridge.

19   Siemens Annual Report (1998) Berlin and Munich, 57.

20   Gow, D. (2006) 'More Pain to Come as Siemens aims to Rival General Electric', The Guardian, 10 July 2006, 23; and Gross, G. (2008) 'Siemens to Cut 3,800 Jobs in Telecom Unit', Washington Post, 26 February 2008, available at <http://www.washingtonpost.com/wp-dyn/content/article/2008/02/26/AR2008022601376.html>.

21   Beese, B. (2008) 'Perceptions of Globalization: Attitudes and Responses in the EU – Germany', European Monitoring Centre on Change, available at <http://www.eurofound.europa.eu/emcc/erm/studies/tn0708016s/de0708019q.htm>.

22   Eichengreen, B. (2006) The European Economy Since 1945: Coordinated Capitalism and Beyond, Princeton: Princeton University Press, 417; and Beese, B., above n21.

23   Spiegel Online (2008) 'Siemens to Cut 16,750 Jobs Worldwide', 7 August 2008, available at <http://www.spiegel.de/international/business/0,1518,564667,00.html>; and Gow, D., above n20.

24   The Economist (1990) 'Restructuring Corporate Germany', 21 November 1998, 63.

Reworking Co-determination

Given these pressures from globalization a key question is what has the institutional response within the German industrial relations system been? A close look at the developments since the 1980s reveals a somewhat mixed picture. For a start collective bargaining is protected by the German constitution and so formal attacks on the institutions through which it takes place have difficulty succeeding.[25] The most significant reformist attack on co-determination institutions was attempted by a coalition led by the political party, *Christlich Demokratische Union* (Christian Democratic Union ('CDU') – CDU being the traditional ally of employer interests against the trade union sponsored *Sozialdemokratische Partei Deutschland* (Social Democratic Party of Germany ('SPD')) – that came into power in 1982 and aimed at the weakening of works councils' influence by containing the dominant role exercised by the DGB within them and by establishing potentially rival firm-level bodies representing middle management. These legislative proposals gave rise to a fierce and prolonged debate among stakeholder representatives and their political counterparts.[26] The outcome of those negotiations was somewhat unexpected given their origin, as employers' fears that as a result of the reforms the intra-firm consensus of the German corporate governance model could break down with severe economic consequences, e.g. by blocking employees' incentives to adapt to technological changes, led them to reverse their position and resist the attack on co-determination, even if ideally they would have preferred it to be a voluntary institution.[27] Thus, once the mandatory co-determination provisions were to remain intact, employers preferred the maintenance of existing workable institutional arrangements despite the disadvantages as they perceived them, as they recognized the superiority of a workable system over an unworkable one. The final version of the reform law which was eventually passed in 1988 was so different from the initial legislative proposal that it barely had any effect on the spirit and function of co-determination or the role of the unions in it.

Path dependence in the development of co-determination, however, did not stop at legislative institutional resistance. Following strong union pressure and the recommendations of a report by *Kommission Mitbestimmung* set up in 1996 by the Bertelsmann and Hans Böckler Foundations, the SPD government that came into

25   Michel, H. (2007) Co-determination in Germany: The Recent Debate Johann Wolfgang Goethe-Universität Frankfurt Working Paper WDW004, <http://www.uclouvain. be/cps/ucl/doc/etes/documents/WDW004.pdf>.
26   For an analytical overview of the events surrounding the debate see Wood, S. (1997) 'Weakening Codetermination? Works Council Reform in West Germany in the 1980s', Discussion Paper FS I 97–302, Wissenschaftszentrum Berlin für Sozialforschung, Berlin.
27   Ibid.

power in 1997 initiated negotiations for strengthening the role of works councils.[28] This time the government succeeded in passing a new Works Constitution Reform Act (*Betriebsverfassungsreformgesetz* ('*BetrVerfReformG*')) which came into effect on 2 July 2001. Among other things, this legislation made possible the formation of inter-group works councils (e.g. a joint works council for several plants or a regional works council for separate parts of a company), increased the number of councillors, included temporary employees and teleworkers in the works council constitution and has strengthened the participation and co-determination rights, particularly with regard to qualification decisions and job security.[29]

In 2004 further formal reinforcement of co-determination occurred when the *Third Part Act* (*Drittelbeteiligungsgesetz*) expanded the application of one-third employee supervisory board representation to private companies with more than 500 employees. Following this, in 2005 the *Biedenkopf Kommission* was appointed to review the operation of supervisory board co-determination rights. In November 2006 it became apparent that labour representatives and employer representatives had reached a deadlock on any reforms. While labour representatives accepted that some minor reforms were needed the employer representatives wished to reduce employee representatives to a minority on the supervisory board. The commission reported at the end of 2006 but without recommending any substantial changes.[30]

Legislative intervention to enhance the role of works councils and expand board level co-determination represents a *formal* protective response to significant changes in the economic context in which co-determination operates. According to Hassel, both firm-level co-determination and macro-level collective bargaining have been losing ground in terms of employee coverage since the 1980s.[31] The coverage of private sector employees by works councils has shrunk from 52.4 percent in 1981 to 45.8 in 2000,[32] although, that figure should be tempered by the presence of works councils in 95 percent of companies with over 500 employees. If one adds in the public sector then 70 percent of the German workforce is still covered by collective bargaining, a decline of only 10 percent since 1980.[33] Part

---

28   Kommission Mitbestimmung (1998) 'Mitbestimmung und neue Unternehmenskulturen: Bilanz und Perspektiven', Gütersloh: Verlag Bertelsmann Stiftung.

29   Addison, J., Bellmann, L., Schnabel, C. and Wagner, J. (2002) 'The Long Awaited Reform of The German Works Constitution Act', Discussion Paper No. 422, Forschungsinstitut zur Zukunft der Arbeit, Bonn.

30   Du Plessis, J. et al. (2007) German Corporate Governance in International and European Context, Springer, 138–139.

31   Hassel, A. (1999), 'The Erosion of the German System of Industrial Relations', British Journal of Industrial Relations, vol. 37(3), 483.

32   Ibid., 488; and Addison, J., Bellmann, L., Schnabel, C. and Wagner, J. (2002) 'German Works Councils Old and New: Incidence, Coverage and Determinants', IZA Discussion Paper No. 495, available at SSRN: <http://ssrn.com/abstract=314220>.

33   OECD (2004) OECD Employment Outlook, Table 3.3; and Ellguth, P. (2003) 'Quantitative Reichweite der Betrieblichen Mitbestimmung', WSI-Mitteilungen, vol. 56(3), 194–199; and Michel, H. above n25, 7.

of the private sector decline is because some employers have been withdrawing from their representative associations and therefore from centralized collective bargaining.[34] Where this has occurred it has often been negotiated with the unions.[35] Similarly, deviations from collective agreements that began in East Germany after reunification and were accepted as necessary by the unions in the context of a very weak East German economy, spread to the west and have been growing since the late 1990's. The unions have largely negotiated these deviations or withdrawals either to save jobs or to prevent jobs leaving Germany.[36] Union membership has also been in decline due to the increase of part-time workers, the rising share of employment in services as opposed to traditional industries and, of course, due to high unemployment.[37] Between 2002 and 2006 trade union membership fell from 7.7 million members to 6.6 million although the decline slowed as the economy has improved.[38] One visible outcome of this membership decline has been a consolidation of unions within sectors. For example, in 2001 the five major services unions facing declining membership and financial problems merged into what is now the *Vereinigte Dienstleistungsgewerkschaft* ('Ver.di') a super union with more than three million members.[39]

In general while domestic legal change was highly path dependent and lead to the fortification of co-determination provisions that were already in place. At the same time functional changes have moved to more flexibility in negotiating on the part of unions. That flexibility has also at times been accompanied by more aggressive targeted strike action. A series of strikes over the course of 2002 and 2003 was successful because it affected some of Germany's most influential industries and companies like Daimler (formerly DaimlerChrysler) and BMW. The strategy has not always been successful as metalworkers striking in 2003

34   Streeck, W. and Rehder, B. (2005) 'Institutionen im Wandel: Hat die Tarifautonomie eine Zukunft?' in Busch, H. et al. (eds) Tarifpolitik Im Umbruch, Cologne: Deutscher Instituts-Verlag, 49–82.

35   Streeck, W. and Hassel, A. (2003) 'The Crumbling Pillars of Social Partnership', West European Politics, vol. 26(4), 101–124 at 113.

36   Gumbrell-McCormick, R. and Hyman, R. (2006) 'Embedded Collectivism? Workplace Representation in France and Germany', Industrial Relations Journal, vol. 37(5), 473–491 at 479, available at SSRN: <http://ssrn.com/abstract=923925>.

37   Schnabel, C. and Wagner, J. (2007) 'Union Density and Determinants of Union Membership in 18 EU Countries: Evidence from Micro Data, 2002/03', Industrial Relations Journal, vol. 38(1), 5–32 at 8, Table 1.

38   Figures from the Confederation of German Trade Unions (Deutscher Gewerkschaftsbund, DGB): Dribbusch, H. (2008) 'Germany: Industrial Relations Developments in Europe', EIRO Online, available at <http://www.eurofound.europa.eu/eiro/studies/tn0803029s/de0803029q.htm>.

39   Prevezanos, K. (2001) 'Stepping Forward: German Trade Unions Prepare for The Future', At Issue Report, American Institute for Contemporary German Studies, Washington.

were defeated.[40] However this pattern of combining flexibility and strategic strike action has continued since then.[41]

A number of corporate scandals have also struck at the credibility of managers and unions.[42] In 2007 two senior executives of Siemens were arrested for their part in a corruption scandal involving the payment of €34 million to one of the unions in order to influence its actions. As the scandal unfolded some 300 Siemens staff came under investigation and it was revealed the Siemens had a slush fund of €1.3 billion to bribe governments and business partners, including unions and worker representatives.[43] The same year a Volkswagen executive was fined €576,000 and received a suspended prison sentence for similar activities involving bribing worker representatives with money, holidays and prostitutes. As we will discuss later in the chapter, a criminal prosecution also occurred as a result of allegations of management and supervisory board bribery during the Vodafone/Mannesmann takeover over the course of 1999/2000. Many other German companies including Deutsche Bahn and Deutsche Post have had the media spotlight shone on questionable practices involving union and management conflicts of interests.[44]

EU developments

The European Union single market project has also affected co-determination. While the European Economic Community has always had the objective of a common market between members states, the collapse of the Soviet Union brought about an acceleration of a single market where goods, capital, people and services could move freely throughout the member states. Between 1986 and 1992 the EU adopted 280 pieces of legislation to open up national markets in order to create one single EU market. By 1993 the single market had been declared

40   Gumbrell-McCormick, R. and Hyman, R., above n36, 479; Williamson, H. (2002) 'German Engineering Union to Strike', Financial Times, 3 June; Whittall, M. (2005) 'Model Deutschland under Pressure: The Growing Tensions Between Works Councils and Trade Unions', Economic and Industrial Democracy, vol. 26(4), 569–592 at 586; and BBC News Online (2002) 'German Strikes to Intensify', 10 June 2002, available at <http://news.bbc.co.uk/1/hi/business/2034755.stm>.

41   Dribbusch, H., above n38.

42   For a good overview of the corruption scandals see Du Plessis, J. et al., above n30, 131–137.

43   Spiegel Online (2008) 'Siemens to Sue Former Top Executives', 22 July 2008, available at <http://www.spiegel.de/international/business/0,1518,567281,00.html>.

44   Sims, T. (2007) 'German Industry Would Alter Law Requiring Labor Seats on Boards', New York Times, 6 April 2007, available at <http://www.nytimes.com/2007/04/06/business/worldbusiness/06seats.html?fta=y>; and Dougherty, C. (2007) 'Germany Battling Rising Tide of Corporate Corruption', New York Times, 15 February, available at <http://www.nytimes.com/2007/02/15/business/worldbusiness/15scandal.html>.

open.[45] One of the effects of this was to bring German companies under increased competitive pressures at home both directly because more competitors from EU states could gain access to German markets but also because the cooperative relationship between German companies came under increased scrutiny from the EU competition authorities.[46]

More specifically with regard to co-determination, with the adoption of the *Societas Europea* (SE) Regulation[47] and its implementation in Germany at the end of 2004, the institutions of co-determination can arguably be diminished.[48] The SE is another form of corporate entity similar to a UK PLC or a German AG. As the name suggests, it is recognized throughout the EU and if it wishes it can move its registered office between member states. It is also designed to easily facilitate EU cross border M&A. For co-determination it has some very specific effects. First, the SE is designed to facilitate the operation of a company in the single market and so can be a single tiered board model or a two-tiered model. Second for SEs the modelling of co-determination is not automatically prescribed by mandatory law as the presumption is that only where no agreement is reached between unions and management does a mandatory regime apply. This negotiation could in theory lead to inferior co-determination outcomes. The mandatory regime in the event of no agreement for a German company is the normal German co-determination regime or the highest level of representation for employees of the two regimes applicable if the SE is formed as the result of a merger of two companies from different EU countries. This might mean that a lower level of representation could be agreed to. Secondly, it is debatable whether co-determination agreements can be renegotiated in order to follow the SE's development in terms of workforce numbers. Thus, if the SE's initial co-determination regime adopts the one-third employee representation and then the company increases its workforce to over 2,000, which for an AG would trigger the full parity provisions of the *Mitbestimmungsgesetz*, it is questionable whether the SE will also have to switch to full parity.[49]

By 2007, 88 SEs had been established throughout the EU with 39 of them established in Germany, although 11 were shelf companies. Of these 39 German SE, 11 were formed with a single tiered board, three of which were shelf companies. While most of these 39 companies are small companies, a few of

---

45   European Commission (2008) Single Market Policies, available at <http://ec.europa.eu/internal_market/top_layer/index_2_en.htm>.

46   Monti, M. (2002) 'Germany and the European Competition Policy', Perspektiven der Wirtschaftspolitik, vol. 3(4), 409–416; and OECD (2004) 'The Role of Competition Policy in Regulatory Reform Regulatory Reform in Germany', available at <http://www.oecd.org/document/24/0,3343,en_2649_34141_32505624_1_1_1_1,00.html>.

47   Regulation 2157/2001/EC of 8 October 2001.

48   Du Plessis, J. et al., above n30, Chapter 6.

49   Wollburg, R (2004) 'Recent Developments in German Corporate Governance', International Financial Law Review 36–40; Noack, U. and Zetzsche, D. (2005) 'Corporate Reform in Germany: The Second Decade', EBLR, 1033–1064.

the largest Germany companies such as Allianz, Fresenius, BASF and Porsche have converted to SE status.[50] Although the co-determination regimes adopted by Allianz, Fresenius, BASF when forming as SEs differ from the German co-determination regime it is not markedly different. The major difference being that they have smaller supervisory boards.[51] In all it is not yet clear if these EU provisions will significantly affect labour co-determination.

Another important EU development has also started to affect co-determination. In a number of judgments beginning with *Centros Ltd. v. Erhvervs- og Selskabsstyrelsen*[52] between 1999 and 2005 the European Court of Justice cleared the way for regulatory competition between member states' corporate forms.[53] As the ECJ observed, the fact that an EU national:

> chooses to form [a company] in the Member State whose rules of company law seem to him the least restrictive and to set up branches in other Member States cannot, in itself, constitute an abuse of the right of establishment. The right to form a company in accordance with the law of a Member State and to set up branches in other Member State states is inherent in the exercise, in a single market, of the freedom of establishment guaranteed by the Treaty.[54]

As a result it is perfectly acceptable to incorporate in another member state with the intention of avoiding your home state's national provisions and your home state must allow you to carry on a legitimate business in your home state free from interference.[55] As a result the UK which is viewed as having the least onerous corporate law has seen a wave of incorporations from German nationals.[56] In 2003 – 3,104 German nationals were listed as directors of UK companies and by 2005

---

50   Reichert, J. (2008) 'Experiences with the SE in Germany', Utrecht Law Review, vol. 4(1), 22–33, available at SSRN: <http://ssrn.com/abstract=1114782>.

51   Teichmann, C. (2004) 'Germany' in Oplustil, K. and Teichmann, C. (eds) The European Company – All Over Europe: A State-by-state Account of the Introduction of the European Company, Walter de Gruyter, 109–131 at 109.

52   (Case C-212/97) [1999] ECR 1459.

53   *Überseering BV v. Nordic Construction Company Baumanagement GmbH* (Case C-208/00) [2002] ECR 9919; *Kamer van Koophandel en Fabrieken voor Amsterdam v. Inspire Art Ltd.* (Case C-167/01) [2003] ECR 10155; *Hughes de Lasteyrie du Saillant v. Ministere de l'Economie, des Finances et de l'Industrie* (Case C-9/02) [2004] RIW 392 and Case C-411/03.

54   *Centros* above n52.

55   Fraudulent or improper use is precluded. Gelter, M. (2005) 'The Structure of Regulatory Competition in European Corporate Law', Journal of Corporate Law Studies, vol. 5, 247–284, available at SSRN: <http://ssrn.com/abstract=742045>.

56   Lowry, J. (2004) 'Eliminating Obstacles to Freedom of Establishment: The Competitive Edge of UK Company Law', Cambridge Law Journal, vol. 63, 331.

that number had risen to 13,450.[57] While most of these incorporations are driven by cost considerations, the attraction of avoidance of co-determination is present in some of these UK incorporations. Alltours and Air Berlin are former high profile AGs that converted to UK PLCs. One of its reasons for this was to avoid board level co-determination. Joachim Hunold, the Chief executive of Air Berlin Plc at the time of the conversion to UK PLC status when asked about this issue replied *Mitbestimmung* 'is no longer competitive internationally'.[58] The German courts have, since the ECJ made its position clear, been very careful to apply its rulings domestically even going so far as to extend it to non-EU companies.[59] In response the German government reformed the incorporation requirements in 2007 to make German corporate form attractive to small and medium sized businesses once again. This reform may stem the flow of cost driven incorporations but will probably not affect those seeking to avoid co-determination.[60]

The SEVIC decision of the ECJ also added to the possibilities for EU erosion of co-determination.[61] The case concerned a German company that was unable to merge with a Luxembourg company because the relevant German statute only provided for merger registration between German companies. Perhaps unsurprisingly given its approach in the *Centros* line of decisions the ECJ found that the difference in treatment between German and foreign companies was contrary to Articles 43 and 48. Although the decision did not deal explicitly with the matter, the implication of the judgement and the *Centros* decision is that if a foreign EU company merged with a German company thus absorbing it, the German authorities would have to register the merger and the merged entity would be subject to the home country's incorporation laws i.e. no co-determination if it was a UK company that absorbed the German Company.

In March 2000 the European Council set out what became known as the Lisbon Agenda aimed at making the European economy the most dynamic and competitive knowledge based economy in the world by 2010. One of the key parts of the Agenda was the promotion and growth of employment in Europe by creating

57   IFLR (2006) 'Will more English PLCs take off in Germany?', International Financial Law Review, available at <http://www.iflr.com/Article.aspx?ArticleID=1977695>.

58   Sims, T., above n44.

59   Judgment of the German Supreme Court in Civil Matters (2005) 60 BB 1016ff and (2006) 61 BB 24ff.

60   Although it's not really clear if these reforms will be successful. Beurskens, M. and Noack, U. (2008) 'Of Tradition and Change – The Modernization of the German GmbH in the Face of European Competition', <http://ssrn.com/abstract=1138704> and Federal Ministry of Justice (2008) 'The Reform of Private Limited Companies', available at <http://www.bmj.bund.de/enid/37496ddf570bf7763771afa1ba7a9342,db5086305f7472636964092d0933343232/Partnership-Company-Law/The_reform_of_private_limited_companies_1ee.html>.

61   SEVIC Systems AG, Judgment of the Grand Chamber of the Court of Justice of 13 December 2005, [2005] ECR I-10805.

greater labour flexibility.[62] As part of this process, the then German Chancellor Gerhard Schröder set out what he called Agenda 2010 to prepare Germany to fulfil its part of the EU Lisbon Agenda. Complicating and to some extent driving both the Lisbon and German 2010 Agenda was the looming enlargement of the EU in 2004 which would likely lead to an influx of workers into western EU members states from new accession former Eastern block countries. The shock of this influx to an economy still struggling with reunification unemployment problems, might have been severe given the nature of German social welfare and employment protections and so the Agenda 2010 reforms should be seen as not solely a response to domestic unemployment but to the EU enlargement issue as well.[63] Agenda 2010 had at the heart of it a plan to cut taxes, reform social welfare and introduce a flexible labour market (known as Hartz I-IV).[64] The core of the social welfare reforms aimed at forcing people on welfare back into work by introducing means testing, a time limit of 12 months on unemployment benefit in most cases, cutting benefits for those refusing to work or retrain and cutting disability benefits in some circumstances. The reforms also aimed at making the labour market more flexible by removing some of the restrictions on the ability of firms to lay workers off.[65] While Schröder managed to ensure his legislation was approved by the German parliament, the Agenda 2010 measures were and continue to be, hugely controversial.[66] Ultimately the reforms cost Schröder his Chancellorship in 2005, damaged the SPD and the unions in particular, who were perceived to have been too weak in opposing the measures.

A flexible form of co-determination?

As we have observed above the situation with regard to institutional changes in the co-determination regime is complex. The rigidity of constitutionally protected

62   Kok, M. (2004) 'Facing the Challenge. The Lisbon Strategy for Growth and Employment', Report from the High Level Group chaired by Wim Kok, November 2004, Office for Official Publications of the European Communities ('the Kok Report').

63   The Czech Republic, Estonia, Hungary, Latvia, Lithuania, Poland, Slovakia, Slovenia, Malta and Cyprus joined on 1 May 2004. Romania and Bulgaria joined in 2007.

64   Buhr, D. and Schmid, J. (2007) 'Big Reform with Little Effect? Labour Market and Employment Policy in Germany', CAP Working Paper, July.

65   Jacobi, L. and Kluve, J. (2006) 'Before and After the Hartz Reforms: The Performance of Active Labour Market Policy in Germany', IZA Discussion Paper No. 2100, April, available at <http://ssrn.com/abstract=900374>. Leschke, J., Schmidt, G. and Griga, D. (2006) 'On the Marriage of Flexibility and Security: Lessons from the Hartz-Reforms in Germany', WZB Discussion Paper: SP I 2006–108; and Deutsche Bank Research (2007) 'Germany Cresting the Wave: A Reform Agenda for the Grand Coalition', Current Issues, 27 September.

66   Konle-Seidl, R., Eichhorst, W. and Grienberger-Zingerle, M. (2007) 'Activation Policies in Germany. From Status Protection to Basic Income Support', IAB-Discussion Paper (Nr.6), Nürnberg.

core statutory co-determination institutions in the face of change illustrates how the formal domestic institutions are subject to strong path dependent forces while other domestic and EU provisions have the potential to produce negative effects on co-determination. Labour co-determination in Germany is therefore under stress and has been reacting but whether it is really threatened is another matter. Path dependency in formal institutions is strong, as we have seen, but it is being negatively affected by market forces and changes in other institutional sub-systems. Many German managers are hostile to it but this is nothing new as the original 1951 Act and the reforms that extended co-determination in 1976 were heavily opposed by management. Indeed, some of the largest German industrial companies (Bayer, Daimler Benz, Hoechst and Bosch) brought a constitutional challenge to the co-determination reforms in 1976 claiming it interfered with their property rights guaranteed under the Federal Constitution. They failed in their challenge and the Supreme Court went on to emphasize the importance of co-determination in serving the nation.[67] Similarly the 1982 attempts at dismantling co-determination were initially, as we discussed earlier in this chapter, promoted by managers. Since then, as Roe has noted, management has done its best to subvert the functioning of the institutions of co-determination both legitimately and illegitimately as we have observed in the recent corruption scandals.[68]

However, while some commentators have described the state of co-determination as one of crisis, others are not so sure.[69] Wever, for example, thinks the model is simply undergoing renegotiation.[70] Behrens and Jacoby similarly don't find much appetite for confrontation on co-determination among employers but that many say they do wish to renegotiate appropriately where possible.[71] Jackson considers that the unique characteristics of representation and collaboration provide the foundations of a flexible system that can adapt to the changing economic circumstances German business operates in.[72] Indeed, the function of co-determination in negotiating solutions between employers and employees appears alive and well even if times are tough. The response from the

---

67   Du Plessis, J. et al., above n30, 122–125.

68   Roe, M. (1998) 'German Codetermination and German Securities Markets' in Hopt, K (ed.) Comparative Corporate Governance: The State of the Art and Emerging Research, Oxford: Oxford University Press, 361–372.

69   For the crisis literature see Streeck, W. and Rehder, B., above n34; Hassel, A., above n31, 484; and Whittall, M., above n40, 586.

70   Wever, K. (1997) 'Renegotiating the German Model: Labor-Management Relations in the New Germany' in Turner, L. (ed.) Negotiating the New Germany, Ithaca: Cornell University Press, 207–225 at 221.

71   Behrens, M. and Jacoby, W. (2004) 'The Rise of Experimentalism in German Collective Bargaining', British Journal of Industrial Relations, vol. 42(1), 95–123.

72   Jackson, G. (2005) 'Contested Boundaries: Ambiguity and Creativity in the Evolution of German Codetermination' in Streeck, W. and Thelen, K. (eds) Beyond Continuity: Institutional Change in Advanced Political Economies, Oxford: Oxford University Press, 229–254 at 245.

co-determination institutions since the turn of the twenty-first century seems to have been to negotiate to find solutions. As we considered earlier in this section in many cases where a move outside of Germany was threatened, unions were willing to relax wage and conditions agreements. For example, Energie Baden-Wurttemberg was a huge loss making company in 2003 that succeeded in turning itself around with the help of the union and employees. It required a reduction of the workforce from 40,000 to 20,000 and wage and conditions reductions but the company survived and was making a profit within 12 months. The managing director Utz Claassen considered that 'without the inclusion and cooperation of the workforce, rationalization would not have been possible'.[73] Similarly, in 2004 when Grohe was purchased by two US private equity firms they intended to relocate 3,200 jobs from a total of 4,500 from Germany to China. The relocation plan became a political football in the 2005 election with the private equity firms involved being described by Franz Munterfering (now Chairman of the SPD) as 'locusts'. The union IG Metall however negotiated an alternative plan and accepted 1,000 job losses in return for securing the future of the remaining employees.[74]

The co-determination regime has a somewhat dual character. On the one hand it aims to protect employees' jobs and conditions, but on the other hand it aims to do so through consensus building. The process of globalization in terms of increased competition and production relocation has however brought a fundamental shift in the bargaining power between management and labour. As such the basis of the consensus has changed over the course of the 1990s and the first decade of the twenty-first century as its function now encompasses minimizing the effect of these changed economic circumstances on jobs and working conditions. To that extent, the negotiation function of co-determination is alive and well but it brings a danger with it. As Jackson puts it:

> [w]hile codetermination continues to provide a number of beneficial economic functions, the legitimacy of an institution cannot rest of functionality alone. Codetermination originated in deep-seated political values, as well as formative experiences of the post-war generation in rebuilding German industry. These value commitments were refreshed during the political climate of the late 1960s and early 1970s where the meaning and boundaries of democracy were again tested by collective action. As codetermination becomes an increasingly professionalized domain of co-management, it is less clearly grounded in broader societal value commitments. In short, by successfully "managing" workplace

---

73   Richards, A. (2007) 'Mitbestimmung: The Future of Co-Determination in a Hostile World', Debatte, vol. 15(3), 343–364 at 353.

74   Madslien, J. (2005) 'Reshaping Germany's Companies', BBC News, 15 September 2005, available at <http://news.bbc.co.uk/1/hi/business/4238438.stm>. Madslien, J. (2005) 'Will "Locusts" Trigger a German Recovery?', BBC News, 16 September 2005, available at <http://news.bbc.co.uk/1/hi/business/4251606.stm>.

conflicts, codetermination may itself erode the preconditions necessary for its own reproduction in the longer term.[75]

There is no doubt that the way consensus building is now operating through flexibility and targeted strike action, indicates that the manner in which labour co-determination has operated in the past has changed. However despite an absolutely fundamental shift in the economic environment in which it operates co-determination does not appear to us to be under threat but is rather being adapted to the circumstances it now finds itself in. That is not to say that it won't change dramatically in the future but for now it remains a reduced but still important institution in the German insider corporate governance system. Perhaps crucially it remains highly valued in the workplace and with the general public, as a 2004 survey conducted by the Hans Böckler Foundation found that 82 percent of respondents had a positive view of co-determination.[76]

Finanzplatz Deutschland: Reforming Germany's Financial Markets

Apart from the challenges with regard to long-established organizational and production-related institutions, Germany has also been facing pressures to reform its financial system as a result of financial globalization. The German economy, being one of the largest in the developed world as well as one that is highly integrated into the international trade regime, could not remain unaffected by the globalization of financial markets that began in the late 1980s. Despite Keynesian concerns about capital movements, post war Germany did not fully use the discretion that the Bretton Woods system allowed for the imposition of capital controls and was one of the first countries to liberalize its capital markets. For example, many capital movement restrictions – e.g. on FDI and on purchases of foreign securities – were largely lifted by the end of the 1950s and interest rates were liberalized as early as 1967. However, as current account surpluses continued, during the late 1960s and early 1970s capital inflows, largely due to speculation about the Deutsch Mark's (DM) revaluation, intensified and Germany was faced with the dilemma of either damaging its export industries by revaluing its currency or imposing capital controls.[77] Initially, the authorities tried to tackle the problem with the imposition of capital controls some of which, as Smith notes, remained in place until as late as the mid 1980s preventing the full integration of

75   Jackson, G. (2004) 'Contested Boundaries: Ambiguity and Creativity in the Evolution of German Codetermination', RIETI Discussion Paper No. 04-E-022, 25–26, available at SSRN: <http://ssrn.com/abstract=569541 or DOI: 10.2139/ssrn.569541>.
76   <http://www.boeckler.de/>.
77   Goodman, J. and Pauly, L. (1993) 'The Obsolescence of Capital Controls? Economic Management in an Age of Global Markets', World Politics, 50.

the German economy into the international capital market.[78] Most importantly, a 25 percent coupon tax on non-residents' income from bonds introduced in 1965 was not abolished until 1984 and until its abolition it restricted outside investment. Moreover, non-residents were not allowed to issue DM denominated bonds unless the lead manager was a German bank and the actual issue took place in Germany. However, as speculative flows into Germany continued to grow, necessitating two consecutive revaluations, in 1973 the government was forced to float the DM.

While the currency's floatation temporarily eased the tensions, the increasing role of the DM in the world economy, not least due to Germany's large surpluses, led to the deregulation and globalization of German financial markets.[79] Remaining direct capital controls were abolished in 1981 in response to short-lived deficits after the second oil shock, but when the current account showed a surplus again in 1982 the liberal policies were not reversed. On the contrary, as the integration of the German economy into international capital markets continued, the pressures for further liberalization intensified. The vast development of the Eurobond markets had by the early 1980s became a direct challenge for German monetary authorities, as a large market for German bonds had been created outside German Government control. For example, by the late 1980s virtually all German government bond transactions took place in London, Luxembourg and Paris.[80] In order to keep their business, German banks established subsidiaries in those less regulated markets from where they conducted those activities that were not permitted in Germany.[81] For instance, in 1984 Deutsche Bank who dominated the German capital market moved all its capital market operations to London, giving a clear signal to German policy makers that something had to be done to prevent large financial institutions' exit.[82]

As a result of these developments, paradoxically the only choice the Bundesbank and the government were left with was to continue the deregulation of financial markets and integrate German markets into the international capital markets in order to bring German bond transactions and financial business in general back under some semblance of domestic control. From April 1984 foreign banks were gradually allowed to underwrite DM Eurobonds, the requirements that all bond issues should be governed by German law and listed on a German stock exchange were abolished, restrictions on different types of bonds were lifted and the restrictive tax regime for securities was reversed. Consequently, financial liberalization made issues of DM Eurobonds more attractive and less costly and

78   Smith, E. (1994) The German Economy, London: Routledge, 366–367.

79   Goodman, J. and Pauly, L., above n77, 62–63.

80   Deeg, R. and Lütz, S. (1998) 'Internationalisation and Financial Federalism – The United States and Germany at the Crossroads?', Working Paper, Max-Planck-Institut für Gesellschaftsforschung, Köln.

81   Smith, E., above n78.

82   Goodman, J. and Pauly, L., above n77, 64.

contributed to the development of Germany as an international bond market and a financial centre in general.[83]

The liberalization and growth of the German bond markets went hand in hand with the development of the equity markets as tax disincentives as well as minimum reserve requirements for equity issues were gradually removed. Stimulants for further development of the stock market have also originated from the increased capital needs of German companies. As we discussed in Chapter 3, the opportunities provided by the opening up of global product markets has resulted in an increased need for capital for companies to expand into those markets. The economic downturn of the 1990s anything but facilitated the ability of German companies to draw sufficient finance in the domestic market. As Waller observed in the early 1990s:

> Germany's traditional capital account surplus has swung into a deficit and companies are realizing that they will be competing with the cash-hungry state for capital throughout the 1990s.[84]

Thus, large German companies could not continue to rely merely on domestic capital markets in their struggle to compete in the global marketplace because, as they pursued their globalization strategies with FDI and cross border M&A, their financial needs had begun to outgrow the potential of German capital markets – neither banks nor the domestic securities markets were able to meet the increased demand of large corporations for capital. In this regard financial liberalization created new financing opportunities for large companies since it enabled them to tap global markets with larger investor bases. Thus, as Deeg and Lütz noted, by 1990 many large German companies had turned to the bond and equity markets in London and New York to provide capital.[85]

Since the liberalization of capital controls, German stock exchanges have been facing direct competition from abroad that they had been unable to cope with so long as the traditional institutions responsible for their underdevelopment remained in place. Plans for the creation of a pan-European equity market based in the City of London intensified the pressures for reform in Germany.[86] The largest German exchanges realized the need for financial change and, thus, began to implement development programmes. At the beginning of the 1990s as the EU moved towards planning for the creation of a single currency, awareness in

---

83   Simmons, B. (1999) 'The Internationalization of Capital' in Kitschelt, H. et al. (eds) Continuity and Change in Contemporary Capitalism, Cambridge: Cambridge University Press, 37–43.

84   Waller, D. (1993) 'Survey of Germany', Financial Times, 11 October.

85   Deeg, R. and Lütz, S., above n80.

86   Story, J. (1997) 'Globalization, the European Union and German Financial Reform: The Political Economy of "Finanzplatz Deutschland"' in Underhill, G. (ed.), The New World Order in International Finance, London: Macmillan, 257 and 265.

Germany that its financial markets needed modernization, if it was to be the host for the European Central Bank (ECB), was acute. As Cioffi describes it:

> [b]y the early 1990s, large segments of the German political and economic elites began to lose faith in the German corporate governance model, which appeared ill-suited to the increasingly market-driven European and international economic orders ... Beginning in the early 1990s, pro-EU CDU and neo-liberal FDP politicians, large financial institutions, and the banking and finance center of Frankfurt overcame the resistance of the parochial interests of the Länder governments, Länder-based (and regulated) stock exchanges, and small firms and banks.[87]

In 1990, in an effort to modernize, the Frankfurt Stock Exchange was turned into an AG which in 1993 became the core subsidiary of Deutsche Börse AG, the holding company of all German exchanges. This provided the basis for major efforts to promote the securities markets as a source of corporate finance in Germany and the emergence of the *Finanzplatz Deutschland* ('Germany as a Financial Centre') concept which was formally announced with a package of reforms in 1992 by the then finance minister Theo Waigel.[88] Fierce competition, not only between different European financial centres, but also between cities and regions within Germany, for the allocation of the European Central Bank (ECB) was also another pressure factor for financial 'modernization'. The final bid for Frankfurt would have been unsustainable without developed and transparent securities markets in place.[89]

However, it was not only German securities markets that were affected as a result of financial globalization and liberalization. The ability of large German companies to draw funds from foreign financial markets, both debt and equity, meant that banks had been losing business from their largest client companies. It also meant that the banks were competing with the former clients for funds in the international debt markets.[90] This is something they could not afford due to the increased competition by foreign banks that financial liberalization brought

---

87   Cioffi, J. (2006) 'Corporate Governance Reform, Regulatory Politics, and the Foundations of Finance Capitalism in the United States and Germany', German Law Journal, vol. 7, 549–550.

88   Financial Times (1992) 'Germany Plans Shake-up of Stock Markets', 24 January 24 1992.

89   New York Times (1992) 'Ambition for Frankfurt', 21 January 1992, available at <http://query.nytimes.com/gst/fullpage.html?res=9E0CE7D8123CF932A15752C0A964958 260>. Keefe, K. (1993) 'Frankfurt: The Gateway to Capital, Commerce, and Communication in the New Europe', Business America, 26 July, available at <http://findarticles.com/p/articles/ mi_m1052/is_n15-16_v114/ai_14412251>.

90   Crane, D. and Schaede, U. (2005) 'Functional Change and Bank Strategy in German Corporate Governance', International Review of Law and Economics, vol. 25, 513–540 at 525–526.

and the decreasing profits from their traditional loan business.[91] To add to the banks' problems, between 1986 and 1992 a wave of EU directives aimed at the harmonization of banking services across the EU were issued. The most important of which was the second banking directive in 1989 which provided for mutual recognition of banks across the EU.[92] This both allowed German banks to do business freely across EU member borders but also introduced competition into the domestic market. As a result a wave of consolidation occurred in the German banking sector. In 1990 there were 4,719 banks in Germany but by 2004 that number had fallen to 2,400 and is likely to fall further given the restructuring necessitated by the sub-prime and global financial market crisis from 2007–2009.[93]

Moreover, because of their increased investment banking needs, non financial companies preferred foreign investment banks to their traditional domestic financial partners who lacked sufficient expertise.[94] In response, and fearing that they were becoming laggards in the global financial markets, German banks began to acquire foreign investment banks, particularly in London and New York. For instance, Deutsche Bank acquired the UK firm Morgan Grenfell in 1992 and the New York investment banking house, Bankers Trust, in 1998. Dresdner Bank similarly bought Kleinwort Benson in London. Thus, German bankers, especially the *Großbanken*, became some of the most committed proponents of stock market modernization as they realized that investment banking was essential to their survival both domestically and abroad due to the increased returns involved compared to their traditional deposit and loan business.[95] In other words they realized that earnings from transactions related advice would be enhanced by the development of the German stock market.

In June 1989, November 1994 and April 1998 the First, Second and Third *Finanzmarktförderungsgesetze* (Financial Market Promotion Acts) were passed with the objective of enhancing the attractiveness of Germany as a place for conducting financial business. The First Act intended to promote the development of a new futures market in Germany, the *Deutsche Terminbröse* (German Futures Market ('DTB')), which started operating in January 1990 and was replaced

---

91   Capital reserve requirements for banks, imposed by the Basle Accord, were also a significant factor constraining the ability of banks to finance 'big business'.

92   Directive 86/566/EEC and 88/361/EEC.

93   Siebert, H. (2005) The German Economy: Beyond the Social Market, Princeton University Press, 226; and Association of German Banks (2008) 'Facts and Figures', available at <http://www.germanbanks.org/html/12_banks_in_facts_figures/sub_01_markt/ban_0501.asp>. See also: Wilson, J. (2008) 'Berlin Poised to Turn Crisis into Opportunity to Shake Up Banks', Financial Times, 22 October, 26.

94   Harris, C. (1998) 'Investment Banking: Foreigners Set the Pace', Financial Times – German Banking and Finance Survey, 24 June, 5; and Fisher, A. (1997) 'Deutsche Bank to Reduce Domestic Shareholdings', Financial Times, 20 May.

95   Cioffi, J., above n87, 549; and Moran, M. (1989) 'A State of Inaction: The State and Stock Exchange Reform in the Federal Republic of Germany' in Bulmer, S. (ed.) Changing Agenda of West German Public Policy, Aldershot: Dartmouth, 110–127.

in 1998 by the EUREX futures market created from the DTB and the Swiss SOFFEX exchanges. The creation of such a market had the dual effect of enabling investors to hedge against risks in the equity market and therefore facilitate investment in stocks. The Second Act was the long-awaited implementation of the EEC Large Holdings and Insider Dealing Directives.[96] This measure tightened disclosure requirements and prohibited insider trading which in 1994 became a criminal offence. The Third Financial Market Promotion Act among other things implemented important amendments to the stock market and securities trading legislation as well as the law governing investment companies ('KAGGs') and venture capital firms ('UBGs').[97] Another important development was the introduction, although short lived as it closed in 2003, of a new market segment, the *Neuer Markt*, at the Frankfurt Stock Exchange in 1997 for small and medium sized innovative companies, thus making access to equity finance for such companies easier.[98] All these measures were intended to promote market finance and investment in equities by increasing the scope, transparency and confidence in the quality of the stock market and, thus, improve the competitiveness of German financial markets as part of the *Finanzplatz Deutschland* project.

The effect of all these developments in corporate finance has been mixed. Bank loans as a source of external financing for German corporations have declined dramatically from the beginning of the twenty-first century as the banks have completed their strategic transformation, to be replaced by a huge increase in internal funding and a wider range of external financing options ranging from equities to other forms of non-bank lending.[99] By 2008 while the number of domestic German companies listed on the German stock exchanges has grown slowly it has been accompanied by an enormous expansion in the number of foreign shares listed in Germany as Frankfurt's position as the financial centre of the Euro Zone was solidified and its stock exchange grew to be the second largest stock exchange in Europe, London being the largest. In 1987 there were 432 foreign shares listed on the various German Stock exchanges, by 1997 that figure had grown to 2,186, by 2000 that figure leapt to 9,812, by 2004 it increased again to 11,525 and by 2006 was 15,051.[100]

---

96   We discuss this further later in this chapter.

97   For comments on the draft law see Baums, T. (1997) 'Der Entwurf eines 3. Finanzmarktförderungsgesetzes: Stellungnahme für den Finanzausschuß des Deutschen Bundestages', Working Paper, Osnabrück Universität, available at <http://www.jura.uni-frankfurt.de/ifawz1/baums/Bilder_und_Daten/Arbeitspapiere/a1297.pdf>.

98   Following the stock markets' collapse in 2001 the Neuer Markt was closed on 1 January 2003. BBC News Online (2002) 'Germany's Neuer Markt to Close', 26 September 2002, available at <http://news.bbc.co.uk/1/hi/business/2283068.stm>.

99   Deutsches Aktieninstitut (2008) DAI Statistics, Table 04–6. We discuss this change in bank behaviour later in this chapter.

100   Deutsches Aktieninstitut (2008) DAI Statistics: Listed Shares in Germany by Market Segment, Table 02–1–1–1.

Despite these regulatory reforms and the dramatic rise in the number of listed companies on German exchanges the development of a German equity culture has been fragile at best. Most of the success of the German Stock exchange has been built on foreign listings as German listed companies only numbered about 1,000 by 2006 and the German public have not wholeheartedly embraced an equity based culture.[101] During the post war period the German public had a general aversion to risky investments, mainly as a result of past monetary instability experiences, which created a preference for fixed-income securities. However, the bullish stock market during the 1990s made investment in equities more attractive and helped to increase the flow of savings directed into shares. Private investors began to buy shares either directly or indirectly though investment funds, so that, as Graph 8.3 shows, in the past decade, in spite of the stock market crash of 2001–2002, the growth of private households' investment has grown to reach €867 billion in 2004 – this is a rise of 332 percent for stock related assets as opposed to a 57 percent increase of bank related assets. On top of this, one should add the large increase (259 percent) of long-term savings related assets of households, such as pension funds, occupational pension schemes, supplementary pension funds etc, over the same period, a large part of which has translated into more savings being directed to the stock market. The move to prepare for the Euro also had a knock on effect on the stock exchange and the level of German shareholdings as privatization became a mechanism for the German government to raise capital to meet the budget requirements for entry to the Euro Zone and to deal with budget restrictions afterwards. Large privatization programmes, such as the Deutsche Telecom, the Deutsche Post and the Post Bank IPOs in 1996, 2000 and 2004 respectively were oversubscribed; the first was five times, the second was eight times and the third by two and a half times despite the stock market downturn since 2001. A large portion of these shares were acquired by retail investors.[102] Further planned privatization programmes – e.g. Deutsche Bahn – may attract more retail investors into the stock market.[103]

---

101   Deutsches Aktieninstitut (2008) DAI Statistics: Table 02–1–1–1.

102   Cant, R. (1996) 'Growing up in Public', Investors Chronicle, available at <http://www.faqs.org/abstracts/Business/Growing-up-in-public-Deutsche-Telekom-its-good-to-privatise.html>.

103   Gow, D. (2008) 'Privatisation Fever Grips La Poste and Deutsche Bahn', The Guardian, 10 September 2008, available at <http://www.guardian.co.uk/business/2008/sep/10/europe1>.

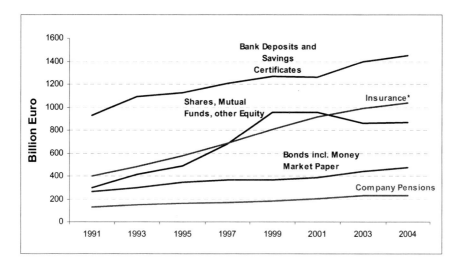

Graph 8.3 Households' financial assets by category, 1991–2004

Note: * Including private pension funds, occupational pension schemes, supplementary pension funds and other claims (including accumulated interest-bearing surplus shares with insurance corporations).

Source: Deutsche Bundesbank.

However a significant dampening effect occurred after the stock market crash in 2001–2002 just as a tentative equity culture was gradually emerging in Germany in which younger Germans were particularly active.[104] In part this activity was driven by uncertainty among younger Germans about the value and availability of retirement income from the state pension in the future.[105] In 1988 3.1 million individual investors owned shares directly, by 2000 at the peak of the dot.com share boom that figure had reached 6.2 million and after the stock market crash in 2001–2002 it has declined back to 4 million in 2007. However, direct holdings do not tell the full story as since 1997 Germans have increasing placed their long-term savings in investment funds of which a part of the investment has gone to the equity markets. In 1997 2.3 million Germans held investments this way, by 2001 9.7 million and by 2007 it had declined to 7.9 million.[106] Again the stock market crash played a large part in the decline. A broader reflection of all this boom and bust can be observed in German stock market capitalization which jumped from just 25 percent of GDP in 1990, to about 68 percent in 1999 near the peak of the stock market boom, and declining to 56.6 percent by 2006. (Graph 8.4).

---

104   Smith, E., above, n78; Deutsche Bank Research (1999) 'Financial Assets in Euro Land: Will Investment Behaviour Converge?', EMU Watch, No. 73, 8 June.

105   See below and BBC News Online (2007) 'German MPs Raise Retirement Age', 9 March 2007, available at <http://news.bbc.co.uk/2/hi/europe/6434929.stm>.

106   Deutsches Aktieninstitut (2008) DAI Statistics: Number of Shareholders.

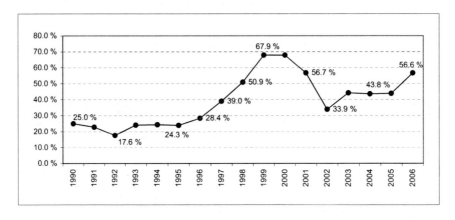

Graph 8.4 Market capitalization as a percentage of GDP in Germany, 1990–2006
Source: DAI Statistics (2008).

Moreover, while until 2002 high tax rates on capital gains (about 52 percent) constituted a major handicap for the development of the stock market, the government abolished it in January 2002 as part of the German tax reform programme (*Steurreform*).[107] In 2008 a further change in the tax regime intended to make investment in Germany more attractive for both overseas and German investors was enacted. The Business Tax Reform Act 2008 and amendments to the German Investment Act are intended to reduce the tax burden on companies and institutional investors operating in Germany by standardizing taxation on interest income, dividends and capital gains on securities from 2009 and in particular reduce the tax burden for foreign investment funds.[108] Similarly, the implementation of the Markets in Financial Instruments Directive ('MiFID') in Germany in 2007 aimed at building a single financial market through removing barriers to cross-border competition in trading and reducing costs for investors may also encourage greater cross border investment.[109]

---

107   On the effects of the capital gains tax abolition on cross-shareholdings see the discussion later in this chapter.

108   Berg, H., Schmich, R. and Enders, B. (2007) 'Analysis of the 2008 German Business Tax Reform and Pending Tax Legislation', Tax Stratagies, vol. 11(16), 12–17; Emde, T. and Wuelfert, K. (2008) 'Germany: Significant Amendments to the German Investment Act', Freshfields Bruckhaus Deringer, 5 June 2008, available at <http://www. mondaq.com/article.asp?articleid=60388>. See also: Böttcher, B. and Deutsch, K. (2007) 'Germany Cresting the Wave: A Reform Agenda for the Grand Coalition', Deutsche Bank Research.

109   2004/39/EC of 21 April 2004 supplemented by EC Directive 2006/73/EC of 10 August 2006.

Pensions reform has also had an impact here. Due to decreasing employment, cutbacks in government spending and demographic reasons – i.e. the pensioner to worker ratio level will more than double in the next 30 years and Germany's birth rate is extremely low – there has been a perceived need for a shift in the government pension from the traditional pay-as-you-go to at least a partially funded pension system.[110] As the increasing value of assets controlled by pension, insurance and mutual investment funds shows, movement in this direction is already underway (Graph 8.3). With regard to this, the Third *Finanzmarktförderungsgesetz* allowed the creation of pension plan investment funds that are obliged by law to invest at least 51 percent of their assets in equities and real estate and thus provided the vehicle for private pensions.[111] In addition, developments at the EU level have also encouraged pension reform. Thus, the EU Pensions Directive, aims to establish pan-European US-style pension funds as part of the internal market initiative and as a solution to the EU-wide pensions' crisis.[112] Following this, a reform of state-pensions has already been enacted and has been introduced in phases from 2002 (the so-called *Riester-Rente*, named after the former employment and social affairs minister). The pension reforms' most important provisions reduce the amount of the state pension and the resulting pension gap is closed by a private pension generated on the capital markets as workers are encouraged to take out private or occupational supplementary pension plans subsidized by the government. Since 2008 employees have been able to put a maximum of four percent of their salary into a private savings account (*Entgeltumwandlung*) provided there is a collective agreement signed by unions and employers (the so-called *Tarifvorrang*).[113] In general, the *Riester* reform constitutes a cautious move from a public pay-as-you-go system towards a privately funded system.

Traditional employer pension coverage has also been in decline. While company pension schemes in 1976 covered two-thirds of the employed, by 1990 their share had decreased to 50 percent and declined further over the course of the 1990s. Moreover, company pension schemes which have traditionally funded pensions directly have also been severely hit by the implementation of cost-cutting policies in German companies which has eroded their value in recent years. Increasingly, external sources of funding have been used, including equities, in a move towards

---

110   Gourevitch, P. and Shinn, J. (2005) Political Power and Corporate Control: The New Global Politics of Corporate Governance, Princeton, 164–165; Harding, L. (2006) 'German Birth Rate Falls to Lowest in Europe', The Guardian, 15 March 2006, available at <http://www.guardian.co.uk/world/2006/mar/15/germany.lukeharding>. See also: Sinn, H. (1999) 'The Crisis of Germany's Pension Insurance System and How It Can Be Resolved', Working Paper, Ludwig-Maximilians Universität and CFSIfo Institute, Munich.

111   Siebert, H (2005) The German Economy: Beyond the Social Market, Princeton: Princeton University Press, 114–121 and 218.

112   Directive 2003/41/EC.

113   Siebert, H., above n111, 116–117.

providing for future employees.[114] Thus, in 1998 the Working Committee on Company Pension Funds proposed that the Act Relating to Company Pension Plans be amended to provide for the creation of 'Investment oriented Pension Funds' which will be governed by the Act on Investment Companies (*Gesetz über Kapitalanlagegesellschaften* ('KAGG')) and be similar to those in Anglo-Saxon countries. In June 2004 Germany adopted a new reform act, the *Alterseinkünftegesetz* (Act Regulating the Taxation of Pensions and Pension Expenses) which became effective on 1 January 2005 and aims, through tax incentives, at enhancing employer-sponsored direct insurance plans (*Direktversicherung*), *Pensionskasse*, and pension funds (*Pensionfonds*). At the moment pension fund assets in Germany compared to the US, Japan and the UK are tiny but may grow in future as these reforms impact (see Chart 8.4).

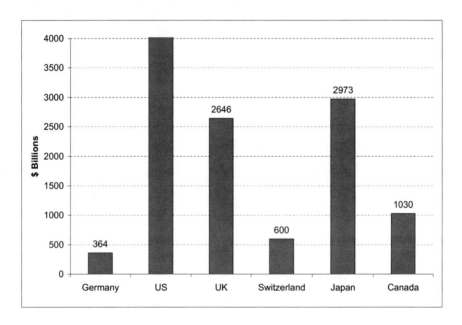

Chart 8.4 Financial assets of pension funds in 2007 (billion dollars)
Source: Watson Wyatt Worlwide (2008) Global Pension Assets Study.

Since the late 1980s Germany has been engaged in a process of developing its financial markets. Increasing exposure of its largest companies and banks to the effects of global capital markets created significant pressures to reform and

---

114   Rhiel, R. (2005) 'Pension Funding in Germany', Mercer, 1 June 2005, available at <http://www.mercer.com/referencecontent.htm?idContent=1181340>. See also: Finanzplatz (1998) The Pension System in Germany, Frankfurt: Finanzplatz.

integrate German capital markets into these global capital markets. Germany's ambitions to be the financial centre of the Euro Zone and have the ECB located in Germany also played a significant part in pushing the development of the financial markets in Germany. Additionally, although not attributable to globalization, the changing demographics of the German population necessitated some tentative pension reform to accommodate an aging population which in turn fed into the need to provide a deeper and more liquid equities market as an outlet for long-term savings provision. In all the direct effect of this has been mixed so far. While the stock exchange has now become a significant European capital market, it has been built on foreign not domestic listings. While initially an equity culture was emerging as individuals invested directly and indirectly through mutual funds, pensions and insurance companies, the stock market crash in 2001–2002 seems to have badly damaged willingness to invest on the German stock exchange. While we will return to the wider effects of the development of the German stock exchange later in this chapter, in the next section we examine the key legal reforms necessitated by *Finanzplatz Deutschland.*

Protecting the Outsider

The effort to transform Germany into a European and global financial centre has also meant that market transparency and outsider investor protection have gradually been introduced primarily to make the investment attractive to foreign institutional investors although, as we will observe in a similar manner to the experience with co-determination, elements of path dependence are also present in key areas. The most important regulatory developments with regard to corporate governance are the amendments to the *Wertpapierhandelsgesetz* (Securities Trading Act ('WpHG')) as part of the second and fourth *Finanzmarktförderungsgesetze,* the *Gesetz zur Kontrolle und Transparenz im Unternehmensbereich* (Act on Control and Transparency in the Enterprise Sector ('KonTraG')) and the *Gesetzes zur Unternehmensintegrität und Modernisierung des Anfechtungsrechts* (Act on the Improvement of Corporate Integrity and on the Modernization of the Regime governing Decision-Directed Suits ('UMAG")) amending the *Aktiengesetz,* the *Deutscher Corporate Governance Kodex* (German Corporate Governance Code ('DCGK')), the passing of the *Kapitalaufnahmeerleichterungsgesetz* (Facilitation of Capital Raising Act ('KapAEG')) amending the *Handelsgesetzbuch* (German Commercial Code ('HGB'), the adoption of a voluntary *Übernahmekodex* for listed AGs (takeover code) later replaced by the controversial *Wertpapiererwerbs- und Übernahmegesetz* (Securities Acquisition and Takeover Act ('WpÜG')), and the *Bilanzrechtsreformgesetz* (Reform Act on Accounting Regulations ('BilReG')). We turn in the next four sections to consider the significance of these and other related measures for German corporate governance.

Takeover regulation

The disadvantageous position of minority shareholders in cases of takeover bids and the ability of blockholders to appropriate benefits as a result of the lack of effective takeover regulation was noted in the previous chapter.[115] As we discussed there, among other institutional factors, insufficient minority shareholder protection in takeovers was associated with the underdevelopment of German securities markets. In moving towards *Finanzplatz Deutschland,* German regulators and policy makers could not ignore this problematic lack of outsider investor protection. Thus, in the mid 1990s the Federal Ministry of Finance assigned the *Börsensachverständigenkommission* (Commission of Stock Exchange Experts (BSK)) the task of devising a code of practice for takeovers. In 1995 the BSK introduced the Kodex which came into force on 1 October 1995, and the implementation of which was based on voluntary adoption by German listed companies. A Takeover Commission, whose members are appointed by the BSK, was created to monitor and promote compliance.[116]

The formulation of the Kodex was along the lines of the London City Code on Takeovers and Mergers and set out four main principles: equal treatment of all shareholders, transparency of the takeover procedure (equal access to information for all shareholders), fair participation for all shareholders in the offer price and the requirement that the *Vorstand* remain neutral during the takeover. In practice, however, the Kodex never fulfilled the expectations the BSK had when the code was adopted. Even though its rules provided satisfactory protection to minority shareholders in takeover transactions and although the Takeover Commission within four years of its inception processed 46 cases involving the code, the problem of enforcement remained. Despite the BSK's persistent efforts and the Deutsche Börse's requirement that all newly listed companies in the DAX and MDAX had to adopt the code, and a joint declaration by German banks not to cooperate with bidders who did not adopt the code, by 1 December 1998 only 348 out of the 758 listed companies had adopted the Kodex. Large companies like BMW, Hoechst, Viag and Volkswagen refused to adopt the code and withstood public criticism for giving priority to specific insider interests.[117] In the words of Dr. Karl-Hermann Baumann, chairman of the BSK, speaking in 1999 'this means that there is no guarantee for a level playing field' in the field of corporate

---

115   See also Hoffmann-Burchardi, U. (1999) 'Corporate Governance Rules and the Value of Control – A Study of German Dual-Class Shares', Discussion Paper No. 315, Financial Markets Group, London School of Economics, available at <http://ideas.repec.org/p/fmg/fmgdps/dp315.html>.

116   Section 20 of the Kodex.

117   Handelsblatt Interactiv (1999) 'Takeover Code to Be Made Law – Commission Disappointed with Acceptance of Voluntary Regulation (English Summary)', 3 February 1999, available at <http://www.handelsblatt.com/>.

takeovers.[118] Consequently, the BSK announced it was abandoning its efforts to gain universal voluntary acceptance of the Kodex and proposed that there should be mandatory legislation regulating takeovers.[119]

In 1999 Vodafone launched a successful but controversial, at least in Germany, hostile bid for Mannesmann, which we will discuss in full later in this chapter, and the situation changed dramatically. Immediately after the takeover, the then Finance Minister, Hans Eichel, urged the EU to implement the Thirteenth Company Law Directive setting out common takeover rules for all Member States.[120] However, the German government badly misjudged the public reaction to the Vodafone/ Mannesmann takeover and more importantly the reaction of the German members of the European Parliament to such a controversial directive on Takeovers. In 1985 the European Commission as a key part of completing its plans for the EU single market proposed drafting a directive, the Thirteenth Company Law Directive, to create a standard set of rules for takeovers in Europe.[121] In January 1989 the Commission put forward its draft directive on European takeovers which became a lightning rod for tensions between the more shareholder oriented Anglo/Saxon outsider corporate system in the UK and the more social market insider Continental Corporate systems within the EU.[122] One of the central points of tension was that the directive had at its heart the UK Takeovers Panel's key Principle 7 (Article 9 of the Directive) that management cannot take defensive action in a takeover without shareholder approval. In essence the directive was viewed as favouring shareholders over social market insider concerns such as employee welfare. As a result of these very different perspectives on the draft directive, it lay dormant for nearly a decade.

By the mid 1990s with an emerging equity culture in many Continental European states, including as we have observed above, Germany, new life was breathed into the draft directive and by 1999 it was re-established within the Commission's plans as possible EU legislation.[123] However, the hostile takeover of Mannesmann by the UK company Vodafone, over the course of 1999/2000, moved the German members of the European Parliament against the takeovers directive because of fears about employee protection, despite the German government

118   Bauman, K. (1999), Takeover Rules Have to Become Binding for All Companies, <www.dai.de>.

119   Börsensachverständigenkommission (1999) 'Standpunkte der Börsensach-verständigen-Kommission zur Künftigen Regelung von Unternehmensübernahmen', Frankfurt.

120   Atkins, R. and Simonian, H. (1999) 'Germans Seek New Bid Rules', Financial Times, 23 November.

121   See Directive 2004/25/EC of 21.04.2004 on takeover bids at <http://ec.europa.eu/internal_market/company/takeoverbids/index_en.htm>.

122   See OJ C 64, 14 March 1989, 8; for the explanatory memorandum, see Bull. EC Supplement March 1989.

123   See OJ C 162, 6 June 1996, 5; for the explanatory memorandum, see COM(95)655 final and OJ C 23, 24 January 2001, 1.

having signed off on the directive at the Council of Ministers level. Subsequently, the draft directive was rejected by the European Parliament in July 2001 in one of the narrowest votes in its history.[124] In response the Commission set up a Group of High-Level Company Law Experts under the chairmanship of Professor Jaap Winter in order to try and navigate a compromise solution.[125] This they achieved and over the course of 2003 the Commission negotiated a new version of the takeovers directive. In April 2004 a much compromised directive was eventually agreed in which, among other changes, Article 9 was made optional for member states.[126] Thus a member state could choose to have takeover defences or not.[127]

While this saga played out at the EU level, the German cabinet approved the draft *Wertpapiererwerbs- und Übernahmegesetz* (Securities Acquisition and Takeover Act ('WpÜG')) which was eventually passed and took effect on 1 January 2002. Although the new law contained a mandatory bid rule once a 30 percent of voting shares threshold is reached, Section 33 enables management to seek shareholder approval for defensive measures, such as the sale of critical assets, the issuance of shares to a third party, the sale or repurchase of assets of the use of authorized capital, that can be applied for a period of 18 months, even if no bid is imminent.[128] Moreover, under the same provision management is granted considerable discretion to employ post-bid defences with the approval of the *Aufsichtsrat*, i.e. without any direct shareholder involvement. For example a post-bid defensive action was taken when Merck extended an offer for Schering, its competitor in the pharmaceuticals industry, in 2006. Schering rejected the offer and using the leeway allowed by the law, which stipulates that even after an offer is made a competing bidder may be called in, found Bayer AG as a white knight who succeeded in outbidding Merck. While such defensive tactics are not always successful, as was the case in Macquarie Group's successive bids for Techem AG over the course of 2006/2008, they can be seriously obstructive and a bidder

---

124   The vote was in fact tied 273 for the directive and 273 against but this amounts to a rejection under the Parliament's rules. On the background to the rejection see Knudsen, J. (2005) 'Is the Single European Market an Illusion? Obstacles to Reform of EU Takeover Regulation', European Law Journal, vol. 11, 510.

125   Report by the Group of High-Level Company Law Experts, European Commission, Brussels, 10 January 2002.

126   See Clarke, B. (2006) 'European Union Articles 9 and 11 of the Takeover Directive (2004/25) and the Market for Corporate Control', Journal of Business Law, June, 374. The directive was required to be implemented by May 2007.

127   The mandatory bid rule, which is the one part of the City Code that is often criticized for distorting the market for corporate control by discouraging takeovers in the UK, was adopted in the Directive. On the role of the mandatory bid rule in protecting managers see Enriques, L. (2004) 'The Mandatory Bid Rule in the Takeover Directive: Harmonization Without Foundation', European Company and Financial Law Review, vol. 4, 448; and Johnson, A. (2007) 'Takeover Regulation: Historical and Theoretical Perspectives On The City Code', Cambridge Law Journal, vol. 66, 451.

128   US-style poison pills diluting the acquirer's stock value are, however, prohibited.

needs to be remarkably determined in order to succeed. In the Macquarie bid, Techem invited the investment company BC Partners to act as a white knight, but Macquarie persisted. BC Partners then switched sides and joined Macquarie's bid for Techem which Techem management fought off. Macquarie returned again in 2007 with a new bid on its own and finally succeeded in 2008.[129]

The much watered down EU Takeovers Directive was eventually implemented in Germany in 2006 by the Act Implementing the Takeover Bids Directive 2004/25/ EC (*Übernahmerichtlinie-Umsetzungsgesetz*). As one would expect given the history of the Directive, Germany opted out of Article 9 (restrictions on defensive action by management) and Article 11 which removed restrictions on voting rights during a bid. However, the amendments to WpÜG provide for companies to apply Articles 9 and 11 if they pass a special resolution amending their articles to this effect and notify the regulator to that effect. As such over time Germany may end up with a complicated two-tiered takeover regime where some companies have restrictions and other do not.

As we discussed in Chapter 2 opposition to takeovers is not surprising when one recognizes that the significant adaptation costs of establishing an active market for hostile takeovers would have to be borne by labour interests in an era of high unemployment – this was something that German politicians, labour and the general public were highly resistant to. As such management and labour have a strong unifying incentive to oppose the development of an active market for corporate control. The area of takeovers is a good example of how securities and corporate reform can move quickly into other institutional sub-systems. In Germany securities market reform quickly touched on takeovers which in turn impacted on the industrial relations system and triggered a strong path dependent reaction not only at the domestic but the EU level. Therefore, it seems that Coffee's argument, discussed in Chapter 4, that convergence of securities regulation involves fewer adaptation costs and thus, as institutional complementarities transmit changes through the system, can drive corporate governance convergence, needs, as we suggested in that chapter, to be qualified. Institutional complementarities between different corporate governance sub-systems – in Germany's case between securities regulation and industrial relations – are also carriers of path dependence and this must be taken into consideration before predicting convergence through stealth.

Reforming disclosure and insider dealing

As we noted above, on 1 January 1995 the second *Finanzmarktförderungsgesetz* came into effect as part of the *Finanzplatz Deutschland* programme. The first purpose of this legal instrument was to transpose the EEC Large Holdings Directive into German law with the enactment of Sections 21–30 WpHG which

---

129 For a discussion of the two bids see BaFin (2007) Annual Report 2006, 182–185; and Dinkloh, P. (2008) 'Macquarie Secures 96 Percent of Techem After Bid', 4 January 2008, available at <http://uk.reuters.com/article/bankingFinancial/idUKL0453774920080104>.

tighten the disclosure requirements with regard to ownership and control.[130] Its second purpose was to make insider dealing a criminal offence and thus bring domestic law in line with the EEC Insider Dealing Directive[131] as transposed in Sections 12–20 WpHG. Moreover, the WpHG provided the legal basis for the creation of the *Bundesaufsichtsamt für den Wertpapierhandel* (Federal Securities Trading Supervisory Office ('BAWe')),[132] which in turn in 2003 became part of the umbrella authority *Bundesastalt für Finanzdienstleistungsaufsich* (Federal Financial Services Supervisory Institution ('BaFin')) with responsibility for the implementation and enforcement of regulations relating to insider trading, ad-hoc disclosure of price relevant information, takeovers and the supervision of securities houses and markets in general.[133] It is noteworthy that the actual implementation deadlines for the two Directives were 1 January 1991 and 1 June 1992 respectively. The gap between these dates and the actual implementation of the WpHG in 1995, due to opposition by entrenched interest groups, indicates that, as with the takeovers provisions, technical securities markets promotion measures are affected by the forces of path dependence. Nonetheless, and despite the three-year delay, German securities markets reform did take place eventually.

The old German regime had been problematic because of the high thresholds for disclosure; the AktG provided for the disclosure of all stakes owned in an AG that are above 20 percent. Moreover, the GWB required the disclosure to the *Bundeskartellamt* (Federal Cartel Office ('BKartA')) of very detailed ownership structure information when companies filed a change in their share or voting control that was above 25 percent or 50 percent of total share capital or votes. It is noteworthy that these provisions applied to all AGs and therefore there was little difference between disclosure rules of listed and non-listed corporations. Moreover, the thresholds for disclosure under the pre-WpHG regime were so high, as we discussed in the preceding chapter, that it was very difficult to determine who controlled German companies. Under the old regime little significance was attributed to the protection of minority investors in the stock market from undisclosed controlling blockholders who could then exploit their dominant position.

---

130   Council Directive 88/627/EEC.
131   Council Directive 89/592/EEC.
132   Following the adoption on 22 April 2002 of the Act on Integrated Financial Services Supervision. With that the German legislator took a similar approach as the UK by creating a single integrated supervisory authority for all financial services.
133   Pursuant to the Anlegerschutzverbesserungsgesetz (Act Improving the Protection of Investors ('AnSVG')) of 2004, implementing the Market Abuse Directive (2003/124/EC), the BaFin has also been given the power to interpret and clarify details of EU and German securities law on a number of issues. On the history of German securities see BaFin (2008) History, available at <http://www.bafin.de/cln_116/nn_721608/EN/BaFin/Legalbasis/History/history__node.html?__nnn=true#doc721614bodyText3>.

In this sense the enactment of the WpHG is an important development in outsider investor protection. Pursuant to Section 21 the disclosure requirement is now triggered when the voting rights owned by a natural or legal person exceed or fall below 3 percent, 5 percent, 10 percent, 15 percent, 20 percent, 25 percent, 30 percent, 50 percent or 75 percent of the total votes of a listed company.[134] Moreover, Section 22 imposes a mandatory disclosure requirement on votes controlled by a person indirectly, e.g. through a company, a voting trust, a family pool etc.[135] Additionally the WpHG was amended in 2007 by the Act for the Implementation of the Transparency Directive Directive 2004/109/EC of 15 December 2004 (*Transparenzrichtlinie-Umsetzungsgesetz* – 'TUG') which introduced a new section 25 of the WpHG which provides for a notification with regard to the holding of financial instruments where a formal entitlement to acquire shares with voting rights arises.

Finally, for the purposes of the WpHG, disclosure means that after receiving the disclosure from the shareholder who acquired the stake in question, the company is required to publish the information in one of the selected newspapers designated by the stock exchange. The BaFin accumulates all publication references and makes them publicly available every two months on its internet site. Additionally, under the EU Prospectus Directive 2003 and its domestic counterpart, the German Securities Prospectus Act (the 'Prospectus Act'), a public offering of securities in Germany requires the publication of a prospectus which is reviewed by BaFin for completeness, consistency and comprehensibility before it will be approved.[136]

As regards the regulation of insider dealing, the WpHG has been a novelty for the regulatory system in German financial markets. The old regulatory regime's deficiencies due to lax provisions on insider trading was briefly mentioned in the previous chapter. Even though the consequences of such activity were recognized in Germany as early as 1968, when the Ministry of Finance instructed the creation of a special committee responsible for tightening the regulatory regime, the adoption of a set of Voluntary Guidelines in 1970[137] was anything but effective in preventing the occurrence of insider dealing. According to section 2 of the old Guidelines, insiders were all the members and legal representatives of the company's *Aufsichtsrat*, its banks and its affiliates, owners of more than 25 percent equity stakes, agents of a corporation who in connection with their agency function in the ordinary course of business obtain inside information, as well as investment

---

134   WpHG as amended in 2007 by the Act for the Implementation of the Transparency Directive, Directive 2004/109/EC of 15 December 2004 (Transparenzrichtlinie-Umsetzungsgesetz – 'TUG') which entered into force 20 January 2007.

135   Banks proxy-voting powers have been reduced by the enactment of KonTraG. We discuss this later in this chapter.

136   European Directive 2003/71/EC.

137   *Insiderhandels-Richtlinien* 1970 as amended in 1976 and 1988.

advisors and consultants.[138] However, as Standen observes, the Guidelines not only did not cover the conduct of two most common inside information traders, namely tippees and secondary insiders, but they were also 'dulled by a host of limitations and exceptions'.[139]

Obviously, this form of insider dealing regulation could not be maintained once the need to reform financial markets and promote the development of the securities markets appeared. The idea of *Finanzplatz Deutschland* was incompatible with the frequent and unpunished occurrence of insider dealing. Moreover, criticisms from international investors and regulators as well as the legal pressures created by the direct effect of the Directive under European law could not be ignored forever by the German authorities, although they were ignored for quite some time. Moreover, the US Securities and Exchange Commission had been challenging the German regulatory regime indirectly by prosecuting a number of US insider dealing violations where the illegal activity originated in Germany, while the German authorities did nothing.[140] Under these direct and indirect pressures, with the passing of the second *Finanzmarktförderungsgesetz* and the amendment of the WpHG, insider dealing became a criminal offence for the first time in Germany bringing past tolerance of such practices to an end despite opposition by entrenched interests.

The scope of the WpHG provisions are much broader than the Voluntary Guidelines and aim to satisfy the Directive's criteria. The sanctions, which go beyond the minimum requirements under the Directive, are strict and the law provides for imprisonment for a maximum of five years or fines up to €1.5 million. Nonetheless they are not without flaw.[141] For example, as Standen notes, the German banks managed to block far-reaching provisions of an early draft of the *Finanzmarktförderungsgesetz* and thus keep their disclosure duties to a minimum.[142] More specifically, secondary insiders who receive inside information from primary insiders who have direct access to it were not caught by the law unless they personally traded on that information. However, pursuant to the AnSVG amendments to the WpHG implementing Art. 9 of the Market Abuse Directive, insider-trading regulation has been strengthened further so that primary and secondary insiders are now treated equally.

---

138   The last category was added by the 1988 amendments to the insider trading guidelines.

139   Standen, D. (1995) 'Insider Trading Reforms Sweep Across Germany: Bracing for the Cold Winds of Change', Harvard International Law Journal, vol. 36(1), 177–206 at 196–197.

140   Pitt, H. and Hardison, D. (1992) 'Games Without Frontiers: Trends in the International Response to Insider Trading', Law and Contemporary Problems, vol. 55(4), 199.

141   Ryan, P. (2003) 'Understanding Director and Officer Liability in Germany for Dissemination of False Information: Perspectives from an Outsider', German Law Journal, vol. 4(5), 439.

142   Standen, D., above n139, 204.

Additional disclosure related protection measures were enacted with the Fourth *Finanzmarktförderungsgesetz* of April 2002, which, among other things, introduced five new provisions to the WpHG.[143] Firstly, the new Sections 37(b) and 37(c) set the conditions for compensation to investors for the damage resulting from the failure of a securities issuer to publish inside information or from the disclosure of false or delayed information directly affecting the stock price. Secondly, implementing the Market Abuse Directive, sections 20(a) and 20(b) contain liability rules for acts amounting to market manipulation and the BaFin has been given the power to investigate and punish such acts.[144] Thirdly, with the addition of a new Section 15 (a) the Act creates an obligation for persons discharging managerial responsibilities and parties related to them to notify their company and the BaFin of their transactions in shares of their company and its affiliates or financial instruments based on them within five business days. This requirement was part of the more stringent disclosure regime of the *Neuer Markt*, but following its closure in 2003 it has been extended to the Regulated and Official Markets of the Stock Exchange. Finally, it is worth noting in this respect that in order to further tighten the corporate disclosure and market manipulation regime, the Government introduced the *Kapitalmarktinformationshaftungsgesetz* (Capital Market Information Liability Act ('KapInhaG')) in 2005 which improves the ability of investors to bring claims for damages due to false, misleading or omitted public capital markets information or a claim to fulfilment of contract based on an offer under the Securities Acquisition and Takeover Act.

On the whole Germany has enhanced its disclosure requirements for the corporate sector, now covering, shareholdings and most kinds of price sensitive information about the financial position or the general business activities of the company. The insider dealing provisions also have criminal and civil sanctions. While the reforms under the WpHG have introduced a range of new provisions designed to protect outsiders, the regulatory structure seems to have a problem with enforcement, particularly in the area of disclosure.[145] Indeed, Porsche's stealth takeover of Volkswagen between 2006 and 2008 and Schaeffler's takeover of Continental in 2008, discussed later in the chapter, using complex derivatives to conceal their stake building seems, much to the disapproval of international investors, to have been outside of BaFin's regulatory capacity.[146]

---

143 The Act also contains provisions related to proxy-voting by investment funds, brokers, lock-up periods, margin trading etc.

144 Directive 2003/6/EC.

145 Zdantchouk, A. and Hackethal, A. (2006) 'Signaling Power of Open Market Share Repurchases in Germany', Financial Markets and Portfolio Management, vol. 20(2), 123–151; and Ehrhardt, O. and Nowak, E. (2002) 'Die Durchsetzung von Corporate-Governance-Regeln', Die Aktiengesellschaft, vol. 47(6), 336–345.

146 Zetzsche, D. (2008) 'Continental AG vs. Schaeffler, Hidden Ownership and European Law – Matter of Law or Enforcement?', CBCRPS No. 0039 <http://ssrn.com/abstract=1170987>. These events are discussed later in the chapter.

Corporate law reform

A series of spectacular corporate crises and collapses during the 1990s, involving high-profile companies, such as Daimler-Benz, Metallgesellschaft, Klocker-Humbolt-Deutz, and the later collapses since 2000 of Holzmann and Kirch, damaged confidence in the German governance model by undermining the credibility of managers and the alleged governance role of universal banks. The case of Metallgesellschaft AG, in particular, apart from questioning the effectiveness of the *Aufsichtsrat* as a governance body, has also been a prime example of how easily the challenges of global financial markets can give rise to corporate control problems due to the increased complexity and magnitude of the risks involved. In the early nineties the New York subsidiary of the company adopted a high-risk strategy involving oil futures contracts in several American exchanges, which eventually by 1993 it could not meet. Due to insufficient understanding of the subsidiary's derivatives strategy, Metallgesellschaft's *Aufsichtsrat* in Germany ordered the premature liquidation of most oil futures resulting in a loss of over $1 billion for the group.[147] Such failures undermined the confidence not only of domestic but also of foreign investors and stirred public criticism regarding the effectiveness of *Aufsichtsräte* and auditors. Simultaneously, German companies and regulators considered that the new financing opportunities arising from the development of domestic and foreign equity markets could not be exploited without 'improving' corporate governance to meet outside investors' demands. As, Ulrich Seibert, of the Federal Ministry of Justice, commented in 1998:

> [t]he turbulence on global financial markets at the end of last year has illustrated to us the extent to which financial markets have grown together. National capital markets are no longer isolated. Our quoted companies raise finance internationally. German stock corporations are in direct competition with other demands for venture capital worldwide. [...] For the legal and political framework, this means that against a background of institutional competition, there is growing pressure for changes and adaptation of our company law, stock market law and accounting law.[148]

Against this background, on 1 May 1998 the KonTraG was enacted amending the AktG and strengthening the governance role of the *Aufsichtsrat*. In particular, this Act amended the rules governing supervisory boards, auditors and managing directors aiming for the improvement of information flows from management to

147   Wenger, E. and Kaserer, C. (1998) 'The German System of Corporate Governance – A Model Which Should Not Be Imitated' in Black, S. and Moersch, M. (eds) Competition and Convergence in Financial Markets: The German and Anglo-American Models, North Holland, 40–47.

148   Seibert, U. (1999) 'Control and Transparency in Business (KonTraG)', European Business Law Review, vol. 10, 70–75.

the *Aufsichtsrat*. The KonTraG also covered other important corporate governance related areas, such as voting rights, share buy-backs and the use of stock options. While not a revolutionary change to the fundamentals of German corporate structure, especially if one considers that the initial reform proposals called for the complete abolition of the two-tier board and its replacement by a unitary one, the KonTraG amendments are nevertheless important as they have played a role in emphasizing the need for monitoring management by the *Aufsichtsrat* and providing the legal basis for enhancing outsider shareholder protection.[149]

Additionally, the *Deutscher Corporate Governance Kodex* (German Corporate Governance Code ('DCGK')[150] was published in 2002 and was the outcome of a government sponsored initiative which began with the establishment of the *Regierungskommission Corporate Governance* (Government Corporate Governance Commission) in 2001.[151] Its task was to examine Germany's corporate governance system and make reform recommendations, the most significant of which was the creation of a permanent commission that would develop a code of best practice.[152] This took the form of the *Deutscher Corporate Governance Kodex Kommission* initially chaired by ThyssenKrupp AG's *Vorstand* Chairman Gerhard Cromme. The first version of the DCGK was published in February 2002 and has been revised regularly since then, the latest revision being June 2008. The *Kommission* specifically set out to address international criticisms of the Germany corporate governance system that it had an inadequate focus on shareholders' interests.[153] With the *Transparenz- und Publizität Gesetz* (Transparency and Disclosure Act ('TransPuG')) of July 2002 the DCGK was incorporated in the AktG so that all listed companies' *Vorstand* and *Aufsichtsräte* have to issue an annual Corporate Governance Report on whether they have complied with the code's provisions, or explain why they do not comply. This was supplemented in 2008 by the *Bilanzrechtsmodernisierungsgesetz* (Accounting Law Reform Act (*BilMoG*)) implementing Directive 2006/46/EC which requires companies to state whether they have complied or not with their national corporate governance code, a description of the senior management structure of the company and a statement as to the company's control and risk management systems with regard to financial reporting.

---

149   Grub, M. (1999) 'A Trend Towards More Shareholder Value in Germany: Recent Developments in German Stock Corporation Law', International and Comparative Company Law Review, vol. 10, 42 and 44.

150   See the Corporate Governance Commission Code: <http://www.corporate-governance-code.de>.

151   Du Plessis, J. et al., above n30, 23–27.

152   Following the proposals by the Commission on Corporate Governance (Regierungkommission Corporate Governance), the German Government announced a 'Ten-Step Program for Corporate Integrity and Investor Protection' on which most of the corporate governance reforms that followed were based. See Noack, U. and Zetzsche, D. (2005) 'Corporate Reform in Germany: The Second Decade', EBLR 1033–1064 at 1040.

153   See Corporate Governance Commission, above n150.

Apart from its statutory status, the DCGK bares strong resemblance, both in terms of its comply or explain enforcement and its content, with the equivalent UK corporate governance code and covers areas such as shareholder voting rights (one vote per share, pre-emption rights), the General Meeting's function, the cooperation between the *Vorstande* and *Aufsichtsräte* and their function, a takeover neutrality principle, the formation of board committees, *Aufsichtsrat* members' independence, remuneration, conflicts of interest, disclosure (equality of information to shareholders), and financial reporting and auditing.

With regard to the *Aufsichtsrat's* operation prior to the KonTraG amendments and the DCGK, there had not been any clear standard practice. Prigge notes that issues such as the frequency of board meetings and the preparation of their agenda, the flow of information from management to the board and the time dedicated by board members to meetings had not been uniformly dealt with by German companies.[154] If anything, the intensity of management monitoring by the *Aufsichtsrat* had been minimal. With the enactment of the KonTraG the German parliament set a minimum standard with regard to the board's operation as a monitoring body. Thus, it provides that in listed AGs the members must meet at least twice each half-year.[155] The total number of board positions that a member could hold was set at ten.[156] However, chairmanships count twice and are thus limited to a maximum of five.[157] Thus, disclosure of mandates in other *Aufsichtsräte* as well as of candidate board members' professional occupation is now mandatory in listed AGs in order to prevent any potential conflicts of interest or the appointment of unqualified members. In this respect, the DCGK recommends that *Aufsichtsrat* members must ensure they devote 'sufficient time to perform [their] mandate', while *Vorstand* members should not have more than five *Aufsichtsrat* mandates in non-affiliated companies[158] and these mandates are subject to the *Aufsichtsrat's* approval.[159] Moreover, the code sets minimum criteria concerning *Aufsichtsrat* members' independence.[160]

Furthermore, even though the establishment of board committees is not a compulsory legal requirement, pursuant to the KonTraG amendments the *Aufsichtsrat* in listed companies has to state whether such committees exist and report in writing to the AGM how many times the board met both as a whole

---

154   Prigge, S (1998) 'A Survey of German Corporate Governance' in Hopt, K., et al. (eds) Comparative Corporate Governance: The State of the Art and Emerging Research, Oxford: Clarendon Press, 961–964.

155   Section 110, para.3 AktG. In unlisted companies the Aufsichtsrat members are advised to meet once a quarter and must meet once each half year.

156   The SPD parliamentary group had proposed the reduction of the number of mandates to five; see SPD (1995) Transparenz- und Wettbewerbsgesetz, Bundestagsdrucksache, 13/367, 30 January.

157   Section 100, para.1 AktG.

158   Rule 5.4.5.

159   Rule 4.3.5.

160   Rule 5.4.2.

and at committee-level.[161] According to Hopt, committee work in Germany has not been as common as in the UK and the US where audit, remuneration and nomination committees are more or less mandatory.[162] However, the introduction of the DCGK meant listed companies were required to form committees with specific tasks depending on the particular requirements of the company. For all listed companies an audit committee became compulsory.[163]

As regards the flow of information, the KontraG requires more detailed *Vorstand* reports which should include matters such as future business prospects and policy, financial planning, investments and personnel. It also requires sufficient risk management and internal control systems be put in place. Similarly, the DCGK contains provisions for such disclosures of the *Vorstand* to the *Aufsichtsrat* concerning important transactions, business planning and risk management.[164] Of particular importance is that, contrary to previous practice, under the Act, the contracts for the audit report are awarded by the *Aufsichtsrat* which now also determines the auditor's remuneration.[165] The DCGK imposes a further requirement that candidate auditors submit a statement disclosing any relationships they may have with the company that could compromise their independence.[166] There is also a requirement for submission of the audit report to each member or to the audit committee and the auditor has to attend the relevant board or committee meeting where the annual and group accounts are discussed.[167] The *Aufsichtsrat* examines the auditor and then reports in writing to the shareholders Annual General Meeting (AGM). The KonTraG also contains provisions governing the form and content of the audit report. It requires that the report must be easily comprehensible, that special emphasis be given to particular risks that could jeopardize the existence of the company, and makes the inclusion of cash flow statements mandatory. Moreover, the person who signs the audit certificate must change every six years and the auditor is excluded altogether if he received more than 30 percent of his total revenue over the previous five years from the company in question.[168] This was subsequently lowered again to 15 percent by the enactment of the *Bilanzrechtsreformgesetz* (BilReG) in 2004.

As we discussed in the previous chapter the position of shareholders *vis-à-vis* management under the old law has been somewhat disadvantageous. The minimum quorum that was required by the old law for the appointment of a special

161 Section 171, para.2 AktG.
162 Hopt, K. (1998) 'The German Two-Tier Board: Experience, Theories, Reforms' in Hopt, K. et al. (eds) Comparative Corporate Governance: The State of the Art and Emerging Research, Oxford: Clarendon Press, 242.
163 Rules 5.3.1 and 5.3.2.
164 Rules 3.3 and 3.4.
165 Section 111, AktG. We discuss the reform of the audit later in this chapter.
166 Rule 7.2.1.
167 Section 171, para.1 AktG.
168 The previous threshold was 50 percent.

representative who would sue the management was very high and prohibitive for small minorities who were the most vulnerable to exploitation by blockholders.[169] With the enactment of the KonTraG, the thresholds were halved, i.e. five percent of the share capital or €500,000 nominal value of shares.[170] However, for an action to be brought there needs to be a well-justified suspicion that management has harmed the company.[171]

In this respect, the enactment in January 2004 of the *Gesetzes zur Unternehmensintegrität und Modernisierung des Anfechtungsrechts* (Act on the Improvement of Corporate Integrity and on the Modernization of the Regime Governing Decision-Directed Suits ('UMAG')) has strengthened even further the position of minority shareholders. So, under the new s.147 (a) AktG, in a similar manner to the UK and US derivative suit, shareholders holding one percent of the share capital or €100,000 nominal value of shares may file a claim for breach of duty against the members of the *Vorstand* or the *Aufsichtsrat* for damages on behalf of the company. To bring such an action they must have acquired their shares prior to their knowledge of the breach, have unsuccessfully asked the company to file a claim, there must be serious suspicion of company loss or gross violation of the law or the company's by-laws, and the claim is not in conflict with the company's interests. The Act also reduced the threshold for shareholders to instigate special audits, from 10 percent of paid up capital or shares of €1 million market value, to one percent or 100,000 respectively. However, the Act also introduces a significant protection of management by codifying the German 'business judgment rule' previously found in German judicial precedent.[172] Thus, where there is an allegation that a management decision gave rise to of breach of duty, there will be no violation if management reasonably believed the decision to be for the benefit of the company and if the decision was based on an appropriately informed business judgment (*Unternehmerisches Ermessen*).

In addition, the UMAG added to the AktG provisions facilitating shareholder coordination for bringing such claims. Thus 127 (a) AktG gives shareholders the right to make known through the electronic edition of the *Bundesanzeiger* (Federal Bulletin) of their intention to file a suit, initiate a special investigation, propose a vote on a specific matter at the General Meeting or call for an Extraordinary General Meeting. In a similar fashion, the *Kapitalanleger-Musterverfahrensgesetz* (Law on Example Procedures for Investor Suits ('KapMuG')) adopted in July 2005 gives shareholders the right to file a claim for damages due to incorrect

---

169   The old law required either a 10 percent stake or DM2 million nominal value of shares.

170   Section 147, para 3 AktG.

171   Grub, M. (1999) 'A Trend Towards More Shareholder Value in Germany: Recent Developments in German Stock Corporation Law', International and Comparative Company Law Review, vol. 10, 42 and 44.

172   E.g. see decision of the BGH in ARAG/Garmenbeck, 135 BGHZ 244 (21 April 1997).

or misleading financial information issued by the company. The court will have to hear the case if a total of eleven suits on the same issue are filed within four months from the first filing, and the person with the highest claim will become the 'sample' plaintiff while the remaining claimants may support the suit as 'additional' claimants. The decision is binding on all claimants, so if the sample suit is successful the court will uphold all other claims too; if the sample claim fails all claimants will have to share costs.

Apart from strengthening the disciplinary mechanisms available to shareholders, legislative reforms have also facilitated the refocusing of managerial incentives. In particular the KonTraG has also brought changes with regard to managerial pay by making the use of Employee Stock Option Plans (ESOPs) awards to managers easier. This form of remuneration is designed to deal with shareholder agency problems as it provides managers with the incentives to maximize shareholder returns as it ties a part of their personal wealth to the price of the companies' shares. Prior to these amendments there were major legal obstacles rendering this form of managerial remuneration very difficult and expensive.[173] Consequently, German companies who wanted to award this kind of (share) performance-related remuneration to their management had to resort to the use of 'phantom' stock option plans, i.e. remuneration packages based on calculation methods that follow an imaginary stock option plan.[174]

Since the passage of the KonTraG, shareholders can approve the disposal of shares outside the stock exchange as part of an ESOP for the company's managers.[175] The change in the law saw the majority of listed German companies tentatively introduce ESOPs.[176] Company size seems to be a significant factor here as the larger the company the more likely the introduction of an ESOP. For instance, by 2002 only 8 of the DAX30 companies had not introduced incentive compensation schemes linked to share price. As ESOPs operate as a tool for aligning management interests with those of current shareholders they were and are still controversial in Germany. In particular the ESOP provisions in the KonTraG ignited a serious debate on whether this type of remuneration can be offered to *Aufsichtsrat* members too.

---

173   Section 71, AktG para.1.

174   Kalisch, I. (1998) 'Stock Options: Will the Upcoming Amendment of the German Stock Corporation Act Facilitate Their Introduction by German Stock Corporations?', *International and Comparative Company Law Review*, vol. 10, 111.

175   Section 192, para.2 No. 3 AktG.

176   Wilhelm, J., Drees, R. and Koeberle-Schmid, A. (2004) Union Investment Studie: Aktienoptionsprogramme der DAX-Unternehmen, Frankfurt am Main: Union Investment; Wilhelm, J., Drees, R. and Koeberle-Schmid, A. (2004) Union Investment Study: Employee Stock Option Programmes of the EuroStoxx 50 Companies 2004, Frankfurt am Main: Union Investment; and Achleitner, A. and Wichels, D. (2002) 'Stock-Option-Pläne als Vergütungsbestandteil Wertorientierter Entlohnungssysteme (Eine Einführung)' in Achleitner, A. and Wollmert, P. (eds) Stock Options, 2nd edition, Stuttgart: Schäffer-Poeschel, 1–24.

Eventually, the matter reached the courts in the case of *Mobilcom AG*.[177] Pursuant to section 71(1) AktG the General Meeting of the company amended the articles of association to grant *Aufsichtsrat* members a number of naked warrants every year as part of their remuneration package. In response, the shareholder association DSW sought to annul this shareholder resolution. When the case reached the *Bundesgerichtshof* (Federal Court of Justice ('BGH')) the court held that the German legislative had not envisaged that a company could repurchase its shares or make a conditional capital increase in order to offer them to its *Aufsichtsrat* members in a stock option plan, while it also considered that even convertible bonds may not be acceptable either. The decision was based on the fact that the Act's final draft uses the term 'members of a company's management' and not 'members of a company's organ/body' as the first draft of the Act had. According to the BGH's opinion that is because *Aufsichtsrat* members should have different incentives from *Vorstand* members, otherwise the legislator would have permitted the alignment of their remuneration with that of management. This decision by the BGH viewed the *Aufsichtsrat* as a body representing and balancing divergent interests within the company and not as simply representing shareholder interests. The impact of this decision was immediate as companies withdrew their plans to award stock options to their *Aufsichtsrat* members. Significantly, Daimler's *Aufsichtsrat* removed from its annual General Meeting's agenda of 7 April 2004 its recommendation to restructure its remuneration packages by including a variable component that would depend on the company's share price. They did this even though it was a phantom stock option plan not expressly covered by the *Mobilcom* decision. The company decided to abandon the idea as it felt its implementation would be controversial. Indeed, even management ESOP plans have been highly controversial, being viewed by the general public as a highly corrupting practice and many companies have discussed withdrawing their plans as a result.[178] As a result the use of this type of compensation measured as a percentage of total outstanding stock by German companies has been relatively limited compared to the US (Table 8.2).

---

177   BGH II ZR 316/02 of 16 February 2004. For an extensive analysis see Reidenbach, D. (2004) 'No Stock Options for Supervisory Board Members of a German Stock Corporation: A Comment on In re Mobilcom AG, BGH II ZR 316/02 of 16 February 2004', German Law Journal, vol. 5(4), 347.

178   Langmann, C. (2007) 'Market Reaction and Stock Options Plans: Evidence from Germany', Schmalenbach Business Review, vol. 59, 85, available at SSRN: <http://ssrn.com/abstract=1000143>. See also: Rosengart, A. and Wetzel, D. (2003) 'Selbstbedienung in Vorstandsetagen', Die Welt, 25 June 2003, 9.

**Table 8.2   ESOPs outstanding as a percentage of total shares outstanding of
DAX-30 and 30 Dow Jones industrial companies in 2001 and 2002
respectively**

DAX-30		30 Dow Jones Industrial	
Company	ESOPs as % of share capital	Company	ESOPs as % of share capital
Adidas-Salomon	1.1	3M	8.8
Allianz	0.3	Alcoa	8.7
Altana	1.7	American Express	11.0
BASF	0.5	AT&T	8.9
Bayer	0.0	Boeing	3.4
Bayerische Hypo-und Vereinsbank	0.0	Caterpillar	9.4
BMW	0.0	Citigroup	7.2
Commerzbank	0.0	Coca-cola	5.7
DaimlerChrysler	4.2	E.I.Dupont de Nemours	6.7
Deutsche Bank	2.7	Eastman Kodak	17.3
Lufthansa	0.4	Exxon Mobil	3.9
Deutsche Post	0.5	General Electric	3.6
Deutsche Telekom	0.2	General Motors	3.7
E.ON	0.6	Hewlett-Packard	11.2
Epcos	0.9	Home Depot	3.0
Fresenius Medical Care	2.6	Honeywell International	6.6
Henkel	0.2	Intel	11.5
Infineon Technologies	1.8	IBM	9.3
Linde	0.0	International Paper	6.0
MAN	0.0	J.P. Morgan Chase	9.8
Metro	0.4	Johnson & Johnson	5.4
MLP	0.0	McDonald's	11.6
Müncher Rückverischerung	0.1	Merck	6.6
RWE	1.0	Microsoft	16.6
SAP	2.2	Philip Morris	6.4
Schering	1.1	Procter & Gamble	7.7
Siemens	1.4	SBC Communications	4.0
ThyssenKrupp	1.5	United Technologies	7.2
TUI	0.0	Wal-Mart Stores	1.1
Volkswagen	1.7	Walt Disney	9.0
Average	**0.9**		**7.7**

Source: Sigurt Vitols, "Negotiated Shareholder Value: The German Version of an Anglo-American Practice" Social Science Research Center Berlin (WZB), December 2003, WZB Markets and Political Economy Working Paper No. SP II 2003–25.

As with the use of stock options, an intense debate has been generated on the issue of managerial pay by the refusal of many German companies to systematically disclose individual compensation packages. Although the DCGK required that individual remuneration figures of *Vorstand* and *Aufsichtsrat* members be detailed in the notes of the consolidated financial statements and the corporate governance statement respectively,[179] compliance was low. For example, a DCGK compliance survey carried out by the Berlin Centre of Corporate Governance reported that in 2004 only a third of the DAX companies disclosed management remuneration on an individual basis compared to 96 percent overall compliance with the codes' provisions.[180] Even for the largest listed companies performance on this issue was poor as in 2005 only 18 of the DAX-30 disclosed individual remuneration packages[181] Hoping to turn around the situation the German Government passed the *Vorstandsvergütungs- Offenlegungsgesetzes* (*Vorstand* Remuneration Disclosure Act ('VorstOG')) in July 2005 which made individual *Vorstand* member remuneration disclosure in the annual statements a legal obligation for listed companies from 2006 unless a 75 percent majority of the General Meeting votes to opt out from the provision for a maximum period of five years.[182] The information includes a breakdown of total compensation into fixed, performance-based, and incentive-based components, as well as pensions and severance payments.[183] Initial resistance to the compulsory disclosures gave way to compliance which in turn caused, as managers suspected, outrage at the size of managerial salaries, from politicians and the general public.[184]

Another change in German company law concerned the ability of companies to engage in share buy-backs. Before the KonTraG amendments the acquisition of own shares by a company, despite it being a common practice in other countries such as the US for some time, was virtually impossible under the old Section 71 AktG.[185] With the amended provision, however, the restrictions have been

179   Rules 4.2.4 and 5.4.8

180   Cromme, G. (2004) 'Status and Development of Corporate Governance in Germany', speech delivered at the third German Corporate Governance Code Conference on 24 June 2004, Berlin.

181   DSW (2005) 'DSW Survey on Directors' Pay 2005', October 2005, available at <www.dsw-info.de>.

182   Du Plessis, J. et al., above n30, 47–50. The DSW (ibid) has been critical of this opt-out provision as it gives companies with concentrated shareholdings the possibility of avoiding the Act's application.

183   The inclusion of severance payments into the VorstOG disclosure requirements was a direct result of the excessive payments to Esser and his management team for accepting Vodafone's bid for Mannesmann AG; see the discussion on this later in the chapter.

184   Baur, D. (2008) 'Decoupling from the Owners and Society? An Empirical Analysis of Executive Compensation in Germany', Working Paper Dublin City University <http://ssrn.com/abstract=1140139>.

185   This section contained a list of circumstances where a share-buy back was allowed, e.g. when it was deemed necessary in order to prevent serious and imminent

significantly eased and the *Aktiengesetz* has been brought in line with 'common international practice'.[186] As such, the conditions under which, subject to General Meeting approval, such transactions are permitted have been widely extended.[187] As early as in October 1998 there were over 50 companies granted authorizations by their shareholder meetings to proceed with share repurchases.[188] By July 1999 this number had risen to 77. However once the initial enthusiasm died down the number of repurchases dropped. For the total period between 1998 and 2003 only 180 companies sought their General Meeting's approval for 240 repurchase programmes.[189]

As we discussed in Chapter 7, some German companies have used multiple or limited voting rights and voting caps as an anti-takeover mechanism with further repercussions for the development of the stock market. Section 5, para. 1 AktG provides that all multiple voting rights shall cease to exist within five years from the date when KonTraG took effect unless the majority of shareholders with no such rights vote to the contrary. Similarly, voting caps and limited voting rights for all listed companies were prohibited from 1 April 2000.[190] The KonTraG, however, did not affect the so-called 'Volkswagen Act', enacted with the privatization of Europe's largest car-maker in 1960, which created a 20 percent voting cap and a 20 percent blocking minority, and gives the Federal and Lower Saxony governments the right to appoint two *Aufsichtsrat* members irrespectively of the number of shares they hold.[191] As such, the State holds about 20 percent of the voting rights which in effect acts as a poison pill for private bidders and to some extent as a guarantor of German and more significantly jobs in Lower Saxony, as the Lower Saxony prime minister occupies one seat on the company's *Aufsichtsrat*. Additionally, special protective voting rights applied to decisions to transfer or establish VW production sites. So, it is not a coincidence that Volkswagen AG has been regarded as a symbol of German business and industrial relations (Germany

harm to the company's interests, to offer shares to its employees or for compensating minority shareholders of subsidiaries wound up or absorbed by the parent. For a detailed analysis of the previous regime see Stawowy, J. (1994) 'The Repurchase of Own Shares by Public Companies and Aktiengesellschaften', Working Paper, Institut für Handels- und Wirtschaftsrecht, Universität Osnabrück.

186   Federal Council (1997) 'Government Statement of Reasons', Publication 892/97, 150.

187   Section 71, para.1 AktG.

188   Frankfurter Allgemeine Zeitung, 31 October 1998, <http://www.faz.net/s/home page.html>.

189   Hackethal A. and Zdantchouk, A. (2006) 'Signaling Power of Open Market Share Repurchases', Fin Mkts Portfolio Management, vol. 20, 123–151.

190   The first draft of KonTraG contained provisions abolishing limitations on voting rights for all companies irrespective of whether they were listed or not.

191   Gesetz über die Überführung der Anteilsrechte an der Volkswagenwerk Gesellschaft mit beschänkter Haftung in private Hand (Act on the transfer of shares in Volkswagenwerk GmbH to private partnership) of 1960 as amended on 31 July 1970.

AG). However, while the German government refused to amend the Volkswagen voting restrictions in the 1998 KonTraG amendments, the European Commission decided to take the matter to the European Court of Justice (ECJ) alleging that the Volkswagen Act contravened Articles 56 and 43 of the EC Treaty which contain the freedom of capital movement and the right of establishment provisions.[192] In 2007 as expected, given the VW Act acted as a takeover barrier and given the ECJ's very restrictive rulings in a stream of cases concerning the use of 'Golden Shares' by member state governments,[193] the Volkswagen Act did not survive European scrutiny.[194] However, in response the German government does not intend to repeal the Act in its entirety but rather to amend it slightly to tackle the issue of the restriction on voting rights. The other protective provisions are intended to remain.[195] Indications are that if the German government persists with its interpretation of the ECJ judgment the European Commission will refer the matter back to the ECJ.[196]

A further modification in the law concerned bank voting. As we discussed in Chapter 7, banks, especially the Big Three, have historically been able to use their position as share custodians for small shareholders to assist managers in insulating themselves from outside shareholder pressures. During the discussions that preceded the passage of the KonTraG, the SPD had proposed the complete abolition of banks' proxy voting rights as well as the limitation of bank shareholdings in industrial and insurance companies to five percent or under. It also recommended a partial deviation from the universal banking system by prohibiting banks from owning mutual funds.[197] However, the KonTraG amendments have been more modest. They have created a new legal requirement that a bank must inform its share depositors about alternative proxy-agents such as shareholder associations. Moreover, banks must disclose to their customers any board memberships and equity participations in the company in question. The most significant legal amendment, however, is Section 135, para.1 AktG which provides that, unless

192   See Commission Press Release IP/04/1209 of 13 October 2004.

193   See *Commission v. Portugal* (C-367/98); *Commission v. France* (C-483/99); *Commission v. Belgium* (C-503/99); *Commission v. Spain* (C-436/00); and *Commission v. UK* (C98/01).

194   Case C-112/05 of 23 October 2007; Zumbansen, P. and Saam, D. (2007) 'The ECJ, Volkswagen and European Corporate Law: Reshaping the European Varieties of Capitalism', German Law Journal, vol. 8(11), 1027–1052; and Bolkestein, F. (2007) 'Decision with Freedom of Europe at its Heart', Financial Times, 23 October 2007, available at <http://us.ft.com/ftgateway/superpage.ft?news_id=fto102320071436459946>.

195   Heym, R. (2008) 'Germany a Complicated Victory', International Financial Law Review: Private Equity and Venture Capital Review, 13–14 April; and Zumbansen, P. and Saam, D., above n194, 1027–1052.

196   Dehnen, P. (2008) 'Germany's VW Law Brought to ECJ Again', GLG, 11 September 2008, available at <http://www.glgroup.com/News/Germanys-VW-Law-brought-to-ECJ-again-27694.html>.

197   SPD, above n156.

they receive specific instructions, banks must choose to exercise their proxy-votes or their own shares in companies where they own more than five percent of the equity outstanding. As Emmons and Schmid point out, this discriminates against banks as voting custodians in favour of other non-bank vote custodians, such as the shareholder association *Deutsche Schutzvereinigung für Wertpapierbesitz e.V.* (DSW), who are not subject to this restriction, and thus further reduces the attractiveness of banks as proxy-holders.[198] It also creates an incentive for banks to reduce any holdings they may have to levels below the five percent threshold. Finally, banks are required to vote in the interests of the 'average customer' and submit their proposals on how they intend to use their voting rights. This requirement serves as a disincentive to the continuation of the management-support approach of banks and combined with the additional obligation to appoint one of their *Vorstand* members as the person responsible for the prompt exercise of proxy-votes, is intended to push banks further towards disengaging with Germany AG . Therefore, despite their relatively modest character, these amendments to the law directly affect the traditional role of banks in the German corporate governance system.

Apart from the power of banks as share-custodians, the KonTraG has also affected cross-shareholdings in that it imposes a limit on the exercise of voting rights by companies with large cross-shareholdings.[199] Thus, a listed AG with a 25 percent cross-shareholding in another company is not permitted to use its voting rights with regard to the election of Aufsichtsrat members in that company and cannot vote more than 25 percent of the voting rights in that company even if its holds more than 25 percent. Indeed, initially after 1998 there seems to have been some unwinding of cross-shareholdings of German companies. In 1995 non financial companies held 45.8 percent of shares in German companies, by 2000 that had declined to 36.2 percent and by 2003 it had reached 32.5 percent. A combination of the KonTraG, strategic factors and capital gains tax reforms (discussed later) may have played a role in this unwinding although as we discuss later in this chapter the outcomes of these changes have been complex as the holdings of non financial companies began to rise again between 2003 and 2007 to reach 39.3 percent.[200]

As we have discussed in Chapters 2 and 6, we view company law as a weak institution in terms of constraining management as it tends to enhance managerial discretion. While corporate scandal and the need to protect outsider shareholders

198   Emmons, W. and Schmid, F. (1998) 'Universal Banking, Control Rights, and Corporate Finance in Germany', Federal Reserve Bank of St. Louis Review, July/August, 19–42 at 27.

199   Sections 19 and 328, para.3 AktG.

200   Vitols, S. (2005) 'German Corporate Governance in Transition: Implications of Bank Exit from Monitoring and Control', International Journal of Disclosure and Governance, vol. 2, 357–367; and Deutsches Aktieninstitut (2008) DAI Statistics: Shareholder Structure in Germany, Table 08–1–3–b.

drove the KonTraG amendments to the AktG, we would observe indications of a similar outcome here. The ability of shareholders to sue managers for breach of duty has been enhanced but management are highly protected by a 'business judgement rule'. Remuneration issues have been reformed but while ESOPs and full disclosure have led to litigation and controversy, the outcome has been increased managerial pay without the hoped for increase in performance.[201] In other words the main beneficiaries of these remuneration changes have been managers rather than shareholders. Accountability to the supervisory board has been enhanced but this does not necessarily protect outsider shareholders as labour, large blockholders and ex-management are likely to dominate the supervisory board. Voting rights for listed companies have been standardized around a one vote per share principle apart from where government interests are involved which does indeed mark an important move to protect outsider shareholders. Share buy backs have increased but are still not common serving often to signal manager frustration at a low share price and a potential opportunity to insider deal than a straightforward return on equity.[202] Incentives for banks to hold proxy voting rights have been affected by the amendments. Cross-shareholdings have also to some extent been affected although their anti-takeover role remains unchanged. As we will observe later in the chapter, the bank proxy changes may have played a role in the withdrawal of the banks from internal influence but without necessarily causing a decline in managerial influence. In all the KonTraG amendments in attempting to enhance protection of outsider shareholders may have succeeded in enhancing managerial discretion in an environment where some blockholders (both directly and indirectly as multiple voting rights have been removed) are reduced in influence but outsider shareholders are still a minority and are largely passive. We will consider further evidence of this phenomenon later in the chapter.

Accounting reform

While some of the KonTraG amendments aim at the improvement of information flows from management to the *Aufsichtsrat*, more important developments have been taking place regarding accounting standards and audit quality. As we discussed in the previous chapter German accounting standards have traditionally been creditor or manager oriented as opposed to shareholder oriented. The ability of German companies in particular to create hidden reserves has been a particular problem as it undermines the level of transparency to outsiders with regard to the real financial position of the company and allows managers increased scope for

---

201 Kaserer, C. and Wagner, N. (2004) 'Executive Pay, Free Float, and Firm Performance: Evidence from Germany' (November). CEFS Working Paper No. 6 <http://ssrn.com/abstract=650621>.

202 German share buy backs have abnormal return patterns attributable to this signalling process as well as having an inadequate disclosure mechanism which provides a strong opportunity to insider deal. Hackethal, A. and Zdantchouk, A. above n189.

deviation from profit maximization in favour of insiders since it constitutes a form of excess cash flow retention.[203] Thus, the German Generally Accepted Accounting Principles (German GAAP) never gained international acceptance and have been a constraint on German companies' ability to raise finance abroad, especially in capital markets with more shareholder oriented accounting principles such as the UK and the US.

Nonetheless, as larger German companies faced the need to tap foreign stock markets in order to finance and realize their global FDI strategies.[204] They began to file their accounts both according to the German GAAP as required under the HGB and according to the US Generally Accepted Accounting Principles (US GAAP) or the International Accounting Standards (IAS).[205] This 'dual reporting' practice, however, meant that German companies that were committing themselves to increased disclosure had to incur substantial additional costs. These costs became the subject of some discontent for larger companies which in turn intensified the pressure for legal reform so that they would not have to bear all adaptation costs themselves due to dual reporting expenses.[206] The dual reporting practice was also embarrassing for large German companies as Daimler Benz found when it listed on the NYSE and used US GAAP for the first time in 1993.[207] According to the German GAAP standards Daimler Benz was a profitable company but under the US GAAP standards it seemed to be making a loss.[208] For example in its 1993 interim report Daimler-Benz AG showed a profit of DM168 million according to German GAAP but a loss of DM949million according to US GAAP.

It was under such pressures from large ambitious German companies that the KapAEG amendments to the HGB took effect in April 1998 changing the situation particularly for those companies seeking finance from foreign securities markets. The amended Section 292(a) HGB provides that listed companies that are the parent of a group may prepare their consolidated accounts solely in accordance

---

203   Keller, E. and Möller, H. (1992) 'Einstufung der Bankbilanzen am Kapitalmarkt infolge von §26 a KWG. Konzeption und Ergebnisse einer Kapitalmarktorientierten Empirischen Untersuchung zum Informationsgehalt der Jahresabschlüsse Deutscher Aktiengesellschaften', Zeitschrift für Bankrecht und Bankwirtschaft, vol. 4, 169.

204   A common 'accounting language' between the merging companies in the case of cross-border M&A is an essential part of the globalization of financial markets.

205   Daimler Benz AG was the first German company to adopt the US GAAP in 1993 when it listed on the NYSE.

206   Leuz, C. and Verrecchia, R. (1999) 'The Economic Consequences of Increased Disclosure', Working Paper, Fachbereich Wirtschaftswissenschaften, Johann Wolfgang Goethe-Universität, Frankfurt am Main, 7, available at SSRN: <http://ssrn.com/abstract =171975>.

207   It was also accused of betraying Germany AG by doing this. Riley, B. (1993) 'Feeling of Betrayal in Corporate Germany', Financial Times, 22 September.

208   Jermakowicz, E., Prather-Kinsey, J. and Wulf, I. (2007) 'The Value Relevance of Accounting Income Reported by DAX-30 German Companies', Journal of International Financial Management and Accounting, vol. 18(3), 151–191 at 161.

with internationally accepted accounting principles, namely the US GAAP or the IAS, as long as the accounting principles followed provide information which is of at least equal value to that under the German GAAP. The fact that the provision only covers consolidated group accounts does not mean that individual company accounts remain unaffected. As Schmidt observes:

> ... the consolidated statements would in most cases not coincide with the financial statements of the corporation as a single entity. The result of this would be that the profit that would be available for dividend distribution would be accounted for by applying accounting standards which would differ significantly from the accounting standards being applied for the consolidated statements. It is difficult to imagine that such a disparity will be accepted by investors over a longer period of time.[209]

Indeed, the scope and effect of Section 292 HGB proved to be broader than it appeared at first sight as the KapAEG amendments had an almost immediate impact on German companies' reporting practices. In 1997 some 80 percent of Dax-30 companies used the German HGB standards, by 1998 that figure had reduced to 50 percent and by 2004 only 6.7 percent used the HGB standards and some 93.3 percent used the International Financial Reporting Standards (IFRS formerly IAS) or US GAAP standards to prepare their accounts (see Table 8.3).[210]

Table 8.3 Number and percentage of DAX-30 companies using German HGB, IAS/IFRS, and US GAAP in consolidated financial statements

Year	German HGB	IAS/IFRS	US GAAP
1997	24 (80%)	3 (10%)	3 (10%)
1998	15 (50%)	10 (33.3%)	5 (16.7%)
2004	2 (6.7%)	19 (63.3%)	9 (30%)

Source: Jermakowicz, E., Prather-Kinsey, J. and Wulf, I. (2007) 'The Value Relevance of Accounting Income Reported by DAX-30 German Companies', Journal of International Financial Management and Accounting, vol. 18(3), 152.

---

209   Schmidt, P. (1998) 'Disclosure and Auditing: A German Auditor's Perspective' in Hopt, K., et al. (eds) Comparative Corporate Governance: The State of the Art and Emerging Research, Oxford: Clarendon Press, 748.

210   Prior to April 2001 when the International Accounting Standards Board (IASB) was formed, the standards were called International Accounting Standards (IAS). Since the formation of the IASB they are called International Financial Reporting Standards (IFRS).

However the KapAEG was intended as transitional in character. The applicability of its provisions had a time limitation fixed on 31 December 2004.[211] This is because by that date new German GAAP were supposed to be implemented. A German Accounting Standards Board (GASB) was established in March 1998 under the provisions of the KonTraG with the task of representing Germany in international accounting standard committees and of formulating new accounting standards for German companies in accordance with established international practice.[212] In the words of Jürgen Krumnow, Chairman of the Committee:

> [i]n Germany itself, it is a matter of bringing German accounting practices up to an international level as soon as possible. It goes without saying that there are no plans to adopt international accounting regulations out of hand. But there is no reason to reinvent good regulations that have already become accepted accounting practice worldwide. It is in this sense that German accounting will then be able to acquire new global recognition.[213]

However, once again EU measures pre-empted German reforms. In February 2001 the European Commission put forward a draft directive on the adoption of certain international accounting standards which resulted in its adoption in June 2002 requiring adoption by listed corporations in European exchanges by 2005.[214] Subsequently, the EU adopted three Regulations, which made it mandatory for all companies with listed securities in organized markets to prepare their accounts in accordance with IFRS by 1 January 2007.[215] As a result the German Accounting Standards Committee's work and intentions were to a great extent superseded by EU legislation. Accordingly, since 2007, all German listed companies have had to prepare their accounts in accordance with the IFRS pursuant to the amended Section 315 (a) HGB by the *Bilanzrechtsreformgesetz* (BilReG) in 2004 and the EU Regulations. However, it is noteworthy that the BilReG has gone even further than the EU instruments as it allows the preparation of consolidated financial statements in accordance with the IFRS even by non-listed companies if they so wish.

Apart from listed companies, the BilReG has also affected the position of auditors as it seeks to strengthen their independence by imposing stricter rules regarding the provision of auditing and consulting services to the same company. In particular, it prohibits the supply of tax or legal consultancy concerning

---

211 Section 5, KapAEG.
212 Sections 342 and 342a, HGB.
213 Krumnow, J. (1998) 'Das Deutsche Rechnungslegungs Standards Committee' in von Rosen, R. (ed.) Neue Bilanzierungsüberlegungen in Deutschland, Frankfurt am Main: Deutsches Aktieninstitut, 8–21.
214 Directive 2003/51/EC of 18 June 2003.
215 Regulation (EC)1606/2002, Regulation (EC) No 1725/2003, Regulation (EC) No. 707/2004.

financial statements by an auditing firm if the latter also participated in the preparation of those statements or in the keeping of the books of the company in question. As we noted earlier in this chapter the BilReG also lowered the threshold of total turnover percentage an auditor may receive from a single client company from 30 percent to 15 percent. Furthermore, the German legislator has enacted two further measures in 2004 aimed at increasing the auditing function's level of integrity. First, pursuant to the *Bilanzrechtskontrollgesetz* (Accounting Control Act ('BilKoG')) an independent enforcement authority, the *Deutsche Pruefstelle für Rechnungslegung* (Financial Reporting Enforcement Panel) was established with a mandate to perform a two-step intervention in the preparation of financial statements. The first step intervention is to perform random checks and reviews of financial statements of behalf of the BaFin and to review financial statements which they suspect of inaccuracy. The second step is where the enforcement authority and the company in question disagree on a certain matter, the BaFin undertakes to further examine the statement and impose penalties if necessary. Second, as an additional scrutiny measure aimed at the accountancy profession, the *Abschlussprüferaufsichtsgesetz* (Accountants' Supervision Act ('APAG')) in 2004 provided for the establishment of another independent body, the *Abschlussprüferaufsichtskommission* (Accounting Supervisory Commission ('APAK')), supervised by the Federal Secretary of Business and Labour, to supervise the work of the *Wirtschaftsprüferkammer* (Certified Accountants Association). These legislative instruments should be seen in combination with the KapInhaG discussed earlier which facilitates the establishment of civil liability for false information included in financial statements an accountant certifies. Additionally the *Bilanzrechtsmodernisierungsgesetz,* Accounting Law Reform Act (*BilMoG*) in 2008 has strengthened auditor independence and simplified the German HGB.[216]

Moreover, as discussed earlier, the KonTraG established a mandatory requirement for all listed AGs to include cash flow statements in their consolidated account statements as of 31 December 1998. Until that date such statements were not compulsory. Nevertheless, a large number of German companies had already begun to include cash-flow statements in their annual reports voluntarily from the early 1990s, mainly in response to foreign and domestic stock market pressures, international standards and business consultants' recommendations.[217] Additionally, apart from upgrading the auditing function, the BilReG also sought to enhance the value of management reporting by including detailed financial and non financial performance information as well as analyses and projections about developments

---

216 Implementing Directive 2006/46/EC.

217 Leuz, C. (1999) 'The Development of Voluntary Cash Flow Statements in Germany and the Influence of International Reporting Standards', Working Paper, Fachbereich Wirtschaftswissenschaften, Johann Wolfgang Goethe-Universität, Frankfurt am Main, available at SSRN: <http://ssrn.com/abstract=171736>.

in the two years following the report.[218] Thus, the KonTraG amendments, while significant, followed on from a clear move by the largest German companies to adopt international disclosure and financial scrutiny standards in a clear example of formal convergence ensuing from functional convergence in a similar manner to Glison's description in Chapter 4. Similarly the example of accounting standards convergence seems a better fit to Roes' claim that 'technical' securities market changes can ensure a sort of stealth convergence as clearly the reforms in Germany did not meet the kind of path dependent resistance securities reforms related to takeovers engaged.

To summarize, the recent changes in the law governing financial statements and accounting in general are all intended to enhance the informational value of German financial reporting from the outside investor's perspective and bring German accounting standards in line with principles accepted by dominant (institutional) investor groups in global financial markets. For example, the ability to create hidden reserves, a significant feature of the German insider corporate governance model, under the US GAAP or the IFRS as opposed to the existing German GAAP is somewhat constrained.[219] This move towards a more outside shareholder oriented accounting regime may also have an impact on labour as in the past a German company with large reserves as a cushion in a downturn could maintain a commitment towards retaining employees in difficult times.[220] Simultaneously, if outsider shareholders are able to so, they can take advantage of the increased transparency by demanding higher returns. Indeed, there is evidence suggesting a positive relationship between enhanced disclosure and dispersed ownership. For example Jermakowicz et al. observed a significant increase in the free float of DAX-30 companies after the adoption of IFRS or US GAAP and that foreign ownership of shares in DAX-30 companies after the adoption of IFRS or US GAAP increased by between 20–30 percent.[221]

---

218   For an analysis of the BilReG impact on management reporting see Buchheim, R. and Beiersdorf, K. (2005) 'New Developments in Management Reporting – The Modernisation of the Annual Report', German Law Journal, vol. 6(5), 861.

219   Historically large reserves could be built up which were not disclosed in the accounts. Fuerbringer, J. (1992) 'World Markets; S.E.C. Says No on German Stocks', New York Times, 26 April 1992 <http://query.nytimes.com/gst/fullpage.html?res=9E0CE7DE1031 F935A15757C0A964958260&sec=&spon=&pagewanted=all> and Deutsche Bank Research (1993) 'US vs. German Accounting Methods', Special Equity Report, Frankfurt: Deutsche Bank.

220   For a case study see Küting, K. (1996) 'Die Talfahrt der Daimler-Benz AG: Neum Jahre Bilanzpolitic des Technologiekonzerns auf dem Prüfstand', Blick durch die Wirtschaft, 12 April, 9.

221   Jermakowicz, E., Prather-Kinsey, J. and Wulf, I., above n208 at 158, 171 and 186; and Leuz, C., above n217.

Finanzplatz Deutschland: A trojan horse?

By the late 1980s the globalization of capital markets meant that large German companies increasingly sought capital in global capital markets and its largest banks were operating increasing outside of Germany. Europe was also moving towards a single currency and Germany was intent on being the financial centre of the Euro Zone. Pension reform also played a role in the drive over the course of the 1990s to build a deep and liquid securities market. In all, as we discussed above, *Finanzplatz Deutschland* became a significant policy imperative for successive German governments. However, with the reform and integration of Germany's capital markets into global capital markets came exposure to outsider norms, primarily from foreign investors. As a result *Finanzplatz Deutschland* has triggered a wave of reforms designed to facilitate outsider shareholders but which also affect traditional relationships within the German insider corporate governance model. These reforms have had a mixed direct effect as the domestic equity culture both in terms of individual and institutional shareholdings remains fragile. Additionally, some significant path dependent reactions occurred particularly on takeovers reforms and the ESOP amendments in the KonTraG. In all while some of the reforms such as the reform of German accounting have potential outsider shareholder benefits others aimed at insider disengagement may, in the absence of outsider shareholder influence and an active market for corporate control, end up benefiting management. Given these development associated with *Finanzplatz Deutschland* we turn in the next three sections of this chapter to try to determine the extent to which the traditional insider German model has been affected by these changes and the degree of penetration of outsider shareholder norms in German corporate governance.

The Changing Nature of Shareholding and the end of the Traditional Role of the Bank

Overall, as Table 8.4 reveals between 1960 and 2007 there have been some major changes in the concentration of shareholdings in Germany companies. A gradual but overall not significant decline in non financial companies holding blocks of shares is observable. Major divesting by private households, mainly family holdings, is present. Public sector holdings have declined to historically low levels. Bank holdings peak in the early 1990s and broadly slowly decline. German institutional and foreign investors have been the major beneficiaries of the decline of other blockholders since the 1960s (Table 8.4). However, a significant step change in the fall and rise of owning sectors seems to relate to the late 1990s and early twenty-first century indicating that the KonTraG and capital gains tax reforms in particular had an effect on shareholdings in their immediate aftermath. It seems a cautious exit by some blockholders occurred immediately after the tax reforms. Given the reforms unfortunately coincided with the aftermath of the stock market crash in over the course of 2001–2002, this may have prevented others from exiting and caused a rethink of blockholder strategy, as contrary to expectations, as the market has recovered the pattern has not been divesting but rather traditional insiders reinvesting between 2003 and 2007. Non financial companies' holdings fell from their peak of 45.8 percent of total in 1995, to 32.5 percent in 2003 but rose again to 39.3 percent in 2007. Banks similarly began strategic unwinding of their shareholdings as well in the aftermath of the KonTraG and capital gains reforms reducing from 12.9 percent in 1995, to 9 percent in 2003 but notably increasing them again to 9.7 percent by 2007. These upsurges in holdings by banks, non financial corporations and the public sector (from 0.6 in 2000 to 1.9 in 2007) in the 2007 figures occurred despite the introduction of outsider oriented provisions which actively sought to reduce their internal influence. This indicates the reforms are not playing out within the institutional sub-systems as had been intended. Private households, including family blockholders also reduced their direct holdings from 18.8 percent in 1995 to 13.9 percent in 2003 and 13.3 percent in 2007. This decline however, is difficult to read as it may indicate that small private shareholders have acquired indirect holdings through collective investment instruments and life assurance, which have increased in step with the private household decline, while larger family shareholders remain stable or indeed may have increased their stakes. Although between 2003 and 2007 as the appetite for equity generally declined in the aftermath of the dot.com crash so too did the holdings of insurance, pension and mutual funds. The major increase in shareholdings in German companies between 1995 and 2007 is by foreign investors who grew significantly from 8.2 percent to 21.3 percent in that 12 year period.

If however we focus in on DAX 100 companies and the years immediately after the tax reforms the impact of the capital gains reforms on bank holdings becomes more obvious. Bank share ownership in non financial companies was stable between 1994 and 2001 at about four percent. However by 2005 it had dropped to 0.4 percent. Additionally other non financial blockholders decline from 55.4 percent in 1994 to 47.7 percent in 2005. This decline though seems less related to the tax reforms as the decline is gradual and not as significant.[222]

---

222 Dittmann, I., Maug, E. and Schneider, C. (2008) 'Bankers on the Boards of German Firms: What They Do, What They Are Worth, and Why They Are (Still) There', ECGI – Finance Working Paper No. 196/2008, 12, available at SSRN: <http://ssrn.com/abstract=1093899>.

**Table 8.4 Structural changes in the ownership of German companies –
percentages of share ownership by sector from 1990 to 2007**

Owning Sector	1960	1970	1980	1990	1992 (1)	1992 (2)	1995	2000	2003	2007
Non-Financial Companies	40.7	37.4	42.8	39.0	41.4	45.8	45.8	36.2	32.5	39.3
Private Households	30.3	31.3	21.2	20.0	17.6	19.8	18.8	16.5	13.9	13.3
Public Sector	12.0	9.6	8.5	4.4	3.9	2.1	1.8	0.6	0.9	1.9
Banks	8.0	9.1	11.6	14.0	14.7	13.0	12.9	11.5	9.0	9.7
Insurance	3.4	4.2	4.8	7.8	9.0	5.1	6.3	8.2	13.2	3.4
Other Financial*	–	–	–	–	–	4.6	6.2	14.4	13.5	11.1
Foreign Investors	5.6	8.5	11.1	14.8	13.2	9.7	8.2	12.5	17.1	21.3

Note: * Due to a classification change in 1992 mutual funds, which were before then accounted for in other groups, from 1992 onwards have accounted for the bulk of 'other financial' owners.
Source: Vitols, S. (2005) 'German Corporate Governance in Transition: Implications of Bank Exit from Monitoring and Control', International Journal of Disclosure and Governance, vol. 2, 357–367 and Deutsches Bundesbank Flow of Funds Data.

The withdrawal of banks

The German banks appear to have been the most significant blockholders affected by the KonTraG proxy reforms and the changes to the tax regime and so in the rest of this section, given the banks historic role in Germany AG, we focus in on the changing nature of the banks role in the German corporate governance model. The *Finanzplatz Deutschland* developments discussed earlier in this chapter although partly driven by the banks ambitions to become global players also affected the relationships between banks and their industrial customers. To some extent, as we discussed earlier, this was because their major clients triggered the change by starting to tap international capital markets because of the inability of German banks to satisfy the corporate finance and investment banking needs of those companies. By turning to foreign investment houses such companies began to break away from their long established relational banking ties. As the liberalization of German financial markets got under way the Banks also faced additional competitive at home from foreign financial institutions. Large German banks who wanted to remain competitive had in turn to reconsider the viability of their close ties with non financial companies. Decreasing profit margins in the traditional deposit and loan business have also been a significant factor as well as new capital requirements imposed on banks under Basel II in 2004 which increased significantly the capital cost of holding equity stakes, which in turn made them a less attractive investment.[223]

One first indication of German banks' changing attitudes is the significant historical reduction and reorganization of their major equity participations in industrial corporations by the mid 1990s as they moved to become global banks. As we observed in the previous section, a number of reforms have encouraged unwinding of their shareholdings which accelerated a pre-existing bank strategy. As Schröder and Schrader found, the ten largest private banks reduced their holdings in non financial companies from 1.3 percent of nominal capital in 1976 to just 0.4 in 1994.[224] Most stakes in the 25 percent – 50 percent range have been significantly reduced, as banks such as Deutsche Bank, Dresdner Bank, Commerzbank, Bayerische Hypotheken- und Wechsel Bank and BHF-Bank have all followed a more diversified strategy with regard to industrial shareholdings.[225] The Big Three, in particular, have been engaged in a process of selling most of their major holdings. Deutsche Bank during the late 1990s significantly reduced its holdings in Daimler AG, Holzmann AG, Karstadt AG, Südzucker AG and Horten AG, all of which have been long-term partners for many decades.[226] It also span off most of its remaining holdings by creating DB Investor AG, a subsidiary company, to undertake the task of professionally managing the bank's portfolio of industrial stakes, focusing on the bank's interest as a shareholder, rather than creditor or strategic partner.[227] Similarly, prior to its takeover by Allianz, Dresdner

223   The Basel II requirements were introduced in 2004 and were followed by two EU directives – Directive 2006/48/EC and Directive 2006/49/EC. The negative effects of the Basle II requirement have been recognized by the European Commission and is intended, indeed is imminent, given the global financial market crisis that emerged in Autumn 2008. EurActiv (2008) Basel II and the Capital Requirements Directive. See <http://www.euractiv. com/en/financial-services/basel-ii-capital-requirements-directive/article-141423>.

224   Schröder, U. and Schrader, A. (1997) 'The Changing Role of Banks and Corporate Governance in Germany: Evolution Towards the Market?', Working Paper, American Institute for Contemporary German Studies, Baltimore: Johns Hopkins University, Washington.

225   Ibid.; and Fohlin, C. (2005) 'The History of Corporate Ownership and Control in Germany' in Morck, R. (ed.) A History of Corporate Governance around the World, Chicago and London: The University of Chicago Press, 223 at 245; and Frankfurter Allgemeine Zeitung (1995) issues 7(6) and (12); (1997) issue 72(24) and 73(23).

226   Fischer, A. (1997) 'Deutsche Bank to Reduce Domestic Shareholdings', Financial Times, 20 May, and 'Banks Sell Karstand Stake', Financial Times, 12 August.

227   Handelsblatt Interactiv (1998) 'Deutsche Bank: No Plans to Sell Industrial Assets', 17 December. See <http://www.handelsblatt.de>. The bank set its policy as follows: 'By the reduction of existing holdings and acquisition of new ones, professional and active portfolio management is to be conducted, but no new holdings accumulated. DB Investor will act, for example, as a kind of midwife in repositioning companies on the basis of value-increasing concepts for companies and industries (e.g. Hapag-Lloyd) or participate in the restructuring and disposal of other companies' holdings which are no longer part of core business, as in the case of DIVAG/Metro' (Deutsche Bank (1999) 'Deutsche Bank Raises Company Value by Industrial Holdings Spin-off'. See <http://www.deutsche-bank.

sold its holdings in Degussa AG and Hapag-Lloyd AG,[228] while Commerzbank sold its stake in Karstadt AG.[229]

So while this trend was part of a long-term strategy of German financial institutions to reorient themselves to play a role in global capital markets, after the 2002 changes in taxation, it intensified. Driven by similar considerations, the insurance giants Allianz and Münchener Rück (Munich Re), owning 24 percent of total holdings in the DAX-30 – mainly in banks – almost immediately after the announcement of the tax reform plans expressed their intention to take advantage of them by selling many of their stakes in other companies.[230] Earlier moves such as the creation of DB Investor, as we noted above, should also be seen in the context of the new tax regime. The pressure for unwinding shareholdings had been such that banks often used derivative instruments in order to sell their stakes tax-free even before 2002. For instance, in 2000 Deutsche Bank used an equity swap to dispose of €2.5 billion of shares in Allianz, which allowed the bank to cash in immediately while for tax purposes the sale was not recorded in the books until after 31 December 2001. Almost simultaneously with the Deutsche transaction, HypoVereinsbank put in place a similar transaction to sell €700 million of shares in the energy and chemicals group E.ON AG. By 2005 Deutsche Bank had reduced almost all of its stakes in other companies including banks to under five percent or had totally sold them off.[231] One of the knock on effects of this disengagement with the banks traditional clients has been the changing role of banks in hostile takeovers.

For reasons already explained hostile bids have not been a feature in Germany so that the market for corporate control has not traditionally exerted significant pressure on German managers. To an extent this is attributable to the fact that banks have historically adopted a supportive approach to management in a hostile bid thus limiting the potential for successful hostile bids. However, the first signs of change began to appear in 1991, when Krupp launched a hostile bid for Hoesch. Even though the target's Chairman was Deutsche Bank's nominee and its CEO had been appointed with the bank's involvement only three months prior to the bid, Hilmar Kopper, Deutsche's CEO at the time, approved of Krupp's move and encouraged Hoesch's chairman not to oppose the takeover irrespective of

---

de>. Deutsche Bank also reduced its 9.3 percent stake in Allianz by 2.3 percent as part of its program to divest shareholdings (Handelsblatt Interactiv (1999) 'Deutsche Bank Earns More than 1bn Euros from the Sale of Allianz Shares' (English Summary), 1 November. See <http://www.handelsblatt.de>.

228   Frankfurter Allgemeine Zeitung (1997) issues 118(17) and 204(25).

229   Fischer, A., above n226.

230   Major, T. (2000) 'Corporate Germany in Preparation for Shake-up', Financial Times, 4 February; (1999) 'Christmas Comes Early for German Boardrooms – Corporate Tax Reform – Abolition of Crippling Capital Gains Levy', Financial Times, 24 December.

231   Vitols, S. (2005) 'German Corporate Governance in Transition: Implications of Bank Exit from Monitoring and Control', International Journal of Disclosure and Governance, vol. 2, 357–367.

the management's opposing view. Deutsche Bank had been Hoesch's *Hausbank* and controlled approximately 12 percent of the votes via proxies in the company. In the end, it was only after intense government pressure that an agreement was reached for a friendly merger between the two companies which took place on 8 December 1992.[232]

An even clearer illustration of the changing attitudes of German banks, however, is provided by their role during Krupp's bid for Thyssen. In spring 1997 the former announced its intentions to acquire its main competitor, which was larger but with diffused ownership, in a hostile bid. Krupp was financially assisted by Deutsche Bank and Dresdner Bank and advised by their investment banking subsidiaries in London – Morgan Grenfell and Kleinwort Benson respectively – with some additional help from Goldman Sachs. At the time of the bid a member of Deutsche's *Vorstand* sat on Thyssen's *Aufsichtsrat* while one active and one retired member of Dresdner's *Vorstand* sat on the *Aufsichtsräte* of both the bidder and the target. The bid caused a huge shock to German industry as Deutsche used its internal board positions to assist the takeover.[233] It should be stressed here that this incident occurred in the most traditional industry in Germany as Thyssen was a steel manufacturer governed by the full-parity co-determination regime under the *Montanmitbestimmungsgesetz*.[234] This of course meant that added to the opposition of management was the resistance of the workforce. The press was also very critical of Krupp's 'wild west' tactics and the bank's role in supporting it.[235] After a decisive intervention by the Northrhine-Westphalia State Government and under heavy pressure from labour representatives from *both* companies and unions, an agreement for a 'friendly' merger was achieved on the basis that no redundancies would take place. Nevertheless, Krupp's attempt was seen as a first significant and direct effect of globalization in the heart of the German system and as a turning point in the way of doing business in Germany. Bendt, commenting on the takeover, considered that the Krupp bid served notice of a change in the way banks had operated historically as:

---

232   Franks, E. and Mayer, C. (1998) 'Bank Control, Takeovers and Corporate Governance in Germany', Journal of Banking and Finance, vol. 22, 1385 at 1392.

233   Höpner, M. and Krempel, L. (2004) 'The Politics of the German Company Network', Competition and Change, vol. 8(4), 339–356 at 352.

234   As a result of the takeover attempt, a stalemate arose in Thyssen's *Aufsichtsrat* for the first time ever, thus breaking a long tradition of decisions based on full consensus.

235   The German newspaper Der Spiegel reported a member of Krupp/Hoesch's works council stating: 'I can't globalize myself, I've got a flat here. Let us therefore march, in order to make sure that Deutsche Bank is no longer able to dominate the country'; cited in Bendt, C., above n18.

[t]he German financial elite almost certainly had greater plans. The whole deal should finally prove that German Banks are just as able as their Anglo-Saxon counterparts to plan and manage such complex financial deals.[236]

Furthermore, banks have also become increasingly unable to keep up with their role as liquidity insurers or corporate rescuers. As we noted earlier in this chapter the external financing arrangements of German companies has changed significantly since 2001. Bank finance, particularly loans from German banks to German corporations, declined dramatically from 2001 when German banks lent €28.2 billion. By 2002 that figure was negative as client companies paid down loans totalling €20.7 billion. In 2003 again it was negative as €41.7 billion was returned. In 2004 similarly it was negative as €40.6 billion was repaid by German companies to German banks. In 2005 €13.4 billion was also paid back and in 2006 €8.1 billion was paid back as lending, particularly long-term lending, revived slightly.[237] Interestingly, the majority of remaining bank finance German companies use is now largely provided by non-German banks.[238] The timing of this financing change also co-insides with the capital gains tax reforms and the unwinding of the banks shareholdings.

The nature of the banks' role in rescues and reconstructions has also been changing. The events during the collapse of Holzmann AG, the second largest and one of the oldest construction group in Germany, provides a prime example of the clash between the formulation of a global strategy and relationship banking engagements. Holzmann's main financial partner had, for almost a century, been Deutsche Bank, who even at the point of Holzmann's collapse, owned a 15.1 percent stake in it.[239] The first problems emerged when Holzmann was unable to make a profit out of a number of projects it had completed in East Germany after reunification. As the debts began to mount – between 1995 and 1998 deficits had reached the level of about DM1.4 billion[240] – Deutsche Bank finally[241] decided to

---

236   Bendt, C., above n18.

237   Data extrapolated from Deutsches Aktieninstitut (2008) DAI Statistics, Table 04–6.

238   Ibid., DAI Table 04–06.

239   Since the beginning of the twentieth century a large number of Holtzmann's projects, from the Baghdad railway (1907) to the new Reichstag building in Berlin, were completed with Deutsche's financial help. Even Deutsche's headquarters building was constructed by Holzmann.

240   Barber, T. (1999) 'Deconstructing Relationships', Financial Times, 23 November.

241   In 1994 a hostile takeover attempt was made for Holzmann by Hochtief with the cooperation of Deutsche Bank who had agreed to sell 15.9 percent out of its 25.9 percent equity stake at that time to the bidder. The takeover, however, was blocked by the Bundeskartellamt on competition law grounds. This indicated that Deutsche Bank's initial intentions were to terminate its longstanding relationship with its old industrial partner. For more details on the bid see Jenkinson, T. and Ljungqvist, A. (1997) 'Hostile Stakes and the Role of Banks in German Corporate Governance', Working Paper, Centre for Economic Policy Research, Oxford, available at SSRN: <http://ssrn.com/abstract=33678>.

intervene in 1997 by placing Carl Boehm-Bezing, a member of its *Vorstand*, as chairman of Holzmann's *Aufsichtsrat* which then undertook the responsibility of appointing a new management team that would restore the company's financial health. Nevertheless, the plan eventually failed and in November 1999 losses of about DM2.4 billion were disclosed which brought the group one step closer to a collapse.[242] At the time Deutsche Bank was severely criticized not only for not using its influence to make sure that the company's turnaround was successful but also for using Holzmann's business dealings for its own benefit rather than for the company's shareholders.[243]

Despite the severe criticism about its level of involvement in the affair, Deutsche Bank was reluctant to engage itself in a fully committed restructuring operation that would rescue the company.[244] It was determined to limit its participation in the rescue plan to only 18.5 percent of the funds needed, which fuelled suspicion on the part of other potential lenders. This resulted in the failure of creditor banks to reach an agreement on their contributions to the rescue plan and to the subsequent initiation of insolvency proceedings in late November 1999. It was only after the direct intervention of the German Federal Government and a DM250 million state subsidy that a last minute agreement on a rescue package was achieved.[245] Again, it was not the banks' commitment to their industrial partner that led to the bailout but direct government intervention.[246] After the rescue Deutsche Bank as well as other major creditor banks of Holzmann planned to disengage from the troubled

---

242   Handelsblatt Interactiv (1999) 'Report Suggests Holzmann's Problems are Recent in Origin' (English Summary), 23 December 1999. See <http://www.handelsblatt.de>.

243   DSW, the German shareholder association, called for Chairman Carl von Boehm-Bezing to resign and called for a special audit investigating Deutsche Bank's dealings with Holzmann. Commerzbank had also considered the possibility of filing a law suit against Holzmann's board. See Handelsblatt Interactiv (1999) 'Creditors Struggle to Agree Rescue Package for Philipp Holzmann', 22 November; Handelsblatt Interactiv (1999) 'Deutsche Bank under Pressure in Holzmann Affair', 29 December; and Handelsblatt Interactiv (1999) 'Deutsche Bank to Face Strong Questioning from Holzmann Shareholders' (English Summary), 30 December. See <http://www.handelsblatt.de>.

244   The initial rescue plan comprised a financial injection of DM1.25 billion through a capital increase and DM1 billion in the form of a syndicated loan.

245   Handelsblatt Interactiv (2000) 'Holzmann to Get Capital Injection in February', 19 January and Handelsblatt Interactiv (1999) 'Chancellor Schröder Makes Holzmann Rescue Top Priority' (English Summary), 24 November. See <http://www.handelsblatt. de>. The final rescue plan would also result in a reduction of the workforce by 3,500 out of a total of 17,000 and additional concessions on the part of employees such as five hours of overtime for free for one and a half years. See Handelsblatt Interactiv (2000) 'Holzmann to extend Job Cutbacks' (English Summary), 12 January. See <http://www.handelsblatt.de>.

246   This was done after intense protests by German building workers outside Holzmann's and Deutsche Bank's headquarters and a threat of a nationwide strike. The coalition government's political instability was a significant factor determining the Chancellor's decision to intervene. See Major, T. (1999) 'Holzmann Insolvency Looms as Talks Founder', Financial Times, 23 November.

company by selling their shareholdings and promoting the possibility of an acquisition.[247] However, a steep downturn in the construction industry led to a new crisis for the group and its eventual collapse in March 2002, as neither its bankers not the government this time were willing make any further contributions.[248]

If banks' attitudes towards their long-term industrial partners have become less supportive, in other cases they have also become aggressive as creditors. Deutsche Bank's stance in the collapse of the Kirch media empire in 2002, the largest in Germany's history so far, is a good example of this change. Although Deutsche Bank was Kirch's second largest creditor with a €715 million secured loan, it effectively welcomed and seemed to precipitate the break up of the group in order to seize one of Kirch's prime assets, a 40 percent stake in publisher Axel Springer worth €880 million. Relations between Deutsche Banks and Kirch became so strained that Leo Kirch, the founder and then CEO of the media group, sued Deutsche's Chairman Rolf Breuer because of negative comments he had made to the media about Kirch's creditworthiness, when it was still struggling to avoid insolvency.[249] In 2006 Kirch's partial success when the lawsuit reached the Supreme Court, forced the resignation of Breuer from Deutsche Bank.[250]

The changing role of banks can also be observed in the changing part they have begun to play in hostile takeovers. For example the hostile bid of the British mobile telecommunications company Vodafone for the German conglomerate Mannesmann (discussed in full in the next section) both illustrated that banks are no longer necessarily supportive of management and that the *Großbanken* have serious competition from overseas banks where German transactions are concerned – in this case launching an unsolicited bid against a German target.[251] When it launched the largest hostile takeover offer in German history, Vodafone employed as its main advisers the US investment banks Goldman Sachs and Warburg Dillon Read. Similarly, in organizing its defence Mannesmann was advised mainly by Morgan Stanley Dean Witter, J.P. Morgan and Merryl Lynch. Deutsche Bank's role in the bid is of particular interest as although it also acted as a financial adviser to Mannesmann, it nevertheless avoided expressing its support for the target's management directly. It refrained from giving a central recommendation to its local investment advisers with regard to whether retail investors should sell their shares to Vodafone or not. Deutsche Bank restricted itself to a careful public relations

---

247   Handelsblatt Interactiv (1999) 'Holzmann Sale Only After Restructuring' (English Summary), 14 December. See <http://www.handelsblatt.de>.

248   Major, T. (2002) 'Holzmann Shares Suspended After Bank Talks Fail', Financial Times, 19 March.

249   Major, T. (2002) 'Leo Kirch Sues Deutsche Bank Chief Breuer', Financial Times, 5 May.

250   Landler, M. (2006) 'Under Fire, Chairman of Deutsche Bank Leaves', International Herald Tribune, 3 April, available at <http://www.iht.com/articles/2006/04/02/business/deutsche.php>.

251   See later in this chapter for a more extensive analysis of the takeover.

comment that it was 'not without emotion' for the particular hostile takeover attempt.[252] Most other major banks (e.g. Commerzbank and Dresdner Bank, but not HypoVereinsbank who issued a clear guideline in favour of Mannesmann's management) followed a similar line and merely recommended that shareholders remain cautious until the last moment.[253] On the other hand WestLB Panmure, Westdeutsche Landesbank's investment banking branch, almost immediately supported Vodafone's offer and described it as attractive to both companies' shareholders.[254]

It seems that German managers are losing both the financing and the unconditional support of their historical financial partners who are increasingly unwilling to use their voting power and overall influence to shield corporate management against hostile takeovers or to finance their rescues in cases of distress. This is also evidenced by the slow but observable decline of bank representation on company boards since the late 1980s. The *Bundesverband Deutscher Banken* (Association of German Banks) found that, in 1993, banks held 99 *Aufsichtsrat* mandates in the 100 largest companies as opposed to 114 in 1986.[255] Deutsche Bank, for example, held board seats in 40 of the top 100 German companies in 1980. By 1990 it had reduced that number to 35 and by 1998 it only held 17 seats. By 2001 Deutsche and Allianz the two key financial institutions in the German board system were formally working towards completely divesting their board positions.[256] In 2008 Dittmann et al. in a survey of bank representation on the boards of the DAX 100 listed companies from 1994–2005 found a decline from 51 percent of companies having a banker on the board in 1994 to 33 percent in 2005. The total number of seats held by bankers in DAX 100 listed companies also declined from 9.6 percent to 5.6 percent. Most of this divesting took place between 2002–2004 after the capital gains tax reforms.[257]

As the possibility of conflicts of interest arising from the banks' complex role as shareholders, providers of credit and investment banking services becomes more visible, it is reasonable to expect that board representation will become increasingly problematic. This issue became very obvious in the case of Krupp's hostile takeover attempt for Thyssen, where bank representatives sat on the boards of both the bidder and the target.[258] As the large financial institutions have divested

252   Financial Times (2000) 'Company Chiefs Speak Out – Domestic Banks Back Mannesmann', 20 January.

253   Ibid.

254   Financial Times (1999) 'Mannesmann Launches Defence: Chairman Claims Superior Growth and Better Value as Single Entity', 30 November.

255   Bundesverband Deutscher Banken (1995) 'Datenbank für Wirtschaftsdaten', cited in Schröder, U. and Schrader, A., above n224.

256   Fohlin, C., above n225, 254.

257   Dittmann, I. et al., above n222, 3 and 12.

258   A similar situation also arose in Pirelli's hostile takeover attempt for Continental in 1990. While Deutsche Bank had advised Pirelli on the potential merger with the German company, it later used Morgan Grenfell, its London-based investment banking

their shareholdings and board seats so, too, has the traditional tightly interlocked German business network begun to disintegrate. As Höpner and Krempel describe it:

> [t]he German company network has not vanished … there still exist capital ties between German companies. But their number has been more than halved, and the function of capital ties between financial companies and industrial companies has changed dramatically. The encompassing company network that provided its core participants with a national perspective now belongs to German economic history. It will never re-emerge on a national basis, and it is an open question whether a network of similar density will ever emerge at the European level.[259]

Large German banks determined to follow a global strategy have been distancing themselves from their old industrial partnerships with German companies over the past two decades.

In all, the shareholding base of the insider German corporate governance landscape seems to be shifting. The most significant observable changes since the 1960s relate to the gradual reduction of banks, families and the state as insiders and the rise of German institutional investors and foreign investors. The late 1990s and early twenty-first century seems to mark a period of acceleration in the decline of banks and non financial corporations as foreign investors and German institutional investors took up significant equity stakes in German companies.[260] However, despite the introduction of a wide range of outsider oriented legislation that pattern was overturned in the aftermath of the stock market crash between 2003 and 2007, when traditional insiders started to rebuild their shareholdings and German institutional investors sold their shares, while foreign shareholdings continued to increase. Perhaps the most dramatic change from the 1960s to 2007 has been the change in the role of the bank in German corporate governance. Banks have moved away from their traditional lending and deposit businesses and no longer operate to supply liquidity insurance or necessarily assist with rescue or reconstruction. Indeed, their role in protecting management from hostile bids has now been reversed as they have sought, like UK or US banks, to generate fees through transactions. Banks have over the past 20 years stopped lending in Germany, divested their shareholdings in client companies and withdrawn from their supervisory boards. As we discuss in the final chapter, the sub-prime and subsequent global financial markets crisis over the course of 2007 – 2009 may

---

subsidiary, to help Continental's management during the takeover battle. At that time the chairman of Continental Ulrich Weiß was also a Vorstand member in Deutsche Bank. See Frankfurter Allgemeine Zeitung (199) 'Pirelli: Weiterhin freundliches Zusammengehen mit Continental', 19 December.

259   Höpner, M. and Krempel, L., above n233, 353.

260   Maurer, R. (2003) 'Institutional Investors in Germany: Insurance Companies and Investment Funds', CFS Working Paper No. 2003/14.

ultimately cause a rethink of this disengagement with Germany AG and the changing shareholder pattern observed in bank holdings between 2003 and 2007 may be an indication of things to come.

The Market for Corporate Control

As we noted in Chapter 7, Germany's market for corporate control has historically been weak. However, the number of M&A transactions has been increasing since the 1970s. In the 1970s there were on average 373 M&A's in Germany. By the 1980s this average had increased to 827 and by the end of the 1990s it averaged 1,479 mostly driven by reunification linked East/West mergers. From 1998 – 2005 that number reached 1,607.[261] Until relatively recently, hostile transactions have not made up more than a very tiny percentage of these M&A deals. Traditionally, hostile takeover bidding has been unacceptable in Germany and has been perceived by managers, labour and the general public, as the unacceptable face of Anglo-American business practices for the benefit of outside shareholders to the detriment of long-term value and stakeholder interests. However, as we discussed in the previous section, hostile takeovers, while still very unpopular with the general public, are not as uncommon as they once were. Even though it would be premature to believe that an active market for corporate control is already in place in Germany, it would not be an exaggeration to claim that managers are no longer as isolated from external financial pressures as they have been in the past.

While some German companies may still regard hostile transactions as controversial, foreign predators have had no such qualms where German target companies are listed on global securities markets. In the past, foreign companies have found it difficult to launch an unsolicited offer for a German listed company as issues ranging from disclosure standards to concentration of ownership prevented such bids.[262] Thus while it would have been unthinkable in the 1980s for a foreign company to launch and win a hostile bid for a German company the globalization of capital markets has now made this possible. Vodafone's bid for Mannesmann in October 1999 represented the point when this became apparent. Not only was it the first time a foreign company's hostile takeover bid for a German listed company ended successfully, but also the target was one of Germany's largest and best performing conglomerate companies based in the 'heart of German capitalism', Nordrhein-Westphalen, home of the most important companies in the steel industry. Vodafone and Mannesmann seemed on paper like a David and Goliath pairing. Mannesmann had been in business for 109 years, while Vodafone

---

261   Höpner, M. and Jackson, G. (2006) 'Revisiting the Mannesmann Takeover: How Markets for Corporate Control Emerge', European Management Review, vol. 3, 142–155 at 143–144.

262   This is exemplified by Pirelli's bid for Continental, which not only lasted for two and a half years but also ended unsuccessfully. See n258 above.

was only 15 years old. Mannesmann had a workforce of 130,860 employees, while Vodafone had 29,465 employees. Mannesmann's turnover was 23 billion, while Vodafone's was 13 billion.[263]

Before Vodafone's bid, Mannesmann had been in the process of restructuring by splitting its unprofitable steel operations from its highly successful fixed-line and mobile telecommunications services to focus on the latter. This strategy, however, gave rise to the possibility of the company becoming a takeover target since a potential buyer could spin off the steel operations more easily.[264] A global issue in 1998 of 20.7 million new shares, 48.4 percent of which were purchased by foreign investors, was also significant, as it contributed to the global dispersal of the company's shareholdings. Subsequently, Mannesmann acquired the British mobile operator Orange in spite of CEO Klaus Esser's public statement that he would 'not be bound in any decisions by consideration of whether they leave [the company] more vulnerable' as it introduced even more outsider oriented shareholders into the company. Obviously, Esser was aware of the possibility of a hostile takeover attempt for his company – Vodafone being the main potential bidder at the time – and thus hoped that the deal with Orange would serve as poison pill for anyone who would try to acquire Mannesmann, as it would trigger potentially prohibitive EU competition and German company law rules.[265]

All this, however, was not sufficient to inhibit Vodafone. On the contrary, the Orange purchase was perceived as an aggressive move against it within its home market, as Orange was a key competitor to Vodafone in the UK. In response, and after the failure of negotiations for a friendly takeover, Vodafone launched a €119 billion all-share offer for the German group.[266] Esser rejected the offer as 'weak and extremely risky for [Mannesmann's] shareholders' and began a defensive campaign.[267] The reaction from politicians as well as employee representatives was immediate and critical of Vodafone's move. IG Metall, Germany's most powerful union, mobilized the workforce through its representative on Mannesmann's *Aufsichtsrat*, while Wolfgang Clement, State Prime Minister, and the German Chancellor Schröder expressed their dismay at the bid. The latter declared that hostile bids destroy the culture of the target company and that hostile bidders

---

263   Höpner, M.and Jackson, G., above n261, 143.

264   Barber, T. (1999) 'Mannesmann Hogs the Limelight', Financial Times, 20 October.

265   Rivlin, R., Larsen, P., Price, C. and Major, T. (1999) 'Mannesmann Eyes two Groups', Financial Times, 20 October; Financial Times (1999) 'Peeling Orange', Lex Column, 20 October; Barber, T., above n264; and Höpner, M. and Jackson, G. (2001) 'An Emerging Market for Corporate Control? The Mannesmann Takeover and German Corporate Governance', Discussion Paper 1/4, Max-Planck-Institut für Gesellschaftsforschung, available at SSRN: <http://ssrn.com/abstract=285232>.

266   Vodafone's takeover of Mannesmann can also be regarded as a defensive acquisition of a competitor.

267   Larsen, P. (1999) 'First Hostile Bid from a Foreigner Launched for a German Concern', Financial Times, 20/21 November.

'underestimate the virtue of co-determination'.[268] Nevertheless, they did nothing to block the bid. For the German corporate governance system this was generally perceived as the point when the implications of exposure to global capital markets really became apparent.

Eventually, on 3 February 2000, Esser gave in under the pressure from the majority of Mannesmann's shareholders[269] and eventually agreed to the takeover after a slight improvement in Vodafone's offer.[270] The role of Canning Fok, managing director of Hutchison Whampoa who earned €5 billion from the transaction as Mannesmann's top shareholder, was of critical importance as he promised €16 million to Esser himself and another €16 million to his team as an 'appreciation award' for accepting Vodafone's offer. In the end, the total cost of the 'appreciation awards' to Mannesmann rose to nearly €57 million in 'golden handshakes' comprising €24 million of special contributions and €32.5 million of 'alternative pensions' to several *Aufsichtsrat* members. The most significant factor, though, in determining the final result of the bid, was Mannesmann's ownership structure, which had been transformed by Mannesmann's tapping of global capital markets and takeovers of other companies. Not only were shareholders dispersed – the largest blockholder owned 10 percent of the shares – but also 62 percent of them were foreign. Most significantly about 40 percent of them were American or British institutional investors as opposed to 39 percent who were German shareholders. Nevertheless, even the latter, most of whom were institutional investors, were not supportive of Esser and his management team's effort to oppose the takeover, as they had begun dumping their shares on the market even before the final agreement was reached.[271] Mannesmann finally 'paid' for the shareholder value orientation it followed, since by separating its profitable telecommunications business from the steel pipes and tubes business in order, to use Esser's words, to 'create value for the shareholders', it became a takeover target.[272] It also paid for the decision to base its expansion upon funds raised in stock markets at home and abroad. In addition, the acquisition of Orange, a company with dispersed foreign shareholders, contributed even further to the globalization of Mannesmann's shareholder base.

---

268   Larsen, P., Atkins, R., Simonian, H. and Cane, A. (1999) 'Schröder Weights into Bid Battle', Financial Times, 20/21 November.

269   Handelsblatt Interactiv (1999)'Vodafone Plans to Force Chief's Resignation' (English Summary), 23 December. See <http://www.handelsblatt.de>.

270   According to the original offer, Mannesmann's shareholders would receive 47.2 percent of the shares in the merged entity. Esser agreed after Vodafone raised its offer by an additional 2.3 percent and agreed to retain the fixed-line operations. See: Handelsblatt Interactiv (2000) 'Vodafone, Mannesmann Agree Merger' (English Summary), 4 February. See <http://www.handelsblatt.de>.

271   Boland, V., Waters, R. and Warlimont, G. (2000) 'Mannesmann Investors Split Over Bid: They Have Only a Week to Decide', Financial Times, 31 January.

272   Cited in Barber, T., above n264.

However, the Vodafone-Mannesmann battle also triggered significant reactions from path dependent forces. As we have already discussed above, the German European parliament members led a successful revolt against the Takeovers Directive. Additionally while on the one hand the elimination of voting rights defences by the KonTraG amendments, the adoption of more transparent accounting standards, enhanced disclosure, the changing role of banks and the abolition of capital gains tax constitute important institutional changes that assist the market for corporate control. On the other hand, however, the WpÜG, takeover reforms and the 2006 amendments implementing the takeovers directive were a significant direct formal managerial and labour protective response to the Vodafone-Mannesmann takeover revealing that the forces of path dependence in the area of takeovers in Germany are still strong.[273] There was also a path dependent reaction for the main German participants as the golden parachute payments were widely perceived as a highly corrupt action. In March 2001 a group of minority shareholders led by Adreas Dimke, a lawyer in Hamburg, filed a criminal lawsuit for perfidy against Esser, the *Aufsichtsrat* chairman Joachim Funk, the *Aufsichtsrat* member and Deutsche Bank CEO Josef Ackermann, and another three employees of the company alleging that they had stolen some €57 million of Mannesmann money. In the trial prosecutors contended that the payments were illegal because they were in effect a bribe to persuade Esser and others to drop their resistance to Vodafone's bid after a long takeover battle. In July 2004 the court of first instance held the defendants were not guilty of a criminal act but found the payments to them were in violation of section 87 AktG as they were inappropriate, contrary to the company's interests and claimable in a civil action by the company, something that naturally the new Vodafone management were unwilling to pursue.[274] However, the saga continued to the Federal level where the Supreme Court overruled the decision and sent it back to the district court for a retrial.[275] In 2006 as the trail began again the defendants agreed a €5.8 million financial settlement to end the trial without admitting guilt.[276]

---

273   The reaction is in many ways is similar to the reaction to hostile takeovers in the US where at an early stage, in the absence of institutional investors as a counterweight as there had been in the UK, managers were able to lobby for protection. Armour, J. and Skeel, D. (2006) 'Who Writes the Rules for Hostile Takeovers, and Why? The Peculiar Divergence of US and UK Takeover Regulation' ECGI – Law Working Paper No. 73/2006, 35, available at <http://ssrn.com/abstract=928928>.

274   For an extensive report of the case see Rolshoven, M. (2004) 'The Last Word? – The July, 2004 Acquittals in the Mannesmann Trial', German Law Journal, vol. 5(8), 935.

275   Morris, C. (2006) 'The Retrial of Mannesmann: Millions for Motivation, Heise Online, 11 March, available at <http://www.heise.de/english/The-retrial-of-Mannesmann-millions-for-motivation--/newsticker/news/80477>.

276   Moore, J. (2006) 'Ackermann Pays €3m to Settle Mannesmann Case', The Independent, 25 November, available at <http://www.independent.co.uk/news/business/news/ackermann-pays-83643m-to-settle-mannesmann-case-425770.html>.

Despite these reactions the Vodafone/Mannesmann takeover has had an effect in that hostile takeovers attempts while nowhere near as active as they are in the UK and US, are now more common. Höpner and Jackson for example, examined hostile takeovers in Germany between 1995–2005. Between 1995 and 1999 when the Vodafone/Mannesmann takeover occurred there were just two hostile bids. After the Vodafone/Mannesmann takeover between 2000 and 2005 there were 13 hostile bids. Of the 15 hostile bids between 1995 and 2005, 9 were successful and 6 unsuccessful.[277] While these figures are still well behind the type of market for corporate control operating in the UK and US, they do represent a small but symbolic change. One of the reasons hostile bids for German listed companies have been increasing is that the trend of shareholdings particularly bank holdings being unwound partly as a result of the capital gains tax reforms has also caused an increase in the free float of DAX 100 companies. In 1994 the free float was 40.5 percent but it had increased to 51.9 percent by 2005.[278] However, whether the free float will continue to increase is questionable given that as we observed earlier the trend of unwinding shareholdings by traditional insiders seems to be ending.

As we noted in Chapter 3 managerial responses to exposure to the global market for corporate control can be defensive as well as aggressive. The case of Daimler Benz' reorganization in the early 1990s and its subsequent merger with Chrysler is a good example of a defensive managerial reaction. Under the leadership of Jurgen Schrempp, who succeeded Edzard Reuter, a long lasting conglomerization strategy of the company came to an end in 1995. The new CEO, with the strong encouragement of Deutsche Bank, one of the main shareholders, implemented a restructuring strategy that would make Daimler Benz leaner and more focused on its main operations by spinning off unprofitable businesses.[279] This process, combined with the company's increased stock liquidity after its listing on the NYSE in 1993 and the reduction of Deutsche Bank's stake in 1994, rendered Daimler-Benz dangerously exposed to the global market for corporate control.[280]

While the goal of capturing the US market should not be ignored, the fear of a takeover was a key reason behind Daimler's merger with the American carmaker Chrysler in 1998, the largest industrial merger in history at the time. The outcome of the merger was DaimlerChrysler, which would, it was hoped stave off any

277 Höpner, M. and Jackson, G., above n261, 152–153.

278 Dittmann, I. et al., above n222, 12.

279 Deutsche Bank, who also faced a performance decline at the time, arguably benefited from Daimler's restructuring and increased profitability. See Logue, D. and Seward, J. (2000) 'Anatomy of a Governance Transformation: The Case of Daimler-Benz', Law and Contemporary Problems, vol. 62(3), 87 at 105. The bank's attitude also signifies the change in relationships between financial and non financial corporations that has been occurring in Germany.

280 The NYSE listing can also be seen in the context of Deutsche Bank wishing to dispose of its shareholding in Daimler.

potential predator and it was anticipated that it would bring economies of scale that would enable it to compete in an increasingly global marketplace. While the transaction was presented as a merger, in reality it represented a takeover by the German company.[281] Daimler's shareholders ended up owning the majority of DaimlerChrysler shares but the largest single group immediately after the merger were American investors owning approximately 44 percent of the outstanding stock, compared to about 37 percent German-owned shares. As a result, a significant consequence of the merger was the dilution and globalization of its share ownership.[282] The merger was though an unhappy one for all concerned, as exposure of US shareholders to German management was not an easy fit particularly in the absence of any threat from the market for corporate control. As a result US institutional shareholders sold their shares in large numbers in the year after the merger and eventually the Chrysler part of the business was sold at a loss in 2007 as the hoped for economies of scale did not emerge.[283]

In Chapter 2 we discussed the link between takeovers and industrial relations as managers and employees tend to have a similar interest in resisting unsolicited bids. Interestingly, fear of a hostile takeover may be one factor in a significant functional path dependent reaction on the part of managers and the institutions of co-determination, where German companies who may be vulnerable to being taken over have sought out an 'anchor' shareholder who intends to be a long-term protective partner for the company. Volkswagon's vulnerability to a hostile takeover, given the likelihood that the ECJ would, and indeed did, end the special voting rights restrictions in the Volkswagen Act, was eliminated by Porsche secretly increasing its stake in the company using derivatives, first to 30 percent over the course of 2006 and 2007 and then to nearly 75 percent in 2008.[284] Additionally, the hostile takeover attempt by Schaeffler KG for Continental AG in

---

281   Logue, D. and Seward, J., above n279, 93.

282   Shields, M. (2008) 'Deutsche Bank's Daimler Stake Falls Below 3 Percent', Reuters, 9 June, available at <http://uk.reuters.com/article/rbssConsumerGoodsAndRetailNews/id UKWEA904020080609>.

283   Ball, J. (1999) 'DaimlerChrysler Frets Over Loss of US Shareholders', Wall Street Journal, 24 March; and Bolger, J. and Bawden, T. (2007) 'Daimler Sells Chrysler to Private Equity', The Times, 14 May, <http://business.timesonline.co.uk/tol/business/industry_sectors/engineering/article1786611.ece>.

284   Atkins, R. and Reed, J. (2006) 'VW Shares Soar on Porsche Move', Financial Times, 15 November, available at <http://us.ft.com/ftgateway/superpage.ft?news_id=fto 111520061450014757>. See also Schafer, D. (2008) 'Bafin to Examine the Volatility of VW Shares', Financial Times, 22 October; and Milne, R. (2007) 'Porsche Boosts Stake in VW', 26 March, available at <http://us.ft.com/ftgateway/superpage.ft?news_id=fto0 32620070303289670>. See also Milne, R. (2008) 'Porsche's Derivative Move Doubles VW's Shareprice', Financial Times, 28 October; Milne, R. and Reed, J. (2008) 'Porsche Accelerates Towards VW Control', Financial Times, 28 October; and Saigol, L. (2008) 'Hedge Funds Rush to Cover Short Positions', Financial Times, 28 October. Although family ownership can have its down side; Betts, P. (2008) 'Volkswagen Caught in Porsche

July 2008 is a good illustration of the complex dynamics of the German market for corporate control. Schaeffler, in a similar manner to Porsche, built up a secret shareholding in Continental before launching a hostile bid for the company. When this was revealed, the bid caused outrage in Germany. However, the bid was ultimately resolved by the Chairman of the Continental supervisory board (who had previously worked for Schaeffler) and the employee representatives on the board, convincing management that in fact a takeover by a family run firm such as Schaeffler was exactly what the company needed to secure the long-term future of the business.[285] This managerial protective reaction to the threat of a hostile takeover may be part of the explanation for the increase in non financial shareholdings, banks and public sector in German companies between 2003–2007 as companies have sought to protect themselves by effectively rebuilding the traditional German insider system to fulfil some of its original managerial protection function (see Table 8.4). Similarly, the withdrawal of banks, who had become less than supportive to German managers as they began to emphasize their transaction driven business models may have been good news for managers. As banks have divested their supervisory board seats those seats have not been filled by independent board members or shareholder representatives but by increasing numbers of former management. For example, Rang found that former managers on supervisory boards increased from 23 percent in 2001 to 36 percent in 2004.[286] Since the 1970s there has been a gradual increase in M&A activity in Germany. For the largest companies the globalization of capital markets has both allowed them to fund their global strategies and made them more vulnerable to being taken over as they have often listed their shares on outsider oriented stock markets in the UK and US or taken over outsider oriented companies from outside Germany and thus inherited outsider oriented shareholders within the merged entity. The Vodafone/Mannesmann hostile takeover was a significant departure in terms of hostile takeovers in Germany and hostile takeovers, while still disapproved of, are no longer as rare as they once were. However, the Vodafone takeover triggered significant path dependent reactions both at the EU level with regard to the Thirteenth Directive and internal German takeovers regulation. Similarly, the Vodafone criminal trial illustrated how outsider remuneration norms could bring about possible criminal consequences in the German context. Managerial defensive reactions were also observed both in the DaimlerChrysler merger and in the phenomenon of German managers seeking protection by finding 'anchor'

Family Feud Crossfire', *Financial Times*, 15 September, available at <http://us.ft.com/ftgateway/superpage.ft?news_id=fto091520081421140517&page=2>.

285 Schäfer, D., Wiesmann, G. and Wilson, J. (2008) 'Schaeffler Deal with Conti Fails to Break German Mould', *Financial Times*, 2 September, available at <http://us.ft.com/ftgateway/superpage.ft?news_id=fto090220081652198254&page=2>.

286 Rang, R. (2004) Ehemalige Vorstände als Kontrolleure. Untersuchung der Zusammensetzung von Aufsichtsräten Mitbestimmter und Börsennotierter Unternehmen im Auftrag der Hans-Böckler-Stiftung, Düsseldorf: Hans-Böckler-Stiftung.

shareholders in a reworking of the traditional insider model where labour, the government, banks, family and cross-shareholdings protected management from hostile takeovers. As we noted in the previous section the breaking of the decline trend with an upsurge in non financial, bank and state shareholding between 2003 and 2007 and the increase in former management on supervisory boards may be an indication that management are having some success in reworking the traditional model.

Outsider Shareholder Influence

Despite the fact that the number of Germany listed companies is still relatively small compared to the US or the UK, the German stock exchange has become an important European stock exchange mostly through foreign listings.[287] In 1990 as *Finanzplatz Deutschland* was beginning, there were 1,392 foreign and domestic listed companies on the German stock exchanges of which approximately 60 percent were German. By 2006 some 16,154 companies were listed there with the vast, vast majority being foreign.[288] As Chart 8.5 reveals IPO's in Germany were few and far between in the 1970s but increased somewhat in the 1980s and reached 34 by 1990. However, towards the end of the 1990s IPOs began to grow significantly in number, fuelled by the demand for high tech shares.[289] By 1999 with the advent of the Euro there were 175 IPOs in Germany. At this point in the late 1990s as one can observe from Chart 8.6 the German stock exchange was beginning to rival and surpass even the US and the UK for new listings. By 2003 the German market had been through the dot.com crash and the *Neuer Markt* had collapsed resulting in a limited appetite for IPOs. Indeed, only three occurred that year. Confidence returned briefly in 2006 as there were 255 IPOs in Germany (Chart 8.5) but they dropped back to 97 in 2007.[290]

---

287   Siebert, H. (2005) The German Economy: Beyond the Social Market, Princeton: Princeton University Press, 228.

288   Data extracted from Deutsches Aktieninstitut (2008) DAI Statistics, Table 02–1–1–1.

289   Deutsche Börse Group (1999) Annual Report, Frankfurt, 25; Handelsblatt Interactiv (1999) 'Neuer Markt Gets Top-50 and All-Share Indices', 1 July. See <http://www.handelsblatt.de>. See also von Rosen, R. (1999) 'Developments in the German Equity Market and Its Regulation', Journal of Financial Regulation and Compliance, vol. 6(3), 238–248.

290   On the effect of the stock market crash on the German appetite for shares see Fohlin, C., above n225, 234.

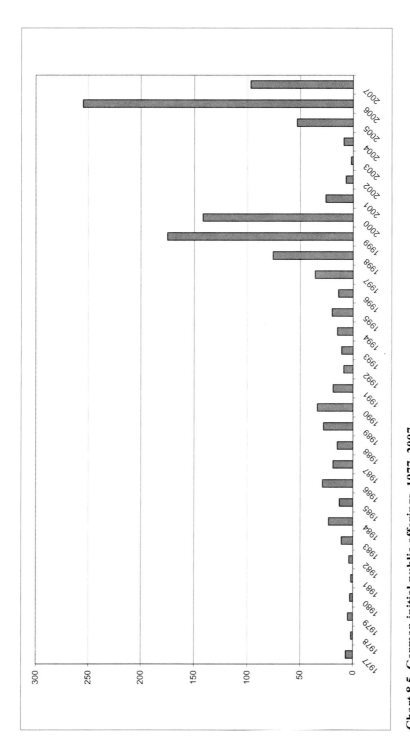

Chart 8.5 German initial public offerings, 1977–2007

Source: Deutsches Aktieninstitut (2008) DAI Statistics: Shareholder Structure in Germany, Table 03–8–b.

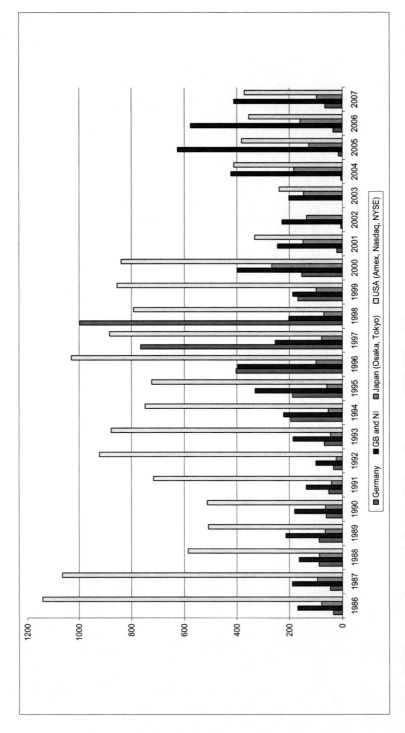

Chart 8.6 Comparative admissions to listing: Germany, UK, US and Japan
Source: Deutsches Aktieninstitut (2008) DAI Statistics: Shareholder Structure in Germany, Table 03–3–3–a.

One can see a reflection of all this activity in the explosion of stock corporations in Germany since 1999. In the post war period the number of AG's in Germany remained consistently between 2–3 thousand until the mid 1990s when the numbers of AGs started to rise slowly. By 1999 there were 7,376 AGs in Germany and by 2004 that number had more than doubled to 16,002 although it has fallen to 14,429 by May 2008.[291] As we have discussed earlier in this chapter the major change in shareholding patterns in Germany since 1998 has been the influx of foreign shareholders. These foreign, mostly institutional investors, increased consistently from 5.6 percent in 1960, to 11.1 percent in 1980, to 12.5 percent in 2000 and 21.3 percent in 2007.[292] US, and in particular UK, institutions account for a vast majority of those funds.[293]

The domestic stock exchanges are not the only exposure some German companies have to capital markets. Many large German companies such as Deutsche Bank, Daimler-Benz, Allianz, Deutsche Telecom, Hoescht and Siemens have exposure to global capital markets through their foreign stock markets listings. In 2006, Abee and Zimmermann found some 46, mostly large German companies, had 100 listings on the world's major stock exchanges. All had a German listing as well and the average number of listings outside of Germany was 2.17. However, 11 companies had more than 3 listings and a few had as many as ten listings outside Germany. One company, Volkswagen, had 13 listings on major capital markets.[294] Some 18 medium sized German companies are listed outside Germany on London's Alternative Investment Market which seems to have benefited from the closure of the *Neuer Markt*.[295] Additionally, the expansion of German companies through cross-border M&As such as the merger of Daimler with Chrysler and the takeover of Mannesmann by Vodafone also contribute to the globalization of shareholdings and the promotion of shareholder norms. As Klaus Esser said at the final shareholder meeting to approve the Vodafone bid, 'Ladies and Gentlemen, what happened here was pure shareholder democracy … Shareholder democracy takes place in the stock market'.[296]

---

291   Deutsches Aktieninstitut (2008) DAI Statistics, Tables 01–1 and 01–1–b.

292   See Table 8.4 above.

293   Deutsche Bundesbank (various years) 'Special Statistical Publication: Balance of Payments by Region', and (2008) 'Foreign Direct Investment Stock Statistics', Frankfurt: Bundesbank, available at <http://www.bundesbank.de/statistik/statistik_veroeffentlichungen_sonderveroeffentlichungen.en.php#sonder11>. See also: Vitols, S. (2005) 'Changes in Germany's Bank-based Financial System: Implications for Corporate Governance', Corporate Governance, vol. 13(3), 386–396 at 391.

294   Abee, S. and Zimmermann, J. (2006) 'Do Cross-Listings Drive Regulatory Convergence? Evidence from Germany', Table 1, available at SSRN: <http://ssrn.com/abstract=902827>.

295   LSE (2008) 'European Globally Focused Companies Continue to Come to AIM', available at <http://www.londonstockexchange.com/NR/exeres/102EC569-0AF9-461D-9C88-71CC7B9F2B83.htm>.

296   Höpner, M. and Jackson, G., above n261, 152.

However as we discussed in Chapter 2, even where a developed stock market is present this does not mean that the outsider shareholders will be able to impose their expectations on management. In Germany although foreign institutional investors have increased their presence in the past decade this does not mean that they have become major players in German corporate governance. Although their holdings have increased significantly in the past decade their holdings have tended to cluster in large numbers in the largest and most influential German companies, as we observed with the Mannesmann takeover and remains the case with companies such as Daimler, Deutsche Telekom, MAN, BASF, Allianz etc where foreign investors hold significant proportions of shares.[297] The *Deutsches Aktieninstitut* 2008 survey of 117 large Germany companies lists only 27 with a significant percentage of foreign ownership. However, where foreign investors are present they tend to hold a very large percentage of the shares in these companies. From the 27 companies that had foreign shareholders the smallest percentage they made up of the company's shareholding was 23.3 percent and the largest was 88.6 percent. The average total percentage combined holdings in those companies of foreign investors was 57.3 percent. If the pattern of influence of institutional investors we observed in Chapters 5 and 6 in the US and the UK is a guide to their behaviour in Germany then they are likely to be mostly passive at the firm level but active at market rules level. Given they hold limited amounts of shares, the absence of a system of self-regulation, a weak market for corporate control and given they are not part of the traditional German business network, imposing their expectations is likely to be significantly more difficult.

The development of the stock market has also led to the development of the private equity industry in Germany, which has grown as private equity investors now have a stock exchange exit available. In 1991 private equity firms both domestic and international had a portfolio of some 2,200 German companies they had invested in employing 273,000 people. By 2000 that figure had increased to 5,500 with 350,000 employees.[298] By the beginning of 2008 private equity investment both international and German reached €24.5 billion worth of investment. This was invested in buyouts of 6,279 mostly medium sized German companies, although some larger companies such as Hypo Real Estate, where JC Flowers bought a 24.9 percent stake in 2008, have attracted private equity investment.[299]

---

297   Handelsblatt, 8 November 1999, reported in Jackson, G., Höpner, M. and Kurdelbusch, A. (2004) 'Corporate Governance and Employees in Germany: Changing Linkages, Complementarities and Tensions', Discussion Paper 04-E-008, Research Institute of Economy, Trade and Industry, Japan, available at SSRN: <http://ssrn.com/abstract=503962>.

298   Ernst and Young (2005) 'German Private Equity Activity: Special Report – The Economic Impact of Private Equity, 12, available at <http://www.ey.com/Global/Assets.nsf/Austria/Studie_PE_Germany_2005/$file/Studie_Private_Equity_2005_Germany.pdf>.

299   Bundesverband Deutscher Kapitalbeteiligungsgesellschaften (BVK) Statistics (2007), available at <http://www.bvkap.de>.

In all by the beginning of 2008, German companies owned by private equity firms employed 1.8 million people.[300] These medium sized companies bought by private equity firms have experienced significant exposure to outsider shareholder expectations as expected shareholder returns on these private equity investments are high. The average fund is expected to return over 11 percent but the best funds invested in Germany already produce returns of 37 percent for buyouts.[301] Private equity has though attracted significant criticism in Germany where these types of returns are obtained by mass lay offs and have led to politicians, as we observed earlier in the chapter, branding private equity firms as 'locusts'.[302]

Hedge funds have also been active in Germany. Prior to 2004 the German government was very keen to reform its tax law to allow hedge funds to operate in Germany and it did so successfully in 2004.[303] Since 2004 hedge fund activity in Germany has increased. By 2006, when two hedge funds, who had become the largest shareholders in Deutsche Börse, effectively stopped its takeover of the London Stock Exchange, removed the board and reportedly extracted some three billion in shareholder returns, the German Government was outraged and its enthusiasm for hedge funds waned.[304] In October 2008 the two hedge funds forced the resignation of the Chairman of Deutsche Borse because of his opposition to the breaking up of Deutsche Börse's business. The situation was heading for a significant clash between the traditional German insider model and the outsider model, as the German State of Hesse (*Hessen*) can remove shareholder voting rights if Frankfurt's position as a financial center is threatened. State intervention was avoided as one of the hedge funds was forced to sell its shares as a result of the global financial crisis.[305] In all, hedge funds have not enjoyed a good press since the original Deutsche Börse

---

300   Ernst and Young, above n298, 12.

301   Bundesverband Deutscher Kapitalbeteiligungsgesellschaften (BVK) (2006) 'Study on the Performance of German Private Equity Funds in 2006', 3, available at <http://www.bvkap.de/media/file/153.BVK-Performance-Study2006_E.pdf>.

302   Deutches Bundesbank (2006) 'The Economic Situation of Small and Medium-sized Enterprises in Germany Since 1997', 30 December, 52, available at <http://www.bundesbank.de/download/volkswirtschaft/mba/2006/200612mba_en_economic.pdf>. See also: Linnemann, C. (2007) 'Germany's Mittlestand: An Endangered Species', Deutsche Bank Research Paper, 6 July 2007, 12, available at <http://www.dbresearch.com/PROD/DBR_INTERNET_EN-PROD/PROD0000000000212667.pdf>.

303   Hedgeweek Special Report (2006) 'Hedge Funds in Germany', available at <http://www.hedgeweek.com/specialreports/listing.jsp?content_id=30133>.

304   Financial Times (2008) 'Deutsche Borse', The Lex Column, 21 October, and International Herald Tribune (2006) 'Germany to Step up Hedge Fund Scrutiny', 4 May, available at <http://www.iht.com/articles/2006/05/03/business/hedge.php>.

305   Mackintosh, J. and Wilson. J. (2009) 'Atticus Signals Halt to D Börse Siege by Selling Most of Stake', Financial Times, 1 April, 23; Financial Times, above n304.

incident in 2006. As a direct result Germany has been campaigning at the EU, G8 and G20 level for international agreement to restrict the activities of hedge funds but without much success as the UK and US were much less keen on introducing regulation of hedge funds.[306] The global financial market crisis from autumn 2008 onwards has brought about a significant international appetite for reform and Germany may get the restriction it wishes over the next few years.

While as we have noted in Chapter 6 institutional investors tend to be generally passive at the firm level some foreign institutional investors such as the California Public Employees Retirement System (CalPERS), who are known for their activist policies in the US have also been active in Germany. Indeed, Bendt identifies CalPERS' proposal at RWE's annual general meeting in 1992 for the abolition of the multiple voting rights owned by German local authorities, as the first significant example of foreign institutional investor activism.[307] Wenger and Kaserer also report that corporate failures in Germany have also generated criticism from Anglo-American investors who have threatened to withdraw their funds unless German companies improved their internal and external controls.[308]

In 1996, having seen the positive results of its governance strategy at home, CalPERS decided to gradually expand its activism in foreign companies too. Thus, it formulated specific corporate governance principles that should be followed by companies in a number of countries, one of which is Germany.[309] Other, American investors have also attempted to intervene from time to time.[310] However, the CalPERS initiative was the first systematic effort to steer established board practices in German companies in order to promote a focus on outsider shareholders. It regularly publishes target-lists of German companies with governance standards that do not satisfy its principles. Most importantly it appears that the US pension fund intends to cooperate with domestic shareholder associations and other activists. In Principle 2 of its International Governance Policy CalPERS calls for German companies to adopt and support the corporate governance recommendations of the German shareholder association DSW, which asks for improvements in the *Aufsichtsrat* and the General Meeting, auditors' independence, transparency in banks' proxy voting, and a focus on shareholder value.[311] Indeed, it was with the help of this particular shareholder association

---

306   Apel, R. and Spannaus, N. (2007) 'G-8 Pass up Opportunity on Hedge Funds', Issue of Executive Intelligence Review, 15 June, available at <http://www.larouchepub.com/other/2007/3424g8_hedges.html>.

307   Bendt, C., above n18. See also Waller, D. and Dickson, M. (1992) 'California Activism Arrives in Germany', Financial Times, 10 December.

308   Wenger, E. and Kaserer, C., above n147.

309   CalPERS (1996) 'Germany Market Principles'. See <http://www.calpers.ca.gov>. Other major countries targeted by CalPERS include Japan, France and the UK.

310   André, T. (1998) 'Cultural Hegemony: The Exportation of Anglo-Saxon Corporate Governance Ideologies to Germany', Tulane Law Review, vol. 73, 69 at 73.

311   See <http://www.dsw-info.de>.

and other local shareholders that CalPERS finally effected the adoption of the one share-one vote principle in RWE.[312]

DSW has itself on a number of occasions filed counter motions against management proposals including the annual general meetings of companies like DaimlerChrysler, Deutsche Telekom, Siemens, Deutsche Bank, Volkswagen, RWE, HypoVereinsbank and even Deutsche Börse AG.[313] There have, of course, been voices for increased shareholder protection and influence before CalPERS' systematic involvement. However, with the exception of DSW, such incidents were isolated and constituted evidence of minority shareholders' aggravation rather than a systematic campaign of outside shareholders to change corporate governance in Germany. However in the last decade, the shareholder movement appears to also involve large investors such as the DWS, Deutsche Bank's powerful mutual fund, which in January 2000 commissioned the creation of a ranking list for German blue chip corporations based on their corporate governance record.[314] The main criteria were quality of disclosure, extent of performance-linked remuneration, *Aufsichtsräte* quality and minority shareholder rights. This initiative constituted a tentative breakthrough for shareholder activism in Germany as it is the first time a domestic target list was formulated and backed by one of the largest mutual funds in Germany.[315] The list is used by DWS and other investors or shareholders' associations as a guide for their investment and targeting strategies. As we observed earlier DSW's successful lawsuit in Mobilcom's case concerning *Aufsichtsrat* remuneration illustrates their targeting policy.[316]

Exposure to capital markets and its outsider norms has also affected managerial goals or at least how they express them. The concept of shareholder value as the primary goal of the corporation is to create financial value for the shareholders. As such it can conflict particularly with employees' interests as it tends to bring a move away from growth strategies which tend to increase employment, ends cross subsidization of loss making units, relates performance to pay and share price, introduces shorter term planning and increased disclosure which removes managements' ability to maintain employee protective reserves. In its pure form it tends to reduce the numbers of employees and create a more insecure working environment for employees as it prioritizes shareholders' interests over all others.[317]

---

312 Atkins, R. (1998) 'RWE Embraces One Share, One Vote – Commitment to Conglomerate Concept Flies in The Face of Fashion', Financial Times, 27 April.

313 DSW (2005) 'Survey on Directors' Pay 2005', reported in the October issue of the 'DSW Newsletter'. See <http://www.dsw-info.de>.

314 Davis Global Advisors (2000) 'Driver Impact', Global Proxy Watch, vol. 4(4), 28 January.

315 Its Global assets exceed €257 billion. See <http://www.dws.com/EN/showpage. aspx?pageID=39>.

316 See the discussion earlier in this chapter.

317 Jackson, G. (2004) 'Contested Boundaries: Ambiguity and Creativity in the Evolution of German Codetermination', RIETI Discussion Paper No. 04-E-022, 23, available at SSRN: <http://ssrn.com/abstract=569541 or DOI: 10.2139/ssrn.569541>.

In Germany shareholder value began to appear in the first half of the 1990s with a number of companies embracing it as a benchmark for their strategies.[318] By 1996 these companies faced severe criticism from labour representatives,[319] the press,[320] academia,[321] but interestingly also some reluctant senior German managers.[322] The case of Daimler is indicative of the general perception of shareholder value as a negative and foreign concept. After its listing on the NYSE in 1993, Daimler-Benz officially announced its commitment to the principle of shareholder value maximization. Under the guidance of a new *Vorstand* chairman, Jürgen Schrempp, the company gradually cut thousands of jobs worldwide, 80,000 of which were in Germany, and transformed itself into a "technology" group by divesting its non-core activities.[323] However, these actions and in particular the company's justification of creating shareholder value attracted severe public criticism and Daimler had to reconsider its new focus. Schrempp then announced that the term shareholder value would not be used by the company in Germany but would be replaced by the more moderate 'company value'.[324] Nonetheless, under Schrempp, Daimler-Benz continued to focus on shareholder value maximization. According to White and Coleman, as the merger with Chrysler was being finalized the 'company value' pretence was dropped with the implementation of $3 billion cost savings involving a contraction of total employment in order to boost the share price.[325] Since then while the use of shareholder value as a goal is not widespread it has become more common.[326]

---

318   Daimler-Benz, Veba, BASF, Bayer and Hoechst were the pioneers. By 1995, they had all undertaken large restructuring programmes aimed at the maximization of shareholder value. See PricewaterhouseCoopers (1997) 'Survey Report: Converging Cultures – Trends in European Corporate Governance', April.

319   Munchau, W. (1997) 'Flexibility the Watchword – The System of Industrial Relations Faces Choice of Change or Extinction', Financial Times, 18 November.

320   See Munchau, W. (1996) 'Minister Calls for Profit Motivation', Handelsblatt Interactiv, 5 November; and Financial Times (1996) 'Workholder Value Carries Equal Weight – German Companies Are Questioning the Automatic Dominance of Shareholders', 23 October, emphasizing the conflict between shareholder value and the interests of the workforce and the society at large.

321   See von Werder, A. (1998) 'Shareholder Value-Ansatz als (einzige) Richtschnur des Vorstandshandelns?' Zeitschrift fuÈr Unternehmens- und Gesellschaftsrecht, 27. Jg., Heft 1, 69–91 for a critical view of the shareholder value concept questioning its legality under German law.

322   Note, for instance, Hermann Franz, Siemens' Aufsichtsrat chairman, who commented: 'All you need to do is announce that you make 20,000 workers redundant and your share price will go up' (author's translation) cited ibid., 70.

323   Logue, D. and Seward, J., above n279.

324   von Werder, A. von, above n321, 69.

325   White, G. and Coleman, B. (1998) 'Chrysler Daimler Focus on Value of Stock', Wall Street Journal, 8 June, cited in Logue, D. and Seward, J., above n279.

326   Vitols, S. (2000) 'The Reconstruction of German Corporate Governance: Reassessing the Role of Capital Market Pressures', Paper for the First Annual Meeting

A factor that may play a part in promoting shareholder value is the changing career paths of German managers. While traditionally managers have been drawn from engineering backgrounds, many German managers, as in the UK and US, now have a finance background. Again traditionally German managers tended to work their way up through the company where they would spend probably a good proportion of their careers. Now however, managers increasingly move between companies and the time spent working in each company has decreased since the 1960s. Indeed, while German managers used to be German, this is no longer necessarily the case at the senior level, as appointments of non-German CEOs are no longer unheard of.[327]

The growth of the MBA qualification in the career path of a German manager may also play a role in detaching German managers from the traditional values associated with the insider German model. While traditionally senior German management viewed a management Ph.D as the postgraduate qualification of choice and to some extent still do, increasingly the MBA is replacing the Ph.D. As a result the University market for MBAs has grown enormously in Germany in the past decade with a number of US universities now offering MBAs in Germany.[328] Klaus Esser, for example, was a pioneer of the new German management career as he had a law and finance background despite working as a manager in the most traditional engineer dominated German industry of all. In 1975/1976 he completed an MBA at the Sloan School of Management at the Massachusetts Institute of Technology in the US, although he completed a traditional Ph.D as well at the University Of Regensburg later in his career.[329] We regard the MBA as playing a role in perhaps moving managers towards outsider shareholder norms because it has had such an effect in the US, the UK and Canada. In a 2002 and 2008 survey of MBA students in the US, the UK and Canada the students observed that the course had an effect on their values making them associate more with shareholder value and less with social goals, customer satisfaction and quality products. Although the survey in 2008 indicated that students were thinking more broadly about issues of quality and customer satisfaction, social goals (employee wellbeing, community,

of the Research Network on Corporate Governance, Wissenschaftszentrum Berlin für Sozialforschung, Berlin, 23–24 June, available at <http://www.wzb.eu/gwd/into/pdf/vitols/vitols00_reconstruction.pdf>. See also Jürgens, U., Naumann, K. and Rupp, J. (2000) 'Shareholder Value in an Adverse Environment: The German Case', Economy and Society, vol. 29, 54–79.

327 Höpner, M. and Jackson, G., above n261, 152.

328 Bergemann, B. (2006) 'The MBA in Germany', Business Leadership Review, vol. 3(4), 1, available at <http://www.mbaworld.com/downloadblrarticle/1022/index.htm>.

329 Business Week (2008) 'Executive Profile: Klaus Esser', available at <http://investing.businessweek.com/research/stocks/private/person.asp?personId=397578&privcapId=20619&previousCapId=20619&previousTitle=Generalpercent20Atlanticpercent20LLC>.

environment and equal opportunities) ranked lowly when the students were asked about a company's responsibilities.[330]

De Jong writing in the late 1990s surveying Anglo-American and Germanic companies in the early 1990s found that in Germanic companies (Germany, Switzerland, the Netherlands and Scandanavia) 86.1 percent of total net added value went to employees while only three percent was paid to shareholders as dividends. Anglo-American companies (UK, US and Ireland) gave 62.2 percent to employees while distributing 15 percent as dividends.[331] This balance of priority, however, seems to be moving in some of the largest companies. Hassel and Beyer in a 2002 survey of 57 large German companies revealed an identifiable reorientation of managerial goals away from employees and towards shareholders in the form of increased dividends.[332] They found that total net value added increased slightly from the early 1990s and the number of employees and employment costs were kept virtually constant. Dividend payments on the other hand increased from the mid-1990s onwards with the effect that the average sum of dividend payments doubled within less than a decade.[333] However, while Kirchmaier and Grant in a study of the 100 largest German companies in 2002 similarly found that dispersed shareholding and better financial performance were connected, overall they found that the private benefits of control available to insiders were significant enough to encourage blockholders to maintain control.[334] Indeed, part of the explanation for the upsurge in shareholdings between 2003 and 2007 may be to do with a realization by insiders that there is an opportunity to increase the private benefits of control. The Porsche and Schaeffler buyouts for example and Susanne Klatten's[335] attempt to buy out all the non-family shareholders in Altana, the specialist chemicals company, in November 2008, were all driven partly by being able to recognize the opportunity to capture very strong internal revenues.[336]

The largest companies are of course the ones most exposed to capital market pressures and the pattern of dividends across all listed German companies shows a more complex picture. From the late 1980s to the mid 1990s there is a discernable rise in dividend yield peaking at four percent in 1994 but then it

---

330   The Aspen Institute (2008) 'Where Will They Lead? MBA Students Attitudes About Business and Society', Centre for Business Education, available at <http://www.aspencbe.org/about/library.html>.

331   De Jong, H. (1997) 'The Governance Structure and Performance of Large European Corporations', The Journal of Management and Governance, vol. 1, 5–27 at 17.

332   Hassel, A. and Beyer, J. (2002) 'The Effects of Convergence: Internationalisation and the Changing Distribution of Net Value Added in Large German Firms', Economy and Society, vol. 31(3), 309–332.

333   Hassel, A. and Beyer, J., above n332.

334   Kirchmaier, T. and Grant, J. (2006) 'Corporate Ownership Structure and Performance in Europe', CEP Discussion Paper No. 0631, 20, available at SSRN: <http://ssrn.com/abstract=616201>.

335   Susanne Klatten is the Quandt family (the family behind BMW) heiress.

336   Lex (2008) No Drama Altana, Financial Times, 7 November, 20.

declines and plateaus to 2004 staying between one and two percent.[337] This may be because a small group of companies have a very high level of exposure to outsider shareholders while others remain largely immune. It may also indicate that a form of profit 'satisficing' similar to that described by managerial theorists and discussed in Chapter 1, is operating whereby managers return just enough of the company's earnings to shareholders to prevent them selling their shares or that insiders are supplementing the dividend income with private rent extraction.

In all, some of the very largest German companies like Siemens, that historically resisted the concept of shareholder value,[338] within the last decade have embraced it as a rule of thumb in introducing a restructuring program aimed at increasing shareholder value.[339] Similarly, Deutsche Telecom, which has a 64 percent foreign shareholder base and a 57 percent institutional shareholding base has distributed dividends of as much as 84 percent of their profits. As we noted above foreign investors have tended to hold a lot of shares concentrated in a small number of the largest German companies and it is these companies that have had the greatest exposure to outsider norms such as shareholder value. However, beyond this group shareholder value has less influence. Indeed, in a 2008 survey of DAX 100 companies with websites in English (a sample biased in favour of those companies with Anglo/Saxon investors) only 30 percent even mention the importance of shareholders in their corporate goals.[340]

German companies' direct exposure to outsider shareholder oriented corporate governance norms such as shareholder value has no doubt increased over the past 20 years as the domestic and global capital markets have become a source of finance, private equity and hedge fund buy outs have appeared and managers are increasingly exposed to shareholder value as a legitimate goal in the exercise of managerial discretion. Most companies, even the majority of the largest companies however, still operate unaffected by norms such as shareholder value, as foreign shareholders remain clustered in a small group of large companies and some medium sized companies owned by private equity firms. Significantly, the incentives for blockholders to retain their shares still seems to be strong.

---

337   Deutsches Aktieninstitut (2008) DAI Statistics, Table 09.2–4 and Table 9.2–3.3.

338   See Hermann Franz's comment, above n322.

339   Handelsblatt Interactiv (1999) 'Siemens to Crown Restructuring with US Stock Market Listing in 2001' (English Summary), February 19. See <http://www.handelsblatt. de>. Intense pressure from shareholders was also an important factor; see Handelsblatt Interactiv (1999) 'Siemens Faces Turbulent AGM' (English Summary), 18 February. See <http://www.handelsblatt.de>.

340   Joerg, P. et al. (2008) 'Shareholder Value. Principles, Declarations, and Actions', ECGI – Finance Working Paper No. 95/2005, available at SSRN: <http://ssrn.com/abstract=1099936>.

Conclusion

We set out in this chapter to examine the interaction between the forces of global corporate governance isomorphism and the traditional German corporate governance institutions described in Chapter 7. We examined in the first section how exposure to increased global and regional competition and the globalization of production were creating simultaneous pressures on management and labour. The result of this has been a formal protective path dependent reaction in Germany to strengthen co-determination while at the same time the participants in the reinforced co-determined system have engaged in negotiating more flexibility. Additionally, developments at the EU level in the availability of the SE, the *Centros* decision and the 2010 agenda aimed at facilitating the single European market may allow some formal erosion of co-determination. In all we considered while co-determination has experienced significant stresses it remains a functioning and important part of the German corporate governance model. Perhaps most significantly it remains highly valued by workers and the general public if not by management, although they may come to value its protective role if the market for corporate control becomes more active.

As the liberalization of capital controls progressed over the 1980s the interaction between domestic and foreign financial markets through regulatory arbitrage, as Germany's largest companies and banks began to increasingly operate outside Germany, created a need for the gradual reorienting of the German financial system. As a result *Finanzplatz Deutschland*, brought capital gains tax changes, accountability and disclosure, insider dealing, prospectus requirements, the KonTraG amendments, the DCGK and accounting reforms which have introduced outsider oriented rules into the German corporate governance system or in the case of the tax changes and voting reforms have actively encouraged insider disengagement. The effects of these reforms on the German corporate governance system have not necessarily been what one would expect. While the accounting reforms seem a clear example of functional leading to formal convergence, managerial power may unintentionally have been enhanced by many of the other reforms. While some blockholders, particularly banks, did disengage after the tax reforms, the reforms coincided with the aftermath of the stock market crash in 2001–2002, resulting in the closing of the *Neuer Markt* in 2003, which may have prevented others from exiting. However, contrary to expectations, as the market recovered the pattern has not been divesting but rather traditional insiders reinvesting between 2003 and 2007.

Similarly while the Vodafone/Mannesmann hostile takeover marked the point at which some of the effects of exposure to global capital markets became apparent, it also brought about a very strong path dependent reaction. Takeover reform as a result at both the EU and domestic level, in the aftermath of the Vodafone/ Mannesmann bid, moved to allow management to protect themselves from hostile bids, while the outsider style remuneration present in the Vodafone/Mannesmann case and ESOP's generally spurred protest and litigation. We have also observed a significant reaction to changing shareholding patterns from German managers who have increased the number of former managers on the supervisory board as banks have given up their places and have been finding 'anchor' shareholders, who are long-term protective investors. The upsurge in government, bank and non financial corporations' shareholdings between 2003 and 2007 may partly be a reflection of this trend.

In one sense the *Finanzplatz Deutschland* reforms have been a success in building up a successful securities market in Germany as some 16,000 companies are now listed there. However, most of the success of the German Stock exchange has been built on foreign listings as German listed companies only numbered about 1,000 of the 16,000 companies listed there by 2006 and the German public have not wholeheartedly embraced an equity based culture having been badly burned by the stock market crash in 2001–2002. While IPOs boomed in the late 1990s they collapsed after the crash reviving briefly in 2006 but retrenching again in 2007. While there has been some pension reform which, initially at least, increased the presence of German institutional investors, the stock market crash also seems to have similarly sparked their withdrawal from German shares.

Overall foreign investor shareholding, most of whom are UK and US institutional investors, has increased significantly but they have tended to cluster in a small number of the largest German companies which does not indicate a high degree of outsider shareholder confidence generally in the German corporate governance system. However, within that small cluster of large German companies, exposure to outsider norms such as shareholder value is high. The availability of an exit through the domestic stock exchange for private equity and hedge funds has also assisted the activities of private equity and hedge funds while simultaneously attracting a huge amount of government and general public disapproval.

One of the purposes of utilizing institutional analysis in this book has been to bring some rigour to the study of change and transformation in corporate governance systems. Simply observing that an antagonistic norm has been introduced from one institutional system into another does not reveal much about the outcomes of such as action, where there are a series of complex institutional interactions as a result. As we have described over the course of this chapter lots of outsider based norms have been introduced into the German corporate system – there is no doubt about this. Observing this has happened though, will not reveal much about whether these norms have had a convergence/transformative effect because institutional sub-systems, as we have discussed in Chapter 4, rearrange themselves in complex ways when pressures are applied. There is little doubt that the traditional insider corporate governance model, described in Chapter 7, has altered. Labour co-determination has had to become more flexible in an environment where production exit offers significant bargaining power to management. In particular, the bank based element of the traditional corporate governance model has changed, as banks have been selling shares, divesting board seats and ceasing to lend to their traditional corporate clients, although that pattern may be changing as bank shareholdings have increased between 2003 and

2007. A small number of the very largest German companies also have high levels of exposure to global capital markets which makes them susceptible to hostile takeovers and norms such as shareholder value. As we described in Chapter 4, and observed in Chapters 5 and 6, corporate governance systems are not static but dynamic and are in a constant state of rearrangement. In most cases systems alter to accommodate change within the general logic of the system. If a change is antagonistic to the systems logic then it may be rejected or neutralized as other systemic forces wield greater influence on the overall systemic outcome. On the other hand, systemic shock such as war – even a destructive victorious one – and economic shock, as we observed in Chapters 5 and 6, can cause destabilization and unworkability until a new systemic equilibrium is found and workability returns. Overall in this chapter we have observed significant reactions within the German corporate governance system as a result of pressures from the process of globalization. Whether this stimuli has amounted to a destabilizing shock leading to convergence/transformation to an outsider system or whether it is simply changing while still moving along its systemic path is a complex issue, as we have already observed, and so we turn to consider it in full along with the parallels with the UK and the US experience in Chapter 9.

Chapter 9
The End of Globalization?

Introduction

In this chapter we consider our findings from Parts I and II on the causes of systemic corporate governance change generally, how globalization causes change, the dynamics of change that led to the UK and US emerging as unique outsider systems and whether the changes we identified in Germany's corporate governance system, resulting from economic globalization, have caused or are likely to cause it to transform/converge to an outsider corporate governance system. To do this we begin by recapping on our conclusions from each chapter and then in the following sections drawing out some remaining issues. In Part 1: Theorizing Corporate Governance Change, we began in the first chapter by setting out the contested theoretical context in which convergence scholarship has occurred. As Anglo/Saxon capitalism has come to dominate global capital markets, so too the domestic Anglo/Saxon conception of accountability whereby divergence from outsider shareholder oriented norms is viewed negatively, has been elevated to the global arena. This has led to claims that insider systems such as Germany are inferior and will converge or be transformed into outsider systems. An understanding of the roots of this corporate theory contest and the ascendance of shareholder oriented theories is important because theory and corporate governance transformation are strongly linked in the UK and US experience. Additionally the shareholder supremacy scholarship has been influential in framing the rules upon which the process of globalizing capital markets has been based. As a result shareholder bias within the convergence scholarship needs, in our view, to be filtered for when considering change and transformation in corporate governance systems.

In Chapter 2 we set out institutional analysis as our preferred method of analysis where change and transformation are at issue in corporate governance systems. We identified (corporate law, the financial system, the industrial relations system, and sub-systems related to the government demand function, particularly competition and effective demand) as institutional sub-systems that were central to corporate governance outcomes. We then went on to illustrate the coherence of both insider and outsider systems as workable combinations of complementary institutional sub-systems at the national level. In Chapter 3 we explained that we viewed globalization as a process that included internationalization and regionalization as part of that process and that we were focusing on economic globalization given its primary effect on corporate governance outcomes. We concluded that globalization through increased product market competition, the globalization of production and the globalization of capital markets was placing significant pressures on key aspects of insider systems that could affect their institutional coherence. In Chapter 4 we continued our use of institutional analysis by examining institutional theories of change that emphasized diversity of response to stimulus within corporate governance systems was likely, rather than uniformity of reaction. In doing so we dismissed convergence arguments of a neoclassical origin that predict a spontaneous outsider shareholder oriented order resulting from the forces of globalization. This was because while the forces of globalization may push towards systemic convergence of some kind, a whole set of other institutional forces may simultaneously pull corporate governance systems towards their original position so that predicting where the resultant force will lead becomes difficult.

We then turned in Part 2: Observing Change and Transformation in the UK, US and Germany, to consider evidence of change and transformation in the UK, US and Germany. In Chapter 5, we considered long run change in the corporate governance systems of the UK and US, up until the 1970s. By analysing long run change in institutions, such as industrial relations, the financial system, corporate law and those related to the government demand function, particularly competition and effective demand, discussed in Chapter 2 as significant for corporate governance change, we demonstrated that institutional change and indeed fluidity of change has been an important feature of both the UK and the US corporate governance systems over time. We noted in particular that in this time period both the UK and US were insider systems and we found that even though there is a shared institutional history, as the US was a former colony of the UK, institutional dynamics in a general sense varied in response to common stimulants. However, both systems underwent an institutional transformation to stronger insider systems as a result of the shock of the Great Depression in the US, and WWII, in Britain

In Chapter 6 we considered the critical period in the transformation of the UK and US into outsider systems as the labour, government and business partnership of the post war period came to an end in both countries. The end of the Bretton Woods Agreement, increasing product market competition and successive shocks from two oil crises led to high inflation and unemployment and the election of two economic radicals in the form of Margaret Thatcher and Ronald Reagan. Initially their economic policies created a further shock, as a deep recession occurred which eliminated further path dependent resistance to radical change. In turn the industrial relations system, financial systems and demand functions of government in both countries were transformed. As a result of the weakness of labour, financial market reform, the emergence of the market for corporate control and the withdrawal of the state, in a self-regulatory environment institutional investors were able to exert themselves as the dominant influence within the corporate governance system, completing both the reorienting of the system to an outsider shareholder focus and in turn setting the rules for nascent global capital markets. In this chapter again we noted the fluidity of response to change within institutional sub-systems in the UK and US and in particular the peculiarity of the common transformative response to change in the 1980s.

In Chapter 7, before examining evidence of change in the German insider model as a result of the process of globalization, we outlined the key elements of the traditional German corporate governance model. Labour co-determination, industry cross-shareholdings, family shareholding, state shareholding and bank shareholding, were significant internal features of the traditional model. Externally a weak securities market, bank based finance, deficient disclosure and minority shareholder protection rules, the absence of a market for corporate control and collusive relationships between companies, were important complimentary aspects of the institutional system sustained historically by a notion of long-term commitment between the company and its various stakeholders. In Chapter 8, we examined the effect of the process of globalization on the traditional German corporate governance system. We observed that global and regional competition, the globalization of production and the globalization of capital markets were having an effect as functional reactions and in some cases formal reactions were altering the strength of labour voice in the co-determination process and securities market reform had promoted outsider shareholder oriented norms within the traditional German corporate governance model. The most dramatic reaction has been in the changing role of banks within the system and the increase in foreign shareholders. On the other hand there was also evidence of formal path dependent reactions in the areas of co-determination, takeover reform and executive remuneration and that many of the norms introduced to promote outsider interests may unintentionally have enhanced managerial discretion. Similarly, we identified a significant reaction by management in replacing bank representatives on the supervisory board and replacing them with former management and management seeking 'anchor' shareholders who are committed to long-term relationships with the company. In all we concluded that reactions to the process of globalization were occurring in important institutional sub-systems. The question remained as to whether these changes had resulted in convergence/transformation to an outsider system or represented an accommodation of the new economic environment according to the German insider system's own internal logic.

Change and Transformation in Corporate Governance Systems

One of the features of our examination of change in the UK, US and Germany is that in general change within corporate governance sub-systems seems to be a constant process of stimuli and reaction within a complimentary workable set of institutional sub-systems. However, as we discussed in Chapter 4 sometimes shocks to individual sub-systems or to the systems as a whole, can align forces for change in a particular direction removing path dependent reactions and pushing it rapidly in a different direction. We observed over the course of Chapters 5 to 8, that wars and economic crises seem to be the major catalysts for change and transformation within our three corporate governance systems. The two world wars of the twentieth century led to the continued rise of government as an influence on corporate behaviour in the victorious UK and US, although in the UK the victory in WWII amounted to a systemic shock, while it led in the aftermath of WWII to the creation of institutional structures designed to minimize the role of the state in the defeated Germany. Similarly, victory in the two world wars of the twentieth century also allowed the UK and US capital markets the luxury of continuity while it destroyed the capital markets of defeated countries such as Germany.[1] Indeed, defeat in two world wars, as we discuss further later in this chapter, meant there was little consistency of institutions design in Germany until after WWII. In the UK, the combined effect of a number of shocks in the interwar years culminating in WWII, did cause unworkability and transformation to a stronger insider model. Economic crises in the interwar years saw systemic transformation in the US as industrial relations, the financial system and the demand function of the state transformed, while in Germany it brought the subjugation of labour and the temporary rise of the Nazi totalitarian state, as the major influence within the corporate governance system. In the initial post war period labour influence was strong in all three countries. The successive economic shocks of the 1970s and early 1980s brought about a period of unworkability for the corporate governance systems of the UK and US as the government, labour and management consensus of the post war years broke down in the face of successive economic shocks. The corporate governance system was then only capable of being transformed as the path dependent forces one would normally expect to resist severe change, were overwhelmed by these shocks. In Germany, as we discuss later in this chapter, exposure to the same economic conditions did not produce the same effect as its corporate governance system seemed to adapt comparatively well to the same economic pressures. This leaves us with two general observations which we need to explore further. While in a general sense within the UK and the US, diversity in reaction to change over time was the norm, as institutional theories of change would suggest, the similarity of reaction in the 1980s indicates to us that rather than this being an example of neoclassical convergence, shared institutions are playing a role in those reactions. We turn then in the next two sections to explore both the commonality of reaction to shock in the UK and US and the diversity of reaction to the same pressures during the 1970s and 1980s in Germany, as well as drawing together the evidence of convergence/transformation of the German insider corporate governance model in response to pressures from economic globalization.

---

1   On the role of war in the development of the victors' securities markets and the lack of development in the defeated powers see Roe, M. (2006) 'Legal Origins and Modern Stock Markets', Harvard Law Review, vol. 120, 460.

Colonialism Matters?

The UK and the US, as we emphasized in Chapters 5 and 6, have a shared colonial history and a subsequent history of strong economic and what we would term, econo-cultural ties i.e. a shared set of economic values. The original colonial relationship despite its revolutionary end is significant, we believe, in that aspects of the institutional structures within the two systems seem to have been formed and reformed by core influences such as a shared central respect for freedom of contract, private property and the value placed on the arm's length nature of economic regulation.[2] As we noted in Chapter 1, La Porta et al. writing on comparative corporate governance, made the observation that legal families make a difference to whether a securities market is central to a corporate governance system or not.[3] They argued that rigid codified civil law systems tend not to have significant securities markets, while common law systems with their independent judge made laws do. This they claim is because the common law protects shareholders to a greater extent than civil law countries i.e. not only does law matter but the legal origin of the system matters.[4] These claims are, as we noted in Chapters 1 and 6, influential but highly controversial. Cheffins critiquing the claims of 'legal origin' scholars has pointed out that matters are considerable more complex than presented by such scholarship. The UK and US, he notes for example, are alone among common law countries in having a securities market as central to their financial systems, civil law systems have had significant stock exchanges in the past and indeed protect shareholders more than has been previously understood.[5]

While we dismissed the 'law matters' aspect of the La Porta et al. claims in Chapter 6 as being unlikely to have played a role in the emergence of the outsider systems in the UK and US, the link they make between outsider systems and the common law has a resonance with the fluidity and commonality of institutional behaviour in the UK and US, observed in Chapters 5 and 6. That is because there is less certainty about institutional arrangements in a common law system, where not only are there areas where the legislature has no role in forming the law (pure judge made common law) but even where the law is produced by the legislature the effects of that legislation is less predictable where the judiciary

---

2   Coffee, J. (2001) 'The Rise of Dispersed Ownership: The Roles of Law and the State in the Separation of Ownership and Control', Yale Law Journal, vol. 111, 56–59; and Jones, W. (1958) 'An Inquiry into the History of the Adjudication of Mercantile Disputes in Great Britain and the United States', University of Chicago Law Review, vol. 25, 445.

3   La Porta, R., Lopez-de-Silanes, F. and Shleifer, A. (1999) 'Corporate Ownership Around the World', The Journal of Finance, vol. 54, 471–517. See also: Glaeser, E. and Shleifer, A. (2002) 'Legal Origins', Quarterly Journal of Economics, vol. 117, 1193–1228.

4   For a good critique of the 'legal origins' literature see Roe, M. (2007) 'Juries and the Political Economy of Legal Origin', Journal of Comparative Economics, vol. 35, 294–308.

5   Cheffins, B. (2008) Corporate Ownership and Control: British Business Transformed, Oxford: Oxford University Press, 52.

retain a discretion to interpret the legislation.[6] As such, institutions in the UK and US remain less fully formed than their counterparts in a civil law system, as they are unable to be rigidly designed and need to be able to respond to a greater degree of change.[7] Additionally, self-regulation is a feature of both the UK and the US, which may be explained both as an institutional design response in a fluid institutional environment and by the value placed on keeping the state at arm's length. As a result when forming institutions the initial instinct in the UK and the US, is not to look to the state to create an institution but to do it privately.[8] The state has been broadly complicit in this, recognizing the difficulty it has in replicating institutions with similar fluidity.[9] That is not to say there are not tensions between the state and the private sector. Britain had a socialist government for significant periods of time until 1979 when Margaret Thatcher was elected.[10] As we discussed in Chapter 5, in the immediate aftermath of the war many industries were nationalized. However, the growth of the state only went so far before finding an accommodation with private sector institutions such as the stock exchange, leaving them their autonomous role.[11] Indeed, even when the state does impose regulation in the economic sphere, as we observed in Chapters 5 and 6 with the US SEC example, it generally does so by taking an oversight function which allows the self-regulatory organization to continue its role, rather than taking that role from them and in a number of crucial examples appointing key members of the regulated community to run the SEC i.e. Joseph Kennedy and

---

6   Zweigert, K. and Kötz, H. (1992) Introduction to Comparative Law, 2nd edition, Oxford: Oxford University Press, 273–278.

7   Grajzl, P. and Murrell, P. (2005) 'Allocating Law-Making Powers: Self-Regulation vs. Government Regulation', Journal of Comparative Economics, vol. 35(3), 520–545 at 538.

8   Wilks, S. (1997) 'The Amoral Corporation and British Utility Regulation', New Political Economy, vol. 2(2), 280.

9   Page, A. (1986) 'Self-Regulation: The Constitutional Dimension', Modern Law Review, vol. 49, 141. The best example of this is the UK Panel on takeovers and mergers which was almost untouchable at the domestic level but was eventually turned into a state body by EU intervention. See: Dignam, A. (2007) 'Lamenting Reform? The Changing Nature of Common Law Corporate Governance Regulation', Company and Securities Law Journal, vol 25, 283–299 at 295.

10   Cheffins, B. (2000) 'Putting Britain on the Roe Map: The Emergence of the Berle-Means Corporation in the United Kingdom', 33, available at <http://ssrn.com/abstract=218655>.

11   Gourevitch, P. and Shinn, J. (2005) Political Power and Corporate Control: The New Global Politics of Corporate Governance, Princeton, 261; Coffee, J. (2001) 'The Rise of Dispersed Ownership: The Roles of Law and the State in the Separation of Ownership and Control', Yale Law Journal. October, vol. 111(1), 1–82; and Roe, M. (2002) 'To Separating Ownership from Corporate Control', Columbia Law and Economics Working Paper No. 155, 573, available at <http://ssrn.com/abstract=165143>.

John Shad.[12] In the UK historically many of the arms of state have viewed their role as representing the interests of those they regulate, in government, rather than having a public service role.[13]

This has some resonance with the German experience after the war where there was a similar need to keep the state at arm's length. Indeed, the German judiciary did come to develop a significant discretion particularly in the commercial context.[14] Crucially however, the difference between the way institutions have been formed in the UK and US, as opposed to Germany, is that the destabilizing effects of two world wars meant that ultimately after WWII externally imposed institutional structures were designed to tightly restrict the role of the state and form stabilizing values, while values in the UK and US, even though their institutional systems may have experienced lower level shocks, in the absence of defeat in wars, formed an unbroken chain of fluid and innovative institutions. What is significant about this observation is that in terms of analysis of change and convergence/transformation generally, institutional rearrangements, particularly self-regulatory rearrangements, that occurred in the UK and US, are unlikely to be easily replicated in insider systems where those types of fluid institutions are not present.

These observations about the common law do not of course explain commonality of reaction in institutional sub-systems to shock in the UK and US. This reaction may not necessarily be strictly about the common law but rather about a cumulative set of shared econo-cultural values that evolved at an early stage in Britain and were transferred to the US through colonization and have been reinforced through trading interaction over time. As we have noted these are often referred to as common law influences or values i.e. a respect for freedom of contract, private property and the arm's length nature of economic regulation. One seeming flaw in this analysis is the revolutionary break between Britain and the US which resulted in a constitutional republic in the US, rather than the Parliamentary monarchy which continued to evolve in Britain. This is problematic because the dominant formal institution in any institutional system is the constitution, which sets the boundaries for the formation of, and influences the shape of, other formal and informal institutions within a system.[15] However, while in one sense the US Constitution

12   Seligman, J. (1995) The Transformation of Wall Street: A History of the Securities and Exchange Commission and Modern Corporate Finance, Northeastern University Press, 575.

13   Dignam, A. (2000) 'Exporting Corporate Governance: UK Regulatory Systems in a Global Economy', Company Lawyer, vol. 21(3), 70–77.

14   Zweigert, K. and Kötz, H. (1998) Introduction to Comparative Law, New York: Oxford University Press, 336 and 442–469; and Beck, T., Demirguc-Kunt, A. and Levine, R. (2003) 'Law and Finance: Why Does Legal Origin Matter?', Journal of Comparative Economics, vol. 31(4), 653–675.

15   North, D. (1990) Institutions, Institutional Change and Economic Performance, Cambridge: Cambridge University Press, 3–4; and Mahoney, P. (2001) 'The Common Law and Economic Growth: Hayek Might Be Right', Journal of Legal Studies, vol. 30, 503–525.

was a reaction against British monarchical tyranny, in another sense it strongly enshrined common law values within it, as the dominant groups in drafting the US Constitution were merchants and lawyers. Indeed, it was a revolution dominated in its formal institutional design by common lawyers.[16] When the Declaration of Independence was signed on 4 July 1776, thirty two of the fifty six signatories were common lawyers. Five of those were English educated and trained lawyers. The next largest group were merchants of which there were eleven. Additionally, seventeen of the fifty six signatories were British born or educated.[17] Similarly of the fifty five delegates who attended the Constitutional convention in 1787 to draft the US Constitution, thirty five were lawyers and of the thirty nine that actually lent their signatures to the agreed Constitution on 17 September 1787, twenty two were lawyers and four of that number were lawyers educated in England. The next largest group were merchants at thirteen. Nine of the signatories were British born or educated.[18] The Constitution eventually agreed, placed checks and balances on Government decision making, established free internal trade between the states and with the bill of rights amendments in 1791, created an arm's length relationship between the state and it citizens. In particular the 'due process' part of the fifth amendment with its roots in *Magna Carta* provides that 'no person shall … be deprived of life, liberty, or property, without due process of law; nor shall private property be taken for public use, without just compensation'. As Siegan considered 'the Constitution created a government without the power to deprive the people of the rights which belong to them under the common law, originally as English citizens and subsequently as American citizens'.[19] As such the US Constitution, rather than marking a break with its common law past, is a document heavily imbued with common law influences, particularly on economic matters, where the values of the common lawyers and the merchant class coincided.

Over time while the two countries have developed differing institutional sub-systems the values upon which they were built were similar and were reinforced over the centuries by the strong trading relationship between the two countries.[20] As we discussed in Chapter 5, the UK was the main trading partner with the US over the nineteenth century and by far and away the major supplier of FDI into the US. In the twentieth century while trade declined between the two countries from

16   Miller, J. (1959) Origins of the American Revolution. Stanford University Press: Stanford, xix.

17   Compiled from the US National Archive: <http://www.archives.gov/national-archives-experience/charters/constitution_founding_fathers.html> and the biographies of the signatories.

18   Compiled from the US National Archive, ibid.

19   Siegan, B. (2001) Property Rights: From Magna Carta to the Fourteenth Amendment, Transaction Publishers, 1; and on the commercial aspects of the Constitution see 65–120.

20   Schweber, H. (2004) The Creation of American Common Law 1850–1880: Technology, Politics and the Construction of Citizenship, Cambridge: Cambridge University Press.

the middle of the century onwards, the UK was the largest European recipient of US FDI over the century and from the 1980s onwards as their capital markets integrated, the world's single largest recipient of US FDI. In a continuation of the nineteenth century pattern, the UK has been the largest supplier of FDI into the US over the twentieth century.[21] A good formal example of this is the dealings between UK and US business leaders, we considered in Chapter 5, in assisting with the coordination of two world wars, which further reinforced common economic values, as did the Anglo-American Council on Productivity in the post WWII period.

In terms of explaining why the UK and US reacted in such similar ways to shocks to their institutional structure over the course of the 1970s and 1980s, we consider that because shared econo-cultural values form the background upon which formal institutions are embedded in both countries, economic institutions when faced with similar shocks end up with similar outcomes because the values underlying the decision making in the realignment process were the same. As we described in Chapter 6, one of the crucial realignments in moving the corporate governance systems to outsider systems was that the self-regulatory systems in the UK and the US, although different from one another, allowed institutional investors to construct an alternative set of norms that focused managerial discretion on them, once the state and labour fell away in influence. In terms of whether the experience of the UK and the US is transferable to the convergence debate generally, we consider that their shared institutional history has played a role in the common response to shock and that transformation, in the way it occurred in the UK and US, is highly unusual as diversity of reaction, in our view, should be regarded as the norm. Indeed, as we will observe in the next section diversity of reaction to similar stimuli has been the outcome in Germany's case.

Transformation in the German Corporate Governance System?

If one takes a snapshot of the traditional German corporate governance model and the UK/US model in the post WWII years up until the 1970s, discussed in Chapter 5, the industrial relations systems in all three countries, although significantly different in each country, aimed in this period at long-term commitment to employees as labour was a significant influence on management discretion. Additionally, while similarly different in orientation, the corporate law of all three countries was managerial in operation. However, while the state was much less proactive in the marketplace in Germany than in the UK and US, the institutional structure created a demand oriented outcome. The UK and Germany have more in common in terms

---

21   Eckes, A. and Zeiler, T. (2003) Globalization and the American Century, Cambridge: Cambridge University Press, 263–267; and Lipsey, R. (1993) 'Foreign Direct Investment in the United States: Changes over Three Decades' in Froot, K. (ed.) Foreign Direct Investment, Chicago: University of Chicago Press, 113–172.

of competition policy as collusion was tolerated in both countries, while in the US collusion was heavily discouraged. The crucial difference between the UK/US and Germany lay in the financial system, in that Germany did not have a significant equities market as a source of finance. This meant the hostile takeover was not a significant pressure on management. Additionally, the lack of a significant equity market, meant that long-term savings were not channelled into equities and in turn institutional investors did not feature within the corporate governance system. If one takes a snapshot of all three corporate governance systems in the 1960s, then all three are clearly insider systems and it is arguable as to which one was the more insider of the three – possibly Britain given its nationalization programme. However, as we have described in Chapter 6, it was the UK and the US, through a combination of withdrawal of the state, industrial relations change and financial market deregulation, that emerged as shareholder oriented outsider systems and Germany did not. This raises the question of course of why it was not affected so dramatically by the same macroeconomic impacts of the 1970s.

After the war Germany faced a bleak future, the country had been devastated, its technology confiscated by the allies, its best engineers and scientists left for the US and reparations payments had to be paid.[22] However, Germany experienced extraordinary growth after WWII. While this growth is often attributed to Marshall Plan funding, which no doubt helped, it was a minor part of the story given the disadvantages Germany faced.[23] Despite these disadvantages the Germany economy expanded rapidly and between 1948 and 1950, the Germany economy grew at a rate of more than 15 percent. From 1950 to 1960, it grew at an average of 8.2 percent and from 1960 to 1973, it averaged 4.4 percent. By comparison from 1950 to 1960, the US grew at 3.3 percent and the UK grew at 2.8 percent. From 1960–1973, the US grew at 4 percent and the UK grew at 3.1 percent.[24] This placed Germany, compared with other major industrialized nations in this period of high growth, at the top of the world growth tables along with Japan, while the UK and the US were consistently at the bottom.

Over the course of the 1970s, as we have described in Chapter 5, the UK and the US experienced destabilizing shock after shock, as a result of the collapse of Bretton Woods and successive oil crises. All of these events affected Germany as well and indeed its growth slowed.[25] However, while the UK and US were affected

---

22   Judt, M. and Ciesla, B. (1996) Technology Transfer Out of Germany After 1945, London: Routledge, 87; Giersch, H. et al. (1992) The Fading Miracle: Four Decades of Market Economy in Germany, Cambridge: Cambridge University Press, 115; Gimbel, J. (1990) Science, Technology, and Reparations: Exploitation and Plunder in Postwar Germany, Stanford University Press; and Naimark, N. (1995) The Russians in Germany; A History of the Soviet Zone of Occupation, 1945–1949, Cambridge, MA: Harvard University Press, 206–207.

23   Reparations payments to the allies outweighed Marshall Plan funding. Giersch, H. et al., above n22.

24   Giersch, H. et al., above n22, 2–3 and 115.

25   Giersch, H. et al., above n22, 3–4.

by unemployment problems, recession, high inflation and balance of payments difficulties, these factors were not present in Germany. Germany's position as one of the worlds leading exporters meant that its current account had a healthy surplus over the 1970s, while the UK current account spent most of that time in deficit and the US dipped in and out of deficit.[26] In the UK and US, unemployment was problematic peaking at 10 percent and 8.5 percent respectively over the 1970s.[27] In Germany unemployment did increase from a very low base, peaking at five percent in 1975 but averaging just over three percent for the decade.[28] Inflation in the UK averaged nearly 16 percent from 1973–1979 and in the US peaked at 26 percent over the course of the decade.[29] By contrast in Germany, inflation averaged less than five percent for the 1973–1979 period. This was both a result of the Bundesbank's historic emphasis on price stability and in part the co-determination aspect of the German insider model.[30] Whereas, in the UK and the US attempts to hold down wages were unsuccessful because there was no way for the state to effectively coordinate wage restraint at the firm level. In Germany industry level coordination was possible between employers and unions because of the collective bargaining structure. Additionally, because of union representation on the boards of companies they had access to information on price increases and its affect on profitability. Management claims for wage restraint could then be evaluated more accurately. In turn coordinated industry wide wage restraint resulted, which played a significant part in keeping inflation under control.[31] For the same reasons working days lost to strike over the 1970s were absolutely minimal in Germany compared to the UK and US.[32] In sum although the experiences of the 1970s had a negative effect on Germany as unemployment rose and growth slowed, the effect

---

26   Giersch, H. et al., above n22, 12–15; Kitson, M. (2004) 'British Economic Growth since 1949' in Floud, R. and Johnson, P. (eds) The Cambridge Economic History of Modern Britain. Volume III: Structural Change and Growth, 1939–2000, Cambridge, 33, Figure 2.2; and U.S. Department of Commerce, Bureau of Economic Analysis, International Transactions Accounts Data, available at <http://www.bea.gov/international/bp_web/simple.cfm?anon=71&table_id=1&area_id=1>.

27   Jones, G. (1997) 'Great Britain: Big Business, Management and Competitiveness in Twentieth Century Britain' in Chandler, A., et al. (eds) Big Business and the Wealth of Nations, Cambridge, 130; and McConnell, C. and Brue, S. (2004) Economics: Principles, Problems, and Policies, McGraw-Hill Professional, 299.

28   Tomlinson, J. (2004) 'Economic Policy' in Floud, R. and Johnson, P. (eds) The Cambridge Economic History of Modern Britain. Volume III: Structural Change and Growth, 1939–2000, Cambridge, 202; and Giersch , H. et al., above n22, 10.

29   Tomlinson, J., above n28, 201; and McConnell, C. and Brue, S., above n27, 300.

30   Smith, O. (1994) The German Economy, London: Routledge, 19; and Eichengreen, B. (2006) The European Economy Since 1945: Coordinated Capitalism and Beyond, Princeton: Princeton University Press, 286.

31   Eichengreen, B., above n30, 268–270.

32   Indeed this is true of the whole post war period. Brown, W. (2004) 'Industrial Relations and the Economy' in Floud, R. and Johnson, P. (eds) The Cambridge Economic

on its economy and in turn on the institutions that influence corporate governance outcomes was nowhere near as dramatic and shocking as that experienced by the US and the UK. As a result any pressures for change that were present were not capable of overwhelming path dependent institutions, while in the UK and US, the same pressures overwhelmed path dependent institutions. Additionally, even had their been a similar shock to the German corporate governance system, the outcome in corporate governance terms, would likely have been different, given the absence of a financial system which allowed institutional investors to emerge as the dominant players. In a nutshell while institution response to shock was similar in the UK and US, the institutional response to the same events was different and not transformative in Germany.

As we observed in Chapter 8, Germany experienced a number of potentially transformative pressures to its traditional insider system of corporate governance from the 1980s onwards. East and West Germany were reunited in October 1990, at the same time as the process of globalization was beginning to exert significant pressures through increased product market competition, the globalization of production and the globalization of capital markets. As a result labour co-determination has been adjusting and securities market reforms and direct exposure by core companies to the global capital markets has introduced outsider norms into the traditional German insider model. The reactions to these pressures have been interesting. Formal responses to the threat to co-determination have occurred to reinforce it, fear of hostile takeovers has spurred a formal protection of management and formal and functional reactions have occurred with regard to outsider based management incentives. One of the most significant changes has been the reaction of banks who have withdrawn from their traditional role as supporters of management and suppliers of liquidity by selling their shares, giving up their board seats and ceasing to lend to client companies. Management has also been reacting by replacing the banks on the supervisory boards with former management and by seeking out 'anchor' shareholders.

We consider this managerial reaction to be a crucial indicator of the rearrangements occurring within the German corporate governance model. The effect of the availability of exit because of the globalization of production has changed the nature of co-determination by weakening labour influence and in turn enhancing management discretion. Simultaneously, while initially banks using their internal influence to encourage takeovers was problematic for managers, the withdrawal of banks from internal governance arrangements, has provided management with an opportunity to increase its power through placing more former management on the supervisory board. Although, foreign investors have been the main beneficiaries of the sale of shares after the capital gains tax reforms in 2002, they have not yet emerged as a significant constraining influence on management or been able to fully orient the market level rules, in the absence of self-regulation

History of Modern Britain. Volume III: Structural Change and Growth, 1939–2000, Cambridge, 403.

and a strong hostile takeovers market, to ensure market enforcement of outsider norms. Indeed, as we considered in Chapter 8, while some of the reforms such as accounting reform, clearly indicate functional and then formal convergence, the rest of the reforms ranging from corporate law reforms to tax reform designed to enhance outsider protection and speed insider disengagement may have had unintended effects by enhancing managerial discretion and insider private rent extraction.[33] The reform of the German pension system has also not moved fully away from a pay as you go system and the stock market crash in 2001–2002, has diminished the appetite of German institutional investors for shares.[34] In all while foreign shareholders may wield influence in a small group of the largest companies, overall they have yet to become a significant presence.

In our view over the course of the 1990s and early twenty-first century the system has rearranged itself to enhance managerial discretion. As we discussed in Chapter 4 in response to Coffee's securities reforms convergence claims, outsider reforms may simply lead to a reorientation of an existing insider corporate governance system, whereby insiders are weakened but outsider shareholders are not significant enough of an influence to restrain management. An indication of this can be observed in the financing rearrangements of German companies since the beginning twenty-first century. The data in Table 9.1 below is drawn from the Bundesbank's Financial Statements Data Pool of over 100,000 financial statements of German companies per year. In terms of turnover, the corporations represented in the Table make up two-thirds of the economic activity of German non financial companies. As such it provides and interesting overview of changing financing pattern in German companies.

---

33   This may explain why Armour et al. found that the introduction of outsider shareholder protection measures does not play a role in stock market development. Armour, J., Deakin, S., Sarkar, P., Siems, M. and Singh, A. (2008) 'Shareholder Protection and Stock Market Development: An Empirical Test of the Legal Origins Hypothesis', University of Cambridge, CBR Working Paper; ECGI – Law Working Paper No. 108/2008 <http://ssrn.com/abstract=1094355>.

34   Bundesbank (2007) 'German Enterprises' Profitability and Financing in 2006', 42, available at <http://www.bundesbank.de/download/volkswirtschaft/mba/2007/200712mba_en_enterprises.pdf>.

Table 9.1 Financing of non financial German corporations, 1991–2006 (amounts in Euro Billions)

	1991	1993	1994	1995	1996	1997	1998	1999	2000	2001	2002	2003	2004	2005	2006
Internal Funds	**132.1**	**132.1**	**149.8**	**168.1**	**185.5**	**174.0**	**189.4**	**154.7**	**154.1**	**175.6**	**209.8**	**192.9**	**221.2**	**218.6**	**235.7**
Net retained income	12.5	(7.5)	0.6	18.8	28.7	17.7	25.4	(11.0)	(19.3)	(3.3)	26.9	10.0	34.7	28.6	46.1
Depreciation allowances	119.6	139.6	149.2	149.3	156.8	156.3	164.0	165.7	173.4	178.9	182.9	182.9	186.5	190.0	189.5
Internal financing ration (in %)	*49.0*	*55.7*	*60.6*	*59.2*	*68.6*	*69.2*	*52.5*	*37.2*	*31.9*	*48.5*	*81.3*	*84.9*	*118.6*	*78.5*	*76.6*
External Financing	**126.9**	**113.7**	**105.3**	**119.6**	**88.6**	**77.2**	**165.6**	**238.7**	**363.9**	**177.5**	**54.2**	**41.3**	**(59.1)**	**19.1**	**82.7**
From banks	**90.1**	**37.0**	**17.2**	**57.9**	**51.0**	**44.0**	**68.9**	**71.2**	**46.6**	**35.4**	**-21.8**	**(44.2)**	**(43.9)**	**(4.2)**	**15.4**
Short-term	*34.3*	*(10.5)*	*0.5*	*19.0*	*13.5*	*7.4*	*19.9*	*10.2*	*13.2*	*2.1*	*(27.4)*	*(25.3)*	*(32.2)*	*(15.8)*	*(3.3)*
In Germany	27.7	(7.9)	3.5	16.5	12.3	4.7	19.1	(5.3)	19.0	6.7	(24.2)	(24.8)	(27.1)	(15.1)	(11.4)
Abroad	6.6	(2.7)	(3.0)	2.5	1.3	2.7	0.8	15.5	(5.7)	(4.6)	(3.2)	(0.5)	(5.2)	(0.7)	8.1
Longer-term	*55.8*	*47.5*	*16.6*	*38.9*	*37.5*	*36.6*	*49.1*	*61.0*	*33.3*	*33.3*	*5.6*	*(19.0)*	*(11.6)*	*11.6*	*18.7*
In Germany	55.5	45.3	15.4	39.1	37.8	36.1	47.3	58.2	31.9	21.5	3.5	(16.9)	(13.5)	1.7	3.3
Abroad	0.3	2.2	1.2	(0.2)	(0.3)	0.5	1.7	2.7	1.4	11.8	2.1	(2.0)	1.9	9.9	15.4
From other lenders	**9.5**	**11.3**	**17.2**	**41.4**	**13.1**	**15.9**	**35.2**	**84.1**	**160.6**	**60.1**	**41.6**	**29.8**	**(40.6)**	**10.3**	**21.0**
In Germany	(2.0)	7.0	6.7	30.1	(3.1)	(0.5)	6.7	17.1	3.4	6.5	21.3	15.4	6.0	(18.4)	(24.6)
Short-term	0.3	0.1	(0.1)	0.0	(0.4)	(0.2)	(1.1)	1.7	5.9	1.3	(0.2)	1.2	1.0	2.2	(1.3)
Longer-term	(2.3)	6.9	6.9	30.1	(2.6)	(0.3)	7.8	15.3	2.6	5.2	21.5	14.2	5.0	(20.6)	(23.3)

Table 9.1 continued

	1991	1993	1994	1995	1996	1997	1998	1999	2000	2001	2002	2003	2004	2005	2006
In the securities market	3.7	46.9	46.3	(3.3)	(4.4)	(3.0)	(3.8)	1.3	9.6	9.8	6.0	27.2	2.1	3.1	17.4
In the form of participating interests	16.5	14.2	19.3	16.5	25.4	16.7	60.7	75.8	138.9	64.1	18.8	21.8	16.6	4.4	23.4
In Germany	14.2	15.8	17.0	14.0	26.2	12.7	58.0	57.1	23.0	51.7	6.3	(11.7)	0.7	(0.1)	2.7
Abroad	2.3	(1.7)	2.3	2.5	(0.8)	4.0	2.7	18.6	115.9	12.4	12.6	33.4	15.9	4.5	20.7
Pension fund provisions	7.2	4.2	5.4	7.1	3.6	3.6	4.5	6.3	8.2	8.2	9.6	6.7	6.7	5.5	5.5
Total	**258.9**	**245.7**	**255.1**	**287.7**	**274.1**	**251.2**	**355.0**	**393.4**	**518.0**	**353.2**	**264.0**	**234.2**	**162.1**	**237.7**	**318.3**

Source: Deutsches Aktieninstitut, DAI statistics, 2008, Table 04–6.

As we can observe from Table 9.1, a significant change occurred from 2002 onwards coinciding with the capital gains tax reforms. German bank funding became negative as companies paid down loans as the banks withdrew from internal corporate governance arrangements. However, perhaps the most striking change in the financing arrangements of German companies has been in the ratio of internal financing to external financing. This has increased significantly since 2002 amounting to 81.3 percent in 2002, 84.9 in 2003, 118.6 percent in 2004 when external financing became a negative figure, 78.5 percent in 2005 and 76.6 percent in 2006 (Table 9.1). The *Bundesbank* also reports that profits have been unusually large in recent years partly driven by wage restraint.[35] The figures suggest to us that management's ability to retain earnings has been enhanced in the absence of traditional stakeholder claims on management discretion, as cost benefits from the effects of the globalization of production have begun to impact over and above the effects of product market competition. Contrary to Glison's expectation, discussed in Chapter 4, that capital markets would impose discipline on management, the influx of foreign mostly institutional shareholders has yet to have that effect.

Change though, is still occurring. As we observed in Chapter 8, from 1995 to 2003 there was a significant shifting of shareholding patterns in German companies as the *Finanzplatz Deutschland* reforms and specifically capital gains tax impacted. However, as we also noted in that chapter, between 2003 and 2007 another significant change in shareholding patterns has been occurring. The data from Chart 9.1 is similarly drawn from the Bundesbank's Financial Statements Data Pool of German companies and gives a good picture of the changing nature of shareholdings since 1991. Again 2002 seems to mark a decisive shift in the changing patterns, as contrary to expectations that the capital gains tax would cause a mass sale of blockholders' shares, private households (including families), non financial corporations holding strategic stakes, government and banks, after an initial sell off, began to build their blocks of shares again. Additionally, investment funds and foreign shareholders also increased their holdings, while insurance companies made a significant exit from shareholdings. Part of this pattern, at least initially, could be explained by the stock market crash in 2002, which meant blockholders held on until more favourable prices were available but it does not explain the recent increase in the shareholdings by banks, government, private households (including families) and non financial corporations. As we suggested in Chapter 8, part of increase in blockholder shares may be to do with a reworking of the traditional German insider model to deal with the threat from outsider shareholders, as management and labour are exposed to a nascent market for corporate control, by seeking 'anchor' shareholders with a long-term commitment to the company. As another sign that traditional insiders are re-engaging, bank lending to German companies begins to revive from 2005 onwards as bank shareholding starts to increase (Table 9.1 and Chart 9.1). Another explanation for the reengagement of blockholders may be to do with exploiting outsider shareholders. It is plausible

---

35   Ibid., on profitability and wage restraint see 37–41.

that blockholders, in particular families and non financial corporations, were content to remain and extract still significant private rents, regardless of the capital gains reforms, or adopt a wait and see attitude with regard to an upsurge in share prices. While doing this they may have become aware that opportunities to extract private rents were increasing in an environment in which labour was more flexible and the banks were withdrawing, outsider shareholders were mostly passive and cost benefits were flowing from the globalization of production. The Schaeffler and Porsche stake building and Susanne Klatten's Altana buyout attempt, we considered in Chapter 8, exhibit elements of these factors. As Enriques and Volpin have argued in the context of EU reforms generally:

> a good part of the European reforms have been patterned after U.S. corporate and securities law. America does have a well-developed legal framework for corporate governance, which has been further improved by the post-scandal reforms. However, the fundamental differences in ownership structure between Europe and the United States mean that emulating laws whose focus is on curbing managerial opportunism may not be an appropriate way to prevent self-dealing by controlling shareholders. Indeed, a cynical observer might argue that when European policymakers adopt U.S.-style solutions designed to tackle managerial agency problems, they can appear to be doing something to reform European corporate governance while actually leaving the rents of Europe's dominant shareholders perfectly intact.[36]

The German insider system has been subject to a number of severe potentially transformative pressures as the result of reunification and the process of globalization. However, it does not look to us as though a move to an outsider system has occurred yet in Germany. As we discussed in Chapters 4 and 5, Amable described institutional rearrangement in terms of 'change' and 'destabilization'. 'Change', he claimed, amounts to instances of institutional alterations that are absorbed without affecting the general logic of relations within that system. 'Destabilization on the other hand amounted to a breakdown in the pattern of a complementary system as a result of a shock. There is some resonance with Amable's analysis in the German experience of exposure to the process of globalization. There is no doubt that the direction of reform and exposure to the pressures of globalization has favoured outsider norms but this has not necessarily had the intended effect, and where it has, say accounting reform, it has not exerted enough influence to transform Germany's insider based system to an outsider system.[37] Co-determination for example has 'changed' but it has always been

---

36 Enriques, L. and Volpin, P. (2007) 'From Corporate Governance Reforms in Continental Europe', Journal of Economic Perspectives, vol. 21(1), 117–140 at 138.

37 Wymeersch, E. (2002) 'Convergence or Divergence in Corporate Governance Patterns in Western Europe?' in McCahery, J. et al. (eds) Corporate Governance Regimes: Convergence and Diversity, Oxford: Oxford University Press.

a resilient part of the German model as it has responded by absorbing adverse economic pressures in the 1970s, the 1980s, during reunification and as a result of the process globalization. In all it is a remarkable resilient institution. Capital markets have become more important but are still not central to German corporate financing or its pension provision. Outsider oriented institutional investors, both foreign and domestic, are similarly not significant enough to reorient the system, as they were able to do in the self-regulatory systems of the UK and US and the market for corporate control despite its high profile in Germany is not yet strong enough to enforce outsider norms. A small group of the very largest German companies may be subject directly to the outsider norms present in global capital markets but outside this small group, in a systemic sense the institutional workability of the German model remains intact. Despite the influx of foreign shareholders and the emergence of German institutional investors, shares are still generally highly concentrated.[38] In all it seems to us that institutional forces are rearranging themselves as formal and function reactions to economic globalization pull and push to find an internal accommodation. Formal protection of co-determination has occurred, while functional and some formal altering has also occurred reflecting part of Glison's argument, discussed in Chapter 4, that functional changes could occur while leaving formal institutions intact. However, contrary to Glison's argument, the functional 'undermining', to use Glison's term, has yet to show signs of real formal convergence, in fact the opposite seems the case with regard to domestic German legislation. The *Finanzplatz Deutschland* reforms encouraged the growth of capital markets and introduced outsider legal norms but the collapse of those markets in the stock market crash of 2001–2002, badly damaged a nascent equity culture in Germany. The major change in the German corporate governance model as a result of the globalization process, has been the withdrawal of banks and the introduction of flexibility in labour co-determination. However, as we described earlier, since the stock market crash in 2002, the traditional insider German corporate governance model seems to be being reworked to reflect this new power differential as outsider norms may not be working in the way they were intended, as they may have simply enhanced managerial discretion and/or given insiders options on how to extract returns from the company.

---

38   Crane, D. and Schaede, U. (2005) 'Functional Change and Bank Strategy in German Corporate Governance', International Review of Law and Economics, vol. 25, 513–540 at 525–526.

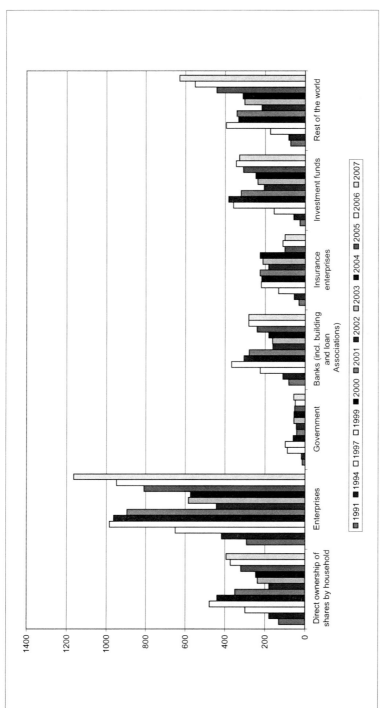

Chart 9.1 Changing shareholding structure, 1991–2007 (billion euros)
Source: Deutsches Aktieninstitut, DAI statistics (2008) Table 08.1–3–a.

As we discussed in Chapter 4, some forces of change can move a system through complimentary alterations, as it evolves according to the general logic of relations within that system. Shocks on the other hand can destabilize the system and move it to change contrary to the general logic of its system. These types of impacts are not simply slow but sustained pressures to change but rather dramatic and severe shock or shocks. As we noted earlier being defeated in a war, even winning a war if the price is high enough, or continued dramatic economic shocks, are the type of disruptive events that have caused systemic transformation. Although the process of globalization has exerted significant pressures on the insider German corporate governance system, even while coinciding with reunification, we don't think it is of the character of a transformative shocking event.

Outside of those events, institutional systems, in our view, tend to find an internal accommodation when presented with pressures to change. Additionally, while there is no doubt outsider norms have been introduced into the sub-systems affecting corporate governance outcomes in German, those norms that operate in the UK and US to protect shareholders may not operate in the same way in Germany. Enhanced disclosure in the absence of a market control, self-regulation and significant institutional investor presence may have little effect. Complementarities between sub-systems that effected their protective operation in the UK and US may not exist and as Enriques and Volpin noted earlier, outsider norms where ownership is still concentrated may in fact work counter to their original purpose, by allowing blockholders to enhance their rent extraction activities and/or enhance managerial discretion.

Where shock occurs and institutions begin a process of possible transformation, this can have a cumulative destabilizing effect on the system as a whole. Two outcomes are then possible. Either the forces of change are strong enough to find a new workable equilibrium or they are not strong enough to find such a workable equilibrium and unworkability becomes a permanent condition, as some institutions have changed and others have not, but the system as a whole has lost its complementarity and workability. The flexibility of co-determination and the reworking of the German corporate governance system since 2002 accompanied by its recent economic resurgence (or rather given the global export contraction as a result of the financial market crisis from 2008 onwards, its resurgence after the major outsider reforms were introduced) is an indication that the system has not become unworkable as it has absorbed outsider norms. It is clearly not the same system as it was twenty years ago, as the dense German corporate board network has been dismantled, but it has managed to retain its own systemic integrity and workability.[39] In other words we consider that it is correct to observe that the German insider system is subject to pressures to change from the process of globalization and indeed that 'change' has occurred. However, convergence/transformation to an outsider system of corporate governance does not seem to

---

39   Höpner, M. and Krempel, L. (2004) 'The Politics of the German Company Network', Competition and Change, vol. 8(4), 339–356 at 353.

be playing out in Germany as a result of the process of globalization. As Vitols describes it '[r]eports of the death of Germany's distinctive corporate governance system are therefore exaggerated'.[40]

Instead, its corporate governance system is altering to accommodate the economic environment in a manner that is consistent with it own internal constraints. Change, as we have observed, is constant within all three systems we examined in this book but movement from one system to another is unusual and predicting the systemic outcome of change is very difficult. Of course, that still leaves the possibility that the process of globalization could produce a future shock which does destabilize the German system and because the system has already borne some of the adaptation costs of change, future transformation may cause less resistance from the forces of path dependent. We have reason to doubt this will occur in this form, as it is more likely that events bringing about the end of the current process of globalization could cause such a destabilizing shock. As James somewhat presciently considered in 2001:

> [a] major financial crisis can have systemic effects and catastrophically undermine the stability of institutions that make global interchange possible. Such a picture, in which financial volatility destroys the system that was built up on the basis of a free flow of capital, has become increasingly worrying to thoughtful analysts. Even thinkers close to the modern consensus about the desirability of liberalization have drawn back and wondered whether there might not be a case for controlling capital flows ... According to this new uneasy critique of financial globalism, continued unregulated capital movements would be the mechanism whereby the liberal international order would destroy itself through its own contradictions (to borrow a phrase widely used in Marxist analysis).[41]

What Happened to Globalization?

Within the past decade the process of economic globalization we described in Chapter 3 has slowed and in 2008 the two pillars upon which it has been built, the liberalization of trade and capital markets, were badly shaken. As we noted in Chapter 3, the globalization of trade has continued apace since the end of WWII and became truly global after the end of the Cold War. However, as inequalities in the global trading system have become more apparent, resistance to any expansion of trade, without addressing inequalities, has been very strong from the developing

---

40   Vitols, S. (2005) 'Changes in Germany's Bank-Based Financial System: Implications for Corporate Governance', Corporate Governance, vol. 13(3), 395.

41   James, H. (2001) The End of Globalization: Lessons from the Great Depression, Cambridge, MA: Harvard University Press, 3–4.

world.[42] Simultaneously, a general sense of disillusionment has also appeared in the developed world as the benefits of globalization have become less clear.[43] At the WTO Ministerial Conference in Seattle in 1999, talks on a new trade round had to be abandoned because of the scale of public protests in the city against global trade.[44] A new round of talks began in Doha in 2001 but failed to reach any agreement as differences between the US, the EU and the developing world proved insurmountable. Similarly talks in Cancun in 2003, Geneva in 2004, Paris in 2005, Hong Kong in 2005, Geneva in 2006, Potsdam in 2007 and Geneva in 2008 all broke down again over developing world concerns about the expansion of trade.[45] In the US, attempts in late 2008 by the outgoing Bush administration to rush through a last minute trade deal before a more protectionist Democratic party took power, facing into the teeth of a recession triggered by the sub prime crisis and subsequent credit crisis over the course of 2007–2009, failed to produce agreement. Democrat control of both houses of Congress and the Presidency from January 2009, has significantly reduced the likelihood of an agreement on the expansion of world trade in the near future.[46] Indeed, the early signals from the Obama administration on trade have already been distinctly protectionist and may trigger a rolling back of trade liberalization as countries generally become much more defensive as the first major global recession since the Great Depression in the 1930s begins to impact.[47]

As we described in Chapter 3, the process of globalizing capital markets began in the aftermath of the Cold War, as significant amounts of capital were allowed

42   Stephens, P. (2008) 'The Blindfolds that Wrecked a Deal to Boost Global Trade', Financial Times, 1 August, 11.

43   Tomkins, R. (2006) 'Profits of Doom', Financial Times Magazine, 14/15 October, 22–25; Gray, J. (1998) 'False Dawn: The Delusions of Global Capitalism', Granta; Friedman, T. (1999) 'The Lexus and the Olive Tree: Understanding Globalization', Farrar Straus; and O'Rourke, K. and Williamson, J. (1999) Globalization and History: The Evolution of a Nineteenth-Century Atlantic Economy, Cambridge, MA: MIT Press.

44   Fergusson, I. (2008) 'World Trade Organization Negotiations: The Doha Development Agenda', Congressional Research Service, available at <http://www.nationalaglawcenter.org/assets/crs/RL32060.pdf>.

45   Ibid. and Rodrik, D. (2007) One Economics, Many Recipes: Globalization, Institutions and Economic Growth, Princeton: Princeton University Press, 213–242.

46   Beattie, A. (2009) 'Legacy of Bitterness and Mistrust on Capitol Hill Points to Stasis on Trade Deals', Financial Times, 16 January, 7; Elliott, L. (2008) 'Meeting Fixed to End Trade Stalemate', The Guardian, 17 November, <http://www.guardian.co.uk/business/2008/nov/17/doha-trade-g20>; and Parker, G. (2008) 'Brown Warns Obama on Trade Protection', Financial Times, 10 November, 2.

47   Webb, T. (2009) 'Indian Elections, likely to reflect Rising Tide of Protectionism', The Guardian, 23 February, 26; Beattie, A, (2009) 'US Signals Tough Stance Over Doha', Financial Times, 3 March, 7; The Economist (2008) 'A Special Report on the World Economy', 11 October, 3–36; and Elliott, L. (2008) 'Winning was the Easy Bit, Mr President', The Guardian, 3 November, 28.

to decouple from the national level. By the 1980s, the removal of capital controls had allowed the Anglo-Saxon capital markets to engage in regulatory arbitrage in the process of becoming global capital markets, as they were deregulated and allowed to decouple from their domestic environment. Stock market crashes in the 1980s, emerging market crises in Asia, Latin America and Russia over the course of 1997 and 1998 and the 'irrational exuberance'[48] leading to the dot.com crash from 2000–2002 did not seem to cause much introspection among policy makers as to systemic causes of instability within deregulated global capital markets.[49] However, the process of globalization of capital markets is under serious review as we write in early 2009, as the effects of the global credit crisis play out into recession in the real global economy. In a very short period of time liberalized global capital markets have had massive and sustained government intervention to stem complete market failure. Property crashes, runs on banks, nationalization and part nationalization of banks, massive coordinated government funding injecting liquidity into capital markets, IMF loans to fund nations in crisis and stock market crashes have all been features of the global economy since autumn 2008 as government intervention and demand management have swung back into vogue to prevent systemic collapse.[50] When the original Bretton Woods institutions were set up in the 1940s capital flows were mostly public. By the twenty-first century, enormous private capital flows had arisen and with no institutional structure to constrain them, near systemic failure occurred. Re-regulation of capital markets as a result of this experience with a new form of Bretton Woods Agreement to build the financial architecture to deal with unregulated capital markets, is now

---

48   This was the phrase used by Alan Greenspan, then Chairman of the US Federal Reserve, to describe the speculative behaviour present in the markets at the time. Greenspan, A. (2007) The Age of Turbulence, Penguin, 164–181.

49   There was plenty of dissent just no-one in power willing to do anything. Krugman, P. (1999) The Return of Depression Economics, Norton, 166; Stiglitz, J. (2003) Globalization and Its Discontents, Penguin, Chapter 4; and Singh, A., Singh, A. and Weisse, B. (2002) 'Corporate Governance, Competition, the New International Financial Architecture and Large Corporations in Emerging Markets', ESRC Centre for Business Research, University of Cambridge Working Paper No. 250, available at <http://ideas.repec.org/p/cbr/cbrwps/wp250.html>.

50   Luce, E. and Freeland, C. (2009) 'Summers Urges Global Boost', Financial Times, 9 March, 1; Lambert, R. (2008) 'Crashes, Bangs and Wallops', Financial Times Weekend Magazine, 19/20 July, 22–27; Bowers, D. (2008) 'Nationalisation of the Banks will Only Harm Globalization', 16 October, available at <http://www.ft.com>. Crook, C. (2008) 'Back in Business', Financial Times, 15 October, available at <http://www.ft.com/cms/s/0/23210f82-9ae2-11dd-a653-000077b07658.html>. England, A. (2008) 'UK Confident Saudis will Help IMF', Financial Times, 3 October, 10; Browning, E., Gullapalli, D. and Karmin, C. (2008) 'Wild Day Caps Worst Week Ever for Stocks', Wall Street Journal, 11 October, available at <http://online.wsj.com/article/SB122368071064524779.html?mod=googlenews_wsj>.

a real possibility.[51] The British Prime Minister, Gordon Brown calling for a new regulatory order said in October 2008 '[w]e now have global financial markets, global corporations, global financial flows. But what we do not have is anything other than national and regional regulation and supervision'.[52]

As governments around the world struggle to contain the impact on their domestic economies of the crisis in integrated global capital markets, the outsider Anglo/Saxon form of capitalism on which it is based, is being questioned. The French President Nicholas Sarkozy, while agreeing that a new regulatory environment was needed considered that the 'Anglo-Saxon model of unrestrained markets has failed'.[53] In a further echo of the 1930s, fears of potentially hostile countries, particularly China,[54] using the market crisis for strategic ends and a general move to protect domestic industry, has led to many countries including Germany, Italy, Russia and Japan, reintroducing controls on foreign investment.[55] China responded to these moves with a defensive reaction by similarly reintroducing capital controls for foreign investors.[56] Iceland and the Ukraine have implemented full foreign exchange controls and the Baltic States may also be forced to do so as the credit crisis increasingly undermines their economies.[57] Developing countries have been turning in large numbers to the World Bank for financial assistance, as

---

51   Editorial (2009) 'What the G20 has to do in London', Financial Times, 30 March, 12; Parker, G., Barber, T. and Dombey, D. (2008) 'European Leaders Back Call for Global Reforms', Financial Times, 16 October, 8.

52   Kirkup, J. and Waterfield, B. (2008) 'Gordon Brown's Bretton Woods Summit Call Risks Spat with Nicholas Sarkozy', The Daily Telegraph, 17 October, available at <http://www.telegraph.co.uk/news/worldnews/europe/france/3205033/Gordon-Browns-Bretton-Woods-summit-call-risks-spat-with-Nicholas-Sarkozy.html>; Tait, N. and Hughes, J. (2009) 'Trichet Calls For Supervision of All Institutions', Financial Times, 24 February, 7.

53   Kirkup, J. and Waterfield, B., above n52; Wolf, M. (2009) 'Seeds of its Own Destruction', Financial Times, 9 March, 13.

54   Tucker, S., Smith, P. and Anderlini, J. (2009) 'Beijing Bars Coke Takeover of Juice Maker', Financial Times, 19 March, 17; Anderlini, J. (2008) 'Secretive Beijing Agency uses Forex Reserves to Target Taiwan', Financial Times, 12 September, 1.

55   DPA (2008) 'Germany Moves to Protect Companies From Foreign Takeovers' DW-World, 20 August, <http://www.dw-world.de/dw/article/0,2144,3580978,00.html>; Financial Times (2008) 'J-Power Failure', 17 April, available at <http://www.ft.com/cms/s/0/6b0efcd0-0caf-11dd-86df-0000779fd2ac.html>; Hooper, J. (2008) 'Italy Moves to Protect Firms from Foreign Hostile Bids', The Guardian, 17 October, 33; Buckley, N. (2008) 'Russia Sets New Rules for Foreign Investors', Financial Times, 6 May, available at <http://www.ft.com/cms/s/0/908b2b4c-1b04-11dd-aa67-0000779fd2ac.html>.

56   Dyer, G. (2008) 'China to Fortify Capital Controls to Clamp Down on "Hot" Cash', Financial Times, 3 July, 1.

57   Gow, D. (2009) 'United they Fall: Post-Communist States Pull EU into the Red', The Guardian, 21 February, 37; Lex (2008) 'Baltic Bust Up', Financial Times, Wednesday 12 November, 16.

the credit crisis has cut their access to private sector funds and recession has badly hit their economies as world trade contracted for the first time since 1982.[58]

Over the past 30 years in particular, the promotion of liberal product and capital markets as part of the process of globalization has featured a strong emphasis on the outsider market and firm level norms of outsider shareholder protection and shareholder value. In particular, insider systems have taken an ideological battering in the past decade at both the academic and policy level as they have been considered inferior models with even well respected historians suggesting that their economic models were outmoded.[59] In turn given the strong link between crisis and change in corporate theory, as real introspection is brought to the process of increased liberalization and globalization of trade and capital markets, the legitimacy of the outsider shareholder model designed by and for this process of globalization also comes into question. As Allen and Gale considered in 2001:

> [i]n Anglo-Saxon countries such as the US and UK good corporate governance is based on the idea that firms should pursue the interests of the shareholders. Traditionally this means firing workers at will and ignoring the needs of other stakeholders in the firm. The intellectual justification for this way of organizing firms is Adam Smith's notion of the invisible hand. If all agents pursue their own interest the resulting outcome will be socially efficient. For firms this means they should pursue the goal of creating value for shareholders. The validity of this argument depends on there being perfect and complete markets. In practice it is not clear that markets are sufficiently perfect and complete for Anglo-Saxon capitalism to be the best way of organizing an economy.[60]

In one very real sense the environment the outsider system has been formed by is likely to change as re-regulation of capital markets and government demand led policies impact.[61] This may provide an opportunity to reassess the virtues of insider based corporate governance systems as the conditions for a neo-Kaldorian model become more favourable. As such there is an opportunity and danger for Germany. On the one hand pressures on the German corporate governance system from global capital markets, private equity and hedge funds, should retreat because of the credit crisis. In their absence traditional insiders may accelerate

---

58   Dombey, D. and MacKenzie, M (2008) 'World Bank to Provide $100bn in Aid for Developing World', Financial Times, 12 November, 5.

59   Hansmann, H. and Kraakman, R. (2001) 'The End of History for Corporate Law', Georgetown Law Journal, vol. 89, 439 at 468; and Eichengreen, B. (2007) 'The European Economy Since 1945: Coordinated Capitalism and Beyond', Heritage Lectures No. 1023, Heritage Foundation, 3.

60   Allen, F. and Dale, G. (2001) 'A Comparative Theory of Corporate Governance', Wharton Business School Financial Institutions Center Working Paper series 03–27.

61   Luce, E. (2008) 'Obama set to push "big bang" reform package', Financial Times, 10 November, 1.

their re-engagement. German banks damaged by their global ambitions, may even rediscover the virtues of their traditional relationships with German companies, as in turn those companies struggle to finance themselves on crisis hit global capital markets.[62] Production exit may also be affected, as global supply chains have already been placed under enormous strain by the global credit crisis, as banks have withdrawn credit lines to the small and medium sized companies that make up the backbone of global just in time production. In the first half of 2008, 67,000 Chinese factories ceased operating and credit insurers have been withdrawing cover even from suppliers to blue chip companies. European manufacturers have over the course of 2008 and 2009 been rethinking their global supply chain as a result of supply chain problems.[63] Governments may also become more protective on trade and capital movement generally as the stalling of trade talks and the introduction of controls on foreign investment discussed above suggests.[64] The German model could even become more influential as economic governance of the Euro Zone, leaving the London markets isolated, is in prospect and regionally the German corporate governance model has strong legal and cultural links particularly with Austria, the Netherlands, Switzerland and the Scandinavian countries.[65] Additionally and somewhat paradoxically, the process of globalization has also played a part in exporting the German corporate governance model, in that many eastern European states, where German companies have located because of lower labour costs, have adopted German corporate and commercial laws rather than its Anglo/Saxon counterpart. In turn as the more advanced of those states have now entered the EU, there is a substantial block of German corporate and commercial influence within the EU.[66]

On the other hand, as we noted in the section on corporate law reform in Chapter 8, the series of financial crises in Asia, Latin America and Russia in 1997 and 1998, spurred not a domestic reflection on the merits of the German model but a domestic policy acceleration away from it in terms of introducing outsider norms. Germany

---

62   Deutsche Bank for example announced its first annual loss in fifty years in January 2009. See Wilson, J. (2009) 'D Bank Set to Unveil €4.8bn Loss', Financial Times, 15 January, 15.

63   Eaglesham, J. and Stacey, K. (2009) 'Mandelson Readies Supply Chain Aid', 15 January, 3; Milne, R. (2008) 'Sum of the Parts', Financial Times, Monday, 17 November, 12.

64   The credit crisis has had a significant impact on trade as finance for trade has become problematic. Blas, J. (2009) 'Nations Barter for Food Amid Credit Crisis', Financial Times, 27 January, 8. The WTO is also extremely concerned about the rapid rise of protectionist policies in response to the credit crisis. Pignal, S. (2009) 'EU Warned on Protectionism', Financial Times, 20 January, 22; and Lex (2009) 'Economic Patriotism', Financial Times, 26 January, 16.

65   Munchau, W. (2008) 'Why the British may Decide to Love the Euro', Financial Times, 17 November, 15.

66   Noack, U. and Zetzsche, D. (2007) 'Germany's Corporate and Financial Law 2007: (Getting) Ready for Competition', CBC-RPS No. 0028, <http://ssrn.com/abstract=986357>; and Dine, J., Koutsias, M. and Blecher, M. (2007) Company Law in the New Europe: The EU Acquis, Comparative Methodology and Model Law, Edward Elgar.

entered a recession in late 2008[67] and as the global recession further impacts in 2009, this will increase unemployment and may in turn increase pressures for production exit (if it is still available), flexible labour markets and to dismantle labour co-determination.[68] Germany may now indeed be at a crossroads as the end of this current process of globalization might be the systemic economic shock that triggers transformation, ironically at a time when the German insider model may have something to offer. These issues are likely to loom large in the German Federal elections in September 2009. Indeed, there already seems to be a deep and wide spread disillusionment with western capitalism generally in Germany, as a poll in October 2008 showed an overwhelming majority of Germans, across all political spectrums, favoured nationalizing large parts of the German economy.[69] Overall there has been a move to the left among the voting public as uncertainty and fears about recession loom large.[70] In response Chancellor Merkel has had to engage much more in consensus building with the Left than her CDU party is necessarily comfortable with. Indeed the SDP have already begun campaigning on the basis that the crisis offers an opportunity for Germany and its economic model.[71] As the German foreign minister and SPD candidate for Chancellor, Frank Walter Steinmeier, said in a speech to his party congress in October 2008, '[t]his upheaval we are going through is the biggest change since the Berlin Wall fell. The rule of the free-market radicals that started with Margaret Thatcher and Ronald Reagan has ended with a big bang'.[72] If that is so, then the price of that bang will be high, indeed the down payment has already by early 2009 been exorbitant, but perhaps in a more regulated demand managed world, stability and incremental innovation may come to be valued once more over excess profitability and in turn the insider corporate governance model may once more have its day in the sun.

---

67   Germany plunged into recession as a result of the credit crisis and the subsequent contraction of world trade in November 2008. Atkins, R. (2008) 'Fast Decline Tips Germany into Recession', Financial Times, 11 November, 11.

68   Benoit, B. (2008) 'Wise Men Predict Flat German Growth' Financial Times, 12 November, 5.

69   Benoit, B. (2008) 'Survey Reveals Germans Back Nationalisation', Financial Times, 30 October, available at <http://www.ft.com/cms/s/0/e7404a9a-a622-11dd-9d26-000077b07658.html>.

70   Benoit, B., Williamson, H. and Barber, L. (2008) '"Secret Chancellor" Steers German Left', 16 June, available at <http://www.ft.com/cms/s/0/31849ccc-3bcb-11dd-9cb2-0000779fd2ac.html>.

71   The current global capital market crisis is a bit of a problem for the CDU as its economic policy has been to move to more free market reforms. In particular it intends to make co-determination optional. Gumbrell-McCormick, R. and Hyman, R. (2006) 'Embedded Collectivism? Workplace Representation in France and Germany', Industrial Relations Journal, vol. 37(5), 473–491 at 480, <http://ssrn.com/abstract=923925>; and Benoit, B. (2009) 'Germany's Tactical "Mutti"', Financial Times, 17/18 January, 11.

72   Bryant, C. (2008) 'SPD Poll Hopes Raised By Crisis, says Steinmeier', Financial Times, 20 October, 10.

Index

foreign exchange markets, globalization of
100–1, **102**
foreign investment in Germany 381–2,
384–5
Franks, J. 220, 277
Freeman, R. 39
Friedman, M. 151–2, 163, 227
Fröbel, F. 131
Fukuyama, Francis 45

Gale, G. 81
Garn-St Germain Depository Institutions
Act 1982 232
Geisst, C. 254
General Agreement on Tariffs and Trade
(GATT) 98, 99, 108, 209–10
Germany
accounting standards 290–1, 354–9,
356
Act on Control and Transparency in the
Enterprise Sector (KonTrag) 333,
342–3, 345, 347, 351–3
Act on the Improvement of Corporate
Integrity and on the Modernization
of the Regime Governing Decision-
Directed Suits (UMAG) 346–7
activism of shareholders 384–5
Agenda 2010 319
anchor shareholders 376–7, 391, 395,
404, 408
Aufsichtsrat 270–1, 292, 342, 344–5
banks
as aggressive as creditors 368
as block holders 294–8
changing role 362–71, 377
as corporate rescuers 366–8
as liquidity insurers 366
proxy-voting function 264–5, 288,
352–3
barriers to hostile takeovers in 285–92
blockholdings 292–4
board structure and composition
269–74, 288, 291–2, 342, 344–5
cartelization pre-WWII 266
co-determination in 270–2, 274–6,
291–2, 304
collective bargaining in 312, 313–14
compared to UK/US 401–2

concentrated ownership 292–4
consensus building through co-
determination 321–2
cooperative corporate governance
267–9
corporate law reforms 342–54
corporate scandals 315
cost-driven FDI 310–11
cross-shareholdings 279–80, 286, 353
decline in exports 304, *305*
deficient outside shareholder protection
289–92
demand oriented institutional structure
298–300
development of equity culture 327–9,
329, 330
disclosure of ownership information
290, 337–9, 341
economy after WWII 402–4
Employee Stock Option Plans (ESOPs)
347
EU impacts on co-determination
315–19
financial system reforms 322–33, *329,
330*
flexibility in co-determination 319–22
foreign investment in 381–2, 384–5
German Corporate Governance Code
(DCGK) 343–5
globalization, first impacts of 307
growth of hostile takeovers in 371, 375
growth of mergers and acquisitions
(M&A) in 377
hedge funds 383–4
impact of increased global
competitiveness 303–11, *305, 307,
308, 310*
inability to adopt new techniques 306
incorporation abroad to avoid co-
determination 317–18
industrial democracy in 267–9, 271–2
industrial relations changes 312–15
insider control 292–8
insider dealing
lack of regulation 290
regulation of 339–40
Law on Example Procedures for
Investor Suits (KapMuG) 346–7